Law of Torts

The
Law of Torts

A Concise Treatise

on the
Civil Liability at Common Law
and under
Modern Statutes for Actionable Wrongs
to Person and Property

By

Francis M. Burdick

Dwight Professor of Law in Columbia University
School of Law
Author of "The Law of Sales", "The Law of Partnership", etc.

BeardBooks
Washington, D.C.

PREFACE.

THE present volume is the result of an endeavor to state, with brevity but with accuracy, the legal principles involved in tort litigations of to-day. While neither the history nor the theory of the subject has been ignored, the discussion of those topics has been subordinated to the exposition of established rules of law.

No attempt has been made at originality in classification. The first six chapters present a sketch of the history of tort development in our law; a statement of the general principles determining tort liability; a brief account of tort remedies, and of the manner in which tort liabilities may be discharged. The remainder of the volume is devoted to a discussion of the most important classes of torts.

The order, in which particular torts have been dealt with, is quite different from that observed by many modern writers. It is not made to depend upon the motive, intent, or state of mind of the wrong-doer, but upon the sort of harm inflicted. Those torts, which are directed principally against the person of the victim, are first considered : then, those which are aimed at his property; and, lastly, those which are clear invasions of both the personal and the property rights of another.

A considerable saving of space has been secured by frequent cross-references. For example, Chapter III, entitled Harms that are not Torts, contains a statement of the principles which excuse or justify acts which are apparently tortious. These principles are not repeated in the chapters, devoted to particular torts, such as Assault and Battery, Trespass and others ; but are referred to in frequent foot-notes. Still, the moderate dimensions of this book are due not so much to the space-saving device, just mentioned, as to the deliberate purpose of the writer to prepare a hand-book; not a series of monographs, nor a collection of commentaries, nor a digest of all reported decisions. He has sought to aid his brethren of the profession by stating, as concisely as possible, the rules of law on this subject; by expounding the reasons for such rules, as these are set forth in judicial decisions; by noting the conflict of opinion which exists on many points, and especially, by referring only to those cases which bear directly and helpfully upon the topics to which they are cited. In order to make these citations as useful as possible, recent cases have been preferred to older ones, whenever the discussion of principles and authorities has been equally valuable; reference has been given not only to the official report, but to unofficial publications in which the case has appeared, and the date of each decision is noted.

COLUMBIA UNIVERSITY,
SCHOOL OF LAW,
March, 1905.

TABLE OF CONTENTS.

INTRODUCTORY CHAPTER.

CHAPTER II.

NATURE OF A TORT.

CHAPTER III.

HARM THAT ARE NOT TORTS.

CHAPTER IV.

PARTIES TO TORT ACTIONS.

CHAPTER V.

REMEDIES.

CHAPTER VI.

DISCHARGE OF TORTS.

CHAPTER VII.

CHAPTER VIII.

ASSAULT AND BATTERY.

CHAPTER IX.

WRONGFUL DISTURBANCE OF FAMILY RELATIONS.

CHAPTER X.

DEFAMATION.

CHAPTER XI.

TRESPASS TO PROPERTY.

CHAPTER XII.

TROVER AND CONVERSION.

CHAPTER XIII.

DECEIT AND KINDRED TORTS.

CHAPTER XIV.

NUISANCE.

CHAPTER XV.

NEGLIGENCE.

TABLE OF CASES.

THE LAW OF TORTS.

INTRODUCTORY CHAPTER.

The Antiquity of Torts:—The Recency of Text Books on Torts. Although the earliest form of legal liability, known to our Anglo-Saxon and Norman ancestors, was quite similar to the present tort,[1] legal text-books upon tort in English law are very modern. The earliest treatise of value was published in this country, in 1859,[2] and was followed the next year in England by a larger work,[3] which still maintains a leading place among the increasing multitude of books on this fascinating topic. It is true that an attempt was made, as early as 1720, to systematize the case law upon the subject, but it was not very successful.[4]

The volume has been dismissed by eminent authors with brief flings.[5] Perhaps it deserves their contemptuous comments. It is serviceable, however, as showing the modernness of this branch of English law and the antiquity of the principles upon which it rests. In comparison with recent treatises on Torts it appears fragmentary in the extreme. Although professing to be " a methodical collection of all the cases concerning actions on the case for torts and wrongs,"

[1] " To exact for all injuries both to person and property, a payment in money to the person injured, appears to have been the first form of legal liability for injuries to private persons alike in Greece, in Rome, and among the Teutonic Tribes." Markby's Elements of Law, § 600.

[2] Hilliard on Torts.

[3] Addison on Torts.

[4] The Law of Actions on the Case, for Torts and Wrongs; Being a Methodical Collection of all the Cases Concerning such Actions. (The name of the author is not given.)

[5] In the dedicatory letter to Justice Holmes, Sir Frederick Pollock refers to this book as " remarkable chiefly for the depths of historical ignorance which it occasionally reveals." The Law of Torts, First Ed., p. vi.

Mr. Bishop expressed the opinion that the book should be passed over as though it did not exist. **Non** Contract Law, § 3, n. 1.

it is limited to five topics. Actions for " Trover and Conversion of Goods," for " Malicious Prosecutions," for " Nuisances," for " Disceits and on Warranties," and " On the Common Custom against Carriers and Innkeepers," cover the entire field of Torts and Wrongs, according to the view of this anonymous author. We know that these were not the only actions for torts which were then in use, and the reports of which were then accessible to the student of English case law. Possibly, however, the five topics discussed in this volume embraced most of the cases which were deemed important, and covered the field of ordinary tort litigation of that period.

Certain it is, that the rules of English law relating to torts had not then been systematized, and that neither the bench nor the bar had any conception of a Law of Torts. They were familiar with various species of civil wrongs, such as assault and battery, false imprisonment, deceit, defamation, nuisance and the like, but they were entirely innocent of any knowledge of legal classification, which would unify these miscellaneous instances and reduce them to a well defined and " individual branch of the law."

Beginning of Modern Theory of Torts. Sir Frederick Pollock, writing in 1886,[6] declared that the really scientific treatment of the principles of torts " begins only with the decisions of the last fifty years." Fifteen years earlier, another writer had asserted that " the English lawyers had not yet made any attempt to define torts." [7] In 1882, an accomplished and learned judge [8] of the New York Court of Appeals opened a notable opinion with these words: " We have been unable to find any accurate and perfect definition of a tort. Between actions plainly *ex contractu* and those as clearly *ex delicto* there exists what has been termed a border-land, where the lines of distinction are shadowy and obscure, and the tort and the contract so approach each other, and become so nearly coincident as to make their practical separation somewhat difficult. The text-writers either avoid a definition entirely, or frame one plainly imperfect, or depend upon one which they concede to be inaccurate, but hold sufficient for judicial purposes."

[6] Pollock on Torts, Dedicatory Letter, p. vi.

[7] Markby's Elements of Law, § 670.

[8] Judge Finch in Rich v. New York Central Ry., 87 N. Y. 382.

Indefiniteness of the Term.　Although, during the last twenty years, text-books on torts have multiplied rapidly, and litigations involving the nature of a tort have been well-nigh innumerable, neither a complete theory of torts nor a perfect definition of a tort has yet been attained.　A very able and original writer thought to clear up all obscurity of the subject, by extending " torts to the natural partition line in the legal field, and making it Non-Contract Law."　In his opinion, " there is not in the entire law any other division so plain and distinct, so completely one subject, so absolutely governed by common fundamental principles, resting in natural reason and recognized by the courts from the earliest dawnings of the common law jurisprudence, and never lost sight of or questioned, as this of non-contract law."　These common fundamental principles he summarizes as follows : " In the whirl of life, each must strive to avoid injuring another ; then, when this endeavor is made, whether successfully or not, every man must bear without compensation whatever sufferings or losses come to him.　Rights of action proceed alone from violations of duty, never from misfortunes." [9]

Non-Contract Law.　Notwithstanding the very positive assurances of the author, the reader of this book, original as it is in many respects and valuable as it is throughout, will not discover that its scope is much more extensive than that of other leading treatises on torts, nor that all obscurity has vanished and a perfect and simple theory of torts has been presented.　Indeed, it is apparent from the author's summary of common, fundamental principles which has been quoted, that simplicity has been attained by resort to vague if not glittering generalities. ·

Thou Shalt Do no Hurt to Thy Neighbor.　Some years before Mr. Bishop set forth his theory of torts, Sir Frederick Pollock had declared that our law of torts, with all its irregularities, has for its main purpose nothing else than the development of this precept of Ulpian, *"alterum non laedere "*—" thou shalt do no hurt to thy neighbor."　At the same time he asserted that " a complete theory of torts is yet to seek."　He was not satisfied with so broad and vague a statement of general principles as that contained

---

[9] Commentaries on the Non-contract Law, and especially as to Common Affairs not of Contract, or the Every Day Rights and Torts. By Joel Prentiss Bishop, 1889, pp. iv., 616.

in Ulpian's precept. In the latest edition of this book,[10] the author discloses his dissatisfaction in the following paragraph, which did not appear in the first edition: "*Alterum non laedere* is to forbear from inflicting unlawful harm in general. As the English Church catechism has adopted Ulpian's words, it belongs to my duty towards my neighbor, to hurt nobody by word or deed. To be true and just in all my dealings. But neither the Latin nor English phrase is clear enough to bring out the real, fundamental distinctions implied in the fact that we recognize torts as forming an individual branch of the law." The distinguished author then proceeds to set forth those distinctions somewhat at length, and concludes his account of them with a summary of the ways in which a right of action for a tort can arise in our law, which covers a page and a half of the text.

Other Attempts at Simplification. Other writers have attempted to simplify this branch of the law by defining a tort as the violation of a right *in rem*,[11] and declaring that to avoid committing a tort one need only to forbear.[12] Such statements, admirable as they are for brevity and comprehensiveness, are inadequate, if not misleading.

Tort may be Negative.—Innkeeper. Not every tort involves an affirmative act. Omission may be tortious as truly as commission.[13] An honest and respectable traveler enters an inn, calls for lodging and refreshment and tenders the proper price therefor. The innkeeper has unoccupied rooms and abundant supplies, but ignores the guest's demand. He takes no affirmative action. He does not eject the guest, nor does he say a word, nor pay any attention to him. He is simply passive. This omission is an actionable tort. The law imposed upon the innkeeper a duty towards guests, which he has violated. That duty was to receive, and furnish food and lodging at reasonable prices to, all travelers presenting

[10] Pollock on Torts, Sixth Ed., pp. 2 and 19.

[11] Innes, Law of Torts, § 6.

[12] Austin, Jurisprudence, Lect. XIV.

[13] United Railways v. Deane, 93 Md. 619, 49 At. 923, 86 Am. St. R. 453 (1901); holding that the negligent failure or omission of railroad servants to protect a passenger from the violence of a drunken fellow-passenger, was an actionable tort. "In such cases," said the court, "the negligence for which the company is liable is not the tort of the fellow-passenger, but the negligent omission of the carrier's servants."

themselves in proper condition, so long as he had room and supplies.[14] It was an affirmative duty; a duty that was violated by omitting to act.[15]

But it may be said, that had the innkeeper forborne from taking up this semi-public vocation, his failure to receive and provide for the traveler would not have been tortious. Undoubtedly. So had he forborne from being born there would have been no tort by him. The act of becoming an innkeeper simply furnished an occasion for his tort. It had no causal connection with it. There was no element of wrongfulness in his taking up the occupation of innkeeper. His tort consisted solely in omitting to perform the affirmative duty of an innkeeper. His forbearance to act was tortious.

Other Examples of Negative Torts of torts of omission as distinguished from torts of commission—are afforded by failures to comply with statutory requirements. For instance, a statute imposes upon factory-owners the duty (which did not exist at common law) of attaching certain fire escapes to factories, that are more than three stories in height. The owner of such a factory makes no change in his building, fails to obey the statute. A fire occurs and some of his employees, who could have escaped without the smell of fire on their garments, had the statutory command been obeyed, are badly burned. His omission is tortious. He is liable to an action at law for damages to each of such injured employees.[16] He committed a tort by forbearing to act.

[14] White's Case, Dyer 158b (1693); Commonwealth v. Mitchell, Parsons' Cases (Pa.), 431 (1850); Watson v. Cross, 2 Duvall (Ky.), 147 (1865). In the last case it is said: "Appellant, being an innkeeper, was legally bound to receive and entertain all guests apparently responsible and of good conduct, who might come to his house, and if he refused to do so, he was liable alike to an indictment and an action by the party aggrieved." Atwater v. Sawyer, 76 Me. 539 (1884). In this case, plaintiff applied for dinner at defendant's inn and was refused. He recovered eight dollars damages.

[15] Hawthorne v. Hammond, 1 C. & P. 404 (1844). This was an action on the case for damages, by reason of not being admitted to defendant's inn at night, after defendant had retired. Plaintiff knocked on the door and called to defendant, who paid no attention to plaintiff's application. Parke, B., in substance charged the jury that if they found the noise was heard by defendant and implied that the persons who made it wanted to be admitted as guests, defendant's failure to admit them was a breach of his common law duty.

[16] Pauley v. Steam Gauge and

Tort may Violate Right in Personam. Equally unsound with the general proposition that we have just considered, is that other, (often linked with it) that a tort is a violation of a right *in rem.* Many, perhaps most, torts are of this character. On the other hand many a tort is a violation of a right *in personam.*[17]

Right of guest against Innkeeper. Such it is submitted is the

Lantern Co., 131 N. Y. 90, 29 N. E. 999 (1892). The court held that the statutory requirements (L. 1887, Ch. 462, § 10) "of fire escapes was for the direct and special benefit of the operatives in such factories, and intended for their protection—that the law of 1887 imposed a duty upon the owners or occupants of the prescribed class of factories, for an *omission* to perform which the operatives injured by the *omission* might recover damages."

In Parker v. Barnard, 138 Mass. 116, 119 (1883), the court said, "When, in the construction of a building the legislature sees fit to direct by statute that certain precautions shall be taken, or certain guards against danger provided, his unrestricted use of his property is rightfully controlled, and those who enter in the performance of a lawful duty, and are injured by the neglect of the party responsible, have just ground of action against him."

In Billings v. Breing, 45 Mich. 65 (1881), it appeared that the law made it incumbent on defendant to exhibit lights on his tugboat at night. He omitted to exhibit them, and such *omission* was held to be actionable negligence. The defendant's tort did not consist in running his tug at night, but in omitting to do what the law commanded him to do.

[17] " There are rights vested in certain determinate persons which are *in personam*, that is, which are available only against a determinate person or persons. Corresponding to them are duties laid on the determinate person or persons against whom the right avails as distinguished from the rest of the community. * * * These rights are sometimes acquired as the immediate consequence of duties imposed on determinate persons towards certain other determinate persons by whom they are acquired. The breach of the duty involves the violation of the right, and is a tort. * * * We have therefore two distinct sets of rights. The first, the three great fundamental rights, which are *in rem;* and which are rights not to be damaged in person, reputation, or property by any wrongful act; the duty being to forbear from violating them. The *injuria* is here found in the violating act causing the damage. The second, the special modifications of the three fundamental rights, which spring out of certain relations in respect of which the law fixes certain duties; the modifications being made in respect of certain given individuals on whom the duties, modified to correspond, are laid; being in respect of certain individuals, they are *in personam*." Piggott's Law of Torts, pp. 6, 13.

tort of the innkeeper in the case mentioned above. The traveler's right to entertainment is not a legal right available against all the world. He may be ever so honest and respectable, his wallet may be overflowing with money. He may be weary and hungry to fainting. But, he has no legal right to demand from any and every householder along his route lodging and refreshment. This right is available only against such persons as have voluntarily become innkeepers. Nor is it an absolute right against every innkeeper. Whether the traveler has a legal right to be received and cared for as a guest, depends upon the plight of the inn when he presents himself. If it is full of guests, the innkeeper may ignore the traveler's request for entertainment, and may even turn him curtly away, without violating any right of the jaded and famished traveler.[18]

Right of Shipper. Again, the tort committed by the common carrier, who neglects to receive or care for goods tendered to him for carriage, is not the violation of a right *in rem*. The right of the owner to have his goods carried is not one available against the world; it is available only against a particular person, who has voluntarily subjected himself to the common-law duty to receive and carry, by holding himself out as a common carrier of such goods.[19] Moreover, the right is not an absolute one, even against such a person. If the latter's means of transportation are fully occupied he may refuse the goods in question, without committing a tort.[20]

Yet again, the innkeeper, who fails to keep safely his guest's property committed to his care, is liable to a tort action, unless the loss is due to an act of God, or to the public enemy or the guest's

---

[18] Atwater v. Sawyer, 76 Me. 539 (1884); Regina v. Ivens, 7 C. & P. 213 (1885); Schouler on Bailments (3 Ed.), § 318.

[19] In Allen v. Sackrider, 37 N. Y. 341 (1867), it is said, " No one can be considered as a common carrier, unless he has in some way held himself out to the public as a carrier in such manner as to render himself liable to an action if he should refuse to carry for anyone

who wished to employ him." " In effect, refusing to enter into the appropriate contract is of itself a tort." Pollock, on Torts (6 Ed.), 513.

[20] Lovett v. Hobbs, 2 Shower, 127 (1681); Schouler on Bailments (3 Ed.) § 377. He may refuse, also, if a mob prevents him from doing business. Pittsburgh & C. Ry. v. Hollowell, 65 Ind. 188 (1879.

fault. Such, too, is the liability of the common carrier for goods which he has received for transportation. Torts of this kind are not violations of rights *in rem*. Neither the guest nor the goods owner has a right against the world, to have his property kept safely. If he delivers it to an ordinary bailee for hire, his right is to have it guarded with ordinary care.[21] Any loss or injury not chargeable to the active misconduct or the ordinary negligence of the bailee, must be borne by himself. On the other hand, the innkeeper or the common carrier who receives this property pursuant to his vocation becomes substantially the insurer of its safety.[22] As soon as the relationship between guest and innkeeper or carrier is created, the guest or shipper acquires a legal right against the particular innkeeper or carrier, to have this property kept safely. This relationship, it is to be borne in mind, is a conventional one; it is the result of a contract between the parties.[23] To say that the right which the common law confers upon the guest or the shipper, as an incident of such contract, is a right *in rem* is certainly to wrench that term from its true signification. The right of the guest or the shipper to have particular property kept safely by a particular innkeeper or carrier with whom he has contracted, partakes far more of the nature of a right *in personam,* than of a right *in rem*. The tort liability of the innkeeper or the carrier of goods insecurely kept, which have been committed to his care, is said to spring out of contract.[24] But for the contract between the parties, the omission of the carrier [25] or the innkeeper to save the property from harm,

[21] Maynard v. Buck, 100 Mass. 40 (1868); Hexamer v. Southal, 49 N. Y. L. 682 (1887).

[22] Mason v. Thompson, 9 Pick. 280, 20 Am. Dec. 471 (1830).

[23] Bradley Livery Co. v .Snook, 66 N. J. L. 654, 50 At. 358 (1901). Said the court in this case: "The liability of the innkeeper for the property of his guest placed in his care arises out of an express or an implied contract of bailment. Such contractual relation can only arise where it is apparent, under the facts, that such was the intention of the parties. A contract, of

course, may be implied from the circumstances, as well as established by an actual agreement. In order to raise an implied contract of liability on the part of an innkeeper for the goods of his guest lost or stolen, it must at least appear that the guest placed the same in his care and keeping."

[24] Rich v. New York Central Ry., 87 N. Y. 382 (1882); Hutchinson on Carriers (2 Ed.), §§ 738-740.

[25] Cf. Turner v. Stallibrass (1895), 1 Q. B. 56, holding that an action founded on the common law liability of a bailee is an action

unless that omission were willful or negligent, would not be tortious.

Agent as Tort Feasor. Of the same character is the tort of an agent who understates the price that has been offered for his principal's property, and appropriates to his own use the difference between the price stated and the price paid. Dealing with a case of this character, Chief Justice Holmes, speaking for the Supreme Judicial Court of Massachusetts, declared: " It is true that, but for the contract of agency, the concealment and misrepresentation might not be a tort. But there are other cases in which a tort is said to spring out of a contract.—Whether an act is tortious or not always depends upon the circumstances of course, and it hardly needs remark that the circumstance of confidential relations should give wrongful character to an act that in a different situation—for instance that of a buyer—would be untouched by the law." [26] In other words, the right of the principal which was violated by the agent was not a right *in rem,* but one *in personam*—a right born of the contract of agency between these two parties.

Torts Springing out of Contract. The same doctrine was

founded on tort, Collins, L. J., said: " An agreement of minds is presupposed in the case of any relation which brings about the common law liability of a bailee to his bailor. Where such relation is established, the result of the cases appears to be that, if the plaintiff can maintain his action by showing the breach of a duty arising at common law out of that relation, he is not obliged to rely on a contract within the meaning of the rule " (relating to costs under a modern statute).

[26] Emmons v. Alvord, 177 Mass. 466, 59 N. E. 126 (1901). In this case the agent told his principal that the best offer he could get for certain real estate of the principal was $3,000 cash and three lots of land. This offer was accepted by the principal, who deeded the real estate to the offerer and received the money and three lots aforesaid. In fact, the offer was $3,000 in cash and six lots, and the three lots not conveyed to the principal were conveyed by the offerer to a third person, who was supposed by the offerer to be an agent of the offeree, but who was a tool of the agent. Chief Justice Holmes' intimation is, that had a purchaser told the seller that he was buying to sell again, and that all he could get from a third party with whom he was treating for its purchase, was $3,000 and three lots, when in fact the third party was ready and willing to give $3,000 and six lots, and did give that price to the first purchaser for the property, such falsehood, though inducing the first seller to transfer the property for less than he could have obtained, had he stood out for more, would not have amounted to a tort.

laid down sixty years earlier, in a leading English case [26] by Chief Justice Tindal. " That there is a large number of cases in which the foundation of the action springs out of privity of contract between the parties, but in which, nevertheless, the remedy for the breach or non-performance is indifferently either assumpsit, or case upon tort, is not disputed. Such are actions against attorneys, surgeons, and other professional men, for want of competent skill or proper care in the service they undertake to render; actions against common carriers, against ship-owners on bills of lading, against bailees of different descriptions; and numerous other instances occur in which the action is brought in tort or contract, at the election of the plaintiff. And as to the objection, that this election is only given when the plaintiff sues for a misfeasance and not for a nonfeasance, it may be answered that in many cases it is extremely difficult to distinguish a mere nonfeasance from a misfeasance. But further, the action of case upon tort very frequently occurs where there is a simple non-performance of the contract, as in the ordinary instance of case against ship-owners, simply for not safely and securely delivering goods according to their bill of lading. * * * The principle in all these cases would seem to be that the contract creates a duty, and the neglect to perform that duty, or the nonfeasance, is a ground of action upon a tort.[28].

[27] Boorman v. Brown, 3 Q. B. (Ad. & E. N. S.) 511 (1842), affirmed in the House of Lords, II Cl. & F. I. (1844); Bretherton v. Wood, 3 Brod. & Bing. 54 (1821), accord.

[28] That the non-performance of a duty, imposed either by statute or by common law, subjects the non-feasor to a tort action was held in the following recent cases: Jones v. Rochester Gas & Electric Co., 168 N. Y. 65, 60 N. E. 1044 (1901),—an action for the statutory penalty, but the court declares that this was not plaintiff's sole means of redress. Defendant's refusal or neglect (see N. Y. Transportation Law § 65), to comply with plaintiff's demand for illuminating gas was a tort. Wamsley v. Atlas Steamship Co., 168 N. Y. 533; 61 N. E. 896 (1901). The Elizabeth, 114 Fed. R. 757 (1902). In St. Louis, Iron Mountain etc., Ry. v. Wilson, 70 Ark. 136; 66 S. W. 661 (1902), defendant's tort consisted in its failure to keep its passenger waiting-room properly heated in winter. In Missouri, Kans. etc. Ry. v. Wood, 95 Tex. 223; 66 S. W. 449 (1902), the company's tort was its failure to prevent a small-pox employee from escaping while delirious and infecting plaintiff. In Western Union Tel. Co. v. Snodgrass, 94 Tex. 284, 60 S. W. 308, 86 Am. St. R. 851 (1901), a telegraph company was held liable for failure promptly to deliver a message, even though no contract obligation was established;

CHAPTER II.

NATURE OF A TORT.

Its Chief Characteristics. Without attempting to frame a perfect definition of tort—a task which appears thus far to have been beyond the power of the English speaking lawyer—we shall be content with describing its leading characteristics. These may be stated briefly as follows:

A tort is an act or omission which unlawfully violates a person's right, created by the law, and for which the appropriate remedy is a common law action for damages by the injured person.

It will be observed that the right violated is private not public. This differentiates tort from crime. Again, the right is created by the law, not by the agreement of the parties. This is the broad distinction between tort and breach of contract. Still again, the violation of this legal right must be remediable by a common law action for damages. If the redress for the unlawful act or omission had to be sought in a court of equity, or of admiralty, or in an ecclesiastical tribunal, and depends upon principles peculiar to those jurisdictions, the wrong was not accounted a tort by English common law.[1] This limitation still attaches to the term, even in jurisdictions where ecclesiastical courts have been shorn of their cognizance of civil wrongs, and where the courts of common law and of equity have been consolidated. Let us consider these three peculiarities of tort more fully.

the court holding that the company was under a legal duty to receive and promptly deliver the message.

[1] Illustrations of such wrongs respectively are afforded by a breach of trust, refusal to pay salvage, adultery of husband or wife. It is to be borne in mind, however, that many torts were, and still are cognizable by admiralty courts, but the legal principles applicable to such cases are those of the common law. Cases of assault and battery, or other personal injury on board a ship on the high seas, are within the jurisdiction of admiralty courts, but they are decided in accordance with common law doctrines. See Stern v. La Campagnie Generale Transatlantique, 110 Fed. R. 996 (1901). The Willamette Valley, 71 Fed. 712 (1896).

Tort is distinguishable from crime. The same act or omission may subject the actor or the omittor to a criminal prosecution and to a civil action for damages. In other words, a single act or omission may unlawfully violate a private right and a public right. Its violation of the former is a tort: its violation of the latter is a crime. For instance, A, without justification or excuse attacks B and knocks him down. He has violated B's right to personal security and is liable to an action by him in tort for damages. He has also violated a right of the State, by his breach of the peace and by the injury inflicted upon one of its citizens, thus rendering himself liable to a criminal prosecution by the State.[2]

This differentiation of the tortious from the criminal characteristics of the same act is comparatively modern. " The early tendency was * * * to treat offenses against individuals, even when, like theft and homicide, they were a serious menace to the general welfare, as merely civil injuries to be compensated for by damages." [3] After the idea was clearly grasped that the same act might be injurious to the State as well as to the individual, and ought to subject the wrongdoer to criminal punishment as well as to the payment of damages to his victim, English Courts found themselves perplexed over the relation of these two sets of proceedings. Should the criminal prosecution have precedence over the civil action, or should each proceeding be allowed to progress without hindrance from the other?

Merger of Tort in Felony: In England. In the earliest reported case,[4] dealing with this question we have the following statement: " If a man beats the servant of J. S. so that he dies of the battery, the master shall not have an action against the other for

---

[2] " It is sometimes alleged by books of authority that the difference between a tort and a crime is a matter of procedure, the former being redressed by the civil, while the latter is punished by the criminal courts. But the distinction lies deeper, and is well expressed by Blackstone, who says that torts are an infringement or privation of the private or civil, rights belonging to individuals; crimes are a breach of public rights and duties which af- fect the whole community. The right which is violated by a tort is always a different right-from that which is violated by a crime. The person of inherence in the former case is an individual, in the latter case is the State." Holland's Jurisprudence, (9th. Ed.) pp. 311, 312.

[3] Holland's Jurisprudence, (9th Ed.) 357.

[4] Higgins v. Butcher, Yelv. 89, (1606).

the battery and loss of the service, because the servant dying of the extremity of the battery it is now become an offense to the crown, being converted into a felony, and that drowns the particular offense and private wrong offered to the master before, and his action is thereby lost." [5]

From this time on we find dicta in judicial opinions, in digests, and in text-books to the effect, that when an act constitutes a felony as well as a tort, the tort is merged in the felony. There is no express decision of an English Court enforcing this doctrine, however, and after undergoing several modifications,[6] " it seems, if not altogether exploded, to be only awaiting a decisive abrogation " in England.[7]

Same in America. It has never received judicial sanction in this country,[8] although judges have shown readiness to adopt a modification of the doctrine, viz. that all civil remedies in favor of a party injured by a felony are suspended until after the termination of a criminal prosecution against the offender.[9] They rested their decisions upon considerations of public policy, asserting that " the public good requires that offenders should be brought to justice; and if a civil remedy in favor of a party injured, is postponed until a public prosecution has terminated, he will be stimulated to effect this as soon as possible." [10] These reasons have not met

---

[5] According to the reports of this case in Noy. 13 and 2 Rolle's Abridg. 575, the only point decided was that an action of trespass for causing the death of plaintiff's wife, could not be maintained by the husband after her death, the cause of action having died with her.

[6] See Lord Blackburn's historical sketch of the doctrine: Wells v. Abrahams, L. R. 7 Q. B. 554, 560–563 (1876).

[7] Pollock On Torts, (6th Ed.) 198.

[8] As early as 1801 the legislature of New York enacted that the private remedy in tort should not be merged in, nor in any way affected by the felony, cl. 60 L. 1801, § 19. Continued in R. S. p. 111, ch. 4, T.

1, § 20, now repealed and continued by Penal Code, § 720, and by § 1899 of the Code of Civil Procedure; Mairs v. Bal. & O. Ry., 175 N. Y. 409, 67 N. E. 901 (1903).

[9] Talbot v. Frederickson, Metcalf's Yelverton, 90 (1813), a *nisi prius* decision of Chief Justice Sewall of Mass. In Boardman v. Gore, 15 Mass. 336, 338 (1819), Chief Justice Parker, doubted the propriety of this rule and in Boston & Worcester Ry. v. Dana, 1 Gray 83 (1854), the rule was rejected in Massachusetts.

[10] Foster v. The Commonwealth, 8 W. & S. (Pa.) 77 (1824); Ballew v. Alexander, 6 Humph. (Tenn.) 433 (1846).

with approval, however, and the great majority of our judicial tribunals have held that " for an act which happens to be both a public and private wrong the public and the party aggrieved each has a concurrent remedy, the former by indictment, and the latter by an action suited to the particular circumstances of his case." [11]

A distinguished Judge of the Court of Appeals of Virginia, after tracing the history of the rule of England, declared;" I am persuaded that the object of promoting the prosecution of crimes, would be more promoted by allowing the injured individual to prosecute his civil action uninterruptedly, and thus expose all the circumstances of the transactions to the officers of the law, who are bound *ex officio* to prosecute for the public, than by holding out strong inducements to both parties, to compound the felony, by throwing impediments in the way of the civil remedy." [12]   The Supreme Court of New Hampshire has characterized the English rule as one having no practical use in any country, and has asserted the belief " that if the civil action and the criminal prosecution go forward together, the public justice will not sustain any detriment whatever from that circumstance;" while " to compel the injured party to wait until the prosecution for the offence is ended before he can commence an action must be, as is very well known, in most cases to deny all remedy."[13]

The distinction between a tort and a breach of contract is broad and clear, in theory.   In practice, however, it is not always easy to determine whether a particular act or course of conduct subjects the wrongdoer to an action in tort, or merely to one for a breach of contract.   The test to be applied is the nature of the right which has been invaded.   If this right was created by the agreement of the parties, the plaintiff is limited to an action *ex contractu*.[14]   If it was created by law he may sue in tort.   A few cases in addition to those cited in the last note, will illustrate the difficulty experienced by lawyers in applying this test.

Plaintiff brought an action of tort in the nature of deceit, al-

---

[11] Boody v. Keating, 4 Greenleaf, (Me.) 164, 166 (1826).   This doctrine was abrogated by legislature in Maine.   See Statutes of Me., for 1844 c. 102.

[12] Allison v. Farmer's Bank, 6 Rand. (Va.) 204, 226 (1828).

[13] Pettingill v. Rideout, 6 N. H. 454, 456 (1833).

[14] Insurance Co. v. Randall, 74 Ala. 170, 178 (1883); Junker v. Fobes, 45 Fed. 840 (1891).

leging that he had been induced by false statements of the defendant to enter into a contract for building thirty miles of the Florida Railway. These statements were, that the defendant had purchased a certain quantity of rails at a certain price, and would sell them to plaintiff at the same price, if the latter would enter into the contract to build this section of the road. Plaintiff further alleged that defendant had not purchased any rails, and did not sell and did not intend to sell any rails to the plaintiff; that by reason of the contract into which the latter was induced to enter, he was obliged to purchase a larger number of rails at a higher price than that named by the defendant, to his great injury. Such allegations, the Court held,[15] did not state a cause of action in tort. The only legal right of plaintiff which defendant invaded was the right to have defendant supply him with the agreed quantity of rails at the agreed price. That was a contract right only. Had defendant supplied the rails at the agreed price, the false statement of defendant that he had bought the rails at a specified price would have worked no injury to the plaintiff. In other words, such statement, when separated from the promise, is seen to be legally unimportant and immaterial and not in any way the cause of damage to the plaintiff. Whatever legal injury the plaintiff sustained was due to defendant's non-performance of his agreement. Such non-performance was the only legal wrong committed by the defendant.

Bigby v. United States: At the opposite extreme from the foregoing case may be placed the following: The plaintiff, while on his way to the marshal's office in the post-office building in Brooklyn, was injured by the incompetence of the person in charge of the elevator. The building and elevator were owned by the United States, and the person in charge of the elevator was an employee of the federal government. Redress was sought against the United States, under a statute which permits recovery " upon any contract

---

[15] Dawe v. Morris, 149 Mass. 188, 21 N. E. 313, 14 Am. St. R. 404 (1889). In Union Pacific Ry. v. Barnes, 64 Fed. 80 (1894), it is said " an action for false and fraudulent representations can never be maintained upon a promise or a prophecy." In Syracuse Knitting Co. v. Blanchard, 69 N. H. 447, 43 At. 637 (1898), defendant's statement " I can safely promise you that our dealings, if you wish to continue them, will be more satisfactory than last season," was held to be a promise and not a tortious misrepresentation, cf. Industrial and General Trust Co. v. Tod, 170 N. Y. 233, 63 N. E. 285 (1902).

expressed or implied, with the government of the United States, or for damages, liquidated or unliquidated, in cases not sounding in tort." Plaintiff's theory was, that the United States entered into an implied contract [16] with him to carry him safely in the elevator, and for a breach of this obligation the government was liable in a contract action. But the court held that the plaintiff was a mere licensee; that the United States entered into no contract either expressed or implied to carry him safely; that whatever duty of care the United States owed to the plaintiff, or whatever right to care the plaintiff possessed against the United States was created by law; that the duty was the same as that imposed by law upon the owner of the building which he permitted the public to enter and use for the purpose for which it was intended—" the duty to use ordinary care that facilities offered to its licensees should be in a state of reasonable safety," that " a breach of such duty would constitute culpable negligence," and hence that plaintiff's cause of action must be in tort; that it could not be for a breach of contract.[17]

Plaintiff's Option to sue in Contract or Tort: Between the classes, of which the two preceding cases are representatives, is a numerous and extensive class, where the plaintiff is entitled to sue either in contract or in tort, because the defendant's act is an unlawful interference with the right of plaintiff which is created by agreement between them, and also with a right which is created by law.

---

[16] In United States v. Lynah, 188 U. S. 445, 23 Sup. Ct. R. 349 (1902), it is held that when the federal government appropriates property which it does not claim to own, there is an implied contract that it will pay the owner its value; while if it claims ownership of the thing appropriated its appropriation is a tort, citing for the last proposition, Langford v. U. S., 101 U. S. 345; Hill v. U. S., 149 U. S. 593, and Schillinger v. U. S., 155 U. S. 163.

[17] Bigby v. United States, 103 Fed. 597 (1900), 188 U. S. 400, 23 Sup. Ct. 468 (1902), cf. Stevenson v. Love, 106 Fed. 466 (1901), in which the court held that plaintiff's cause of action was for slander of title and not for breach of contract. So, if a common carrier receives A as a passenger and his luggage, pursuant to a contract with B for their transportation, A's action against the carrier for the loss of his luggage is properly in tort. Marshall v. York, Newcastle, Etc., Ry., 11 Com. Bench 655 (1851), cf. Gladwell v. Steggale, 5 Bing. N. C. 733 (1889), holding that an action by an infant against a physician for mal-practice, where the hiring was by the infant's mother, was properly *ex delicto.*

Several examples of this class have been given already, in discussing the liability of common carriers,[18] innkeepers,[19] and agents,[20] These could be multiplied many times; but a few additional illustrations will suffice for the present.

The bailee of a horse, which is injured through his negligence, may be sued either for breach of his contract to treat the horse with ordinary care or for breach of his legal duty to so treat him.[21] A bank, which fails to honor its customer's check without lawful excuse, breaks its contract with the customer and also violates a duty imposed upon it by law. Accordingly the customer may sue either on the contract or for the tort.[22] A grantee of land who, after giving a bond and mortgage on the premises to the grantor to secure a part of the purchase price, sells and conveys the land to a *bona fide* purchaser as unencumbered, and thus enables the latter to hold it free from the mortgage which had not been recorded, is of course liable in contract on the bond; but he is also liable in tort to the mortgagee for wrongfully depriving him of his lien on the land.[23] Yet again, the payee of a note induces the plaintiff to sign it as a co-principal with the original maker by promising not to so use it as to make plaintiff liable for its payment. Thereafter he does negotiate it before due to a *bona fide* purchaser, who compels plaintiff to pay the note. The payee has broken his promise to plaintiff, but he is also liable in tort for his fraudulent use of the note with its consequent damage to plaintiff.[24]

Advantage of Suing in Tort: When a person is entitled to the option of suing another either in contract or in tort, it is ordi-

---

[18] *Supra*, p. 7, citing Boorman v. Brown, 3 Q. B. (Ad. & E. N. S.) 511 (1842); Holden v. Rutland Ry., 72 Vt. 156, 47 At. 403 (1900).

[19] *Supra*, p. 4, citing Bradley Livery Co. v. Snook, 66 N. J. L. 654, 50 At. 358 (1901).

[20] *Supra*, p 9, citing Emmons v. Alvord, 177 Mass. 466, 59 N. E. 126 (1901).

[21] Pelton v. Nichols, 180 Mass. 345, 62 N. E. 1 (1902); Turner v. Stallibrass (1898), 1 Q. B. 56, 67 L. J. Q. B. 52.

[22] Davis v. Standard Nat. Bank, 50 App. Div. (N. Y.) 210 (1900); Atlanta Nat. Bank v. Davis, 96 Ga. 734, 23 S. E. 190, 51 Am. St. R. 139 (1895); Schaffner v. Ehrman, 139 Ill. 109, 28 N. E. 917 (1891); Patterson v. Marine Nat. Bk., 130 Pa. St. 419, 18 At. 632 (1889); Marzetti v. Williams, 1 B. & Ad. 415 (1830).

[23] Conley v. Blinerby, 20 Misc. (N. Y.) 371 (1899).

[24] Jones v. Crawford, 107 Ga. 325, 33 S. E. 51 (1889), cf. Met. Elevated Ry. v. Kneeland, 120 N. Y. 134, 24 N. E. 381 (1890); Nashville Lumber Co. v. Fourth Nat. Bk., 94 Tenn. 374, 29 S. W. 368 (1895).

narily to his advantage to elect the tort action. In the case of the bank above referred to, if the customer sues in tort, he is entitled to substantial damages without proof of actual damage [25] certainly if he is a trader,[26] while if he sues for a breach of contract to honor his check, his recovery will be limited to a nominal sum, unless he proves actual damage.[27] A plaintiff, suing in tort, may be entitled to arrest the defendant, or to attach his property, and, after judgment, to issue an execution against his body, when he could not have had recourse to any of these remedies, had he elected to sue in contract. Moreover, his right of action for breach of contract may be limited by some stipulation in the contract, which limitation he may escape by resorting to a tort action. For example, plaintiff shipped certain goods by an express company to one who had bought them on credit, accepting a bill of lading which limited the company's liability in case of loss to fifty dollars, at which the property, it was expressly declared, was valued by the contracting parties.[28] Learning that the consignee was insolvent, plaintiff gave notice of stoppage *in transitu* to the express company, but by reason of its negligent failure to properly notify the connecting carrier to whom it delivered them, the goods were not stopped and returned to plaintiff, but were handed over to the insolvent pur-

[25] Atlanta Nat. Bank v. Davis, 96 Ga. 334, 23 S. E. 190, 51 Am. St. R. 139 (1895), in which case plaintiff was awarded $200 as damages for the bank's careless refusal to pay a check of $12.48, although he gave no evidence of actual damage to his credit.

[26] Bank v. Milvain, 10 Vict. L. R. 3 (1884); Bank of Commerce v. Goos, 39 Neb. 437, 445, 23 L. R. A. 190 (1894); Svendsen v. State Bank, 64 Minn. 40, 65 N. W. 1086, 58 Am. St. R. 523 (1896); J. M. James Co. v. Continental Nat. Bank, 105 Tenn. 1, 58 S. W. 261 (1900); American Nat. Bank v. Morey, (Ky.), 69 S. W. 759 (1902). In the last case, the court held that plaintiff was not entitled to punitive damages, in absence of proof that the bank acted malici-ously.

[27] Brooke v. Tradesman's Nat. Bk., 69 Hun (N. Y.) 202 (1893); Buroughs v. Tradesman's Nat. Bk., 87 Hun 1 (1895).

[28] Rosenthal v. Weir, Pres'dt 170 N. Y. 148, 63 N. E. 65 (1902). It is to be noted that defendant's tort in this case was negative. "Defendant's line did not extend to Dallas, but ended at Kansas City, and the delivery complained of was made by the connecting company. Therefore, there was in fact no conversion by the defendant, but its fault lay in its failure to properly notify the connecting carrier. The action was, therefore, necessarily brought in its present form and not for conversion," (170 N. Y. p. 154).

chasers. For the damages thus sustained plaintiffs sued the company in tort, and were met with the limitation clause of the contract. But the court held, that as plaintiffs had founded their action on the tortious negligence of the defendant, and not on the contract of carriage, the contract limitation did not modify plaintiff's common law right to recover the actual value of the goods.

Disadvantage of Suing in Tort. While it is ordinarily advantageous to the plaintiff to elect a tort rather than a contract remedy, it is not always so. In some jurisdictions, it is held that a person, who has the option to sue a telegraph company in contract or in tort, for its failure to deliver a message, may recover damages for mental suffering and anguish if he chooses the contract action; while he may not, if he sues in tort, unless in the latter case he alleges and proves actual injury to his person, reputation or property.[29]

Again, a plaintiff may have greater difficulty in establishing his cause of action in tort, than in contract. Such was the experience of the plaintiff in a leading New York case [30]—a case worthy of careful study, not only because of this element, but because of its clear analysis of the nature of a tort. While the facts of the case are many and complicated, the following statement is believed to be full enough to bring out the point now under consideration.

Rich v. Railroad. Plaintiff was the owner of land near defendant's depot on Main Street in the City of Yonkers; and also of land on the Nepperhan river. Defendant changed its depot to another part of the City, thus depreciating the value of plaintiff's Main Street property, which was heavily mortgaged. It wished to dispense with a draw over the Nepperhan and substitute for it a solid bridge. Plaintiff objected to this unless defendant paid him for the damage the bridge would inflict upon his Nepperhan property. Defendant informed plaintiff that unless he consented to the construction of the permanent bridge, it would continue its depot at the new site. Plaintiff was thus forced to choose between surrendering his riparian rights on the Nepperhan, and allowing his Main Street property to be lost by depreciation and mortgage

[29] Western Union Tel. Co. v. Krichbaum, 132 Ala. 535, 31 So. 607 (1902); West. U. T. Co. v. Wilson, 93 Ala. 32, 9 So. 414, 30 Am. St. R. 23 (1890). This is another example of a negative tort.

[30] Rich v. New York & C. Ry., 87 N. Y. 382 (1882), cf. Marten v. Reilly, 109 Wis. 464, 84 N. W. 840 (1901).

foreclosure. He chose the former alternative, and entered into a contract with defendant, by which he surrendered all riparian rights, in consideration of its agreement, " as soon as practicable, and within a reasonable time to build and forever maintain its principal passenger depot for Yonkers " on the Main Street site. Defendant proceeded to build the depot, and, a few months later had it ready for use. Meantime, it had asked the City of Yonkers for permission to close Main Street and to fence in its new depot. Plaintiff insisted that this change would damage his property to the extent of fifty thousand dollars, and the City refused defendant's request, because of the heavy damages the City would have to pay. Defendant then announced, that it would never occupy the new depot for passenger use, until the permission was granted. It then, according to plaintiff's allegations, planned a fraudulent scheme for the accomplishment of its purpose. This scheme included a deliberate breach of its contract to restore the depot to Main Street; a public refusal to occupy and use it in order to depreciate plaintiff's mortgaged property and make the mortgagee feel insecure; and also a direct instigation of the latter, by the defendant, to foreclose the mortgage, cut off plaintiff's interest in the property and execute a release from damages. As soon as this scheme was consummated, and the permission was granted by the City of Yonkers, defendant opened and used its new depot.

That the defendant had broken its contract with plaintiff was clear. Had the latter sued for such a breach, the task of proving his case would have been easy. He chose, however, to sue in tort, and found his way beset with difficulties. The trial court refused to permit him to prove the contract or its breach, because he was not suing on the contract. This ruling was approved by the general term. It was declared erroneous, however, by the Court of Appeals, which explained the theory of the Complaint and set forth the plaintiff's right thereunder as follows: " There was here, on the theory of the Complaint, something more than a mere breach of contract. That breach was not the tort; it was only one of the elements which constituted it. Beyond that and outside of that, there was said to have existed a fraudulent scheme and device by means of that breach to procure the foreclosure of the mortgage at a particular time and under such circumstances as would make that foreclosure ruinous to the plaintiff's rights, and remove him as an obstacle by causing him to lose his property, and thereby his means of resistance to the purpose ultimately sought. In other words, the necessary theory of the complaint is, that a breach of contract may be so intended and planned; so purposely fitted to time, and circumstances, and conditions; so inwoven into a scheme of oppression and fraud; so made to set in motion innocent causes which otherwise would not operate, as to cease to be a mere breach of contract, and become, in its association with the attendant circumstances, a tortious and wrongful act or omission. It may be granted that an omission to perform a contract obligation is never a tort, unless that omission is also an omission of a legal duty.[31] But such legal duty may arise, not merely out of certain relations of trust and confidence, inherent in the nature of the contract itself, but may spring from extraneous circumstances, not constituting elements of the contract as such, although connected with and dependent upon it, and born of that wider range of legal duty which is due from every man to his fellow, to respect his rights of property and person, and refrain from invading them by force or fraud. The duty and the tort grow out of the entire range of facts of which the breach of contract was but one."

Extending the Area of Tort. The case, which we have stated thus at length, marks an important advance in the progress of the law of torts.[32] Had it come before a common law tribunal, a century ago, there is little doubt that the ruling of the trial Court would have been affirmed. Certainly the decision of the Court of Appeals would have amazed the anonymous author of " The Law of Actions on the Case for Torts and Wrongs.[33] The lack of precedent coupled with plaintiff's acknowledged right of action ᐟ for breach of contract would have been powerful arguments against the plaintiff.[34] At present, neither lack of precedent nor the fact that

---

[31] In Jones v. Stanly, 76 N. C. 355 (1877), a recovery was allowed against the defendant for $3,000 damages, for maliciously inducing a railroad corporation, of which he was President, to break the contract to transport certain freight for plaintiff.

[32] Oliver v. Perkins, 92 Mich. 304, 52 N. W. 609 (1892), accord.

[33] Referred to *supra*, p. 1, as published A. D. 1720.

[34] Cf. Sheehorn v. Darwin, 1 Treadway (S. C.) 196 (1812), in which the judge said, " I have never read or heard of such an action; though such occurrences must frequently take place, nor does it bear any analogy to cases quoted. * * * The Court will not be induced to

plaintiff may bring a contract action is considered a serious obstacle to the maintenance of an action in tort.

For example, plaintiff was induced to marry a woman by defendant's representations that she was virtuous and respectable. In fact she was pregnant at the time by defendant, and, within a few months after the marriage, gave birth to a child of which defendant was the father. Plaintiff sued defendant for damages, and was met with the defense, among others, that no precedent could be cited for the action. This was admitted, but the New York Court of Appeals declared, " If the most that can be said is that the case is novel, and is not brought plainly within the limits of some adjudged case, we think such fact is not enough to call for a reversal of the judgment." The Court then proceeded to sustain plaintiff's recovery on the ground that his right as husband to the conjugal fellowship and society of a virtuous wife had been wrongfully invaded by defendant; that such conduct by defendant was a fraud upon plaintiff resulting in damage to him.[35]

Plaintiff Must Show Breach of Legal Duty. While Courts are not dismayed by a want of precedent from sustaining novel tort actions, they do insist, that the plaintiff's statement of his cause of action shall disclose a legal right on his part which has been wrongfully invaded by the defendant. Or, to put it in another way, they insist upon the plaintiff's showing that defendant's alleged misfeasance or nonfeasance was a breach of legal duty which he owed to plaintiff. Accordingly, a servant cannot maintain a tort action against his master for refusing to continue him in his employ, after the expiration of their contract, nor for refusing to give him a

---

establish a new form of action, without manifest necessity, and none such appears in this case." In Murray v. South Car Ry., McMullan Law, (S. C.) 385, 36 Am. Dec. 268, the majority opinion bases the decision (that a master is not liable to a servant for the injuries of a fellow servant) chiefly upon want of precedent.

[35] Kujek v. Goldman, 150 N. Y. 178, 44 N. E. 773, 34 L. R. A. 157, 55 Am. St. R. 670 (1896). The reason-

ing of this case is adopted and followed in Graham v. Wallace, 63 N. Y. Supp. (97 N. Y. St. Rep.) 372 (1900), where a female ward, on attaining her majority, was allowed to maintain an action in her own behalf against her personal guardian for damages for her seduction by him, when she was under the statutory age of consent, although the court found " the action without precedent." p. 373.

certificate of character.[36] In another case, plaintiff gave to an officer a valid process to serve on an actor. The officer entered defendant's theater for the purpose of serving the process, but defendant forbade his going to the stage to make personal service, and he returned the process unserved. It was held[37] that as the officer had the legal right to break the door to the stage as well as to command sufficient force to enter, the cause of the plaintiff's injury, if any, was not defendant's refusal, but the officer's failure to do his duty.

Still again, it is not the legal duty of a steam surface railroad company to expressly notify passengers that a train has stopped. If notice is given that a train is approaching a station, which is its "last stop," and where all passengers are to alight, anyone leaving the train before it stops acts at his peril. It is the duty of the Company not to mislead the passenger, by announcing that it is safe for him to alight when in fact it is unsafe;[38] but it is the passenger's duty to discover whether the train has come to a stop or not.

False Statements Causing Damage. Not every false statement, made by one person which causes injury to another, constitutes an actionable tort. If it did, "a man might sue his neighbor for any mode of communicating erroneous information, such for example, as having a conspicuous clock too slow, since plaintiff might be thereby prevented from attending to some duty or acquiring some benefit." A class of false representations which have been held to have no legal effect, are those by which one excites "another to believe that he intends to make him his heir and then leaves his property away from him. Though such conduct may

---

[36] Cleveland & C. Ry. v. Jenkins, 174 Ill. 398, 51 N. E. 811 (1898); New York & C. Ry. v. Schaffer, 65 Ohio St. 414, 62 N. E. 1034 (1902). Nor does the law impose upon an employer the duty of protecting his employee from the violence of a mob of strikers, Lewis v. Taylor Coal Co., 112 Ky. 845, 66 S. W. 1044 (1902).

[37] Paulton v. Keith, 23 R. I. 164, 49 At. 635 (1901), cf. Clark v. Gay, 112 Ga. 777, 38 S. E. 81 (1901), where plaintiff sued for the value of

a house, which he declared had become worthless to him, because defendant had murdered one of plaintiff's servants in it; and the complaint was held not to state a cause of action.

[38] Mearns v. The Central Ry. of N. J., 163 N. Y. 108, 57 N. E. 292 (1900), cf. Bridges v. North London Ry. Co. L. R., 7 H. L. 213 (1874); Filer v. N. Y. Cent. Ry., 49 N. Y. 47 (1872); Robson v. North Eastern Ry. Co., 2 Q. B. D. 85 (1876).

inflict greater loss on the sufferer than almost any breach of contract, and may involve greater moral guilt than many common frauds, it involves no legal consequences, unless the person making the representation not only excites an expectation that it will be fulfilled, but legally binds himself to fulfill it." [39]   Much less will blundering but honest advice, given gratuitously to one who is erecting a structure, create a legal liability against the adviser who acts as a mere volunteer.[40]   Breach of moral duty may not be a tort.   It is a breach of legal duty only which gives rise to a tort action.   And this is much narrower than moral duty.   " If I know that a villain intends to defraud or in any way injure my neighbor, it is doubtless my duty, as a good citizen, and as a Christian man, to put him on his guard.   But there is no rule of law which renders me liable for his loss in case of my neglect of duty.   It is a moral duty simply; not one recognized and enforced by law." [41]

Waiving Tort and Suing in Contract.   In certain cases the victim of a tort may sue the wrongdoer in a contract action, although no contract exists between them.   For example X takes Y's horse and sells it without the latter's consent.   Y has his option to sue X in tort for the conversion of the animal, or to waive the tort and sue in contract for the proceeds of the sale.[42]   The latter form of action was devised for " the undisguised purpose of giving a better and more convenient remedy " [43] to the injured person than his

---

[39] Alderson v. Maddison, 5 Exch. D. 293, 296 (1880), cf. Hutchins v. Hutchins, 7 Hill (N. Y.) 104 (1845). Here the defendants, by false representations concerning the plaintiff, induced a third party to revoke his will, devising valuable property to plaintiff, and to execute another, depriving him of all the benefits which would have accrued under the first will. Yet it was held that the plaintiff had sustained no legal harm—he had no legal interest in the property mentioned in the first will—nothing but a mere naked possibility " which is altogether too shadowy and evanescent to be dealt with by courts of law." Also, Dudley v. Briggs, 141 Mass. 582

(1886), defendant falsely represented that plaintiff would not publish a directory of Bristol County in 1885, and thus induced third persons to advertise in and subscribe for defendant's directory. As a result plaintiff gave up the publication of the directory, *held* plaintiff's intention to publish a directory was not property, and no legal right of his was invaded by defendant.

[40] McCausland v. Cresap, 3 Greene (Ia.) 161, 169 (1851).

[41] Ohio & C. Ry. Co. v. Kasson, 37 N. Y. 218, 224 (1867).

[42] Howe v. Clancy, 53 Me. 130 (1865).

[43] Pollock on Torts (6th Ed.) 520.

tort action. If X died after converting the horse and before suit was brought by Y, the latter would be met in a tort action with the defense that the wrong done by X had died with him.[44] Y was therefore allowed to sue the personal representative of X in a contract action for the value of the horse, upon the fiction of an implied promise by X to pay the amount, as money had and received by him to Y's use. Speaking of this form of action, Lord Mansfield laid down the rule in a leading case [45] as follows; " If the defendant be under an obligation, from the ties of natural justice, to refund; the law implies a debt and gives this action, founded in the equity of the plaintiff's case as it were upon a contract, *quasi ex contractu,* as the Roman law expresses it."

Some of the reasons for encouraging this form of action are stated by Lord Mansfield as follows:[46] " One great benefit which arises to suitors from the nature of this action is that the plaintiff need not state the special circumstances from which he concludes that, *ex aequo et bono,* the money received by the defendant, ought to be deemed as belonging to him: that he may declare generally that the money was received to his use; and make out his case at the trial. This is equally beneficial to the defendant. It is the most favorable way in which he can be sued; he can be liable no further than the money he has received; and against that may go into every equitable defense upon the general issue; he may claim every equitable allowance; he may prove a release without pleading it; in short, he may defend himself by everything which shows that the plaintiff *ex aequo et bono,* is not entitled to the whole of his demand or to any part of it."

Distinction between Quasi-Contract and True Contract. The cases in which an injured party has an option to sue in tort or in quasi-contract, are to be distinguished from those where his option is between a tort action and one for the breach of a true contract.[47] Failure to observe this distinction has led some eminent

[44] This defense was based on the common law maxim; *Actio personalis moritur cum persona.*

[45] Moses v. Macferlan, 2 Burr. 1005, 1008 (1760). The plaintiff in this case had been compelled, by defendant's fraudulent use of promissory notes made by plaintiff, to pay a certain sum of money to defendant, and the court held that he was entitled to maintain this action for the recovery of the money so paid.

[46] Ibid. 1010.

[47] Supra p. 16, and Boorman v. Brown, 3 Q. B. (Ad. & E. N. S.) 511 (1842), there cited.

judges to unsound conclusions. For example, it has been held that if an owner of goods, wrongfully converted by several persons, sues one of them in quasi-contract for their value, he thereby makes a final election to treat the transaction as a sale of the goods to such defendant, and cannot subsequently sue the others for "conversion."[48] In such a case the conversion ought not to be deemed any the less a tort, because a legal fiction permits the owner to sue in assumpsit. There was in fact no sale to the defendant. Indeed, the plaintiff in his quasi-contract action alleges and proves conversion by the defendant. The tort is the very foundation of the action, and what the plaintiff waives, when suing in assumpsit, is more properly described as damages for the conversion, than the tort itself. His election is simply between remedies against this defendant for an act done, and should leave his rights against the other wrongdoers unimpaired, until he has obtained legal satisfaction for the wrong.[49]

It will be noticed that Lord Mansfield limited the right to waive tort and sue in contract to cases where the defendant is bound by "the ties of natural justice to refund" to the plaintiff. He does not intimate that the obligation of a tort-feasor to compensate his victim for injuries inflicted, can be treated as implying a promise to pay damages, and thus be made the basis of a contract action. Nor has a plaintiff ever succeeded in waiving a pure tort, which did not in any way unjustly enrich the defendant, and in maintaining a contract action for the damages.[50] In the Louisiana and Missouri cases,

---

[48] Terry v. Munger, 121 N. Y. 161; 24 N. E. 272 (1890); Carroll v. Fethers, 102 Wis. 436; 78 N. W. 604 (1889).

[49] Huffman v. Hughlett, 11 Lea (Tenn) 549 (1883). Keener, Quasi Contracts, Chapter 3. The learned author in criticising Terry v. Munger, *supra*, says: "Now, every one knows that when one man tortiously takes the goods of another, there is no sale between the parties; and yet the highest court of New York gravely asserts that there was. In other words, a fiction to which it was no longer necessary to resort in

New York, in order to give a remedy, is there resorted to, to deny a right; and the court says there is no tort where but for the proof of a tort there could have been no recovery against anyone. The decision will probably never be cited as illustrating the maxim, *In fictione juris subsistit equitas*," at p. 212.

[50] Bigby v. United States, 188 U. S. 400, 23 Sup. Ch. 468 (1902). At p. 409, Harlan, J. says. "The plaintiff cannot by the device of waiving the tort committed by the elevator operator make a case against the

cited in the last note, the plaintiff had been induced by the false representations of defendant's intestate, that he was unmarried, to marry him and live with him as his wife. Discovering the deceit after the wrongdoer's death, the plaintiff was held entitled to maintain an action against his estate for the value of the services rendered him, to the extent that she could show that " he was made richer, or his circumstances improved " thereby.[51]

Quasi-Delict. The law of Scotland, founded as it is upon the civil law, recognizes not only quasi-contracts, but also quasi-delicts. " Delicts proper," said Lord Watson, in deciding a Scotch case at the bar of the House of Lords, " embraces all breaches of the law which expose their perpetrator to criminal punishment. The term quasi-delict is generally applied to any violation of the common or statute law, which does not infer criminal consequences, and does not consist in the breach of any contract express or implied. Cases may and do often occur in which it is exceedingly difficult to draw the line between delicts and quasi-delicts. The latter class, as it has been developed in the course of the present century, covers a great variety of acts and omissions, ranging from deliberate breaches of the law, closely bordering upon crime, to breaches comparatively venial and involving no moral delinquency."[52]

In Louisiana, whose legal rules are also founded on those of the civil law, quasi-offense is used in much the same sense as quasi-

Government of implied contract. A party may in some cases waive a tort * * * but it has been well said that a right of action in contract cannot be created by waiving a tort; and the duty to pay damages for a tort does not imply a promise to pay them, upon which assumpsit can be maintained," citing Cooper v. Cooper, 147 Mass. 370, 373 (1888). The decision in the latter case is ably criticized in Keener's Quasi Contracts, pp. 321–325; and is *contra* to Fox v. Dawson, 8 Martin, 94 (4 La. 47) (1820), and Higgins v. Breen, 9 Mo. 493 (1845); but the language, quoted by Mr. Justice Harlan, is unexceptionable when applied to such a case as he was considering. See the facts stated *supra*, p. 15.

[51] In some states, legislation has authorized persons injured by the fraud or deceit of another to sue in assumpsit, for the damages caused by the injury, and expressly declares, " that a promise to pay such damages shall be implied by law." See Mich. Compiled Laws, §§ 10, 421, applied in In re Pennewill, 119 Fed. 139 (1902).

[52] Palmer v. Wick &c. Company (1894), A. C. 318, 326; 6 Rep. 245; 71 L. T. 168. In this case the quasi delict consisted in negligently supplying and using a defective tackle-block.

delict in Scotland. "Offenses," said the Supreme Court of the State, "are those illegal acts which are done wickedly and with the intent to injure, while quasi-offenses are those which cause injury to another, but which proceed only from error, neglect or imprudence." [53]

Quasi-Tort. The term quasi-tort appears to be finding its way into our legal nomenclature, but not at all as a synonym of quasi-delict or quasi-offense. In a recent English text-book [54] it is said "Suppose a solicitor be employed to transact certain business, and he does not transact it, or does it negligently. In that case the action aganist him might be either an action *ex contractu,* for breach of contract, or an action *ex delicto,* for breach of duty in not transacting, or in transacting negligently, the business which he had undertaken. Cases of this kind are classified by some writers as quasi torts." In this sense the term has been used by Lord Justice Lindley, in a case where he was called upon to decide whether the action was founded upon contract or tort.[55] This usage, however, has not commended itself to the judiciary either in England or in the United States.

---

[53] Edwards v. Turner, 6 Rob. (La.) 382 (1844). The quasi-offense in this case was the wrongful seizure, under a writ of attachment against a third party of plaintiff's steamboat.

[54] Ringwood, Outlines of the Law of Torts, p. 6 (London, 1898).

[55] Taylor v. Manchester & C. Ry. 11 Times Law Rep. 27 (1894), 43 W. R. 120, 71 L. T. 596, 64 L. J. Q. B. 6 (1895), 1 Q. B. 134.

CHAPTER III.

HARMS THAT ARE NOT TORTS.

§ I. HARM MUST BE UNLAWFUL.

If the gist of tort consists in the unlawful invasion of a legal right,[1] we shall not be surprised to find that one person may inflict harm upon another, without committing a tort. The famous maxim of the Roman Law—*sic utere tuo ut alienum laedas*—is not a prohibition of every sort of harm, but only of unlawful harm.[2] A learned English judge once characterized the maxim as " mere verbiage," adding: " A party may damage the property of another when the law permits; and he may not when the law prohibits; so that the maxim can never be applied till the law is ascertained; and when it is, the maxim is superfluous." [3] Whether this irreverent fling at a time-honored maxim was justified or not, the learned judge was quite right in asserting that a party may damage another in person or property without liability to a tort action, provided the law permits it. Let us consider, briefly, some of the typical classes of harm that are not torts.

Arrest of Innocent Person. We shall see in a later chapter, that our law guards with special jealousy the right of personal liberty; yet frequently it permits an innocent person to be arrested and imprisoned, and denies him any redress for the harm thus inflicted. For example, a murder has been committed, and X has reasonable cause to believe that Y is the murderer; the common law permits X to arrest Y and hale him before a magistrate, in the character of imprisoned murderer. Even though Y is absolutely innocent, and though such arrest and charge may cause Y a heavy money loss as well as injure his standing in the community, X has not committed a tort against him.[4] He must bear the loss, as one

---

[1] *Supra*, chap. 11 § 1. [2] *Ante* p. 4.
[3] Bonomi v. Backhouse, E. B. & E. 622 (1858); Erle, J. at p. 643.
[4] Beckwith v. Philby, 6 B. & C. 635 (1827). The common law rule stated in the text has been modified

of the incidents of life in organized society. His right to personal liberty is temporarily sacrificed to the higher right of the public security.

§ 2. DEFAMATION BY LEGISLATORS.

Members of Parliament in England, and Members of Congress and of State Legislatures in this country, are not to be questioned in any other place, for any speech or debate.[5] While this exemption from liability for the defamation of another is guaranteed to legislators by constitutional provisions in express terms, it rests upon well-established principles of the common law. It is not accorded to legislators for their individual benefit, " but to support the rights of the people, by enabling their representatives to execute the functions of their office without fear of prosecution, civil or criminal." [6] The privilege may be abused, and a private citizen may have his reputation basely defamed without any pecuniary recompense or legal redress. It is true, the house of which the defaming speaker is a member, may force him to retract the slanderous statement on pain of expulsion. But even if it takes no such action, and leaves the private citizen to bear without mitigation the stigma cast upon him, and to sustain any special damage caused to him, it is but one of many cases where " a private benefit must submit to the public good. The injury to the reputation of a private citizen is of less importance to the commonwealth, than the free and unreserved exercise of the duties of a representative, unawed by the fear of legal prosecution."

§ 3. JUDICIAL OFFICERS' EXEMPTION.

Similar considerations of public policy operate to exempt judicial

in some of our states by statute. For example in New York, a private person may arrest another only " for a crime committed or attempted in his presence; or when the person arrested has committed a felony, although not in his presence." Code of Crim. Proc. § 183.

[5] Bill of Rights, 1 W. & M. Sess. 2 c. 2; U. S. Const. Art. 1, § 6; see similar clauses in various state constitutions.

[6] Coffin v. Coffin, 4 Mass. 1, 28 (1808). In this case defendant charged plaintiff with having robbed a bank. As this charge was not made while acting as a member of the Massachusetts legislature, it was held that defendant was not within the exemption.

officers from tort liability to persons, harmed by their mistakes, and even by their corrupt misconduct [7] in the performance of their judicial function. "Such an exemption is absolutely essential to the very existence, in any valuable form, of the judicial office itself; for a judge could not be either respected or independent, if his motives or conclusions, could be put in question at the instance of every disappointed suitor." [8]

In order to entitle a judicial officer to this exemption, however, it must apear that his mistake or misconduct occurred during a judicial proceeding and was a part of it. If a magistrate should of his own motion, without oath or complaint being made to him, and without color of legal authority, issue a warrant and cause the arrest of an innocent person, the one so illegally imprisoned could maintain a tort action against him. [9] The act would not be a judicial act. It is the individual and not the magistrate who acts in such a case. "When there is no jurisdiction at all, there is no judge: the proceeding is as nothing" [10] has long been the accepted rule.

[7] Anderson v. Gorrie, (1895), 1 Q. B. 668. "By the common law of England no action will lie against a judge for acts done in the exercise of his judicial office." Dixon v. Cooper, 109 Ky. 29, 58 S. W. 437 (1900).

[8] Grove v. Van Duyn, 44 N. J. L. 654, 42 Am. R. 648 (1900). In Yates v. Lansing, 5 Johns, (N. Y.) 282, 291 (1810), Kent. Ch. J. said: "The doctrine which holds a judge exempt from civil suit or indictment, for any act done or omitted to be done by him, sitting as judge, has a deep root in the common law. It is to be found in the earliest judicial records, and it has been steadily maintained, by an undisturbed current of decision, in the English courts, amid every change of policy, and through every revolution of government." This view was approved by the court of errors, in the same case on appeal, 9 Johns. 395 (1811), and the following American

decisions in accord were cited: Lining v. Bentham, 2 Bay (S. C.), (1796). Brodie v. Rutledge, 2 Bay (S. C.) 69 (1796); Phelps v. Sill, 1 Day, (Conn.) 315 (1804). In a few states there is a disposition to limit judicial immunity to mistakes made in good faith. See Gregory v. Brown, 4 Bibb. (Ky.) 28 (1815); Morgan v. Dudley, 18 B. Mon. 711 (1857); Hoggett v. Bigley, 6 Humph. (Tenn.) 236 (1845); Cope v. Ramsey, 2 Heisk. (Tenn.) 197 (1870). The last two cases have recently been limited to justices of peace, and applied to them because they are not subject to impeachment,in Tennessee: Webb v. Fisher, 109 Tenn. 101; 72 S. W. 110, 60 L. R. A. 791 (1903).

[9] Glazer v. Hubbard, 102 Ky. 69, 42 S. W. 1114 (1897); State v. McDaniel, 78 Miss. 1, 27 So. 994 (1900).

[10] Perkins v. Proctor, 2 Wils, 382. 384 (1768), S. P. in Church v. Fearne

Lange v. Benedict. A modern case declares: " It is plain that the fact that a man sits in the seat of Justice, though having a clear right to sit there, will not protect him in every act which he may choose or chance to do there: Should such an one, rightfully holding a court for the trial of a civil action order the head of a bystander to be stricken off, and be obeyed, he would be liable." [11] But, in actual practice, the question is not often as simple as in the supposititious case, just put. While it is generally agreed that the test of a judicial officer's liability to civil suit is, whether the act complained of was a matter within his jurisdiction as judge, the courts have had no little difficulty in applying the test.[12] However, the view which prevails generally has been set forth in a well considered opinion of the New York Court of Appeals as follows: In order to exempt a judge from tort liability for misconduct, it must appear that when he acted, " he had judicial jurisdiction of the person acted upon, and of the subject matter as to which it was done. Jurisdiction of the person is when the individual acted upon is before the judge, either constructively or in fact, by reason of the service upon him of some process known to the law, and which has been duly issued and executed." Jurisdiction of the subject matter is the power to inquire and adjudge, whether the facts of a particular case make that case a proper one for judicial consideration by the judge before whom it is brought.[13]

Applying that view to the case then before the court it was held

---

75 Conn. 350; 53 At. 955 (1903).

[11] Lange v. Benedict, 73 N. Y. 12, 29 Rm. R. 80, 18 A. L. J. 11 (1878); citing Beaurain v. Sir William Scott, 3 Camp. 338 (1813), where a judge of the ecclesiastical court in England, excommunicated one for refusing to obey an order made by him, that the person become guardian *ad litem* for an infant son.

[12] Piper v. Pearson, 2 Gray (Mass.) 120 (1854); Pratt v. Gardner, 2 Cush. (Mass.) 63 (1848); Holden v. Smith, 14 Q. B. (A. & E. N. S.) 841 (1850); Patzack v. Von Gerichten, 10 Mo. App. 424 (1891; Vaughan v. Congdon, 56 Vt. 111,

48 Am. R. 758, 30 A. L. J. 289 (1883)—see dissenting opinion in this case; Austin v. Vrooman, 128 N. Y. 229, 28 N. E. 477, 44 A. L. J. 424, 14 L. A. 138, and note (1891).

[13] Lange v. Benedict, 73 N. Y. 12, 29 Am. R. 80, 18 A. L. J. 11 (1878). The decision is criticised in a learned article on the " Liability of Officers acting in a judicial capacity," by Arthur Biddle, Esq. 15 Am. L. Rev. 427 (1881). Mr. Biddle contends that the true rule is that a judge enjoys immunity from action only so long as he does not exceed his jurisdiction.

that the defendant was exempt from liability to the plaintiff in tort, although the Supreme Court of the United States had ruled, that defendant had imposed the sentence of imprisonment for one year upon plaintiff without authority; and had discharged plaintiff from such erroneous imprisonment. As Judge Benedict imposed the sentence while holding a term of the United States Circuit Court; as plaintiff was before the court under a valid process, and as the question, whether any sentence could be pronounced against him by that court, at that time, was one that he was then and there bound by his judicial duty to decide, his decision was a judicial act, and although erroneous and harmful to plaintiff was not an actionable tort.

Grove v. Van Duyn. The same doctrine was applied by the Court of Errors & Appeals of New Jersey, in a carefully reasoned case already cited.[14] Plaintiff was arrested under a warrant issued by defendant Stout, as justice of the peace, and was committed to jail by the justice on a sworn complaint charging him with forcibly and unlawfully carrying off a quantity of corn stalks from certain lands. The complaint was made under a statute which declared it to be an indictable offense to willfully, unlawfully and maliciously carry off any barrack, cock, crib, rick or stacks of hay, corn, wheat, barley, oats or grain of any kind, but which said nothing of cornstalks. Later, plaintiff was discharged from the imprisonment, and sued the justice for assault and unlawful imprisonment. He was nonsuited, and this judgment was affirmed, although the court of errors declared that the misconduct described in the complaint before the justice was not the misconduct described in the . statute. The justice it was held, was called upon by the facts laid before him, to decide whether his authority extended over the act complained of, and over the person who was charged with doing that act. In making that decision, he was doing a judicial act, and therefore, was not liable in a suit to any person affected by his decision, whether such decision was right or wrong.

Judges of Inferior Courts. The case, it will be observed, gives no countenance to the distinction recognized by some authorities, between the liability of judges of courts of general jurisdiction and those of inferior courts.[15] On grounds of public policy, both

[14] Grove v. Van Duyn, 44 N. J. L. 654; 42 Am. R. 648 (1882).

[15] De Courcey v. Cox, 94 Cal. 665, 30 Pac. 95 (1892); Truesdell v.

classes are entitled to equal protection, and the most recent and best considered cases in this country, as well as in England, accord that protection.[16] If either class is in greater need of this protection than the other, it is the judges of inferior courts such as justices of the peace. As pointed out by a distinguished judge: " They stand nearer to the people than the judges of the superior courts, and are more liable to be influenced by popular feeling; and it is therefore even more important that the rule should be enforced, so that they may be accorded that immunity from suit which will lead to independence of action. Nor is there any danger that this immunity from suits for damages will leave the judges superior to the law, or as feeling that they are above the law," [17] For malicious or corrupt misconduct they are liable to removal from office and to criminal prosecution. Even though individuals may be forced to suffer harm at the hands of a corrupt judge, without obtaining pecuniary compensation from him, his immunity, as already pointed out, does not proceed from a rule of law established for his benefit, but " for the benefit of the public, whose interest it is that the judges should be at liberty to exercise their functions with independence, and without fear of consequences." [18]

Arbitrators: Military and Naval Courts. The same principle operates to exempt an arbitrator from liability to answer in damages for an erroneous award, even though it be also malicious and corrupt.[19] In England it is settled that members of military

---

Combs, 33 O. St. 186 (1877). In these cases it is said: " Inferior tribunals, invested with special jurisdiction only, and persons clothed with limited authority, such as justices of the peace, must at their peril keep within their prescribed jurisdiction; and if they transcend the limits of their authority, they are answerable to anyone whose rights are thereby invaded."

[16] Allec v. Reece, 39 Fed. 341, 40 A. L. J. 226 (1889) (Defendant was a justice of the peace). Haggard v. Pelicier Frères (1892), A. C. 61. (Defendant was a judge of a consular court). Garnett v. Ferrand, 6 B. & C. 619 (1827). (Defendant

was a coroner); State v. Wolever, 127 Ind. 306, 26 N. E. 762 (1890). (Defendant was a Mayor); Bannister v. Wakeman, 64 Vt. 203 (1891). (Deft. was a justice of the peace); Rudd v. Darling, 64 Vt. 456, 25 At. 479 (1892); (Deft. was judge of city court).

[17] Brewer, J., in Cooke v. Bangs, 31 Fed. 640, 642 (1887).

[18] Scott v. Stansfield, L. R. 3 Exch. 220 (1869). (Defendant was a county judge).

[19] Jones v. Brown, 54 Ia. 74 (1880). Such misconduct, however, may defeat an action by him for fees as arbitrator. Bever v. Brown, 56 Ia. 565 (1881).

or naval courts are entitled to the same exemption that is accorded to judges of civil tribunals.[20] Indeed the rule we have been considering should be applied, whenever the officer in question is acting in a judicial capacity, under legal authority to hear and determine matters of dispute between individuals; and the cases cited in the last paragraph support this view.

Quasi-Judicial Officers. When persons are legally empowered to deal with and determine questions, which call for the exercise of deliberation, judgment, and discretion, but which do not involve the administration of justice between individuals,[21] they are said to occupy a quasi-judicial position. Municipal officers belong to this class, when engaged in determining whether a sewer is necessary in a particular locality,[22] or who is the " lowest responsible bidder giving adequate security."[23] So do assessors, in determining whether a particular person is entitled to exemption from assessment, as a minister of the gospel, or in estimating the value of taxable property.[24] School trustees and members of boards of education often act in a quasi-judicial capacity in deciding what children are entitled to attend school.[25] The Postmaster-General of the United States, although ordinarily an executive officer, performs quasi-judicial functions, in settling the accounts of contractors with his department.[26] County boards of supervisors are legislative bodies, but in examining and approving the sureties on official bonds, they act in a quasi-judicial capacity.[27]

In all such cases, the quasi-judicial officer is exempt from liability for the consequences of honest mistakes and errors of judgment, however harmful these may be to innocent persons. According to the weight of authority, his immunity does not extend beyond this,[28] although in some jurisdictions the full immunity of judi-

[20] See Dawkins v. Lord Rokeby, L. R. 7. H. L. 744, 45 L. J. Q. B. 8 (1875); Dawkins v. Prince Edward (1876), 1 Q. B. D. 499, 45 L. J. Q. B. 567.

[21] Mills v. City of Rochester, 32 N. Y. 489, 495 (1865).

[22] Johnston v. District of Columbia, 118 U. S. 19, 6 Sup. Ct. 923 (1885).

[23] East River Gas Light Co. v. Donelly, 93 N. Y. 557 (1883).

[24] Weaver v. Devendorf, 3 Den. (N. Y.) 117 (1846); Stearns v. Mills, 25 Vt. 20 (1852).

[25] Stewart v. Southard, 17 Ohio, 402 (1848).

[26] Kendall v. Stokes, 3 How. (U. S.) 87, 98 (1845).

[27] Wasson v. Mitchell, 18 Ia. 153 (1864).

[28] Cases in the last three notes;

cial officers has been accorded to him.[29] In a leading case of the latter class it is said: "He is exempt from all responsibility by action for the motives which influence him, and the manner in which such duties are performed. If corrupt he may be impeached or indicted, but the law will not tolerate an action to redress the individual wrong which may have been done."[30] The reason for the prevailing view has been stated by a learned author[31] as follows: "By the express or implied terms of the officer's authority, he is to act honestly, carefully, and after the dictates of his own judgment, which, of necessity, being a human judgment, may err: therefore, when he has done what is thus commanded, whether the result is correct or not, he has exactly discharged his duty, and the law, which compelled this of him, will protect him, whatever harm may have befallen individuals. * * * It follows that if the quasi-judicial act is corrupt, or even if it is negligent, it will not be protected."[32]

---

also, Pikes v. Megoun, 44 Mo. 491 (1869); Gregory v. Brooks, 37 Conn. 365 (1870); Black v. Linn, 16 S. D. —; 96 N. W. 697 (1903).

[29] Weaver v. Devendorf, 3 Den. (N. Y.) 117 (1846); Mills v. City of Brooklyn, 32 N. Y. 489 (1865); East River Gas-Light Co. v. Donnelly, 93 N. Y. 557 (1887); Seifert v. City of Brooklyn, 101 N. Y. 139 (1896).

[30] Wilson v. Mayor, etc., of New York, 1 Den. (N. Y.) 595 (1845). Cf. Dillingham v. Snow, 5 Mass. 547 (1809), whore quasi-judicial officers are likened to judges of inferior courts, but their liability for malicious acts is left undecided.

[31] Bishop, Non Contract Law, § 787.

[32] In the famous case of Bernardiston v. Soame, (2 Lev. 114, 6 Howell's State Trials, 1092-1120 (1674 and 1689), the plaintiff charged the defendant, as sheriff, with maliciously making a false return of an election, which plaintiff claimed had resulted in his election to the House of Commons, while according to the sheriff's return he had been defeated. At the trial, Twysden, Rainsford, and Wylde, judges of the King's Bench, charged the jury, that if they believed the return was made maliciously, they should find for the plaintiff. A verdict was given in plaintiff's favor for £800. On motion in arrest of judgment, it was held by Hale, C. J., and Twysden and Wylde, JJ., (Rainsford, J., doubting) that "for as much as the return is said to be false and malicious and with intent to put the plaintiff to charge and expense to prove his election, and so found by the jury, the action lay and judgment was given for the plaintiff." This decision was reversed by the Exchequer Chamber, and the reversal was affirmed by the House of Lords. The principal ground of reversal is stated by North, C. J., as follows: "The sheriff, as to the declaring the

§ 4. HARMS INFLICTED BY ACTS OF STATE.

Another class of harms, which are not torts, are those inflicted by acts of State. They are not of frequent occurrence, being limited to injuries done to the subjects of one nation by the sovereign authority of another, or by the subjects of that other and ratified by it. A typical example is supplied by Buron v. Denmam.[33] The defendant, a captain in the British navy caused certain barracoons on the west coast of Africa to be burned and the slaves contained in them to be released. His conduct, although not authorized by previous orders, was approved and ratified by the British government. Thereafter, the owner of the slaves sued the captain for their loss, but it was held that the action would not lie because the captain's acts were acts of State. The principle underlying this and similar decisions has been stated in various forms. One statement is "that the acts of a sovereign State are final and can be called in question only by war or by an appeal to the justice of the State itself. They cannot be examined into by the courts of the State which does them." [34] Another form of statement is: "The transactions of independent States between each other are governed by other laws than those which municipal courts administer; such courts have neither the means of deciding what is right, nor the power of enforcing any decision which they may make." [35] The principle has been stated in still another form as follows: "When an act, injurious to a foreigner, and which might otherwise afford a ground of action, is done by a British subject, and the act is adopted by the British government, it becomes an act of the State, and the pri-

---

majority is judge; and no action will lie against a judge, for what he does judicially, though it be laid *falso, malitiose et scienter*." Lord North refers to the fact that the sheriff often acts ministerially, and declares that when acting in that capacity, a different rule of liability applies. When acting quasi-judicially, however, he asserts, the sheriff should have the same protection that is accorded to any judge in Westminster Hall.

[33] 2 Exch. 167, 188--9 (1847). The same principle is applied in Lamar v. Brown, 92 U. S. 187 (1875), and The Paquette Habana, 189 U. S. 453, 465, 23 Sup. Ct. 593 (1902).

[34] Stephen, History of the Criminal Law of Eng. Vol. 11 p. 64.

[35] Secretary of State in Council of India v. Kamachee Boye Sahaba 13 Mo. P. C. 22, 75 (1859).

vate right of action becomes merged in the international question which arises between the British government and that of the foreigner." [36]

Similar considerations have led to the adoption of the rule that neither the sovereign prince of an independent power, nor its duly accredited representative, is liable in tort for harm inflicted upon individuals, while sojourning in a foreign country. Redress for such an injury must be sought not in the ordinary courts of justice, but through the channels of international diplomacy. The principle deducible from the cases on this topic has been judicially declared to be " that, as a consequence of the absolute independence of every sovereign authority, and of international comity, which induces every sovereign State to respect the independence and dignity of every other sovereign State, each and every one declines to exercise, by means of its courts, any of its territorial jurisdiction over the person of any sovereign or ambassador, of any other

---

[36] Cockburn, C. J., in Feather v. The Queen, 6 B. & S. 257, 296 (1865), cf. People v. McLeod, 25 Wend. 483; 1 Hill, 377 (1841), in which the Supreme Court of New York refused to adopt this view. Mr. Webster declared in the U. S. Senate, that the opinion in that case was "not a reputable opinion, either on account of the results reached, or the reasoning on which it proceeds." In his letter of instruction to the Atttorney-General concerning the McLeod case, Mr. Webster wrote· "If the attack on the Caroline was unjustifiable, as this Government has asserted, the law which has been violated is the law of Nations; and the redress which is to be sought is the redress authorized in such cases by the provisions of that code." After remarking, that if McLeod had been arrested by a United States officer, he would have been discharged by the Federal Government, while had he been sued for damages in a civil action he must have availed himself of his defense in judicial proceedings, Mr. Webster added: " But whether the process be criminal or civil, the fact of having acted under public authority and in obedience to the order of lawful superiors, must be regarded as a valid defense; otherwise, individuals would be holden responsible for injuries resulting from the acts of government and even from the operations of war." Curtis' Life of Webster pp. 66--69. At that time, the Federal Government was unable to take McLeod from the jurisdiction of the State Court, but serious international difficulty was avoided by the verdict of acquittal. By an act of Congress, passed Aug. 29, 1842, (now a part of § 753, U. S. R. S.), authority, in such a case was given to the Federal courts to remove the foreign subject from the jurisdiction and control of the State tribunals and officers.

State, or over the public property of any ambassador, though such sovereign, ambassador or property be within its territory, and therefore, but for the common agreement, subject to its jurisdiction." [37]

Liability of Government Officials to Fellow Citizens. The immunities, which we have been considering, do not extend to government officials and agents, in their dealings with fellow citizens or subjects. It is true, the sovereign cannot be made a defendant in an action for a tort against a subject, nor in this country, can the government of the Union or of a State be proceeded against in such an action, unless it consents to be so sued. [38]   Even

[37] The Parliament Belge, 5 Probate Div. 197, 214 (1880). Cited and followed in Mighell v. Sultan of Johore (1894), 1 Q. B. 149, 159, 63 L. J. Q. B. 593, in which the defendant was sued for a breach of promise to marry the plaintiff. At the time he engaged to marry plaintiff, he was residing in England under the name of Albert Baker, and represented himself to be a private individual and subject of the Queen. Yet the court held that he could not be called to answer in the courts of England, for the breach of this promise, although it was accompanied by deceit; that there could be no inquiry by the court into his conduct, he being an independent sovereign and not submitting to the jurisdiction.

[38] The Federal Government has provided a court of claims for the decision of many cases which it consents may be brought against it. The principal classes of demands which may be litigated in that court, are claims founded on laws of Congress, on regulations of executive departments, on contracts express and implied and on claims specially referred to the court by Congress. See U. S. R. S. § 1059 *et seq.* This court has no jurisdiction of claims against the government for a mere tort. Schillinger v. U. S. 155 U. S. 163, 15 Sup. Ct. R. 85 (1894); Bigby v. U. S. 188 U. S. 400, 23 Sup. Ct. 468 (1902). Most of our states have created similar tribunals, in which they permit themselves to be sued upon specified causes of action. As this permission is altogether voluntary, on the part of the sovereignty, it follows that it may prescribe the terms and conditions on which it can be sued, and the manner in which the suit shall be conducted, and may withdraw its consent whenever it may suppose that justice to the public requires it. Beers v. Arkansas, 20 How. (U. S.) 527, 529 (1857); Locke v. State, 140 N. Y. 480, 482; 35 N. E. 1076 (1894); Troy, Etc. Ry. v. Commonwealth, 127 Mass. 43 (1879). Virginia prides herself on her early adoption of the policy "to allow to the citizen the same use of her courts against herself which she has against the citizen; the largest liberty of suit." Higginbotham's executors v. Commonwealth, 25 Gratt. 627, 639 (1874).

In United States v. Lee, 106 U. S. 196, 206, 1 Sup. Ct. R. 240 (1882), Justice Miller expressed the opinion that "As no person in this govern-a petition of right will not lie, in England, for the redress of such a tort,[39] because "the King can do no wrong." From this maxim, it follows as a necessary consequence that the king cannot authorize a wrong; for to authorize a wrong to be done is to do a wrong. As in the eye of the law no such wrong can be done so, in law, no right to redress can arise, and the petition which rests on such a foundation falls at once to the ground.[40]

But, while the injured subject or citizen has no remedy against the crown in England, or the State in this country, it follows from the maxim that the King can neither do nor authorize a wrong, that the authority of the king (the government with us), will afford no defense to an action, brought by a fellow subject or citizen, for an illegal act committed by a government officer. This position it has been judicially declared rests " on principles which are too well settled to admit of question, and which are alike essential to uphold the dignity of the Crown on the one hand and the rights and liberties of the subject on the other."[41] Accordingly if government officials acting under orders from the President of the United States take and hold possession of land without lawful authority, they are liable as trespassers, and the owner may have them ejected and recover possession.[42] If the commandant of a

ment exercises supreme executive power, or performs the public duties of a sovereign, it is difficult to see on what solid foundation of principle the exemption from liability to suit rests. It seems most probable that it has been adopted in our courts as a part of the general doctrine of publicists, that the supreme power in every state, wherever it may reside, shall not be compelled by process of courts of its own creation, to defend itself from assaults in those courts." In Nichols v. United States, 7 Wall. 122, 126 (1868), Justice Davis said: "The principle (of immunity from suit) is fundamental, applies to every sovereign power, and, but for the protection which it affords, the government would be unable to per-

form the various duties for which it was created."

[39] The Queen v. Lords Commissioners of the Treasury, 1 Eng. Ruling Cases 802, English Notes p. 815. The petition lies for breach of contract, for restitution of lands or compensation in money, or for the fair value of services rendered to the government, but not for a pure tort, done by a person in the government service.

[40] Feather v. The Queen, 6 B. & S. 257, 295 (1865).

[41] Cockburn, C. J., in Feather v. The Queen, 6 B. & S. 257, 297 (1865).

[42] United States v. Lee, 106 U. S. 196, 1 Sup. Ct. R. 240 (1882). This suit was brought against the officers in possession of the Arlington Es-

national armory [43] or a commodore in the navy [44] is guilty of the infringement of a patent he is liable to an action in tort therefor, although he has acted under the orders of the Secretary of the Navy, and has used the patent only for the benefit of the United States. So, the sergeant-at-arms of a legislative body is liable for false imprisonment, if he arrests a person upon an order of that body, which it has not lawful authority to make.[45] Still again, the

tate, but the United States intervened, and prosecuted the appeal to the Supreme Court. In the prevailing opinion, Justice Miller declares: "No man in this country is so high that he is above the law. All the officers of the government, from the highest to the lowest, are creatures of the law, and are bound to obey it. * * * Shall it be said, in the face of all this and of the acknowledged right of the judiciary to decide, in proper cases, statutes to be unconstitutional which have been passed by both branches of Congress and approved by the President, that the courts cannot give a remedy when the citizen has been deprived of his property by force, his estate seized and converted to the use of the government without lawful authority, without process of law, and without compensation, because the President has ordered it, and his officers are in possession? If such be the law of this country, it sanctions a tyranny which has no existence in the monarchies of Europe, nor in any other government which has a just claim to well regulated liberty and the protection of personal rights" pp. 220–1.

[43] Head v. Porter, 48 Fed. 481, 45 A. L. J. 205 (1891).

[44] Belknap v. Schild, 161 U. S. 10, 16 Sup. Ct. R. 443 (1895). In this case, the doctrine of former decisions was approved, that the United

States have no more right than any private person to use a patented invention without license of the patentee, or making compensation to him. It was also held that a suit would not lie against the United States for the infringement, as such suit sounded in tort, and the United States have not consented to be liable to suits founded in tort, for wrongs done by their officers, though in the discharge of their official duties. "But," it was declared, "the exemption of the United States from judicial process does not protect their officers and agents, civil or military, in time of peace, from being personally liable to an action of tort by a private person, whose right of property they have wrongfully invaded or injured, even by the authority of the United States;" citing Little v. Barreme, 2 Cranch, (U. S. Sup. Ct.) 169 (1804), and Bates v. Clark, 95 U. S. 204 (1877). At p. 209 of last cited case, Miller, J., says: "Whatever may be the rule in time of war and in the presence of actual hostilities, military officers can no more protect themselves than civilians in time of peace, by orders emanating from a source which is itself without authority."

[45] Kilbourne v. Thompson, 103 U. S. 168, 2 Transcript R. 56, 23 A. L. J. 227 (1881). The members of the House of Representatives who

unlawful order of a State Board of Health will not protect a person against a suit for damages, brought by one who has been injured by the enforcement of the order. Regard must be had to the maxim, " *Salus populi suprema lex*," but regard must also be had to the liberty of the citizen, and both principles must be given reciprocal play.[46]

Acts of Military and Naval Officers. These may be divided into two classes: First; Those of superior officers towards their subordinates. If acts of this class are of a kind, which would subject the actor to tort liability, were he not an official, he must be prepared to justify them on one of two grounds, viz.: (1) the express or implied assent of the plaintiff, or (2) valid authority conferred upon him by the government.[47] Second. Acts done by subordinates under the command of superior officers. If these acts are such as the superior had no legal authority to command, his orders will not excuse the subordinate.[48] If, however, they are of a kind which the superior is generally empowered to command, and the facts do not clearly disclose to the subordinate the illegality of the acts, the order of a superior officer will protect him.[49]

§ 5. HARMS DONE UNDER THE POLICE POWER.

The State, in the proper exercise of its police power, may and often

caused the issue of the order of arrest, were not liable, because of the Constitutional provision of Art. 1, § 6, *supra*, p. 30; but the plaintiff recovered a judgment for $37,500 against the serjeant-at-arms. On appeal, the court ordered the verdict to be reduced to $20,000, or to be set aside as excessive. The reduced sum was paid by a congressional appropriation. The subject of "Legislative Inquiries " is carefully considered in 1 Political Sc. Quar. 84.

[46] Wilson v. Alabama, Etc, Ry., 77 Miss. 714, 28 So. 568 (1900), cf. Hurst v. Warner, 102 Mich. 238, 60 N. W. 440, 26 L. R. A. 484 (1894); Brown v. Murdock, 140 Mass. 314 (1885).

[47] Wilson v. Mackenzie, 7 Hill (N. Y.) 95, 42 Am. Dec. 54, with note (1845).

[48] *Ex parte* Milligan, 4 Wall. (71 U. S.) 3, 18 L. Ed. 28 (1886).

[49] Riggs v. State, 3 Cold. (Tenn.) 85, 91 Am. Dec. 272 (1866); McCall v. McDowell, 1 Abb. (U. S.) 212; Fed. Cas. No. 8,673 (1867); Ford v. Surgat, 87 U. S. 594, 24 L. Ed. 1018 (1878); U. S. v. Clark, 31 Fed. 710 (1887); Commonwealth v. Shorthall, 206 Pa. 165, 55 At. 952 17 L. L. R. 87 (1903), Dicey's Law of the Constitution, (1 Ed.) 308–9, " A soldier may be liable to be shot by a court-martial if he disobeys an order, and to be hanged by a judge and jury, if he obeys it."

does inflict serious hardships upon individuals.[50] For these, the victims have no redress either against the State, or against its officers, agents, or servants, who act under its command. Accordingly, if the State orders all rags coming from certain regions, to be disinfected and the expense thereof to be paid by the owner, a particular owner has no right of action against the persons taking the rags for disinfection, though he may be able to prove that the rags in question were not infected.[51] If the State prohibits the use of nets in fishing, and authorizes the seizure and destruction of the nets so used, its agents are not liable in trover to the owners of the nets thus destroyed.[52] " To justify the State in thus interposing its authority in behalf of the public," said the court in the last cited case, " it must appear first, that the interests of the public generally, as distinguished from those of a particular class, require such interference; and, second, that the means are reasonably necessary for the accomplishment of the purpose, and not unduly oppressive upon individuals. The legislature may not, under the guise of protecting the public interests, arbitrarily interfere with private business, or impose unusual or unnecessary restrictions upon lawful occupations." " Under this (the police) power it has been held that the State may order the destruction of a house falling to decay or otherwise endangering the lives of passers-by:[53] the demolition of such as are in the path of a conflagration;[54] the slaughter of diseased

---

[50] California Reduc. Co. v. Sanitary Reduc. Co., 126 Fed. 29 (1903). The second head-note is as follows: " Laws or ordinances enacted under the police power for the protection of the public health, reasonably adapted to that end, are not unconstitutional because they may incidentally operate to deprive individuals of their property or its use without compensation, or interfere with their personal liberty, nor because they may give one person a monopoly of a certain business or occupation, private rights being required to yield in such case to the public good."

[51] Train v. Boston Disinfecting

Co., 144 Mass. 523, 11 N. E. 116 (1887); cf. Los Angeles County v. Spencer, 126 Cal. 670, 59 Pac. 202 (1889), where a statute was held constitutional, that authorized State agents to abate insect pests in orchards, nurseries and like places, and which made the expense of the abatement a lien on the premises thus disinfected.

[52] Lawton v. Steele, 152 U. S. 133, 136, 137, 14 Sup. Ct. 499 (1893), affirming same case in 119 N. Y. 226, 23 N. E. 878 (1890).

[53] Dewey v. White, M. & M. 56, (1827); Fields v. Stokely, 99 Pa. St. 306 (1882).

[54] Malever v. Spink, Dyer, 36 Pl. 40

cattle:[55] the destruction of decayed or unwholesome food,[56] the prohibition of wooden buildings in cities,[57] the regulation of railways and other means of public conveyance,[58] and of interments in burial grounds:[59] the restriction of objectionable trades to certain localities:[60] the compulsory vaccination of children:[61] the confinement of the insane or those afflicted with contagious diseases:[62] the restraint of vagrants, beggars and habitual drunkards[63] the suppression of obscene publications [64] and houses of ill fame:[65] and the prohibition of gambling houses [66] and places where intoxicating liquors are sold." [67]   So, the State may compel real-estate owners to bridge ditches which would otherwise obstruct the free passage or use of streets.[68]

Harms Inflicted by Neighboring Land Owners.

At common law, a man has a right to build a fence or other structure

(1838); Surocco v. Geary, 3 Cal. 69 (1853); Bowditch v. Boston, 101 U. S. 16 (1879).

[55] Loesch v. Koehler, 144 Ind. 278, 41 N. E. 326 (1895); Newark, Etc. Co. v. Hawk, 50 N. J. L. 308, 12 At. 697 (1888). So, the killing of dogs, which are not put on the assessment rolls by their owners, may be authorized by statute; Sentell v. New Orleans Ry., 166 U. S. 698, 17 Sup. Ct. 693 (1896).

[56] Dunbar v. City of Augusta, 90 Ga. 390, 17 S. E. 907 (1892); Munn v. Corbin, 8 Colo. App. 113, 44 Pac. 783 (1896).

[57] First Nat. Bank of Mt. Vernon v. Sarlis, 129 Ind. 201, 28 N. E. 434, 28 Am. St. R. 85 (1891).

[58] Bluedorn v. Missouri Pac. Ry., 108 Mo. 439, 18 S. W. 1103, 32 Am. S. R. 615 (1891); cf. N. W. Tel. Co. v. Minneapolis, 81 Minn. 140, 83 N. W. 527 (1900), applying city ordinance regulating telegraph and telephone poles and wires.

[59] Mayor, Etc. of Newark v. Wilson, 56 N. J. L. 667, 20 At. 487 (1894); Humphrey v. Church, 109 N. C. 13, 18 S. E. 793 (1891).

[60] City of Newton v. Joyce, 166 Mass. 83, 44 N. E. 116 (1896); Comm. v. Hubley, 172 Mass. 58, 51 N. E. 448 (1898); Weir's Appeal, 74 Pa. 230 (1873); Butcher's Union Co. v. Crescent City, C. 111 U. S. 746, 4 Sup. Ct. 652 (1883).

[61] Morris v. City of Columbus, 102 Ga. 792, 30 S. E. 850, 66 Am. St. R. 243 (1897).

[62] Compagnie Francaise v. State Board of Health, 51 La. Ann. 645, 25 So. 591, 72 Am. St. R. 458 (1899).

[63] Comm. v. Morrisey, 157 Mass. 471, 32 N. E. 664 (1892).

[64] Willis v. Warren, 1 Hilton, (N. Y.) 590 (1859); Comm. v. Sharpless, 2 S. & R. (Pa.) 91 (1815).

[65] L'Hote v. City of New Orleans, 51 La. Ann. 93, 24 So. 608 (1899).

[66] Mugler v. Kansas, 123 U. S. 623, 8 Sup. Ct. 273 (1887).

[67] U. S. v. Dixon, 4 Cranch, (U. S. C. C.) 107 (1830); Ex parte Tattle, 91 Cal. 589, 27 Pac. 933 (1891); Booth v. People, 186 Ill. 43, 57 N. E. 798, 78 Am. St. R. 229 (1900).

[68] Boise City v. Boise City Rapid Transit Co., (Idaho); 59 Pac. 716 (1899).

on his own land as high as he pleases, even though this is done for the sole purpose of annoying a neighbor, or shutting the sunlight from his windows or garden.[69] This right may be modified by legislation, however. A statute which declares that " a fence unnecessarily exceeding six feet in height, maliciously erected or maintained for the purpose of annoying the owners or occupants of adjoining property, shall be deemed a private nuisance," is a proper exercise of the police power.[70] So is a statute which compels a land owner to plug abandoned oil-wells,[71] or to refrain from the use of artificial means to increase the natural flow of gas from a well.[72]

Legalizing Nuisances—Britain. As the State may declare property to be a nuisance, so, on the other hand, it may legalize a nuisance. In Great Britain, the power of parliament is unlimited in this direction. Accordingly, if an act of parliament authorizes a railroad to construct and maintain a station for loading and unloading cattle, the company will not be liable to those owning property near the station, though the latter be of such a character as to amount to a nuisance, at common law. " No doubt, * * *

---

[69] Letts v. Kessler, 54 Ohio St. 73, 42 N. E. 765 (1896); Mahan v. Brown, 13 Wend. (N. Y.) 261 (1835); Falloon v. Schilling, 29 Kan. 292; 44 Am. R. 642 (1883); *contra*, Burke v. Smith, 69 Mich. 380, 37 N. W. 838 (1888); Flaherty v. Aloran, 81 Mich. 52, 45 N. W. 381, 21 Am. St. R. 510 (1890).

[70] Ridehout v. Knox, 148 Mass. 368, 19 N. E. 390 (1888); Smith v. Morse, 148 Mass. 407, 19 N. E. 393 (1888); Lord v. Langdon, 91 Me. 221, 39 At. 552 (1898); Karasek v. Peier, 22 Wash. 4, 19, 61 Pac. 33 (1900). The tendency appears to be towards a strict construction of such a statute. In Brostrom v. Lauppe, 179 Mass. 315, 60 N. E. 785 (1901), it was held not applicable to a fence located wholly on defendant's land, from three to ten feet from the line.

[71] Hague v. Wheeler, 157 Pa. 324, 27 At. 714 (1893).

[72] Ohio Oil Co. v. Indiana, 177 U. S. 190, 20 Sup. Ct. 576 (1900), affirming S. C. in 150 Ind. 698, 50 N. E. 1125 (1898); Manufacturers' Gas Co. v. Indiana Natural Gas Co., 156 Ind. 679, 57 N. E. 912 (1901).

[73] London and Brighton Ry. Co. v. Truman, 11 App. Cases, 45 (1885); cf. Metropolitan Asylum District Co. v. Hill, 6 App. Cases, 193 (1881). The distinction between the two cases is stated by Lord Chancellor Halsbury as follows: " A small-pox hospital might be built and maintained, if it could be done without creating a nuisance, whereas the Railway Acts are assumed to establish the proposition that the railway might be made and used, whether a nuisance were created or not."

when compensation is not given to those interested in the neighboring land, this is, as against them, harsh legislation;" but it is valid legislation.[73]

In the United States. Such is not the rule, however, in this country. Legislation of the sort just referred to is unconstitutional with us, because falling within the prohibition against depriving a person of his property without due process of law, or against taking private property for public use without just compensation.[74] Accordingly, a federal statute, authorizing a railroad corporation to bring its track within the city limits of Washington, and construct such works as were necessary and expedient for the completion and maintenance of its road, is not to be construed as authorizing the erection and maintenance of an engine house and repair shop, so near to a church edifice as to render it unfit for use as a place of public worship. Such a construction would render the statute unconstitutional. Said the United States Supreme Court, " whatever the extent of the authority conferred, it was accompanied with this qualification, that the works should not be so placed as by their use to unreasonably interfere with and disturb the peaceful and comfortable enjoyment of others in their property."[75] It was held, therefore, to be no answer to the action by the religious corporation, whose church was rendered uncomfortable and almost unendurable as a place of worship, that defendant was authorized by act of Congress to construct its line and terminal facilities within the city of Washington, nor that its engine-house and repair shop were properly built and conducted without negligence, nor that the chimneys were of the height required by the city ordinances.[76]

---

[74] See United States Constitution Amendments 5 and 14, Constitution of N. Y. Art. 1, §§ 6, 7. See United States v. Lynah, 188 U. S. 445, 23 Sup. Ct. 349 (1902), holding the United States liable for property taken by it. Constitution of Penn. Art. 1, § 10 and Art. 16, § 8, Const. of Va. Art. 5, § 14. See Williams v. Parker, 188 U. S. 491, 23 Sup. Ct. 440 (1902), holding the Massachusetts high building statute constitutional, as it provides for compensating property owners, who are prohibited from building above a specified height.

[75] Baltimore and Potomac Ry. v. Fifth Baptist Church, 108 U. S. 317, 2 Sup. Ct. 719 (1883).

[76] Cf. Georgia Ry. Etc. Banking Co. v. Maddox, 116 Ga. 64, 42 S. E. 315 (1902), holding that injuries and inconveniences to persons residing near a terminal yard, located

The same doctrine has been maintained by the State courts; and private corporations[77] as well as municipal corporations[78] have been held liable to neighboring property owners for nuisances in connection with works which they were expressly authorized by statute to construct. In Cogswell v. New York, New Haven & Hartford Railway Company,[79] the trial court found that defendant's engine-house practically deprived the plaintiff of the use of her dwelling-house, by filling it with smoke and dust, and by corrupting and tainting the atmosphere with offensive gases; but it denied relief to her on the ground that defendant, as a railroad corporation was authorized by statute to acquire real estate for an engine-house; that an engine-house at the point where this one was erected, was necessary for the operation of the road: that in the construction and use of the engine-house and coal-bins, it had exercised all practicable care, and, therefore, the harm sustained by plaintiff was *damnum absque injuria*. This decision was sustained by the General Term, but was reversed by the Court of Appeals, on the ground that the State legislature had not authorized the wrong of which the plaintiff complained; and this rule of statutory construction in

at a point authorized by statute, and operated in a proper manner, are not actionable. The smoke, noises and the like are not nuisances, but the necessary concomitants of the franchise.

[77] Brown v. Cayuga, Etc. Ry. Ct., 12 N. Y. 486 (1885); Cogswell v. New York, Etc. Ry. Co., 103 N. Y. 10, 8 N. E. 537 (1886); Boham v. Port Jervis Gas Light Co., 122 N. Y. 18, 25 N. E. 246 (1890); Garvey v. Long Island Ry., 159 N. Y. 323, 54 N. E. 57 (1899); Evans v. Chicago, Etc. Ry., 86 Wis. 597, 57 N. W. 354 (1893); Shively v. Cedar Rapids, Etc. Ry., 74 Ia. 169, 37 N. W. 133, 7 Am. St. R. 471 (1887); Lexington & Ohio Ry. v. Applegate, 8 Dana. (Ky.) 289 (1839); Jeffersonville, Etc. Ry. v. Esterle, 13 Bush. (Ky.) 675 (1878); Cleveland v. Bangor Street Ry., 86 Me. 232, 29

At. 1005 (1894); Adams v. Chicago, Etc. Ry., 39 Minn. 286, 39 N. W. 629 (1888); Village of Pine City v. Munch, 42 Minn. 342, 44 N. W. 197 (1890); Pennsylvania Ry. v. Angel, 46 N. J. Eq. 316, 7 At. 432, 56 Am. R. 6 (1886); cf. Hammersmith, Etc. Ry. v. Brand, L. R. 4 H. L. 171, (1868).

[78] Proprietors of Locke v. Lowell, 7 Gray, (Mass.) 223 (1856); Haskell v. New Bedford, 108 Mass. 208 (1871); Bacon v. City of Boston, 154 Mass. 100, 28 N. E. 9 (1891); Edmondson v. City of Moberly, 98 Mo. 523, 11 S. W. 900 (1889); Nevins v. Fitchburg, 174 Mass. 545, 55 N. E. 321 (1899); Hill v. The Mayor, Etc., 139 N. Y. 501, 34 N. E. 1098 (1893); Morton v. The Mayor, Etc., 140 N. Y. 207, 35 N. E. 490 (1893).

[79] 103 N. Y. 10, 8 N. E. 537 (1886).

such cases was announced: "The statutory sanction, which will justify an injury to private property, must be express or must be given by clear and unquestionable implication from the powers expressly conferred, so that it can fairly be said that the legislature contemplated the doing the very act which occasioned the injury."

Even had express authority been given by statute to build and maintain the engine-house, it would have afforded the defendant no protection.[80]   In the language of the Supreme Court of Massachusetts, "the legislature may authorize small nuisances, without compensation, but not large ones."[81]   Hence a statute, expressly authorizing the ringing of bells, and the use of steam whistles and of gongs by employers to give notice to their workmen, will protect the employers from actions by neighbors, although such noises have been adjudged common law nuisances and enjoined as such by the courts, before the statute is passed.[82]

---

[80] Bellinger v. New York Central Ry., 23 N. Y. 42, 48 (1861). In this case the defendant was expressly authorized to build a particular bridge, which plaintiff claimed caused injury to his land by choking the throat of the stream and throwing back a flood upon his premises.   The court said: "If a corporation or an officer should be authorized by statute to take the property of individuals for any purpose, however public or generally beneficial, without compensation, or for a private use making compensation, the pretended authority would be wholly void, and of course could afford no protection. But this limitation has no application to cases where property is not taken, but only subjected to damages consequential upon some act done by tht State or pursuant to its authority." The damage, in the case then before the court, was declared to be consequential.

[81] Bacon v. City of Boston, 154 Mass. 100, 28 N. E. 9 (1891).

[82] Sawyer v. Davis, 136 Mass. 239 (1884). The court said: "It is then argued that the legislature cannot legalize a nuisance, and cannot take away the rights of defendant as they have been ascertained and declared by the court; and this is undoubtedly true, so far as such rights have become vested. For instance, if the plaintiff under an existing rule of law has a right of action to recover damages, for past injury suffered by him, his remedy cannot be cut off by an act of legislature. So also, if, in a suit in equity to restrain the continuance of a nuisance damages have been awarded to him, or costs of suit, he would have an undoubted right to recover them, notwithstanding the statute. But, on the other hand the legislature may define what in the future shall constitute a nuisance, such as will entitle the person injured thereby to a legal or requitable remedy, and may change the existing law rule on the subject. This legislative power is not wholly be-

Taking Private Property. On the other hand, the legislature can neither authorize the total destruction of property without making compensation, nor can it authorize permanent and substantial injury to such property without making compensation.[83] Whether the authorized nuisance amounts to a taking of property of the victim, or inflicts but trifling, indirect or consequential injury, may be a difficult question of fact, in a particular case,[84] but the rule of law, to be applied when the fact is determined, is clear and unquestioned.

In several states, the constitution provides that " private property shall not be taken or damaged for public use without just compensation.[85] Under such a provision, recovery may be had whenever

yond the control of the courts, because it is restrained by the constitutional provision limiting it to wholesome and reasonable laws, of which the court is the final judge; but within this limitation, the exercise of the police power of the legislature will apply to all within the scope of its terms and spirit: " Cf. Tyler v. City of Lansingburgh, 37 Misc. (N. Y. Sup. Ct.) 604 (1902), holding that when the legislature abolishes a village, against which a person has a cause of action, the municipal corporation, into which the village is merged, becomes liable and is properly substituted as defendant.

[83] Lexington & Ohio Ry. v. Applegate, 8 Dana (Ky.) 289 (1839); Hill v. Mayor, Etc., 139 N. Y. 501, 34 N. E. 1098 (1883). Said Judge Finch, in this case: " Obviously the general doctrine which levies upon individuals forced contributions for the benefit of the public, and denies compensation for the injury done, is vulnerable at two points. It is defeated by construing the harm inflicted into the taking of private property, for which compensation must be made, and sometimes by a

rigid construction of the authority claimed. Both methods indicate a lurking doubt of the equity of the general doctrine, and a disposition to narrow the field of its operation." Garvey v. Long Island Ry., 159 N. Y. 323, 54 N. E. 57 (1889).

[84] Beidman v. Atlantic City Ry., 19 At. 731 (N. J. Ch.) (1890); American Bank Note Co. v. New York El. Ry., 129 N. Y. 252, 29 N. E. 302 (1891); Marchant v. Pennsylvania Ry., 153 U. S. 380, 14 Sup. Ct. 894 (1894); Gibson v. United States, 166 U. S. 269, 17 Sup. Ct. 578 (1897); Meyer v. City of Richmond, 172 U. S. 95, 19 Sup. Ct. 106 (1898); Long v. City of Elberton, 109 Ga. 28, 34 S. E. 333 (1899); (A Prison; No recovery), Frazer v. City of Chicago, 186 Ill. 480, 57 N. E. 1055 (1900); (A small-pox hospital. No recovery), Muhlker v. N. Y. & H. Ry., 173 N. Y. 549, 66 N. E. 558 (1903); (Changing grade of railway track in a city street); Bedford v. U. S., 192 U. S. 217, 24 Sup. Ct. 238 (1904); (Damage, to land as the result of revetments along the Mississippi are consequential).

[85] Osborne v. Missouri Pac. Ry., 147 U. S. 248, 13 Sup. Ct. 299 (1892),

the plaintiff's property has been damaged by any public improvement, whether the damage is caused by an actual physical invasion of the property, or indirectly by diminishing its saleability or its rental value.[86]

Destruction of Property Under the Police Power: In the exercise of its police power, the State may authorize the summary destruction of private property, as we have seen. An officer who seizes and destroys property under such authority has the burden of proving a justification.[87] If the statute authorizes the summary killing of animals having the glanders, an adjudication by the local cattle commissioners that a horse had the glanders, is not conclusive against the owner of the animal. Such an adjudication is not a defense to those killing the horse pursuant to an order thereunder, if in fact the horse did not have the disease.[88] "Of course," said the Court, "there cannot be a trial by jury before killing an animal, supposed to have a contagious disease, and we assume that the legislature may authorize its destruction in such emergencies without a hearing beforehand. But it does not follow that it can throw the loss on the owner without a hearing. If he cannot be heard beforehand, he may be heard afterward. The statute may provide for paying him in case it should appear that his property was not what the Legislature has declared to be—a nuisance, and may give him his hearing in that way. If it does not do so, the statute may leave those who act under it to proceed at their peril, and the owner gets his hearing in an action against them."

Whether the destruction of property by public officers, under the authority of a statute, as a means of preventing the spread of fire or

applying Art. 11, § 21, of Mo. Const; City Council of Montgomery v. Townsend, 80 Al. 489, 2 So. 155 (1886); Hot Springs Ry. v. Williamson, 45 Ark. 429 (1885); Weyl v. Sonoma Valley Ry., 69 Cal. 202, 206 (1886); City of Atlanta v. Green, 67 Ga. 386 (1881); Gottschalk v. Chicago, Etc. Ry., 14 Neb. 550 (1883); Reading v. Althouse, 93 Pa. 400 (1880); Spencer v. Mount Pleasant Ry., 23 W. Va. 406 (1884); DeGeofroy v. Merchant's Bridge Co., 179 Mo. 698, 79 S. W. 387, 64 L. R. A. 959 (1903).

[86] Chicago v. Taylor, 125 U. S. 161, 8 Sup. Ct. 820 (1888), applying the provision of Ill. Const., and following Rigney v. Chicago, 102 Ill. 64 (1882).

[87] Lawton v. Steele, 152 U. S. 133, 142, 14 Sup. Ct. 499 (1893).

[88] Miller v. Horton, 152 Mass. 540, 26 N. E. 100 (1891). Such an officer acts in a ministerial capacity, and is answerable for negligence: Bair v. Struck, 29 Mont. 45, 74 Pac. 69, 63 L. R. A. 481 (1903).

disease, is merely the regulation of rights created by necessity, which properly is referable to the police power, and which requires no provision for compensation, or whether it can be done only in the right of eminent domain, and with a provision for compensation, is a question upon which authorities differ. Recent legislation, however, generally makes provision for compensation when valuable property is destroyed to stay fires.[89]

§ 6. defense of self and property.

Inevitable Accident.   A person, who inflicts harm upon another, in the defense of himself or his property, or by inevitable accident, is not liable therefor in tort. This has not always been the rule of English law. Anciently, our law, like every other primitive legal system, imposed an absolute responsibility upon the voluntary doer of harm. We have the record of a case, early in the fourteenth century, brought for battery of the plaintiff, in which the jury found, " that the plaintiff was beaten, but this was because of his own assault, since the defendant could not otherwise escape. It was nevertheless adjudged that the plaintiff should recover his damages * * * and the defendant to go to prison." [90]   The Statute of Gloucester [91] had already provided that the King should pardon one, who had been found by a jury to have killed another in self-defense or by misadventure, but a plea of self-defense does not seem to have been successfully interposed to a civil action for damages, until the opening of the fifteenth century: [92] while the plea of misadventure or inevitable accident in civil cases, did not gain clear recognition for a century thereafter.[93]   Even in the seventeenth century, we find eminent judges declaring that, " in all civil acts the law doth not so much regard the intent of the actor as the loss and damage of the party suffering, * * *   And the reason is because he that is damaged ought to be recompensed." [94]

---

[89] Bates v. Worcester Protection Department, 177 Mass. 130, 58 N. E. 274 (1900).

[90] Anonymous, Year Book, Ed. 2, f. 381 (1319).

[91] 6 Ed. 1, Ch. 9 (1278).

[92] Chapleyn of Greye's Inne v. —— Year Book, H. 4, f. 8, pl. 40 (1400).

[93] Responsibility for Tortious Acts, VII Harvard Law Review, pp. 442–445, by Professor John W. Wigmore.

[94] Bacon's Maxims, 7 (1630); Lambert v. Bessey, T. Raym, 421 (1691).

Defense of Family. Not only in defense of oneself, may a person inflict harm upon another without committing a tort, but he is equally privileged in defending his master,[95] or his servant,[96] or spouse,[97] or child,[98] or parent,[99] or brother.[100] In all such cases, the law treats plaintiff's harm as attributable to his own misconduct. In the language of Chief Justice Holt " If A strike B, and B strikes again, and they close immediately, and in the scuffle M mayhems A, that is *son assault.*"[101] A brings the harm upon himself and has no cause of action against B, so long as the latter uses no more violence than a reasonable man would, under the circumstances, regard necessary to his defense.[102] Whether a person acted reasonably in repelling an assault, or in believing that an assault was threatened, is a question for the jury. The one assailed " judges at the time, upon the force of the circumstances, when he forms and acts upon his belief, at the peril that a jury may think otherwise and hold him guilty. But he will not act at the peril of making that guilt, if appearances prove false, which would be innocence if they proved true.[103] He need not wait until his assailant has given a blow, for perhaps it will come too late afterwards." [104] On the other hand, he is not entitled to a verdict simply because he testifies that he believed he was about to be attacked.[105] He must

[95] Year Book, 14 H. 6, 24, pl. 72 (1436); Anonymous, Year Book, 21 Hy. 7, 39, pl. 50 (1505); Barfoot v. Reynolds, 2 Strange 953 (1734).

[96] Seaman v. Cuppledick, Owen 150, (about 1610); Orton v. State, 4 Greene, (Ia.) 140 (1853).

[97] Leward v. Basely, 1 Lord Raym, 62 (1695); Staton v. State, 30 Miss. 619 (1856); Biggs v. State, 29 Ga. 723, 76 Am. Dec. 630 (1860).

[98] Commonwealth v. Malone, 114 Mass. 295 (1873); Higgins v. Minaghan, 76 Wis. 301, 45 N. W. 127 (1890).

[99] Obier v. Neal, 1 Houst. (Del.) 449 (1857); State v. Johnson, 75 N. C. 174 (1876).

[100] State v. Melton, 102 Mo. 683, 15 S. W. 139 (1880).

[101] Cockroft v. Smith, 2 Salk. 642 (1705).

[102] Dole v. Erskine, 35 N. H. 503 (1857); Ogden v. Claycomb, 52 Ill. 365 (1869).

[103] Shorter v. People, 2 N. Y. 193 (1849); Morris v. Platt, 32 Conn. 75, 83 (1864).

[104] Chapleyn of Greye's Inne v. —— Y. B., 2 H. 4, f. 8, pl. 40 (1400); State v. Sherman, 16 R. I. 631 (1889).

[105] State v. Bryson, 2 Winston Law (N. C.) 86 (1864). In this case, the court said: " A prayer for instruction, which assumed that one's personal feelings and apprehensions, however eccentric or morbid these might be, determined the character of his conduct, was properly refused."

convince a jury that his belief was honest and well-founded.[106]
" In other words, the law of self-defense justifies an act done in
honest and reasonable belief of immediate danger.   It does not
rest on the actual, but on the apparent facts and the honesty of
belief in danger.[107]   When one is attacked by a number of persons, he may act with more promptness, and resort to more forcible
means to protect himself or his family, than in the case of attack
by a single person.[108]

In defense of person or family, one may destroy animals or other
noxious property without liability to the owner.[109]

Defense of Property.   The right to defend one's property,
without liability for damages, necessarily inflicted upon others as an
incident of the defense, has long been recognized.   In one of the
earliest reported cases on this topic, the defendant, in an action for
assault, justified on the ground that the plaintiff came and took certain goods of the defendant, who bade him leave the goods, but he
would not, whereupon defendant took them out of his possession,
which was the assault complained of.   Chief Justice Newton said:
" If a man will take my horse from me, or anything which belongs
to me, and I will not suffer him to do it, although he is hurt, in this
case I shall be excused. * * *   For, since he was about to injure me,
this malfeasance shall be said to be an assault upon me begun by him,
and all this shall be said to be in defense of the goods and chattels of
the defendant." [110]   During the period which has passed since that
decision, (nearly five centuries) it has remained undoubted law, that
a man is justified in using whatever force is reasonably necessary to
protect and maintain his rightful possession of property.[111]

---

[106] Rippy v. State, 2 Head (Tenn)
217 (1858).

[107] New Orleans, Etc. Ry. v. Jopes,
142 U. S. 18, 23, 12 Sup. Ct. 109
(1891), holding the following
charge erroneous: " If the conductor shot, when there was in fact
no actual danger, although from
the manner, attitude and conduct
of the plaintiff, the former had reasonable cause to believe, and did believe, that an assault upon him with
a deadly weapon was intended, and
only fired to protect himself from

such apprehended assault, the company was liable for compensatory
damages."

[108] Higgins v. Minaghan, 78 Wis.
602, 47 N. W. 941 (1891); Thornton
v. Taylor, 54 S. W. 16, (Ky.)
(1899).

[109] Keck v. Halstead, 3 Lutwyche,
481 (1699); see Police Power, *supra*,
p. 50; and Nuisance, *infra*, ch. 14.

[110] Anonymous, Year Book, 19 H.
6, f. 31, pl. 59 (1440).

[111] Anonymous, Year Book, 9 Ed.
4, f. 28, Pl. 42 (1470); Taylor v.

Recaption : Whether he is also justified in recapturing his property by force, is a question upon which the courts are not agreed. If the property can be considered as still in the owner's legal possession, although within the physical grasp of the wrong-doer; or if legal possession has been gained by force or fraud, and the owner makes fresh pursuit and promptly demands return of the property, the owner may safely use all reasonably necessary force to regain it.[112] Some courts have held that whenever a person has wrongful possession of the chattels of another, and refuses to surrender them upon the demand of the owner, the latter is justified in using force sufficient to defend his right and retake the chattels. If the owner was compelled by law to seek redress by action, for a violation of his right of property, say these courts, the remedy would often be worse than the mischief.[113]

The weight of authority, however, favors a distinction between cases where violence is used to retain possession; and where it is employed to regain possession; holding it lawful in the former and unlawful in the latter.[114] According to this view "the law does not permit parties to take the settlement of conflicting claims, into their own hands. It gives the right of defense but not of redress. The circumstances may be exasperating; the remedy at law may seem to inadequate; but still the injured party cannot be arbiter of his own claim. Public order and the public peace are of greater consequence than a private right or an occasional hardship. Inadequacy of remedy is a frequent occurrence, but it cannot find its complement in personal violence." [115]

Markham, Cro. Jac. 224 (1535); Alderson v. Waistell, 1 C. & K. 358 (1844); Motes v. Berry, 74 Ala. 374 (1883); Bliss v. Johnson, 73 N. Y. 529 (1878).

[112] State v. Elliot, 11 N. H. 540 (1841); Gyre v. Culver, 47 Barb. (N. Y.) 592 (1867); Anderson v. State, 6 Baxt. (Tenn.) 608 (1872); Johnson v. Perry, 56 Vt. 703 (1884).

[113] Anonymous, Keilwey, f. 92, pl. 4 (1506); Blades v. Higgs, 10 C. B. N. S. 713, 30 L. J. C. P. 347 (1861); Rex v. Milton, M. & M. 107 (1827); Baldwin v. Hayden, 6 Conn. 453 (1827); Comm. v. Donahue, 148 Mass. 529, 20 N. E. 171 (1889).

[114] Story v. State, 71 Ala. 328, 338 (1882); Sabre v. Mott, 88 Fed. 780 (1898); Andre v. Johnson, 6 Blackf. (Ind.) 375 (1843); Bobb v. Bosworth, 2 Littell (Ky.) 81 (1808); Watson v. Rheinderknecht, 82 Minn. 235, 84 N. W. 798 (1901); Bliss v. Johnson, 73 N. Y. 529 (1878); Harris v. Marco, 16 S. C. 575 (1881).

[115] Kirby v. Foster, 17 R. I. 437, 22 At. 1111, (1891).

Reasonable Force :—In defense of property, as in defense of person, one must act in a reasonable manner; and what is reasonable depends largely upon the circumstances of each case. One may go to much greater lengths in repelling another from his house, or in ejecting one therefrom, than in dealing with a trespasser to other parts of his premises, or to his personal property. In an early case, Chief Justice Fineux said: "If a man is in his house, and hears that such a one is coming to his house to beat him, he may well collect his friends and neighbors to help in the defense of his person. * * * One's house is his castle and defense, where he may properly abide." [116] Two centuries later it is laid down as settled law that one may defend his house against a burglar by returning violence with violence.[117] Even the killing of a person, in the actual resistance of an attempt to commit a felony upon or in a dwelling or other place of abode in which the slayer is, has long been deemed justifiable homicide.[118] In defense of other property, however, the owner is not justified in taking life or in using dangerous weapons. If he stones [119] or shoots [120] a trespasser he is liable for assault and battery. While he may repel with force [121] an attempt to wrongfully enter upon his land or take chattels from his possession, yet, if the wrongdoer has peacefully gained entrance or pos-

---

[116]Anonymous, Year Book, 21 H. 7, f. 39, pl. 50 (1505). In Lawrence's Case, 2 Rolle's Abridgment, 548 (1609), it was held by the whole court, "One may justify the battery of another who will enter my house, for it is my castle." According to State v. Patterson, 45 Vt. 308, 12 Am. R. 200 (1873): "The idea embodied in the expression that a man's house is his castle, is not that it is his property, and, as such, he has the right to defend and protect it by other and more extreme means than he might lawfully use to defend and protect his shop, his office or his barn. The sense in which the house has a peculiar immunity is, that is is sacred for the protection of his person and of his family," Hollingsworth v. Fitzgerald, 16 Neb. 499 (1884).

[117] Breen v. Goddard, 2 Salk. 641 (1705), Cf. When a Man's House is His Castle, 10 Al. L. J. 241.

[118] Carrol v. The State, 23 Al. 28, 58 Am. Dec. 282 (1853); Wharton Criminal Law, (7 Ed.) Vol. 2, § 1024. Bishop's New Criminal Law, § 858, New York Penal Code, § 205.

[119] Cole v. Maunder, 2 Rolle's Abridgment, 548 (1635); Conners v. Walsh, 131 N. Y. 590, 30 N. E. 59 (1892).

[120] Everton v. Ergati, 24 Neb. 235 (1888); Bloom v. State, 155 Ind. 292, 58 N. E. 81 (1900).

[121] Harrison v. Harrison, 43 Vt. 417 (1871); Hannabalson v. Sessions, 116 Ia. 457, 90 N. W. 93 (1902); Montgomery v. Comm., 98 Va. 840, 36 S. E. 371 (1900).

session, the owner cannot justify forcible ejection without first requesting him to depart.[122] Even then, he must use no more force than is necessary to overcome the wrongdoer's resistance.[123]

Defense Against Animals : A person's property is often injured or threatened by animals belonging to another. Here, again, in defense of his property, one may do what is reasonably necessary for its protection, and no more. If a dog is in the act of destroying a fowl or sheep, the owner of the latter may kill the dog, if he has reason to believe that such killing is necessary to save his property.[124] He is not entitled, however, to destroy valuable animals of his neighbor, simply because they are trespassers, even though they are habitual trespassers, and he has warned their owner to keep them at home or he will kill them.[125] His remedy is to impound them or sue for the damage done by them.[126] Generally, the killing of a trespassing domestic animal is not justifiable, unless it is engaged at the time in the destruction of property ;[127] but wild animals,[128] or domestic animals which, because of mischievous habits, are a common enemy and nuisance,[129] may be killed, though the

[122] McCarthy v. Fremont, 23 Cal. 196 (1863); Tullay v. Reed, 1 C. & P. 6 (1823); Thompson v. Berry, 1 Cranch, C. C. 45 (1801); Britenbach v. Trowbridge, 64 Mich. 393, 31 N. W. 402 (1887); Lichtenveller v. Lanbach, 105 Pa. 366 (1884).

[123] Collins v. Renison, Sayer 138 (1754); Comm. v. Clark, 2 Met. (Mass.) (1840); State v. Lazarus, 1 Mill (S. C.) 34 (1817).

[124] Leonard v. Wilkins, 9 Johns, (N. Y.) 233 (1812); Livermore v. Batcheller, 141 Mass. 179, 5 N. E. 275 (1886); Morse v. Nixon, 8 Jones' Law, (N. C.) 35 (1866); McChesney v. Wilson, — Mich. —, 93 N. W. 627 (1903). In the last case the majority of the court held that the question of necessity was for the jury.

[125] Johnson v. Patterson, 14 Conn. (1840); Chapman v. Decrow, 93 Me. 378, 45 At. 295 (1899); Hodges v. Causey, 77 Miss. 353, 26 So. 445 (1900); Harris v. Eaton, 20 R. I. 81, 37 At. 308 (1897).

[126] Ulvey v. Jones, 81 Ill. 403 (1876); Clark v. Keliher, 107 Mass. 406 (1871); Matthews v. Tiestee, 2 E. D. Smith, (N. Y.) 90 (1853); Ford v. Taggart, 4 Tex. 492 (1849). See note on this topic in 67 Am. St. R. pp. 293-295.

[127] Protheroe v. Matthews, 5 C. & P. 581 (1833); Bowers v. Horen, 93 Mich. 420, 53 N. W. 535, 32 Am. St. R. 513, 17 L. R. A. 773 (1892); Ten Hopen v. Walker, 96 Mich. 236, 55 N. W. 657, 35 Am. St. R. 598 (1893); Bost v. Mingness, 64 N. C. 44 (1870).

[128] Aldrich v. Wright, 53 N. H. 398, 16 Am. R. 339 (1873).

[129] Hubbard v. Preston, 90 Mich. 221, 51 N. W. 209, 15 L. R. A. 259, with valuable note; 30 Am. S. R. 426 (1892); Brill v. Flagler, 23 Wend. (N. Y.) 354 (1840); Fisher v. Badger, 95 Mo. App. 209, 69 S. W. 26 (1902). In this case the dog had broken into plaintiff's house and emptied a crock of milk. He

killing is not necessary to prevent any mischief impending at the moment. Ordinarily a landowner is not liable to the owner of trespassing animals, which have eaten poisoned food on the former's premises, unless he placed it there for the purpose of injuring them.[130] In some jurisdictions, statutory authority is given to kill dogs that are in the habit of worrying sheep,[131] or that are found doing mischief of any kind.[132]

Accidental Harm: Primitive Rule. As stated on a former page, early English law did not recognize misadventure or accident as a defense to a criminal prosecution,[133] or a civil action.[134] Its doctrine was that " a man acts at his peril * * * If the act was voluntary, it was totally immaterial that the detriment which followed from it was neither intended nor due to the negligence of the actor.[135] Such was the current opinion of English lawyers, until about a century ago, if not later.." [136] In an early case [137] Justice Littleton is reported as assenting to the statement of counsel: " If one

was killed by defendant, the householder, as he jumped out of the house to escape. The court expressed the opinion that the killing was reasonably necessary to protect plaintiff's property from future dep-. redations by the dog; and also that the dog was a nuisance.

[130] Gillum v. Sisson, 53 Mo. App. 516 (1893); Dudley v. Love, 60 Mo. App. 420 (1894); Stansfeld v. Bolling, 22 Law Times, N. S. 799 (1870); Cobb v. Cater, 59 S. C. 462, 38 S. E. 114 (1901). The court was evenly divided in this case, two members approving the charge of the trial judge that, " If a man puts out poison to protect his property, and a dog invades his premises and gets the poison, the man would not be liable, but if he puts out the poison not for the protection of his property, but with the intent to kill his neighbor's dog he would be liable for damages." The other two judges thought the correct rule to

be this: " That a person, exercising the right to put out poison on his premises, shall act with such care as shall reasonably be expected of a man possessing ordinary prudence under the circumstances."

[131] Marshall v. Blackshire, 44 Ia. 475 (1876); Hinckley v. Emerson, 4 Cow. (N. Y.) 351, 15 Am. Dec. 383 (1825).

[132] Simmonds v. Holmes, 61 Conn. 1, 23 At. 702, 15 L. R. A. 253 (1891).

[133] Select Pleas of the Crown, Vol. 1, pl. 114 (1214), " Roger of Stainton was arrested because in throwing a stone he by misadventure killed a girl. And it is testified that this was not by felony. And this was shown to the King, and the King, moved by pity, pardoned him the death. So let him be set free."

[134] *Supra*, p. 51.

[135] Holmes, The Common Law, 82.

[136] Pollock, The Law of Torts, (6th Ed.) 134, 139 .

assaults me and I cannot escape, and in self-defense I lift my stick to strike him, and in lifting it hit a man who is behind me, in this case he shall have an action against me, yet my act was lawful, and I hit him, *me invito:*" and as adding, " If a man is damaged he ought to be recompensed." Nearly four hundred years later, a learned English judge [138] declared: " Looking into all the cases from the Year Book in 21 H. 7 down to the latest decision on the subject, I find the principle to be, that if the injury be done by the act of the party himself at the time, or he be the immediate cause of it, though it happen accidentally or by misfortune, yet he is answerable in trespass." Not until the case of Stanley v. Powell,[139] was this doctrine squarely rejected by an English Court, and the rule laid down that a person is not legally wronged, who suffers harm through the doing of a lawful act, in a lawful manner, by lawful means, and with due care and caution.

Modern Doctrine : In this country, such rule received judicial sanction at a much earlier day.[140] The case of Brown v. Kendall,[141] contains a full exposition of the principles upon which the rule rests. Two dogs, belonging to the plaintiff and the defendant were fighting, when the defendant took a stick about four feet long and commenced beating the dogs in order to separate them. In raising the stick to strike the dogs he accidentally hit the plaintiff in the eye, inflicting a severe injury. It was held that " if, in doing this act, using due care and all proper precautions necessary to the exigency of the case to avoid hurt to others, in raising the stick for that purpose, he accidentally hit plaintiff in the eye, and wounded him, this was the result of pure accident, or was involuntary and unavoid-

---

[137] Anonymous, Y. B., 6 Ed. 4, f. 7, pl. 18 (1466).

[138] Grose, J., in Leame v. Bray, 3 East, 593 (1803).

[139] (1891), 1 Q. B. D. 86, 60 L. J. Q. B. 683.

[140] Vincent v. Stinehour, 7 Vt. 62, (1835): " The result of our examination is, that we think that there must be some blame or want of care and prudence to make a man answerable in trespass: " Harvey v. Dunlap, Hill & Den. (N. Y.) 193

(1843). " If not imputable to the neglect of the party by whom it was done, or to his want of caution, an action of trespass does not lie, although the consequences of a voluntary act."

[141] Brown v. Kendall, 6 Cush. (Mass.) 292 (1850); Brown v. Collins, 53 N. H. 442, (1873); Spade v. Lynn, Etc. Ry., 172 Mass. 488, 52 N. E. 747, 70 Am. St. R. 298, (1889); Dunton v. Allan Line S. S. Co., 115 Fed. 250 (1902), *accord.*

able, and therefore the action would not lie. * * * To make an accident, or casualty, or as the law sometimes states it, inevitable accident," declared Chief Justice Shaw, "it must be such an accident as the defendant could not have avoided by the use of the kind and degree of care necessary to the exigency, and in the circumstances in which he was placed." [142]

Applying these principles, other courts have held that a person, who, in lawfully defending himself against an attack of A, accidentally and without negligence, harms B, is not liable to B for the harm.[143] Undoubtedly, when one is using fire-arms [144] or other dangerous instruments,[145] even though he is using them lawfully, he is bound to exercise a degree of care commensurate with the risk, and conduct will be deemed negligent and, therefore, tortious, which would be treated as not tortious, and hence not actionable, had the instrument been harmless.

When a person is suddenly and unexpectedly confronted by a terrible and impending danger, "the law presumes that an act or omission done or neglected under the influence of the danger is involun-

---

[142] In Feary v. Met. Street Ry., 162 Mo. 75, 99, 62 S. W. 452, 459 (1901), it was held unnecessary to use "inevitable" or "unavoidable" in connection with accident, and that a charge, "that if the jury believed the injuries sustained by the plaintiff were merely the result of accident, their verdict should be for the defendant," was correct.

[143] Paxton v. Boyer, 67 Ill. 132 (1873). Defendant was knocked down by plaintiff's brother, and, on rising, struck plaintiff with a knife, wounding his arm. The jury found, by special verdict, that "the blow complained of was struck by the defendant without malice, and under circumstances which would have led a reasonable man to believe it was necessary to his proper self-defense:" Cf. James v. Campbell, 5 C. & P. 372 (1832); Peterson v. Hafner, 59 Ind. 130, 26 Am. R. 81, and

note on p. 93 (1877); Cogdell v. Yett, 1 Cold. (Tenn.) 230 (1860), where defendant did not intend to harm plaintiff, but his act was voluntary and unlawful. In Wright v. Clark, 50 Vt. 130, 135 (1877), defendant killed plaintiff's dog, unintentionally, as the result of shooting at a fox. The court held that as defendant was under no obligation to shoot at the fox, he was answerable for any injury which might happen from his voluntary shooting, either by carelessness or by accident. Morris v. Platt, 32 Conn. 75 (1864), follows Brown v. Kendall, *supra*, p. 58.

[144] Castle v. Duryee, 2 Keyes, (N. Y.) 169, 175 (1865); Knott v. Wagner, 16 Lea. (Tenn.) 481 (1886).

[145] Peterson v. Haffner, 59 Ind. 130, 26 Am. R. 81 (1877); Bullock v. Babcock, 3 Wend. (N. Y.) 391 (1829).

tary." Any harm, therefore, which his involuntary act or omission inflicts upon others is deemed accidental.[146]

Harm Inflicted by Lunatics. So long as the primitive notion prevailed that the doer of harm was absolutely responsible therefor, the insanity of the doer could afford no defense, either to a criminal prosecution or a civil action.[147] When this notion was so far modified, that misadventure or accident on the part of the doer became a defense, it would have been entirely logical for the courts to treat the acts or the omissions of lunatics as involuntary, and, consequently, not tortious but accidental.[148] This was not done, however, and the general rule is, to-day as it was centuries ago, that " if a lunatic hurt a man he shall be answerable in trespass." [149] An exception has been suggested in the case of torts, " in which malice and therefore intention is a necessary ingredient."[150] Again, in actions for slander, if it is shown that the defendant's insanity " was great and notorious, so that the speaking the words could produce no effect on the hearers," the plaintiff should fail, because it is manifest that he has sustained no legal damage.[151] It has been held that, " the doctrine which renders an insane person responsible for what in a sane person would be called willful or negligent conduct, does not apply to the personal conduct of the master of a vessel, in case his incapacity to care for and navigate the ship resulted solely from exhaustion caused by his efforts to save the vessel during a storm," which continued for three days and nights.[152] The Court asks,

---

[146] Laidlaw v. Sage, 158 N. Y. 73, 52 N. E. 679, 44 L. R. A. 216 (1899), S. P. in Cleveland City Ry. v. Osborn, 66 Ohio. St. 45, 63 N. E. 604 (1902).

[147] 7 Harvard Law Review, 446.

[148] Bishop, Non Contract Law, §§ 505-507; Piggott, Principles of the Law of Torts, 215.

[149] Weaver v. Ward, Hob. 134, (1616); Cross v. Andrews, Cro. Eliz. 622 (1599); Taggard v. Innes, 12 U. C. C. P. 77 (1862); McIntyre v. Sholty, 121 Ill. 660, 13 N. E. 239, 2 Am. St. R. 140 (1887); Cross v. Kent, 32 Md. 581 (1870); Morain v. Devlin, 132 Mass. 87, 42 Am. R. 423

(1882); Jewell v. Colby, 66 N. H. 399, 24 At. 902 (1890); Krom v. Schoonmaker, 3 Barb. (N. Y.) 647 (1848); Williams v. Hays, 143 N. Y. 442, 38 N. E. 449, 42 Am. St. R. 743, 26 L. R. A. 153 (1894).

[150] Jewell v. Colby, 66 N. H. 399, 400, *supra*, Williams v. Hays, 143 N. Y. 442, 446, *supra*.

[151] Yeates v. Reed, 4 Blackf. (Ind.) 463, 32 Am. Dec. 43 (1838); Dickinson v. Barber, 9 Mass. 225, 228, 6 Am. Dec. 58 (1812); Bryant v. Jackson, 6 Humph. (Tenn.) 199 (1845); Irvine v. Gibson, — Ky. —, 77 S. W. 1106 (1904).

[152] Williams v. Hays, 157 N. Y. 541,

" What careful and prudent man could do more than to care for his vessel until overcome by physical and mental exhaustion?" Grant that no careful and prudent man could do more, does it follow that the master, rendered insane by such overwork, is not liable for the destruction of the vessel caused by acts or omissions due to his insanity, when it is admitted by the Court that he would have been liable, had his insanity come upon him in any other way? The distinction taken by the Court seems to indicate a lurking suspicion of the unsoundness of the general rule, and its willingness to evade it, whenever evasion is possible.

Unsatisfactory Reasons: If we examine the reasons assigned for the rule, we shall not find them very satisfactory. One reason is that, " the law looks to the person damaged by another and seeks to make him whole, without reference to the purpose or the condition, mental or physical, of the person causing the damage." [153] But we have seen that the law abandoned that ground long ago.

Another reason is that " where a loss must be borne by one of two innocent persons it shall be borne by him who occasioned it." [154] This would render the defense of inevitable accident futile.

Still another reason is that public policy requires the enforcement of the rule, so that tort-feasors may not simulate insanity as a defense to their harmful acts. [155] There would seem to be less danger of successful perjury by the defendant here, than in many accident cases. The rule is also supported on the ground of public policy, as tending to make a lunatic's relatives more careful about guarding him. But the occasional benefits derived from this tendency are small in comparison to the hardships resulting from the rule. [156]

The tort liability of insane persons has rarely come before the courts of England for adjudication, but the dicta in reported cases [157] are generally in accord with the decisions in this country,

---

43 L. R. A. 253, 52 N. E. 589 (1899). (A second hearing in the Court of Appeals.)

[153] Williams v. Hays, 143 N. Y. 442, 447, 42 Am. St. R. 743, 745, 26 L. R. A. 153, 38 N. E. 449 (1894).

[154] Beals v. See, 10 Pa. 56, 61, 49 Am. Dec. 573 (1848); Karow v. Continental Ins. Co., 57 Wis. 56, 46 Am. R. 17 (1883).

[155] McIntyre v. Sholty, 121 Ill 660, 13 N. E. 239, 2 Am. St. R. 140, (1887).

[156] On the second trial of Williams v. Hays, the trial court spoke of this rule as enunciating a " cruel doctrine " 157 N. Y. at p. 547.

[157] See those cited in preceding notes; and Mordaunt v. Mordaunt, L. R. 2 P. & D. 103, 142, 39 L. J. P.

as are also the few decided cases in the Colonial courts.[158]   Text-writers, however, are disposed to favor the view that the act or omission of an insane person, which he has not the power of willing or intending, are to be looked upon in law as involuntary or acciden-tal, and, therefore, acts or omissions which subject him to no tort liability.[159]

§ 7. CONFLICTING RIGHTS.

Neighboring Land Owners. We have seen that the common law permits a land owner to build a fence or other structure on his own land as high as he pleases, even though the erection cuts off his neighbor's view, or shades his garden, or otherwise harms his property.[160]   It also allows him to make excavations on his land, although these may result in the destruction of valuable springs or wells on his neighbor's premises, or may intercept or draw off bene-ficial subterranean waters.[161]   In such cases it is declared the land owner is exercising a right which the law accords to him as owner, without invading any legal rights of the neighbor.   The maxim, *Sic utere tuo ut alienum non leadas*, it is said " should be limited to causing injury to the right of another, rather than the property of another."   Or to put it in another way, the common law secures to the land owner certain absolute rights of dominion; that is, rights which he may exercise without incurring legal liability, how-

& D. 57, 59 (1870). A dictum that a lunatic is civilly answerable for a libel.

[158] Taggard v. Innes, 12 U. C. C. P. 77 (1862); Donagby v. Brennan, 19 N. Z. L. R. 289 (1901).

[159] Clerk and Lindsell, The Law of Torts, pp. 39, 40; Piggott, Princi-ples of the Law of Torts, pp. 215, 216. Pollock, The Law of Torts, (6th Ed.) Ch. 3, § 1. Lunacy in Re-lation to Contract; Tort and Crime, 18 Law, Quar. Rev. 21 (1902); Ren-ton, on Lunacy, pp. 64, 65.

[160] *Supra*, p. 45.

[161] Greenleaf v. Francis, 18 Pick. (Mass.) 117 (1836); Acton v. Blun-dell, 12 M. & W. 324, 13 L. J. Ex. 289 (1843); Chasemore v. Richards, 7 H. L. C. 349, 29 L. J. Ex. 81 (1859); Mayor of Bradford v. Pick-les, (1895), A. C. 587, 64 L. J. Ch. 759; Roath v. Driscoll, 20 Conn. 533 (1850); Chatfield v. Wilson, 28 Vt. 49 (1855); Phelps v. Nowlen, 72 N. Y. 39; Miller v. Black Rock Springs Co., 99 Va. 747, 40 S. E. 27 (1901); Cf. Smith v. City of Brooklyn, 160 N. Y. 357, 54 N. E. 787, 45 L. R. A. 664 (1899), and Forbell v. City of New York, 164 N. Y. 522, 58 N. E. 644, 51 L. R. A. 695, 79 Am. St. R. 666 (1900).

ever harmful their exercise may prove to his neighbor, or however malevolent may be the spirit with which he exercises them. It gives to him all that lies beneath the surface, whether it is solid rock or porous ground, or venous earth, or part soil and part water. It permits him to dig indefinitely downwards and apply all that is there found to his own purposes at his free will and pleasure.[163] It also permits him to rear structures indefinitely upwards.[164]

Limits of Land Owner's Privileges. If however, he exceeds these privileges and invades a legal right of his neighbor, as by maintaining a nuisance [165] or by diverting or unreasonably using a flowing stream,[166] or by accumulating water which percolates beneath the surface into his neighbor's land to its harm,[167] or by withdrawing the lateral support from his neighbor's land [168] he is liable to respond in damages for the injury.

It has been held, also, that a land owner invades a legal right of his neighbor, when, by means of wells and pumping stations, he forces the under-ground water from the neighbor's land into his wells, and thus deprives the neighbor of the natural supply of sub-surface water.[169]

---

[163] Acton v. Blundell, 12 M. & W. 324, 13 L. J. Ex. 289 (1843).

[164] Mahan v. Brown, 13 Wend. (N. Y. 261 (1835); Ridehout v. Knox, 148 Mass. 368, 19 N. E. 390, 2 L. R. A. 81, 12 Am. St. R. 560 (1889); Lovell v. Noyes, 69 N. H. 263, 46 At. 25 (1898).

[165] Aldred's Case, 9 Co. 59a (1610); Simmons v. Everson, 124 N. Y. 319, 26 N. E. 911 (1891); Hanck v. Tidewater Pipe Line Co., 153 Pa. 366, 20 L. R. A. 642, 26 At. 644 (1893); Wilson v. Phoenix Powder Co., 40 W. Va. 413, 52 Am. St. R. 890, 21 S. E. 1035 (1895); Townsend v. Epstein, 93 Md. 537, 49 At. 629, 86 Am. St. R. 441 (1901); Davis v. Niagara Falls Co., 171 N. Y. 336, 64 N. E. 4, 89 Am. St. R. 817, 57 L. R. A. 545 (1902).

[166] Watson v. New Milford Water Co., 71 Conn. 442, 42 At. 265 (1899).

[167] Cooper v. Barber, 3 Taunt, 99 (1810); Pixley v. Clark, 35 N. Y. 520, 91 Am. Dec. 72 (1866).

[168] Thurston v. Hancock, 12 Mass. 220 (1815); Humphries v. Brogden, 12 Q. B. 739 (1850).

[169] Forbell v. City of New York, 164 N. Y. 522, 51 L. R. A. 695, 58 N. E. 644, 79 Am. St. R. 666 (1900). Said the Court: "In the cases in which the lawfulness of interfering with percolating waters has been upheld, either the reasonableness of the acts resulting in the interference, or the unreasonableness of imposing an unnecessary restriction upon the owner's dominion of his own land has been recognized. In the absence of contract or enactment, whatever it is reasonable for the owner to do with his sub-surface water, regard being had to the definite rights of others, he may do.

It has also been held [170] that a land owner invades a legal right of his neighbor, by using in his gas-wells pumping machinery or other devices, by which the natural flow is greatly increased, and the common supply is injured or threatened with destruction. Said the court: " The right of each owner to take the gas from the common reservoir is recognized by the law, but this right is rendered valueless if one well owner may so exercise his right as to destroy the reservoir, or to change its condition in such manner that the gas will no longer exist there." * * * " The surface proprietors have the right to reduce to possession the gas found beneath. They could not be absolutely deprived of this right without a taking of private property. But there is a co-equal right in all of such owners to take the gas from the common source of supply. The use by one of his power to seek to convert a part of the common fund to actual possession may result in an undue proportion being attributed to one of the possessors of the right, to the detriment of others."

In Pennsylvania,[171] however, the courts have declared that a land owner has the absolute right not only to sink wells for water, gas or oil, but to use the most effective machinery possible for the

---

He may make the most of it that he reasonably can. It is not unreasonable, so far as it is now apparent to us, that he should dig wells and take therefrom all the water that he needs in order to the fullest enjoyment and usefulness of his land as land, either for purposes of pleasure, abode, productiveness of soil, trade, manufacture, or for whatever else the land as land may serve. He may consume it, but may not discharge it to the injury of others. But to fit it up with wells and pumps of such pervasive and potential reach that from their base the defendant can tap the water stored in the plaintiff's land, and in all the region thereabout, and lead it to his own land, and by merchandising it, prevent its return, is, however reasonable it may appear to the defendant and its customers, unrea-

sonable as to the plaintiff and the others whose lands are thus clandestinely sapped, and their value impaired: " Followed in Katz v. Walkinshaw, 141 Cal. 116, 70 Pac. 663 (1903); Cf. Fisher v. Feige, 137 Cal. 39, 69 Pac. 618 (1902); denying injunction to restrain upper riparian owner from denuding his land of forest, for the malicious purpose of diminishing the flow of a stream, and thus harming lower proprietor. *Contra*, Huber v. Merkel, 117 Wis. 355, 94 N. W. 354, 62 L. R. A. 589 (1903).

[170] Manufacturers' Gas & Oil Co. v. Ind. Nat. Gas Co., 156 Ind. 679, 57 N. E. 912, (1900).

[171] Westmoreland, Etc., Gas. Co. v. De Witt, 130 Pa. 235, 18 At. 724, 5 L. R. A. 731 (1889); Jones v. Forest Oil Co., 194 Pa. 379, 44 At. 1074, (1900).

extraction of the largest possible product, even though such use diminishes the product of his neighbor's wells. According to this view: " the property of an owner of land in oil, water and gas is not absolute until it is actually within his grasp and brought to the surface." Until then, the water, oil and gas are declared to be " minerals *feræ naturae,* belonging to the land owner so long as they are on or in it and subject to his control, but when they escape and go to the land of another or come under another's control, the title of the former owner is gone."

Test of Permissible Use of Land. On the other hand, it has been held that a land owner may blast rock, in the ordinary improvement of his premises, without liability to his neighbor for consequential harm; provided he acts with due care [172] and does not commit trespass.[173] According to these authorities, " The test of permissible use of one's own land is not whether the use or the act causes injury to his neighbor's property, or that the injury was the natural consequence, or that the act is in the nature of a nuisance, but the inquiry is, was the act or use a reasonable exercise of the dominion which the owner of property has by virtue of his ownership over his property having regard to all interests affected, his own and those of his neighbors, and having in view, also, public policy." [174]

---

[172] Booth v. R. W. O. Ry., 140 N. Y. 267, 24 L. R. A. 105, 35 N. E. 592, (1893); Holland House Company v. Baird, 169 N. Y. 136, 62 N. E. 149 (1901). There are dicta in Fitzsimons v. Braun, 199 Ill. 390, 65 N. E. 249, 59 L. R. A. 59 (1902), which are inconsistent with the foregoing doctrine, but the decision is not, nor are any of the cases, cited in the opinion, irreconcilable with it. In every one, there was actual trespass by the defendant, or the source of injury was held to be a nuisance for which the defendant was responsible: Cf. Quinn v. Crimmings, 171 Mass. 255, 50 N. E. 624, 68 Am. St. R. 420, 42 L. R. A. 101 (1898), in which Holmes, J., declares, " It is for the public welfare that buildings be put up, and here, as elsewhere public policy and custom have to draw the line between opposing interests."

[173] Hay v. Cohoes Co., 2 N. Y. 159 (1849); Sullivan v. Dunham, 161 N. Y. 290, 55 N. E. 923, 76 Am. St. R. 274, 47 L. R. A. 715 (1900). In Middlesex Co. v. McCue, 149 Mass. 103, 21 N. E. 230, 14 Am. St. R. 402 (1889), it was held that the owner of a garden upon a slope of a hill may cultivate and manure it, without liability for damages to a pond at the foot of the hill.

[174] Andrews, C. J., in Booth v. R. W. & O. R., 140 N. Y. 267 (1893).

Conditional Privilege of Defamation. The principle underlying the land owner cases is one of extensive and frequent application. In the law of defamation we shall find it playing an important part, under the title of " Conditional or qualified privilege."
Not only may counsel, and witnesses, during the progress of a litigation, defame a person with impunity, as we have seen in a former
connection;[175] but so may an employer in giving a character to a
servant,[176] or any person in the discharge of a legal or moral
duty,[177] or in the pursuance of a right.[178] The right to enjoy a good
reputation, until forfeited by his misconduct, is accorded to every
one by our law; and yet, " for the convenience and welfare of society," [179] our law refuses to treat this as an absolute right. It
balances " the needs and good of society against this right of the individual," [180] and, in cases where it deems the former to outweigh
the latter, grants the privilege of defamation. The courts have declared that " the business of life could not be well carried on," [181] if
this privilege were not granted. To its exercise, however, are an-
nexed certain conditions, which we shall consider more fully under
the topic of defamation; the person making the defamatory statement must honestly believe that it is true,[182] and must not make it

[175] *Supra*, p. 30; also Hartung v.
Shaw, 130 Mich. 177, 89 N. W. 701
(1902).

[176] Child v. Afflick, 9 B. & C. 403
(1829); Fresh v. Cutter, 73 Md. 87,
20 At. 774, 10 L. R. A. 67, 25 Am.
St. R. 577 (1890).

[177] Harrison v. Bush, 5 E. & B. 344,
25 L. J. Q. B. 25 (1855); Stuart v.
Bell, 2 Q B. 341 (1891); Deals v.
Thompson, 149 Mass. 405, 21 N. E.
932 (1889); Bayssett v. Hire, 49 La.
Ann. 904, 22 So. 44, 62 Am. St. R.
675 (1897); Redgate v. Roush, 61
Ks. 480, 59 Pac. 1050 (1900).

[178] Blackham v. Pugh, 2 C. B. 611
(1836); Baker v. Carrick, 1 Q. B.
838, 63 L. J. Q. B. 399 (1894); Caldwell v. Story, 107 Ky. 10, 52 S. W.
850, 45 L. R. A. 735 (1899); Hebner v. Great Northern Ry., 78 Minn.
289, 80 N. W. 1128, 79 Am. St. R.

387 (1899); Western Union Tel. Co.
v. Pritchett, 108 Ga. 411, 34 S. E. 216
(1899).

[179] Parke, B., in Toogood v. Spyring, 1 Cr. M. & R. 181 (1834).

[180] Post Publishing Co. v. Hallam,
59 Fed. 530 (1893).

[181] Parke, B., in Toogood v. Spyring, 1 Cr. M. & R. 181 (1834); Cf.
Blackburn, J., in Davies v. Snead,
L. R. 5 Q. B. 608, p. 611 (1870);
" Where a person is so situated that
it becomes right in the interests of
society that he should tell to a third
person certain facts, then, if he,
bona fide and without malice, does
tell them, it is a privileged communication."

[182] Jackson v. Hopperton, 16 C. B.
N. S. 829, 10 L. T. N. S. 529, 12 W.
R. 913 (1864).

with a malicious intention to injure its victim,[183] nor give it an unnecessarily wide publication.[184]

Modern Industrial Competition. The adjustment of conflicting rights, in cases growing out of modern business practices, is proving to be a very difficult task; but the principle, upon which the courts generally profess to rest their opinions, is that which we have been considering. The right to make contracts, or to labor or to build up a business is not an absolute right. It is qualified by a like right in others. Hence it should not be accounted a tort for A to buy goods from B, which he knows B has contracted to sell to C; and, in the absence of fraud [185] or some other independent wrong [186] by A, the weight of judicial authority is in favor of treating such a purchase as not tortious towards C. The same rule should be applied to interferences with contracts for personal services or with opportunities to labor. In the absence of a statute on the subject, the fact, that the offer of high wages of one employer induces the servants of another to quit him and enter the service of the former, ought not to subject the offerer to an action in tort.[187] If the offer is *bona fide,* and is limited to persons not under contract

[183]Carpenter v. Bailey, 53 N. H. 590 (1873); Clark v. Molyneux, 3 Q. B. D. 237, 47 L. J. Q. B. 230, 37 L. T. N. S. 694 (1877); Buisson v. Huard, 106 La. Ann. 768, 31 So. 293 (1901).

[184]King v. Patterson, 49 N. J. L. 417, 9 At. 705, 60 Am. R. 622 (1887); Redgate v. Roush, 61 Ks. 480, 59 Pac. 1050 (1900).

[185]Rice v. Manley, 66 N. Y. 82 (1876). In this case, plaintiffs had agreed to buy a quantity of cheese of S. Defendant, knowing of this agreement, caused a telegram to be sent to S., purporting to come from plaintiffs, to the effect that they did not want the cheese, and that S could sell it to others. Defendant took the telegram to S, who, supposing it genuine, sold and delivered the cheese to defendant. This fraudulent conduct by defendant was held to be a tort towards plaintiffs, who would have made a profit out of the transaction, but for defendant's interference: Angle v. Chicago, Etc. Ry., 151 U. S. 1, 13, 14 Sup. Ct. 240, 38 L. Ed. 55 (1893), is also a case of fraud on the part of defendant: Cf. Nashville C. & Gt. L. Ry. v. McConnell, 82 Fed. 65 (1897).

[186]Boysen v. Thorn, 98 Cal. 578, 33 Pac. 492, 21 L. R. A. 233 (1893); Pollock on Torts (6th Ed.) 232; Morasse v. Brochu, 151 Mass. 567, 25 N. E. 74, 8 L. R. A. 524 (1890); Ratcliffe v. Evans, (1892) L. R. 2 Q. B. 524, 61 L. J. Q. B. 535.

[187] See Chambers v. Baldwin, 91 Ky. 121, 15 S. W. 57, 11 L. R. A. 545, 34 Am. St. R. 171 (1891); May v. Wood, 172 Mass. 11, 51 N. E. 191 (1898); Kline v. Eubanks, 109 La. 241, 33 So. 211 (1902); Cf. Jones v. Stanley, 76 N. C. 355 (1877), holding that an action for damages lies

to others, there is no semblance of authority for holding the offerer liable in tort to employers, who find themselves forced thereby to pay higher wages or lose their workmen. Nor is it tortious for a laborer, or body of laborers, to refuse to work with specified individuals, or with a particular class, and to follow that refusal with a peaceful strike, although such conduct may result in the tabooed laborers' losing employment and wages which they would have secured, but for this interference.[188]

Rival Business. Again, it is not an actionable tort, to set up a rival business and thereby reduce the profits of an established proprietor, or even drive him out of trade. This has been the settled rule of English law for five centuries. In 1410, two masters of a grammar school at Gloucester " brought a writ of trespass against another master, and counted that the defendant had started a school in the same town, so that whereas the plaintiffs had formerly received 40d. or two shillings a quarter from each child, now they got only 12d. to their damage &c." But the Court of Common Pleas were unanimous in holding that the plaintiffs should take nothing by this writ. Said Hill, J.: " There is no ground to maintain this action, since the plaintiffs have no estate, but a ministry for the time; and though another equally competent with the plaintiffs comes to teach the children, this is a virtuous and charitable thing, and an ease to the people, for which he cannot be punished by our law." [189] In other words, English law has encouraged free competition, holding that it is worth more to society than it costs.[190]

Mogul Steamship Case. This is brought out very clearly in a modern English case.[191] An associated body of traders endeavored to get the whole of a limited trade (the tea carriage from certain Chinese ports) into their own hands, by offering exceptional and

against a person for maliciously persuading another to break any contract with plaintiff.

[188] National Protective Association v. Cumming, 170 N. Y. 315, 63 N. E. 369, 88 Am. St. R. 648, 58 L. R. A. 135 (1902). This is admitted in the dissenting opinion.

[189] Anonymous, Y. B. 11 H. 4, f. 47, pl. 21.

[190] Holmes, J., in Vegelahn v. Gunter, 167 Mass. 92, 44 N. E. 1077, 57 Am. S. R. 443, 35 L. R. A. 722 (1896), citing Comm. v. Hunter, 4 Met. (Mass.) 111, 134 (1842).

[191] Mogul Steamship Co. v. McGregor, 15 Q. B. D. 476, 54 L. J. Q. B. 540, S. C. Again 21 Q. B. D. 544, 57 L. J. Q. B. 541, S. C.; again 23 Q. B. D. 598, 58 L. J. Q. B. 465; still again (1892), A. C. 25, 61 L. J. Q. B. 295, 66 L. T. 1, 40, W. R. 337.

very favorable terms to customers who would deal exclusively with them; so favorable that but for the object of keeping the trade to themselves they would not offer such terms; and if their trading were confined to one particular period they would be trading at a loss, but in the belief that by such competition they would prevent the plaintiffs, as rival traders, competing with them, and so receive the whole profits of the trade to themselves.[192] The plaintiffs, who were thus driven out of the tea carrying trade with China, insisted that the associated traders had acted unlawfully toward them and should respond in damages. Lord Chief Justice Coleridge, before whom the case was tried, ruled against the plaintiffs, and his view was sustained by the successive appellate tribunals.

In the Court of Appeal, Lord Justice Bowen,[193] after calling attention to the fact that the case presented an apparent conflict between two rights that are equally regarded by the law—the right of the plaintiffs to be protected in the legitimate exercise of their trade, and the right of the defendants to carry on their business as seems best to them, provided they commit no wrong to others, said. " The acts of the defendants which are complained of here were intentional, and were also calculated, no doubt, to do the plaintiffs damage in this trade. But in order to see whether they were wrongful we have still to discuss the question whether they were done without any just cause or excuse. * * * They have done nothing more against the plaintiffs than pursue to the bitter end a war of competition waged in the interest of their own trade. * * * I can find no authority for the doctrine that such a commercial motive deprives of just cause or excuse, acts done in the course of trade, which would, but for such motive, be justifiable. So to hold would be to convert into an illegal motive the instinct of self-advancement and self-protection, which is the very incentive of all trade. To say that a man is to trade freely, but to say that he is to stop short at any act which is calculated to harm other tradesmen, and which is designed to attract business to his own shop, would be a strange and impossible course of perfection. But we are told

---

[192] See Lord Chancellor Halsbury's statement of facts, (1892), A. C. at p. 35. This offer of low freights is popularly styled " smashing rates." See Bowen, L. J., in 23 Q. B. D. at p. 611.

[193] L. R. 23 Q. B. 598 (1889). This opinion received the express approval of Lord Chancellor Halsbury, in the House of Lords.

that competition ceases to be the lawful exercise of trade, and so to be a lawful excuse for what will harm another, if carried to a length which is not fair or reasonable. The offering of reduced rates by the defendants in the present case is said to have been unfair. This seems to assume that, apart from the fraud, intimidation, molestation, or obstruction of some other personal right *in rem* or *in personam,* there is some natural standard of ' fairness ' or ' reasonableness ' (to be determined by the internal consciousness of juries) beyond which competition ought not in law to go. There seems to be no authority, and I think, with submission, that there is no sufficient reason, for such a proposition. It would impose a novel fetter upon trade."

Unfair Competition. In the same Court, Lord Justice Fry declared: " To draw a line between fair and unfair competition, between what is reasonable and unreasonable, passes the power of the courts. Competition exists where two or more persons seek to possess or to enjoy the same thing; it follows that the success of one must be the failure of another, and no principle of law enables us to interfere with or to moderate that success or that failure so long as it is due to mere competition."

When the case was before the House of Lords, one learned Lord [104] asserted that " there is no restriction imposed by law on competition by one trader with another with the sole object of benefiting himself." Another [105] expressed the opinion that all trade competition is " fair," which is " neither forcible nor fraudulent." The Lord Chancellor [106] declared: " The whole matter comes around to the original proposition, whether a combination to trade, and to offer, in respect of prices, discounts, and other trade facilities, such terms as to render it unprofitable for rival customers to pursue the trade is unlawful, and I am clearly of the opinion that it is not."

Fraudulent Injury to Business. This case has been cited frequently by American judges [197] and carefully followed by a number of courts.[198]

[194] Lord Hannen, (1892), A. C. p. 59.

[195] Lord Bramwell, *Ibid.* p. 47.

[196] *Ibid.* p. 40.

[197] Van Horn v. Van Horn, 52 N. J. L. 284, 10 L. R. A. 184, 20 At. 485 (1890); Barr v. Essex Trades Council, 53 N. J. Eq. 101, 30 At. 881, (1894).

[198] Continental Ins. Co. v. Board

It is generally agreed in this country, that a person, whose business is seriously injured, or destroyed by the fraudulent conduct of another deliberately planned to accomplish that end, has sustained an actionable tort.[199]

Intimidation of Third Persons. There is also substantial unanimity of opinion that physical intimidation or molestation of third persons, resorted to for the purpose of coercing them to abstain from business relations with another, is tortious towards the one who is damaged by such coercion.[200] Whether the peaceful persuasion, or even the moral intimidation of third persons, intending to result, and actually resulting in damage to another, amounts to a tort toward him, is a question upon which judges differ. On the one hand, it is said that a threat of workmen to strike, or to boycott, having business ruin behind it for the person threatened, " may be as coercive as physical force; " [202] that the anathemas of a secret organization of men appointed for the purpose of controlling the industry of others by a species of intimidation, that works upon the mind rather than the body, are quite as dangerous and, gener-

---

of Fire Underwriters, 67 Fed. 310 (1895); Macauley v. Tierney, 19 R. I. 255, 33 At. 1, 37 L. R. 455 (1895); Transportation Co. v. Standard Oil Co., 50 W. Va. 611, 40 S. E. 591 (1901).

[199] Rice v. Manly, 66 N. Y. 82 (1876); Angle v. Chicago, Etc. Ry., 151 U. S. 1, 14 Sup. Ct. 240, 38 L. Ed. 55 (1893); defendant by bribery and corruption got control of the stock of the Omaha Company, and caused the latter's officers to break a contract with plaintiff to latter's serious damage. Van Horn v. Van Horn, 52 N. J. L. 284, 20 At. 485, 10 L. R. A. 184 (1890); 56 N. J. L. 318, 28 At. 669 (1893). Defendant's broke up plaintiff's business by fraudulent and deceitful statements about his personal and business character.

[200] Quinn v. Leathem, (1901), A. C. 495, and cases cited therein;

Vegelahn v. Gunter, 167 Mass. 92, 44 N. E. 1077 (1896), prevailing and dissenting opinions; Kernan v. Humble, 51 La. Ann. 389, 25 So. 451 (1899); Southern Ry. Co. v. Machinite Local Union, 111 Fed. 49 (1901); National Protective Association v. Cumming, 170 N. Y. 315, 58 L. R. A. 135, 63 N. E. 369, 88 Am. St. R. 648 (1902), prevailing and dissenting opinions.

[201] Vann, J. in Nat. Protective Assoc. v. Cumming, 170 N. Y. at p. 343. In London Guarantee Co. v. Horn, 206 Ill. 493, 69 N. E. 526 (1903), the Court held that one who induces an employer to discharge an employee, by the threat to cancel an accident policy issued to the employer, unless he discharged the employee, was liable in tort to the latter—But see dissenting opinion.

[202] State v. Stewart, 59 Vt. 273, 9 At. 559 (1887). Similar views are

ally altogether more effective than acts of actual violence;[202] that
" when the will of the majority of an organized body in matters involving the rights of outside parties, is enforced upon its members by
means of fines and penalties, the situation is essentially the same as
when unity of action is secured among unorganized individuals by
threats or intimidation."[203]

On the other hand, it is declared that threats to withhold or withdraw patronage; to strike, or even to peacefully boycott or picket,
cannot be regarded as coercive in a legal sense:[204] that intimidation
or molestation to be legally coercive must have " an element of violence, or threat of violence, or actual trespass upon the person or
property, or the threat of it;"[205] that " the policy of allowing free
competition justifies the intentional inflicting of temporal damage,
including the damage of interfering with a man's business by some
means, when the damage is done, not for its own sake, but as an
instrumentality in reaching the end of victory in the battle of trade.
* * * If it be true that workingmen may combine, with a view
among other things, to getting as much as they can for their labor,
just as capital may combine with a view to getting the greatest
possible return, it must be true that, when combined, they have the
same liberty that combined capital has to support their interests by
argument, persuasion and the bestowal or refusal of those advantages, which they otherwise lawfully control."[206]

Difference of View Accounted for: The difference of view
brought out in the foregoing extracts is attributable in part perhaps,

expressed in Lucke v. Clothing Cut-
ters, 77 Md. 396, 26 At. 505 (1893);
Jackson v. Stanfield, 137 Ind. 592,
36 N. E. 345, 23 L. R. A. 588 (1894);
Barr v. Essex Trades Council, 53 N.
J. Eq. 101, 30 At. 881 (1894); Vegelahn v. Gunter, 167 Mass. 92, 44 N.
E. 1077, 57 Am. St. R. 443, 35 L. R.
A. 722 (1896); Hopkins v. Oxley
Stave Co., 83 Fed. 912 (1897); Webb
v. Drake, 52 La. Ann. 290, 26 So. 791
(1899); Gatzow v. Buening, 106 Wis.
1, 81 N. W. 1003, 80 Am. St. R. 17
(1900).

[203] Boutwell v. Marr, 71 Vt. 1, 42
At. 607, 43 L. R. A. 803, 76 Am. St.
R. 746 (1899).

[204] Macauley v. Tierney, 19 R. I.
255, 33 At. 1, 37 L. R. A. 455 (1895).

[205] Caldwell, J., in Hopkins v. Oxley Stave Co., 83 Fed. at p. 935.

[206] Holmes, J., dissenting opinion
in Vegelahn v. Gunter, 167 Mass. 92,
44 N. E. at p. 1081. Similar views
are expressed in Allen v. Flood,
(1898) A. C. I; Baker v. Metropolitan Life (Ky.), 64 S. W. 913 (1901),
and other Kentucky cases therein
cited; National Protective Association v. Cumming, 170 N. Y. 315
(1902). Guether v. Altman, 26 Ind.
App. 587, 60 N. E. 355 (1901).

to the different economic sympathies and political ideals of individual judges.[207]

Moreover, if, in all cases where one party, in the use of his property, or in the prosecution of his business, or in the exercise of his calling, intentionally so acts as to inflict loss upon another, the true inquiry is, was the act or use a reasonable exercise of defendant's legal rights, having regard to all interests affected, and having in view also public policy, we should expect different judges to answer the inquiry differently, even upon an agreed state of facts.[208]

Again, though the evidence be not conflicting, different judges will draw different inferences of fact therefrom. This is shown in Vegelahn v. Gunter,[209] where Allen J., writing for the majority, draws the inference from the report of the trial judge, that defendants indulged in threats of personal injury; while Holmes J. (who made the report) declared such inference unwarranted.

Unlawful Combinations. Still again, many cases containing conflicting dicta are easily reconcilable when tested by the inquiry above set forth. A combination of persons for the purpose of destroying the business of another or preventing his obtaining employment, and which accomplishes its object, without subserving any legitimate interests of its members or of the public, is clearly unlawful and is responsible for the harm which it inflicts.[210]

---

[207] See, a suggestive article by Mr. Justice Holmes, 8 H. L. R. I. (1893), entitled Privilege, Malice and Intent. At p. 8, dealing with the Mogul Steamship Company's Case, he says: "The ground of decision really comes down to a proposition of policy of rather a delicate nature, concerning the merit of the particular benefit to themselves intended by the defendants, and suggests a doubt whether judges with different economic sympathies might not decide such a case differently when brought face to face with the issue." Compare also the majority and minority opinions in Allen v. Flood and Hopkins v. Oxley Stave Co., *supra.*

[208] In Hopkins v. Oxley Stave Co.,

83 Fed. 912 (1897), the majority opinion lays stress upon the fact that defendant's combination and boycott were intended "to deprive the public at large of advantages to be derived from the use of" a labor saving invention. On the other hand the minority opinion asserts that the defendants had not exceeded the lawful limits of competition; that "products of labor-saving machinery are no more exempt from competition than hand-made products."

[209] 167 Mass. 92; 44 N. E. 1077, 57 Am. St. R. 443, 35 L. R. A. 722 (1896), cf. the references to Allen v. Flood, in the Lord Chancellor's Opinion in Quinn v. Leathem (1901), A. C. 495.

[210] Ertz v. Produce Exchange, 79

Such conduct is often characterized as malicious; but the use of that term has proved to be a source of confusion, and judges and text-writers are discarding it for less ambiguous terms, such as " unlawful," " wrongful," " bad faith." [211]

§ 8. ASSENT OF PLAINTIFF.

Contract Exemption from Tort Liability. If the essence of a tort is the unlawful violation of a person's right created by the law, it must follow that an act or omission of A, to which B has consented, is not tortious towards B, unless the consent is of a kind that the law will not countenance. As a rule, the law does not force a person to stand upon his rights. It permits him to waive, release or sell them. Accordingly, by a contract freely and fairly made, he may limit his right of recovery,[212] for what would otherwise be an actionable tort, or he may forego that right altogether.[213] This doctrine has been modified in some jurisdictions by statutes, which invalidate contracts by common carriers,[214] or by certain classes of employers,[215] exempting them from liability for negligence or other torts.

Invalid in Some Cases. Even in the absence of a statute, many courts have held that contract " exemptions limiting carriers from responsibility for the negligence of themselves or their serv-

Minn. 140, 48 L. R. A. 90, 81 N. W. 737 (1900), distinguishing Bohn Manufacturing Co. v. Hollis, 54 Minn. 223, 55 N. W. 1119, 21 L. R. A. 337 (1893); Martens v. Reilly, 109 Wis. 464, 84 N W. 840 (1901); Transportation Co. v. Standard Oil Co., 50 W. Va. 611, 40 S. E. 591 (1901).

[211] See Allen v. Flood (1898), A. C. 1; Pollock, Torts (6 Ed.) 272; Macauley v. Tierney, 19 R. I. 255, 33 At. 1, 37 L. R. A. 455, 61 Am. St. R. 770 (1895).

[212] Alair v. Northern Pac. Ry., 53 Minn. 160, 54 N. W. 1072, 19 L. R. A. 763, 39 Am. St. R. 588 (1893); O'Malley v. Great Northern Ry., 86 Minn. 380, 90 N. W. 974 (1902); Jacobs v. Central Ry. of N. J., 208 Pa. 535, 57 At. 982 (1904).

[213] Hartford Fire Ins. Co. v. Chicago, Mil. & St. P. Ry., 175 U. S. 91, 20 Sup. Ct. 33 (1899), aff'g S. S. in 70 Fed. 201, 17 C. C. A. 62, 62 Fed. 904, 36 U. S. App. 152; Griswold v. Illinois Cen. Ry., 90 Ia. 265, 24 L. R. A. 647, 57 N. W. 834 (1894).

[214] Norfolk & Wes. Ry. v. Tanner, 100 Va. 379, 41 S. E. 721 (1902); Postal Tel. Cable Co. v. Schaefer, 110 Ky. 907, 62 S. W. 1119 (1901).

[215] Rev. Laws, Mass. C. 106, § 16, and other statutes cited in Dresser, Employers Liability Acts, pp. 149-151.

ants are both unjust and unreasonable and will be deemed as wanting in the element of voluntary assent; and, besides, that such conditions are in conflict with public policy," [216] and "invalid for the reason that they tend to promote negligence on the part of corporations in respect to the personal safety of their employees "[217] and passengers.[217] Some of these courts, however, permit common carriers to exempt themselves from tort liability by contracts with other corporations, such as express companies. In cases of this kind the contracting parties are deemed to stand on a footing of equality, and the consent of the express company is entirely voluntary. No rule of public policy, therefore, it is said, requires a court to invalidate the contract.[319] The same doctrine has been applied to contracts between circus proprietors and railroad companies for the transportation of circus property and employees.[220] In short, contract exemptions of common carriers are generally upheld unless these "amount to a denial or repudiation of duties which are of the very essence of their employment." [221] Hence, when a common carrier becomes a private carrier or bailee, and undertakes a service which is not imposed upon it as " a public or a quasi public duty, such as that owing by a common carrier to an ordinary shipper, passenger or servant,"[222] but which it is at liberty to undertake or to decline, and with respect to which the bailor or patron is at no disadvantage in bargaining, the carrier is allowed to contract for exemption from tort liability.[223]

[216] The Kensington, 183 U. S. 263, 268, 22 Sup. Ct. 102 (1902), and cases therein cited.

[217] Tarbell v. Rutland Ry., 73 Vt. 347, 51 At. 6 (1901).

[218] Railroad Company v. Lockwood, 17 Wall. (U. S.) 357 (1873); Carroll v. Missouri Ry., 88 Mo. 234, 57 Am. R. 382, with valuable note pp. 388--398 (1885).

[219] Baltimore and Ohio S. W. Ry. v. Voigt, 176 U. S. 498, 20 Sup. Ct. 385, 44 L. Ed. 560 (1899), distinguishing New York Cen. Ry. v. Lockwood, 17 Wall 357 (1873), and citing Bates v. Old Colony Ry., 147 Mass. 255, 17 N. E. 633 (1888); Griswold v. N. Y. & N. E. Ry., 53 Conn. 371, 4 At. 261 (1885), Pittsburg C. C. & St. L. Ry. v. Mahoney, 148 Ind. 196, 40 L. R. A. 101, 47 N. E. 464, 62 Am. St. R. 503 (1897); Poucher v. N. Y. C. Ry., 49 N. Y. 263, 10 Am. R. 364 (1872).

[220] Robertson v. Old Col. Ry., 156 Mass. 535, 31 N. E. 650 (1892); Coup v. Wabash St. L. & C. Ry., 56 Mich. 111, 22 N. W. 215 (1885).

[221] Louisville Railway Co. v. Faylor, 126 Ind. 126, 25 N. E. 869 (1890).

[222] Pittsburg, C. C. & C. Ry. v. Mahoney, 148 Ind. 196 *supra.*

[222] Russell v. Pittsburgh & C. Ry., 157 Ind. 305, 61 N. E. 678, 87 Am. St. R. 214, 55 L. R. A. 253 (1901); a

Conflicting Views. Whether a common carrier may exempt itself from such liability to a passenger riding on a free pass, is a question upon which courts differ. In England, and in some of our jurisdictions, it has received an affirmative answer. Courts, holding this view, declare that such person is not "in the position of one who at common law, was entitled to the rights of a passenger, and became so entitled because of the obligation of the carrier to perform the duties resting upon it by virtue of the public nature of its employment;" and, therefore, "there is no principle of public policy" prohibiting him and the carrier from making a valid contract of exemption.[224]

On the other hand, courts which answer the question in the negative declare: "The ground upon which such agreements are held to be invalid is that they violate public policy. Is the State solicitous only for the safety of those who pay their fare? How does the fact that the passenger is being transported for hire, or as a mere gratuity, interest or affect the State? The policy of the State is to enforce, with an equal hand, the performance of those duties upon which the safety of her citizens depends."[225]

Leave and License by Plaintiff. Thus far we have been considering cases, where the plaintiff's exoneration of the defendant has taken the form of a contract. It is not necessary, however, that it should take this form. Most frequently it consists in an agreement without consideration, commonly characterized as "leave and license," or of conduct which falls under the maxim *volenti non fit injuria,* or the phrase "assumption of risk."

A physician, who forcibly or fraudulently makes an examination of another's person without his consent or other lawful authority, commits an aggravated assault.[226] If, however, the examination is assented to, though the assent be reluctant, he will be exempt from tort liability.[227] Persons, taking part in lawful sports, assent

well reasoned decision citing many authorities.

[224] Duncan v. Maine Cent. Ry., 113 Fed. 508 (1902). Those who accept gratuities and acts of hospitality are bound by the conditions on which they are granted, at p. 514. Rogers v. Kennebec Steamboat Co., 86 Me. 261, 29 At. 1069 (1894).

[225] Norfolk & C. Ry. v. Tanner, 100 Va. 379, 41 S. E. 721 (1902).

[226] Reg v. Flattery, 2 Q. B. D. 410 (1877); Agnew v. Johnson, 13 Cox C. C. 625 (1877).

[227] Latter v. Braddell, 50 L. J. Q. B. 166, 44 L. T. 369, 29 W. R. 366 (1880).

to the harsh treatment which they had good reason to believe would be accorded them in such play, but to nothing more than this.[228] Nor does one assent to being made the victim of a college rush by becoming a student of the college, or a spectator of the rush.[229] Moreover, plaintiff's assent will not exonerate the defendant from tort liability, if the acts assented to are such as the law will not countenance. Hence " one may recover in an action for assault and battery, although he agreed to fight with his adversary; for such an agreement to break the peace being void, the maxim *volenti non fit injuria* does not apply."[230] An assent to a form of initiation [231] into a society or of expulsion therefrom,[232] which subjects the victim to " appreciable bodily harm for the mere pleasure " [233] of the participants, has been held invalid.

Deception of Plaintiff. If the plaintiff's assent is secured by fraud or deception on the part of defendant the assent is vitiated by the fraud, and will not avail as a defense; [234] unless the deceit practised relates to something of such an illegal or clearly immoral character, that the law raises no duty of disclosure on the part of the deceiver.[235]

In the last cited case, the plaintiff sued the defendant for assault upon her person. Upon the trial, it appeared that, for about two years illicit intercourse subsisted between the parties and, during

[228] Fitzgerald v. Cavin, 110 Mass. 153 (1872); Peterson v. Hoffner, 59 Ind. 130, 26 Am. R. 81 (1877).

[229] Markley v. Whitman, 95 Mich. 236, 54 N. W. 763, 35 Am. St. R. 558, 20 L. R. A. 55 (1893), cf. Reid v. Mitchell, 12 R. (Sessions Cases Fourth Series), 1129 (1885), and Reynolds v. Pierson, 29 Ind. App. 273, 64 N. E. 484 (1902).

[230] Bell v. Hausley, 3 Jones (N. C.) 131 (1855), citing and following Boulter v. Clark Buller's N. P., 16 (1747); Barholt v. Wright, 45 Ohio St. 177 (1887), citing Stout v. Wren, 1 Hawks (N. C.) 420 (1821); Adams v. Waggoner, 33 Ind. 531 (1870); Shay v. Thompson, 59 Wis. 540 (1883); Logan v. Austin, 1 Stewart (Al.) 476 (1828); Comm. v. Colberg, 119 Mass. 350 (1876), *Contra*, Bishop, Non Contract Law, § 196, approved and followed in Goldnamer v. O'Brien, 98 Ky. 569, 33 S. W. 831, 56 Am. St. R. 378, 36 L. R. A. 715 (1896).

[231] Kniver v. Phoenix Lodge, 7 Ont. (Q. B.) 377 (1885).

[232] State v. Webster, 75 N. C. 134 (1876).

[233] Pollock on Torts (6 Ed.) 158.

[234] Reg. v. Flattery, 2 Q. B. D. 410 (1877); Comm. v. Stratton, 114 Mass. 303, 19 Am. R. 350 (1873); McCue v. Klein, 60 Tex. 168, 48 Am. R. 260 (1883).

[235] Hegarty v. Shine, L. R. 4 Irish, 288 (1878).

its continuance the defendant infected plaintiff with venereal disease. The trial judge charged the jury that " If the defendant, knowing he had venereal disease, and that the probable and natural effect of his having connection with the plaintiff would be to communicate to her venereal disease, fraudulently concealed from her his condition, in order to induce, and did thereby induce her to have connection with him; and if but for the fraud she would not have consented to have such connection, he had committed an assault, and one for which they might, on the evidence, award substantial damages." This charge was held by the appellate tribunals to be erroneous. " In the present case," said Lord Chancellor Ball, " the fraud relied upon to annul the plaintiff's consent, is the concealment of a fact which if known would have induced her to withhold it: but before this effect is attributed to such concealment, it seems to me reasonable to demand—what is required in contract—that from the relation between the parties there should have arisen a duty to disclose, capable of being legally enforced. And how can this be, when the relation is itself immoral and for the indulgence of immorality: the supposed duty with the object of aiding its continuance? To support obligation founded upon relation, it appears to me the relation must be one that we can recognize and sanction. The consequence of an immoral act—the direct consequence—is the subject of the complaint. Courts of justice no more exist to provide a remedy for the consequences of immoral or illegal acts and contracts, than to aid or enforce those acts or contracts themselves." [236]

Volenti Non Fit Injuria. The maxim *volenti non fit injuria* seems to be peculiarly applicable to cases, where the plaintiff, not having expressly consented to defendant's exemption from tort liability, has sustained harm by voluntarily encountering a source of danger due to the conduct of another. It is effective as a defense on the ground that, in the circumstances of a given case, the defendant's conduct is not the violation of a legal duty to the plaintiff. A land owner sets spring-guns,[237] or discharges fire-arms into the air,[238] to frighten off trespassers. Towards them his duty is only

[236] Hamilton v. Lomax, 26 Barb (N. Y.) 615 (1858), *accord*.

[237] Ilott v. Wilkes, 3 B. & Ald. 304, 22 R. R. 400 (1820); State v. Barr,

11 Wash. 481, 39 Pac. 1080, 48 Am. St. R. 890, 29 L. R. A. 154, with note (1895).

[238] Magar v. Hammond, 171 N. Y.

to abstain from inflicting willful or wanton injury. A person, who, with knowledge of the land owner's habits, voluntarily enters upon the premises thus protected, and sustains harm from the known source of danger, has only himself to blame. The consequences are only those which he courted. In his situation, the land owner owed him no duty of care which has been violated. The injury is legally chargeable to his own act, and not to that of the land owner.

The principle underlying the foregoing and similar cases has been stated as follows: " One, who, knowing and apprehending a danger, voluntarily assumes the risk of it, has no just cause of complaint against another who is primarily responsible for the existence of the danger. As between the two, his voluntary assumption of the risk absolves the other from any particular duty to him in that respect, and leaves each to such chances as exist in the situation, without right to claim anything from the other. In such a case there is no actionable negligence on the part of him who is primarily responsible for the danger. If there is a failure to do his duty according to a high standard of ethics, there is, as between the parties, no neglect of legal duty." [239] A briefer statement is found in a modern English decision: " The duty of an occupier of premises, which have an element of danger upon them, reaches its vanishing point in the case of those who are cognizant of the full extent of the danger and voluntarily run the risk." [240]

Limitations upon Maxim. It is apparent from these statements of the principle, that it is subject to various limitations. First the defendant is bound to show that the plaintiff knew and apprehended the danger in question. If it is not clearly apparent, notice of the danger must be given, and this notice must be brought home to the plaintiff.[241] Whether the plaintiff has been thus noti-

---

377, 64 N. E. 150, 59 L. R. A. 315 (1902). The Court of Appeals declared that if the defendants were free from " willfulness, malice, intention to injure, or desire or motive to do so, they were entitled to have the jury instructed that, if the plaintiff voluntarily exposed himself to a known danger, he could not recover for the act of the watchman in shooting, though this act, in the defense of the master's

property was without due care."

[239] O'Maley v. Gaslight Co., 158 Mass. 135, 32 N. E. 1119, 47 L. R. A. 161, with valuable note (1893). Quoted with approval in Drake v. Auburn City Ry., 173 N. Y. 466, 66 N. E. 121 (1903).

[240] Bowen, L. J., in Thomas v. Quartermaine, 18 Q. B. D. 685, 56 L. J. Q. B. 340 (1887).

[241] Bird v. Holbrook, 4 Bing. 628, 22 R. R. 657 (1828). Plaintiff,

fied, or has in truth known and apprehended the danger, is a question of fact, and, usually for the jury;[242] although when the evidence is not conflicting and warrants but one inference, the question may be disposed of by the court.[243]

Positive Duty imposed by Law. Another limitation upon the principle appears in cases, where the common law or a statute imposes upon the defendant a positive duty not to cause or permit the danger in question. If a person creates or maintains a nuisance, he is liable for all the direct consequences thereof: [244] and cannot be heard to say that one who has been subjected to a risk by such nuisance has voluntarily courted it, and thus has absolved him from tort liability. For example, defendant unlawfully dug a trench along the driveway from plaintiff's livery-stable to the street, making

though a trespasser, had no notice of spring guns on defendant's land, and recovered damages: Sarch v. Blackburn, 4 C. & P. 297 (1830). Defendant had posted a notice in large letters, "Beware of dog;" but plaintiff could not read, and entered defendant's premises in ignorance of the danger: Dowd v. N. Y. O. & W. Ry., 170 N. Y. 459, 63 N. E. 541 (1902), holding that it is no part of the plaintiff's case to show that he did not assume the risk, but that the burden of showing such assumption is on the defendant: Cf. Choctaw, Etc., Ry v. McDade, 191 U. S. 64, 24 Sup. Ct. 24 (1903). Upon this question the true test is not in the exercise of care to discover dangers, but whether the defect is known or plainly observable by the employee: Texas, Etc. R. Co. v. Archibald, 170 U. S. 665, 42 L. Ed. 1188, 18 Sup. Ct. 777 (1898).

[242] Osborne v. London & N. W. Ry., 21 Q. B. D. 220 (1888); Fitzgerald v. Conn. River Paper Co., 155 Mass. 155, 29 N. E. 464, 31 Am. St. R. 537 (1891).

[243] Juchatz v. Michigan Alkali Co.,

120 Mich. 654, 79 N. W. 907 (1899); Howey v. Fisher, 122 Mich. 43, 80 N. W. 1004 (1899); Roberts v. Missouri, Etc., Co., 166 Mo. 370, 66 S. W. 155 (1901); Ball v. Hanser, 129 Mich. 397, 89 N. W. 49 (1902); Martin v. Chicago, Etc. Ry., 118 Iowa 148, 91 N. W. 1034 (1902); George Fowler Sons & Co. v. Brook, 65 Ks. 861, 70 Pac. 600 (1902); Drake v. Auburn City Ry., 173 N. Y. 466, 66 N. E. 121 (1903).

[244] Muller v. McKesson, 73 N. Y. 195 (1878); Missouri & c. Ry. v. Burt, (Tex. Civ. App.) 27 S. W. 948 (1894); Davis v. Rich, 180 Mass. 285, 62 N. E. 375 (1902); Kleebauer v. Western Fuse Co., 138 Cal. 497, 69 Pac. 246 (1902). In the last cited case, the court approved the rule laid down in Kinney v. Koopman, 116 Ala. 310, 22 So. 593, 67 Am. St. R. 119, with note (1896), and Tuchachinsky v. Lehigh, Etc. Co., 199 Pa. 515, 49 At. 308 (1901), holding that whether a store-house of gunpowder or of dynamite is a nuisance, is a question for the court, where the facts are undisputed.

it dangerous for plaintiff to take his horses out. The latter attempted to lead one of his horses along the dangerous path, when it fell over the rubbish, thrown up by defendant, and into the trench and was killed. The Court charged the jury "that it could not be the plaintiff's duty to refrain altogether from coming out of the stable merely because the defendant had made the passage in some degree dangerous: that the defendant was not entitled to keep the occupier of the stable in a state of siege until the passage was declared safe, first creating a nuisance and then excusing himself by giving notice that there was some danger; though, if the plaintiff had persisted in running upon a great and obvious danger, his action could not be maintained." [245]

Again, defendant, a manufacturer, permitted the steps leading from his mill to the street, to become coated with ice. Plaintiff, an employee, in going from her work, fell on the icy steps and was injured. It was the duty of the defendant to provide a reasonably safe passage way for plaintiff, and he was not absolved from this duty by plaintiff's attempt to go down these icy steps, such being her only way of leaving the mill. [246]

Spectators at Unlawful Exhibitions. It is submitted that the foregoing doctrine should have been applied in Scanlon v. Wedger [247] and Frost v. Josselyn. [248] The defendants, in those cases, discharged fire-works in public highways without a lawful license. The plain-

---

[245] Clayards v. Dethick, 12 Q. B. 439 (1848). The last clause of the instruction is sustained in Kriwinski v. Penn. Ry. Co., 65 N. J. L. 392, 47 At. 447 (1900); cf. Lax v. Corporation of Darlington, 5 Ex. D. 28, 49 L. J. Ex. 105 (1879); Osborne v. London, Etc. Ry., 21 Q. B. D. 220, 57 L. J. Q. B. 618 (1888); Yarmouth v. France, 19 Q. B. D. 647, 57 L. J. Q. B. 7 (1887). In the last two cases it is said that the plaintiff is not precluded from recovering by the fact that he knew there was some danger. In order to bar a recovery, the defendant must show that "the plaintiff freely and voluntarily, with full knowledge of the nature and extent of the risk he ran, impliedly agreed to incur it."

[246] Fitzgerald v. Connecticut River Co., 155 Mass. 155, 29 N. E. 464, 31 Am. St. R. 537 (1891). The Court laid much stress upon the fact that it was not shown that plaintiff knew and appreciated the extent of the danger, to which defendant's misconduct subjected her, as the English Court did in the cases cited in the last preceding note. English v. Amidon, 72 N. H. 361, 56 At. 548 (1902).

[247] 156 Mass. 462, 31 N. E. 642, 16 L. R. A. 395 (1892).

[248] 180 Mass. 389, 62 N. E. 469 (1902).

tiffs, while lawfully upon the highway as spectators, and in the exercise of due care, were injured by the fire-works. There was no evidence of negligence on the part of defendants. It was held by a divided court, in the former case, (and this decision was followed in the latter) that " the plaintiffs were content to abide the chance of personal injury not caused by negligence;" that " a voluntary spectator, who is present merely for the purpose of witnessing the display, must be held to consent to it, and he suffers no legal wrong, if accidentally injured without negligence on the part of any one, although the show was unauthorized." [249] In the minority opinion, Morton J. said: " It is carrying the doctrine of assumption of risk further than I think it has ever been carried to say that one who, being lawfully on the highway, and in the exercise of due care, observes as a spectator an unlawful and dangerous exhibition in it, assumes the risk. The exhibitor is bound at his peril to see that he has a valid license. If he selects the highway for an unlawful and dangerous display designed or calculated to attract the public, he, and not the spectator, assumes the risk of injury. It is of no consequence that the defendant exercised reasonable care in firing the bomb. It is a contradiction of terms to say of one engaged in an unlawful, dangerous, wrongful and unjustifiable business that he used due care in it. Due care is predicated of something which a person may lawfully do, but which, by his negligent manner

---

[249] Pollock on Torts, (1st Ed.) 138-144 is cited in support of this view, But the learned author's statements are predicated upon lawful conduct on the part of the defendant. In the sixth edition at p. 497, it is said that voluntary exposure to danger will not excuse the breach of a positive statutory duty. This doctrine has been applied frequently by American courts in fire-escape cases. See Corrigan v. Stilwell, 97 Me. 247, 54 At. 389, 61 L. R. A. 163 (1903), and authorities there cited.

In Evans v. Waite, 83 Wis. 286, 53 N. W. 445 (1892), defendant, a minor, armed with a revolver in violation of a statute accidentally shot plaintiff. The latter recovered as compensatory damages $375. Lyon, C. J., said, " It was unlawful for the defendant to be armed with a revolver when the plaintiff was injured, and hence he is liable for any injury inflicted by him with such weapon. It is immaterial that the plaintiff was consenting to the defendant being so armed, and to his use of the revolver. The question of negligence (on defendant's part) is immaterial." Followed in Horton v. Wylie, 115 Wis. 505, 92 N. W. 245 (1902); Osborne v. Vandyke, 113 Ia. 557, 85 N. W. 784, 54 L. R. A. 367 (1901); accord. Gilmore v. Fuller, 198 Ill. 130, 65 N. E. 84 (1902), contra.

of doing it, may become injurious to others; not of something which he has no right to do."

Assumption of Risk as an Absolvent from Statutory Duty. In England it is well settled that a defendant is not absolved from a positive statutory duty by plaintiff's assumption of the risk: and, unless the latter's conduct is altogether unreasonable, in taking the risk thus unlawfully thrust upon him by the defendant, he is entitled to recover.[250] In this country, the decisions are conflicting, but the weight of authority is opposed to the English view.[251]

Assumption of Risk a Term of Servant's Contract. Most of the American cases, in which this question has been considered, have arisen between employee and employer, and the discussion has been further complicated by a difference of opinion concerning the basis of the assumption of risk by the employee. On the one hand, it is said, that "assumption of risk is a term of the contract of employment, by which the servant agrees that danger of injury, obviously incident to the discharge of his duty, shall be at his risk * * and the only question is whether the courts, will enforce or

[250] Clarke v. Holmes, 7 H. & N. 937, 31 L. J. Ex. 356 (1862); Baddeley v. Earl of Granville, 19 Q. B. D. 423, 56 L. J. Q. B. 501 (1887); Clerk & Lindsell, On Torts, (2 Ed.) 441-446; Pollock On Torts, (6 Ed.) 497.

[251] In accord with the English cases are Narremore v. Cleveland & C. Ry., 96 Fed. 298, 37 C. C. A. 499, 48 L. R. A. 68 (1899); Carterville Coal Co. v. Abbott, 181 Ill. 495, 55 N. E. 131 (1899); Godfrey v. Coal Co., 101 Ky. 339, 41 S. W. 10 (1897); Love v. American Manufacturing Co., 160 Mo. 608, 61 S. W. 678 (1900); Chattanooga Rapid Transit Co. v. Walton, 105 Tenn. 415 (1900); Davis Coal Co. v. Polland, 158 Ind. 607, 62 N. E. 492, 92 Am. St. R. 319 (1901); Troxler v. Southern Ry., 124 N. C. 189, 32 S. E. 550, 44 L. R. A. 315, 70 Am. S. R. 580 (1899); Elmore v. Seaboard Ry., 132 N. C. 865, 44 S. E. 620 (1903); Evans v.

Waite, 83 Wis. 286, 53 N. W. 465 (1892). *Contra.* Birmingham Electric Co. v. Allen, 99 Al. 359, 13 So. 8, 20 L. R. A. 457 (1892); St. Louis Cordage Co. v. Miller, 126 Fed. 495, 63 L. R. A. 551 (1903); Glenmont Lumber Co. v. Roy, 126 Fed. 524 (1903); but see dissenting opinion by Thayer, J., in these two cases; Martin v. Chicago, Etc. Ry., 113 Ia. 148, 91 N. W. 1034 (1902); Keenan v. Edison, Etc. Co., 159 Mass. 379, 34 N. E. 366 (1893); Anderson v. C. N. Nelson Lumber Co., 67 Minn. 79, 69 N. W. 630 (1896); Kinsley v. Pratt, 148 N. Y. 372, 42 N. E. 986, 32 L. R. A. 367 (1896); Wellston Coal Co. v. Smith, 65 Ohio St. 71, 61 N. E. 143, 87 Am. St. R. 546 and note, p. 587 (1901); Langlois v. Dunn Worsted Mills, 25 R. I.—, 57 At. 910 (1904); Dressler, Employers' Liability, § 116, and authorities cited.

recognize as against a servant an agreement, express or implied on his part, to waive the performance of a statutory duty of the master, imposed for the protection of the servant and in the interest of the public. We think they will not." [252]

Assumption of Risk versus Public Policy. Other courts declare that assumption of risk by the servant is not a term of his employment, but has its origin in the legal relations of the parties, precisely as in the case of the land owner and an invited guest; that when a servant voluntarily assents to a known risk, no cause of action in his behalf arises against the statute-violating employer and "hence there is none from which the contract exempts;" that "it is quite as obnoxious to public policy, independent of the penalty imposed, for the employee to aid and encourage the employer to violate it;" [253] that the statute "does not deprive laborers of their free agency and the right to manage their own affairs." [254] Even these courts admit that statutes may be so framed as to prevent any assumption of risk by employees; and such statutes have been enacted in several jurisdictions. [255]

Distinguishable from Contributory Negligence. The conduct of the plaintiff which we have been considering under the various headings of leave and license, *volenti non fit injuria* and assumption of risk, is to be sharply distinguished from contributory negligence on his part. This distinction has not always been observed, [256] and

---

[252] Narremore v. Cleveland, Etc. Ry., 96 Fed. 398, 37 C. C. S. 499, 48 L. R. A. 68 (1899); Evans Laundry Co. v. Crawford, — Neb. —, 93 N. W. 177 (1903).

[253] Martin v. Chicago, Etc. Ry., 113 Ia. 148, 91 N. W. 1034 (1902).

[254] Kinsley v. Pratt, 148 N. Y. 372, 42 N. E. 986, 32 L. R. A. 367 (1896).

[255] Coley v. North Car. Ry., 128 N. C. 534, 39 S. E. 43 (1901), applying ch. 56 Priv. Laws 1897, §§ 1 and 2. The latter section is as follows: "That any contract or agreement, expressed or implied, made by an employee of said company to waive the benefit of the aforesaid section shall be null and void." See other statutes referred to in Dresser, Employer's Liability, pp. 248, 249, 604.

[256] In David v. New York, On. Etc. Ry., 170 N. Y. 459, 63 N. E. 541 (1902); Vann, J., says: "Nearly all Courts recognize the doctrine of assumed risks as resting upon implied contract, although in applying it, they frequently refer to the result, without discussion, as contributory negligence." See 8 Harv. L. R. 457, "*Volenti non fit injuria,*" by Charles Warren, (1895); Dresser, Employers' Liability, §§ 84, 86 (1902). This distinction is fully discussed in St. Louis Cordage Co. v. Miller, 126 Fed. 495, 63 L. R. A. 551 (1903).

no little confusion has resulted from the failure of judges in this respect. Under the statutes referred to in the last paragraph the distinction comes out very clearly.

A railroad employee does not assume the risk incident to the employer's violation of a statute, requiring grab-irons on all cars, where the statute expressly invalidates any contract or agreement, expressed or implied, to waive the benefit of the statute. But he may be guilty of contributory negligence in taking hold of the drain-pipes of an engine-tender, knowing that they were not put there to be used as grab-irons.[257] In that event, his contributory negligence will bar a recovery.

Not a few of the cases often cited for the proposition that a defendant is absolved from the performance of a statutory duty, by the plaintiff's assumption of the risk, have decided only, that contributory negligence of the plaintiff may bar his action, although the defendant is guilty of a breach of statutory duty towards plaintiff.[258]

§ 9. PLAINTIFF A WRONGDOER.

Not an Outlaw. We have seen that a person, who is injured while engaged in an illegal fight, may recover against his assailant, although he voluntarily assented to the assailant's conduct. This is not the result of unfair discrimination between the parties, but of various considerations of public policy.

Illegality of Conduct as a Bar to Recovery. In some instances, however, the illegality of the plaintiff's conduct, at the time of his injury, bars a recovery, but to have this effect, his illegal conduct must form a part of his cause of action, or must be a contributing cause of his injury. "While this principle is universally recognized, there is a great practical difficulty in applying it. The best minds often differ upon the question whether in a given case, illegal conduct of a plaintiff was a direct and proximate cause contributing with others to his injury, or was a mere condition of it; or

---

[257] Coley v. North Car. Ry., 128 N. C. 534, 39 S. E. 43 (1901).

[258] Victor Coal Co. v. Miner, 20 Colo. 320, 38 Pac. 378, 46 Am. St. R. 299 (1894); Godfrey v. Coal Co., 101 Ky. 339, 41 S. W. 10 (1897); Queen v. Dayton Coal Co., 95 Tenn. 458, 32 S. W. 460, 49 Am. St. R. 935 (1895).

[259] Newcomb v. Boston Protective Dep., 146 Mass. 596, 4 Am. St. R. 354, 16 N. E. 555 (1888).

to state the question in another way, appropriate to the reason of the rule, whether or not his own illegal act is an essential of his case as disclosed by all the evidence." [259]

Difficulty in Applying the Principle. The practical difficulty referred to in the foregoing extract is aptly illustrated by two lines of Massachusetts decisions. As great a Judge as Chief Justice Shaw ruled that the act of a plaintiff (injured by reason of a defect in a highway) in driving for pleasure on Sunday in violation of the statute, was " a species of fault on his part that concurred in causing the damage complained of." [260] Justice Morton, approving this view declared: " Whoever travels on the Lord's day, except for necessity or charity is acting in violation of the law. Such act of traveling itself is unlawful, and if, in the course and as an incident of such traveling, the traveler sustains an injury his unlawful act necessarily is a contributing cause of the injury."[261] In another line of cases, the same Court has sustained recoveries by plaintiffs who were injured, while traveling in violation of the Sunday law, by an attacking dog,[262] or negligent fellow-traveler.[263]

Violation of Sunday Laws. The ruling of Chief Justice Shaw has not commended itself to judges outside of Massachusetts, and, in that State, it has been negatived by statute.[264] According to the prevailing view, a traveler in violation of the Sunday law is not a trespasser upon the highway. If he brings an action for injuries, caused by the defective street or bridge, " the fault which prevents a recovery is one which directly contributes to the accident: as carelessness in driving, either a vicious or unmanageable horse, or at an improper rate of speed, or without observation of the road, or in an insufficient vehicle, or with a defective harness, or in a state of intoxication, or under some other condition of driver, horse or carriage, which may be seen to have brought about the injury." [265] If, in a given case, " the same causes would have produced the

---

[260] Bosworth v. Inhabitants of Swansey, 10 Met. (Mass.) 363 (1845).

[261] Lyons v. Desotelle, 124 Mass. 387 (1878).

[262] White v. Lang, 128 Mass. 598 (1880).

[263] Wallace v. Merimack, Etc. Co., 134 Mass. 95 (1883).

[264] Gen. Laws, Mass. L. 1884, C. 37, § 1. " The provision of C. 98 of the Public Statutes, relating to the observance of the Lord's Day shall not constitute a defense to an action for a tort or injury suffered by a person on that day."

[265] Danforth, J., in Platz v. City of Cohoes, 89 N. Y. 219 (1882).

same result upon any other day, the fact that the accident occurred on Sunday is immaterial in considering the cause of it, or the question of contributory negligence;"[266] and plaintiff's violation of the law is only a condition and not a cause of his harm.[267]

Illegal Conduct an Element in the Cause of Action.

On the other hand, if the plaintiff's illegal conduct is an essential element of his case when all the facts appear, a court will not lend him its aid. His harm is not a legal injury. This is admirably illustrated by three cases tried at the same term in North Carolina. In the first of these,[268] it appeared that plaintiff, a soldier in the Confederate service, was injured in a railroad accident, while being carried by the defendant's company to the field of hostile operations against the United States.

"If the rebellion had been successful," said the Court. "And a government had been founded upon that success, it would doubtless have been legitimate for the courts of such a government to adjust the rights of those who had been engaged in establishing it. But will the courts of the government which was attempted to be destroyed, interfere to redress one of the insurgents who was disabled in the very act of hostility to the government whose aid he now seeks? It will consult its dignity and not interfere in this dispute. The act of going to the field of operations was illegal, and the contract of the defendant to aid him by carrying him to the field was an illegal contract, and there can be no recovery."

[266] Ill. Railroad Co. v. Dick, 91 Ky. 434, 15 S. W. 665 (1891).

[267] Phil. Etc. Ry. v. Phil. Etc. Towboat Co., 23 How. (U. S.) 209 (1859); Black v. City of Lewiston, 2 Idaho 254, 13 Pac. 80 (1887); Schmid v. Humphrey, 48 Ia. 652, 30 Am. R. 414 (1878); Bigelow v. Reed, 51 Me. 325 (1863); Sharp v. Evergreen Township, 67 Mich. 443, 35 N. W. 67 (1887); Opsahi v. Judd, 30 Minn. 126, 14 N. W. 575 (1883); Woodman v. Hubbard, 5 Fost. (N. H.) 67 (1852); Carroll v. Staten Island Ry., 58 N. Y. 126, 17 Am. R. 221 (1874); Kerwhacker v. Cleveland, Etc. Ry., 3 Ohio St. 172 (1854); Mohney v. Cook, 26 Pa. 342 (1855); Baldwin v. Barney, 12 R. I. 392, 34 Am. R. 670 (1879); Eagan v. Maguire, 21 R. I. 189, 42 At. 506 (1890); Sutton v. Wanwatosa, 29 Wis. 21, 9 Am. R. 534 (1871); cf. Harrington v. Los Angeles Ry., 140 Cal. 514, 74 Pac. 15, 63 L. R. A. 238 (1903). A bicycle rider injured while racing, in violation of a city ordinance. Judgment for $10,000, affirmed.

[268] Turner v. North Car. Ry., 63 N. C. 522 (1869); Wallace v. Cannon, 38 Ga. 199 (1868); accord. S. P. Fivas v. Nicholls, 2 M., G. & S. 500, 52 Eng. C. L. 501 (1846).

In the second case,[269] growing out of the same accident, the defendant failed to show that the plaintiff was then going in order to take part in the confederate service, and he recovered a verdict of $2,000. In the third case,[270] the plaintiff's " intestate was an officer of the Confederate States army at home on a furlough, and was killed by the negligence of officials of the defendant, while returning home from a visit to friends. Plaintiff recovered a verdict for $3,000."

Duty Towards a Law Breaker : — It is thus apparent that a law-breaker is not an outlaw. The fact that one has committed larceny gives no legal warrant to a mob to seize and threaten him with hanging.[271] It "would work a confusion of relations and lend a very doubtful assistance to morality to allow an offender against the law, to the injury of another, to set off against the plaintiff that he too is a public offender."[272] But the illegal conduct of the plaintiff, though not directly contributing to his injury in a particular case, may modify the defendant's duty towards him. A land owner has no right to treat a trespasser as an outlaw, and proceed to shoot,[273] or dynamite[274] or stone[275] him. On the other hand, he is not liable to such an one for mere negligence. The extent of his duty is to abstain from inflicting upon him willful or wanton injury.[276]

---

[269] Ireland v. North Car. Ry., 63 N. C. 526n. (1869).

[270] Clark v. Raleigh, Etc. Ry., 63 N. C. 526n. (1869); S. P. Gross v. Miller, 93 Ia. 72, 26 L. R. A. 605, 61 N. W. 385 (1894). It is no defense to an action for negligent shooting, that, at the time of the injury, plaintiff and defendant were violating a statute prohibiting shooting on Sunday.

[271] Stallings v. Owen, 51 Ill. 92 (1869).

[272] Mohney v. Cook, 26 Pa. 342 (1855).

[273] Bird v. Holbrook, 4 Bing. 628, 29 R. R. 657 (1828).

[274] Carter v. Columbia, Etc. Ry., 19 S. C. 20 (1883).

[275] Conners v. Walsh, 131 N. Y. 590, 30 N. E. 59 (1892).

[276] Carter v. Columbia, Etc. Ry., 19 S. C. 20 (1883); Condran v. Chicago, Etc. Ry., 67 Fed. 522, 32 U. S. App. 182, 14 C. C. A. 506, 28 L. R. A. 749 (1895); Way v. Chicago, Etc. Ry., 64 Ia. 48, 19 N. W. 828 (1884); Bullard v. Mulligan, 69 Ia. 416, 29 N. W. 404 (1886); Purple v. Union Pac. Ry., 114 Fed. 123, 51 C. C. A. 564, and cases cited (1902). The same principle has been applied in cases brought by persons injured through a carrier's negligence, while riding on a free pass, given and used in violation of a statute; McNeill v. Durham, Etc. Ry., 132 N. C. 510, 44 S. E. 34,

Illegal Business outside the Pale of the Law.   While a law-breaker is not an outlaw, the business which he carries on, or the property which he owns may be outside the pale of the law. For example, the author of a copyrighted book, which is under the ban of the law as indecent or immoral, cannot maintain an action against one who pirates it, or otherwise interferes with its sale.[277] Nor can a person who, under the guise of conducting a drugstore, carries on an illicit traffic in intoxicating liquors, be heard to complain that he has been forced to discontinue this illegal business and has lost the profits thereof, by reason of threats of the defendant, that if he did not discontinue it, he must take the consequences. To such a case the maxim applies, *ex dolo malo non oritur actio.*[278]

Doctrine Misapplied : — This maxim was misapplied, it is submitted, in a recent Illinois case.[279]   Plaintiff was negligently shot by defendant, while they with others were engaged in " a charivari of a young married couple."   The transaction being an illegal one, the plaintiff's cause of action was held to be within the maxim.   His unlawful act, in becoming a member of the party, was declared to concur in causing his damage, and thus to bar his recovery.   Indeed, the Court went so far as to assert that as plaintiff and defendant were members of a party engaged in breaking the law, the plaintiff was responsible for every act of the defendant in carrying on the charivari, and, hence, the shooting was as much the act of the plaintiff as of any other person engaged in the enterprise. It would seem that his membership in this party was merely a condition and not a cause of the injury.

§ 10. REMOTENESS OF DAMAGE.   PROXIMATE CAUSE.

Statement of Rule.   Persons often escape legal liability for the

(1903); State v. Southern Ry., 122 N. C. 1052, 30 S. E. 133, 41 L. R. A. 246 (1898).

[277] Lawrence v. Smith, Jacob, 471 (1622); Stockdale v. Onwhyn, 5 B. & C. 173, 7 D. & R. 625, 2 C. & P. 163 (1826).   So, one, who fraudulently mingles his chattels with those of another, loses all legal right to them, and is remediless against

him, who appropriates the whole mass; Stephensen v. Little, 10 Mich. 434 (1862).

[278] Prude v. Sebastian, 107 La. 64, 31 So. 764 (1902).

[279] Gilmore v. Fuller, 198 Ill. 130, 65 N. E. 84, 60 L. R. A. 286 (1892). Reversing same case in 99 Ill. App. 272 (1901); Cf. Evans v. Waite, 83 Wis. 286, 53 N. W. 445 (1892); Hor-

results of their wrongful conduct, on the ground that the plaintiff's harm was too remote. " A man's responsibility for his negligence." it is said, " must stop somewhere."[280] Although the general rule is, undoubtedly, that a wrongdoer must answer for the damages caused by his misconduct, our law strives to apply this rule in a practical and reasonable manner. " It is impossible to trace any wrong to all its consequences. They may be connected together and involved in an infinite concatenation of circumstances. As said by Lord Bacon, ' it were infinite for the law to judge the cause of causes, and their impulsion one of another. Therefore, it contenteth itself with the immediate cause, and judgeth of acts by that, without looking to any further degree.' [281] The best statement of the rule is that a wrongdoer is responsible for the natural and proximate consequences of his misconduct."[282]

Line is Sometimes Arbitrary. Even in this form, the rule has proved difficult of application.[283] In some cases, the difficulty has been surmounted by arbitrarily drawing a line beyond which all consequences are ticketed " remote." For example, a person slanders another. Nothing is more natural than the repetition of that slander by the hearer. And yet, though this natural consequence follow immediately with serious pecuniary harm to the victim, the author of the slander is not legally answerable for the harm. His liability is limited to damage done by his original utterance. For the harm inflicted by the repetition only the repeater is liable.[284] His misconduct is the proximate cause of this harm.

ton v. Wylie, 115 Wis. 505, 93 N. W. 245 (1902); Osborne v. Van Dyck, 113 Ia. 557, 85 N. W. 784, 54 L. R. A. 367 (1901).

[280] Hoag v. Lake Shore, Etc. Ry., 85 Pa. 293 (1877).

[281] Maxims of the Law, Reg. 1.

[282] Ehrgott v. Mayor, Etc., 96 N. Y. 264 (1884).

[283] Perhaps this difficulty is best disclosed by comparing cases, in which the facts are substantially the same, but the conclusions are opposed e. g., cf. Seale v. Gulf, Etc. Ry., 65 Tex. 274 (1886); negligent fire by defendant not the proximate cause of injury to

person attempting to put it out, with Glanz v. Chicago, Etc. Ry., 119 Ia. 611, 93 N. W. 575 (1903), it is the proximate cause. Stone v. Boston, Etc. Ry., 171 Mass. 536, 51 N. E. 1, 41 L. R. A. 794 (1898), with Pittsburgh, Etc. Ry v. Wood, 94 Fed. 618 (1899). The prevailing and dissenting opinions in Seifter v. Brooklyn, Etc. Ry., 169 N. Y. 254, 62 N. E. 349 (1901); Brown v. Chicago, Etc. Ry., 54 Wis. 342, 11 N. W. 356, 911, 41 Am. R. 41 (1882); with Snow v. N. Y., Etc. Ry., 185 Mass. 321, 70 N. E. 205 (1904).

[284] Elmer v. Fessenden, 151 Mass. 359, 5 L. R. A. 724, 24 N. E. 208

A like arbitrary line has been drawn by the New York Court of Appeals in cases of negligent fires.[285] The proximate consequence is restricted to damage inflicted upon an abutting owner. If the fire extends beyond his premises, whether they be ten feet or ten miles in breadth, its destruction is too remote to make the negligent originator of the fire liable therefor. This limitation is admitted to be arbitrary, " but," it is claimed, " it recognizes the principle that we should live and let live. Fires often occur from the trivial acts of the most prudent persons. Great conflagrations are daily reported. Not long since one of our largest cities substantially disappeared within a single day. No person, however cautious, is exempt: misfortune may overtake him in a forgetful moment, or through fault in the members of his family or servants. No man is able to answer for all the remote consequences of his acts and those for whom he is responsible."[286]

The Opposite View : — In reply to this reasoning, other courts have said,[287] that it is better and more in accordance with the relative rights of others, that he should be ruined through whose negligence a number of buildings are burned, than that the various owners should suffer a loss which is in no way attributable to fault on their part. The assumption that, if a great loss is to be borne, it would better be distributed among many innocent victims than wholly visited upon the wrongdoer, does not seem either reasonable or just.

Leaving Remoteness to the Jury. Another way of surmounting the difficulty, inherent in this rule, is to leave the question of remoteness to the jury. It is frequently resorted to by American courts [288]

(1890). If the first speaker authorized the repetition of the slander such repetition is virtually his act through an agent, and he must answer for it. Washington Gas Light Co. v. Lansden, 172 U. S. 534, 19 Sup. Ct. R. 296 (1899).

[285] Ryan v. New York Central, 35 N. Y. 210, 91 Am. Dec. 49 (1866); Hoffman v. King, 160 N. Y. 618, 55 N. E. 401, 73 Am. St. R. 715, 46 L. R. A. 672 (1899). See able· dissenting opinion of Vann, J., in which Parker, C. J., concurred

[286] Haight, J., in Hoffman v. King, *supra.* Similar views are expressed in Kerr v. Penn. Ry., 62 Pa. 353 (1870).

[287] Hoyt v. Jeffers, 30 Mich. 181 (1874); Lillibridge v. McCann, 117 Mich. 84, 75 N. W. 288, 41 L. R. A. 381 (1898); Fent v. Toledo, Etc. Ry., 59 Ill. 349 (1871); Milwaukee, Etc. Ry. v. Kellogg, 94 U. S. 469 (1876).

[288] Milwaukee, Etc. Ry. v. Kellogg, 94 U. S. 469 (1876): " The true rule is, that what is the proximate cause

although it has been criticised by eminent judges in this country,[289] and is under the ban of judicial opinion in England.[290] Lord Blackburn, after commenting on the vagueness of the rule, and comparing the line which has to be drawn, in these cases, to that between night and day, declared: " I do not think it is any one's fault that the rule cannot be put any more definitely. I think it must be left as vague as ever as to where the line must be drawn—but I think, in each case, the Court must say whether it is on the one side or the other; and I do not think the question of remoteness ought ever to be left to the jury. That would be in effect to say that there shall be no such rule as to damages being too remote; and it would be highly dangerous if it was left generally to the jury to say whether the damage was too remote or not."[291]

Even in this country when the question of remoteness is raised by the pleadings,[292] or when it arises upon agreed or undisputed facts from which but one inference can be drawn by reasonable men, it is to be determined by the court.[293]

---

of an injury is ordinarily a question for the jury. It is not a question of science or of legal knowledge. It is to be determined as a fact, in view of the circumstances of fact attending it." S. P. in Pastene v. Adams, 49 Cal. 87 (1874); Village of Carterville v. Cook, 129 Ill. 152 (1889); Lane v. Atlantic Works, 111 Mass. 136 (1872); Bishop v. St. Paul City Ry., 48 Minn. 26, 50 N. W. 927 (1892); Dickson v. Omaha, Etc. Ry., 124 Mo. 140, 27 S. W. 476 (1894); Gilman v. Noyes, 57 N. H. 627 (1876); Wiley v. West, J. Ry., 44 N. J. L. 247 (1882); Ehrgott v. Mayor, Etc., 96 N. Y. 264 (1884); Thomas v. Central Ry., of N. J., 194 Pa. 511, 45 At. 344 (1900); Harrison v. Berkley, 1 Strobhart Law, (S. C.) 525 (1847).

[289] In Gilman v. Noyes, 57 N. H. 627 (1876); Ladd, J., said: " The question is, whether courts can relieve themselves from troublesome inquiries of this description, by

handing them over to the jury for determination. I am not prepared to admit that they can."

[290] Scott v. Shepherd, 2 W. Bl. 892, 3 Wils. 403 (1773); Rommey Marsh v. Trinity House, L. R. 5 Exch. 204 (1870); Lynch v. Knight, 9 H. L. C. 477 (1861); Clerk & Lindsell on Torts, p. 116.

[291] Hobbs v. London, Etc. Ry., L. R. 10 Q. B. 11, 122 (1875), cited approvingly in Glassey v. Worcester Consol. Co., 185 Mass. 315, 70 N. E. 199 (1904).

[292] Bosch v. Burlington, Etc. Ry., 44 Ia. 402 (1876); McDonald v. Snelling, 14 Allen (Mass.) 290 (1867); Molbus v. Town of Waitsfield, 750 Va. 122, 53 At. 775 (1902).

[293] Goodlander Mill Co. v. Standard Oil Co., 63 Fed. 400 (1894); Scheffer v. Washington, Etc. Ry., 105 U. S. 249 (1881); Thomas v. Lancaster Mills, 71 Fed. 481 (1896); Mayor, Etc. of Macon v. Dykes, 103 Ga. 847, 31 S. E. 443 (1898); Alex-

Usual Instruction to the Jury. In case the question is left to the jury, the court instructs them that they are to find for the plaintiff, if, in their opinion, there was an unbroken connection between the defendant's wrongful act and the plaintiff's injury, so that the injury was a result naturally and reasonably to be expected, either as the sole consequence of that and of other causes, which might reasonably have been expected to be set in motion by it, or to act in concurrence with it.[294] On the other hand, if in their opinion, the injury would not have happened, but for the intervention of some new cause, which could not have been reasonably anticipated,[295] the defendant's act is to be deemed the remote and not the proximate cause, and they should find for the defendant.[296] At times, the court contents itself with instructing the jury more briefly, that the

---

ander v. Town of Newcastle, 115 Ind. 51, 17 N. E. 200 (1888); Bentley v. Fisch Lumber Co., 51 La. Ann. 451, 25 So. 262 (1899); Martinez v. Bernhard, 106 La. 368, 30 So. 901 (1901); Maryland Steel Co. v. Marney, 88 Md. 482, 42 At. 60 (1898); Loker v. Damon, 17 Pick. (Mass.) 284 (1835); Carter v. Towne, 103 Mass, 507 (1870); Salisbury v. Herchenroder, 106 Mass. 458 (1871); Daniels v. N. Y., Etc. Ry., 183 Mass. 393, 67 N. E. 424 (1903); Dickson v. Omaha Etc. Ry., 124 Mo. 140, 27 S. W. 476 (1894); Meyer v. King, 72 Miss. 1, 16 So. 245, 35 L. R. A. 474 (1894); Rooks v. Alabama, Etc. Ry., 78 Miss. 91, 28 So. 821 (1900); Ward v. West Jersey Ry., 65 N. J. L. 383, 47 At. 561 (1900); Mars v Del. & Hud. Ry., 54 Hun. (N. Y.) 625 (1889); Mitchell v. Rochester Ry., 151 N. Y. 107, 45 N. E. 354, 34 L. R. A. 781 (1896); Ewing v. Pittsburgh Ry. Co., 147 Pa. 40, 23 At. 340 (1892); Willis v. Armstrong Co., 183 Pa. 184, 38 At. 621 (1897); Isham v. Dow's Estate, 70 Vt. 588, 41 At. 585, 45 L. R. A. 87 (1898).

[294] Milwaukee, Etc. Ry. v. Kellogg, 94 U. S. 469 (1876); Binford v. Johnson, 82 Ind. 426 (1882); Lane v. Atlantic Works, 111 Mass. 136 (1872).

[295] An example of such a cause is found in Afflick v. Bates, 21 R. I. 281, 43 At. 539 (1899). Explosion of percussion caps by trespassing boy. An intervening cause fairly to be anticipated is found in Owen v. Cook, 9 N. D. 134, 81 N. W. 285, starting a "back fire." In Daniels v. N. Y., Etc. Ry., 183 Mass. 393, 67 N. E. 424 (1903); an act of suicide by one whose mind was disordered by sickness caused by defendant's negligence, was held to be a new and independent as well as the efficient cause of the death, and defendant's negligence was too remote to render it liable for the death.

[296] Gilman v. Noyes, 57 N. H. 627 (1876). An excellent statement of the proper charge in these cases is found in Meyer v. Milwaukee, Etc. Ry., 116 Wis. 336, 93 N. W. 6, (1903), and in Andrews v. Chicago, Etc. Ry., 96 Wis. 348, 71 N. W. 372 (1897).

rule of law applicable to the case is, that plaintiff's injuries must be the natural and proximate consequences of defendant's misconduct; explaining that the term " natural " imports that the consequences are such as might reasonably have been foreseen, such as occur in an ordinary state of things; while the term " proximate " indicates that there must be no other culpable and efficient agency intervening between the defendant's dereliction and the loss.[297]

§ 11. MENTAL ANGUISH; WOUNDED FEELINGS; FRIGHT; NERVOUS SHOCK.

Mental Anguish not a Cause of Action. " It is undoubted law that mental pain or anxiety alone, unattended by any injury to the person, cannot sustain an action."[300] But, suppose such mental suffering cause physical sickness, disabling the sufferer from attending to his ordinary business and compelling him to incur expense for medical treatment: has the victim a cause of action against the wrongful disturber of his peace of mind?

Origin of Doctrine: — This question appears to have presented itself first for judicial decision in defamation cases, and that, too, in quite recent times. The answer of the New York Court of Appeals[301] is as follows: " It would be highly impolitic to hold all language, wounding the feelings and affecting unfavorably the health and ability to labor of another, a ground of action; for that would be to make the right of action depend often upon whether the sensibilities of a person spoken of are easily excited or otherwise; his strength of mind to disregard abusive, insulting remarks concerning him; and his physical strength and ability to bear them. * * * * In the present case the words were defamatory,[302] and the illness and physical prostration of the plaintiff may be assumed to have been actually produced by the slander: but, this consequence was not, in

---

[297] Wiley v. West Jersey Ry., 44 N. J. L. 247 (1882); Ehrgott v. Mayor, Etc., 96 N. Y. 264 (1884); Harrison v. Berkeley, 1 Strob. L. (S. C.) 525 (1847); Isham v. Davis Estate, 70 Vt. 588, 41 At. 585, 45 L. R. A. 87 (1898).

[300] Beven on Negligence (2d Ed.) 77 (1895).

[301] Terwilliger v. Wands, 17 N. Y. 53, 72 Am. Dec. 420 (1858), overruling Bradt v. Towsley, 13 Wend. (N. Y.) 253 (1835), and Fuller v. Fenner, 16 Barb. (N. Y.) 333 (1853).

[302] The words imputed incontinency to the plaintiff, but were not actionable *per se*.

a legal view, a natural and ordinary one, as it does not prove that the plaintiff's character was injured. * * * Such an effect may, and sometimes does, follow from such a cause, but not ordinarily; and the rule of law was framed in reference to common and usual effects, and not those which are accidental or casual."

Two years later a similar case [302 1-4] came before the English Court of Exchequer and evoked the same answer. Pollock, C. B. said: "This particular damage depends upon the temperament of the party affected, and it may be laid down that illness arising from the excitement which the slanderous language may produce is not that sort of damage which forms a ground of action." Bramwell, B. said: "The question seems to me one of some difficulty, because a wrong is done to the female plaintiff who becomes ill, and therefore there is damage alleged to be following from the wrong; and I think it did in fact so flow. But I am struck by what has been said as to the novelty of this declaration, that no such special damage ever was heard of as a ground of action. * * * There is certainly no precedent for such an action, probably because the law holds that bodily illness is not the natural consequence of the speaking of slanderous words. Therefore, on the ground that the damage here alleged is not the natural consequence of the words spoken by the defendant, I think the action will not lie." [302 1-2]

Mental Anguish Accompanying Actionable Defamation.

While the doctrine of the foregoing decisions has been accepted, generally, both in England and in this country, it is also agreed that in case of libel, or of slander actionable *per se,* sickness due to the plaintiff's mental distress, and even the injury to her feelings though not causing sickness, may be taken into account by the jury in assessing damages.[303]

[302 1-4] Allsop v. Allsop, 5 H. & N. 534, 29 L. J. Exch. 315 (1860); Lynch v. Knight, 9 H. L. C. 577 (1861), *accord.*

[302 1-2] In McQueen v. Fulgham, 27 Tex. 463, 469 (1864), a case also of slanderous words not actionable *per se;* the Court declared that it could not "say as a matter of law, that the words of a ribald and malign slanderer may not prey like a can-

cer upon the mind and health of a sensitive and nervous female, until the one is unsettled and the other impaired and destroyed, much less that pecuniary injury would not result from the loss of health and the inability to discharge her ordinary and accustomed domestic labor."

[303] Odgers, Libel and Slander (3d Ed.) 353; Johnson v. Robertson, 8 Port. (Al.) 486 (1839); Swift v.

Soliciting Sexual Intercourse. A similar distinction has been made in cases where sexual intercourse has been solicited. An action will not lie, it is said, in favor of a woman against a man, who, without trespass or assault, solicits her to illicit intercourse, though the humiliation and mental distress " unnerved and damaged her." [304] But it will lie, if his solicitation amounts to a technical assault or trespass; and, in the latter case, the injury to feelings, the mental distress, as well as the physical sickness induced thereby may be taken into account by the jury in assessing damages.[305]

Worry and Fright Caused by Defendant's Misconduct. Where the consequences of the defendant's wrongdoing are limited to the mental disturbance of the plaintiff, and the wrongdoing is not actionable in behalf of the plaintiff, apart from such consequences, any harm sustained by the plaintiff is deemed *damnum absque injuria.* Thus far there is entire unanimity of decision.[306] When, however, the worry or fright causes physical derangement, differences of opinion immediately develop, and it becomes impos-

---

Dickerman, 31 Conn. 285 (1863); Pugh v. McCarty, 40 Ga. 444 (1869); Dufort v. Abadie, 23 La. Ann. 280 (1871); Wilson v. Noonan, 35 Wis. 321 (1874); Zeliff v. Jennings, 61 Tex. 458 (1884).

[304] Reed v. Maley, —— Ky.——, 74 S. W. 1079 (1903).

[305] Newell v. Whitcher, 53 Vt. 589, 38 Am. R. 703 (1830). The court charged the jury that, if the plaintiff was so frightened and shocked in her feelings as to injure her health, by defendant's conduct, she should receive damages for such injury. The defendant's counsel asked the court to charge, in substance, that if defendant's acts and conduct would not have injured a person of ordinary nerve and courage, then there can be no recovery. On appeal, the Supreme Court upheld the charge and the refusal of defendant's request, declaring that as defendant's conduct amounted to

an assault he must answer for all actual injuries, and affirmed a judgment for $225, including $100 for exemplary damages. Bruske v. Neugent, 116 Wis. 488, 93 N. W. 454 (1903). Verdict for $500 upheld, the court saying: " The mere physical or pecuniary injury was, of course, insignificant; but the outrage to the feelings of a modest and chaste woman, resulting from the immoral solicitation which she testifies accompanied the assault, is such that we cannot feel justified in deeming the allowance of $500 so grossly excessive as to justify this court in interfering."

[306] Beven on Negligence (2d Ed.) 77. Kalen v. Terre Haute Ry., 18 Ind. App. 202, 47 N. E. 694, 63 Am. St. R. 343 (1897); Wyman v. Leavitt, 71 Me. 227, 36 Am. R. 303 (1880); Turner v. Great Nor. Ry., 15 Wash. 213, 46 Pac. 243 (1896).

sible to reconcile the various judicial views of the wrongdoer's liability.

Physical Derangement Caused by Fright. At one extreme, are the cases which deny the right to recover for a physical injury, resulting from fright or mental anguish alone. " Assuming that fright cannot form the basis of an action," say these authorities, " it is obvious that no recovery can be had for injuries resulting therefrom. That the result may be nervous disease, blindness, insanity, or even a miscarriage, in no way changes the principle. These results merely show the degree of fright, or the extent of the damages. The right of action must still depend upon the question whether the recovery may be had for fright." [306 12]

At the other extreme, are the cases which hold that a recovery may be had for sickness, physical derangement or physical pain, resulting directly from fright or mental anguish, caused by the defendant's wrongdoing; provided that the defendant would have been liable, had his misconduct caused the sickness, derangement or pain, without the intervention of the fright or mental disturbance.[307] In order to bring a case within the foregoing proviso the

---

[306 1,2] St. Louis, etc., Ry. v. Bragg, 69 Ark. 402, 64 S. W. 226, 86 Am. St. R. 206 (1901); Braun v. Craven, 175 Ill. 401, 51 N. E. 657, 42 L. R. A. 199 (1898); Kansas City Ry. v. Dalton, 65 Ks. 661, 70 Pac. 645 (1902); Morse v. Chesapeake Ry., ——, Ky., —— 77 S. W. 362 (1903); Spade v. Lynn, etc., Ry. 168 Mass. 285, 47 N. E. 88, 38 L. R. A. 512 (1897); Trigg v. St. Louis, etc., Ry., 74 Mo. 147, 41 Am. R. 305 (1881); Ward v. West Jersey Ry., 65 N. J. L. 383, 47 At. 561 (1900); Mitchell v. Rochester Ry. Co., 157 N. Y. 107, 45 N. E. 354, 34 L. R. A. 781, 56 Am. St. R. 604 (1896); Ewing v. Pittsburgh, etc., Ry., 147 Pa. St. 40, 23 At. 340, 14 L. R. A. 666, 30 Am. St. R. 709 (1892); Victorian Ry. Commissioners v. Coultas, 13 App. Cas. 222, 57 L. J. P. C. 69 (1888).

[307] Fitzpatrick v. Great Western Ry., 12 Up. C. Q. B. 645 (1854);

Bell v. Great Nor. Ry., 26 L. R. Ir. 428 (1890); Dulieu v. White (1901), 2 K. B. 669, 70 L. J. K. B. 837; Sloane v. Southern Cal. Ry., 111 Cal. 668, 44 Pac. 320, 32 L. R. A. 193 (1896). Defendant's misconduct consisted in tortiously ejecting (without using physical force) the plaintiff from a train. Insomnia and paroxysms resulted from humiliation and indignity. Watson v. Dills, 116 Ia. 249, 89 N. W. 1068 (1902). Defendant wrongfully entered the house of plaintiff's husband, which was her house, and to the peaceful and quiet enjoyment of which she was legally entitled, and this invasion " produced physical injury to her through fright resulting in nervous prostration." Cf. Ford v. Schlimman, 107 Wis. 479, 83 N. W. 761 (1900), limiting recovery to trespass to house; Purcell v. St. Paul, etc., Ry., 48 Minn. 134, 50

plaintiff must show, not only that defendant's conduct was wrongful towards some one, but that it was a breach of legal duty owing to him by the defendant. Accordingly, if A is made sick by the shock of seeing another person maltreated, or of seeing his own property negligently injured,[308] he has no cause of action against the wrong-doer, as these facts fall short of establishing a breach of legal duty to the plaintiff by the wrongdoer.[309] For the law to furnish redress for mental suffering or its physical consequence, "there must be an act which, under the circumstances, is wrongful; and it must take effect upon the person, the property, or some other legal interest of the party complaining. Neither one without the other is sufficient. This is but another way of saying that no action for damages will lie for an act which, though wrongful, infringed no legal right of the plaintiff, although it may have caused him suffering."[310]

Reasons for Denying Remedy. Courts which deny all remedy for fright, or like disturbance of the mind and nerves, assign one or both[311] of the following reasons for their holdings. First: That physical suffering, sickness or permanent harm is not the probable or natural consequence of fright or nervous shock, in the case of a person of ordinary physical and mental vigor.[312] Hence,

N. W. 1034, 16 L. R. A. 203 (1892); Mack v. South, etc., Ry., 52 S. C. 323, 29 S. E. 905, 40 L. R. A. 679, 68 Am. St. R. 913 (1898); Gulf Col., etc., Ry. v. Hayter, 93 Tex. 239, 54 S. W. 944, 77 Am. St. R. 856, 47 L. R. A. 325 (1900).

[308] This doctrine has been applied in a case where the dead body of plaintiff's child was negligently, but not wantonly, thrown from a wagon, by a collision between a train and the wagon. Hackenhammer v. Lex. & E. Ry. (Ky.), 74 S. W. 222 (1903).

[309] Smith v. Johnson & Co., unreported but cited and approved in (1901) 2 K. B. at p. 675; Mahoney v. Dankwort, 108 Ia. 321, 79 N. W. 134 (1899); Kansas City Ry. v. Dalton, 65 Ks. 661, 70 Pac. 645 (1902); Buckman v. Great Nor. Ry., 76

Minn. 373, 79 N. W. 98 (1899); Sanderson v. Nor. Pac. Ry., 88 Minn. 162, 92 N. W. 542 (1902).

[310] Larson v. Chase, 47 Minn. 307, 50 N. W. 238, 28 Am. St. R. 370, 14 L. R. A. 85 (1891), holding that the surviving wife has the legal right to the possession of the dead body of her husband, and may recover damages for injuries to her feelings caused by defendant's wrongful mutilation of the body. S. P. in Meigher v. Driscoll, 99 Mass. 281, 96 Am. Dec. 759 (1868).

[311] Mitchell v. Rochester Ry., 151 N. Y. 107, 45 N. E. 354, 34 L. R. A. 781, 56 Am. St. R. 604 (1896). See Chicago, etc., Ry. v. Caulfield, 63 Fed. 396, 11 C. C. A. 552, with valuable note, pp. 556–583 (1894).

[312] Victorian Ry., Commiss. v. Coultas, 13 App. Cas. 222, 57 L. J. P.

plaintiff's injury is declared to be, as a matter of law, not the proximate, but the remote result of defendant's wrongdoing. Second: That damages sustained by fright or nervous shock must be refused, because of the impracticability of satisfactorily administering any other rule.[313]

An Arbitrary Test. It is quite apparent that the courts which adopt the first of these reasons prefer an arbitrary rather than a logical test of remoteness. Even though it is admitted by the pleadings that by reason of defendant's negligence, plaintiff was subjected to great danger of being run down and killed by a railroad train, and by reason of the danger to which he was thus exposed, he was shocked, paralyzed and otherwise injured, these courts declare that the paralysis is a remote result of the negligence.[314] If, when subjected to such danger, plaintiff had jumped and fallen, and the fall had shocked his nervous system so as to impair his health,[315] or had resulted in serious harm to his knee,[316] the same courts would declare the injury not remote. That serious physical disorder is the every-day consequence of fright or nervous shock is a fact not only established by modern science, but one which has long been accepted by the ordinary man.[317] It would seem, therefore, to fall within the category of natural and probable consequences.

Unsatisfactory Test. The second reason assigned for denying recovery, in cases now under consideration, does not appear to be entirely satisfactory, even to the courts which continue to apply it. The Supreme Court of Massachusetts has declared recently:[318] " It

---

C. 69 (1888); Atchison T. etc. Ry. v. McGinnis, 46 Ks. 100, 26 Pac. 453 (1891); Kansas City Ry. v. Dalton, 65 Ks., 661, 70 Pac. 645 (1902); Ward v. West Jersey Ry., 65 N. J. L. 383, 47 At. 561 (1900); Ewing v. Pittsburgh Ry. Co., 147 Pa. 40, 30 Am. St. R. 709, 14 L. R. A. 666, 23 At. 340 (1892).

[313] Brown v. Craven, 175 Ill. 401, 51 N. E. 657, 42 L. R. A. 199 (1898); Spade v. Lynn, etc. Ry., 168 Mass. 285, 47 N. E. 88, 38 L. R. A. 512 (1897); Homans v. Boston Elevated Ry., 180 Mass. 456, 62 N. E. 737 (1902).

[314] Ward v. West Jersey Ry., 65 N. J. L. 383, 47 At. 561 (1900).

[315] Tuttle v. Atlantic City Ry., 66 N. J. L. 327, 49 At. 450, 88 Am. St. R. 491, 54 L. R. A. 582 (1901).

[316] Buchanan v. West Jersey Ry., 52 N. J. L. 265, 19 At. 254 (1890).

[317] Gulf, Col. etc. Ry. v. Hayter, 93 Tex. 239, 54 S. W. 944, 77 Am. St. R. 856, 47 L. R. A. 325 (1900), and authorities therein cited. Watson v. Dilts, 116 Ia. 249, 89 N. W. 1068 (1902).

[318] Homans v. Boston El. Ry., 180 Mass. 456, 62 N. E. 737, 91 Am. St. R. 324 (1902).

is an arbitrary exception, based upon a notion of what is practicable, that prevents a recovery for visible illness resulting from nervous shock alone. But where there has been a battery and the nervous shock results from the same wrongful management as the battery, it is at least equally impracticable to go further and to inquire whether the shock comes through the battery or along with it. Even were it otherwise, recognizing as we must the logic in favor of the plaintiff when a remedy is denied because the only immediate wrong was a shock to the nerves, we think that when the reality of the case is guaranteed by proof of a substantial battery of the person there is no occasion to press further the exception to general rules. The difference between this case and the Spade Case[319] in its second presentation is that in the latter the defendant's wrong, if any, began with the battery, and it was not responsible for the previous sources of fear, whereas here the defendant was responsible for the trouble throughout."

Law Values Feelings. Moreover, all courts agree that when the defendant's misconduct causes a physical injury to plaintiff,[320] however slight, or, without physical harm, wrongfully invades his right of personal security,[321] or liberty,[322] or reputation,[323] he is entitled to have the jury estimate and assess the damages which he has sustained by reason of injured feelings. The objection, therefore, that the law cannot value mental pain or anxiety,[324] and that

[319] Spade v. Lynn Ry., 172 Mass. 488, 52 N. E. 747, 43 L. R. A. 832, 70 Am. St. R. 298 (1899).

[320] Canning v. Inhabitants of Williamstown, 1 Cush. (Mass.), 451, (1848); Warren v. Boston, etc. Railway Co., 163 Mass. 484, 40 N. E. 895, (1895); Consolidated Traction Co. v. Lambertson, 59 N. J. L. 297, 36 At. 100, (1896). This doctrine seems to have been overlooked in Gulf, etc. Ry. v. Trott, 86 Tex. 412, 25 S. W. 419, 40 Am. St. R. 866, (1894).

[321] Head v. Georgia, etc. Ry., 79 Ga. 358, 7 S. E. 217, 11 Am. St. R. 434, (1887); Mabry v. City Elec. Ry., 116 Ga. 624, 42 S. E. 1025, 59 L. R. A. 590, (1902); Kline v. Kline, 158 Ind. 602, 64 N. E. 9, 58 L. R. A. 397, (1902); Shephard v. Chicago, etc., Ry. Co., 77 Ia. 54, 41 N. W. 564, (1884); Craker v. Chicago & N W. Ry. Co., 36 Wis. 657, 17 Am. R. 504, (1875); Williams v. Nor. Pac. Ry., 5 Wash. 621, 32 Pac. 468, (1893).

[322] Gibney v. Lewis, 68 Conn. 392, 36 At. 799, (1896); Young v. Gormley, 120 Ia. 372, 94 N. W. 922, (1903).

[323] Swift v. Dickerman, 31 Conn. 285, (1863); Cole v. Atlantic, etc. Ry., 102 Ga. 474, 31 S. E. 107, (1897); Magonrick v. W. U. Tel. Co., 79 Miss. 632, 31 So. 206, (1901).

[324] Lynch v. Knight, 9 H. L. C. 577, (1861).

a claim for injury to feelings is purely transcendental, belonging to the realm of fancy rather than of fact,[325] seems open to criticism. While damages for injury to feelings are frequently too shadowy and speculative to be properly measured,[326] this is no reason for denying their recovery in all cases. It may well be urged by defendant's counsel as a powerful reason for a verdict in his favor, or for a sharp scrutiny by an appellate court of a verdict against him. Beyond this, it should have no effect.[327]

Mental Anguish Caused by Illegal Conduct. In most cases of this kind, the defendant commits a tort towards the plaintiff to which the mental anguish is incidental, such as an assault[328] or false imprisonment; and the courts are substantially agreed in granting a recovery.[329] Occasionally, however, the very gist of the defendant's wrongdoing, as far as the plaintiff is concerned, is in frightening the plaintiff, or in causing him either mental or nervous disturbance. Here, too, the courts are disposed to uphold verdicts for damages, when the evidence shows clearly that the defendant acted willfully or wantonly.[330]

---

[325] Western Union Tel. Co. v. Ferguson, 157 Ind. 64, 60 N. E. 674, 54 L. R. A. 846 (1901), and cases cited.

[326] Mahony v. Dankwart, 108 Ia. 321, 79 N. W. 134, (1899); Wyman v. Leavitt, 71 Me. 227, 36 Am. R. 303, (1880); Fox v. Bradley, 126 Pa. 604, 17 At. 604, (1889); Bovee v. Town of Danville, 53 Vt. 183, 190, (1880); Turner v. Great Nor. Ry., 15 Wash. 213, 46 Pac. 243, (1896).

[327] Western U. T. Co. v. Ferguson, 157 Ind. 64, 78. (Dissenting opinion), 60 N. E. 1080, (1901), Mentzer v. W. U. Tel. Co., 93 Ia. 752, 62 N. W. 1, 28 L. R. A. 72, 57 Am. S. R. 294, (1895).

[328] Barbee v. Reese, 60 Miss. 906, (1883). (Defendant, while intoxicated, threatened to shoot plaintiff who fled and suffered miscarriage because of her fright). See cases cited in preceding paragraph.

[329] Razzo v. Varni, 81 Cal. 289, 22 Pac. 848, (1889); Preiser v. Wielandt, 48 App. Div. 569, 62 N. Y. Supp. 890 (1900); Williams v. Underhill, 63 App. Div. 223, 71 N. Y. Supp. 29 (1901); Hill v. Kimball, 76 Tex. 210, 13 S. W. 59, 7 L. R. A. 618 (1890).

[330] Wilkinson v. Downton, (1897), 2 Q. B. 57, 66 L. J. Q. B. (Defendant falsely told plaintiff that her husband had broken both legs, intending her to believe it. She did believe it, and became seriously ill from the nervous shock). Cf. Nelson v. Crawford, 122 Mich. 466, 81 N. W. 335, (1899), where defendant was held not liable for frightening plaintiff, by way of a joke. He was harmlessly insane and acted without malicious motives or the intent to harm any one. Rice v. Rice, 104 Mich. 371, 62 N. W. 834 (1895). At p. 381, the court approved the charge of the trial Judge, that plaintiff in a suit for the alienation of her husband's affections "was entitled to

Punishing the Wrongdoer. In some jurisdictions, these damages are awarded as a punishment of the defendant rather than as compensation of the plaintiff.[331] The prevailing view, however, is that these damages, though not measurable by market values or price lists, are compensatory, and that the " amount is to be left to the sound discretion of the jury." [332]

Mental Anguish Caused by the Negligence of Telegraph Companies. In many jurisdictions, this is recognized as a distinct cause of action, independent of any physical injury to the plaintiff or of any malicious intent of the defendant, although the courts are not entirely agreed as to the ground upon which the right to damages is based. The pioneer case[333] on this topic declares: that when a telegraph message announces the death of the plaintiff's parent, or other near and dear relative, the natural result of negligence in delivering it, is to " inflict upon the mind the sorest disappointment and sorrow," and that the damages " resulting therefrom constitute general damages, recoverable under a general averment of damage." Emphasis was also laid upon the fact that telegraph companies exercise and enjoy special franchises and privileges under the law, which ought to subject them to a duty of care, over and above their contract obligation. A breach of this duty, it is declared by most courts which have followed this Texas decision, is a com-

recover for mental anguish and suffering, mortification, and embarrassment " due to defendant's misconduct. In Conklin v. Thompson, 29 Barb. (N. Y.) 218 (1859), defendant willfully, and without a license, exploded firecrackers in a public street, intending to frighten plaintiff's horse. It was frightened, and died immediately. A verdict for plaintiff was sustained on appeal. In Lee v. City of Burlington, 113 Ia. 356, 85 N. W. 618 (1901), a demurrer was sustained to plaintiff's complaint, which sought recovery for the value of a horse frightened to death by defendant's negligent management of a steam roller in a city street. See Watkins v. Kaolin Manf. Co., 131 N. C. 536, 42 S. E.

983, 60 L. R. A. 617 (1902).

[331] Chappell v. Ellis, 123 N. C. 259, 31 S. E. 709, 68 Am. St. R. 822 (1898).

[332] Young v. Gormley, 120 Ia. 372, 94 N. W. 922 (1903), and cases cited. In McChesney v. Wilson, 132, Mich. 252, 93 N. W. 627 (1903), the court said: " Our understanding is that the rule in this state limits exemplary damages to the aggravation of the injury to feelings which arises from malice, and does not permit damages for the purpose of punishment: " Gillespie v. Brooklyn Heights Ry., 178 N. Y. 347, 70 N. E. 857 (1904).

[333] So Relle v. W. U. T. Co., 55 Tex. 308, 40 Am. R. 805 (1881).

mon law tort, subjecting the tort-feasor to at least nominal damages; and, when the message is such as fairly to apprise him of the mental suffering which will naturally follow the failure to deliver it, damages for such suffering are recoverable upon the same principle that gives them in cases of wrongful ejection from a train, or of false imprisonment, or of assault, unattended with actual bodily injury or pain.[334]

Whether the message does fairly apprise the telegraph company that mental anguish will naturally and approximately follow negligence of delivery, is often a troublesome question.[335] The practical difficulties attendant upon answering it have led some courts to retreat from the Texas leadership, and join the more conservative side.[336] A few courts permit a recovery for mental suffering only when the conduct of the telegraph company is wanton or grossly negligent.[337]

A nice question, in the conflict of laws, has arisen in some of these cases. In the State where the telegram is received for transmission, the law does not allow damages for mental anguish; while they are allowed in the State where the message is deliverable. If the failure to deliver causes the sender mental anguish, and he sues in the jurisdiction where the message was deliverable, is his right of action determined by the law of the first or the second jurisdiction?

[334] Western U. T. Co. v. Henderson, 89 Al. 510, 7 So. 419 (1889); Mentzer v. W. U. T. Co., 93 Ia. 752, 62 N. W. I., 28 L. R. A. 72 (1895); Chapman v. W. U. T. Co., 90 Ky. 265, 13 S. W. 880 (1890); Graham v. W. U. T. Co., 109 La. 1069, 34 So. 91 (1903); Young v. W. U. T. Co., 107 N. C. 384, 11 S. E. 1044, 9 L. R. A. 669, 22 Am. St. R. 883 (1890); Wadsworth v. W. U. T. Co., 86 Tenn. 695, 8 S. W. 574, 6 Am. S. R. 864 (1888); Stuart v. W. U. T. Co., 66 Tex. 580, 18 S. W. 351, 59 Am. R. 623 (1886). This doctrine has received legislative sanction in some states. See Marsh v. W. U. T. Co., 65 S. C. 430, 43 S. E. 953 (1903), applying the statute of 1901, Sess. L. p. 693.

[335] In W. U. T. Co. v. Ayers, 131 Al. 391, 31 So. 78, 90 Am. St. R. 92 (1901), a message calling an uncle to the death bed of a nephew was not notice that damages would ensue; while in W. U. T. Co. v. Crocker, 135 Al. 492, 33 So. 45, 59 L. R. A. 398 (1902), a message to a grandmother was notice. Cf. Robinson v. W. U. T. Co., ——, Ky. ——, 68 S. W. 656, 57 L. R. A. 611 (1902), message related to sending money; mental anguish not recoverable.

[336] W. U. T. Co. v. Ferguson, 157 Ind. 64, 60 N. E. 674, 54 L. R. A. 846 (1901).

[337] W. U. T. Co. v. Lawson, 66 Ks. 660, 72 Pac. 283 (1903); Butler v. W. U. T. Co., 62 S. C. 223, 40 S. E. 162 (1901); and see W. U. T. Co. v. Seed, 115 Al. 670, 22 So. 474 (1896).

The law of the latter jurisdiction has been held to govern, and this decision seems to be correct.[338]

Texas Doctrine Generally Rejected. The weight of judicial authority is opposed to the Texas doctrine, and denies a recovery for damages for mental anguish only, resulting from negligent failure to deliver a telegraphic message. The principal reasons assigned for this view are: that damages for mental suffering alone were never allowed at common law: that such damages must be uncertain, indefinite and speculative, and open " into a field without boundaries," and that " the mental anguish doctrine awards damages for a state of mind, that is not at all dependent upon or measurable by a cause of action, existing outside the mental contemplation of the plaintiff, and provable by evidence of both parties.[339]

---

[338] Gray v. W. U. T. Co., 108 Tenn. 39, 64 S. W. 1063, 56 L. R. A. 301 (1901), and valuable note on the topic, cf. W. U. T. Co. v. Waller, 96 Tex. 589, 74 S. W. 751 (1903), holding that such damages are recoverable in the state from which the message was sent, although the law of state in which the message was deliverable did not allow them.

[339] Peay v. W. U. T. Co., 64 Ark. 538, 43 S. W. 965, 39 L. R. A. 463 (1898); Russell v. W. U. T. Co., 3 Dak. 315, 19 N. W. 408 (1884); Internat. O. T. Co. v. Saunders, 32 Fla. 434, 14 So. 148, 21 L. R. A. 810 (1893); Chapman v. W. U. T. Co., 88 Ga. 763, 15 S. E. 901, 30 Am. St. R. 183, 17 L. R. A. 430 (1892); W. U. T. Co. v. Ferguson, 157 Ind. 64, 60 N. E. 674, 54 L. R. A. 846 (1901), overruling Reese v. W. U. T. Co., 123 Ind. 294, 24 N. E. 163, 7 L. R. A. 583 (1889); Francis v. W. U. T. Co., 58 Minn. 252, 59 N. W. 1078, 49 Am. St. R. 507, 25 L. R. A. 406 (1894); W. U. T. Co. v. Rogers, 68 Miss. 748, 9 So. 823, 13 L. R. A. 859, and note, 24 Am. St. R. 300 (1891); Connell v. W. U. T. Co., 116 Mo. 34, 22 S. W. 345, 20 L. R. A. 172, 38 Am. St. R. 575 (1893); Morton v. W. U. T. Co., 53 Ohio St. 431, 41 N. E. 689, 32 L. R. A. 735, 53 Am. St. R. 648 (1896); Butner v. W. U. T. Co., 2 Okl. 234, 37 Pac. 1087 (1894); Connelly v. W. U. T. Co., 100 Va. 51, 40 S. E. 618, 56 L. R. A. 663 (1902); Davis v. W. U. T. Co., 46 W. Va. 48, 32 S. E. 1026 (1899); Summerfield v. W. U. T. Co., 87 Wis. 1, 57 N. W. 973, 41 Am. St. R. 17 (1894); W. U. T. Co. v. Wood, 57 Fed. 471, 13 U. S. App. 317, 6 C. C. A. 432, 21 L. R. A. 706 (1893); Stansell v. W. U. T. Co., 107 Fed. 668 (1901); Western U. T. Co. v. Sklar, 126 Fed. 295 (1903), a case containing a valuable collection of authorities on this topic.

CHAPTER IV.

PARTIES TO TORT ACTIONS.

§ 1. CORPORATIONS.

The State May be Plaintiff. We have seen that an action of tort cannot be maintained against the State, nor against the sovereign or diplomatic representative of a foreign State, without its permission.[1] Such action may be brought by the State, however, in its corporate capacity. Accordingly, if timber is wrongfully taken from its land, it may prosecute the wrongdoers criminally, or it may proceed against them in trover.[2] It may also sue another State or a public corporation created by another State for diverting or fouling streams accustomed to flow through its territory.[3]

Political Subdivisions of the State. At present, these are, as a rule, public corporations, with power to acquire, hold and use property, as well as to sue and be sued. It does not follow from this, [3 1-2] however, that they are liable to tort actions for injuries done by their officials or employees to individuals. Whether they are so liable depends upon two questions: First: What functions are they performing through their wrongdoing representatives? Second: To what extent has their common-law liability been modified by statute?[4]

---

[1] *Supra*, 38; Bigby v. U. S. 188 U. S. 400, 23 Sup. Ct. 468 (1902).

[2] Wooden Ware Co. v. U. S., 106 U. S. 432, 1 Sup. Ct. 398 (1882).

[3] Missouri v. Illinois, 180 U. S. 208, 21 Sup. Ct. 331 (1900); Kansas v. Colorado, 185 U. S. 126, 22 Sup. Ct. 552 (1901).

[3 1-2] Markey v. County of Queens, 154 N. Y. 675, 49 N. E. 71, 39 L. R. A. 46, with note (1898). By the County Law (ch. 686 L. 892), a county is declared to be a "municipal corporation" and "an action * * to enforce any liability * * shall be in the name of the County." School District v. Williams, 38 Ark. 454 (1882).

[4] For an excellent discussion of this topic, see Goodnow, Municipal Home Rule, Chaps. vii and viii. (New York, 1895).

Government and Private Functions. Most modern municipal corporations possess " two kinds of powers; one governmental and public, and, to the extent they are held and exercised, the corporation is clothed with sovereignty; the other private, and, to the extent they are held and exercised, it is a legal individual. The former are given and used for public purposes; the latter for private purposes. While in the exercise of the former the corporation is a municipal government, and while in the exercise of the latter it is a corporate legal individual."[5] When the corporation is exercising a power of the first class—is performing a purely political function —it is entitled, at common law, to the same exemption from suit that is enjoyed by the State in the performance of the same function. It is a mere " instrumentality of government,"[6] an " agency of the State,"[7] and the same reasons which prevent recovery from the State for injuries inflicted in its behalf by its officers or agents, should save the public corporation from actionable liability.

Counties, Parishes, Townships, School Districts, and similar subdivisions of the State are rarely liable for the misconduct of their officers or servants. This freedom from tort liability has been declared by some courts[8] to rest upon the genesis of these corporations. They are " created by the sovereign power of the State, of its own sovereign will, without the particular solicitation, consent, or concurrent action of the people who inhabit them. The organization is superimposed by a sovereign and permanent authority." Being such " involuntary incorporations organized as political subdivisions of the State for governmental purposes, they are not liable for the negligence of their officers or servants any more than the State would be liable."

Quasi-Municipal Corporations : Other courts have preferred to rest the non-liability of these corporations solely upon the nature of their functions. At first, these were exclusively political, or governmental. The county,[9] the township,[10] and the parish[11] were

---

[5] Lloyd v. The Mayor, 5 N. Y. 369, 55 Am. Dec. 347 (1851).

[6] Summers v. Daviess County, 103 Ind. 262, 2 N. E. 725 (1885).

[7] Jones v. City of Williamsburg, 97 Va. 722, 34 S. E. 883 (1900).

[9] Commissioners of Ham. Co. v. Mighels, 7 Ohio St. 109 (1857);

Board, etc. v. Dailey, 132 Ind. 73, 31 N. E. 531 (1892); Bailey v. Lawrence County, 5 S. D. 393, 59 N. W. 219, 49 Am. St. R. 881 (1894).

[9] Markey v. County of Queens, 154 N. Y. 675, 49 N. E. 71, 39 L. R. A. 46 (1898), containing an excellent sketch of the legal status of coun-

established for the more convenient administration of government. Their duties were public,[12] and were apportioned among them by the State with a view to the convenience and benefit of its citizens. Although certain officers were chosen by the electors of each subdivision, they were not its servants or special representatives, but officers of the public at large, and were charged with the performance of public duties, not with the conduct of the corporate affairs of the county, or the township, or the parish. Accordingly, injuries inflicted by them, in the performance of their duties, did not render the *quasi* corporations liable as their master.[13]

In many of our States, privileges and powers have been granted to these political subdivisions to be exercised by them for their corporate advantage. For injuries inflicted by their representatives in the exercise of such powers and privileges, their liability is that of a private corporation.[14] It is to be noted, too, that modern statutes impose upon the county, the parish, and the township a duty of responding for the torts of their officers and servants, which was not imposed by common law.[15] Such statutory provisions,

---

ties in New York. Lafrois v. County of Monroe, 162 N. Y. 563, 57 N. E. 185, 50 L. R. A. 206 (1900).

[10] Hill v. Boston, 122 Mass. 344 (1877). On p. 349, Gray J., says: "At the first settlement of the colony, towns consisted of clusters of inhabitants dwelling near each other, which by the effect of legislative acts, designating them by name, and conferring upon them the powers of managing their own prudential affairs, electing representatives and town-officers and making by-laws, and disposing, subject to the paramount control of the Legislature, of unoccupied lands within their territory, became in effect municipal or *quasi* corporations, without any formal act of incorporation." On p. 351 he declares: "A private action cannot be maintained against a town or other *quasi* corporation for a neglect of corporate duty, unless the action be given by statute."

[11] Sherman v. Parish of Vermilion, 51 La. Ann. 880, 25 So. 538 (1899), tracing the history of the parish in La.

[12] Russell v. The Men of Durham, 2 Durn. & E. 667 (1788).

[13] Cases cited in the last seven notes; also, Prichard v. Commissioners of Morganton, 126 N. C. 908, 36 S. E. 353 (1900).

[14] Moulton v. Scarborough, 71 Me. 267, 36 Am. R. 308 (1880); Waldron v. Hoverhill, 143 Mass. 582, 10 N. E. 481 (1887); Collins v. Greenfield, 172 Mass. 78, 51 N. E. 454 (1898); Butman v. Newton, 179 Mass. 16, 60 N. E. 401 (1901); Hannon v. St. Louis Co., 62 Mo. 313 (1876).

[15] Hill v. Boston, 122 Mass. 344 (1877); Medina v. Perkins, 48 Mich. 67 (1882); Bryant v. Town of Randolph, 133 N. Y. 70, 30 N. E. 657 (1892); McCalla v. Multunoah Co., 3 Or. 424 (1869).

however, are generally subjected by the courts to a strict construction.[16]

Cities, Villages, and Specially Incorporated Towns. These are often described by judges and text-writers as true municipal corporations, in contra-distinction to the *quasi* corporations, which we have just been dealing with. They possess political or governmental powers, it is true; but they possess also many of the powers of a private corporation. As a rule, their organization is solicited by their inhabitants, for the promotion of local interests and the betterment of community conditions, quite as much as for the discharge of governmental functions. Accordingly, it is held that they are subject to an implied liability for the torts of their representatives, which does not attach to the *quasi* corporation. If those torts are inflicted in connection with the business affairs of the municipality, the persons harmed are not required to show a statute expressly imposing liability upon it: they are entitled to recover against it, whenever a recovery would be allowed against a private corporation.

For example, a city engages in carrying on gas works,[17] or water works,[18] or in the ownership and management of wharves,[19] or in the towing of vessels,[20] for profit. It must respond in damages for the wrongs of its officers, agents or servants, provided these wrong-doers were acting within the scope of their apparent authority, or their misconduct has been ratified by the municipality. In other words, their liability depends upon the rules relating to master and servant, which we shall consider hereafter.

While this doctrine is generally accepted by the courts, they have experienced no little difficulty in applying it. Many activities of

---

[16] Bartram v. Sharon, 71 Conn. 686, 43 At. 143, 46 L. R. A. 144 (1899); Spencer v. Freeholders of Hudson, 66 N. J. L. 301, 306, 49 At. 482 (1901); Chick v. Newberry Co., 27 S. C. 419 (1887); Schaffer v. Fond du Lac, 99 Wis. 333, 74 N. W. 810, 41 L. R. A. 287 (1898).

[17] Scott v. Manchester, 2 H. & N. 204 (1857); Shuter v. The City, 3 Phil. (Pa.), 228 (1858).

[18] Logansport v. Dick, 70 Ind. 65, 36 Am. R. 308 (1880); Stock v.

Boston, 149 Mass. 410, 21 N. E. 871, 14 Am. St. R. 430 (1889); Bailey v. Mayor, 3 Hill (N. Y.) 531, 38 Am. Dec. 669 (1842); Aldrich v. Tripp, 11 R. I. 141, 23 Am. R. 434 (1875).

[19] Kennedy v. Mayor, etc., of New York, 73 N. Y. 365 (1878); Willey v. Alleghany, 118 Pa. 490 (1888); City of Petersburg v. Applegart, 28 Gratt (Va.), 321, 26 Am. R. 387 (1877).

[20] City of Philadelphia v. Gavagnin, 62 Fed. 617 (1894).

the modern municipality have at once a private and a public character. They minister to the public welfare as well as contribute to the private benefit of the corporation. In conducting them, the city or village is discharging a governmental function as a deputy of the State, while it is also relieving the inhabitants of the locality of a burden they would otherwise be compelled to bear as individuals. An example of this class is the work of the street cleaning department. In view of its mixed character, it is not surprising that some courts hold the municipality liable [21] for the torts of this department's officers and servants, while other courts hold that it is not liable.[22]

Non-Liability of City. There is substantial agreement that it is not liable for the torts of its fire [23] or police [24] departments, nor for those of its boards of health [25] or of education; [26] nor for those

[21] Barney Dumping Boat Co. v. New York, 40 Fed. 50 (1889); Quill v. Mayor, etc., 55 N. Y. Supp. 889, 36 App. Div. 476 (1899); Missano v. Mayor, 160 N. Y. 123, 54 N. E. 744 (1899).

[22] Love v. Atlanta, 95 Ga. 129, 22 S. E. 29 (1894); McFadden v. Jewell, 119 Ia. 321, 93 N. W. 302 (1903); Condict v. Jersy City, 46 N. J. L. 157 (1884); Connelly v. Nashville, 100 Tenn. 262, 46 S. E. 565 (1898).

[23] Wilcox v. Chicago, 107 Ill. 334, 47 Am. R. 434 (1883); Saunders v. City of Ft. Madison, 111 Ia. 102, 82 N. W. 428 (1900); Davis v. Lebanon, 108 Ky. 698, 57 S. W. 471 (1900); Burrill v. Augusta, 78 Me. 118, 3 At. 177 (1886); Grube v. St. Paul, 34 Minn. 402, 26 N. W. 228 (1886); Heller v. Sedalia, 53 Mo. 159, 14 Am. R. 444 (1873); Alexander v. Vicksburg, 68 Miss. 564, 10 So. 62 (1891); Gillespie v. Lincoln, 35 Neb. 34, 52 N. W. 811, 16 L. R. A. 349 (1892); Smith v. Rochester, 76 N. Y. 506 (1879); Frederick v. Columbus, 58 Ohio St. 538, 51 N. E. 35 (1898); Fire Ins. Patrol v. Boyd, 120 Pa.

624, 15 At. 553, 1 L. R. A. 417 (1888); Lawson v. Seattle, 6 Wash. 184, 33 Pac. 347 (1893). In Workman v. Mayor, 179 U. S. 552, 21 Sup. Ct. 212, 45 L. Ed. 314 (1900), the Supreme Court of the United States held the City liable in an admiralty proceeding, although admitting that the City was not liable at common law. Both the prevailing and dissenting opinions are worthy of careful study.

[24] Masters v. Bowling Green, 101 Fed. 101 (1899); Bartlett v. City of Columbus, 101 Ga. 300, 28 S. E. 599, 44 L. R. A. 795, with note (1897); Lahner v. Williams, 112 Ia. 428, 84 N. W. 506 (1900); Craig v. City of Charleston, 180 Ill. 154, 54 N. E. 184 (1899); Butterick v. Lowell, 1 Allen (Mass.) 172, 79 Am. Dec. 721 (1861); Tomlin v. Hildreth, 65 N. J. L. 438, 47 At. 649 (1900); Petersfield v. Vickers, 3 Cold. (43 Tenn.) 205 (1866).

[25] Nicholson v. City of Detroit, 129 Mich. 246, 88 N. W. 695 (1902); City of Richmond v. Long, 17 Grat. 375, 94 Am. Dec. 461, (1867).

[26] Hill v. Boston, 122 Mass. 344

of any other officers, agents or servants in the discharge of functions, which primarily belong to the State, but the performance of which it has delegated to the municipality. Neglect of officers in guarding prisoners,[27] or in caring for jurymen,[28] or in keeping court houses, town houses, jails and other public buildings in repair,[29] will not subject the corporation to legal liability. Nor will the negligence of an employee of a charity hospital render the city, which maintains it, liable to damages.[30]

Legislative, Judicial and Quasi-Judcial Powers. As a rule, a municipality is not liable in tort for the nonfeasance or the misfeasance of its officers, in the exercise of these powers. Hence, the failure of a city council to pass ordinances prohibiting the use of sidewalks by bicycles,[31] or the use of streets for coasting,[32] or providing for the suppression of nuisances,[33] will not subject the city to a tort action. Nor will it be liable for injuries done to individuals by the enforcement of unconstitutional and void ordinances,[34] except where these are enacted for the private benefit of the corporation.[35] The blunders or even the willful misconduct of its judicial officers

(1887); Ford v. School District, 121 Pa. 543, 15 At. 812, 1 L. R. A. 607 (1888); Wixon v. Newport, 13 R. I. 454 (1881); Folk v. City of Milwaukee, 108 Wis. 359, 84 N. W. 420 (1900).

[27] Davis v. Knoxville, 90 Tenn. 599, 18 S. W. 254 (1891).

[28] Sherman v. Parish of Vermillion, 51 La. Ann. 880, 25 So. 538 (1899).

[29] Kincaid v. Harden Co., 53 Ia, 430, 5 N. W. 589 (1880); Eastman v. Meredith, 36 N. H. 284, 72 Am. Dec. 302 (1858).

[30] Maxmillian v. Mayor, etc., 62 N. Y. 160, 20 Am. R. 468 (1876); Tarbutton v. Tenville, 110 Ga. 90, 35 S. E. 282 (1899).

[31] Jones v. City of Williamsburg, 97 Va. 722, 34 S. E. 883, 47 L. R. A. 294 (1900), contra, Hagerstown v. Klotz, 93 Md. 437, 49 At. 836, 54 L. R. A. 940 (1901).

[32] City of Lafayette v. Timberlake,

88 Ind. 330 (1882), contra, Taylor v. Mayor, 64 Md. 68, 54 Am. R. 759 (1885); Cochrane v. Mayor of Frostburg, 81 Md. 54, 31 At. 703, 48 Am. St. R. 479, 27 L. R. A. 728 (1895). These cases proceed upon the theory that the duty to prevent nuisances is imperative, not legislative or discretionary.

[33] James v. Harrodsburg, 85 Ky. 191, 3 S. W. 135 (1887); Cain v. Syracuse, 95 N. Y. 83 (1884); Leonard v. Hornellsville, 41 App. Div. 106, 58 N. Y. Supp. 266 (1899); McDade v. Chester City, 117 Pa. 414, 12 At. 421, 2 Am. St. R. 681 (1888); Smith v. Selings-grove Borough, 199 Pa. 615, 49 At. 213 (1901); Hubbell v. City of Viroqua, 67 Wis. 343, 30 N. W. 847 (1886).

[34] Taylor v. City of Owensboro, 98 Ky. 271, 32 S. W. 948 (1895).

[35] McGraw v. Town of Marion, 98 Ky. 673, 34 S. W. 18, 47 L. R. A. 593 (1896).

cannot be charged to its account:[36] nor will it be made to respond in damages for injuries caused by mistaken plans for street sewers and similar works.[37]

Moreover, it is not responsible for an abuse by its officers of a discretionary power vested in them by law, such as the appointment of unfit men to office.[38]

Statutory Liability of Municipal Corporations.   In the absence of constitutional prohibitions, the State may impose upon public corporations of every kind, any of the liabilities from which they are free at common law. Whether such a liability has been imposed in a particular case depends upon the existence and the construction of statutory enactments. If the terms of the statute are clear and unequivocal, there is no difficulty; but oftentimes the legislature does not impose a liability in express terms, while its language indicates an intent to impose it. The canon of construction to be applied in such a case in England has been judicially stated as follows: " In the absence of something to show a contrary intention, the legislature intends that the body, the creature of the statute, shall have the same duties, and that its funds shall be rendered subject to the same liabilities as the general law would impose on a private person doing the same thing." [39]

In this country, various canons of construction have been suggested,[40] but that which seems to be sustained by the weight of authority, as well as by sound legal principle, is this: In the absence of an express statement of its intention, the legislature must be presumed to impose upon a public corporation liability for injuries inflicted by its officers or servants, within the scope of their authority, when the authority given or the duty enjoined by statute relates

---

[36] Duke v. Rome, 20 Ga. 635 (1856); Gray v. Griffin, 111 Ga. 361, 36 S. E. 792, 51 L. R. A. 131 (1900).

[37] City of Chicago v. Seben, 165 Ill. 37, 46 N. E. 244 (1897); Mills v. City of Brooklyn, 32 N. Y. 489 (1865); Hughes v. City of Auburn, 161 N. Y. 96, 55 N. E. 389 (1899); Cf. Stone v. City of Seattle, 30 Wash. 65, 70 Pac. 249 (1902), holding the city liable for damages caused by defect in plan of side walk, and repudiating the doctrine

that the duty of devising a proper plan is *quasi* judicial.

[38] Craig v. City of Charleston, 180 Ill., 154, 54 N. E. 184 (1889).

[39] Blackburn, J., in Mersey Dock Trustees v. Gibbs, L. R. I. H. L. 93, 110, 35 L. J. Exch. 225 (1866).

[40] See Hill v. Boston, 122 Mass. 244, 23 Am. R. 332 (1877); Detroit v. Blackeby, 21 Mich. 84 (1870); Weet v. Brockport, 16 N. Y. 161 (1857).

to the local or special interests of the corporation, and is ministerial or imperative, and ample means are provided for the exercise of the authority or the performance of the duty.[41]

Liability of Municipality as Property Owner. For the wrongful use and management of property which it holds and enjoys in its private corporate capacity, or for the proper management of which it is made liable by statute, it is subject to the same liability that attaches to individual ownership.[42] Such is not the rule, however, in the case of property acquired and controlled by it for the public, or in the discharge of governmental functions.[43] Still, if such property is so used as to become a private nuisance to adjoining property owners, the corporation may be liable for the damages inflicted,[44] unless its conduct is constitutionally authorized by the State.[45] It seems to be well settled in most jurisdictions that a public corporation may be liable for trespass and other injuries directly inflicted, while not liable for consequential damages.[46]

Liability of Municipal Officers and Servants. In many cases where the municipal corporation escapes liability, under the rules which we have been considering, the injured party is not without redress. If the wrongdoing officers or servants were performing executive or ministerial functions, as distinguished from those that are judicial, or *quasi*-judicial, they are personally liable to those who have sustained legal harm.[47]

---

[41] 2 Dillion, Municipal Corporations, (4 Ed.) § 967, 980–983, and authorities cited.

[42] Brown v. Atlanta, 66 Ga. 71 (1880); Moulton v. Scarborough, 71 Me. 267 (1880); Thayer v. Boston, 19 Pick (Mass.) 511 (1837); Mackey v. Vicksburg, 64 Miss. 777, 2 So. 178 (1887); Carrington v. St. Louis, 89 Mo. 208, 1 S. W. 240 (1886).

[43] Hill v. Boston, 122 Mass. 344, 23 Am. R. 332 (1887), and cases cited supra, p. 106.

[44] Platt Brothers & Co. v. Waterbury, 72 Conn. 531, 45 At. 154, 48 L. R. A. 691, and note (1900); Winchell v. Waukesha, 110 Wis. 101, 85 N. W. 668 (1901).

[45] Marcus Sayre Co. v. Newark, 60 N. J. Eq. 361, 45 At. 985, 48 L. R. A. 722 (1900); Valparaiso v. Hagen, 153 Ind. 337, 54 N. E. 1062, 48 L. R. A. 707 (1899); Lefrois v. County of Monroe, 162 N. Y. 563, 57 N. E. 185 (1900); Smith v. Sedalia, 152 Mo. 283, 53 S. W. 907 (1899). The constitution of Missouri prohibits the taking or damaging of private property for public use, without compensation. Hence the city was held liable.

[46] Hughes v. City of Auburn, 161 N. Y. 96, 55 N. E. 389, 46 L. R. A. 630 (1892); 2 Dillion Mun. Corp. (4 Ed.) § 987.

[47] School District v. Williams, 38 Ark. 454 (1882); Tomlin v. Hildreth, 65 N. J. L. 438, 47 At. 649

Charitable Corporations. When these institutions are a part of the governmental machinery of the State, or of one of its political subdivisions, they are not liable for the torts of their officers or servants. The same reasons which exempt the municipality exempt them.[48]

Frequently, however, they are founded by the gifts of individuals, and are not in any sense State institutions. In such circumstances, what is their liability? It must be admitted that the judicial answers are quite at variance.[49] They fall into three classes, in this country. According to one class, the liability is that of the ordinary private corporation.[50] According to another class, there is no corporate liability for the negligence of the officers or servants. If there were, say these courts, the trust funds of the corporation would be diverted from the purposes to which they were devoted by the donors. Charitable bequests would be thwarted, and trustees, by their negligence, or other wrongdoing, would be able to waste the funds which have been dedicated to charitable purposes. Those who accept the ministrations of such establishments, it is declared, assent to the condition imposed by law, that they shall look to the individual wrongdoers for redress of wrongs done to them by the

(1900); Bennett v. Whitney, 94 N. Y. 302 (1884); Lefrois v. County of Monroe, 162 N. Y. 563, 57 N. E. 185 (1900); *semble.* Workman v. New York, 179 U. S. 552, 21 Sup. Ct. 212, 45 L. Ed. 314 (1900).

[48] Williamson v. Louisville Indus. School, 95 Ky. 251, 24 S. W. 1065, 23 L. R. A. 200, 44 Am. St. R. 243 (1894); Perry v. House of Refuge, 63 Md. 20, 52 Am. R. 495 (1885); MacDonald v. Massachusetts Hospital, 120 Mass. 432, 21 Am. R. 529 (1876); Overholser v. Nat. Home, etc., 68 Ohio St. 286, 67 N. E. 487 (1903); Maxmilian v. Mayor, etc., of New York, 62 N. Y. 160 (1875); Richmond v. Long, 17 Grat. (Va.) 375, 94 Am. Dec. 461 (1867).

[49] In England, the question has not received an authoritative answer. 1 Beven on Negligence (2 Ed.) 290.

[50] Donaldson v. Commissioners, 30 New Brunswick, 279 (1890); Glavin v. Rhode Island Hospital, 12 R. I. 411, 34 Am. R. 675 (1879). In the last cited case, Durfee, C. J., in reply to the argument that if such corporations are held liable for the negligence of their physicians or attendants, people will be discouraged from contributing to their support, says: " The public is doubtless interested in the maintenance of a great public charity, such as the Rhode Island Hospital is; but it is also interested in obliging every person and every corporation which undertakes the performance of a duty to perform it carefully, and therefore it has an interest against exempting any such person or corporation from liability for its negligence."

officers, agents or employees. The wrongdoer, but not the trust fund, must respond in damages.[51]

The intermediate view, and that which seems to be supported by the weight of authority as well as by the weight of argument, is, that a charitable organization is not liable in tort for injuries done by physicians, employees or servants, when it has exercised due care in their selection,[52] but that it is liable for corporate misconduct or negligence.[53]

What Organizations are Charitable? The distinguishing characteristics of these institutions are: First: Their origin, in the donations of benevolent persons or in grants from the State. Second —the manner in which they are conducted—not for the pecuniary profit of their managers or owners, but for the promotion of the welfare of others.[54] A railroad or steamship company, which maintains a hospital for the gratuitous treatment of its injured or sick employees, or provides a surgeon for the gratuitous treatment of passengers, is subject to the rule governing charitable corporations. It is liable only for failure to use reasonable care in selecting surgeons, nurses, and other assistants.[55] The fact that those receiving treatment make contributions to the hospital or similar institution, will not change its character,[56] unless these contributions are required and received as a source of profit to the proprietors.[57] It

[51] Downes v. Harper Hospital, 101 Mich. 555, 45 Am. St. R. 427, 60 N. W. 42 (1894); Insurance Patrol v. Boyd, 120 Pa. 624, 15 At. 553, 6 Am. St. R. 745 (1888).

[52] Hearns v. Waterbury Hospital, 66 Conn. 98, 33 At. 595, 31 L. R. A 224 (1895); Powers v. Mass. Hospital, 109 Fed. 294, 47 C. C. A. 122, and note (1901); Conner v. Sisters of the Poor, 10 Ohio S. C. P. Dec. 86, 7 Ohio N. P. 514 (1900); Corbett v. St. Vincent's Industrial School, 79 App. Div. (N. Y.) 334 (1903).

[53] The first two cases in the preceding note. In Herr v. Central Ky. Asylum, 97 Ky. 458, 30 S. W. 97, 28 L. R. A. 394 (1895), an injunction was granted against a charitable corporation for a nuisance as this would not deplete the funds, although damages, it was said, should not be awarded.

[54] Sherman v. Cong. Miss. Soc. 176 Mass. 349, 57 N. E. 702 (1900); Corbett v. St. Vincent's Industrial School, 79 App. Div. (N. Y.) 334 (1903).

[55] Eighney v. Ry. Co., 93 Ia. 538, 61 N. W. 1056, 27 L. R. A. 296 (1895); Galveston, etc., Ry. v. Hanway (Tex. Civ. App.) 57 S. W. 695 (1900); Laubheim v. DeKoninglyke, etc., Co., 107 N. Y. 228, 13 N. E. 781, 1 Am. St. R. 815 (1887).

[56] Richardson v. Coal Co., 10 Wash. 648, 39 Pac. 95 (1895).

[57] Hanway v. Galveston, etc., Ry., 94 Tex. 76, 58 S. W. 724 (1900).

has been held that a Young Men's Christian Association is not a public charitable organization. "The report shows," said the court, "that while much of the work of the defendant corporation is of a charitable nature, its purposes are also social, and include the giving of lectures, and of theatrical and other entertainments for the benefit of its members." Hence, the Court declared, it was not entitled to exemption from liability for the negligence of its servants.[58]

Private Corporations. These may sue and be sued for torts, and the rules which govern such actions are substantially those which apply to like actions by or against natural persons.[59]

Such corporation is entitled to sue for damages inflicted by a libel, provided the defamation is against it as an artificial person,[60] and not against its officers or agents as individuals.[61]

Its liability for torts was formerly denied, or confined to narrow limits. This denial appears to rest upon a dictum of Thorpe, C. J.,[62] which was misunderstood. "In terms it applied to municipal corporations only," but many writers and judges treated it as applicable to all corporations aggregate.[63] It is now well settled, however, that if a corporation has no body to be seized by *capias* or *exigent*, it has property which may be attached or levied upon.[64] Some eminent judges have declared that it is not liable for a tort which involves actual malice.[65] Their view is that a corporation aggregate has not a "mind," and, therefore, cannot entertain malice. "If malice in law," said an English judge in rejecting this view, "were synonymous with malice in French—a sort of *esprit* tinged with ill-nature, I should entirely agree. In such a sense a corporation would be as incapable of malice as of wit. But of actual malice in

[58] Chapin v. Holyoke Y. M. C. A., 165 Mass. 280, 42 N. E. 1130 (1896).
[59] Phil. W. & B. Ry. v. Quigley, 21 How. (U. S.) 202 (1858).
[60] Martin County Bank v. Day, 73 Minn. 195, 75 N. W. 1115 (1898); Trenton Mutual Life, etc., Co. v. Perrine, 23 N. J. L. 402 (1852); Morrison Jewell Co. v. Lingane, 19 R. I. 316, 33 At. 452 (1895).
[61] Mayor of Manchester v. Williams (1891), 1 Q. B. 94, 60 L. J. Q. B. 23.
[62] 29 Ass. f. 100, Pl. 67 quoted in Bro. Abr. Corporations, 43.
[63] See note by Serj. Manning, in 4 Man & G. at pp. 453–455.
[64] Maund v. Monmouthshire Canal Co., 4 Man. & G. 452 (1842); Trespass for breaking and entering locks on a canal; Central of Ga. Ry. v. Brown, 113 Ga. 414, 38 S. E. 989, 84 Am. St. R. 250 (1901).
[65] Baron Alderson, in Stevens v. Midland Counties Ry., 10 Ex. 352 (1854); Lord Bramwell, in Abrath v. N. E. Ry., 11 App. Cas. 247 (1886).

a legal sense, I think a corporation is capable." [66]   This is the prevailing view both in England and in this country.   Accordingly, a corporation is liable for malicious prosecution,[67] or for libel,[68] or for fraud,[69] although the malicious acts were done, as of course they could only be done, by its agent or servant; provided, those acts were done in the course and within the apparent scope of his authority in the business of his principal; and provided further, that, if the acts were not strictly within the corporate powers, they were assumed to be performed for the corporation, and by one who was competent to employ the corporate powers actually exercised.[70]

Liability for Slander.   The suggestion has been made that a corporation is not liable for slander spoken by its agents.[71]   It is believed that there is no judicial decision declaring such doctrine, while there are numerous judicial dicta to the contrary.[72]   The view seems to rest upon the idea that as a corporation has no voice it cannot commit slander.   Such a notion belongs to the same category with those which have been exploded: that a corporation has no body, and hence cannot commit a trespass; that it has no mind, and hence can entertain no malice.   It can speak only through its agents; and their voice, when used in compliance with its orders, or with its

[66] Cornford v. Carlton Bank (1899), 1 Q. B. 392.

[67] Cornford v. Carlton Bank (1901), 1 Q. B. 22, 68 L. J. Q. B. 1020. Hussey v. Norfolk, etc., Ry., 98 N. C. 34, 3 S. E. 923, 2 Am. St. R. 312 (1887), semble.

[68] Fogg v. Boston, etc., Ry., 148 Mass. 513, 20 N. E. 100, 12 Am. St. R. 583 (1889); Hussey v. Norfolk, etc., Ry., 98 N. C. 34, 3 S. E. 923, 2 Am. St. R. 312 (1887); Miss. Pac. Ry. v. Richmond, 73 Tex. 568, 11 S. W. 555, 4 L. R. A. 280 (1889).

[69] Fitzgerald v. Fitzgerald Co., 41 Neb. 374, 59 N. W. 838 (1894); Erie City Iron Works v. Barber, 106 Pa. 125 (1884).

[70] Washington Gas Light Co. v. Lansden, 172 U. S. 534, 19 Sup. Ct. 296 (1898).

[71] Townshend, Slander and Libel § 265, citing Mahoney v. Bartley, 3 Camp. 210 (1812), and Toll v. Thomas, 15 How. Pr. 314 (1857). Neither case deals with this question. The holding of each is that if an agent publishes a libel or a slander he is personally liable therefor. To infer from these decisions, that a corporation is not liable for slander uttered by its authorized agents, is warranted only upon the theory, that a principal is never liable in tort for his agent's acts, if the agent is personally liable.

[72] Palmeri v. Man. Ry. Co., 133 N. Y. 261, 30 N. E. 1001 (1892). Action was for false imprisonment accompanied by slanderous words, and recovery was sustained. Hussey v. Norfolk, etc., Ry., 98 N. C. 34, 3 S. E. 923, 2 Am. St. R. 312 (1887).

approval,[73] or, it is submitted, within the scope of their authority as its agents, is its voice.

§ .2. MEMBERS OF THE FAMILY.

Married Women. The common law did not permit a married woman to sue or be sued alone. If she were a proper party to the action, her husband must be joined with her. For torts committed by her in his presence or by his order,[74] or at least under his coercion,[75] he alone was responsible, and suit was properly brought against him alone. The rule, requiring him to be joined as a party with the wife, in other tort actions, rested upon the fact that he was entitled to her property. Unless he could be made a party defendant, one who had suffered wrong at the hands of the wife would be without remedy.[76] On the other hand, any recovery for injury to his wife's person or estate would belong to the husband, and should be prosecuted by him,[77] either as sole plaintiff,[78] or joined with his

---

[73] Behre v. National Cash Reg. Co., 100 Ga. 213, 27 S. E. 986, 62 Am. St. R. 320 (1896), *dictum* adopting statement of Odgers on Libel & Slander (1 Am. Ed. 368, 3 Eng. Ed. 435), that a corporation is not liable for slander uttered by its officers, unless the corporation ordered and directed the utterence of the very words.

[74] 2 Kent's Commentaries, 149; Dailey v. Houston, 58 Mo. 361 (1874); Edwards v. Wessinger, 65 S. C. 161, 43 S. E. 518 (1903).

[75] Marshall v. Oakes, 51 Me. 308 (1864); Handy v. Foley, 121 Mass. 259 (1876); Kosminsky v. Goldberg, 44 Ark. 401 (1884).

[76] Hawk v. Harman, 5 Binney (Pa.) 43 (1812); Head v. Briscoe, 5 Car. & P. 484 (1833); Capel v. Powell, 17 C. B. N. S. 743 (1864), said Erle, C. J., at p. 748: "Seeing that all her personal property is vested in the husband it would be idle to sue the wife alone, the action would be fruitless."

In some cases the view has been expressed that the common law required the husband to be joined, because the wife had in law no separate existence, and torts committed by her were his torts. Flesh v. Lindsay, 115 Mo. 1, 21 S. W. 907, 37 Am. St. R. 374 (1892); Wainford v. Heyl, L. R. 20 Eq. 321, 324 (1875). But this is inconsistent with the established doctrine that after divorce, the husband cannot be sued for torts of the wife during coverture, Capel v. Powell, 17 C. B. N. S. 743 (1864), as well as with the doctrine, that for her personal torts, " such as assault and battery, libel, slander and the like," judgment could be rendered against her jointly with her husband. Flesh v. Lindsay, *supra* (115 Mo. at p. 13, 14 and cases cited).

[77] Pollock, Torts (6 Ed.) p. 56.

[78] Smith v. City of St. Joseph, 55 Mo. 456 (1874).

wife.[79]   If the cause of action were one which would die with the person, the death of the wife, even after action brought by the husband with her, was good ground for arresting judgment in his favor.[80]   The husband could not join a cause of action in his own right for a tort to himself, with one as co-plaintiff with his wife for a tort to her.   Accordingly, if A slandered both husband and wife, the husband was required to bring an action in his own behalf, and a distinct action as co-plaintiff with the wife for the slander to her.[81]

Modern Legislation.   In nearly every jurisdiction, statutes have been passed modifying the husband's common law rights to his wife's property and his marital authority.   As a rule, this legislation has been strictly construed, so far as its effect upon the doctrines which we have been considering is concerned.   Its primary object was to exempt the wife's property from the husband's control and from liability for his debts, not to exempt him from his common law liability for her torts.[82]   Hence, his liability continues, save where the statute expressly changes it, as by declaring that he shall not be liable for her wrongful or tortious acts.[83]

---

[79] Laughlin v. Eaton, 54 Me. 156 (1866).

[80] Stroop v. Swarts, 12 Ser. & R. (Pa.) 76 (1824). So, if the action were brought against the husband and wife for her tort, his death would not abate the action, Douge v. Pearce, 13 Ala. 127 (1845); Smith v. Taylor, 11 Ga. 20 (1852); Baker v. Braslin, 16 R. I. 635; but her death would. Willis, J., in Wright v. Leonard, 11 C. B. N. S. 258 at p. 266 (1861); Rapallo, J., in Kowing v. Manly, 49 N. Y. 192, at p. 201, 10 Am. R. 346 (1872).

[81] Ebersoll v. Krug, 3 Binney (Pa.) 555 (1811). On the other hand, if the husband and wife slandered plaintiff, he could not join the action against the husband for his slander with that against husband and wife for her slander. Penters v. England, 1 McCord Law (S. C.) 14 (1821); Malone v. Stilwell, 15 Abb. Pr. 421 (1863).

[82] Seroka v. Kaltenburg, 17 Q. B. D. 177 (1886); Henley v. Wilson, 137 Cal. 273, 70 Pac. 21, 58 L. R. A. 941, 92 Am. St. R. 160 and note (1902); McElfresh v. Kerkendall, 36 Ia. 224 (1872); Wolf v. Banereis, 72 Md. 481 (1890). Such legislation does not relieve the wife from the necessity of joining her husband as plaintiff in a suit for injuries to her person. Hill v. Duncan, 110 Mass. 238 (1872); Morgan v. Kennedy, 62 Minn. 348, 64 N. W. 912, 54 Am. St. R. 647, 30 L. R. A. 521 and note (1895); Flesh v. Lindsay, 115 Mo. 1, 21 S. W. 907, 37 Am. St. R. 374 (1893); Fitzgerald v. Quann, 109 N. Y. 441, 17 N. E. 354 (1888).

[83] Strouse v. Leiff, 101 Al. 433, 14 So. 667, 46 Am. St. R. 122 (1893); Austin v. Cox, 118 Mass. 58 (1875), applying c. 312, St. of 1871, that a husband shall not be held liable for a wife's tort, unless he aided or encouraged it; Burt v. McBain, 29

A different view of these statutes obtains in some States, and they have been held to abolish by implication the common law rule of a husband's liability for his wife's torts. As they have destroyed the common-law theory of legal unity of husband and wife, have secured to her the full control and sole ownership of her property, have enabled her to carry on a separate business, and accorded her "the right to control her own time," courts have declared that they have destroyed the reason for the husband's liability for her misdeeds.[84]

Double Action for Injury to Wife.　When the wife sustains a personal injury through the tort of another, two distinct rights of action may accrue against the wrongdoer; one to the wife,[85] and one to the husband. The gist of the former is the injury itself, including her "potentiality to earn for herself and her expectation of life." [86]　The gist of the latter is, "the consequence of the injury, in depriving the husband of his common-law right to her society or services, or in imposing on him the common-law duty to care for her." [87]

Mich. 260 (1874); Mason v. Mason, 66 Hun (N. Y.) 386 (1892), applying statute now embodied in Domestic Relations Law, ch. 272, L., 896 § 27: "A married woman has a right of action for an injury to her person, property or character, or for an injury arising out of the marital relation, as if unmarried. She is liable for her wrongful or tortious acts: her husband is not liable for such acts unless they were done by his actual coercion or instigation: and such coercion or instigation shall not be presumed, but must be proved." Vacht v. Kenklence, 119 Pa. 365, 13 At. 198 (1888); Storey v. Downey, 62 Vt. 243, 20 At. 321 (1890).

[84] Martin v. Robinson, 65 Ill. 132, 16 Am. R. 578 (1872); Norris v. Corkill, 32 Ks. 409, 4 Pac. 862, 49 Am. R. 489 (1884); Lane v. Bryant, 100 Ky. 138, 37 S. W. 584, 36 L. R. A. 709 (1896); Culmer v. Wilson,

13 Utah, 129, 44 Pac. 833, 57 Am. St. R. 713 (1896).

[85] At common law, this action must be brought in the names of the wife and husband. Such is still the rule in some jurisdictions: Wolf v. Bauersis, 72 Md. 481 (1890). In others, the wife may sue alone. See cases in next note.

[86] Texas, etc., Ry. v. Humble, 181 U. S. 57, 63, 21 Sup. Ct. 526 (1900); Atlantic, etc., Ry. v. Percy, 73 Ga. 479 (1884); Chic., etc., Ry. v. Dunn, 52 Ill. 260 (1869); Pancoast v. Burnell, 32 Ia. 394 (1871); Townsdin v. Nutt, 19 Ks. 282 (1877); Harmon v. Old Col. Ry., 165 Mass. 100, 42 N. E. 505 (1896); Omaha, etc., Ry. v. Doolittle, 7 Neb. 481 (1878); Norfolk, etc., Ry. v. Dougherty, 92 Va. 372, 23 S. E. 777 (1895); Stevenson v. Morris, 37 O. St. 10, 41 Am. R. 481 (1881).

[87] Skoglund v. Minn. Street Ry., 45 Minn. 330, 47 N. W. 1071 (1891);

In some States the damages recovered for personal injuries to the wife are " community property of the husband and wife, of which the husband has the management, control and absolute power of disposition other than testamentary." [88]

Tort Actions between Husband and Wife. At common law, neither spouse could maintain a tort action against the other. This rule is sometimes said to be based on the doctrine that husband and wife " being one person, one cannot sue the other."[89] At other times, it is declared to rest upon considerations of public policy. Unless " marriage acts as a perpetually operating discharge of all wrongs between man and wife," it is said, each party will be tempted to take all petty domestic difficulties into court. It is thought to be wiser " to draw the curtain, shut out the public gaze, leave the parties to forget and forgive." [90]

The Injured Spouse is not without Remedy, however. In case of a serious assault and battery, the wrongdoer may be punished criminally.[91] If unlawfully deprived of liberty, the victim is entitled to a writ of *habeas corpus*.[92] There is also the resort of divorce, with the right to alimony in case of an abused wife.

Modern Statutes give a Right of Action in Tort Between Husband and Wife in some Cases. The English Married Woman's Property Act permits the wife to sue her husband for a tort to her separate estate,[93] but does not accord the reciprocal privilege to him. The statutes of Iowa and Illinois authorize an action by either spouse to recover his or her property from the other.[94] Such legislation has not given rise to many reported decisions, and is generally subjected to a strict construction.[95] The prevailing

Smith v. City of St. Joseph, 55 Mo. 456 (1874); Kelly v. N. Y., etc., Ry., 168 Mass. 308, 46 N. E. 1063 (1897); Hyatt v. Adams, 16 Mich. 180 (1867); Shanahan v. City of Madison, 57 Wis. 276 (1883); Southern Ry. Co. v. Crowden, 135 Al. 417, 33 So. 335 (1902).

[88] McFadden v. Santa Anna Ry., 87 Cal. 464 (1891).

[89] Blackburn, J., in Phillips v. Quarnet, 1 Q. B. D. 435, 45 L. J. Q. B. 277 (1876).

[90] Abbott v. Abbott, 67 Me. 304, 24 Am. R. 27 (1877); Bandfield v. Bandfield, 117 Mich. 80, 75 N. W. 287, 40 L. R. A. 757 (1898).

[91] State v. Oliver, 70 N. C. 60 (1874).

[92] Reg. v. Jackson (1891), 1 Q. B. 671, 60 L. J. Q. B. 346.

[93] 45 & 46 Vict. c. 75, § 12 (1882).

[94] Porter v. Goble, 88 Ia. 565, 55 N. W. 530 (1893); Larison v. Larison, 9 Brad. (Ill. App.) 27 (1881).

[95] Johnson v. Johnson, 72 Ill. 489 (1874); Chestnut v. Chestnut, 77 Ill. 347 (1875).

view is that all disabilities which the common law imposes upon husband and wife by reason of the marriage status still exist, except in so far as they have been modified or changed by express statutory enactment.[96]

Still, when the statutes secure to the wife the ownership and control of her separate estate, and give her the right to sue and be sued with respect to such property, as though she were a *feme sole*, it would seem that she should be accorded all actions, both equitable and legal, which are necessary to secure her in the possession or recovery of her property, even though her husband has to be made a party defendant, and thereby becomes liable to a judgment for money. And such seems to be the doctrine of the best considered cases.[97]

Tort Liability of Infants. It has never been doubted in English law that an infant is answerable for his torts, which are unconnected with his contracts.[98] If he is very young, however, his harmful acts may fall within the category of accident, instead of that of tort.[99] The command of his parents to commit a tort will not absolve him from liability,[100] although it will render the parent also liable.[101]

---

[96] Heacock v. Heacock, 108 Ia. 540, 79 N. W. 353 (1899). Cf. Abbe v. Abbe, 22 App. Div. 483, 48 N. Y. Supp. 25 (1897); State ex rel. Lasserre v. Michel, 105 La. Ann. 741, 30 So. 122 (1901).

[97] Crater v. Crater, 118 Ind. 521 (1888); White v. White, 58 Mich. 546, 25 N. W. 490 (1885); Whitney v. Whitney, 49 Barb. (N. Y.) 319 (1867); Berdell v. Parkhurst, 19 Hun (N. Y.) 358 (1879); Wood v. Wood, 83 N. Y. 575 (1881); McKendry v. McKendry, 131 Pa. 24, 18 At. 1078, 6 L. R. A. 506 and note (1890).

[98] Y. B. 35 Hen. VI. f. 11, pl. 18 (1456), holding an infant four years old liable for putting out an eye: Hodsman v. Grisell, Noy, 129; Barnard v. Haggis, 14 C. N. B. S. 45 (1863); Neal v. Gillett, 23 Conn. 437 (1855); Peterson v. Haffner, 59 Ind.

130, 26 Am. R. 81 and note (1877); Shaw v. Coffin, 58 Me. 254, 4 Am. R. 290 (1870); Sikes v. Johnson, 16 Mass. 389 (1820); McCabe v. O'Conner, 4 App. Div. 354, 38 N. Y. Supp. 572 (1896), affd. 162 N. Y. 600, 57 N. E. 1116 (1900); Fry v. Leslie, 78 Va. 269, 12 S. E. 671 (1891); Humphrey v. Douglass, 10 Vt. 71, 33 Am. Dec. 180 and note (1838); Hutching v. Engel, 17 Wis. 230 (1863).

[99] Harvey v. Dunlop, Hill & Den. (N. Y.) 193 (1843).

[100] Scott v. Watson, 46 Me. 362, 74 Am. Dec. 457 (1819); School Dist. v. Bragdon, 23 N. H. 507, 516 (1851); Humphrey v. Douglas, 10 Vt., 71, 33 Am. Dec. 180 and note (1838).

[101] Teagarden v. McLaughlin, 86 Ind. 476 (1882); Hower v. Ulrich, 156 Pa. 410, 27 At. 37 (1893).

Even when his tort is connected with a contract, it ought not to be difficult to determine whether a tort action will lie against him: and yet judicial decisions are quite in conflict on this point. Undoubtedly, the courts ought not to permit a plaintiff to turn a contract obligation into a tort liability by a mere trick of pleading, and thus recover against an infant in an action *ex delicto* for what is in reality the breach of a contract, which the law permits him to repudiate. For example, an infant contracts to act as plaintiff's agent,[102] or as bailee of his property.[103] He comes under a common-law duty to obey instructions and to exercise due skill and care in the performance of his contract. For a breach of such duty an adult may be sued in an action *ex delicto;* but if the infant is so sued, his infancy is a defense. The same proof, which would establish the cause of action in the tort suit, would have established a cause of action in a suit for breach of the contract. A release of the infant's liability for breach of the contract would operate as a release from the tort.[104] Hence the rule of law which releases the infant from liability upon the contract must operate to release him from the alternative liability for the tort.

The same doctrine has been applied in cases for false warranty by infants on the sale of goods. It has been declared that "the substantial ground of action rests on promises;" that "the assumpsit" in such cases "is clearly the foundation of the action."[105] If the warranty is an engagement collateral to the sale contract, and proof of damage cannot be made without referring to and proving the contract, then the courts are right in holding that the infant cannot be made liable by framing the action for damages in tort.[106]

Deceit by Infant.   If, on the other hand, the false statement

---

[102] Vasse v. Smith, 6 Cranch (U. S.) 226 (1810).

[103] Young v. Muhling, 48 App. Div. 617, 63 N. Y. Supp. 181 (1900).

[104] Bishop, Non-Contract Law, § 566.

[105] Green v. Greenbank, 2 Marsh. 485, 4 E. C. L. 375 (1816). This was a special action on the case. In Howlett v. Haswell, 4 Camp. 118 (1814), the action was assumpsit. In Brown v. Dunham, 1 Root (Conn.) 272 (1791), the declaration was "for fraud in the sale of a horse;" plea, that defendant was under age when the sale was made: reply, that defendant had the appearance of a man of full age and was allowed by his father to trade. Judgment—"The defendant being a minor under the care of his parent, was incapable of making a contract, therefore could not be guilty of fraud in contracting."

[106] Gilson v. Spear, 38 Vt. 311, 88 Am. Dec. 659 (1865).

as to the quality, condition or title of the article is made by the infant with knowledge of its falsity and with the intention to induce the buyer to act upon it, and the latter does act upon it to his damage, we have the common-law tort of deceit, and the infant should be held liable in a tort action for damages.[107]

Certainly, the weight of authority in this country is in favor of holding the infant liable for damages caused by inducing the plaintiff to sell him goods upon credit, by false representations that he was of age,[108] or that he intended to pay for the goods, when he did not,[109] or by inducing the seller to deliver to him goods sold for cash by giving a check for the price, which he knew to be worthless.[110] The doctrine of these authorities is, that an infant is liable for his tort, to the extent of the loss actually sustained, although it be connected with his contract, where a recovery can be had without giving effect to his contract. " The test," it is declared, " is supplied by answer to the question: Can the infant be held liable without directly or indirectly enforcing his promise? There is no enforcement of a promise where an infant, who has been guilty of a positive fraud, is made to answer for the actual loss his wrong has caused to one who has dealt with him in good faith and has exercised due diligence. Nor does such a rule open the way for a designing man to take advantage of an infant, for it holds him to the exercise of good faith and reasonable diligence, and does not enable him to make any profit out of the transaction with the infant, because it allows him compensation only for actual loss sustained." [111]

False Representations as to Age. In England, and in some of our States,[112] false representations as to his age by an infant

---

[107] The following language in a recent decision is applicable, it is submitted: " The right not to be led by fraud to change one's situation is anterior to and independent of the contract. The fraud is a tort. Its usual consequence is that as between the parties, the one who is defrauded has a right, if possible, to be restored to his former position." Nat. Bank Loan Co. v. Petrie, 189 U. S. 423, 425, 23 Sup. Ct. 512 (1902). The bank had not legal capacity to sell in this case.

[108] Fitts v. Hall, 9 N. H. 441 (1838); Wallace v. Morss, 5 Hill (N. Y.) 391 (1843).

[109] Ashlock v. Vivell, 29 Ill. App. 388 (1888).

[110] Mathews v. Cowan, 59 Ill. 341 (1871).

[111] Rice v. Boyer, 108 Ind. 472, 9 N. E. 420, 58 Am. R. 53 (1886).

[112] Johnson v. Pie, 1 Lev. 169, 1 Sid. 258, 1 Keb. 965 (1665); Bartlett v. Wells, 1 B. & S. 836, 31 L. J. Q. B. 57 (1862); Monumental Building Assoc. v. Herman, 33 Md. 128

do not subject him to a tort action by one who has been damaged thereby. The rule that infants are liable for their torts, it is said, "is to be applied with due regard to the other equally well settled rule that, with certain exceptions, they are not liable on their contracts; and the dominant consideration is not that of liability for their torts, but of protection from their contracts."[113] Accordingly, in the case just cited, it was held that one who had been induced to sell goods to a minor, by his false and fraudulent representation that he was of age, could not recover either for deceit or trover, although the infant had refused to pay the agreed price because of his infancy, and had disposed of the goods to third persons unknown to plaintiff. The court declared that plaintiff could not maintain his action without showing that there was a contract, which he was induced to enter into by the defendant's fraudulent representations in regard to his capacity to contract, and that pursuant to that contract there was a sale and delivery of the goods in question.

This reasoning ignores the fundamental doctrine that an agreement which has been procured by fraud may be treated by the defrauded party as void.[114]

Liability of Infant for Trover. The reasoning appears to ignore, also, previous decisions of the same court. As early as 1819,[115] that court declared in a case where the infant had induced the plaintiff to sell and deliver goods, by the misrepresentation that he was of age, and when sued for the price successfully interposed the defense of infancy: " The basis of this contract has failed from

---

(1870); Nash v. Jewett, 61 Vt. 501, 18 At. 47, 4 L. R. A. 561, 15 Am. St. R. 931 (1889).

[113] Slayton v. Barry, 175 Mass. 513, 56 N. E. 574, 49 L. R. A. 560 (1900).

[114] Nolan v. Jones, 53 Ia. 387, 5 N. W. 572 (1880); Kilgore v. Jordan, 17 Tex. 341, 350 (1856).

[115] Badger v. Phinney, 15 Mass. 359, 8 Am. Dec. 105. See Walker v. Davis, 1 Gray, 506 (1854), where the infant got plaintiff drunk and bought from him a cow for $26, giving his note for the price. When sued on the note, he pleaded his infancy and defeated the action. Then plaintiff sued the infant for the conversion of the cow, and recovered. Said the Court: "If the defence to the action on the contract had been one, which admitted its validity and then sought to discharge it, the judgment in the case would have concluded the parties"; but the defendant in the original action on the note having elected to avoid the contract, "the contract never became complete: the title to the cow did not pass. The tort was not waived."

the fault, if not the fraud, of the infant; and on that ground, the property may be considered as never having passed from, or as having revested in, the plaintiff." Accordingly, the plaintiff was allowed to maintain an action for replevin of the property.[116] Again, in Hall v. Corcoran,[117] the court ruled that an action of tort for the conversion of property is not founded on the contract under which the defendant obtained possession. It would seem to follow from those decisions, that when an infant is sued for conversion, in such a case as Slayton v. Barry,[118] his false representations and avoidance of his contract are such a fraud upon the adult, as enables him to treat the contract as void, and to reclaim the property if it is still in the infant's hands, or if he has disposed of it to sue him in trover. Such is the right generally accorded in this country.[119]

The same right is accorded in almost every jurisdiction, when an infant bailee does a positive and willful act to the property bailed, which amounts to a disaffirmance of the contract of bailment.[120] Hence, if an infant has money or property in his hands which he is bound to return to plaintiff, but which he willfully converts to his

[116] Similar actions of replevin were sustained in Bennett v. McLaughlin, 13 Ill. App. 349 (1883); Nolan v. Jones, 53 Ia. 387, 5 N. W. 572 (1880); Wheeler & Wilson Co. v. Jacobs, 2 Misc. 236, 21 N. Y. Supp. 1006 (1893); Robinson v. Berry, 93 Me. 320, 45 At. 34 (1899); Neff v. Landis, 110 Pa. 204, 1 At. 177 (1885).

[117] 107 Mass. 251 (1871).

[118] Slayton v. Barry, 175 Mass. 513, 56 N. E. 574, 49 L. R. A. 560 (1900).

[119] Ashlock v. Vivell, 29 Ill. 388 (1888); Eckstein v. Frank, 1 Daly (N. Y.) 335 (1863). In some States, infants are prohibited by statute from disaffirming contracts induced by their false representations that they are of age. See Iowa Code (1897), § 3190; Kansas Gen. St. (1901) § 4184; Utah R. S. (1898) § 1543; Wash. Ballinger's Codes and Statutes § 4582.

[120] Furnes v. Smith Rolle Abr. 530

(1635); Burnard v. Haggis, 14 C. B. N. S. 45 (1863); Vasse v. Smith, 6 Cranch (U. S.) 226 (1810); Homer v. Thwing, 3 Pick (Mass.) 492 (1826); Campbell v. Stokes, 2 Wend. 137, 19 Am. Dec. 561 (1828); Churchill v. White, 58 Neb. 22, 78 N. W. 369 (1899); Peigne v. Sutcliff, 4 McCord L. (S. C.) 387, 17 Am. Dec. 340 (1827); Freeman v. Boland, 14 R. I. 39, 51 Am. R. 340 (1882); Towne v. Wiley, 23 Vt. 355, 56 Am. Dec. 85 (1851). Contra, Penrose v. Curran, 3 Rawle (Pa.) 351 (1832); Wilt v. Welsh, 6 Watts (Pa.) 9 (1837). In Schink v. Strong, 4 N. J. L. 87 (1818), plaintiff counted on the contract and defendant's willful breach, and was defeated. A similar blunder in the nature of his action defeated plaintiff in Studwell v. Shapter, 54 N. Y. 249 (1873), a case of fraudulent representation by defendant inducing credit.

own use, he is liable in tort;[121] while if, by the transaction, he becomes a debtor only to the plaintiff,[122] or his loss of the property is due to negligence or disobedience of orders and not to willful misconduct,[123] a tort action is not maintainable.

Infant's Liability for Negligence.   As soon as a minor becomes capable of exercising care towards others, he is liable for negligence,[124] although regard is always to be had for the rule that a child is to be held to such care and prudence only, as is usual among children of his age, experience and capacity.[125]

When the negligence of the minor amounts to a breach of contract, and subjects him to legal liability only because of the contract relation, his infancy is a defense, as we have seen, whether the form of action be in contract or in tort.   In a recent Tennessee case,[126] this doctrine was held to exempt an infant from liability in the following circumstances: He had contracted to thresh a quantity of grain for the plaintiff, and while engaged in performing the contract he negligently set fire to certain of plaintiff's property, whereby it was destroyed.   When sued for the damage, he pleaded his infancy. The trial court struck out the plea, and plaintiff had a verdict.   On appeal, the Supreme Court reversed the judgment, holding that " the gravamen of the action is that the defendant's negligence constituted a breach of the contract."   It is submitted that the view of the trial court is not only preferable to that of the Supreme Court, but is in entire accord with the test laid down by the latter tribunal for such cases, viz.: " Whether a liability can be made out without taking notice of the contract."   It was immaterial whether the defendant was running an engine pursuant to a contract with plain-

---

[121] Bristow v. Eastman, 1 Esp. 172, Peake 223 (1794); Re Seager: Seeley v. Briggs, 60 L. T. N. S. 660 (1889); Mills v. Graham, 1 N. R. 140 (1804); Lewis v. Littlefield, 15 Me. 233 (1839); Catts v. Phalen, 2 How. (U. S.) 376 (1844); Baxter v. Bush, 29 Vt. 465, 70 Am. Dec. 429 (1857).

[122] Root v. Stevenson, 24 Ind. 115 (1865); Munger v. Hess, 28 Barb. (N. Y.) 75 (1858).

[123] Caswell v. Parker, 96 Me. 39, 51 At. 238 (1901); Stack v. Cavanaugh, 67 N. H. 149, 30 At. 350 (1891); Saum v. Cofflet, 79 Va. 510 (1884).

[124] Neal v. Gillet, 23 Conn. 437 (1855); Baker v. Morris, 33 Ks. 580, 7 Pac. 267 (1885); Conway v. Reed, 66 Mo. 346, 27 Am. R. 354 (1877).

[125] Haynes v. Gas Co., 114 N. C. 203, 19 S. E. 344, 26 L. R. A. 810, 41 Am. St. R. 786 (1894); Lexington Ry. v. Fain, — Ky.—, 71 S. W. 628 (1903).

[126] Lowry v. Cate, 108 Tenn. 54, 64 S. W. 1068, 57 L. R. A. 673 with valuable note (1901).

tiff or not. Being upon plaintiff's land with this dangerous instrument, he was under a common-law duty to use due care to prevent the escape of sparks and resulting injury to plaintiff's property. The plaintiff does not sue for injury to his grain from improper threshing, but for injury to property wholly disconnected with the contract. It was not necessary for him to show any contract between himself and the defendant, and if proved by the defendant, upon cross-examination of plaintiff's witnesses or otherwise, it had nothing to do with plaintiff's cause of action, save as a bit of history.[127]

Parent's Liability for the Child's Tort. Allusion has already been made to the fact, that a parent is liable for a tort which he directs his child to commit.[128] He is also liable for torts committed by his children as his agents or servants;[129] and, it has been held, that he must answer for damage resulting from the discharge of firearms by his young children and other misconduct on their part, on his premises and with his permission.[130] He is answerable, also, for a child's tort, when the circumstances warrant the inference that he was a party to it, either by precedent approval or by continuing to enjoy its fruits with knowledge of the material facts.[131]

Beyond this, his liability does not extend. The mere relationship of parent does not subject him to legal responsibility for his child's torts.[132] If a parent puts a dangerous instrument into the hands of his young child, and " encourages, countenances and consents to its negligent use " by him, he may well be held liable for the injurious consequences.[133] But he would have been equally liable

[127] Hall v. Corcoran, 107 Mass. 251, 257 (1871).

[128] Supra, p. 121.

[129] Teagarden v. McLaughlin, 86 Ind. 476, 44 Am. R. 332 (1882); Lashbrook v. Patten, 1 Duv. (Ky.), 317 (1864); Strohl v. Levan, 39 Pa. 177 (1861); Andrus v. Howard, 36 Vt. 248, 84 Am. Dec. 680 (1863); Schaefer v. Osterbrink, 67 Wis. 495, 58 Am. R. 875 (1886).

[130] Hoverson v. Noker, 60 Wis. 511, 50 Am. R. 381 (1884).

[131] Dunks v. Grey, 3 Fed. 862 (1880); Beedy v. Reding, 16 Me. 362 (1839); Hower v. Ulrich, 156 Pa. 410, 27 At. 37 (1893).

[132] Moon v. Tower, 8 C. B. N. S. 611, 98 E. C. L. 611 (1860); Hagerty v. Powers, 66 Cal. 368, 56 Am. R. 101 (1885); Smith v. Davenport, 45 Ks. 423, 25 Pac. 851, 11 L. R. A. 429, 23 Am. St. R. 737 (1891); Paul v. Hummell, 43 Mo. 119, 97 Am. Dec. 381 (1868); McCalla v. Wood, 1 Pen. (2 N. J. L.) 85 (1806); Tifft v. Tifft, 4 Den. 175 (1847); Kumba v. Gilham, 103 Wis. 312, 79 N. W. 325 (1899).

[133] Johnson v. Glidden, 11 S. Dak. 237, 76 N. W. 232, 74 Am. St. R. 795 with note (1898).

had the youngster been the child of another person.[134]   In other words, his liability in such cases turns not upon his relationship to the minor, but upon his own exercise of due care.[135]

Parent's Right to Sue for Injury to his Child.   The rule in this country upon this subject has been judicially declared as follows: " A parent, whose infant child has been injured by the tort of a third person, has a right of recovery to the extent of his own loss.   He cannot recover for the immediate injury to the child.   His action rests upon his right to the child's services, and upon his duty of maintenance.   When he is deprived of the right or put to extra expense in fulfilling the duty, in reason and justice he ought to be permitted to have recourse to the wrongdoer for indemnity." [136]   In England, this right of recovery does not exist, unless the child is old enough to render some act of service.[137]   The loss of service is the very gist of the action there.

It follows from the American rule, that a recovery by the parent, as guardian or next friend of the child, for damages to the latter, will not bar the parent's action on his own behalf.[138]   It follows also from the rule, that the tort to the child, in order to be actionable by the parent, must be harmful to him in one of two ways: it must diminish the child's ability to render service, or it must cause extra expense to the parent.[139]   In case the tort consists in the seduction and debauchment of a female child, the parent may recover more than compensatory damages.   In fact, the action is now treated, both in England and in this country, as " one to redress a moral outrage and punish libertinism under the form of a remedy for the

---

[134] Dixon v. Bell, 5 M. & S. 198, 17 R. R. 308 (1816).

[135] Chaddock v. Plummer, 88 Mich. 225, 50 N. W. 135, 26 Am. St. R. 283, 14 L. R. A. 675 (1891); Harris v. Cameron, 81 Wis. 239, 51 N. W. 437, 29 Am. St. R. 891 (1892).

[136] Nederlandsch, etc., Co. v. Hollander, 20 U. S. App. 225, 59 Fed. 417 (1894).

[137] Hall v. Hollander, 4 B. & C. 600, 10 E. C. L. 436, 7 D. & R. 133, 28 R. R. 437 (1825); Sir Frederick Pollock notes that " this case does not

show that, if a jury chose to find that a very young child was capable of service, their verdict would be disturbed."   Pollock, Torts (6 Ed.) 228n. (b).

[138] Wilton v. Middlesex Ry. Co., 125 Mass. 130 (1878); McGarr v. Nat. & Prov. Mills, 24 R. I. 447, 53 At. 320, 60 L. R. A. 122 (1902).

[139] Donahoe v. Richards, 38 Me. 376 (1854); Dennis v. Clark, 2 Cush. (Mass.) 347, 48 Am. Dec. 671 (1848); Cuming v. Brooklyn Ry., 109 N. Y. 95, 16 N. E. 65 (1888).

loss of manual services." [140] The jury, in assessing damages, " may consider not only that the plaintiff has a daughter disgraced in the eyes of the neighbors, but that there is a living memorial of the disgrace " (where such is the fact) " in a bastard grandchild." [141]

While the father is the only parent [142] ordinarily entitled to maintain an action for a tort to a child, if he is dead,[143] or, if he relinquishes his duty to support and provide for his children,[144] the widow or the wife, as the case may be, may bring the action, in most of our jurisdictions. So, a person standing *in loco parentis* may recover for expenses and loss of service resulting to him from tort to a minor.[145]

Tort Actions by Child against Parent. The law imposes upon the parent the duty of caring for, guiding, and controlling his children, and clothes him with the power of enforcing discipline in a reasonable manner. If he exercises this authority with cruelty, he may subject himself to criminal punishment,[146] and forfeit his right to the custody and services of the maltreated child.[147] There is some authority for the proposition that the cruel parent may be sued in a tort action by the injured child; [148] but the better view seems to be that " the peace of society, and of the families composing society, and a sound public policy, designed to subserve the repose of families, and the best interests of society, forbid to the minor child a right to appear in court in the assertion of a claim to civil redress for personal injuries suffered at the hands of the parent." [149]

[140] Lipe v. Eisenlerd, 32 N. Y. 229 (1865). Verdict for $1,000, sustained.

[141] Terry v. Hutchinson L. R. 3 Q. B. 559, 603 (1868). Verdict for £150 sustained.

[142] Geraghty v. New, 27 N. Y. Supp. 403, 7 Misc. 30 (1899); Worcester v. Marchant, 14 Pick. (Mass.) 510 (1833).

[143] Horgan v. Pacific Mills, 158 Mass. 402, 33 N. E. 581, 35 Am. St. R. 504 (1893); Gray v. Durland, 50 Barb. 100, 211 (1867); Aff'd. 51 N. Y. 424 (1873); Furman v. Van Sise, 56 N. Y. 435, 15 Am. R. 441 (1874); Villepigue v. Shular 3 Strobh. L. (S. C.) 462 (1849).

[144] McCarr v. Nat. & Prov. Mills, 24 R. I. 447, 53 At. 329, 60 L. R. A. 122 (1902).

[145] Manvel v. Thompson, 2 Car. & P. 303 (1826); Whitaker v. Warren, 60 N. H. 20, 49 Am. R. 302 (1880).

[146] Hinkle v. State, 127 Ind. 490, 26 N. E. 777 (1890); State v. Jones, 95 N. C. 588 (1886).

[147] Cunningham's Case, 61 N. J. Eq. 454, 48 At. 341 (1901); Farnham v. Pierce, 141 Mass. 203 (1886).

[148] Reeve's Domestic Relations (4 Ed.) 357; Treschman v. Treschman, 28 Ind. App. 206, 61 N. E. 961 (1901); Clasen v. Pruhs, — Neb. —, 95 N. W. 640 (1903).

[149] Foley v. Foley, 61 Ill. App. 577

The parental power of discipline may be delegated, either expressly to a specified person,[150] or impliedly, as to schoolmasters.[151] Such persons, however, are liable in tort to the child, if they exercise their delegated power in an unreasonable manner, or with malice.[152]

§ 3. ACTIONS INVOLVING THE RELATION OF MASTER AND SERVANT.

Terms Used in their Generic Sense. The terms master and servant, in this connection, will be used in their early and generic sense,[153] and not with the specific signification which differentiates them from principal and agent. While the agent as distinguished from the servant, is employed to represent his principal in creating contract obligations,[154] many, perhaps most, agents are also employed to do acts for their principal which are not to subject him to contract liability, but may make him answerable in tort.[155] And it is the liability to a tort action, growing out of the relation of employer and employed, that we are to consider in this section.

The Master's Liability for the Servant's Tort. Its Basis. The liability of a master extends beyond those wrongs done by his authority, or on his behalf and ratified by him. Speaking generally, he is answerable also for the wrongs of his servant, whether authorized or ratified by him or not, which are done in the course of the servant's employment and of the master's business.[156]

(1895); Hewlette v. George, 68 Miss. 703, 9 So. 885, 13 L. R. A. 682 (1891); McKelvey v. McKelvey, 111 Tenn. —, 77 S. W. 664, 64 L. R. A. 991 (1903).

[150] Harris v. State, 115 Ga. 578, 41 S. E. 983 (1902).

[151] Heritage v. Dodge, 64 N. H. 297 (1886); Cleary v. Booth (1893) 1 Q. B. 465.

[152] Lander v. Seaver, 32 Vt. 114 (1859).

[153] In Bacon's Abridgment, under the title of Master and Servant, it is said: "The relationship between a master and a servant is in many respects applicable to other relationships, such as lord and bailiff, principal and attorney, owners and mas-

ters of ships, merchants and factors." Bacon has no topic of "Principal and Agent."

Blackstone divides servants into four classes: Menial Servants; Apprentices; Laborers, and a "fourth species such as Stewards, factors and bailiffs, whom the law considers as servants *pro tempore*, with regard to such of their acts as affect their master's or employer's property." Vol. 1, pp. 425–428.

[154] Dwight, Persons and Personal Property, p. 323. Huffcut on Agency, Chap. 1 (2d Ed.).

[155] Singer Manufacturing Co. v. Rahn, 132 U. S. 518, 10 Sup. Ct. 175 (1889).

[156] Pollock on Torts (6th Ed.), pp.

Doubt has been expressed by a learned author and judge,[157] whether, if we were contriving a new code to-day, we would impose so extensive a liability on the master. He finds it hard to explain why the master is subjected to this liability, save upon the theory that it is a survival from the far-off time when the servant was a slave,[158] and, by a fiction of law, he and his master were "feigned to be all one person." [159]

Different Historical Stages of Liability. This theory does not seem to accord with the facts of English legal history. They indicate that the master's liability for his servant's torts has passed through distinct stages of development, and that the present rule rests not on grounds of policy which belonged to a different state of society, nor does it result from "a fiction which is an echo of *patria potestas* and the English frank-pledge," [160] but was slowly and cautiously evolved, and did not take its present form until the nineteenth century.[161] It was deliberately based upon considerations of practical expediency; and upon such considerations its continuance has been repeatedly rested. Lord Brougham declared that the reason for the master's liability for his servant's torts is, that by employing him, the master "sets the whole thing in motion." [162]

Chief Justice Shaw defended the rule as "obviously founded on the great principle of social duty that every man in the management of his own affairs, whether by himself or by his agents or servants, shall so conduct them as not to injure another,[163] and if he does not, and another thereby sustains damage, he shall answer for it." [164] Judge Grier, writing for the Supreme Court of the United States, said: "We find no case which asserts the doctrine that a master

---

573, 574. Huffcut on Agency (2d Ed.) 295.

[157] Holmes, J., in Dempsey v. Chambers, 154 Mass. 330, 28 N. E. 279, 13 L. R. A. 219, 26 Am. St. R. 249 (1891).

[158] Holmes Common Law, p. 228.

[159] Ibid. Lect. 1: 4 Harvard L. Rev. 350.

[160] Dempsey v. Chambers, 154 Mass. 330, 28 N. E. 279, 13 L. R. A. 219, 26 Am. St. R. 249 (1891).

[161] Responsibility for Tortious Acts, by Prof. John H. Wigmore, 7 Harv. L. Rev. 315, 383, 441; Helms v. Nor. Pac. Ry., 120 Fed. 389 (1903).

[162] Duncan v. Findlater, 6 Cl. & F. 894, 910 (1839).

[163] Of course, if the harm done by the servant is the result of inevitable accident, as when the servant stumbles, without negligence, and knocks plaintiff down, the master is not liable. Wall v. Lit, 195 Pa. 375, 46 At. 4 (1900).

[164] Farwell v. Boston, etc., Ry., 4 Met. (Mass.) 49 (1842).

is not liable for the acts of a servant in his employment, when the particular act causing the injury was done in disregard of the general orders or special command of the master. * * * If such disobedience could be set up by a railroad company as a defense, when charged with negligence, the remedy of the injured party would in most cases be illusive, discipline would be relaxed and the danger to life and limb of the traveler greatly enhanced. Any relaxation of the stringent policy and principles of the law affecting such cases, would be highly detrimental to the public safety." [165]

Who is a Servant? The rule stated above assumes that the relation of master and servant exists between the defendant and the wrongdoer. Ordinarily, the question whether this relation exists in a particular case is not a difficult one, for it results from the voluntary agreement of the parties. We have seen that the husband was liable at common law for his wife's torts, but that his liability in such a case was not that of a master for his servant's wrongdoing.[166] To subject him to hesponsibility in that character, it was necessary to show that she was in fact a servant or agent of her husband in the particular transaction.[167] We have also seen that similar proof was necessary to render the parent liable for his child's torts.[168]

Compulsory Pilot. Again, a person is not liable at common law for the wrongdoing of one whose services are forced upon him by the State. If a pilot is employed by the master or owner of a ship, we have the ordinary case of master and servant; [169] but if the law compels the employment of a particular pilot, or takes from the shipowner or master the right of choosing his pilot, the relation of master and servant does not exist, and for the fault of such a pilot the shipmaster or owner is not responsible.[170] Such is also

---

[165] Philadelphia, etc., Ry. v. Derby, 14 How. (U. S.) 468, 487, (1852).

[166] Supra, 118.

[167] Taylor v. Green, 8 C. & P. 316 (1837).

[108] Supra, 127.

[169] "And it will make no difference in the case that the pilot, if any is employed, is required to be a licensed pilot; provided the master is at liberty to take a pilot or not at his pleasure." Story on Agency (2d Ed.) § 456a. Cf. Consolidated Coal Co. v. Seniger, 179 Ill. 370, 53 N. E. 733 (1899), and Durkin v. Kingston Coal Co., 171 Pa. 193, 33 At. 237 (1895).

[170] Homer Ramsdell Tr. Co. v. La Compagnie Trans., 182 U. S. 406, 21 Sup. Ct. 831 (1901); The Halley L. R. 2 P. C. 193 (1868).

the English rule in Admiralty, but in this country, the Admiralty doctrine is [171] that the vessel " is in some sense herself a principal, and anyone having lawful command of her is, for the time being, her agent, for whose conduct she is herself responsible, both in contract and in tort." Hence in a proceeding *in rem* the vessel may be held liable for the consequences of a collision through the negligence of a pilot compulsorily taken on board.

Independent Contractors. The liability of a master for the torts of his servant rests, as we have seen, upon considerations of practical expediency. A man is bound to manage his affairs with a due regard for the safety of the persons and property of his fellows. But suppose he turns over the management of certain of his transactions to persons, who undertake to accomplish a prescribed result, but who are not otherwise subject to his control. Must he answer for their torts which are incident to the transaction? He does, indeed, " set the whole thing in motion; " but such persons are not his servants in the ordinary sense of that term. He does not direct and control their acts, and has no right to command obedience from them. They are the principals in the work which they have in hand. For damages inflicted by their misconduct, or the misconduct of those under their control, they are liable, and the law does not permit the injured person to go back of them in the line of causation,[172] save in exceptional cases, to be noted hereafter.

Who are Independent Contractors? The test generally applied in answering this question is " independence of control in employing workmen and in selecting the means of doing the work." [173] If the employer retains the right to determine and direct the manner in which the work is to be done, to point out the

---

[171] The China, 7 Wall. (U. S.) 53, 19 L. Ed. 67 (1868); Ralli v. Troop, 157 U. S. 386, 15 Sup. Ct. 657, 39 L. Ed. 742 (1894).

[172] In Murray v. Currie, L. R. 6 C. P. 24, 40 L. J. C. P. 26 (1870), Willes, J., said: " In ascertaining who is liable for the act of a wrongdoer, you must look to the wrongdoer himself, or to the first person in the ascending line, who is the employer and has control over the work. You cannot go further back

and make the employer of that person liable." In Painter v. Mayor, 46 Pa. 213 (1863), and Heidenaag v. City of Philadelphia, 168 Pa. 72, 31 At. 1063 (1895), it is said: " There cannot be more than one superior legally responsible."

[173] Uppington v. City of New York, 165 N. Y. 222, 59 N. E. 91, 53 L. R. A. 550 (1901); Wright v. Big Rapids Co., 124 Mich. 91, 82 N. W. 829, 50 L. R. A. 495 (1900).

dangers to be avoided and to fix the extent to which the work shall be carried on, it does not matter that the work is let out by the job to one who supplies laborers and materials. The principal is the employer, and not the contractor, and the latter and his laborers are the servants of the former.[174] It is not necessary in such a case, that the employer should actually guide and control the contractor. It is enough that the contract vests him with the right of guidance and control.[175]

On the other hand, an independent contractor is not converted into a servant by provisions in the contract which reserve to the employer certain rights of supervision and approval, during the progress of the work.[176] If these stipulations are for the purpose of securing faithful compliance with the specifications on the part of the contractor, the relation remains that of employer and independent contractor, though the stipulations give the employer the right to reject work or material which does not conform to the specifications, or to stop the work,[177] or even to insist upon the dismissal of incompetent workmen.[178]

Determined by the Contract. It is apparent from what has been said, that whether the relation in a particular case is that of employer and independent contractor, or of master and servant, depends upon the terms of the contract, in the absence of legislation.[179] If this is in writing, or though it be oral, if but one inference can be drawn from the evidence, the question is presented for the court;[180] while if more than one inference can fairly be drawn,

---

[174] Atlantic Transport Co. v. Coneys, 83 Fed. 177, 51 U. S. App. 570 (1897); Railroad Co. v. Hanning, 15 Wall. (U. S.) 649 (1872).

[175] Linnehan v. Rollins, 137 Mass. 123 (1884); Barg v. Bonsfield, 65 Minn. 355, 68 N. W. 45 (1896); Congregation v. Smith, 163 Pa. 561, 30 At. 279 (1894).

[176] Steel v. Southeastern Ry., 16 C. B. 550 (1855); Casement v. Brown, 148 U. S. 615, 13 Sup. Ct. 672 (1893). Thomas v. Altoona, etc., Ry., 191 Pa. 361, 43 At. 215 (1899).

[177] Stephen v. Commissioners, 3 Sess. Cases (4th Series) 535, 542

(1876); Vosbeck v. Kellogg, 78 Minn. 176, 80 N. W. 957 (1899); Blumb v. City of Kansas, 84 Mo. 112 (1884).

[178] Uppington v. City of New York, 165 N. Y. 222, 59 N. E. 91, 53 L. R. A. 550 (1901); Reedin v. London, etc., Ry., 4 Exch. (W. H. & G.) 244 (1849).

[179] Cargill v. Duffy, 123 Fed. 721 (1903). The driver of a licensed cab in New York city, is the servant of the owner, towards the public, although a bailee of the horse and vehicle.

[180] Sadler v. Henlock, 4 E. & B.

the question should go to the jury.[181] A physician whose services are supplied by common carrier to an employee,[182] or to a passenger,[183] or by another physician to the latter's patient,[184] or who is sent by one who has injured the plaintiff to examine the latter,[185] is an independent contractor. "There is no more distinct calling than that of the doctor," said Holmes, C. J., in the last cited case, "and none in which the employee is more distinctly free from the control of his employer." The only duty, resting upon the one who supplies the physician, is to use proper care in selecting him.

A mason, a carpenter, or other mechanic, whose business is recognized as a distinct trade,[186] or a truckman [187] or livery stable

570 (1855); Adams Express Co. v. Schofield, 111 Ky., 832, 64 S. W. 903 (1901); Leavitt v. Bangor, etc., Ry., 89 Me. 509, 36 At. 998, 36 L. R. A. 382 (1897); Boomer v. Wilbur, 176 Mass. 482, 57 N. E. 1004, 53 L. R. A. 172 (1899); Vosbeck v. Kellogg, 78 Minn. 176, 80 N. W. 957 (1899); Allen v. Willard, 57 Pa. 374 (1868); Sanford v. Pawtucket, etc., Ry., 19 R. I. 537, 35 At. 67, 33 L. R. A. 564 (1896); Singer Manufacturing Co. v. Rahn, 132 U. S. 518, 10 Sup. Ct. 175 (1889).

[181] Driscoll v. Towle, 181 Mass. 416, 63 N. E. 922 (1902). In Dutton v. Amesbury Nat. Bank, 181 Mass. 154, 62 N. E. 405 (1902), the majority thought but one inferences was warrantable, while one judge thought two could be drawn; Klages v. Gillette-Herzog Co., 86 Minn. 458, 90 N. W. 1116 (1902); Howard v. Ludwig, 171 N. Y. 507, 64 N. E. 172 (1902); Wallace v. Southern Cotton Oil Co., 91 Tex. 18, 40 S. W. 399 (1897); Emerson v. Fay, 94 Va. 60, 26 S. E. 386 (1896).

[182] York v. Chicago, etc., Ry., 98 Ia. 544, 67 N. W. 574 (1896).

[183] Obrien v. Cunard, S. S. Co., 154 Mass. 272, 28 N. E. 266 (1891); Allan v. State Steamship Co., 132 N. Y. 91, 30 N. E. 482, 15 L. R. A. 166, 28 Am. St. R. 556 (1892).

[184] Myers v. Holborn, 58 N. J. L. 193, 33 At. 389 (1895).

[185] Pearl v. West End Ry., 176 Mass. 177, 57 N. E. 339, 49 L. R. A. 826, 79 Am. St. R. 309 (1900).

[186] Lawrence v. Shipman, 39 Conn. 586 (1873).

[187] Murray v. Dwight, 161 N. Y. 301, 55 N. E. 901, 48 L. R. A. 673 (1900). The prevailing opinion says: "The relation of master and servant is often confused with some other relation. The mere fact that some person renders some service to another for compensation, expressed or implied, does not necessarily create the legal relation of master and servant. There are many kinds of employment which are peculiar and special, where one person may render service to another without becoming his servant in the legal sense. A servant is one who is employed to render personal services to his employer, otherwise than in the pursuit of an independent calling. The truckman who transports the traveler's baggage or the merchant's goods to the railroad station, though hired and paid for the service by the owner of the bag-

proprietor,[188] renders service to his employer, ordinarily, as an independent contractor and not as a servant. However, the employer may estop himself from showing that such a mechanic is an independent contractor, when he holds himself out as the master.[189]

A Servant with Two Masters. It often happens that a man is hired and paid by A, and thus becomes his servant, but, for certain transactions is transferred by A to the service of B. While thus engaged about B's affairs, he tortiously injures a third person. Is A or B to respond as master for the damage? Upon principle, the answer would seem not to be difficult, and that A or B should be liable, according as the one or the other had the right to control the act or omission which caused the harm. And such seems to be the answer given by the best considered cases. Accordingly, if A lends[190] or leases[191] his servant to B, or places him upon B's premises,[192] pursuant to an arrangement by which B is to have the right to direct the acts or control the conduct of the servant, B must respond for the torts of the servant, while thus engaged. On the

gage or the goods, is not the servant of the person who thus employs him. He is exercising an independent and *quasi* public employment in the nature of a common carrier, and his customers, whether few or many, are not generally responsible for his negligent or wrongful acts, as they may be for those of other persons in their regular employment as servants. A contract, whether express or implied, under which such special jobs are done or such special services rendered, is not that of master and servant, within the law of negligence."

[188] Quarmann v. Burnett, 6 M. & W. 499 (1840); Jones v. Corporation, 14 Q. B. D. 890 (1885); Joslin v. Grand Rapids Ice Co., 50 Mich. 516 (1883); Driscoll v. Towle, 181 Mass. 416, 63 N. E. 922 (1902); Little v. Hackett, 116 U. S. 366, 6 Sup. Ct. 391, 23 L. Ed. 655 (1885).

[189] Hannon v. Siegel-Cooper Co., 167 N. Y. 244, 60 N. E. 597, 52 L. R.

A. 429 (1901).—Defendant held itself out as practicing dentistry, in one of the departments of its store, and was declared liable for the malpractice of the dentists, although they were in fact practicing on their own account.

[190] Rourke v. White Moss. Colliery Co., 2 C. P. D. 205, 46 L. J. C. P. 283 (1877); Grace & Hyde Co. v. Probst, 208 Ill., 147, 70 N. E. 12 (1904).

[191] Donovan v. Lang (1893), 1 Q. B. 629, 63 L. J. Q. B. 25; Delory v. Blodgett, 185 Mass. 126, 69 N. E. 1078, 64 L. R. A. 114 (1904); Roe v. Winston, 86 Minn. 77, 90 N. W. 122 (1902); McInerney v. Del. & Hud. Ry., 151 N. Y. 411, 45 N. E. 848 (1897); Higgins v. West Un. Tel. Co., 156 N. Y. 75, 50 N. E. 500, 66 Am. St. R. 537 (1898).

[192] Atwood v. Chicago, etc., Ry., 72 Fed. 447 (1896); Brady v. Chicago, etc., Ry., 114 Fed. 100, 52 C. C. A. 48 (1902).

other hand, if, in the transaction, A sustains the relation of independent contractor to B, so that the latter's right of control is limited to indicating the work to be done, and does not extend to directing how it shall be done, then A and not B is answerable for the servant's torts.[193]

It often happens that there is a sort of duality of service.[194] With respect to certain acts, A retains the right of control, while with respect to others, the right of control is vested in B. In such cases A or B will be liable according as the negligent act belongs to the one or the other class. For example, if A lets his horses, wagon and driver to a city which is engaged in paving a street, and through the negligence of the driver, in looking after the shoeing of the horses and driving them, a horse kicks a loose shoe through the plaintiff's plate glass window, A and not the city is liable.[195] Had the plaintiff been injured, however, by the negligent manner in

---

[193] Jones v. Mayor, etc., of Liverpool, 14 Q. B. D. 890, 54 L. J. Q. B. 345 (1885); Cameron v. Nystrom (1893), A. C. 308, 62 L. J. P. C. 85; Stewart v. Calif. Imp. Co., 131 Cal. 125, 63 Pac. 177 (1900); Wood v. Cobb, 13 Allen (95 Mass.) 58 (1866); Murray v. Dwight, 161 N. Y. 301, 55 N. E. 901, 48 L. R. A. 673 (1900). The dissenting opinion in this case is based upon the view that the servant of the contractor was subject to the control of the defendant; Quinn v. Complete Electric Company, 46 Fed. 506 (1891).

[194] D. L. & W. Ry. v. Hardy, 59 N. J. L. 35, 37, 34 At. 986 (1896).— "Doubtless, no man can serve two masters, yet the law recognizes a sort of duality of service. A general servant of one person may, for a particular work, or for a particular occasion become, *pro hac vice*, the servant of another person." In Atwood v. Chicago, etc., Ry., 72 Fed. 447, 454 (1896), Phillips, J., said: "*It is a doctrine as old as the Bible itself, and the common law of the land follows it, that a man cannot serve two masters at the same time; he will obey the one, and betray the other.* He cannot be subject to two controlling forces which may at the time be divergent. So the English courts, which are generally apt to hit the blot in the application of fundamental rules, hold that there can be no application of the doctrine of *respondeat superior* in its application to two distinct masters; that the servant must be subject to the jurisdiction of one master at one time." Of course the same person may be acting in a particular transaction as the servant of two masters, as when the affairs of two corporations are carried on at the same place and by the same employees. If it is found as a matter of fact that the tort was committed by one while rendering service to both corporations, both will be liable. Diethers v. St. Paul Gas Light Co., 86 Minn. 474, 91 N. W. 15 (1902).

[195] Huff v. Ford, 126 Mass. 24, 30 Am. R. 645 (1878); Delory v. Blodgett, 185 Mass. 126, 69 N. E. 1078, 64

which the servant carried out an order which the city had a right to give him, the city would have been liable.[196]

Temporary Transfer of Service: An admirable statement of the principles applicable to these cases of temporary transfer of service, is found in a recent Massachusetts decision:[197] " In such cases the party who employs the contractor indicates the work to be done, and in that sense controls the servant, as he would control the contractor if he were present. But the person who receives such orders is not subject to the general orders of the party who gives them. He does his own business in his own way, and the orders which he receives simply point out to him the work which he or his master has undertaken to do. There is not that degree of intimacy and generality in the subjection of one to the other which is necessary in order to identify the two and to make the employer liable under the fiction that the act of the employed is his act.

" Of course the chances are that some orders will be given which are not strictly within the contract of the master. That is to be expected from the relative positions of the servant and the other party. If the latter has something that he wants done and sees a working man at hand, he is likely to ask him to do it, and if it is within the penumbra of his business the servant is likely to obey. While he thus goes outside his master's undertaking and his own contract with his master, he ceases to represent him,[198] and he may make the other liable for his acts,[199] but he does not on that account become the servant of his master's contractee for all purposes, or when he returns to the work which his master agreed to perform."

If the evidence does not show clearly that A's servant has been put, for the time being, under B's control, a question of fact for the jury as to whether A or B is the master seems to be presented,[200]

L. R. A. 114 (1904); Consolidated Fireworks Co. v. Kiehl, 190 Ill., 145, 60 N. E. 87 (1901).

[196] Donovan v. Lang (1893), 1 Q. B. 629; Driscoll v. Towle, 181 Mass. 416, 63 N. E. 922 (1902); Roe v. Winston, 86 Minn. 77, 86, 90 N. W. 122 (1902).

[197] Driscoll v. Towle, 181 Mass. 416, 63 N. E. 922 (1902).

[198] Brown v. Engineering Co., 166 Mass. 75, 43 N. E. 1118, 32 L. R. A.

605, 55 Am. St. Rep. 382 (1896); Wyllie v. Palmer, 137 N. Y. 248, 33 N. E. 381, 19 L. R. A. 285 (1893).

[199] Kimball v. Cushman, 103 Mass. 194, 4 Am. Rep. 528 (1869).

[200] Howard v. Ludwig, 171 N. Y. 507, 64 N. E. 172 (1902). The minority of the court thought the evidence in this case did not warrant the inference that the wrong-doer was the servant of the defendant, but showed clearly that he re-

although the burden seems to be on B of showing that one who is rendering service to him is not his servant, but the servant of A.[201]

Right of Selecting and Discharging Servant: In some cases the test of liability for the servant's torts, in such cases as we have been considering, has been declared to be, Who has the right of selecting and discharging him? If this test is applied, the liability will be thrown in almost every case upon the general master.[202] But it is submitted that the true test is that set forth in a preceding paragraph, and tersely stated by an eminent English judge: "The true principle of law is that if I lend my servant to a contractor, who is to have the sole control and suiperintendence of the work contracted for, the independent contractor is alone liable for any wrongful act done by the servant while so employed. The servant is doing, not my work, but the work of the independent contractor."[203]

Exceptional Liability of Employer for Torts of Independent Contractor: In some cases, as already noted, a person harmed by the tort of an independent contractor is allowed to go beyond this principal, and seek redress from the contractor's employer. The extent of this exceptional liability is a question upon which the courts of this country are not agreed. Its narrowest limits are those fixed by the New York decisions. "Where the employer personally interferes with the work and the acts performed by him occasion the injury; where the thing contracted to be done

---

mained the servant of his general master, the University Express Co.; Ward v. New England Fibre Co., 154 Mass. 419, 28 N. E. 299 (1891).

[201] Taylor, etc., Ry. Co. v. Warner, 88 Tex. 642, 648, 32 S. W. 868 (1895).

[202] New Orleans, etc., Ry. v. Norwood, 62 Miss. 565 (1885); Michael v. Stanton, 3 Hun (N. Y.) 462 (1875); Burton v. Galveston, etc., Ry., 61 Tex. 526 (1884); The Slingsley, 120 Fed. 748 (1903). In this case the court said: "Of all the tests which have been suggested, and the authorities are far from

uniform, it would seem that this, the power of substitution of one man for another, is the most satisfactory. It may not in all cases be as apparent as it is in this one that B. has no power to remove or differently employ the individual whom A. has selected and assigned to a special line of work, but when it does appear, the amount of control which B. exercises over the individual is surely insufficient to establish, even *pro hac vice*, the relation of master and servant."

[203] Brett, J., in Murray v. Currie, L. R. 6 C. P. 24 (1870).

is unlawful;[204] where the acts performed create a public nuisance;[205] and where an employer is bound by a statute to do a thing efficiently, and an injury results from its inefficiency,"[206] are the only cases "where a person employing a contractor" is liable for his torts.[207]

On the other hand, the broadest statement of this exceptional liability is found in a recent Ohio decision,[208] as follows: "The weight of reason and authority is to the effect that, where a party is under a duty to the public or third person to see that work he is about to do, or have done, is carefully performed, so as to avoid injury to others, he cannot by letting it to a contractor, avoid his liability, in case it is negligently done to the injury of another."

[204] Ellis v. Sheffield Gas Co., 2 E. & B. 767, 23 L. J. Q. B. 42 (1853); Spence v. Schultz, 103 Cal. 208, 37 Pac. 220 (1894); McDonnell v. Rifle Boom Co., 71 Mich. 61, 38 N. W. 681 (1888); Crisler v. Ott, 72 Miss. 166, 16 So. 416 (1894); Ketcham v. Newman, 141 N. Y. 205, 209, 36 N. E. 197, 24 L. R. A. 102 (1894).

[205] Hole v. Railway Co., 6 H. & N. 488 (1861); Deford v. State, Use of Keyser, 30 Md. 179 (1863); Woodman v. Met. Ry., 149 Mass. 335, 21 N. E. 482, 4 L. R. A. 213 (1889; Thomas v. Harrington, 72 N. H. 45, 54 At. 285 (1903).

[206] Smith v. Milwaukee, etc., Exchange, 91 Wis. 360, 64 N. W. 1041, 51 Am. St. R. 912, 30 L. R. A. 504 (1895).

[207] Berg v. Parsons, 156 N. Y. 109, 50 N. E. 957, 41 L. R. A. 391, 66 Am. St. R. 542 (1898). The New Jersey courts seem to hold this view. See Cuff v. Newark, etc., Ry., 35 N. J. L. 1, 10 Am. R. 205 (1870); Schutte v. United Electric Co., 68 N. J. L. 435, 53 At. 204 (1902). See Hoff v. Shockley, 122 Ia. 720, 98 N. W. 573, 64 L. R. A. 538 (1904).

[208] Covington, etc., Co. v. Steinbock, 61 Ohio St. 215, 55 N. E. 618, 76 Am. St. R. 375 (1899), with note citing: "Bower v. Peate, 1 Q. B. D. 321; Tarry v. Ashton, Id. 314 (1876); Hughes v. Percival, 8 App. Cas. 443 (1883); Dalton v. Angus, 6 App. Cas. 829 (1881); Hole v. Railway Co., 6 Hurl. & N. 488 (1861); Gray v. Pullen, 5 Best & S. 970 (1864); Hardaker v. Idle Dist. (1896), 1 Q. B. 335; Storrs v. City of Utica, 17 N. Y. 104 (1858); Spence v. Schultz, 103 Cal. 208, 37 Pac. 220 (1894); Sturges v. Society, 130 Mass. 414 (1881); Gorham v. Gross, 125 Mass. 232 (1878); Mechem, Ag. § 747, 748; Whart. Neg. § 185; Wood, Mast. & Serv. § 316; Shear. & R. Neg. § 176; Pickard v Smith, 10 C. B. (N. S.) 470 (1861); Penny v. Council (1898), 2 Q. B. 212, 217; Halliday v. Telephone Co., (1899) 2 Q. B. 392; Lawrence v. Shipman, 39 Conn. 586, 589 (1873); Stevenson v. Wallace, 27 Grat. (Va.) 77 (1876); Water Co. v. Ware, 16 Wall. 566, 21 L. Ed. 485 (1872); Black v. Finance Co. (1894), App. Cas. 48."; Pittsfield, etc., Co. v. Shoe Co., 71 N. H. 522, 53 At. 807, 60 L. R. A. 116 (1902); Davis v. Summerfield, 133 N. C. 325, 45 S. E. 654, 63 L. R. A. 492 (1903).

It will be observed that the New York doctrine recognizes and expresses such a duty—a duty which the employer cannot assign to a contractor—in three classes of cases: (1) where the work contracted for is unlawful, (2) where it amounts to a public nuisance, and (3) where a statute imposes the duty. To this extent, then, all authorities are agreed. Undoubtedly, the weight of authority favors the recognition and enforcement of such a duty, also, when " according to previous knowledge and experience the work to be done is in its nature dangerous to others, however carefully performed." [209] The negligence of the contractor or his servants, in such a case, is often spoken of as not collateral to the work, but directly involved in it.[210]

Collateral and Direct Negligence : Two recent cases well illustrate the distinction between " collateral " and " direct " negligence above referred to. In one case,[211] the owner of property employed an independent contractor to repair certain chimnies, by taking off a few feet and relaying the brick. Such work, the court declared, was not such as would necessarily endanger persons in the street. It did not involve throwing brick into the street, or causing or allowing them to fall so as to endanger persons traveling therein. The negligence of the contractor's servants in handling bricks, was a mere detail of the work. The work itself could not be classed as dangerous. Any negligence of the contractor's serv-

---

[209] Cf. Ridgeway v. Downing Co., 109 Ga. 591, 34 S. E. 1028 (1900), applying the following § 3819 of the Civil Code: " The employer is liable for the negligence of the contractor; (1) when the work is wrongful in itself, or, if done in the ordinary manner, would result in a nuisance; (2) or, if according to previous knowledge and experience, the work to be done is in its nature dangerous to others, however carefully performed; (3) or, if the wrongful act is in violation of a duty imposed by express contract upon the employer; (4) or, if the wrongful act is violation of a duty imposed by statute; (5) or, if the employer retains the right to direct or control the time and manner of executing the work; or interferes and assumes control, so as to create the relation of master and servant, or so that an injury results which is traceable to his interference; (6) or, if the employer ratifies the unauthorized wrong of the independent contractor."

[210] Hole v. Ry. Co., 6 H. & N. 488 (1861); Bower v. Peate, 1 Q. B. D. 321, 45 L. J. Q. B. 446 (1876); Pye v. Faxon, 156 Mass. 471, 31 N. E. 640 (1892); Water Co. v. Ware, 16 Wall. (U. S.) 566 (1872).

[211] Booveer v. Wilbur, 176 Mass. 482, 57 N. E. 1004, 53 L. R. A. 172 (1900).

ants was merely "collateral" to the work, and did not render the owner of the chimnies liable.

In the other case, the owner of property, who had been ordered by the inspector of buildings to remove the walls of a ruined building, as a nuisance to the public as well as to adjoining property, let the job of removal to an independent contractor, who had agreed to save the owner harmless for injuries done to others in the performance of the contract. Plaintiff was injured, through the negligence of the contractor and his servants. The court held the owner liable for the injury, on the ground that "the doing of the work necessarily involved danger to others, unless great care was used, and the injury resulted from negligence in doing the work. It was not collateral to the employment, as would have been the case had a servant of the contractor, while at work, negligently let fall a brick upon a person passing by." [212] In reply to the argument that it is "unreasonable that one who has work to perform, that he himself cannot perform from want of knowledge or skill, should be held liable for the negligence of one whom he employed to do it, since, if he did reserve control, it would avail nothing, from his own want of knowledge and skill," the court said: "There is seeming force in this, but only so. It is not agreeable to the principles of distributive justice; for it is equally a hardship that one should suffer loss by the negligent performance of work which another procured to be done for his own benefit, and which he in no way promoted and over which he had no control. Hence, where work is to be done that may endanger others, there is no real hardship in holding the party, for whom it is done, responsible for neglect in doing it. Though he may not be able to do it himself, or intelligently supervise it, he will nevertheless be the more careful in selecting an agent to act for him. This is a duty which arises in all cases where an agent is employed, and no harm can come from stimulating its exercise, in the employment of an independent contractor, where the rights of others are concerned." [213]

[212] Covington, etc., Co. v. Steinbrock, 61 Ohio St. 215, 55 N. E. 618, 76 Am. St. R. 375 and note (1899).

[213] Cf. Cork v. Blossom, 162 Mass. 330, 38 N. E. 495, 26 L. R. A. 256, 44 Am. St. R. 362 (1894), where the owner of a chimney was held liable for its fall, although he had hired an independent contractor to inspect it, who had pronounced it safe.

What Work is Intrinsically Dangerous? This is a question which has proved troublesome even for the courts which recognize and enforce the distinction taken in the cases last cited. A contract to burn brush on the defendant's land calls for the doing of intrinsically dangerous work,[214] in the opinion of some courts, while others entertain a contrary opinion.[215] Blasting with dynamite,[216] or excavating adjoining land,[217] or digging trenches in highways or across foot-paths,[218] is considered by most courts so dangerous an undertaking, as to impose upon the landowner or employer the non-assignable duty of seeing that the work is carefully conducted; while some courts refuse to recognize such a duty, unless the work is unlawful, or a nuisance, or the duty is imposed by statute.[219]

There is substantial unanimity in the view, that when a valid statute or municipal ordinance commands the observance of certain precautions in doing particular work, the work is to be deemed inherently dangerous, unless those precautions are taken. In such cases the employer is bound to see that the precautions are taken, and cannot escape responsibility by letting the work to ever so skillful or careful a contractor.[220] The same result follows, in

---

[214] Black v. Christchurch Finance Co. (1894) A. C. 48; Cameron v. Oberlin, 19 Ind. App. 142, 48 N. E. 386 (1897).

[215] St. Louis Iron Mt. Ry. v. Yonly, 53 Ark. 503, 14 S. W. 831, 9 L. R. A. 604 (1900). The court intimated that such a work might be intrinsically dangerous in some circumstances; but that the burden of showing that it was so dangerous was on the plaintiff.

[216] Norwalk Gaslight Co. v. Borough of Norwalk, 63 Conn. 495, 28 At. 32 (1893); Juliet v. Harwood, 86 Ill., 110, 29 Am. R. 17 (1877). Dissenting opinion of Dwight C., in McCafferty v. Spuyten Duyvil, etc., Ry., 61 N. Y. 178, 185 (1874).

[217] Bonaparte v. Wiseman, 89 Md. 12, 42 At. 918, 44 L. R. A. 482 (1899).

[218] Spence v. Schlutz, 103 Cal. 208, 37 Pac. 220 (1894); Curtis v. Kiler, 153 Mass. 123, 26 N. E. 421 (1891);

McCarrier v. Hollister, 15 S. D. 366, 89 N. W. 862, 91 Am. St. R. 695 (1902).

[219] Myer v. Hobbs, 57 Al. 175 (1876); Mayor of Birmingham v. McCary, 84 Ala. 469, 4 So. 630 (1887); Scammon v. Chicago, 25 Ill., 424, 79 Am. Dec. 334 (1861); Kepperly v. Ramsden, 83 Ill., 354 (1876); Tibbetts v. Knox, etc., Ry., 62 Me. 437 (1873); Blumb v. City of Kansas, 84 Mo. 112 (1884); Cuff v. Newark, etc., Ry., 35 N. J. L. 17, 10 Am. R. 205 (1870); Blake v. Ferris, 5 N. Y. 48, 55 Am. Dec. 304 (1851); Hackett v. West. Un. Tel. Co., 80 Wis. 187, 49 N. W. 822 (1891).

[220] Gray v. Pullen, 5 B. & S. 970 (1864); Wilson v. White, 71 Ga. 506, 51 Am. R. 269 (1883); Atlanta, etc., Ry. v. Kimberley, 87 Ga. 161, 13 S. E. 277, 27 Am. St. R. 231 (1891); Hinde v. Wabash, etc., Ry., 15 Ill.,

every case where the law, whether statute or common law, imposes a special duty on the employer; such as the duty of municipal corporations to keep their streets in a reasonably safe condition for those entitled to use them,[221] or the duty of common carriers to transport safely their passengers or freight,[222] or the duty of a party to a contract to take agreed precautions in doing certain work,[223] or the duty of the owner of highly dangerous things to see that they are properly used.[224]

Incompetent or Unfit Contractor.   There are many *dicta* to the effect that the employer is under a legal duty to exercise due care in selecting a contractor, and that he will be answerable for the contractor's torts if the latter is known to him to be unfit or incompetent for the proper execution of the work in hand, or if his manner of doing the work is known to the employer to be negligent.[225]   This doctrine has received the express approval of at least one court of last resort,[226] but appears to have been rejected by another.[227]

72 (1853); Brannock v. Elmore, 114 Mo. 55, 21 S. W. 451 (1892); Houston, etc., Ry. v. Meador, 50 Tex. 77 (1878); Smith v. Milwaukee Builders, etc., Exch. 91 Wis. 360, 64 N. W. 1041, 51 Am. St. R. 912 (1895).

[221] Mayor of Birmingham v. McCary, 84 Ala. 469, 4 So. 630 (1887); Wiggin v. St. Louis, 135 Mo. 558, 37 S. W. 528 (1896); Omaha v. Jensen, 35 Neb. 68, 37 Am. St. R. 432 (1892).

[222] Barrow Steamship Co. v. Kane, 88 Fed. 197, 59 U. S. App. 674 (1898). The carrier's "obligation to transport the passenger safely cannot be shifted from himself by delegation to an independent contractor, and it extends to all agencies employed, and includes the duty of protecting the passenger from any injury caused by the act of any subordinate or third person, engaged in any part of the service required by the contract of transportation. The present case is quite analogous to those in which it

has been held that a railroad company is responsible for the neglect or misconduct of the servants of a sleeping-car company, whereby a passenger sustains loss or injury, while being transported under a contract with the railroad company. Pennsylvania Company v. Roy, 102 U. S. 451; Dwinelle v. N. Y. Central & Hud. Riv. R. Co., 120 N. Y. 117; Railroad Co. v. Walrath, 38 Ohio St. 461; Kinsley v. Lake Shore and Michigan Southern Railroad Company, 125 Mass. 54."

[223] Water Co. v. Ware, 16 Wall. (U. S.) 566 (1872).

[224] Salisbury v. Erie Ry., 66 N. J. L. 233, 50 At. 117, 88 Am. St. R. 480 (1901).

[225] Dillon v. Hunt, 82 Mo. 155 (1884); Brannock v. Elmore, 114 Mo. 55, 21 S. W. 451 (1892), and authorities there cited.

[226] Norwalk Gaslight Co. v. Norwalk, 63 Conn. 495, 28 At. 32 (1893).

[227] Berg v. Parsons, 156 N. Y. 109,

Sub-Contractor's Torts. These are governed by the rules applicable to the original contractor. The sub-contractor becomes the principal in the execution of that part of the work committed to him, and for his torts, neither the original contractor, nor his employer, is liable save in the excepted cases already discussed.[228]

Adoption of Torts done on One's Behalf. Although the relation of master and servant does not exist when a particular tort occurs, that tort may be adopted by a third person, on whose behalf it is committed, so that he will be answerable therefor, precisely as though he had previously commanded it.[229] But the tort must have been committed on the adopting person's behalf,[230] or he must have received and retained the profits of it, with knowledge of all the material facts,[231] or with an intention to adopt it at all events,[232] in order to subject him to liability therefor. It is not necessary, however, that the ratification be directed specifically to the tort in question, nor that the tort taken by itself be beneficial to the adopting party.[233] In the case last cited, one McCullock took upon himself to deliver a load of defendants' coal to plaintiff, but without authority from defendant. By McCullock's carelessness in driving, a light of plate glass in plaintiff's window was broken. Thereafter, with knowledge of these facts, defendant presented a bill for the coal to the plaintiff and claimed that the plaintiff owed him for the same. This conduct, it was held, amounted to a ratification of McCullock's employment; established the relation of master and

[228] Overton v. Freeman, 11 C. B. 867, 21 L. J. C. P. 52 (1852); Beberick v. Ebach, 131 Pa. 165, 18 At. 1008 (1890); Powell v. Construction Co., 88 Tenn. 692, 13 S. W. 691, 17 Am. St. R. 925 (1890).

[229] Serle De Lanlarazon's Case, Y. B. 30 Ed. 1, (Roll's Series) 129 (1302); Anonymous, Godbolt, 109 pl. 129 (1586); Foster v. Bates, 12 M. & W. 226 (1843); Brown v. City 50 N. E. 957, 41 L. R. A. 391, 66 Am. St. R. 542 (1898), reversing S. C. in 84 Hun. 60, 51 N. Y. Supp. 1091 (1895), where it was expressly held that the employer is bound to select a suitable and competent contractor for blasting.

of Webster City, 115 Ia. 511, 88 N. W. 1070 (1902).

[230] Anonymous, Y. B. 7 H. IV, 34, pl. 1 (1405–6); Wilson v. Tumman, 6 M. & G. 236 (1843); Hyde v. Cooper, 26 Vt. 552 (1854).

[231] Dunn v. Hartford, etc., Ry., 43 Conn. 434 (1876); Beberick v. Ebach, 131 Pa. 165, 18 At. 1008 (1890); Singer Man'fg. Co. v. Stephens, (Ky.), 53 S. W. 525 (1899).

[232] Freeman v. Rosher, 13 Q. B. 780 (1849); Lewis v. Read, 13 M. & W. 834 (1845.

[233] Dempsey v. Chambers, 154 Mass. 330, 28 N. E. 279, 13 L. R. A. 219, 26 Am. St. R. 249 (1891).

THE LAW OF TORTS.

servant from the beginning, with all its incidents, and rendered the defendant liable for McCullock's negligence.

Evidence of Ratification. It is sometimes said that but slight evidence will be required to establish the ratification of a tort.[234] The statement does not seem to be a very helpful one, for the courts, which are responsible for it, have held that the retention of a servant, with knowledge of his misconduct, does not amount to an adoption of that misconduct, if it was not such as to render the master liable when it occurred.[235]

Scope of Servant's Authority. We have stated that the master is generally answerable, not only for the wrongs done by his express authority, or on his behalf and ratified by him, but also for the wrongs of his servant which are done in the course of the servant's employment and of the master's business, whether authorized or not. Let us now consider these two phrases, " course of employment " and " the master's business."

In many cases, the servant's acts are so clearly within the rule that the courts have no trouble in deciding them. For example, he is sent by his master to a certain place at a certain time to kill a beef. Finding but one animal there, he kills it. The animal turns out to be a valuable thoroughbred Shorthorn bull owned by plaintiff, which the master knew nothing about. The latter had no reason to believe that this particular animal was at the place in question, but supposed a different animal would be there. Still, as the servant " killed this bull while in the execution of his master's business, and within the scope of his employment," the master is liable to the plaintiff.[236]

On the other hand, many acts of the servant fall so far outside the rule as to occasion the courts little if any trouble. Clearly a teamster is not acting in the course of his employment, or in his master's business, when he invites a boy nine years old, to ride with him and

---

[234] Perkins v. Mo., etc., Ry., 55 Mo. 201, 214 (1874); Brown v. City of Webster City, 115 Ia. 511, 88 N. W. 1071 (1902); *Contra*, Williams v. Pullman Palace Car Co., 40 La. Ann. 87, 3 So. 631, 8 Am. St. R. 512 (1888), holding that ratification can only be inferred from acts which clearly and unequivocally evince the intention to ratify.

[235] Eidelmann v. St. Louis Co., 3 Mo. App. 503 (1877); Gulf, etc., Ry. v. Kirkbride, 79 Tex. 457, 15 S. W. 495 (1891).

[236] Maier v. Randolph, 33 Ks., 340 (1885); Maier v. Hopkins, 16 Ill., 313 (1855); Wilson v. Noonan, 27 Wis. 598 (1871), *accord*.

take the reins, while he goes to sleep; and the master is not liable for injuries sustained by the boy while thus assisting the teamster.[237] Nor is a car conductor so acting when he leaves his car and assaults one with whom he has had an altercation, but who is no longer a passenger,[238] or assaults boys at a distance from the road, who have placed obstructions on the track.[239] Nor is the janitor of a building,[240] or the watchman of an ice-factory,[241] or the fireman of a railroad crew,[242] so acting, when playing a practical joke on other employees of his master, or on persons invited to the premises by the servant.[243]

Not quite so clear a case is presented, where a servant, who is set to guard property and furnished with firearms by the master, shoots without legal excuse a person who is near the property. If the person shot is not molesting the property,[244] or if he is retreating from it,[245] or if the shooting occurs after the property has been injured and not with a view to protecting or regaining it,[246] the master is not liable. On the other hand, if the shooting is incident to measures taken by the servant for the protection of property

---

[237] Driscoll v. Scanlon, 165 Mass. 348, 43 N. E. 100, 52 Am. St. R. 523 (1896). Houston, etc., Ry. Co. v. Bolling, 59 Ark. 395, 27 S. W. 492, 27 L. R. A. 190, 43 Am. St. R. 38 (1894); Keating v. Mich. Cent. Ry., 97 Mich. 154, 56 N. W. 346, 37 Am. St. R. 28 (1893); Schulwitz v. Delta Lumber Co., 126 Mich. 559, 85 N. W. 1075 (1901); Parent v. Nashua Mfg. Co., 70 N. H. 199, 47 At. 261 (1900); Faust v. Phila. & Reading Ry., 191 Pa. 420, 43 At. 329 (1899,) *accord.* Had the boy negligently injured a third person, while driving for the teamster, such negligence might properly be deemed the teamster's negligence in the course of his employment. See Englehart v. Farrant & Co. (1897), 1 Q. B. 240, 66 L. J. Q. B. 122; Tuller v. Talbot, 23 Ill. 357, 76 Am. Dec. 695 (1860).

[238] Palmer v. Winston-Salem Electric Ry., 131 N. C. 250, 42 S. E. 604 (1902).

[239] Dolan v. J. C. Hubbinger Co., 109 Ia. 108, 80 N. W. 514 (1899).

[240] Gibson v. International Trust Co., 177 Mass. 100, 58 N. E. 278, 52 L. R. A. 928 (1900).

[241] Canton Cotton Warehouse Co. v. Pool, 78 Miss. 147, 28 So. 823, 84 Am. St. R. 620 (1900).

[242] Sullivan v. Louisville & N. Ry. 115 Ky. 447, 74 S. W. 171 (1903).

[243] Western Ry. of Ala. v. Milligan, 135 Ala. 205, 33 So. 438 (1902).

[244] Davis v. Houghtellin, 33 Neb. 582, 50 N. W. 765, 14 L. R. A. 737 (1891); Holler v. P. Sanford Ross, 68 N. J. L. 324, 53 At. 472 (1902).

[245] Turley v. Boston Ry., 70 N. H. 348, 47 At. 261 (1900); Golden v. Newbrand, 52 Ia. 59, 2 N. W. 537, 35 Am. R. 257 (1819).

[246] Candiff v. Louisville, etc., Ry., 42 La. Ann. 477, 7 So. 601 (1890).

against the person shot, the master may be liable, though the servant acted recklessly or maliciously in shooting.[247]

A Question for the Jury. Whether the tortious conduct of a servant is within the scope of his employment and in his master's business is a question of fact, a question at times so clear and easy as to admit of but one answer. It is then disposed of by the court, as we have seen in the last paragraph.[248] Generally, however, the evidence is conflicting, or warrants more than one inference, and the question is then to be submitted to the jury with proper instructions.[249]

In the Pennsylvania case, cited in the last note, " a boy eight years of age climbed on a moving wagon belonging to defendant and held on to the standard. Defendant's driver struck the boy with his whip on the hand which grasped the standard and the boy fell and was injured." The trial court nonsuited the plaintiff, on the ground that whipping the boy was an unauthorized act of defendant's servant. On appeal the judgment was reversed, the court saying: " It was for the jury to determine, under proper instructions, whether the act of the driver in causing the boy to fall from the wagon was negligent, and whether it was in the line of his duty and within the scope of his employment, so as to render his employer responsible for the act. At the time of the accident, Larkins had the custody and management of the wagon, and was driving it for the owner, the defendant company. The driver's control of the wagon carried with it the employer's authority to protect it and to prevent persons from getting on it, as well as to remove persons from it. It was not only the right of the driver to remove trespassers from the wagon, but also his duty to his employer to do so. He therefore was authorized to eject the boy from the wagon, and could use the necessary force for that purpose. If his act in striking

[247] Railway Co. v. Hackett, 58 Ark. 381, 24 S. W. 881 (1894); Haehl v. Wabash Ry., 119 Mo. 325, 24 S. W. 737 (1893).

[248] Steele v. May, 135 Ala. 483, 33 So. 30 (1902); Simonton v. Loring, 68 Me. 164, 28 Am. R. 29 (1878); Marshall v. Cohen, 44 Ga. 489, 9 Am. R. 170 (1871).

[249] Brennan v. Merchant & Co., 205 Pa. 258, 54 At. 891 (1903); and cases in last preceding note: Bergman v. Hendrickson, 106 Wis. 434, 82 N. W. 304, 80 Am. St. R. 47 (1900); Rounds v. D. L. & W. Ry., 64 N. Y. 129, 21 Am. R. 597 (1876); Baltimore Consol. Ry. v. Pierce, 89 Md. 495, 43 At. 940, 45 L. R. A. 527 (1899).

the boy was intended to remove him by force from the wagon, it would be the act of his employer, for which the latter would be responsible. If, on the other hand, the purpose of the driver was not to cause the boy to leave the wagon, but to inflict punishment upon him, to gratify the ill will of the driver, the defendant company is not responsible for the wrongful or tortious act. It would not be an act done by the employee in the execution of his employer's business, although it was performed while he was in the service of the employer. It would be an act of the employee directed against the boy, independently of the driver's contract of service, and in no way connected with or necessary for the accomplishment of the purpose for which the driver was employed. The negligent performance of the act, therefore, would impose no liability on the employer." [250]

Acts not Within the Particular Servant's Course of Employment. Rarely does a servant's employment extend to every branch and ramification of his master's business. Ordinarily, it is limited to a specific class of acts or line of work.[251] A "barman and cellarman in a public house," in England, is not the general manager of the master's business there carried on, and is not acting in the course of his employment in causing the arrest of one whom he suspects of having stolen whisky from the cellar.[252] Nor, it has been held, is a clerk in a store so acting, when he orders the arrest of a customer on suspicion of theft.[253] The prevailing view in this country, however, is that, if the master's manner of conducting his business justifies the jury in believing that the servant, in causing the arrest, was acting within the scope of his employment, and dis-

---

[250] Pierce v. N. C. Ry. Co., 124 N. C. 83, 32 S. C. 399, 44 L. R. A. 316 (1899); Cook v. Southern Ry., 128 N. C. 333, 38 S. E. 925 (1901), *accord*.

[251] Graham v. St. Charles, etc., Ry., 47 La. Ann. 1656, 49 Am. St. R. 436, 18 So. 707 (1895). A foreman of a railroad company, employed to hire, oversee and discharge laborers, is not acting in the course of his employment in inducing employees to withdraw their trade from plaintiff.

See Western U. Tel. Co. v. Mullins, 44 Neb. 733, 62 N. W. 880 (1895); Western U. T. Co. v. Foster, 64 Tex. 220, 53 Am. R. 754 (1895); Baker v. Kinsey, 38 Cal. 631, 99 Am. Dec. 438 (1869); Weldon v. Harlem Ry. Co., 5 Bosw. (N. Y.) 576 (1859); Aldrich v. Boston, etc., Ry., 100 Mass. 31, 1 Am. R. 76 (1868).

[252] Hanson v. Waller (1901), 1 Q. B. 390, 70 L. J. Q. B. 231.

[253] Mali v. Lord, 39 N. Y. 381, 100 Am. Dec. 448 (1868).

charging the ordinary duties imposed upon him, the master is liable.[254]

It has also been held that the section foreman of a railway company is not acting within the scope of his employment in lending a hand-car to boys, for the purpose of going along the track to a swimming place, and hence the company is not liable for injuries sustained by the boys while using it.[255] Had a third person been run over by the car through the boys' negligence, the company might well have been held liable; for guarding such an instrument of danger and keeping it from the hands of untrained boys was within the course of the foreman's employment.[256]

Again, a person's servant is not acting within the scope of his employment when lighting a pipe which he is accustomed to smoke while working; and for damage caused by the servant's negligence in lighting his pipe, the master is not answerable.[257]

Acts not Done in the Master's Business. Harm is often inflicted upon third persons by acts of a servant, which are within the course of his particular employment, and yet for this harm the master is not answerable. For example, A is the coachman of defendant. It is therefore within the course of his employment to drive defendant's horses. Plaintiff is injured by reason of A's negligent driving of defendant's horses. Whether he has a cause of action against defendant for the damages depends upon whether A was engaged in defendant's business at the time. If it appears that A took the horses out and was driving them for his own purposes,

---

[254] Craven v. Bloomingdale, 171 N. Y. 439, 64 N. E. 169 (1902); Pennsylvania Co. v. Weddle, 100 Ind. 138 (1884); Stephen v. Schmid, 18 R. I. 207, 26 At. 193, 19 L. R. A. 824 (1893).

[255] Robinson v. McNeil, 18 Wash. 163, 51 Pac. 355 (1897).

[256] Erie Ry. Co. v. Salisbury, 66 N. J. L. 233, 50 At. 187, 55 L. R. A. 578 (1901). "When the company placed the push car in the hands of the foreman, it was the duty of the foreman to use it with reasonable care to prevent injury to anyone lawfully on the tracks, and to keep it under his own supervision until it was returned. * * * * The obligation to see that this duty is performed is cast upon the railroad."

[257] Williams v. Jones, 3 H. & C. 256, 602, 33 L. J. Exch. 297, 13 L. T. N. S. 300 (1864). S. P., Walton v. N. Y., etc., Co., 139 Mass. 556 (1885). Defendant not liable for damages done to a person who was hit by a bundle thrown by a car porter; the bundle belonging to the porter and being thrown for his own purposes. S. P., Walker v. Hannibal, etc., Ry., 121 Mo. 575, 26 S. W. 360, 42 Am. St. R. 547 (1894).

and without authority from defendant, the latter is not liable to plaintiff.[258] If, on the other hand, A was driving them,[259] or charged with their custody,[260] in the business of defendant,[261] the latter is liable, although the particular conduct of A, causing the harm, was in violation of the defendant's orders,[262] or was even willful and malicious.[263]

The principles laid down in the decisions just referred to, are applicable to all cases involving the liability of the master for the wrongful and unauthorized acts of his servant. Although those acts are done while the actor is engaged in the master's employment, they will not render the master liable, unless they were done in his business. A few examples will suffice to illustrate this proposition. A railroad conductor strikes a passenger unnecessarily as he is attempting to board the train. If the force is used in the management of the passengers in leaving and entering the train, the master will be liable,[264] although, by misjudgment or violence

[258] Rayner v. Mitchell, 2 C. P. D. 357 (1877); Fiske v. Enders, 73 Conn. 338, 47 At. 681 (1900); Maddox v. Brown, 71 Me. 432, 36 Am. R. 336 (1880); Campbell v. Providence, 9 R. I. 262 (1869); Way v. Powers, 57 Vt. 135 (1884).

[259] Ritchie v. Walker, 63 Conn. 156, 28 At. 29, 27 L. R. A. 161, 38 Am. St. R. 361 (1893). Cf. Stone v. Hills, 45 Conn. 44, 29 Am. R. 635 (1877), where the servant, after driving to the destination named by the master, took new directions from a third party, and, while doing the business of such third party, negligently injured plaintiff. The master was not liable therefor.

[260] Whatman v. Pearson, L. R. 3 C. P. 422, 37 L. J. C. P. 156 (1868); Englehart v. Farrant & Co. (1897), 1 Q. B. 240, 66 L. J. Q. B. 122.

[261] In some jurisdictions, a temporary departure from the master's business, such as driving to a saloon for a drink, instead of returning to the master's stable, relieves the master from liability for the driver's negligence, during such period. McCarty v. Timmins, 178 Mass 378, 59 N. E. 1038, 86 Am. St. R. 490 (1901); Perlstein v. Am. Ex. Co., 177 Mass. 530, 59 N. E. 184, 52 L. R. A. 959 (1901); Sheridan v. Charlick, 4 Daly (N. Y.) 338 (1872); Cavanagh v. Dinsmore, 12 Hun (N. Y.) 465 (1878).

[262] Limpus v. London, etc., Co., 1 H. & C. 526, 32 L. J. Exch. 34 (1862).

[263] Cohen v. Dry Dock Ry., Co., 69 N. Y. 170 (1877); Baltimore Consol. Ry. v. Pierce, 89 Md. 495, 43 At. 940, 45 L. R. A. 527; Southern Bell Tel. Co. v. Francis, 109 Ala. 224, 231–235, 19 So. 1, 31 L. R. A. 193, 55 Am. St. R. 930 (1895); City Delivery Co. v. Henry, 139 Ala. 161, 34 So. 389 (1903).

[264] McFarlan v. Penn. Ry., 199 Pa. 408, 49 At. 270 (1901). He may be liable though the assault is upon a trespasser. Rowell v. Boston, etc., Ry., 68 N. H. 358, 44 At. 486 (1895).

of temper, the servant goes beyond the necessity of the occasion.[265]
On the other hand, if force is applied as an incident to reckless
horse-play between the conductor and a third person, the master
will not be liable.[266]

Again, the ticket agent of a railroad company causes the arrest
of a ticket purchaser, for passing counterfeit money for the ticket.
It turns out that the money was genuine. The railroad company
will be liable if the arrest is made in the prosecution of the master's
business,[267] but not if it is made for the purpose of aiding the public
authorities in bringing a supposed criminal to justice.[268] The same
doctrine applies to assaults made by servants while in the defendant's employ. If committed in prosecuting the defendant's business, he is liable, although he may have forbidden such conduct,
and although the servant's dominant motive at the moment of
assault was to inflict harm on the plaintiff, rather than to benefit the
defendant.[269] But if the servant commit the assault to redress a
personal grievance, or to save himself from loss, the master will
not be liable.[270]

[265] Rounds v. D. L. & W. Ry., 64 N.
Y. 129, 21 Am. 8. 597 (1876). S. P.,
Evans v. Davidson, 53 Md. 245, 36
Am. R. 300 (1880); Nelson Business
College v. Lloyd, 60 Ohio St. 448, 54
N. E. 471, 71 Am. St. R. 729, 46 L.
R. A. 314 (1899).

[266] Goodloe v. Memphis, etc., Ry.,
107 Ala. 233, 18 So. 166, 29 L. R. A.
729, 54 Am. St. R. 67 (1894): S. P.,
Lynch v. Florida Central Ry., 113
Ga. 1105, 39 S. E. 411, 54 L. R. A.
810 (1901). A quarrel between
plaintiff and defendant's station
agent grew out of, but was directly
connected with the agent's discharge of his duties to the defendant; Little Miami Ry. Co. v. West-
more, 19 Ohio St. 110, 2 Am. R. 373
(1869).

[267] Palmeri v. Manhattan Ry. Co.,
133 N. Y. 261, 30 N. E. 1001, 28 Am.
St. R., 632, 16 L. R. A. 136 (1892);
McDonald v. Franchere Brothers,
102 Ia. 496, 71 N. W. 427 (1897).

[268] Mulligan v. N. Y., etc., Ry., 129

N. Y. 506, 29 N. E. 952, 26 Am. St.
R. 539, 14 L. R. A. 791 (1892); Tol-
chester, etc., Co. v. Steinmeir, 72
Md. 313, 20 At. 189, 8 L. R. A. 846
(1890); Lafitte v. New Orleans, etc.,
Ry., 43 La. Ann. 34, 8 So. 701, 12 L.
R. A. 337 (1891).

[269] Williams Adm'r. v. Southern
Ry. Co., 115 Ky. 320, 73 S. W. 779
(1903). "The instructions were erroneous and misleading in the use
of the words 'not done in the interest and business of the defendant,'
instead of the words 'not done in
the line of his employment,' and
while acting within the scope of his
authority.'" Smith v. L. & N. Ry.,
95 Ky. 11, 23 S. W. 652, 22 L. R. A.
72 (1893); Dorsey v. Kansas, etc.,
Ry., 104 La. 478, 29 So. 177, 52 L. R.
A. 92 (1900); Girvin v. N. Y. C., etc.,
Ry., 166 N. Y. 289, 59 N. E. 921
(1901); Bergman v. Hendrickson,
106 Wis. 434, 82 N. W. 304, 80 Am.
St. R. 47 (1900).

[270] McDermott v. Am. Brewing Co.,

Willful, Malicious and Fraudulent Acts of Servant. There is much authority in the earlier cases for the view, that such acts do not subject the master to liability. Lord Kenyon declared [271] that " when a servant quits sight of the object for which he is employed, and, without having in view his master's orders, pursues that which his own malice suggests, he no longer acts in pursuance of the authority given him, and his master will not be answerable for such act." Judge Cowen asserted,[272] " all the cases agree that a master is not liable for the willful mischief of his servant, though he be at the time, in other respects, engaged in the service of the former." The tendency of later decisions, both in England and in this country, has been to discard this doctrine, and to hold the master answerable for the servant's willful, malicious and fraudulent misconduct, provided it was in the course of his employment and in the master's business.[273] The foundation of the modern doctrine is the principle that " if one of two innocent persons must

---

105 La. 124, 29 So. 498, 83 Am. St. R. 428 (1901); Williams v. Pullman Car Co., 40 La. Ann. 89, 3 So. 635, 8 Am. St. R. 512 (1888).

[271] McManus v. Crichett, 1 East 106, 5 R. R. 518 (1800).

[272] Wright v. Wilcox, 19 Wend. (N. Y.) 343, 32 Am. Dec. 507 (1838).

[273] This has appeared in the preceeding pages. Additional cases might be cited in great numbers. In the following, the topic is well discussed: Strang v. Bradner, 114 U. S. 555, 29 L. Ed. 248, 5 Sup. Ct. 1038 (1884), innocent partner liable in deceit for fraudulent misrepresentations of a co-partner. For other cases in accord, see Burdick on Partnership, pp. 203–214; Bank of Cal. v. West. U. Tel. Co., 52 Cal. 280 (1877); McCord v. W. U. T. Co., 39 Minn. 181, 39 N. W. 315, 1 L. R. A. 143, 12 Am. St. R. 637 (1888); Elwood v. W. U. T. Co., 45 N. Y. 549, 6 Am. R. 140 (1871); Bank of Palo Alton v. Pac. Postal Tel. Co., 103 Fed. 841, holding the telegraph company liable for willful and fraudulent acts of its servant in sending telegrams; Wheeler v. Baars, 33 Fla. 696, 15 So. 584 (1894); McArthur v. Home Life Assurance, 73 Ia. 36, 35 N. W. 540, 5 Am. St. R. 684 (1887); Rhoda v. Annis, 75 Me. 17, 46 Am. R. 354 (1883); Haskell v. Starbird, 152 Mass. 117, 25 N. E. 14, 23 Am. St. R. 809 (1890); Busch v. Wilcox, 82 Mich. 336, 47 N. W. 328, 21 Am. St. R. 563 (1890), innocent master held liable in tort for fraudulent misrepresentations of servant; Stranahan Bros. Catering Co. v. Coit, 55 Ohio St. 398, 45 N. E. 634 (1896), holding the master liable for the servant's adulteration of milk, although the latter adulterated it to gratify his malice against the master and to injure him. This decision is rested in part upon the fact, that the master had contracted with the plaintiff to supply pure milk; Dyer v. Munday (1895), 1 Q. B. 742, 64 L. J. Q. B. 448, holding master liable for servant's assault, although the latter had been punished as a criminal offense.

suffer loss by the act of a third, he who put it in the power of the third person to do such act should be compelled to sustain the loss occasioned by its commission." [274]

False Imprisonment and Malicious Prosecution by Servant. Applying the doctrine in the foregoing paragraph, the master has been held liable for the false imprisonment of persons by his servant, and for the malicious prosecution instituted in his name by his servant, not only when such proceedings were expressly authorized or ratified, but also when the servant's authority to act was fairly inferable from the nature and scope of his employment.[275] On the other hand, the master has escaped liability, where it appeared that the servant was not acting in the course of his employment, or in a manner ordinarily conducive to his master's interests, but was performing the functions of a citizen in seeking to bring the criminals to punishment.[276]

Master's Liability for Torts of Servant, which are not in the Course of His Employment. This exceptional liability of the master results from a special legal duty resting upon him, in certain circumstances. In some cases, that duty is imposed upon him by contract. A master who contracts to deliver pure milk to a cheese and butter factory, is liable in damages to the factory proprietor for the adulteration of the milk by a servant, although the latter adulterated it for the sole purpose of gratifying his spite against the master.[277] A common carrier contracts not only to

[274] Pac. Postal Tel. Co. v. Bank of Palo Alto, 109 Fed. 369, 48 C. C. A. 413 (1901).

[275] Krulevitz v. Eastern Ry., 140 Mass. 573, 5 N. E. 500 (1886); Palmeri v. Manhattan Ry., 133 N. Y. 261, 30 N. E. 1001, 16 L. R. A. 136, 54 Am. St. 632 (1892); Kelly v. Traction Co., 132 N. C. 368, 43 S. E. 923 (1903); Staples v. Schmid, 18 R. I. 224, 26 At. 193, 19 L. R. A. 824 (1893); Eichengreen v. Louisville Ry., 96 Tenn. 229, 34 S. W. 219, 31 L. R. A. 702, 54 Am. St. R. 833 (1896); Moore v. Met. Ry. L. R. 8 Q. B. 36, 42 L. J. Q. B. 23 (1872).

[276] Page v. Citizens Banking Co., 111 Ga. 73, 36 S. E. 418, 51 L. R. A. 463, with valuable note (1900); Tolchester Co. v. Steinmeir, 72 Md. 313, 20 At. 188, 8 L. R. A. 846 (1890); Mulligan v. N. Y. & R. Ry., 129 N. Y. 506, 29 N. E. 952, 14 L. R. A. 791, 26 Am. St. R. 539 (1892); Croasdale v. Van Boyneburg, 206 Pa. 15, 55 At. 770 (1903); Markley v. Snow, 207 Pa. 447, 56 At. 999 (1904); Abraham v. Deakin (1891), 1 Q. B. 516, 60 L. J. Q. B. 238.

[277] Stranahan Bros. Co. v. Coit, 55 Ohio St. 398, 45 N. E. 634 (1896). The court expressed the opinion that the servant's act in adulterating the milk was within the scope of his employment; but it also declared that the master's contractual

transport hi. passengers, but to use every reasonable effort to transport them safely. This contract, and the common law duty incident thereto, often render the carrier liable for his servant's torts, which are committed without a shadow of authority, and wholly outside of the master's business. Nothing could be further removed from the course of a railroad conductors' employment, or from the carrier's business, than the kissing of female passengers, and yet the carrier must answer in tort for the assault and battery of a conductor who kisses a female passenger against her will.[278] So he must answer for any tortious conduct of his servants towards passengers, which violates his duty towards them.[279] This duty extends to the exercise of a high degree of care in guarding them against the assaults of strangers.[280] He is not an insurer of their safety[281] against other passengers, or outsiders, nor even against his servants, but he is bound to use every reasonable effort to maintain order and discipline among his servants, as well as among passengers and those who are upon his premises and conveyances.[282]

relations with plaintiff determined the scope of the employment. Pittsfield Cottonware Co. v. Pittsfield Shoe Co., 71 N. H. 522, 53 At. 807, 60 L. R. A. 116 (1902); Steele v. May, 135 Ala. 483, 33 So. 30 (1902).

[278] Croaker v. Chicago & N. W. Ry., 36 Wis. 657, 17 Am. R. 504 (1875).

[279] Birmingham Ry. v. Baird, 130 Ala. 334, 30 So. 456, 89 Am. St. R. 43 (1901); Savannah, etc., Ry. v. Quo, 103 Ga. 125, 29 S. E. 607, 68 Am. St. R. 85 (1897); Keokuk, etc., Co. v. True, 88 Ill., 608 (1878); Chicago, etc., Ry. v. Flexman, 103 Ill., 546, 42 Am. R. 33 and note (1882); McKinley v. Chicago & N. W. Ry., 44 Ia. 314, 24 Am. R. 748 (1876); Wabash Ry. v. Savage, 110 Ind. 156, 9 N. E. 85 (1886); Missouri Pac. Ry. v. Divinney, 66 Ks. 776, 71 Pac. 855 (1903); Spangler v. St. Joseph, etc., Ry., 68 Ks.   , 74 Pac. 607, 63 L. R. A. 634 (1903); Shirley v. Billings, 8 Bush (71 Ky.) 147, 8 Am. R. 451 (1871); Goddard v. Grand Tk. Ry., 57 Me. 202, 2 Am. R. 39

(1869); Bryant v. Rich, 106 Mass. 180, 8 Am. R. 311 (1870); New Orleans, etc., Ry. v. Burke, 50 Miss. 200 (1874); Dwinell v. N. Y. C. Ry., 120 N. Y. 117, 24 N. E. 319, 8 L. R. A. 224, 17 Am. St. R. 611 (1890); Haver v. Cent. Ry., 62 N. J. L. 282, 41 At. 916, 43 L. R. A. 84, 72 Am. St. R. 647 (1898); White v. Norfolk, etc., Ry., 115 N. C. 631, 20 S. E. 191, 44 Am. St. R. 489 (1894); Seawell v. Car. Cent. Ry., 133 N. C. 515, 44 S. E. 610 (1903); Dillingham v. Russell, 73 Tex. 47, 11 S. W. 139, 15 Am. St. R. 753, 3 L. R. A. 634 (1889); Knoxville Traction Co. v. Lane, 103 Tenn. 376, 53 S. W. 557, 46 L. R. A. 549 (1899).

[280] Chic. & A. Ry. v. Pillsbery, 123 Ill., 9, 14 N. E. 22, 5 Am. St. R. 483 (1887); Snow v. Fitchburg Ry., 136 Mass. 552, 49 Am. R. 40 (1884); Carpenter v. Boston & A. Ry., 97 N. Y. 494, 49 Am. R. 540 (1884).

[281] Fritz v. Southern Ry., 133 N. C. 725, 44 S. E. 613 (1903).

[282] Mullan v. Wis. Ry. Co., 46

A similar duty rests upon the proprietor of a liquor saloon, or other place where intoxicants are publicly sold.[283] He has " the undoubted right to exclude therefrom drunken and disorderly persons, and the right to remove and expel them when they become in that condition and disorderly, and likely to produce discord and brawls. Being clothed with such power, a corresponding duty to do so in the interests of law and order, and for the protection of his other guests, should be imposed as a matter of law." [284]

Again, a person who puts into the hands of a servant a dangerous instrumentality, is under a common-law duty to see that the servant properly guards or uses it.[285] A parent is under a similar duty when he places dangerous instruments in the hands of his children, although they are not his servants in dealing with them.[286]

Tort Liability of Master to Servant. This is measured by the master's legal duty towards his servant. For any unjustifiable invasion of the servant's personal rights, the master is answerable precisely as he would be to a stranger.[287] In some cases,—rather

Minn. 475, 49 N. W. 249 (1891); New Orleans, etc., Ry. v. Burke, 53 Miss. 200, 24 Am. R. 689 (1876).

[283] Curran v. Olson, 88 Minn. 307, 92 N. W. 1124, 60 L. R. A. 733 (1903).

[284] Mustad v. Sweedish Brethren, 83 Minn. 40, 85 N. W. 913, 53 L. R. A. 803 (1901); Roumel v. Schambacker, 120 Pa. 579, 11 At. 779 (1887). *Contra* Belding v. Johnson, 86 Ga. 177, 12 S. E. 304, 11 L. R. A. 53 (1800).

[285] Tex., etc., Ry. v. Scoville, 62 Fed. 730, 23 U. S. App. 506, 10 C. C. A. 479, 27 L. R. A. 179 (1894); Alsever v. Minn., etc., Ry., 115 Ia. 338, 88 N. W. 841, 56 L. R. A. 748 (1902); Pittsburg, etc., Ry. v. Shields, 47 O. St. 387, 24 N. E. 658, 8 L. R. A. 464, 21 Am. St. R. 840 (1890); Cobb v. Columbia, etc., Ry., 37 S. C. 194, 15 S. E. 878 (1892); Erie Ry. Co. v. Salisbury, 66 N. J. L. 233, 50 At. 117, 55 L. R. A. 578 (1901); Enting v. Chic. & N. W. Ry., 116 Wis. 13, 42

N. W. 358, 60 L. R. A. 158 (1902), holding master liable for servant's misconduct with torpedos, locomotive whistle, with push-car, etc. *Contra*, Stephen v. So. Pac. Ry., 93 Cal. 558, 29 Pac. 234, 27 Am. St. R. 223 (1892). And when the servant takes possession of such dangerous instrumentality and uses it without the master's authority, the latter is not liable: Sullivan v. Louisville & Nashville Ry., 115 Ky. 447, 74 S. W. 171 (1903).

[286] Chaddock v. Plummer, 88 Mich. 225, 50 N. W. 135, 14 L. R. A. 675 with note (1891).

[287] Loveless v. Standard Gold Min. Co., 116 Ga. 427, 42 S. E. 741 (1902); Odin Coal Co. v. Denman, 185 Ill., 413, 57 N. E. 192, 76 Am. St. R. 45 (1900); Lorentz v. Robinson, 61 Md. 64 (1883); Troxler v. Sou. Ry., 124 N. C. 189, 32 S. E. 550, 44 L. R. A. 313, 70 Am. St. R. 580 (1899); Russell v. Dayton Coal Co., 109 Tenn. 43, 70 S. W. 1 (1902); Norfolk, etc., Ry.

rare at the present time,—the master is entitled to discipline a servant,[288] and, within certain limits, to defame him.[289] But, as a rule, a master is under the same legal duty to refrain from harming his servant that rests upon him towards strangers.[290]

SPECIAL DUTIES OF MASTER TOWARDS SERVANT.

(1) **To Employ Suitable Fellow Servants.** The relationship between them imposes upon the master certain special duties towards the servant, which may be classified as follows: First, to use reasonable care in selecting suitable and sufficient co-servants, including superintendents. He is not a guarantor of their competency and fitness. He is bound to exercise due care, however, in securing a sufficient number of competent servants; [291] but if, after such due care, injury happen to a servant through the unfitness or negligence of a fellow servant, the master is not liable therefor.[292] Of course, if the master is informed of a servant's incompetency, and thereafter retains him, he is violating his duty towards other servants and may be liable to them in damages; [293] provided, the injury is due to the incompetence or unfitness of the servant in

v. Houchins, 95 Va. 398, 28 S. E. 578, 46 L. R. A. 359, 64 Am. St. R. 791 (1897).

[288] The Agincourt, 1 Hagg. 271 (1824); Butler v. McClellan, 1 Ware (U. S.) 220 (1831); The Stacy Clarke, 54 Fed. 533 (1892). See Masters of Vessels, 20 Am. & Eng. Cyc. of Law, pp. 203–207 (2d Ed.).

[289] Child v. Affleck, 9 B. & C. 403 (1829).

[290] In some cases, the fact of an accident carries with it no presumption of negligence on the part of the master towards his injured servant, although it would towards certain others, such as passengers, in whose behalf there is *prima facie* a breach of his contract to carry safely. Patton v. Texas, etc., Ry., 179 U. S. 658, 21 Sup. Ct. 275 (1900).

[291] Louisville, etc., Ry. Co. v. Davis,

91 Ala. 487, 8 So. 552 (1890); Kelly v. New Haven Steamboat Co., 74 Conn. 343, 50 At. 871 (1902); Louisville, etc., Ry. v. Semonis, (Ky.), 51 S. W. 612 (1899); Cheney v. Ocean Steamship Co., 92 Ga. 726, 19 S. E. 33, 44 Am. St. R. 113 (1893); Portance v. Lehigh Valley Co., 101 Wis. 574, 579, 77 N. W. 875, 70 Am. St. R. 932 (1899).

[292] The Antonio Zambrana, 89 Fed. 60 (1898); Weeks v. Sharer, 111 Fed. 330, 49 C. C. A. 372 (1901); Relyea v. Kansas City Ry., 112 Mo. 86, 20 S. W. 480 (1892); Reichel v. N. Y. Cent. Ry., 130 N. Y. 682, 29 N. E. 763, 42 N. Y. St. R. 510 (1892).

[293] Metropolitan, etc., Co. v. Fortin, 203 Ill., 454, 67 N. E. 977 (1903); Brown v. Levy, 108 Ky. 163, 55 S. W. 1079 (1900); Norfolk & W. Ry. v. Hooven, 79 Md. 253, 29 At. 994, 25 L.

question.[294]   The burden of proof, however, is upon the plaintiff
to show the master's negligence in selecting or continuing incompetent servants.   The mere fact that they turn out to be incompetent
does not tend to establish a *prima facie* case of negligence on the
master's part.[205]

(2) **Duty to Establish and Promulgate Proper Rules.**
That this duty rests upon the master, whenever such rules are
feasible and will serve to minimize the risk of a hazardous employment, is well settled.   If the business involves no exercise of peculiar
skill, nor the use of dangerous machinery, nor extra hazard to the
servant, rules for the performance of the work are unnecessary.[296]
In other lines of business it may be a question for the jury, whether
rules and regulations should be made and enforced.[297]   In still
others, the conditions may be so complex and the hazard to the
servant so great, that the master's failure to establish proper rules
and to insist upon their observance will amount to a clear violation
of his legal duty.[298]   Perhaps no better statement of the principles,
defining and regulating this duty, has been made than the following: [299]   " The duty of a master in making rules is measured by the
law of ordinary diligence.   That law varies with the situation, for
what would be ordinary diligence under one set of facts would be
negligence in another.   If, however, under the circumstances of a

R. A. 710 and note, 47 Am. St. R.
392 (1894); Lamb v. Littman, 128
N. C. 361, 38 S. E. 911, 53 L. R. A.
852 (1901).

[204] Norfolk, etc., Ry. v. Phillips,
100 Va. 362, 41 S. E. 726 (1902).

[295] Stafford v. Chicago B. & T. Ry.,
116 Ill., 244 (1885); Roblin v. Kansas City, etc., Ry., 119 Mo. 476, 24 S.
W. 1011 (1894).

[296] Texas, etc., Ry. v. Echos, 87
Tex. 339, 27 So. 60 (1894); Olsen v.
Nor. Pac. L. Co., 40 C. C. A. 427, 100
Fed. 384 (1900); Gila Valley, etc.,
Ry. v. Lyon (Ariz.), 71 Pac. 957
(1903); Morgan v. Hudson, etc.,
Ore Co., 133 N. Y. 666, 31 N. E. 234
(1892).

[297] McGovern v. Central Vt. Ry.,
123 N. Y. 280, 25 N. E. 373 (1890);

Ford v. Lake Shore, etc., Ry., 124
N. Y. 493, 26 N. E. 1101, 12 L. R. A.
454 (1891).

[298] Kansas City Ry. v. Hammond,
58 Ark. 324, 24 S. W. 723 (1894);
Judkins v. Maine Central Ry., 80
Me. 417, 14 At. 735 (1888); Lake
Shore, etc., Ry. v. Lavalley, 36 O.
St. 221 (1880); Hartvig v. Nor. Pac.
L. Co., 19 Or. 522, 25 Pac. 358
(1890); Lewis v. Seifert, 116 Pa.
628, 647, 11 At. 514, 2 Am. St. R. 631
(1887); Madden v. Cheseapeake Ry.,
28 W. Va. 610, 57 Am. R. 695
(1886); Smith v. Baker (1891), A.
C. 325.

[299] Devoe v. New York, etc., Ry.,
174 N. Y. 1, 66 N. E. 568 (1903).
Consult also Nolan v. N. Y. & C. Ry.,
70 Conn. 159, 39 At. 115, 43 L. R. A.

particular case, the master has met the obligation of ordinary diligence in making and enforcing a rule, he is free from liability,[300] even if some other rule would have been safer and better. The law requires him to make and promulgate reasonably safe and proper rules, and if he does so he is not liable, even if he might have made safer and more effective rules."

Test of Sufficiency of Rules: If a rule is actually made, the question still remains whether it is proper and sufficient under the circumstances, for due diligence is not satisfied by an insufficient and inadequate rule.[301] " There is an essential difference between rules made by a master for his own protection and the regulation of his business in his own interest, and those made for the protection of his servants ; for, in the one case, the sufficiency affects no one but himself, while in the other, the lives and limbs of his servants are involved. * * * It may be that where the situation is simple and entirely free from complications the sufficiency of the rules made even to protect employees would be a question of law. When, however, the situation is complicated, the question of sufficiency " of the rules, as well as of the manner of their promulgation, " is for the jury. * * * What is reasonable and proper under a complicated state of facts permitting diverse inferences, is a question of fact."

For Court or Jury? It must be confessed, that the diversity of judicial opinion upon the last point in the foregoing extract is irreconcilable. In the case quoted from, a minority of the court dissented, holding[302] that " the question as to whether a rule is reasonable and proper is a question for the court, and not for the jury." " Of course," said the dissenting judges, " in cases where the facts with reference to the nature and contents of the rule are not clearly established, or are to be determined from controverted

305 with full note (1898), and Hill v. Boston & M. Ry., 72 N. H. 578, 57 At. 924 (1904).

[300] Smith v. Chic., etc., Ry., 91 Wis. 503, 65 N. W. 183 (1895); Ball v. Hauser, 129 Mich. 397, 89 N. W. 49 (1902).

[301] Vose v. Lancashire, etc., Ry., 2 H. & N. 728 (1858); Memphis, etc., Ry. v. Graham, 94 Ala. 545, 10 So. 283 (1891); Dowd v. N. Y. O. & W. Ry., 170 N. Y. 459, 63 N. E. 541

(1902); Willis v. Atlantic, etc., Ry., 122 N. C. 905, 29 S. E. 941 (1898). Nor is the master protected if he sanctions the habitual disregard of the rules by his servants. Hunn v. Mich. Cent. Ry., 78 Mich. 513, 526, 44 N. W. 502, 7 L. R. A. 500 (1889); McNee v. Coburn, etc., Co., 170 Mass. 283, 49 N. E. 437 (1898).

[302] Devoe v. N. Y., etc., Ry., 174 N. Y. pp. 12, 13.

facts, the question must be submitted to the jury as to what the rule promulgated was, under proper instructions from the court as to what is necessary to constitute a reasonable and proper rule." The minority view seems to be supported by the weight of authority in other jurisdictions.[303] Some courts have declared that the reasonableness of the master's rules is a question for the court, while their sufficiency is for the jury.[304] Whether rules have been fairly brought to the notice of the servant is generally a question of fact.[305] The presumption is that necessary rules have been made and duly promulgated.[306]

(3) **Duty to Provide a Safe Place to Work.** Closely connected with the master's duty, which we have just discussed, is his duty to provide a reasonably safe place for the servant while prosecuting his work. It is not to be understood that a master who carries on an extra-hazardous business is an insurer of his servants' safety. When they enter such employment they assume its necessary risks; but risks which can be obviated by reasonable care on the part of the master are not necessary risks.[307] A master maintaining electrical wires over which a high voltage of electricity is conveyed, rendering them highly dangerous, is bound to inspect such wires with a care commensurate with the risk, and to use proportionate efforts to keep them properly insulated and to prevent their doing harm to his servants.[308]

---

[303] Little Rock, etc., Ry. v. Barry, 84 Fed. 949, 56 U. S. App. 37 (1898), approving and following Kansas, etc., Ry. v. Dye, 36 U. S. App. 23, 70 Fed. 24, 16 C. C. A. 604 (1895); St. Louis, etc., Ry. v. Adcock, 52 Ark. 406, 12 S. W. 874 (1889); South Fla. Ry. v. Rhodes, 25 Fla. 40, 5 So. 633, 23 Am. St. R. 506, 3 L. R. A. 733 (1889); Reagan v. St. Louis, etc., Ry., 93 Mo. 348, 6 S. W. 371, 3 Am. St. R. 542 (1887).

[304] Chicago B. & Q. Ry. v. McLallen, 84 Ill., 109 (1876).

[305] McNee v. Coburn Trolley Co., 170 Mass. 283, 49 N. E. 437 (1898).

[306] Hill v. Boston & Me. Ry., 72 N. H. 518, 57 At. 924 (1904); Brady v.

Chicago, etc., Ry., 114 Fed. 100, 52 C. C. A. 48, 57 L. R. A. 712 (1902).

[307] Rockport Granite Co. v. Bjornholm, 115 Fed. 947, 53 C. C. A. 429 (1902).

[308] Myhan v. Louisiana, etc., Co., 41 La. Ann. 964, 11 So. 51, 16 L. R. A. 43, 32 Am. St. R. 348 (1889). In Union Pac. Ry. v. Jarvi, 53 Fed. 65, 3 C. C. A. 433 (1892), it is said: " The care and diligence required of the master is such as a reasonably prudent man would exercise under like circumstances, in order to protect his servants from injury. It must be commensurate with the character of the service required, and with the dangers that a reason-

At the other extreme, is the master whose business involves no unusual hazard to the servant, such as the ordinary householder or farmer. Here, the duty to provide a safe place to work reaches its lowest limit, extending no farther, probably, than the use of reasonable care to prevent harm to the servant from unusual danger, which the master knows or ought to know.[309]

In deciding cases which fall between these extremes, the greatest source of difficulty has been, in determining whether the servant's harm was due to the master's fault, in not providing a safe place to work, or to a fellow servant's fault in carrying on the work. The principles to be applied in such cases have been well stated in a recent decision [310] as follows: " It is the master's duty to exercise reasonable care in furnishing those things which go to make up the plant and appliances, so as to have them at the outset reasonably safe for the work of the servants who are engaged in the general employment, and further, to exercise reasonable care, by means of inspections and repairs, when needed, to keep the plant and appliances reasonably safe. These duties the master cannot avoid by employing others for their performance. If the negligence of those who are charged with such performance results in injury to one of those servants for whose safety the precautions are required, the master is liable, unless by reason of the obvious character of the consequent risk, or otherwise, it is assumed by the injured employee, or unless the injury is brought about by contributory negligence."

It will be observed that the master, who has provided a safe plant for his workmen, is not bound absolutely to keep it safe. He is under a legal duty to properly inspect it,[311] and, if such inspection

---

ably prudent man would apprehend under the circumstances of each particular case."

[309] Indemauer v. Dames, L. R. 1 C. P. 274, 35 L. J. C. P. 184, L. R. 2 C. P. 311, 36 L. J. C. P. 181 (1867); Eastland v. Clarke, 165 N. Y. 420, 428, 59 N. E. 202 (1901). In Collins v. Harrison, 25 R. I. ——, 56 At. 678, 64 L. R. A. 156 (1903), it is held to be the duty of the employer to furnish the domestic servant with a lodging room in such repair as not to endanger his health.

[310] Smick v. Erie Ry. Co., 67 N. J. L. 636, 52 At. 634 (1902). Master held liable to servant for injuries caused by defective roadbed, negligently allowed to remain in bad repair; Potter v. Detroit, etc., Ry., 122 Mich. 179, 81 N. W. 80 (1899), accord.

[311] Chicago, etc., Ry. v. Kneirin, 152 Ill., 458, 39 N. E. 324, 43 Am. St. R. 259 (1894); Simone v. Kirk, 173 N. Y. 7, 65 N. E. 739 (1902). It is the duty of a master whose servants are excavating materials from a

disclosed or would have disclosed defects or dangers, to use reasonable effort to repair, or remove, or warn against them.[312]

Safety of Place Dependent upon Co-Servants. At times, the safety of the place where the servants are employed does not depend upon the plant furnished by the employer, but upon the conduct of the employees.[313] The conditions of the place are constantly changing. " The work and the place of working are coincident." [314] In such cases, if the master has supplied a reasonably safe plant, with appliances for working and repairing it; has made, promulgated and enforced reasonable rules, and has exercised due care in selecting and continuing fellow servants, he has discharged his entire legal duty. For the negligence or misconduct of servants in carrying on the work—in executing a detail of operation—the master is not answerable to a fellow servant. That is an ordinary risk of the employment.[315] It must be admitted, however, that

bank of ashes, where lumps, partially undermined are liable to fall, to so inspect the place as to keep it reasonably safe. Three judges dissented on the ground that the negligence of the foreman related to a matter of detail.

[312] Hanley v. California, etc., Co., 127 Cal. 232, 59 Pac. 577, 47 L. R. A. 597 (1899). Defective roof of tunnel in which plaintiff was working; Toledo Brewing, etc., Co. v. Bosch, 101 Fed. 530, 41 C. C. A. 482 (1899). Defect caused by independent contractor, but reasonable inspection would have disclosed it; Belleville Stone Co. v. Mooney, 60 N. J. L. 323, 38 At. 835, 61 N. J. L. 253, 39 At. 764, 39 L. R. A. 834 (1897); Kelly v. Fourth of July Co., 16 Mon. 484, 41 Pac. 273 (1895).

[313] Coal Mining Co. v. Clay, 51 Ohio St. 542, 38 N. E. 610 (1894).

[314] Curley v. Hoff, 62 N. J. L. 758, 42 At. 731 (1899).

[315] Callan v. Bull, 113 Cal. 593, 604, 45 Pac. 1017 (1896). " The making of this bent was a part of the work to be done by the laborers themselves," not a " place furnished by their employer; " Angel v. Jellico Coal Co., 115 Ky. 728, 74 S. W. 714 (1903). " The negligence of fellow servants who placed dynamite before the furnace fire " was held a breach of the master's duty to provide a safe place to work; Holden v. Fitchburg Ry., 129 Mass. 268, 37 Am. R. 343 (1880); O'Connor v. Rich, 164 Mass. 560, 42 N. E. 111, 40 Am. St. R. 486 (1895). A scaffold made by servant in prosecuting the work is a detail of operation; Lindvall v. Woods, 41 Minn. 212, 42 N. W. 1020, 4 L. R. A. 793 (1889); McLaughlin v. Camden Iron Works, 60 N. J. L. 557, 38 At. 677 (1897); Loughlin v. State, 105 N. Y. 159, 11 N. E. 371 (1887); Cullen v. Norton, 126 N. Y. 1, 26 N. E. 905 (1891); Perry v. Rogers, 157 N. Y. 251, 51 N. E. 1021 (1899); Capasso v. Woolfolk, 163 N. Y. 472, 57 N. E. 760 (1900); Lambert v. Missisquoi Co., 72 Vt. 278, 47 At. 1085 (1900); Okouski v. Penn., etc., Co., 114 Wis.

courts are not agreed as to what is a detail of operation, as distinguished from an act which renders the working plant unsafe.[316]

Court and Jury. Nor are they agreed as to whether the question of what constitutes a reasonably safe place to work is one for the court or for the jury. The weight of authority favors the view, that it is not proper to submit to a jury the question whether a particular place of work was reasonably safe. To do that, it is said, would be to substitute the varying opinion of juries, as to how a business should be conducted, for the lawful judgment of the employer, and would prevent the formation of a rule of law upon the subject.[317] " Reasonably safe," it has been judicially declared, " means safe according to the usages, habits and ordinary risks of the business. * * * No jury can be permitted to say that the usual and ordinary way " of preparing a place of work is an unsafe way.[318]

In a recent New Hampshire case the majority of the court declared that " when the danger arises, not from the place itself, but from the use of it for the work, and no special skill or experience beyond that involved in doing the work is required to maintain the safety of the place, the maintenance of such safety is the duty of the servant, because it is a part of the work." [319]

(4) **Duty to Furnish Safe Appliances.** By some courts the term " safe appliances " is used in a very extensive sense, includ-

448, 90 N. W. 429 (1902); Wilson v. Merry, L. R. 1 Sc. & D. 326, 19 L. T. R. 30 (1868).

[316] With cases in the last note, Cr. Chic., etc., Ry. v. Maroney, 170 Ill., 520, 48 N. E. 953, 62 Am. St. R. 396 (1897); McBeath v. Rawle, 192 Ill., 626, 61 N. E. 847 (1901), holding that a scaffold used in prosecuting the work is a " place to work," not a detail of operation. The New York Labor Law (Chap. 415 L., 1897) has adopted the Illinois rule, and imposes upon the master the duty of providing safe scaffolding for employees; Stewart v. Ferguson, 164 N. Y. 553, 58 N. E. 662 (1900).

[317] Bethlehem Iron Co. v. Weiss, 100 Fed. 45, 40 C. C. A. 270 (1900).

[318] Titus v. Bradford, etc., Ry., 136 Pa. 618, 20 At. 517, 20 Am. St. R. 944 (1890).

[319] McLaine v. Head & Dowst Co.,. 71 N. H. 294, 52 At. 545, 15 L. R. A. 462, 93 Am. St. R. 522 (1902). The dissenting opinion will repay a careful examination. This declares that " the law now is, that the master by the contract of employment assumes certain personal duties to the servant, not only in respect to original equipment, but subsequent maintenance and management, and that whoever represents him in the discharge of any of these duties, whatever his title or rank, is to that extent the master's agent, for whose negligence the master is responsible.

ing a safe place in which to work.[320] It will be employed in this section to designate machinery, tools and contrivances, which do not form part of the employer's permanent plant, but are used in the business there carried on.

The employer's duty with respect to appliances is substantially the same as his duty with respect to a safe place in which to work. It is not absolute, in the sense that he is an insurer of their perfection.[321] On the other hand, it is a duty which he cannot assign or delegate so as to free himself from liability for its non-performance.[322] The degree of care, which this duty imposes upon the employer, varies with the character of the appliances. Some kinds are much more dangerous than others, and require greater skill in selecting and installing, as well as greater watchfulness of their condition. If the master exercises such care and skill in furnishing

to the servant, just as he would be responsible if the negligence were directly his own."

[320] Hess v. Rosenthal, 160 Ill., 621, 43 N. E. 743 (1896).

[321] In Hough v. Texas, etc., Ry. Co., 100 U. S. 213 (1879), it is said: "To guard against the misapplication of these principles, we should say that the corporation is not to be held as guarantying or warranting the absolute safety, under all circumstances, or the perfection in all its parts, of the machinery or apparatus which may be provided for the use of employees. Its duty in that respect to its employees is discharged when, but only when, its agents whose business it is to supply such instrumentalities exercise due care, as well in their purchase originally, as in keeping and maintaining them in such condition as to be reasonably and adequately safe for use by employees." The general rule is that a master is not liable for a mere error of judgment in selecting appliances. Negligence, or culpable ignorance, must be shown. O'Neill v. Chic., etc., Ry.,

62 Neb. 358, 86 N. W. 1098, 60 L. R. A. 443 (1901), and cases cited therein.

[322] In Balt. & Ohio Ry. v. Baugh, 149 U. S. 368, 13 Sup. Ct. 914 (1893), the court said: "That positive duty does not go to the extent of a guaranty of safety, but it does require that reasonable precautions be taken to secure safety, and it matters not to the employee by whom that safety is secured, or the reasonable precautions therefor taken. He has a right to look to the master for the discharge of that duty, and if the master, instead of discharging it himself, sees fit to have it attended to by others, that does not change the measure of obligation to the employee, or the latter's right to insist that reasonable precaution shall be taken to secure safety in these respects." Noble v. Bessemer Co., 127 Mich. 103, 86 N. W. 520, 89 Am. St. R. 461 (1901); Orr v. Sou. Tel. Co., 132 N. C. 691, 44 S. E. 401 (1903); Port Makely Mill Co. v. Garrett, 97 Fed. 537 (1899); Ry. Co. v. Peterson, 162 U. S. 353, 16 Sup. Ct. 842 (1896), *accord.*

appliances, and in inspecting and repairing them,[323] he has performed his whole duty in this respect towards his servants; and for any injury sustained by one servant, through the negligent use or care of such appliances by a fellow servant, the master is not answerable.[324] In some jurisdictions, however, the master's duty seems to extend to securing the proper use of safe appliances,[325] but this view does not appear to accord either with sound principle or the weight of authority.[326]

Safety of Appliances and Fellow Servants. When the master does not personally superintend and direct the selection, repair and custody of appliances, the extent of his liability for injuries due to their defects, unfitness or dangerous condition, is a a matter upon which the courts are not agreed. In England, the master appears to discharge his full duty towards servants, in such cases, when he uses due care in selecting proper representatives to act in his stead, and supplies them with adequate materials and resources.[327] Such is not the doctrine in any of our jurisdictions. Almost without exception, our courts declare that a master cannot escape liability for injuries to a servant by unsafe appliances, by showing that he delegated their selection to a thoroughly competent and experienced agent. The duty of selecting them with reasonable care—a care proportionate to their dangerous character—cannot be shifted to a delegate. It remains upon the master, no matter who is employed by him to perform it.[328] To be sure, the agent is under

---

[323] Byrne v. Eastmans Co., 163 N. Y. 461, 57 N. E. 738 (1900); Kelly v. N. H. Steamboat Co., 74 Conn. 343, 50 At. 871, 92 Am. St. R. 220 (1902).

[324] Trimble v. Whithin Mach. Wks., 172 Mass. 150, 51 N. E. 463 (1898); master furnished a suitable gangplank which was improperly placed by a fellow servant; following Robinson v. Blake Mnfg. Co., 143 Mass. 528, 10 N. E. 314 (1887); Ashley v. Hart, 147 Mass. 573, 18 N. E. 416 (1888); Thyng v. Fitchburg Ry., 156 Mass. 13, 30 N. E. 169 (1892); Carroll v. W. U. T. Co., 160 Mass. 152, 35 N. E. 456 (1893); Allen v. Smith Iron Co., 160 Mass. 557, 36

N. E. 581 (1893); Anderson v. Erie Co., 68 N. J. L. 647, 54 At. 830 (1903); car of another railroad, whose defects were not discoverable by ordinary inspection.

[325] John S. Metcalf Co. v. Nystedt, 203 Ill., 333, 67 N. W. 764 (1903).

[326] Jennings v. Iron Bay Co., 47 Minn. 111, 49 N. W. 685 (1891); Steamship Co. v. Ingebregsten, 57 N. J. L. 400, 31 At. 619 (1895).

[327] Wilson v. Merry, L. R. 1 Sc. & D. 326, 19 L. T. R. 30 (1868). This seems to be the rule in Maryland. Nat. Enam. Co. v. Cornell, 95 Md. 524, 52 At. 588 (1902).

[328] In addition to cases cited in previous notes, see Nor. Pac. Ry. v.

no greater duty of care than his employer. He is not bound to select the very best appliances discoverable. It is enough that he selects such as are in ordinary use, and are reasonably safe.[329] But if he fails to do this, his negligence is that of his employer.[330]

Keeping Appliances Safe. After the master has selected and installed reasonably safe appliances, what is his duty with respect to keeping them safe?[331] It must be confessed that the judicial answers are not harmonious. In a recent case,[332] after allusion to the "incongruous decisions" upon this topic, the court suggested, that "a rational distinction would seem to be that, when the employee's duty to inspect or repair the apparatus is incidental to his duty to use the apparatus in the common employment, then he is not intrusted with the master's duty to his fellow servant, and the master is not responsible to his fellow servant for his fault, but

Herbert, 116 U. S. 642, 6 Sup. Ct. 590 (1885); Cincinnati, etc., Ry. v. McMullen, 117 Ind. 439, 29 N. E. 287, 10 Am. St. R. 67 (1888); Toy v. U. S. Cartridge Co., 159 Mass. 313, 34 N. E. 461 (1893); Morton v. Detroit Ry. Co., 81 Mich. 423, 46 N. W. 111 (1890); Bailey v. R. W. & O. Ry., 139 N. Y. 302, 34 N. E. 918 (1893); Ell v. Nor. Pac. Ry., 1 N. Dak. 336, 26 Am. St. R. 621 with note, 48 N. W. 222 (1891); Gunter v. Graniteville Co., 18 S. C. 262 (1882).

[329] Louisville, etc., Ry. v. Hall, 91 Ala. 112, 8 So. 371, 24 Am. St. R. 863 (1891); Little Rock, etc., Ry. v. Eubanks, 48 Ark. 460, 3 S. W. 808, 3 Am. St. R. 245 (1886); Gurneau, etc., Co. v. Palmer, 28 Neb. 207 (1889); Bohn v. Chicago, etc., Ry., 106 Mo. 429, 17 S. W. 580 (1891); Carlson v. Phoenix, etc., Co., 132 N. Y. 273, 30 N. E. 750 (1892); Nix v. Tex. Pac. Ry., 82 Tex. 473, 18 S. W. 571, 27 Am. St. R. 897 (1891); Humphreys v. Newport, etc., Ry., 33 W. Va. 135, 10 S. E. 39 (1889); Keeler v. Schwenk,

144 Pa. 348, 22 At. 910, 27 Am. St. R. 633 (1891).

[330] Myers v. Hudson Iron Co., 150 Mass. 125, 29 N. E. 631, 15 Am. St. R. 176 (1889); Johnson v. Spear, 76 Mich. 139, 42 N. W. 1092, 15 Am. St. R. 298 (1889); Carter v. Oliver Oil Co., 34 S. C. 211, 13 S. E. 419, 27 Am. St. R. 815 (1891); Galveston, etc., Ry. v. Garrett, 73 Tex. 262, 13 S. W. 62, 15 Am. St. R. 781 (1889).

[331] Trigg W. R. Co. v. Lindsay, 101 Va. 193, 43 S. E. 349 (1903). "Though a master is liable for failure to use ordinary care to provide reasonably safe machinery, he is not liable for unsafe conditions existing while the machinery is in process of erection; and where an emery wheel exploded because of the improper arrangement of the pulleys, resulting from the fault of a fellow servant of plaintiff, who was injured thereby before the machine was ready for operation, the master was not liable."

[332] Steamship Co. v. Ingebregsten, 57 N. J. L. 400, 31 At. 619 (1895).

that, if the master has cast a duty of inspection or repair upon an employee, who is not engaged in using the apparatus in a common employment with his fellow servant, then that employee, in that duty, ˜presents the master, and the master is chargeable with his default." Although this distinction has been recognized and followed in other jurisdictions,[333] it has not found acceptance in all.[334] And even the courts which have adopted the distinction do not seem to apply it consistently. The inspection of cars which the servants of a railroad company are to handle, is a task allotted to employees who are not engaged in using them. For their negligent inspection, the master should be held liable;[335] but in Alabama, Massachusetts and Michigan, such inspectors are deemed fellow servants of those managing the cars, for the faithful performance of whose duty the employer is not liable.[336]

(5) **Duty to Warn of Danger.** Still a fifth duty, which the law imposes upon the master towards his servant, is that of warning him of danger in certain circumstances. It does not rest upon every master, nor does it exist in favor of every servant. If the danger is one of which the master, without negligence, is ignorant, there can be no obligation on his part to disclose it.[337] A

[333] Moynihan v. Hills Co., 146 Mass. 586, 16 N. E. 574 (1888); Drum v. New England Co., 180 Mass. 113, 61 N. E. 812 (1901); Creagan v. Marston, 126 N. Y. 568, 27 N. E. 952, 22 Am. St. R. 851 (1891).

[334] Buck v. New Jersey Zinc Co., 204 Pa. 132, 53 At. 740, 60 L. R. A. 453 (1902); Wachsumth v. Shaw Co., 118 Mich. 275, 76 N. W. 497 (1898).

[335] Baltimore & P. Ry. v. Mackay, 157 U. S. 572, 15 Sup. Ct. 491, 39 L. Ed. 624 (1895); Felton v. Bullard, 94 Fed. 781, 37 C. C. A. 1 (1899); Eaton v. N. Y. C. Ry., 163 N. Y. 391, 57 N. E. 609, 79 Am. St. R. 600 (1900); Anderson v. Erie Co., 68 N. J. L. 647, 54 At. 830 (1903); Dooner v. D. & H. Canal Co., 164 Pa. 17, 30 At. 269 (1894); Jones v. N. Y., etc., Ry., 20 R. I. 210, 37 At. 1033 (1897).

[336] Smoot v. Mobile, etc., Ry., 67 Ala. 13 (1880); Mackin v. B. & A. Ry., 135 Mass. 201, 46 Am. R. 201 (1883); Lellis v. Mich. Cent. Ry., 124 Mich. 37, 82 N. W. 828 (1900); Dewey v. Detroit, etc., Ry., 97 Mich. 334, 52 N. W. 942, 22 L. R. A. 294, 37 Am. St. R. 348 (1893).

[337] Walkowski v. Penokee, etc., Mines, 115 Mich. 629, 73 N. W. 895, 41 L. R. A. 33, with note (1898); Burns v. Pethcal, 75 Hun (N. Y.) 437 (1894). "The master must warn his servants of all dangers to which they will be exposed in his employment, * * * except such as he cannot be deemed to have foreseen:" Wagner v. Jayne Chem. Co., 147 Pa. 475, 479, 23 At. 772, 30 Am. St. R. 745 (1892); Gay v. So. Ry., 101 Va. 466, 44 S. E. 707 (1903).

servant who knows and appreciates the danger attending his master's business is not entitled to be warned of its existence.[338] The law does not command impossibilities nor stipulate for superfluities.

In cases, however, where the master knows, or, had he used due care, would have discovered, that the employment is dangerous, and has reason to believe that his servant does not know the danger and will not discover it in time to protect himself from injury, he is under a legal duty to give proper warning [339] and instructions to the servant.[340] The warning should be unequivocal,[341] and the instructions should be such as are suited to the circumstances of the particular case.[342] If the servant is young and inexperienced, the instructions should be more minute than in case of an adult, and especial care should be taken to make them intelligible.[343] Still, even toward minors, the master is "only required to do what a prudent master would naturally do under like circumstances." [344]

Court and Jury: — Whether the warning and instructions in

---

[338] Rooney v. Sewall, etc., Co., 161 Mass. 153, 36 N. E. 789 (1894); Yeager v. Burlington, etc., Ry., 93 Ia. 1, 61 N. W. 215 (1894); Reynolds v. Boston, etc., Ry., 64 Vt. 66, 24 At. 134, 33 Am. St. R. 908 (1891).

[339] Baxter v. Roberts, 44 Cal. 187, 13 Am. R. 160 (1872); Holshouser v. Denver Gas Co., 32 Col. ——, 72 Pac. 289 (1903). Danger of being shot by neighbors or strikers.

[340] Tedford v. Los Angelos Co., 134 Cal. 76, 66 Pac. 76 (1901); Ingerman v. Moore, 90 Cal. 410, 27 Pac. 306, 25 Am. St. R. 138 (1891); Daly v. Kiel, 106 La. 170, 30 So. 254 (1901); Stuart v. West End Ry., 163 Mass. 391, 393, 40 N. E. 180 (1895).

[341] Myhan v. La. Elec. Co., 41 La. Ann. 964, 6 So. 799, 7 L. R. A. 172, 17 Am. St. R. 436 (1889).

[342] Tagg v. McGeorge, 155 Pa. 368, 26 At. 671, 35 Am. St. R. 889 (1893). "It is the duty of the employer to give suitable instructions as to the manner of using dangerous machines." Davis v. Augusta Factory, 92 Ga. 712, 18 S. E. 974 (1893): "much depends upon the nature of the machinery, the age, capacity, intelligence and experience of the employee, as well as all the surounding circumstances and facts:" Davis Coal Co. v. Polland, 158 Ind. 607, 62 N. E. 492, 92 Am. St. R. 319 (1901).

[343] O'Connor v. Golden Gate Co., 135 Cal. 537, 67 Pac. 966, 87 Am. St. R. 127 (1902); Newburg v. Getchel, etc., Co., 100 Ia. 441, 69 N. W. 743, 62 Am. St. R. 582 (1896); Chicago etc., Co. v. Reinneiger, 140 Ill. 334, 29 N. E. 1106, 33 Am. St. R. 249 (1892); Brazil Block Co. v. Young, 117 Ind. 520, 20 N. E. 423, 12 Am. S. R. 422 (1889); James v. Rapides Lumber Co., 50 La Ann. 717, 23 So. 469, 44 L. R. A. 33, with full note (1898); Bohn Mn'fg Co. v. Erickson, 55 Fed. 943, 12 U. S. App. 260, 5 C. C. A. 341 (1893).

[344] Omaha Bottling Co. v. Theiler, 59 Neb. 257, 80 N. W. 821, 80 Am. St. R. 673.

a particular case are those which a prudent master would naturally give, is generally a question for the jury; [345] although, if the evidence is undisputed, and fairly warrants but one inference, it will be disposed of by the court.[346] And wherever it clearly appears that the servant was fully aware of the dangers of his employment, and fully informed as to his proper course of conduct, the master, as we have seen, is under no duty to give warning or instruction. The servant takes the risk of the situation.[347]

Moreover, even when the master has violated his duty of warning and instructing the servant, the latter has no right of action, unless such violation was the proximate cause of his injury.[348]

Assumption of Risk and Contributory Negligence of Servant: The master who has performed the various duties enumerated above, is not chargeable at common law [349] for the injuries sustained by a servant in his employment. They are to be ascribed to the risks of the business, which the servant impliedly engages to assume, or to his contributory negligence. Either is a perfect defense for the master when sued by the servant, but they ought not to be confused.

Assumption of risk is an affirmative defense which must be

---

[345] Hartrich v. Hawes, 202 Ill. 334, 67 N. E. 13 (1903); James v. Rapides Lumber Co., 50 La Ann. 717, 23 So. 469, 44 L. R. A. 33, with note (1898); De Costa v. Hargraves Mills, 170 Mass. 375, 49 N. E. 735 (1898); Addicks v. Cristoph, 62 N. J. L. 786, 43 At. 196, 72 Am. St. R. 687 (1899); Dresser Employer's Liability, p. 470.

[346] Carrigan v. Washburn, etc., Co., 170 Mass. 79, 48 N. E. 1079 (1898); Juchatz v. Michigan Alkali Co., 120 Mich. 645, 79 N. W. 907 (1899).

[347] Staldter v. City of Huntington, 153 Ind. 354, 55 N. E. 88 (1899); McClusky v. Garfield Co., 180 Mass. 115, 61 N. E. 804 (1901); Roberts v. Missouri Tel. Co., 166 Mo. 370, 66. S. W. 155 (1901); Maltbie v.

Belden, 167 N. Y. 307, 60 N. E. 645, 54 L. R. A. 52 (1901); Drake v. Auburn City Ry., 173 N. Y. 466, 66 N. E. 121 (1903); Erdman v. Ill. Steel Co., 95 Wis. 6, 69 N. W. 993, 60 Am. St. R. 66 (1897); Anderson v. C. N. Nelson Lumber Co., 67 Minn. 79, 69 N. W. 630 (1896); Lally v. Crockston Lumber Co., 82 Minn. 407, 85 N. W. 187 (1901).

[348] Henderson v. Williams, 66 N. H. 405, 23 At. 365 (1891); Buckley v. Gutta Percha Co., 113 N. Y. 540, 21 N. E. 717 (1889); Same principle Morrison v. Whittier Mach. Co., 184 Mass. 39, 67 N. E. 646 (1903).

[349] The most important statutory changes upon this topic will be noted hereafter.

pleaded [350] and proved [351] by the defendant. Moreover, it rests
upon a valid contract of the plaintiff, while contributory negligence
is a question of plaintiff's conduct in particular circumstances. The
distinctions have been stated very satisfactorily in a recent Indiana
decision.[352] The plaintiff sued his employer, a coal mining company, for damages sustained by the falling of slate from the roof
of the mine. Defendant claimed that plaintiff had not only assumed
the risk of employment in the mine in question, but was also guilty
of contributory negligence. Referring to the arguments in defendant's behalf, the court said: " Counsel are confusing the doctrines
of contributory negligence and assumption of risk. Assumption of
risk is a matter of contract. Contributory negligence is a question
of conduct. If appellee were to be defeated by the rule of assumed
risk, it would be because he agreed, long before. the accident happened, that he would assume the very risk from which his injury
arose. If appellee were to be defeated by the rule of contributory
negligence, it would be because his conduct, at the time of the
accident, under all the attendant circumstances, fell short of ordinary care. If the one circumstance of the employee's knowledge of
the employer's failure to provide the statutory safeguards were held,
as a matter of law, always to overcome the other circumstances
characterizing the employee's conduct at the time of the accident,
assumption of risk would be successfully masquerading in the guise
of contributory negligence. If the assumption of risk is the issue,
knowledge of defective conditions and acquiescence therein are
fatal. If contributory negligence is the issue, knowledge of defect-

---

[350] Oregon, etc., Ry. v. Tracy, 66
Fed. 931, 14 C. C. A. 199 1895);
Nicholaus v. Chicago, etc., Ry., 90
Ia. 85, 57 N. W. 694 (1894); Faulkner v. Mammoth Min. Co., 23 Utah
437, 66 Pac. 799 (1901): " As assumed risk is an affirmative defense, essentially different in its
character from the defense of contributory negligence, it should
therefore be treated as an implied
contract in bar and as a waiver
of the plaintiff's right to recover."
Cf. Miller v. Detroit, etc., Ry.,—
Mich—; 95 N. W. 718 (1903); and

De Cair v. Mainstee Ry. Mich.
—, 95 N. W. 726 (1903).

[351] Dowd v. N. Y., etc., Ry., 170 N.
Y. 459, 63 N. E. 541 (1902), " We
think that the burden of showing
that the servant assumed the risk
of obvious dangers rests upon the
master." Welle v. Celluloid Co., 175
N Y. 401, 67 N. E. 609 (1903).

[352] Davis Coal Co. v. Polland, 158
Ind. 607, 62 N. E. 492, 92 Am. St. R.
319 (1901). It was held in this
case, that the risks, arising from
an employer's disregard of specific
statutory requirements for the safe-

ive conditions and acquiescence therein may be fatal, or may not be, depending upon whether a person of ordinary prudence, under all the circumstances, would have done what the injured person did. If the risk is so great and immediately threatening that a person of ordinary prudence, under all the circumstances, would not take it, contributory negligence is established. If the risk is not so great and immediately threatening but that a person of ordinary prudence, under all the circumstances, would take it, contributory negligence is not established." [353]

Servant Remaining after Knowledge of Danger :— When a servant is fully aware that his master has violated any of his duties towards him, and appreciates, or should appreciate, the attendant risks, he is entitled to leave the employment. If he voluntarily remains and continues in the hazardous work, he assumes the risk, or may even be guilty of contributory negligence,[354] as we have seen. Nor will it avail him, that he continued in the hazardous position through fear of being dismissed if he protested against his master's negligence. But a different situation exists, when he is

ty of employees, cannot be assumed by the servant. See supra, p. 83.

[353] Similar views are maintained in the following cases: Lunberg v. Glenwood Lumber Co., 127 Cal. 598, 60 Pac. 176, 49 L. R. A. 33, with extensive note (1900); O'Maley v. So. Boston Co., 158 Mass. 135, 32 N. E. 1119, 47 L. R. A. 161 with note (1893); Fitzgerald v. Conn. Co., 155 Mass. 155, 29 N. E. 464, 31 Am. St. R. 537 (1891); Mennier v. Chemical Co., 180 Mass. 109, 61 N. E. 810 (1901), plaintiff held guilty of contributory negligence upon his own evidence; St. Louis, etc., Ry. v. Irwin, 37 Ks. 701, 16 Pac. 146, 1 Am. St. R. 266 (1887); Atchinson, etc., Ry. v. Bancord, 66 Ks. 81, 71 Pac. 253 (1903); Alcorn v. Chic., etc., Ry. 108 Mo. 81, 18 S. W. 188 (1891); Dowd v. N. Y. etc., Ry., 170 N. Y. 459, 63 N. E. 541 1902); Texas, etc., Ry. v. con-

roy, 83 Tex. 214, 18 S. W. 609 Faulkner v. Mammoth Min. Co., 23 Utah 437, 66, Pac. 799 (1901); Tuttle v. Detroit etc., Ry., 122 U. S. 189, 7 Sup. Ct. 1116, 30 L. Ed. 1114 (1887), assumption of risk; Southern Pac. Ry. v. Seley, 152 U. S. 145, 14 Sup. Ct., 530, 38 L. Ed. 391 (1894), both assumption of risk and contributory negligence involved.

[354] In some jurisdictions, as we have seen (supra p. 83) when the negligence of the master consists in the violation of a statutory duty of care, there can be no contributory negligence by the servant, "because the continuing negligence of the defendant up to the moment of the injury is subsequent to the plaintiff's negligence, if any, and is the proximate cause of the injury." Troxler v. Southern Ry. 124 N. C. 189, 32 S. E. 550, 44 L. R. A. 313, 70 Am. St. R. 580 (1899.

induced to go on by the master's promise to remove the danger. In such a case, "the risk during the running of the promise and for a reasonable time thereafter is that of the master and not of the servant," [355] according to the weight of authority in this country.[356]

The Risk from Fellow-Servant's Misconduct :— This is one of the most important risks which a servant assumes. The general rule applicable to it may be stated briefly in these terms: "One who enters the service of another takes upon himself the ordinary risks of the negligent acts of his fellow-servants in the course of the employment." [356 1-2] The earliest case in which the existence of this rule was suggested, is that of Priestly v. Fowler,[357] although "all the case actually decided was that a master does not warrant to his servant the sufficiency and safety of a carriage in which he sends him out." [358] A few years later, it was formally announced by a divided court in South Carolina,[359] and, a year there-

[355] Rice v. Eureka Paper Co., 174 N. Y. 385, 66 N. E. 979 (1903); Dowd v. Erie Ry., 70 N. J. L. ——, 57 At. 248 (1904).

[356] Hough v. Texas, etc., Ry., 100 U. S. 213, 225, 25 L. Ed. 612 (1879); Birmingham Ry. v. Allen, 99 Al. 359, 13 So. 8, 12, 20 L. R. A. 457 (1892); Standard Oil Co. v. Helmick, 148 Ind. 460, 47 N. E. 14 (1897), servant was induced by the promise, as defect was not to be remedied until after the injury happened; Swift v. O'Neill, 187 Ill. 337, 58 N. E. 416 (1900); Illinois Steel Co. v. Mann, 170 Ill. 200, 48 N. E. 417, 62 Am. St. R. 370, 40 L. R. A. 781 (1897); Stoutenbourgh v. Plow, Gilman etc. Co., 82 Ia. 179, 47 N. W. 1039 (1891); Brown v. Levy, 108 Ky. 163, 55 S. W. 1079 (1900); Roux v. Blodgett, etc., Co., 85 Mich. 519, 48 N. W. 1092, 24 Am. St. R. 102, 13 L. R. A. 728 (1891); Snowbrog v. Nelson-Spencer Co., 43 Minn. 532, 45 N. W. 1131 (1890); Conroy v. Vulcan Iron Works, 62 Mo. 35 (1876); Manufacturing Co. v. Morrissey, 40 Oh. St. 148, 48 Am. R.

669 (1883); Patterson v. Pittsburgh etc., Ry., 76 Pa. 389, 18 Am. R. 412 (1874); Gulf, etc., Ry. v: Donnelly, 70 Tex. 371, 8 S. W. 52, 8 Am. St. R. 608, (1888); Dresser, Employer's Liability § 115.

[356 1-2] Randall v. Bal. & O. Ry., 109 U. S. 478, 483 (1883).

[357] 3 M. & W. 1, 49 R. R. 495 (1837).

[358] Pollock on Torts (6 Ed.) p. 95 note.

[359] Murray v. South Car. Ry.,1 McMullan Law, 385, 36 Am. Dec. 268 (1841); Evans, J., said: " If this plaintiff is entitled to recover, a new class of liabilities would arise, which I do not think has ever heretofore been supposed to exist. It is admitted no case like the present has been found, nor is there any precedent suited to the plaintiff's case. . . With the plaintiff, the defendants contracted to pay for his services. Is it incident to this contract that the company should guarantee him against the negligence of his co-servant. It is admitted he takes upon himself the

after, received a statement and exposition by Chief Justice Shaw, which have become classical.[360]   In each of the cases named above, stress was laid upon the fact, that no precedent could be found for an action, by a servant against his master, for injuries due to the misconduct of a fellow-servant.

From this admitted lack of precedent, different conclusions have been drawn. It has been inferred, on the one hand, that these decisions " ingrafted into English law a new rule." [361]   On the other hand, the inference has been drawn that the law had always been in accordance with these decisions, and that not until these actions were brought had an attempt been made to hold the master liable to a servant for harm due to a co-servant.[362]   Whichever inference may be the correct one, the rule established by these cases was accepted with a unanimity quite unusual, and has been enforced in a manner which shows that not only the legal profession, but the community at large, agree with Chief Justice Shaw in the conviction, that the rule results " from considerations as well of justice as of policy." The statutory modifications, whether in England or

ordinary risks of his vocation; why not the extraordinary ones? Neither are within his contract."

[360] Farwell v. Boston, etc., Ry., 4 Met. (Mass.) 49, 38 Am. Dec. 339 (1842).

[361] See note on this topic in 75 Am. St. R. 584 *et. seq.* This seems to be Sir Frederick Pollock's view. " Our law," he writes, " can show no more curious instance of a rapid modern development. The first evidence of any such rule is in Priestly v. Fowler, decided in 1837. * * It was not only adopted by the House of Lords for England, but forced by them on the reluctant Courts of Scotland to make the jurisprudence of the two countries uniform." Torts, (6 Ed.), pp. 95, 97. Referring to the rule, in another connection he writes: " Its history is certainly not a favorable one. It appears to be rejected by continental jurisprudence, and re-

cent legislation in Germany has deliberately increased employers' liabilities in the case of railways and other specified industries. In England and the United States, it is modern." Essays in Jurisprudence pp. 114, 115. It does not exist in Mexico, Mexican Cent. Ry. v. Sprague, 114 Fed. 544, 52 C. C. A. 318 (1902).

[362] Pollock, C. B., in Vose v. Lancashire, etc., Ry., 2 H. & N. 728, 734 (1858), said: " the law must have been the same long before it was enunciated in Priestly v. Fowler. If not, such actions would have been of frequent occurrence. No such action appears to have been brought before that case. We ought not to allow so important a decision to be frittered away by minute distinctions or the ingenuity of advocates." Similar views are expressed by Judge Dillon, in 24 Am. L. Rev. 180.

in this country, do not evince a disposition to abolish the rule, although they show dissatisfaction with some of its consequences.

Reasons for the Rule: — In the Farwell case, plaintiff's counsel based his claim on the ground of contract—an implied contract of indemnity arising out of the relation of master and servant. The existence of such a contract was repudiated by the court, which declared that " the rule resulting from considerations as well of justice as of policy is, that he who engages in the employment of another for the performance of specified duties and services, for compensation, takes upon himself the natural and ordinary risks and perils incident to the performance of such services, and, in legal presumption, the compensation is adjusted accordingly. And we are not aware of any principle which should except those perils arising from the carelessness and negligence of those who are in the same employment. These are perils which the servant is as likely to know, and against which he can as effectually guard, as the master. They are perils incident to the service, and which can be as distinctly foreseen and provided for in the rate of compensation as any others."

Not a True Contract Provision: — This form of statement, that the master's exemption from liability in these cases rests upon the implied contract between servant and master, has been adopted by most courts.[363] It is open to criticism,[364] perhaps, unless we

---

[363] In Hutchinson v. York, etc., Ry., 5 Exch. 343, 19 L. J. Exch. 296 (1850), it is said: " The principle is that a servant when he engages to serve a master undertakes, as between himself and his master, to run all the ordinary risks of the service, and this includes the risk of negligence upon the part of a fellow-servant, when he is acting in the discharge of his duty as servant of him who is the common master of both." In Morgan v. Vale of Neath Ry., 5 B. & S. 570, 578, 33 L. J. Q. B. 260 (1866), Lord Blackburn used this language: " A servant who engages for the performance of services for compensation does, as an implied part of the contract, take upon himself, as between himself and his master, the natural risks and perils incident to the performance of such services: the presumption of law being that the compensation was adjusted accordingly, or in other words, that these risks are considered in the wages." In Boswell v. Barnhoot, 96 Ga. 521, 23 S. E. 414 (1895), the court said: " The ground upon which a master is relieved from liability to a servant for injuries resulting from negligence of a fellow-servant is that the servant, when he enters the employment of the master, impliedly contracts to assume the risk of negligence, as one of the risks incident to the service, and that his compensation is fixed with reference to this: and, clearly, this reas-

bear in mind that the contract here referred to is not a true consensual agreement, but an obligation imposed by law. That this is the sense in which Chief Justice Shaw employed the term is apparent from the following extract: " In considering the rights and obligations arising out of particular relations, it is competent for courts of justice to regard considerations of policy and general convenience, and to draw from them such rules as will, in their practical application, best promote the safety and security of all parties concerned. This is, in truth, the basis on which implied promises are raised, being duties legally inferred from a consideration of what is best adapted to promote the benefit of all persons concerned, under given circumstances."

If a true contract were necessary to exempt the master, he would be liable to one who voluntarily " associates himself with a master's servants in the performance of his work; " but he is not so liable.[365] Moreover, if the exemption of the master rested upon an actual stipulation in the contract of hiring, a servant who hired to a master, in a jurisdiction where the fellow-servants rule existed, would be barred from recovery, although he was injured in a jurisdiction where the rule did not obtain; but he is not so barred.[366]

Who Are Fellow-Servants? Various Tests: While the rule of exemption, which we have been considering, seems a simple

---

on cannot apply in the case of one not voluntarily in the service, but merely a prisoner, serving out his sentence for a violation of the law. Indeed, it can hardly be seriously contended that a chain-gang boss is in any sense a fellow-servant of a prisoner working under him. The boss, while acting in that capacity, is the *alter ego* of his employer, and the latter is responsible for any wrongful or negligent acts on the part of such employee by which a prisoner is deprived of his life."

[364] In 24 Am. L. Rev., p. 180, Judge Dillon, after quoting the language of Chief Justice Shaw, adds: " A modern jurist would probably prefer to say that the relation was one wherein the duties and liabilities of the parties were fixed by law."

[365] Potter v. Faulkner, 1 B. & S. 800, 31 L. J. Q. B. 30 (1861); Swainson v. North E. Ry., 3 Exch. Div. 341, 47 L. J. Exch. 372 (1877); Stevens v. Chamberlain, 100 Fed. 384, 40 C. C. A. 421, 51 L. R. A. 513 (1900); Osborne v. Knox, etc., Ry., 68 Me. 49 (1877); Barstow v. Old Col. Ry., 143 Mass. 535 (1887).

[366] Boston, etc., Ry. v. McDuffy, 79 Fed. 934 (1897). The contract of hiring was in Vermont, where the fellow-servant rule existed, while the injury happened in Lower Canada, where the rule did not obtain; and recovery was allowed in the U. S. court for the district of Vermont.

one, the courts have experienced no little difficulty in discovering the true test of fellow-service, within the meaning of this rule, as well as in determining the proper limits of the rule itself.

" Speaking generally," to quote from a recent decision, " two rules, applied as tests in questions of this kind, have obtained a wide acceptance. Under one, the test is whether the duty violated by the offending servant was one resting upon the master, or solely upon the offending servant; while under the other, the test is whether the offending servant, in what he did or omitted to do, was or was not *pro hac vice* the master. Under the first rule, the test is mainly the nature and character of the duty violated by the offending servant. If it was a duty resting upon the master, he is liable to the injured servant for the negligence of the offending servant; if it was not such a duty, he is not. Under this rule, the rank or grade of the offending servant in the master's business or the department of it in which he is employed, as compared with that of the injured servant, is not of primary importance in determining the master's liability. Under the second rule, the test is mainly the relation of the offending servant to the master and to the injured servant. If in what he does he acts for and represents the master, and therefore *pro hac vice* is the master, then his negligence is the master's negligence. Under this rule, the rank or grade of the offending servant in his master's business and the department in which he works are regarded as of primary importance in determining the master's liability." [367] It may be noted in passing that the burden is upon the plaintiff to prove that he and the servant, by whose negligence he was injured, were not fellow-servants.[368]

Nature and Character of the Negligent Act. In jurisdictions where this test prevails, a servant may occupy a dual position. If employed to perform an act, incident to any of the five classes of duties which the law imposes upon the master, and which we have considered at length, he is, as to that act, a vice-principal—a true representative of his master—and his negligence is the master's negligence. If employed to do any other act, he is a mere servant, no matter what his rank, and for injuries resulting to fellow-

[367] Kelley v. New Haven Steamboat Co., 75 Conn. 42, 50 At. 871 (1902).

[368] Chicago City Ry. v. Leach, 208 Ill., 198, 70 N. E. 222 (1904).

servants from his misconduct, the master is not liable. Accordingly, the superintendent of a manufactory was held a fellow-servant, in letting steam on an engine and starting a wheel, which other servants were at the moment lifting off its centre.[369] On the other hand, the storekeeper of a steamship line was held a vice-principal, in providing apparatus for use in putting the stores on board the ship.[370]

Nature of the Act: — The test adopted in the foregoing cases, that the responsibility of the master to a servant for misconduct of another servant is determined by the nature of the act in question, and not by the rank or grade of the actor, has been accepted by the United States Supreme Court,[371] after some hesitation,[372] and by most of the state courts.[373]

---

[369] Crispin v. Babbitt, 81 N. Y. 516, 37 Am. R. 521 (1880); S. P. McLaine v. Head, etc., Co., 71 N. H. 294, 52 At. 545, 58 L. R. A. 462 (1902); O'Neil v. Great Nor. Ry., 80 Minn. 27, 82 N. W. 1086, 51 L. R. A. 532 (1900).

[370] Nordt Deutscher Co. v. Ingebregsten, 57 N. J. L. 400, 31 At. 619 (1895); S. P. Olney v. Boston, etc., Ry., 71 N. H. 427, 52 At. 1097 (1902).

[371] Baltimore, etc., Ry. v. Baugh, 149 U. S. 368, 13 Sup. Ct. 914, 37 L. Ed. 772 (1893); New Eng. Ry. v. Conroy, 175 U. S. 323, 20 Sup. Ct. 85, 44 L. Ed. 181 (1899); Weeks v. Schorer, 111 Fed. 330, 49 C. C. A. 372 (1901); Lafayette Bridge Co. v. Olsen, 108 Fed. 335, 54 L. R. A. 33, with full note (1901).

[372] Chicago, etc., Ry. v. Ross, 112 U. S. 377, 5 Sup. Ct. 184, 28 L. Ed. 787 (1884).

[373] Mobile, etc., Ry. v. Smith, 59 Al. 245 (1877), modified by Statute. See Civil Code of 1896, §§ 1749–1751; Nixon v. Selby Smelting Co., 102 Cal. 458, 36 Pac. 803 (1894); Kelley v. New Haven Steamboat Co., 74 Conn. 343, 50 At. 871 (1902); McElligott v. Randolph, 61 Conn. 157, 22 At. 1094, 29 Am. St. R. 181 (1891); Carleton Mining Co. v. Ryan, 29 Col. 401, 68 Pac. 279 (1902); Camp & Bros. v. Hall, 39 Fla. 535, 22 So. 492 (1897), modified by Chap. 4071 L. 1891; New Pittsburgh Co. v. Peterson, 136 Ind. 398, 35 N. E. 7, 43 Am. St. R. 327 (1893); Peterson v. Whitebreast Coal Co., 50 Ia. 673, 32 Am. R. 143 (1879), modified by § 1307 of Code; Blake v. Maine C. Ry., 70 Me. 60, 35 Am. R. 297 (1879); Norfolk v. Hoover, 79 Md. 263, 29 At. 994, 47 Am. St. R. 392, 25 L. R. A. 770 (1894); Moody v. Hamilton Mn'fg Co., 159 Mass. 70, 34 N. E. 185, 38 Am. St. R. 396 (1893); Schroeder v. Flint, 103 Mich. 213, 61 N. W. 663, 50 Am. St. R. 354, 29 L. R. A. 321 (1894); Brown v. Winona Ry., 27 Min. 162, 38 Am. R. 285, 6 N. W. 484 (1880), modified by Chap. 13 L. 1887, and § 2701 Gen'l. St. 1894; McMaster v. Ill. C. Ry., 65 Miss. 264, 4 So. 59, 7 Am. R. 653 (1887), modified by § 193 Const. of 1890, and §3559 Code of 1892; Goodwell v. Mont., etc., Ry.,

Superior Servant Test : This test has been applied by the Ohio courts from the beginning; those courts characterizing the test which prevails generally in this country as " contrary to the general principles of law and justice." [374] According to these tribunals: " The implied obligation of the servant to assume all risk incident to the employment, including that of injury occasioned by the negligence of a fellow-servant, has no application where the servant, by whose negligent conduct or act the injury is inflicted, sustains a relation of superior in authority to the one receiving the injury ; " but the true rule is, " that where one servant is placed by his employer in a position of subordination to, and subject to the orders and control of another, and such inferior servant, without fault, and while in the discharge of his duties, is injured by the negligence of the superior servant, the master is liable for such injury." [375]

This test, with varying modifications, has been adopted by the courts of several states,[376] and by legislation in others.[377]

---

18 Mont. 293, 45 Pac. 210 (1896); Galvin v. Pierce, 72 N. H. 79, 54 At. 1014 (1903); Knutter v. N. Y., etc., Tel. Co., 67 N. J. L. 646, 52 At. 565 (1902); Hankins v. N. Y., etc., Ry., 142 N. Y. 416, 37 N. E. 466, 40 Am. St. R. 616, 25 L. R. A. 396 (1894); Ell v. Nor. Pac. Ry., 1 N. Dak. 336, 48 N. W. 222, 26 Am. St. R. 621, 12 L. R. A. 97 (1891); Matt. v. Kern, 34 Or. 247, 54 Pac. 950, 75 Am. St. 580, with extensive note (1898); Casey v. Penn. Asphalt Co., 198 Pa. 348, 47 At. 1128 (1901); Milhench v. E. Jenckes Mn'fg. Co., 24 R. I. 131, 52 At. 687 (1902); Davis v. Cent. Vt. Ry., 55 Vt. 84, 45 Am. R. 590 (1883); Norfolk, etc., Ry. v. Phillips, 100 Va. 362, 41 S. E. 726 (1902); Trigg W. R. Co. v. Lindsay, 101 Va. 193, 43 S. E. 349 (1903); Jackson v. Norfolk, etc., Ry., 43 W. Va. 280, 27 S. E. 278, 31 Id. 258, 46 L. R. A. 337 (1897); Wiskie v. Montello Granite Co., 111 Wis. 443, 87 N. W. 461, 87 Am. St. R. 885 (1901).

[374] Little Miami Ry. v. Stevens, 20 Ohio 415 (1851).

[375] Berea Stone Co. v. Kraft, 31 Ohio St. 287, 27 Am. R. 510 (1877).

[376] Fort Smith Oil Co. v. Slover, 58 Ark. 168, 24 S. W. 106 (1893); St. Louis, etc., Ry. v. Thurmond, 70 Ark. 411, 68 S. W. 488 (1902). See Const. 1874, Art. 17, § 12 and § 6247 Sand & H. Dig.; Taylor v. Geo. Marble Co., 99 Ga. 512, 27 S. E. 768, 59 Am. S. R.238, (1896). See Code of 1882, §§ 2083, 2202, 3033, 3036; Chicago, etc., Ry. v. Kelly, 127 Ill. 637, 21 N. E. 203 (1889); St. Louis, etc., Ry. v. Weaver, 35 Ks. 412, 11 Pac. 408 (1886); Volz v. Chesapeake Ry., 95 Ky. 188, 24 S. W. 119 (1893); Edmonson v. Ken. Cen. Ry., 105 Ky. 479, 49 S. W. 200 (1899); Illinois Cent. Ry. v. Josey, 110 Ky. 342, 61 S. W. 703, 54 L. R. A. 78 (1901); Dobson v. N. O., etc., Ry., 52 La. Ann. 1127, 27 So. 670 (1900); Shervin v. St. Jos., etc., Ry., 103 Mo. 378, 15 S. W. 442, 23 Am. St. R. 881 (1890); New Omaha

Injuries Due to Negligence of Master and Fellow-Servant: Whenever a servant's injury is legally traceable to the master's negligence, the latter cannot escape liability by showing that the harm was due in part to the negligence of a fellow-servant.[378] If, however, the master's negligence has only a remote connection with the harm, while the efficient, proximate negligence is wholly that of a fellow-servant, the master will not be liable.[379]

Limitations of the Fellow-Servant Rule. It is quite apparent from the statement of the rule and the reasons in support of it, that it does not apply to a servant who, at the time of the injury, is not serving his master, or at least is not in a position of danger by reason of his contract of service. Accordingly, a railroad employee, who has finished his day's work, and is moving along a highway near his employer's road, is not subject to the fellow-servant rule when hurt by the careless throwing of wood from the train by a trainman.[380] Nor is such an employee, when riding as

---

Co. v. Baldwin, 62 Neb. 180, 87 N. W. 27 (1901). "Our court has said the satisfactory evidence of vice principalship is his supervision, control and subjection to his orders and directions." Mason v. Richmond, etc., Ry., 111 N. C. 482, 16 S. E. 698, 18 L. R. A. 845, 32 Am. St. R. 814 (1892); Lamb v. Littman, 131 N. C. 978, 44 S. E. 646 (1903); Jenkins v. Richmond, etc., Ry., 39 S. C. 507, 18 S. E. 182, 39 Am. St. R. 750 (1893); Illinois Cent. Ry. v. Spence, 93 Tenn. 173, 23 S. W. 211 (1893); Sweeny v. Gulf, etc., Ry., 84 Tex. 433, 19 S. W. 555, 31 Am. St. R. 71 (1892); Reddon v. Union Pac. Ry., 5 Utah, 344, 15 Pac. 262 (1887); Pool v. Southern Pac., 20 Utah 210, 58 Pac. 326 (1899); Keating v. Pac. Steamship Co., 21 Wash. 415, 58 Pac. 224 (1899); Allend v. Spokane Falls Ry., 21 Wash. 324, 58 Pac. 244 (1899).

[377] Several of these statutes have been referred to in previous notes. See also Mass. R. L. 1901, ch. 106;

Colorado Sess. L. 1901 ch. 67, Sess. L. N. Y. 1902, ch. 600. Bailey, Personal Injuries Relating to Master and Servant (Chicago, 1897); Dresser, Employer's Liability (St. Paul 1902).

[378] Grand Trunk Ry. v. Cummings, 106 U. S. 700, 1 Sup. Ct. 493 (1883); Loveless v. Standard Gold Co., 111 Ga. 427, 42 S. E. 741 (1902); Chicago, etc., Ry. v. Gillison, 173 Ill. 264, 50 N. E. 657, 64 Am. St. 117 (1898); Towns v. Vicksburg, etc., Ry., 37 La. Ann. 630, 55 Am. R. 508 (1885); Ellis v. N. Y., etc., Ry., 95 N. Y. 546 (1884); Bodie v. Charleston, etc., Ry., 66 S. C. 302, 44 S. E. 943 (1903); Sroufe v. Moran Bros. Co., 28 Wash. 381, 68 Pac. 896, 92 Am. St. R. 847 (1902).

[379] Carter v. Lockey Piano Case Co., 177 Mass. 91, 58 N. E. 476 (1900); Philadelphia Iron Co. v. Davis, 111 Pa. 597, 56 Am. R. 305 (1886); Fowler v. Chicago, etc., Ry., 61 Wis. 159 (1884).

[380] Fletcher v. Baltimore, etc., Ry.,

a gratuitous passenger, after his working hours.[381]   If, however, the employee is a passenger, or otherwise upon the master's vehicles or premises, in the course of his employment, he is subject to the fellow-servant rule.[382]   Which of these positions a servant occupies, at a particular time, is a question of fact, and if the evidence warrants more than one inference, the question is for the jury.[383]

There Must be a Common Master: This is quite apparent from the very terms of the fellow-servant rule.   In the language of Lord Herschell: " It is obvious that if the exemption results, as it does according to the authorities, from the injured person having undertaken, as between himself and the person he serves, to bear the risks of his fellow-servant's negligence, it can never be applicable when there is no relation between the parties from which such an undertaking can be implied." [384]   Hence, the employees of an independent contractor are not the fellow-servants of the employee of him for whom the contractor is working; [385] nor are palace-car company employees fellow-servants with the trainmen of the railroad company hauling the cars; [386] nor are the employees of different

168 U. S. 135, 18 Sup. Ct. 35 (1897).

[381] Dickinson v. West End Ry., 177 Mass. 365, 59 N. E. 60, 52 L. R. A. 328 (1900); McNulty v. Penn. Ry., 182 Pa. 479, 38 At. 524, 38 L. R. A. 376, 61 Am. St. R. 721 (1897); Chatanooga, etc., Co. v. Venable, 105 Tenn. 460, 58 S. W. 861, 51 L. R. A. 886 (1900); Peterson v. Seattle Co., 23 Wash. 615, 63 Pac. 539, 53 L. R. A. 586, containing a full review of the authorities (1900). *Contra*, Innone v. N. Y., etc., Ry., 21 R. I. 452, 44 At. 592, 79 Am. St. R. 812 (1899).

[382] Gillshannon v. Stony Brook Ry., 10 Cush (64 Mass.) 228 (1852); Boyle v. Columbian, etc., Co., 182 Mass. 93, 102, 64 N. E. 726 (1902); Russell v. Hudson Ry., 17 N. Y. (1858); Wright v. Northampton, etc., Ry., 122 N. C. 852, 29 S. E. 100 (1898); Holmes v. Great Nor. Ry. (1900), 2 Q. B. 409, 69 L. J. Q.

B. 854. See 3 Col. L. Rev. 49–51, note on Orman v. Salvo, 117 Fed. 233 (1902).

[383] Northwestern Pack. Co. v. Mc-Cue, 17 Wall (U. S.) 508 (1873).

[384] Johnson v. Lindsay (1891), A. C. 371, 65 L. T. 97.

[385] Cameron v. Nystrom (1893), A. C. 308, 63 L. J. P. C. 85; The Victoria, 69 Fed. 160 (1895); Louthan v. Hewes, 138 Cal. 116, 70 Pac. 1065 (1902); Cruselle v. Pugh, 67 Geo. 430, 44 Am. R. 724 (1881); Lake Super. Co. v. Erickson, 39 Mich. 492, 33 Am. R. 423 (1878); Jansen v. Mayor Jersey City, 61 N. J. L. 243, 39 At. 1025 (1898); Hallett v. N. Y. C. Ry., 167 N. Y. 543, 60 N. E. 653 (1901); Noll v. Phil. Ry., 163 Pa. 504, 30 At. 157 (1894); Cunningham v. Int. Ry., 51 Tex. 503, 32 Am. R. 632 (1879).

[386] Jones v. St. Louis, etc., Ry., 125 Mo. 666, 28 S. W. 883, 46 Am. St. R.

railroad companies using the same track or premises.[387] When the servant of A is put under the temporary control of B, in order to render him subject to the fellow-servant rule, it must appear that the servant has assented to the transfer of his services to B, and that he has in fact submitted himself to the direction and control of this new master. "This assent may be established by direct proof that he agreed to accept the new master and to submit himself to his control, or by indirect proof of circumstances justifying the inference of such assent. Such evidence may be strong enough to justify a court in removing the question from the jury, or it may require to be submitted to the jury."[388]

The Servants Must be Engaged in a Common Employmen: It is not enough to bring employees within the fellow-servant rule that they have a common master. They must be so associated in his employment, "that the safety of the one servant must in the ordinary and natural course of things depend on the skill and care of the other."[389] Accordingly, it has been held that the crews of different vessels of the same owner are not necessarily within the fellow-servant rule.[390] Whether they are subject to it, depends upon the question, Does the safety of one crew depend upon the skill and care of the other? Or, to put it in another way, Is injury by the negligence of one crew an ordinary risk of the service of the other? Applying the same test, there can be no doubt that a telegraph operator who transmits the orders for trains is a fellow-servant with a trainman;[391] nor that the crews of different

514, 26 L. R. A. 718 (1894), S. P. applied to an express agent, Yeomans v. Contra Costa Co., 44 Cal. 71 (1872); Blair v. Erie Ry., 66 N. Y. 313, 23 Am. R. 55 (1876).

[387] Zeigher v. Danbury, etc., Ry., 52 Conn. 543 (1885); Wabash, etc., Ry. v. Peyton, 106 Ill. 534, 46 Am. R. 705 (1883); Phil., etc., Ry. v. State, 58 Md. 372 (1882); Penn. Ry. v. Gallagher, 40 Ohio St. 637, 48 Am. R. 689 (1884); Phillips v. Chic., etc., Ry., 64 Wis. 475 (1885); Bosworth v. Rogers, 82 Fed. 975 (1897).

[388] Del. L. & W. Ry. v. Hardy, 59

N. J. L. 35, 38, 34 At. 986 (1896); Morgan v. Smith, 159 Mass. 570, 35 N. E. 101 (1893). Cf. Ewan v. Lippincott, 47 N. J. L. 192, 54 Am. R. 148 (1885); Murray v. Dwight, 161 N. Y. 301, 55 N. E. 901, 48 L. R. A. 673 (1900); Union Steamship Co. v. Claridge (1894), A. C. 185, 63 L. J. P. C. 56.

[389] Blackburn, J., in Morgan v. Vale of Neath Ry., 5 B. & S. 736, L. R. I Q. B. 149, 35 L. J. Q. B. 23 (1864).

[390] The Petrel (1893), P. 320, 62 L. J. P. 92, 1 R. 651.

[391] Slater v. Jewwett, 85 N. Y. 61,

trains are fellow-servants, whenever the safety of the one depends upon the conduct of the other; [392] nor that the mate of a vessel is a fellow-servant of a table-waiter; [393] nor that a railroad track laborer is a fellow-servant of a conductor on a train going over the same track; [394] nor that a carpenter at work on an elevator shaft is a fellow-servant of the the one operating the elevator.[395]

Different Department Doctrine; Habitual Association :— In a few States, the fellow-servant rule is subject to what is known as the " different department limitation." Where this doctrine prevails, " in order that one servant should be a fellow-servant of another, their duties must be such as to bring them into habitual association, so that they may exercise a mutual influence upon each other promotive of proper caution," [396] or they must be actually co-operating with each other in the line of employment.[397]

The Servant's Liability for his Torts. Although the master is liable for his servant's torts, within the limits heretofore described, and is the one against whom the injured party ordinarily proceeds, the servant is also liable. The law does not permit a tort-feasor to shield himself behind the command of his master.[398] In a limited class of cases, it is true, a servant's or agent's conduct is not treated as a tort, although it assists the principal or master in perpetrating an actionable wrong; as where the servant receives property from the master, honestly believing that it belongs to the

39 Am. R. 627 (1881). *Contra,* East Tenn. Ry. v. De Armond, 86 Tenn. 73, 5 S. W. 600, 6 Am. S. R. 816 (1887), applying the different department test.

[392] Oakes v. Mase, 165 U. S. 363, 17 Sup. Ct. 345 (1897); Van Avery v. Union Pac. Ry., 35 Fed. 40 (1888).

[393] Livingston v. Kodiak Packing Co., 103 Cal. 263, 37 Pac. 149 (1894).

[394] Fagundes v. Cent. Pac. Ry., 79 Cal. 97, 21 Pac. 437 (1889).

[395] Mann v. O'Sullivan, 126 Cal. 61, 58 Pac. 375 (1899).

[396] Edward Hines Lumber Co. v. Ligas, 172 Ill. 315, 50 N. E. 225, 64 Am. St. R. 38 (1898); Chic., etc., Ry. v. Moranda, 93 Ill., 302, 34 Am. R. 168 (1879); Louisville, etc., Ry.

v. Collins, 2 Duv. (63 Ky.) 114, 87 Am. Dec. 486 (1865); Angel v. Jellico Coal Co., 115 Ky. 728, 74 S. W. 714 (1903); Cooper v. Mullins, 30 Ga. 146, 76 Am. Dec. 638 (1860); Krogg v. Atlantic, etc., Ry., 77 Ga. 202, 4 Am. St. R. 79 (1886); Coal Creek Mining Co. v. Davis, 90 Tenn. 711, 18 S. W. 387 (1891).

[397] Illinois Steel Co. v. Bauman, 178 Ill. 351, 53 N. E. 107, 69 Am. St. R. 316 (1899).

[398] Perkins v. Smith, 1 Wil. 328 (1752); Stephens v. Elwall, 4 M. & S. 259 (1815): " It is no answer that he acted under authority from another who had no authority to bestow." Rice v. Yocum, 155 Pa. 538, 26 At. 698 (1893).

latter, and delivers it to another without notice that the master has no right to it.[399] As a rule, however, the servant is liable *ex delicto* (for conversion, trespass, or other tort) when he invades a legal right of the true owner or other person, though his act be innocent of intentional wrong, and be done under the master's command.[400]

Again, a servant whose willful or negligent misconduct causes injury to a fellow-servant is liable to the latter therefor, although the victim may not be able to recover from the master, because of the fellow-servant rule.[401]

Servant's Liability for Non-Feasance. While the authorities are agreed that an agent or servant is individually responsible for his misfeasance, they are at variance regarding his liability for non-feasance. The theory that he is not liable seems to have been first suggested in an argument by Coke,[402] and to have received the first judicial sanction in a dictum of Lord Holt.[403] It was accepted by Judge Story, who urged in its support, that the agent's or servant's liability in such "cases is solely to his principal, there being no

[399] Burditt v. Hunt, 25 Me. 419 (1845); Gurley v. Armstead, 148 Mass. 267, 19 N. E. 389 (1889); Leuthold v. Fairchild, 35 Minn. 99, 27 N. W. 503, 28 N. W. 218 (1886); Walker v. First Nat. Bank, 43 Ore. 102, 72 Pac. 635 (1903); Hodgson v. St. Paul Plow Co., 78 Minn. 172, 80 N. W. 956, 50 L. R. A. 644, with valuable note (1899).

[400] Swim v Wilson, 90 Cal. 126, 27 Pac. 33, 13 L. R. A. 605, 25 Am. St. R. 110 (1891); Kimball v. Billings, 55 Me. 147 (1867); Robinson v. Bird, 158 Mass. 357, 33 N. E. 391 (1893); Bercich v. Marye, 9 Nev. 312 (1874); Donahue v. Shippee, 15 R. I. 453 (1887); Doliff v. Robbins, 83 Minn. 498, 86 N. W. 772, 85 Am. St. R. 464 (1901); Johnson v. Martin, 87 Minn. 370, 92 N. W. 221 (1902).

[401] Davis v. Southern Pac. Ry., 98 Cal. 19, 32 Pac. 708 (1893); Miller v. Staples, 3 Col. App. 93, 32 Pac.

81 (1893); Hinds v. Harbon, 58 Ind. 121 (1877); Martin v. Louisville, etc., Ry., 95 Ky. 612, 26 S. W. 801 (1894); Osborne v. Morgan, 137 Mass. 1 (1884); Steinhauser v. Spraul, 114 Mo. 551, 21 S. W. 515 (1892); Schunpert v. Southern Ry., 65 S. C. 332, 43 S. E. 813 (1903); Greenberg v. Whitcomb Lumber Co., 90 Wis. 225, 63 N. W. 93, 28 L. R. A. 439, 48 Am. St. R. 911 (1895); Warax v. Cincinnati, etc., Ry., 72 Fed. 637 (1896); Helms v. Nor. Pac. Ry., 120 Fed. 389 (1903).

[402] Marsh v. Astry Cro. Eliz. 175 (1590).

[403] Lane v. Cotton, 12 Mod. 472, 488 (1701): "A servant or deputy, as such, cannot be charged for neglect, but the principal only shall be charged for it; but for a misfeasance, an action will lie against a servant or deputy, but not as a deputy or servant, but as a wrongdoer."

privity between him and such persons, but the privity exists only
between him and his principal." [404]

Undoubtedly, when the servant or agent owes no legal duty to a
third person, such person cannot make out a cause of action in tort
against him, by showing that his neglect to perform a duty, owing
to the master, has been followed by injury to himself, the third
person.[405] If the master owed such person a duty, his neglect to
perform it would render him answerable for injury caused thereby;
and such liability is all that the injured party needs or can claim.
But when the servant or agent has taken full possession of his
master's or principal's property, and has agreed to keep it in repair,
or to do other acts upon or about it, whose performance is necessary
to the safety of third persons, it would seem that he has voluntarily
assumed a duty towards such persons, as well as towards his employer; and must respond accordingly for its non-performance.
This view is sustained by the weight of modern authority,[406] although
some courts have felt constrained to characterize such misconduct
of the agent or servant as misfeasance [407] rather than non-feasance.
Other courts prefer the views of Holt and Story, that agents or
servants are not liable to third persons for mere omissions of duty,
but only for the actual commission of some positive wrong.[408]

Tort Liability of Servant to Master.   If the agent or
servant unjustifiably assaults his employer, or wrongfully injures [409]

[404] Story on Agency, § 308.

[405] Hill v. Caverly, 7 N. H. 215
(1834); Calvin v. Holbrook, 2 N. Y.
126 (1848).

[406] Mayer v. Thompson-Hutchin-
son Co., 104 Al. 611, 16 So. 620, 28
L. R. A. 433, 53 Am. St. R. 88
(1894); Baird v. Shipman, 132 Ill.
16, 23 N. E. 384, 7 L. R. A. 128, 22
Am. St. R. 504 (1890); Lough v.
John Davis, etc., Co., 30 Wash. 204,
70 Pac. 491 (1902). See 3 Col. Law
Rev. 116–118, for an excellent discussion of this topic.

[407] Osborne v. Morgan, 130 Mass.
102, 39 Am. R. 437 (1881); Ellis v.
McNaughton, 76 Mich. 237, 42 N. W.
1113, 15 Am. St. R. 308 (1889);

Lottman v. Barnett, 62 Mo. 159
(1876); Horner v. Lawrence, 37 N.
J. L. 46 (1874).

[408] Dean v. Brock, 11 Ind. App.
507, 38 N, E. 829 (1894); DeLaney
v. Rochereau, 34 La. Ann. 1123, 44
Am. R. 456 (1882); Feltus v. Swan,.
62 Miss. 415 (1884); Denny v. Manhattan Ry., 5 Den. (N. Y.) 639
(1848); Van Antwerp v. Linton, 89
Hun. 417 (1895); Drake v. Hogan,
108 Tenn. 265, 67 S. W. 470 (1902);
Lobadie v. Hawley, 61 Tex. 177, 48
Am. R. 278 (1884); Carey v. Rochereau, 16 Fed. 87 (1883); Bryce v.
Southern Ry., 125 Fed. 958 (1903).

[409] Mobile, etc., Ry. v. Clanton, 59
Al. 392, 31 Am. R. 15 (1877); Zul-

or converts [410] his property, he is liable to him in tort, precisely as he would be to any other person. But in many cases, the master has the option to proceed against the servant or agent in tort, when but for the relationship between them he would be limited to an action for a breach of contract. Even in the absence of an express stipulation on the subject, it is an implied term of the contract of employment, that the employee will be loyal to his employer, and abstain from misconduct harmful to him. For a breach of these engagements, the master has a remedy either in a contract [411] or a tort action,[412] as he may prefer.[413] Ordinarily, he prefers the latter; and if his property has been damaged by the servant's misconduct,[414] or if he has been compelled to pay damages to third persons,[415] because of such misconduct, he proceeds in tort against the servant.

Joint Actions Against Master and Servant. Whenever the master is an active participant with the servant in the commission of a tort, or has actually authorized, commanded or ratified it, he may be joined with the servant in a tort action for redress.[416] Thus far, all authorities are agreed. If, however, the servant is the

---

kee v. Wing, 20 Wis. 498, 91 Am. Dec. 425 (1866).

[410] Scott v. Rogers, 31 N. Y. 676 (1864); Laverty v. Sneathen, 68 N. Y. 522, 23 Am. R. 184 (1877).

[411] Bixby v. Parsons, 49 Conn. 483, 489, 44 Am. R. 246 (1882): "The plaintiff seeks to recover the wages on the contract of hiring. The cases show that the seducer of defendant's daughter broke that contract, and these damages resulted to the defendant in consequence of the breach. This gives the defendant the same right to recoup the damages that he would have had, if the servant (the plaintiff) had intentionally killed the defendant's horse, or burned his dwelling, for in such cases the contract of hiring would be broken."

[412] Greenfield Savings Bank v. Simons, 133 Mass. 415 (1882).

[413] See supra, p. 17 and Industrial

& Gen. Trust v. Tod, 170 N. Y. 233, 63 N. E. 285 (1902), holding the agent liable only for breach of contract.

[414] Mobile, etc., Ry. v. Clanton, 59 Al. 392, 31 Am. R. 15 (1877); Odd Fellows' Assoc., 63 Cal. 598, 49 Am. R. 107 (1883); Zulkee v. Wing, 20 Wis. 408, 91 Am. Dec. 425 (1866).

[415] Smith v. Foran, 43 Conn. 244, 21 Am. R. 647 (1875); Georgia Southern Ry. v. Jossey, 105 Ga. 271, 31 S. E. 179 (1898); Grand Trunk Ry. v. Latham, 63 Me. 177 (1874); Costa v. Yoachim, 104 La. 170, 28 So. 932 (1900).

[416] Petrie v. Lamont, 1 Car. & M. 93, 96 (1841); Hill v. Caverly, 7 N. H. 215, 26 Am. Dec. 735 (1834); Caldwell v. Sacra, Littell's Select Cases (Ky.) 118, 12 Am. Dec. 285, and cases cited in note thereto (1811); Hewlett v. Swift, 3 Allen (85 Mass.) 420 (1862).

only actual wrongdoer, and the master's liability is due solely to his position as master, the right of the injured party to join them as defendants is a question upon which the authorities differ.

In England, this right seems to be unquestioned,[417] although a learned writer has suggested that " it is better generally to sue only the master." [418] The weight of authority in this country seems to accord with the English decisions. In the leading case on this side of the controversy, the learned judge said: [419] " In a case of strict negligence by a servant while employed in the service of his master, I see no reason why an action will not lie against both jointly. They are both guilty of the same negligence, at the same time, and under the same circumstances; the servant in fact, and the master constructively, by the servant, his agent." This doctrine has been repeatedly approved in New York,[420] and has been accepted in many other jurisdictions.[421]

The Opposite View. The leading case, in opposition to this view, is that of Parsons v. Winchell.[422] According to this decision, " the act of the servant is not the act of the master, even in legal intendment," in cases such as we are now considering. " The mas-

---

[417] Michael v. Alestree, 2 Lev. 172, S. C. *sub nom*. Mitchell v. Alestree, 1 Vent. 295; Mitchell v. Alestry, 3 Keb. 650 (1687); Moreton v. Hovdern, 4 B. & C. 223, 10 E. C. L. 316 (1825); Steel v. Lester, 3 C. P. D. 121 (1877).

[418] Smith, Master and Servant (5 Ed.), 285, note t.

[419] Cowen, J., in Wright v. Wilcox, 19 Wend (N. Y.) 343, 32 Am. Dec. 507 (1838).

[420] Suydam v. Moore, 8 Barb. (N. Y.) 358 (1850); Montfort v. Hughes, 3 E. D. Smith (N. Y.) 591 (1854); Phelps v. Wait, 30 N. Y. 78 (1864).

[421] Chicago & A. Ry. v. Wise, 206 Ill. 453, 69 N. E. 500, 503, (1903); Chesapeake & O. Ry. v. Dixon, 104 Ky. 608, 47 S. W. 615 (1898); S. C. in 179 U. S. 131, 21 Sup. Ct. (1900), but this point left undecided by the Supreme Court. Winston's Adm'r.

v. Ill. Cent. Ry., 111 Ky. 954, 65 S. W. 13, 55 L. R. A. 603, (1901); Wright v. Compton, 53 Ind. 337 (1876); Schumpert v. Southern Ry., 65 S. C. 332, 43 S. E. 813 (1903): " Both are liable jointly, because from the relation of master and servant they are united or identified in the same tortious act resulting in the same injury." Howe v. Northern Pac. Ry., 30 Wash. 569, 70 Pac. 1100, 60 L. R. A. 949 (1902); McHugh v. Nor. Pac. Ry., 32 Wash. 30, 72 Pac. 450 (1903); Greenberg v. Whitcomb Lumber Co., 90 Wis. 225, 63 N. W. 93, 28 L. R. A. 439, 48 Am. S. R. 911 (1895); Charman v. Lake Erie Ry., 105 Fed. 449 (1900); Riser v. Southern Ry., 116 Fed. 215 (1902).

[422] 5 Cush. (59 Mass.) 592, 52 Am. Dec. 745 (1850).

ter is liable not as if the acts were done by himself, but because the law makes him liable," while the servant is liable because of his personal act in doing the wrong. Liabilities created on two such wholly different grounds, it is declared, cannot and ought not to be joint.[423]   Moreover, it is urged, " if the master and servant were jointly liable to an action, the judgment and execution would be against them jointly as joint wrongdoers, and the master, if he alone should satisfy the execution, could not call on the servant for reimbursement, nor even for contribution." [424]

The last objection seems to be without force; for the master could certainly obtain reimbursement from the negligent servant if himself free from actual fault. Even as between joint tort-feasors, contribution is allowed, if they are not intentional wrongdoers.[425]

---

[423] Warax v. Cincin., etc., Ry., 72 Fed. 637 (1896); Helms v. Nor. Pac. Ry., 120 Fed. 389 (1903); Mulchey v. Methodist Relig. Soc., 125 Mass. 487 (1878); Clark v. Fry, 8 Ohio St. 385 (1858).

[424] Campbell v. Portland Sugar Co., 62 Me. 553, 16 Am. R. 503 (1873); Page v. Parker, 40 N. H. 47 (1860).

[425] Palmer v. Wick, etc., Co. (1894), A. C. 318; Armstrong County v. Clarion County, 66 Pa. 218 (1870).

CHAPTER V.

REMEDIES.

§ I. DEVELOPMENT OF REMEDIES.

Historical Sketch. — The history of remedies for torts presents four stages of development. In primitive ages, the law, so far as it deals at all with this topic, throws upon the victim the duty of redressing his injuries—it " expects men to help themselves when they have been wronged." [1] It is true that " self-help " of this sort more frequently resulted in punishing the wrongdoer than in compensating the party who had been wronged. It took the form of the right of " feud," or private warfare, to revenge an injury, rather than the right of distraining property of the wrongdoer as a means of coercing him to pay money or do an act. And yet, the right of " distress " is probably as old as the right of " feud." [2]

Undoubtedly, this policy of early law is due, in part, to the weakness of the primitive state. As government becomes more powerful, and as experience discloses the wastefulness and inefficiency of " self-help," courts of justice are opened for the settlement of private disputes, and the law-suit is offered to the disputants as " an alternative to private reprisals, a mode of stanching personal or hereditary blood-feuds other than slaughter or plunder." [3] During this second stage of legal development, the law-suit is only an alternative. The person harmed is not bound to seek redress in a court of justice. Private warfare may still be waged. Even if the wrongdoer is brought into court and a judgment rendered against him, he can refuse to abide by the decision. The court, at that time, " had no power of directly enforcing its decrees. The man who disobeyed the order of the court went out of the law: his kinsmen

[1] Pollock and Maitland, History of English Law (1st Ed.), 572.

[2] Ibid., p. 573; Markby, Elements of Law (5 Ed.), 826–830; Furbush v. Fisher, 16 Phil. (Pa.) 170 (1883).

[3] Maine, Early Law and Custom, p. 381.

ceased to be responsible for his acts, and the kinsmen of those who injured him became also irresponsible; and thus he carried his life in his hand." The earliest service of courts of justice "to mankind was to furnish an alternative to savagery, not to suppress it wholly." [4]

The third stage of development is marked by a stringent prohibition of "self-help" in almost every direction. It is thought of as "an enemy of the law, a contempt of the King and his court. * * * The man who is not enjoying what he ought to enjoy should bring an action; he must not disturb an existing seizure, be it of land, of chattels, or of incorporeal things, be it of liberty, of serfage or of the marital relationship." [5]

During the later middle ages, according to the authority just quoted, the law became laxer on this topic, and at present is "permanently lax. * * * In our own day, our law allows an amount of quiet self-help that would have shocked Bracton. It can safely allow this, for it has mastered the kind of self-help that is lawless."

§ 2. SELF-HELP.

Defense of Self and Property. This form of self-help, which the early common law discountenanced, but which the law now tolerates, has been considered to some extent already,[6] and will be referred to hereafter, in connection with trespass to person and to property. It is sufficient, at this time, to state very briefly the rules relating to forcible re-entry upon lands, and to forcible recaption of chattels.

Forcible Entry and Detainer. Prior to 1381, the common law permitted a man to regain by force lands of which he was forcibly disseized. Under pretense of enforcing this right, powerful men forcibly ejected their weaker neighbors and retained possession of lands thus acquired. To remedy this evil, statutes were enacted in the latter part of the fourteenth century, prohibiting, under pain of criminal punishment, the forcible entry into [7] and the detainer of [8] lands, except in cases where the entry or detainer was given by law. These statutes, as subsequently amended in England,[9] have become

---

[4] Ibid., p. 387.

[5] Pollock & Maitland, History of Eng. Law (1 Ed.), p. 572.

[6] Ante, ch. III.

[7] 5 Ric. II, c. 7 (1381).

[8] 15 Ric. II, c. 2 (1391).

[9] Hen. VI. c. 9 (1430); 31 Eliz. c. 11 (1589); 21 Jac. I. c. 15 (1623).

a part of the common or statute law of most of our States. Their object, it has been declared, is " to prevent any and all persons, with or without title, from assuming to right themselves with the strong hand, after feudal fashion, when peaceable possession cannot be obtained, and to compel them to the more pacific course of suits in court, where the weak and strong stand upon equal terms." [10]

The statute of Henry VI provided that the person forcibly turned out or kept out, in violation of the statutes of Richard II, should be restored to his possession. It followed, therefore, that if a person, rightfully entitled to possession, gained such possession by forcible entry, he should be punished for the breach of the peace by a fine to the King, *and* by losing the possession thus illegally acquired; [11] but he was not liable in damages to the wrongful occupant whom he had forcibly ejected or repelled, [12] except " for an independent wrong; some act which could be justified only if he was in lawful possession." [13]

In this country, neither the statutes nor the decisions are uniform upon these points. Some States punish forcible entry and detainer as crimes, but do not give a civil action against one guilty of these offenses, if he was entitled to possession, either for trespass, *quare clausum fregit*, or for damages to the wrongful occupant. [14]   But, in

[10] Vinson v. Flynn, 64 Ark. 453, 43 S. W. 146, 39 L. R. A. 415 (1897).

[11] Pollock, Torts (6 Ed.), p. 370.

[12] Ibid., Clerk and Lindsell, Torts (2 Ed.), 286–8. Harvey v. Brydges, 14 M. & W. 437 (1845).

[13] Beddall v. Maitland, 17 Ch. D. 174, 50 L. J. Ch. 401 (1881), holding that the wrongful occupant could not recover damages for forcible eviction, but could for injury to his furniture which was put out of the house.

[14] Page v. Dwight, 170 Mass. 29, 48 N. E. 850, 39 L. R. A. 418 (1897): "Upon the whole, we think the better view is that the legislature, after making first trial of the ancient system under which a possession ended by force might be restored without regard to title or right of possession, thought it better to provide that those only who had a right of possession should be put in by the courts, and to leave to the criminal law the acts of one who, being entitled to possession, takes it by prohibited force." Low v. Elwell, 121 Mass. 309, 23 Am. R. 272 (1876), "landlord not liable for force upon person of tenant necessary to effect his removal, after the termination of his tenancy." Mugford v. Richardson, 6 Allen (88 Mass.) 76 (1863), landlord is not liable for assault and battery, who uses only such force as is necessary to subdue resisting tenant who is wrongfully in possession. See Sterling v. Warden, 51 N. H. 217, 12 Am. R. 80 (1871); Gillespie v. Beecher, 85 Mich. 347,

most jurisdictions, even the owner of land who is entitled to immediate possession is not allowed to take the law into his own hands, and gain possession by the exercise of force which amounts to a breach of the peace. If he acquires possession in that way, he may be compelled to restore it and pay damages for trespass upon the property, as well as for injuries inflicted upon the persons of the wrongful occupants who resist the wrongful entry.[15] If, however, he can gain possession peaceably, he may resort to force to retain it, without being chargeable with wrongful detainer.[16]

Forcible Recaption of Chattels. In England, there seems to be no doubt that he who is entitled to the immediate possession of a chattel is legally justified in using whatever force is reasonably necessary to recover it, either from a trespasser, or from an innocent third person claiming under the trespasser.[17] There is no statute relating to such forcible recapture, similar to those prohibiting forcible entry and detainer, in the case of lands; and it has been judicially declared that, " if the owner was compelled by law to seek redress by action for a violation of his right of property, the remedy would be often worse than the mischief, and the law would aggravate the mischief instead of redressing it." [18]

Many courts in this country have taken the same view.[19] On the

48 N. W. 561 (1891); Allen v. Keily, 17 R. I. 731, 24 At. 776, 16 L. R. A. 798 (1892); Stearns v. Sampson, 59 Me. 568, 8 Am. R. 442 (1871); Manning v. Brown, 47 Md. 506 (1877).

[15] Denver, etc., Ry. v. Harris, 122 U. S. 597, 607, 7 Sup. Ct. 1286 (1886); Ely v. Yore, 71 Cal. 130 (1886); Larkin v. Avery, 23 Conn. 304 (1854); Reeder v. Purdy, 41 Ill. 279 (1866); Bristor v. Burr, 120 N. Y. 427, 24 N. E. 937 (1890); Sinclair v. Stanley, 69 Tex. 718 (1888); Dustin v. Cowdry, 23 Vt. 631 (1851).

[16] Bliss v. Johnson, 73 N. Y. 529, 534 (1878).

[17] Clerk and Lindsell, Torts (2 Ed.), p. 124, Pollock, Torts (6 Ed.), p. 372.

[18] Blades v. Higgs, 10 C. B. N. S. 713, 30 L. J. C. P. 347 (1861); Anonymous, Keil f. 92 pl. 4 (1506), accord.

[19] Baldwin v. Hayden, 6 Conn. 453 (1827). In Heminway v. Heminway, 58 Conn. 443, 19 At. 766 (1890), the right of forcible recaption seems to be limited to cases of " momentarily interrupted possession," cases where there is ground for saying that the recaptor is virtually exercising the right of defense; Comm. v. Donahue, 148 Mass. 529, 20 N. E. 171, 2 L. R. A. 623, 12 Am. S. R. 591 (1889); Same doctrine, Hopkins v. Dickson, 59 N. H. 235 (1879); Moore v. Shenk, 3 Pa. 13, 45 Am. Dec. 618 (1846), semble; Anderson v. State, 6 Baxt. (65 Tenn.) 608 (1872); Hodgeden v.

other hand, it has been held that the use of force, amounting to a breach of the peace, is justifiable in defending one's possession against a wrongdoer, but not in regaining a possession which he has lost. "There is no doubt," it is said by these courts, "that one having either the general or special right of property in personal chattels, may, if wrongfully dispossessed thereof, retake them wherever he can find them, provided he can obtain peaceable possession; [20] but the law more highly regards the public peace than the right of property of a private individual, and therefore forbids recaption to be made in a riotous or forcible manner." [21]

Even in jurisdictions holding this doctrine, the right of the owner to forcibly rescue his property from a thief is recognized.[22] Such force is employed, it is said, in defense of the owner's legal possession, and not to regain a possession which has been lost. And some of the authorities cited above, as following the English decisions, may not have been intended to stand for any broader doctrine than the right of defending legal possession, as distinguished from physical custody.[23]

Hubbard, 18 Vt. 504, 46 Am. Dec. 167 (1846); Hite v. Long, 6 Rand. 457 (Va.), 18 Am. Dec. 719 (1828); State v. Dooley, 121 Mo. 591, 26 S. W. 558 (1894). At p. 599, the court says: "Where one's property is taken with felonious intent * * * great force may be resorted to with propriety; but where there is clearly no felony, but mere dispute as to legal ownership, a resort to violence, disproportionate to the value of the property, and where peaceful remedies would prove equally efficacious, should not be sustained."

[20] Stanford v. Howard, 103 Tenn. 24, 52 S. W. 140 (1899); recapture of money lost at poker.

[21] Bobb v. Bosworth, 2 Littell, (Ky.) 81, 12 Am. Dec. 273 (1808); Story v. State, 71 Al. 329, 338 (1882); Winter v. Atkinson, 92 Ill. App. 162 (1899); Andre v. Johnson,

6 Blackf. (Ind.) 375 (1843); Stuyvesent v. Wilcox, 92 Mich. 233, 239, 52 N. W. 465, 31 Am. St. R. 580 (1892); Bowman v. Brown, 55 Vt. 184 (1882); Barnes v. Martin, 15 Wis. 240, 82 Am. Dec. 670 (1862); Bliss v. Jonson, 73 N. Y. 529, 534 (1878); Davis v. Whitridge, 16 S. C. 575 (1881); Kirby v. Foster, 17 R. I. 437, 22 At. 1111, 14 L. R. A. 317, with note (1892); Sabre v. Mott, 88 Fed. 780 (1898).

[22] Gyre v. Culver, 47 Barb. (N. Y.) 592 (1867).

[23] In Johnson v. Perry, 56 Vt. 703, 48 Am. R. 826, (1884), the court said: "We should not be disposed to extend the law of the Hodgeden v. Hubbard case (18 Vt. 504). But we are not disposed to overrule it; or to adopt a rule, that when one man goes on to another's premises, without leave or license, and undertakes to carry away his prop-

Entering Another's Premises to Retake Property. If A's chattels have been wrongfully placed by B, or with his consent, upon his premises, or if B has sold to A personal property thus located, the law creates a license in A's favor to enter and take the property.[24] Such a license exists also in favor of the owner of cattle, driven along the highway, when they wander upon adjoining lands without the owner's fault.[25] As this license is created by the law, it cannot be revoked by the land owner.[26] While, however, he has no legal authority to rovoke the license, if he does prohibit A from entering, the latter is not justified in resorting to force and violence to overcome B's opposition, but must resort to legal process,[27] except in those jurisdictions which permit one to use force in retaking his property.[28]

Distress as a Form of Self-Help. This ancient remedy of the common law, " whereby a party in certain cases is entitled to enforce a right or obtain redress for a wrong in a summary manner by seizing chattels and detaining them as a pledge until satisfaction is obtained," still exists; [29] but, in this country, its exercise is regulated with much particularity by statute.[30] At present, therefore,

erty, the latter cannot interfere to stop it."

[24] Chapman v. Thumblethorp, Croke Eliz. 329 (1594); Patrick v. Colerick, 3 M. & W. 483 (1838); Cuningham v. Yeomans, 7 Sup. Ct. Rep. (N. S. Wales) 149 (1868); Wheeldon v. Lowell, 50 Me. 499 (1862); McLeod v. Jones, 105 Mass. 403, 405 (1870); Chambers v. Bedell, 2 W. & S. (Pa.) 225 (1841).

[25] Goodwyn v. Chevely, 4 H. & N. 631, 28 L. J. Ex. 298 (1859); Hartford v. Brady, 114 Mass. 466, 19 Am. R. 377 (1874).

[26] Wood v. Manley, 11 A. & E. 34 (1839); White v. Elwell, 48 Me. 360, 77 Am. Dec. 231 (1861); Emerson v. Shores, 95 Me. 237, 239, 49 At. 1051 (1901); McLeod v. Jones, 105 Mass. 403, 406 (1870).

[27] Herndon v. Barttell, 4 Porter (Al.) 481, 494 (1837); Chase v. Jefferson, 1 Houst. (Del.) 257 (1856);

Blount v. Mitchell, 1 Taylor (N. C.) 131 (1798); Salisbury v. Green, 17 R. I. 758, 24 At. 787 (1892); Roach v. Damon, 2 Humph. (21 Tenn.) 425 (1841).

[28] Lambert v. Robinson, 162 Mass. 34, 37 N. E. 753, 44 Am. S. R. 326 (1894); " A person who has a right to enter upon the land of another, and there do an act, may use what force is required for that purpose, without being liable to an action. If he commits a breach of the peace, he is liable to the commonwealth. If he uses excessive force, he is liable to a personal action for an assault." Yale v. Seely, 15 Vt. 221 (1843); Mills v. Wooters, 59 Ill. 234 (1871).

[29] Clerk & Lindsell, Torts (2 ed) chap. 12; Stewart v. Benninger, 138 Pa. 437, 21 At. 159 (1891).

[30] See 9 Am. & Eng. Enc. of Law (2 ed.), title Distress.

194 THE LAW OF TORTS.

it partakes far more of the nature of legal process than of " self-
help." [31]   In not a few jurisdictions, as a means of collecting rent—
its most important function at common law—it has been abolished
by statute, or is treated as obsolete.[32]   What has been said of distress for rent is substantially true of the right to distrain trespassing
cattle.   It is in the main a statutory right.[33]

Abatement of Nuisances.   This is not only one of the most
ancient [34] forms of " self-help," but also one of the most important
at the present time.   If A permits trees to grow upon his land so
near B's line that the boughs overhang, or the roots penetrate the
soil of B's premises, the latter may abate the nuisance by cutting off
the boughs and the roots.[35]   Some courts declare that B ought to
content himself with this remedy, and, if he brings an action for
damages, when the injury to his property is nominal, should be
turned out of court because he is prosecuting a vexatious and groundless suit.[36]   Such is not the prevailing view, however.   He may

[31] Flury v. Grimes, 52 Ga. 342
(1874); Patty v. Bogle, 59 Miss. 491,
(1882).

[32] Herr v. Johnson, 11 Col. 393, 18
Pac. 342 (1888); Garrett v. Hughlett, 1 Har. & J. (Md.) 3 (1800);
Dutcher v. Culver, 24 Minn. 584,
594 (1877), referring to C. 140 L.
1877; Marye v. Dyche, 42 Miss.
347 (1869); Hosford v. Ballard, 39
N. Y. 150 (1868), referring to ch.
274 L. 1846; Crocker v. Mann, 3
Mo. 472 (1834); Utah, Genl. Laws
1898, §§ 1407, 1408, substitute a
landlord's lien on the tenant's property for the right of distress; Wis.
Gen. Laws 1898, § 2181, abolishes
distress for rent.

[33] Oil v. Rowley, 69 Ill. 469
(1873); Frazier v. Nortinus, 34 Ia.
82 (1871); Northcote v. Smith, 4
Ohio C. C. R. 565 (1890); Mooney
v. Maynard, 1 Vt. 470 (1829).

[34] Bracton, DeLegibus Angliae,
Lib. 3, f. 233: "But those things
which have thus been raised to
cause a tortious nuisance* * * may
be immediately and recently, whilst
the misdeed is flagrant (as in the
case of other disseysines) demolish-
ed and thrown down, * * if the complainant is sufficient to do it; but,
if not, he must have recourse to
him who protects rights."   At p.
234 the learned author advises the
victim of a nuisance to proceed by
an assize of nuisance rather than
by abatement by his own act.

[35] Lemmon v. Webb, 63 L. J. Ch.
570 (1894), 3 ch. 1, 12, Lindley, L. J.
"This has been declared to be the
law for centuries," citing 2 Brooke
Abr. "Nuisances" p. 105, pl. 28
(1493); Norris v. Baker, 1 Roll. 293
(1617), and later authorities; S. C.
affirmed (1895) A. C. 1, 64 L. J. Ch.
205; Hickey v. Mich. Cen. Ry., 96
Mich 498, 55 N. W. 989, 21 L. R. A.
729, with note, 35 Am. S. R. 621
(1893).

[36] Countryman v. Lighthill, 24
Hun. (N. Y.) 405 (1881) cf.; Gran-
dona v. Lovdal, 78 Cal. 611, 11 Pac.
623, 12 Am. St. R. 121 (1889).

abate the action by his own act; but he is not bound to pursue this course.[37]   He is entitled to go into a court of justice for the recovery of damages.

Risk of Abating.   Indeed, a person takes no little risk when he ventures upon abating a nuisance by his own act.[38]   While he is not bound to save the property which constitutes the nuisance,[39] he is bound to exercise a care, commensurate with the exigencies of the situation, and if valuable property is destroyed by reason of his failure to exercise such care, he is liable to its owner for damages.[40] " The true theory of abatement of nuisance is that an individual citizen may abate a private nuisance injurious to him, when he could also bring an action; [41] and also when a common nuisance obstructs his individual right, he may remove it to enable him to enjoy that right, and he cannot be called in question for so doing.   As in the case of obstruction across a highway, and an unauthorized bridge over a navigable watercourse, if he has occasion to use the way, he may remove the obstruction [42] by way of abatement."   But this principle does not justify private citizens in breaking into a saloon where spirituous liquors are sold in violation of law, and destroying the liquors and saloon fixtures.   The illegal business " is exclusively

[37] Buckingham v. Elliott, 62 Miss. 296, 52 Am. R. 188 (1884); Missouri, etc., Ry. v. Burt, (Tex. Civ. App.), 27 S. W. 948 (1894).

[38] People ex rel. Copcutt v. Board of Health, Yonkers, 140 N. Y. 1, 35 N. E. 320, 23 L. R. A. 481, 37 Am. S. R. 522 (1893); Hicks v. Dorn, 42 N. Y. 47 (1870.)   Defendant, the state superintendent of canal repairs, had to pay $1,856.14 and costs for destroying plaintiff's canal boat although it was an obstruction to canal navigation: Bowden v. Lewis, 13 R. I. 189, 43 Am. R. 21 (1881).

[39] McKeesport Sawmill Co. v. Penn. Co., 122 Fed. 184 (1903); Kendall v. Green, (N. H.) 42 At. 178, 183 (1896); Mark v. Hudson River Bridge Co., 103 N. Y. 28, 8 N. E. 243 (1886); Philiber v. Matson, 14 Pa. 306 (1850); Harrington v.

Edwards, 17 Wis. 586, 86 Am. Dec. 768 (1863).

[40] Gumbert v. Wood, 146 Pa. 370, 23 At. 404 (1891).

[41] Anonymous, Y. B. Ed. IV. f. 34, pl. 10 (1469); Amoskeag Mfg. Co. v. Goodale, 46 N. H. 53 (1865); California Civil Code, §§ 3495, 3502, modifying Gunter v. Geary, 1 Cal. 462 (1851).

[42] James v. Hayward Croke, Charles, 184 (1631); Hubbard v. Deming, 21 Conn. 356 (1851); Marcy v. Taylor, 19 Ill. 634 (1858); Brown v. DeGroff, 50 N. J. L. 409 (1887); State v. Parrott, 71 N. C. 311, 17 Am. R. 5 (1874); Lancaster T. Co. v. Rogers, 2 Pa. 114, 44 Am. Dec. 179 (1845); Selman v. Wolfe, 27 Tex. 68 (1863); Larson v. Furlong, 63 Wis. 323, (1885).

a public nuisance; and the fact that the husbands, wives, children, or servants of any persons do frequent such a place and get intoxicating liquor there, does not make it a special nuisance or injury to their private rights, so as to authorize and justify such persons in " forcibly abating it.[43]

Even when a public nuisance causes such special damage to individuals as to give them a civil action against the wrongdoer, they must be careful, in attempting to abate it by their own acts, not to go further than is necessary to protect themselves. The fact that a nuisance is maintained in a particular building, does not authorize the destruction of the building,[44] unless that is essential to the abatement of the nuisance.[45]

Notce of intention to abate a nuisance is rarely necessary,[46] except when entry must be made upon the wrongdoer's land to effect the abatement, or human life will be endangered if notice is not given.[47] Vicious animals, whose continued existence endangers human life, may be killed by anyone without notice.[48]

Action for Damages is the Ordinary Tort Remedy. Although the victim of a tort may resort to " self-help," as we have seen, and, in some cases, may appeal to a court of equity [49] for relief, his ordinary remedy is a common-law action for damages. If the wrong is a maritime tort, that is, a wrong committed upon public navigable waters of the United States, but of such a character as had it been committed upon the land, it would have been remedi-

---

[43] Brown v. Perkins, 12 Gray (78 Mass.) 89 (1858); Goodsell v. Fleming, 59 Wis. 52 (1883); Ely v. Supervisors, 36 N. Y. 297 (1867); Moody v. Supervisors, 46 Barb. (N. Y.) 659 (1866); State v. Paul, 5 R. I. 185 (1858); State v. Keeran, 5 R. I. 497 (1858).

[44] Brightman v. Inhabitants of Bristol, , 65 Me. 443, 20 Am. R. 711 (1876); Clark v. Ice Co., 24 Mich. 508 (1872); Griffith v. McCullum, 46 Barb. (N. Y.) 561 (1866).

[45] Meeker v. VanRensselaer, 15 Wend. (N. Y.) 397 (1836), cited with approval in Lawton v. Steele,

119 N. Y. 226, at 236 (1890); Fields v. Stokely, 99 Pa. 306, 44 Am. R. 109 (1882).

[46] Jones v. Williams, 11 M. & W. 176 (1843); Estes v. Kelsey, 8 Wend. (N. Y.) 555 (1832).

[47] Jones v. Jones, 1 H. & C. 1, 31 L. J. Exch. 506 (1845); Lane v. Copsey (1891), 3 Ch. 411; Cal. Civil Code § 3503.

[48] Woolf v. Chalker, 31 Conn. 121, 129 (1862); Brill v. Flagler, 23 Wend. (N. Y.) 354 (1840); Brown v. Carpenter, 26 Vt. 638 (1854).

[49] Keeners' Cases on Equity Jurisdiction, Vol. 1, Chaps. 5, 6 and 7;

able by a common-law action for damages,[50] it is within the jurisdiction of the Federal Admiralty Courts; although the injured party
may have the option of bringing a common-law action.[51] If he
proceeds in admiralty, not only will the litigation be conducted in
accordance with the rules of practice [52] of that tribunal, but will be
governed by the peculiar rules of the substantive law of admiralty.
One of these is that admiralty will not entertain a suit for merely
nominal damages for a personal tort.[53] Another is that a public
corporatic is answerable for the torts of the master and crew of a
vessel which it owns, although it is employed in the performance
of police duties; and, by the rule of the common law, in the jurisdiction where the torts were committed, the doctrine of *respondeat
superior* does not apply to such a corporation.[54] On the other hand,
if a valid claim for maritime tort exists, it may be pursued in admiralty by proceedings *in rem*, and the claimant is not limited to an
action *in personam*,[55] while, if the injured party goes into a common-
law court for redress, his action must be *in personam*.

Damages are of Three Sorts. The common law recognizes
three species of damages in tort actions; (1) nominal, (2) compensatory or ordinary, and (3) punitive or exemplary. In a few jurisdictions, the third class has been placed under statutory or judicial
taboo. "It is not the province of the jury," according to the view
prevailing in these jurisdictions, "after full damages have been
found for the plaintiff, so that he is fully compensated for the wrong
committed by the defendant, to mulct the defendant in an additional
sum to be handed over to the plaintiff, as a punishment for the wrong
he has done to the plaintiff." [56]

Pomeroy's Equity Jurisprudence,
§§ 1346-1358; Story's Equity, §§ 909-
950.

[50] Holmes v. Oregon, etc., Ry., 5
Fed. 75 (1880); Waring v. Clarke,
5 How. (U. S.) 451 (1847).

[51] Schooner Robt. Lewis v. Kekanoha, 114 Fed. 849, 52 C. C. A. 483
(1902).

[52] Wm. Johnson & Co. v. Johansen,
86 Fed. 886 (1898); The Saginaw,
95 Fed. 703 (1899); In re Cent. Ry.
of N. J. 95 Fed. 700 (1899).

[53] Barnett v. Luther, 1 Curtis C.

C. 434 (1853); In re Calif. Nav. and
Imp. Co., 110 Fed. 670 (1901).

[54] Workman v. New York City, 179
U. S. 552, 21 Sup. Ct. 212, 45 L. Ed.
314 (1900).

[55] The Albert Dumois, 177 U. S.
240, 20 Sup. Ct. 595, 44 L. Ed. 751
(1900); The Northern Queen, 117
Fed. 906 (1902).

[56] Wilson v. Bowen, 64 Mich. 133,
141 (1877); Lucas v. Mich. Cen.
Ry., 98 Mich. 1, 56 N. W. 1039
(1893); Barnard v. Poor, 21 Pick.
(38 Mass.) 378 (1838); Riewe v.

Nominal Damages. Tort actions are often brought for the purpose of securing a judicial vindication of a right, rather than a money compensation. In such cases, the plaintiff claims and is awarded only nominal damages, such as a penny or a shilling, or six cents or a dollar. Actions for the diversion of a water course,[57] for the trespass [58] to person or to property, or for wrongful interference with one's right to vote,[59] are the most common examples. When " a clear legal right of a party is invaded, in consequence of another's breach of duty," the former is entitled to an action against the latter for at least nominal damages.[60] Nor can this action be defeated by proof that such invasion has actually benefited the plaintiff.[61]

In the foregoing cases, the trifling amount of damages awarded to the plaintiff casts no reflection upon him. When, however, his action is brought not simply for a judicial affirmance of his legal right which has been invaded, but for substantial money damages, and only a nominal sum is given, the verdict is clearly disparaging. A typical example of this kind is an action for defamation, where the wrongdoing is clearly established, but the jury award six cents damages. Clearly they believe that plaintiff's reputation was too bad to be appreciably injured by the utterance. They are forced to find in his favor,[62] for an absolute right—the right of reputation—

McCormick, 11 Neb. 261 (1881); Fay v. Parker, 53 N. H. 342 (1873); Spokane Truck Co. v. Hoefer, 2 Wash. 45, 25 Pac. 1072 (1891.)

[57] Webb v. Portland Manufacturing Co., 3 Sumn. (U. S. Cir. Ct.) 189, Fed. Cases, No. 17, 322 (1838); Blodgett v. Stone, 60 N. H. 167 (1880).

[58] Leonard v. Castle, 78 Cal. 454 (1889), damage fixed by jury at one dolar; Wartman v. Swindell, 54 N. J. L. 589, 25 At. 356 (1892); Dixon v. Clow, 24 Wend. (N. Y.) 188 (1840); Casebeer v. Mowry, 55 Pa. 419, 93 Am. Dec. 766 (1867), jury assessed damages at three cents.

[59] Ashby v. White, 2 Ld. Raymond, 938 (1703).

[60] Clifton v. Hooper, 6 Ad. & E. (N. S.) 468, 14 L. J. Q. B. 1 (1837); Texarkana, etc., Ry. v. Anderson, 67 Ark. 123, 53, S. W. 673 (1899), passenger negligently carried beyond her station, but no actual damage shown; Fullman v. Stearns, 30 Vt. 454 (1858); Slingerland v. Int. Contg. Co., 169 N. Y. 60, 61 N. E. 995, 56 L. R. A. 499 (1901).

[61] Jewett v. Whitney, 43 Me. 242 (1857); Stowell v. Lincoln, 11 Gray (77 Mass.), 434 (1858); Jones v. Hannovan, 55 Mo. 462 (1874); Murphy v. Fond Du Lac, 23 Wis. 365, 99 Am. Dec. 181 (1868).

[62] In Jones v. King, 33 Wis. 422 (1873), the court admited that the verdict should have been in plain-

has been invaded without justification; but whether he shall receive nominal damages or a substantial sum is for them to decide.[63]

Ordinary or Compensatory Damages. In the ordinary tort action, damages are sought and awarded with a view of compensating the plaintiff for the pecuniary injury which he has sustained. If the sod or tillable soil of land has been wrongfully carried off, the owner is not entitled to the cost of actually replacing the sod or the soil, but to the difference between the value of the land before and after the injury.[64] So, if fruit or shade trees or fences are destroyed, the wrongdoer is not bound to replace them, nor to pay the cost of planting like trees or of rebuilding the fences with the same sort of material, but to fairly compensate the injured owner for the damage done to his realty.[65] It is true that this is not always measured by the difference in the market value of the land before and after the injury. " The owner of property has a right to hold it for his own use as well as to hold it for sale, and if he has elected the former, he should be compensated for an injury wrongfully done him in that respect, although that injury might be unappreciable to one holding the same premises for purposes of sale." [66]

Punitive or Exemplary Damages. In some jurisdictions, as we have seen already, these damages are not awarded. " The aim of the law which gives redress for private wrongs is compensation to the injured, rather than the prevention of a recurrence of the wrong." And yet, say the courts, holding this view, " The law recognizes the fact that an injury may be intensified by the malice or willfulness or oppressiveness or recklessness of the act, and allows damages commensurate with the injury when these elements are present." [67] Hence any manifestation of malevolent motives on the

tiff's favor, for nominal damages, yet refused to set aside a verdict for the defendant.

[63] Gray v. Times Publishing Co., 74 Minn. 452, 77 N. W. 204 (1898).

[64] Witham v. Kershaw, 16 Q. B. D. 613 (1885).

[65] Dwight v. El. C. & N. Ry., 132 N. Y. 199, 30 N. E. 398, 15 L. R. A. 612, 28 Am. St. R. 563 (1892); Norfolk, etc., Ry. Co. v. Bohannon, 85 Va. 293, 297, 7 S. E. 236 (1888).

[66] Gilman v. Brown, 115 Wis. 1, 91 N. W. 227 (1902); Montgomery v. Lock, 72 Cal. 75, 13 Pac. 401 (1887); Ohio & M. Ry. v. Trapp, 30 N. E. 812, 4 Ind. App. 69 (1891); McMahon v. City of Dubuque, 107 Ia. 62, 77 N. W. 517, 70 Am. St. R. 143 (1898).

[67] Lucas v. Michigan Cent. Ry., 98 Mich. 1, 56 N. W. 1039 (1893); People v. Pearl, 76 Mich. 207, 42 N. W. 1109 (1889).

part of the defendant may enhance damages, not by way of punishing him, but as a compensation for the plaintiff's injured feelings.[68] As damages of this sort are deemed punitive or exemplary by other courts,[69] the results reached in the different jurisdictions are not very dissimilar.

In a few States, the doctrine obtains, that, if the tort is one which is criminally punishable, punitive damages are not recoverable in a civil action,[70] or that a criminal conviction and fine may be considered by the jury in mitigation of civil damages.[71] In support of this view it is said that " punishment for offenses should be inflicted only by public prosecution in due course of the law of the land, under those safeguards which are rooted and grounded in the maxims of the common law, and guaranteed by the constitution of our political government; " that if punitive damages are recoverable in a civil action, in such cases, " the defendant might be punished twice for the same act." [72]

To this, it is answered, that the constitutional provision, that no person for the same offense shall twice be put in jeopardy, applies only to strictly criminal prosecutions; that the judgment in the criminal action is for the wrong to the State, while the judgment in the civil suit is for the private wrong to the plaintiff; that if a criminal conviction and fine is a bar to the victim's claim to punitive damages, it is equally a bar to any tort action for the wrongdoing.[73]

[68] Morgan v. Kendall, 124 Ind. 454, 24 N. E. 143, 9 L. R. A. 445 (1890). Mahony v. Belford, 132 Mass. 393 (1882); Burt v. Advertiser Co., 154 Mass. 238, 28 N. E. 1 (1891); Bixby v. Dunlop, 56 N. H. 456, 22 Am. R. 475 (1875).

[69] Chappell v. Ellis, 123 N. C. 259, 31 S. E. 709, 68 Am. St. R. 822 (1898); in Runyan v. Cent. Ry. of N. J., 65 N. J. L. 228, 47 At. 422 (1900), damages for injured feelings are held compensatory.

[70] Wabash Printing Co. v. Crumrine, 123 Ind. 89, 21 N. E. 940 (1889).

[71] Thamagan v. Womack, 54 Tex. 45 (1880); Rhodes v. Rogers, 151 Pa. 634, 24 At. 1044 (1892).

[72] Austin v. Wilson, 4 Cush. (58 Mass.) 273, 50 Am. Dec. 766 with note (1849); Boyer v. Barr, 8 Neb. 68, 30 Am. R. 814 (1878); Riewe v. McCormick, 11 Neb. 264, 9 N. W. 88 (1881); Fay v. Parker, 53 N. H. 342, 16 Am. R. 270 (1873); Huber v. Teuber, 3 McAr. (D. C.) 484, 36 Am. R. 110 (1879).

[73] Smith v. Bagwell, 19 Fla. 117, 45 Am. R. 12 (1882); Phillips v. Kelly, 29 Al. 628 (1857); Bundy v. Maginess, 76 Cal. 532, 18 Pac. 668 (1888); Hause v. Griffith, 102 Ia. 215, 71 N. W. 223 (1897); Chiles v. Drake, 2 Met. (59 Ky.) 146 (1859); Pike v. Dilling, 48 Me. 539 (1861); Boetcher v. Staples, 27 Minn. 308, 38 Am. R. 295 (1880); Cook v. Ellis,

Against Whom Punitive Damages Allowable? As these damages are given not by way of compensation to the plaintiff, but by way of punishment to the defendant, they are allowable, as a rule, against those only who have committed a tort, deliberately or recklessly. A wrong due to ordinary negligence merely will not justify the award of punitive damages.[74] The defendant's conduct must have been actually malicious or wanton, displaying a spirit of mischief towards the plaintiff, or of criminal indifference to his rights. Examples of this class of torts are assault and battery of a brutal character, or attended with insulting or indecent language;[75] false imprisonment, where the plaintiff has been improperly treated, or has been subjected to unnecessary indignity, or the defendant's motives were actually malicious;[76] defamation of a serious character recklessly or wickedly uttered,[77] and trespass to person or property where the injury is wanton and malicious, or the result of gross negligence, or of a reckless disregard of the rights of others.[78]

6 Hill. (N. Y.) 466 (1844); Hoadly v. Watson, 45 Vt. 289, 12 Am. R. 197 (1872); Brown v. Swineford, 44 Wis. 282, 28 Am. R. 582 (1878).

[74] Walker v. Fuller, 29 Ark. 448 (1874); Chesapeake, etc., Ry. v. Judd, 106 Ky. 364, 50 S. W. 539 (1899); Louisville, etc., Ry. v. Creighton, 106 Ky. 42, 50 S. W. 227 (1899); Sinclair v. Tarbox, 2 N. H. 135 (1819); Hansley v. Jamesville, etc., Ry., 117 N. C. 565, 23 S. E. 443 (1895); Mil. etc., Ry. v. Arms, 91 U. S. 489, 23 L. Ed. 374 (1875).

[75] Bundy v. Maginess, 76 Cal. 532, 18 Pac. 668 (1888); Smith v. Bagwell, 19 Fla. 117, 45 Am. R. 12 (1882); Berkner v. Dannenberg, 118 Ga. 888, 43 S. E. 463, 60 L. R. A. 559 (1903); Wood v. Young (Ky.) 50 S. W. 541 (1899).

[76] Raza v. Smith, 65 Fed. 592 (1895); Thorpe v. Wray, 68 Ga. 359 (1882); Hewlette v. George, 68 Miss. 703, 9 So. 885, 13 L. R. A. 682 (1891); Craven v. Bloomingdale, 171 N. Y. 439, 64 N. E. 169 (1902);

Lewis v. Clegg, 120 N. C. 292, 26 S. E. 772 (1897); Taylor v. Coolidge, 64 Vt. 506 24 At. 656 (1892); Bolton v. Vellines, 94 Va. 393, 26 S. E. 847 (1897); Fenelon v. Butts, 53 Wis. 344 (1881); Spear v. Hiles, 67 Wis. 350, 30 N. W. 506 (1886).

[77] Rutherford v. Morning Journal, 51 Fed. 513, 1 U. S. App. 296, 2 C. C. A. 354, 16 L. R. A. 803 (1892); Cahill v. Murphy, 94 Cal. 29, 30 Pac. 195 (1892); Hintz v. Granpner, 138 Ill. 158, 27 N. E. 935 (1891); Lehner v. Elmore, 100 Ky. 56, 37 S. W. 292 (1896); Callahan v. Ingram, 122 Mo. 355, 26 S. W. 1020 (1894).

[78] Sears v. Lyons, 2 Stark. 317 (1818); Emblem v. Myers, 6 H. & N. 54, 30 L. J. Ex. 71 (1860); Parker v. Mise. 27 Al. 480 (1855); Merrills v. Tariff Mfg. Co., 10 Conn. 384, 27 Am. Dec. 682, with note (1835); Illinois C. Ry. v. Stewart, (Ky.) 63 S. W. 596 (1901); Smalley v. Smalley, 81 Ill. 70 (1876); Garland v. Wholeham, 26 Ia. 185 (1868); Storm v. Green, 51 Miss. 103

Damages Recoverable from Joint Wrong Doers. If several persons are engaged in committing a tort, the victim may bring one action against all. If he proceeds in this manner, and any of the defendants is not liable for punitive damages, his recovery in the action will be limited to compensatory damages. If he would obtain a judgment for punitive damages he must bring a several action against those wrongdoers whose misconduct renders them liable thereto.[79]

Whether a principal or master is liable to punitive damages for a malicious or wanton tort of his agent or servant, committed within the scope of the latter's authority, is a question upon which the decisions are not entirely agreed. If the principal or master takes an active part with the agent or servant in the commission of the tort, or if he orders or ratifies it, he is liable to punitive damages in every jurisdiction where such damages are recoverable.[80] If, however, he is not thus connected with the tort, and his liability therefor is due solely to his relationship to the tort-feasor, or, as it is often put, to the doctrine of *respondeat superior,* many courts hold that recovery against him must be limited to compensatory damages, and if the injured person would secure punitive damages, he must proceed against the servant or agent alone. " Examplary or punitive damages," it is said by these authorities,[81] " being awarded not by

---

(1876); Work v. Jenkins, 14 Johns. (N. Y.) 352 (1817); Polk v. Francher, 1 Head. (Tenn.) 336 (1858); Thirkfield v. Mountain View Cemetery, 12 Utah, 76, 41 Pac. 564 (1895); Day v. Woodworth, 13 How. (U. S.) 363 (1851); Morgan v. Barnhill, 118 Fed. 24 (1902). In the last cited case, the court charged the jury to return a verdict for both actual and exemplary damages, under sec. 26 of Art. 16 of the Texas Const. and Arts. 3017, 3018 and 3019 of the R. S. of Texas.

[79] Cunningham v. Underwood, 116 Fed. 803, 53 C. C. A. 99 (1902); Krug v. Pitass, 162 N. Y. 154, 56 N. E. 526, 76 Am. St. R. 317 (1900).

[80] Denver, etc., Ry. v. Harris, 122 U. S. 597, 7 Sup. Ct. 1286, 30 L. Ed.

1146 (1887), the corporation was an active wrong-doer, through its managing agents; Wheeler & Wilson Co. v. Boyce, 36 Kan. 350, 13 Pac. 609 (1887), similar to preceding case; Stevens v. O'Neill, 64 N. Y. Supp. 663 (1900) affd. 169 N. Y. 375, 62 N. E. 424 (1902); Bingham v. Lipman, Wolf & Co. 40 Or. 363, 67 Pac. 98 (1901), the wrong-doers were the officers of the corporation.

[81] Lake Shore, etc., Ry. v. Prentice, 147 U. S. 101, 13 Sup. Ct. 261, 37 L. Ed. 97, with note (1893); Maisenbacker v. Society Concordia, 71 Conn. 369, 42 At. 67, 71 Am. St. R. 213 (1899); Trabing v. Cal. Nav. Co., 121 Cal. 137, 53 Pac. 644 (1898); Augusta Factory v. Barnes, 72 Ga. 217, 53 Am. R. 838 (1884); Detroit

way of compensation to the sufferer, but by way of punishment to the offender, and as a warning to others, can only be awarded against one who has participated in the offense. A principal, therefore, though of course liable to make compensation for injuries done by his agent within the scope of his employment, cannot be held liable for exemplary or punitive damages merely by reason of wanton, oppressive, or malicious intent on the part of the agent. * * * Actual guilty intention on the part of the defendant is required to charge him with exemplary or punitive damages." [82]

The Majority View: — The weight of authority, however, or at least the majority view, is in favor of according punitive damages against the principal or master, wherever the malicious or grossly negligent act of the agent or servant is within the scope of his authority. It is said by the courts and writers maintaining this doctrine, that the rule of punitive damages is not the result of logic, but of public necessity; that such damages are imposed to deter persons from gross misconduct towards others, and that where anyone, whether a natural or artificial person, transacts his business by agents or servants, the same considerations of public policy apply to him as to one who transacts his business in person. Either he or the injured person must take the risk of the infirmities of temper, the maliciousness and gross misconduct of his agent or servant, and it is but just that he should bear the risk. Especially, say these authorities, is this true in the case of passenger carriers, whose servants have unusual opportunities of abusing and insulting their passengers. Only by a strict enforcement of the rule of punitive damages, it is declared, can these great employers of servants be forced to exercise proper care in the choice, discipline and management of their representatives. [83]

Daily Post v. McArthur, 16 Mich. 447 (1868); Forham v. Consolidated Trac. Co., 63 N. J. L. 391, 43 At. 892 (1899); Krug v. Pitass, 162 N. Y. 154, 56 N. E. 526, 76 Am. S. R. 317 (1900); Craven v. Bloomingdale, 171 N. Y. 439, 64 N. E. 169 (1902); Staples v. Schmid, 18 R. I. 224, 26 At. 196, 19 L. R. A. 824 (1893); Ricketts v. Chespeake, etc., Ry., 33 W. Va. 433, 10 S. E. 801, 7 L. R. A. 354, 25 Am. St. R. 901 (1890); Eviston v. Cramer, 57 Wis. 570, 15 Am. R. 560 (1883); Robincon v. Superior Rapid Transit Ry. 94 Wis. 345, 68 N. W. 961, 34 L. R. A. 205 (1896).

[82] Northern Cen. Ry. v. Newman, Md. , 56 At. 973 (1904).

[83] Highland Ave. Ry. v. Robinson, 125 Al. 483, 25 So. 28 (1900); St. Louis, etc., Ry. v. Wilson, 70 Ark.

Punitive Damages Against Muncipal Corporations. are rarely, if ever, allowed, even in jurisdictions where business corporations are amenable to such damages. Public policy, it is thought, does not require that they be punished for the misdeeds of their representatives.[84] Very large verdicts against them for personal injuries have been sustained, however, but upon the theory that they represented the honest estimate by a jury of the plaintiff's actual damages, including the pain and suffering incidental to physical injuries.[85]

Punitive Damages for Conversion of Propeity. The ordinary measure of damages for the conversion of property is its value, at the time and place of its conversion. This is all that can be recovered, where the conversion is due to an honest mistake of the defendant, or to his negligence.[86] If, however, it is the result of the defendant's willful or dishonest conduct, he will be compelled, in most jurisdictions, to pay the value of the property at the time and place of the owner's demand for it, even though that has been greatly enhanced by the defendant's expenditure of labor and money

136, 66 S. W. 661 (1902); Chic. B. & Q. Ry. v. Bryan, 90 Ill. 126 (1878); Citizen, etc., Ry. v. Willoeby, 134 Ind. 563, 33 N. E. 627 (1892); Southern Kan. Ry. v. Rice, 38 Ks. 398, 16 Pac. 817 (1888); Atchinson, etc., Ry. v. Henry, 55 Ks. 715, 41 Pac. 952 (1895); Louisville, etc., Ry. v. Balard, 85 Ky. 307, 3 S. W. 530, 7 Am. St. R. 600 (1887); Lexington Ry. Co. v. Cozine (Ky.) 64 S. W. 848 (1901); Goodard v. Grand Trunk Ry., 57 Me. 202 (1869); Balt., etc., Ry. v. Blocher, 27 Md. 277 (1867); Pullman Palace Car Co. v. Lawrence, 74 Miss. 803, 22 So. 53 (1897); Hopkins v. Railroad, 36 N. H. 9 (1857); Purcell v. Richmond, etc., Ry., 108 N. C. 414, 12 S. E. 954, 12 L. R. A. 113 (1891); At. & Great W. Ry. v. Dunn, 19 Ohio St. 162, 2 Am. Rep. 382 (1869); Phil. Tract. Co. v. Orbann, 119 Pa. 37, 12 At. 816 (1888); Mack v. South Bound Ry., 52 S. C. 323, 29 S. E. 905, 40 L. R. A. 679 (1898); Knoxville Tract. Co. v. Lane, 103 Tenn. 376, 53 S. E. 557 (1899).

[84]Dillon Municipal Corporations (4 ed.) § 1020; Bennett v. City of Marion, 102 Ia. 425, 71 N. W. 360, 63 Am. St. R. 454 (1897); Wilson v. Wheeling, 19 W. Va. 350, 42 Am. R. 780 (1877); Costich v. City of Rochester, 68 App. Div. (N. Y.) 623, 73 N. Y. Supp. 835 (1902).

[85]Collins v. Council Bluff, 32 Ia. 324 (1871), verdict for $15,000; Shartle v. Minneapolis, 17 Minn. 308 (1871), verdict for $4,000.

[86]Central Coal Co. v. John Henry Shoe Co., 69 Ark. 302, 69 S. W. 49 (1901); Livingston v. Rawyards Coal Co., 5 App. Cas. 25, 42 L. T. N. S. 334 (1880); McLean County Coal Co. v. Long, 81 Ill. 359 (1876); Beede v. Lamprey, 64 N. H. 510, 15 At. 133 (1888); Forsyth v. Wells, 41 Pa. 291, 80 Am. Dec. 617 (1861).

upon it.[87] This rule is applied, by many courts, to an innocent purchaser from a fraudulent converter. He must pay the value of the property at the time he took title,[88] although, for expenditures subsequently made upon the property, he is to be reimbursed, if the owner takes it from him;[89] and he is not to be charged with such enhancement of value, if sued for damages.[90]

Conversion of Property of Fluctuating Value. The measure of compensatory damages for the conversion of such property varies in different jurisdictions.[91] Most of the cases fall within one of three classes. According to one class, the true measure of damages is the value of the property at the time of conversion, with interest from that date.[92] According to a second class, " Where either party is to be injured by the casual rise or fall of converted property, it ought to be he who is in the wrong; " [93] hence the correct measure of damages is the highest market value to the time of trial.[94] The rule laid down in a third class of cases is, that the converter

[87] Martin v. Porter, 5 M. & W. 351 (1839); Trotter v. McLean, 13 Ch. D. 574, 42 L. T. N. S. 118 (1879); Ellis v. Wire, 33 Ind. 127, 5 Am. R. 189 (1870); Tuttle v. White, 46 Mich. 485, 41 Am. R. 175 (1881); Hughes v. United Pipe Lines, 119 N. Y. 423, 23 N. E. 1042 (1890); Benson Mining Co. v. Alta., etc., Co., 145 U. S. 428, 12 Sup. Ct. 877 (1892).

[88] Birmingham Min. Ry. v. Tenn. Co. 127 Al. 137, 28 So. 679 (1900); Bolles Wooden Ware Co. v. United States, 106 U. S. 432, 1 Sup. Ct. 398 (1882); Tuttle v. White, 46 Mich. 487, 41 Am. R. 135 (1881); contra, Railroad Co. v. Hutchins, 32 Ohio St. 571, 30 Am. R. 629 (1877).

[89] Contra, Wing v. Milliken, 91 Me. 387, 40 At. 138, 64 Am. S. R. 238 (1898); " The law neither divests him of his property, nor requires him to pay for improvements made without his authority: " Gaskins v. Davis, 115 N. C. 85, 20 S. E. 88, 44 Am. S. R. 439, 25 L. R. A. 813 (1894).

[90] Fisher v. Brown, 70 Fed. 570, 17 C. C. A. 225 (1895).

[91] For a full discussion of the cases, see Joyce on Damages, chap. 47.

[92] Peterson v. Gresham, 25 Ark. 380 (1869); Continental Co. v. Bliley, 23 Col. 160, 46 Pac. 633 (1896); Sturgis v. Keith, 57 Ill. 451, 11 Am. R. 28 (1870); Gravel v. Clough, 81 Ia. 272, 46 N. W. 1092 (1890); Freeman v. Harwood, 49 Me. 195 (1859); Whitfield v. Whitfield, 40 Miss. 352 (1866); Walker v. Borland, 21 Mo. 289 (1855) Boylan v. Huguet, 8 Nev. 345 (1873); Pennsylvania Co. v. Phil., etc., Ry. 153 Pa. 160, 25 At. 1043 (1893).

[93] Ked v. Mitchell, 1 N. & Mc. C. (S. C.), 202, 9 Am. Dec. 702 (1818).

[94] Burks v. Hubbard, 69 Al. 384 (1884); Moody v. Caulk, 14 Fla. 50 (1872); Jaques v. Stewart, 81 Ga. 81, 6 S. E. 815 (1888); Stephenson v. Price, 30 Tex. 715 (1868).

is liable for the highest value of the property between the time of its conversion and a reasonable time after the owner has notice of it. This rule rests upon the theory that the owner, when notified of the conversion, is bound to use reasonable efforts to minimize his damages. He is entitled, therefore, to only a reasonable time within which to replace the property.[95]

Damages Against Independent but Concurrent Wrong-Doers. It often happens that the consequences of several independent torts are so mingled that it is quite impossible to measure accurately the damages caused by each. What are the injured person's rights in such cases?

It is certainly unfair to leave him without redress, simply because he cannot disentangle the consequences of the several torts, and trace with exactness each line of causation. Accordingly, if either of the wrongdoers committed his tort in circumstances which would fairly apprise a reasonably careful person that it would co-operate with the tort of another, he is answerable for the entire damage.[96] Otherwise, the extent of liability will be left " to the good sense of the jury, as reasonable men, to form, from the evidence, the best estimate that can be made under the circumstances " of the damage caused by each wrongdoer.[97]

Interest as an Element of Damages in Tort Actions This topic has received but little attention from the courts until quite recent times. It was assumed, formerly, that interest could be recovered only when the defendant had expressly or impliedly

---

[95] Galligher v. Jones, 129 U. S. 193, 9 Sup. Ct. 335, 32 L. ed. 658 (1888); Citizens Ry. v. Robbins, 144 Ind. 671, 42 N. E. 916 (1896); Dimock v. U. S. Nat. Bk., 55 N. J. L. 296, 25 At. 926, 9 Am. St. R. 643 (1893); Wright v. Bank of Met. 110 N. Y. 237, 18 N. E. 79, 6 Am. S. R. 356, 1 L. R. A. 289 (1888); Morris v. Wood, (Tenn.) 35 S. W. 1013 (1896); substantially the same rule is laid down by statute in California, North Dakota, and South Dakota. See Ralston v. Bank of Cal. 112 Cal. 208, 44 Pac. 476 (1896); First Nat. Bank v. Minn.,

etc., Elec. Co., 8 N. D. 430, 79 N. W. 874 (1899); Golden Reward Co. v. Buxton Co., 97 Fed. 423, 38 C. C. A. 228 (1889).

[96] Byrne v. Wilson, 15 Ir. C. L. 332 (1862); Kansas City v. Slangstrom, 53 Ks. 431, 36 Pac. 706 (1894); Slater v. Mersereau, 64 N. Y. 138 (1876).

[97] Jenkins v. Penn. Ry., 67 N. J. L. 331, 334, 51 At. 704, 57 L. R. A. 309 (1902); Ogden v. Lucas, 48 Ill. 492 (1868); Washburn v. Gilman, 64 Me. 163, 18 Am. R. 246 (1873); Auchmuty v. Ham. 1 Den. (N. Y.) 495 (1845).

promised to pay it. In 1833, this doctrine was modified by a statute in England, which enacted that the jury might " give damages in the nature of interest, over and above the value of the goods at the time of the conversion or seizure, in all actions of trover, or trespass *de bonis asportatis.*" [98] In no other tort actions is interest recoverable in England.[99]

In this country, the courts and legislatures have virtually discarded the common-law rule, and have adopted the principle " that wherever a claim for damages exists, no matter what the cause of action, if it represents a loss of pecuniary value ascertainable with reasonable certainty, as of a definite time, interest should be recoverable from that time. If the claim is at large and for the discretion of the jury; if it is unliquidated, and involves non-pecuniary elements, such as pain and suffering, it should not be allowed." [100] Applying this principle, it is generally held in this country, that in actions for personal injury, such as assault and battery, defamation, false imprisonment, seduction, and the like, interest is not allowable as a separate item of damages.[101] In such actions the jury are at liberty to award, as general damages, such sum as will fully compensate the plaintiff for the wrong inflicted. To supplement that with interest, would be " to add damages to damages." [102] By statute, in a few states, interest is discretionary with the jury in such cases.[103]

In actions for the conversion of personal property, as well of trespass and replevin, where plaintiff's damages are easily ascertainable by reference to fairly fixed and well known values, interest is allowable as a matter of law, from the date of the injury.[104] In

[98] Chap. 42, § 29, 3 & 4 W. 4.

[99] Mayne, On Damages, (7 ed.) p. 174, 176.

[100] Sedwick, Elements of Damages p. 129.

[101] Western, etc., Ry. v. Young, 81 Ga. 397, 7 S. E. 912 (1888); Pittsburg, etc., Ry. v. Taylor, 104 Pa. 306, 49 Am. R. 580 (1883); Texas, etc., Ry. v. Carr, 91 Tex. 332, 43 S. W. 18, (1897); Nichols v. Union Pac. Ry., 7 Utah 570, 27 Pac. 693 (1891); in Wash. & Geo. Ry. v. Hickey, 12 App. (D. C.) 269 (1895);

interest was held allowable on money expended by reason of a personal injury.

[102] Louisville, etc., Ry. v. Wallace, 91 Tenn. 35, 17 S. W. 882, 14 L. R. A. 548 (1891).

[103] King v. Southern Pac. Ry., 109 Cal. 96, 41 Pac. 786, 29 L. R. A. 755 (1895), applying § 3288 of Civil Code; Ell v. Nor. Pac. Ry. 1 N. D. 336, 48 N. W. 222, 12 L. R. A. 97, 26 Am. S. R. 631 (1891) applying § 4578 Comp. Laws.

[104] St. Louis, etc., Ry. v. Lyman,

admiralty cases, the rate allowed in this country is six per cent.[105] In common-law actions, the local rate, at the time and place of the injury, is allowed.[106] Some courts do not recognize this right to interest as one definitely accorded by law, but as one depending upon the circumstances of each case, and thus determinable by the jury.[107]

A third class of cases, according to the prevailing view, includes injuries to property which do not amount to conversion or destruction. Here the jury, in assessing damages, are " to take into account the lapse of time, and put the plaintiff in as good a position in reference to the injury, as if the damages directly resulting from it had been paid immediately." If the circumstances are such as to show that interest at the legal rate is not necessary to fully compensate the plaintiff, the jury can withhold it.[108] In some jurisdictions, the power to give interest in this class of cases is denied to the jury.[109]

Avoidable Damages. The law does not hold even a willful wrongdoer to liability for all the consequences of his misconduct. It compels him to answer only for the proximate result. It casts upon the injured party the duty of using reasonable care and effort to minimize his damages. He is not allowed to " stand by and suffer the injury to continue and increase without reasonable efforts to prevent further loss." [110] If A breaks down B's fence, the latter

57 Ark. 512   22 S. W. 170 (1893); Oviatt v. Pond, 29 Conn. 479 (1861); Wood v. Conn. Pipe Co., 71 Conn. 345, 41 At. 1057, 42 L. R. A. 706, 71 Am. S. R. 207 (1889); Union Pac. Ry. v. Ray, 46 Neb. 750, 65 N. W. 773 (1896); City of Allegheny v. Campbell, 107 Pa. 530 (1884); Walkins v. Junker, 90 Tex. 584, 40 S. W. 11 (1897); Sherwin v. McKie, 51 N. Y. 180 (1872).

[105] The Aleppo, 7 Ben. 120, Fed. Cases No. 158 (1874); The Oregon 89 Fed. 520 (1898); Parquette Habana, 189 U. S. 453, 467, 23 Sup. Ct. 593 (1903).

[106] Machette v. Wamless, 2 Col. 170 (1873); New Dunderburg Co. v. Old, 97 Fed.. 150, 38 C. C. A. 89 (1889); Miller v. Express Propeller Line, 61 N. Y. 313 (1874).

[107] Eddy v. Lafayette, 49 Fed. 807, 4 U. S. App. 247 (1892); Frazer v. Bigelow Carpet Co., 141 Mass. 126, 4 N. E. 620 (1886).

[108] Ainsworth v. Lakim, 180 Mass. 397, 402, 62 N. E. 746 (1902); Wilson v. City of Troy, 135 N. Y. 96, 32 N. E. 44, 18 L. R. A. 449, 31 Am. S. R. 817 (1892); Richards v. Citizens Nat. Gas Co., 130 Pa. 37, 18 At. 600 (1889).

[109] Meyer v. A. & P. Ry., 64 Mo. 542 (1877); New York, etc., Ry. v. Estill, 147 U. S. 591, 622, 13 Sup. Ct. 444, 37 L. Ed. 305 (1893).

[110] Brant v. Gallup, 111 Ill. 487, 53 Am. R. 638 (1888); Simpson v. Keo-

cannot deliberately leave it unrepaired and recover from A the damages caused by cattle which get into his field through the opening. Such damage is too remote. It is the result of B's folly.[111] A person, who is unlawfully ejected from a train, or who is wrongfully prevented from boarding it, is bound to act reasonably, although he has been wronged. If, instead of waiting for the next train, or hiring a conveyance, he walks to his destination in extremely cold weather and injures his health, such injury is chargeable to his imprudence and not to the railroad company's misconduct.[112] Had he hired a conveyance, he would have been bound to act prudently in so doing.[113] In case of personal injury, the victim must exercise reasonable care in mitigating the consequences.[114] He is not bound, however, to engage the services of the most skillful physician;[115] and if he uses ordinary care in employing medical advisers, he is not chargeable with their errors.[116] In the case of willful torts, it

kuk, 34 Ia. 568 (1872). "If the plaintiffs by the use of ordinary diligence and efforts, and at a moderate expense, might have prevented the damages, by filling in the lots near the ally, it seems to follow that their negligence contributed to the injury."

[111] Loker v. Damon, 17 Pick. (34 Mass.) 284, 288 (1835). "So if one throw a stone and break a window, the cost of repairing the window is the ordinary measure of damages. But if the owner suffers the window to remain without repairing a great length of time after notice of the fact, and his furniture, or pictures, or other valuable articles sustain damage, this damage would be too remote."

[112] Ind. B. & W. Ry. v. Birney, 71 Ill. 391 (1847); Bader v. Southern Pac. Ry. 52 La Ann. 1060, 27 So. 584 (1900).

[113] LeBanche v. Lon. & N. W. Ry. 1 C. P. D. 286, 45 L. J. C. P. 521 (1876). "The question then is, whether, according to the ordinary habits of society, a gentleman in the position of the plaintiff, who was going to Scarborough for the purpose of amusement, and who missed his train at York, would take a special train at York to Scarborough at his own cost, in order that he might arrive at Scarborough an hour and a half sooner than he would do if he waited at York for the next train."

[114] Fullerton v. Fordyce, 144 Mo. 519, 44 S. W. 1053 (1898); Sullivan v. Tioga Ry., 112 N. Y. 643, 20 N. E. 569, 8 Am. S. R. 793 (1899); Salladay v. Dodgeville, 85 Wis. 318, 55 N. W. 696, 20 L. R. A. 541 (1893).

[115] Selleck v. Jamesville, 100 Wis. 157, 75 N. W. 975, 41 L. R. A. 563, 69 Am. S. R. 906 (1898).

[116] McGarrahan, v. N. Y., etc., Ry., 171 Mass. 211, 50 N. E. 610 (1898); Reed v. Detriot, 108 Mich. 224, 65 N. W. 967 (1896); New York, etc., Co.v. Bennett, 62 N. J. L. 742, 42 At. 759 (1899); Sauter v. N. Y. C. Ry., 66 N. Y. 50, 23 Am. R. 18 (1876).

has been held that ordinary negligence on the part of the victim will not bar a recovery.[117]

The Functions of Court and Jury. To the court belongs the power of announcing and explaining the rule of law relating to damages in a particular case, while to the jury belongs the power of determining the facts. If the evidence is undisputed and warrants but one inference, the court may properly direct the jury to find a verdict in accordance with that inference. Accordingly, when a plaintiff, injured by the defendant's negligence, asks damages for loss of time, while confined to his house, but offers no evidence showing the character or extent of such damages, the court should direct the jury to bring in a verdict for nominal damages only.[118] When the evidence is undisputed, it is also a question for the court whether the plaintiff is entitled to exemplary damages or to compensatory damages.[119] And, generally, it is the duty of the court to state the rule which the jury are to apply in fixing the damages in the case before them.[120]

Amount of Damages is Ordinarily for the Jury. While the amount of damages in a particular case is generally left to the discretion of a jury, their power, even here, is not arbitrary. It is subject to considerable supervision by the court. For a time after the institution of trial by jury was established, the answer of a jury to the question of damages appears to have been final,[121] especially in cases of trespass to property, where the facts were within the personal knowledge of the jurors;[122] or of defamation, where the injury sustained depended much upon the quality of the persons and the

---

[117] Chicago, etc., Co. v. Meech, 163 Ill. 305, 45 N. E. 290 (1896); Galveston, etc., Ry. v. Zantzinger, 92 Tex. 365, 48 S. W. 563, 44 L. R. A. 553, 71 Am. S. R. 859 (1898).

[118] Leeds v. Met. Gas Light Co., 90 N. Y. 26 (1882).

[119] Louisville, etc., Ry. v. Fox, 11 Bush. (74 Ky.) 495, 516 (1876); Spokane Truck Co. v. Hoefer, 2 Wash. 45; 25 Pac. 1072 (1891); Ward v. Blackwood, 41 Ark. 295 (1883); Goldsmith's Adm'r. v. Joy, 61 Vt. 488; 17 At. 1010 (1889).

[120] Balt. & Ohio Ry. v. Carr, 71 Md. 135, 17 At. 1052 (1889); Knight v. Egerton, 7 Exch. 407 (1852).

[121] Sedgwick, Elements of Damages p. 2. Sedwick On Damages, (8th Ed.) § 1316.

[122] Delves v. Wyer, 1 Brownl. 204 (1605); the jury assessed the damages at £40 for cropping 200 pear trees and 100 apple trees, and the court said it could not diminish the "damages in trespass which was local and therefore could not appear to them."

local situation.[123]   But it is to be borne in mind that " courts existed before juries," and have never " allotted all questions of fact to the jury." [124]   Accordingly, when the matter of damages depends on a " cause which appears in sight of the court, so that they may judge of it as in mayhem, etc.; "[125] or upon undisputed evidence, which shows that if the plaintiff is entitled to recover anything he is entitled to recover a specific sum, or a sum much larger than the jury have awarded, the court has the right to set aside the verdict.[126]

At present, therefore, the jury have not unlimited authority over the assessment of damages.   As early as 1695, Lord Holt, in setting aside a verdict for £2,000 damages for false imprisonment, said: " The jury were very shy of giving a reason of their verdict, thinking they have an absolute, despotic power; but I did rectify that mistake, for the jury are to try causes with the assistance of the judges, and ought to give reasons when required, that if they go upon any mistake they may be set right." [127]   Accordingly, if the verdict is the result of casting lots, or of any other improper practice; [128] or if the jury have refused to apply the measure of damages properly stated to them by the court,[129] or if their verdict shows that they adopted an erroneous theory of liability,[130] or that their

[123] Hawkins v. Sciet, Palmer, 314 (1622). In this case the court at first reduced the damages from £150 to £50, " but afterwards on great consideration revoked this and resolved to leave such matters to the jury." Lord Townsend v. Hughes, 2 Mod. 150 (1677). Verdict for £4,000 was left undisturbed.

[124] Thayer, "Law and Fact in Jury Trials," 4 Harv. L. Rev. 147; Cases on Evidence Ch. I, Sec. VI.

[125] Hawkins v. Sciet, Palmer 314 (1622).

[126] Richards v. Sanford, 2 E. D. Smith (N. Y.) 349 (1854); verdict for $10.00 was set aside and new trial ordered, unless defendant would consent to its being raised to $100.00; Phillips v. Lon., etc., Ry., 5 C. P. D. 78 (1874); verdict for £7,000 was set aside as inadequate, the evidence showing that the plaintiff as a physician had been earning from £6,000 to £7,000 a year and was incapacitated for life. On a second trial, the verdict was for £16,000, and the court refused to disturb it, as being excessive: Carter v. Wells, Fargo & Co., 64 Fed. 1005 (1894).

[127] Ash v. Lady Ash, Com. 357; plaintiff was confined two or three hours and forced to take physic.

[128] Mellish v.   Burnb. 51 (1719); verdict set aside because " jury threw up cross or pile for £300 or £500." Falvey v. Stanford L. R. 10 Q. B. 54, 44 L. J. Q. B. 7 (1874).

[129] Limburg v. Germ. Fire. Ins. Co., 90 Ia. 709; 57 N. W. 626 (1894).

[130] Louisville, etc., Ry. v. Minogue, 90 Ky. 369, 14 S. W. 357 (1890); Moseley v. Jamieson, 68 Miss. 336

minds were influenced by some improper motives or feelings or bias,[131] the court has the power and will not hesitate to set the verdict aside, unless the prevailing party assents to its reasonable modification.

Damages not to be Split Up.   The victim of a tort is not allowed to bring a separate suit for each item of damage which results from a single wrongdoing. " It is ofr the public good that there be an end of litigation," is an ancient and honored maxim of the common law.[132]   Accordingly, in a suit for personal injuries, the plaintiff not only may claim prospective damages, in addition to those already developed, but must claim them then, if he would recover them at all.[133]   So, if the action is brought for injury to property, the plaintiff must unite all the items of damage both present and prospective.[134]

Thus far, there is no difference of opinion and no difficulty.   But suppose a single tortious act of the defendant invades distinct legal rights of the plaintiff,—does the common-law maxim apply?   Is the plaintiff bound to bring a single action for all the damages suffered?   The answers are discordant.   In England, and in some of our jurisdictions, the courts declare that the single act may result in more than one tort.   If it causes harm to the plaintiff's person and also to his property, he has two causes of action, although the several injuries are inflicted at the same moment.   His right to personal security, it is said, is wholly distinct from his right of property,[135]

(1890)).   Church v. Ottawa, 25 Ont. R. 298 (1894).

[131] Thurston v. Martin, 5 Mason (U. S.), 497 (1830).

[132] Wichita, etc., Ry. v. Beebe, 39 Ks. 465, 18 Pac. 502 (1888).

[133] Fetter v. Veal, 1 Salk. 11, 12 Mod. 542 1 Ld. Raymond, 339; (1703); recovery had been had for assault and battery. Upon reopening of wound, second action was brought but held not to lie; Hodsoll v. Stallebrass, 11 Ad. & E. 301, 3 P. & D. 200, 9 C. & P. 63 (1839); Fox v. St. John, 23 New Bruns. 244 (1883); Stodghill v. Chic., etc., Ry., 53 Ia. 341; 5 N. W. 495 (1880);

Howell v. Goodrich, 69 Ill. 556 (1873); Richmond Gas. Co. v. Baker, 146 Ind. 600; 45 N. E. 1049, 36 L. R. A. 683 (1897); Kansas, etc., Ry. v. Mihlman, 17 Ks. 224 (1876); Thompson v. Ellsworth, 39 Mich. 719 (1878); Warner v. Bacon, 8 Gray, (74 Mass.) 397 (1857); Filer v. N. Y. C. Ry., 49 N. Y. 42 (1872); Goodhart v. Penn. Ry. 177 Pa. 1; 35 At. 191 (1896); Whitney v. Clarendon, 18 Vt. 252 (1846).

[134] Wheeler Savings Bank v. Tracy, 141 Mo. 252, 42 S. W. 446; 64 Am. S. R. 505 (1897), and cases cited in preceding note.

[135] Brunsden v. Humphrey, 14 Q.

and "the essential difference between an injury to the person and an injury to property makes it impracticable, or at least very inconvenient in the administration of justice, to blend the two." [136]

This view seems to the writer correct. It must be admitted, however, that the weight of judicial decision and *dicta* in this country is opposed to it. According to these authorities, "the cause of action consists of the wrongful act which produced the effect, rather than in the effect of the act in its application to different primary rights; and the injury to the person and property, as a result of the original cause, gives rise to different items of damage." [137]

§ 4. Local Actions for Tort.

Early Law : Modern Doctrine. Originally, all actions at common law were local, because the issue of fact in every common-law action was to be tried by a jury of the vicinage. This rule was modified by degrees, until the modern doctrine was established, "that actions are deemed transitory when the transactions on which they are founded might have taken place anywhere; but are local when their cause is in its nature necessarily local." [138] The most common example of a local action for tort is that of trespass to land. As this tort can occur only in the country where the land is situated,

B. D. 141, 53 L. J. Q. B. 476, 51 L. T. R. 529, 31 A. L. J. 329 (1884); Watson v. Tex., etc., Ry., 8 Tex. C. App. 144, 27 S. W. 924 (1894).

[136] Reilly v. Sicilian Asphalt Co., 170 N. Y. 40, 62 N. E. 772, 88 Am. S. R. 636, 57 L. R. A. 176 (1902). In this case, stress was laid upon the fact that different periods of limitation apply to the two injuries; that the right of action for injury to property is assignable, and that for injury to person is not; that the former is seizable by creditors and would pass to an assignee in bankruptcy, while the latter is not seizable and would not pass. This decision overruled S. C. in 31 App. Div. 302, 52 N. Y. Supp. 817 1898).

[137] King v. Chic., etc., Ry., 80 Minn. 83, 82 N. W. 1113, 81 Am. S. R. 238, 50 L. R. A. 161, with note (1900); Segar v. Bookbamsted, 22 Conn. 295 (1853). Cf. Boerum v. Taylor, 19 Conn. 122 (1848), holding that plaintiff had two distinct causes of action against defendant for putting poison in rum; one for spoiling the rum, and another for injury to the plaintiff from drinking the rum; Doran v. Cohen, 147 Mass. 342, 17 N. E. 647 (1888); Hatchell v .Kimbrough, 4 Jones L. (N. C.) 163 (1856); Cox v. Crumley, 5 Lea (Tenn.), 529 (1880); Hazzard Powder Co. v. Volger, 3 Wyo. 189, 18 Pac. 636 (1888).

[138] Livingston v. Jefferson, 1 Brock. (U. S. C. C.) 203, 209 (1811).

the action must be brought there. The court of no other country has jurisdiction of the cause of action. Although it is admitted that this doctrine is highly technical, and, at times, works a hardship to the injured party, it is still maintained in England and in most of our States.[139]

Applying this doctrine, it has been held that an action for cutting and tapping trees is local, but one for slander of title to the land on which the trees stood is transitory.[140] An action for the conversion of timber which has been cut, or of oysters which have been taken "from their beds," is transitory.[141] It has been held that an action for damages caused by a nuisance may be brought in the jurisdiction where it is situated, although the damages are inflicted in a different jurisdiction.[142] If, however, the action is for injury to the land, the suit is to be brought there, although the act causing the injury, such as the diversion of a stream, takes place in another state.[143]

§ 5. CONFLICT OF LAWS IN TRANSITORY ACTIONS.

What Actions are Transitory. For torts of a personal character, the victim is not limited to a local action. His right to a remedy is transitory, accompanying him into other "venues" of the same country, and oftentimes into foreign jurisdictions.[144] In case he seeks redress in another country from that in which the injury was inflicted, various questions in the conflict of laws may arise. We shall not be able to discuss these questions with fullness in this connection, but must be content with stating the leading

[139] Doulson v. Matthews, 4 D. & E. 503 (1792); British South Africa Co. v. Companhia de Mocambique (1893), A. C. 602, 63 L. J. Q. B. 70, 69 L. T. 604; Allen v. Conn. Ry. Co., 150 Mass. 560, 23 N. E. 581, 6 L. R. A. 416 (1890); Watts v. Kinney, 23 Wend. (N. Y.) 485, 6 Hill, 82 (1840); Cragin v. Lovell, 88 N. Y. 258 (1882); Ellenwood v. Marietta Co., 158 U. S. 105, 15 Sup. Ct. 771, 39 L. Ed. 913 (1895); Niles v. Howe, 57 Vt. 388 (1885).

[140] Dodge v. Colby, 108 N. Y. 445, 15 N. E. 703 (1888).

[141] Makely v. A. Boothe Co., 129 N. C. 11, 39 S. E. 582 (1901).

[142] Rundle v. Del. & Raritan C. Co., 1 Wall. Jr. (U. S. C. C.) 275 (1849).

[143] Thayer v. Brooks, 17 Ohio, 489, 49 Am. Dec. 474 (1848).

[144] In Rafael v. Vevelst, 2 W. Bl. 1055, 1058 (1776), De Gray, C. J., said, "Crimes are in their nature local, and the jurisdiction of crimes is local. And so as to the rights of real property, the subject being fixed and immovable. But personal injuries are of a transitory nature, and *sqeuuntur forum rei*."

principles applicable to such cases, referring the reader to treatises upon the conflict of laws, for more detailed information.

A Tort by Lex Loci and Lex Fori. When the wrong complained of is an actionable tort by the law of both jurisdictions, the suit will be sustained by any competent tribunal which has obtained jurisdiction of the defendant's person. This rule has been adopted as a matter of international comity and with a view to promote justice.[145] In this class of cases, the only question of difficulty relates to the measure of damages. Upon principle it would seem that this is determinable by the law of the place where the injury is done;[146] unless the *lex fori* limits the recovery to a fixed sum.[147]

Injury which is not Tortious by the Lex Loci. If the act complained of was not wrongful by the law of the place where it occurred, it will not be actionable in any other jurisdiction, although had the act occurred in the latter country it would have constituted a tort.[148] "If no cause or right of action for which redress may be had exists in the country where the personal injury was received, then there is no cause of action to travel with the person claimed to be in fault, which may be enforced in the State where he may be found."[149]

In England, however, it is held that if the act is wrongful by the *lex loci,* although not remediable in a civil action *ex delicto,* but only

[145] Mexican Nat. Ry. v. Jackson, 89 Tex. 107, 37 S. W. 861, 31 L. R. A. 276, 59 Am. St. R. 28 (1896); Williams v. Pope Mfg. Co., 52 La. Ann. 1417, 27 So. 851, 50 L. R. A. 816 (1900); Morisette v. Canadian Pac. Ry., 76 Vt.—, At. 1102 (1904).

[146] Pullman Car Co. v. Lawrence, 74 Miss. 782, 22 So. 53 (1897). But see Carson v. Smith, 133 Mo. 606, 34 S. W. 855 (1896).

[147] Wooden v. Western, etc., Ry., 126 N. Y. 10, 26 N. E. 1050, 13 L. R. A. 458, 22 Am. St. R. 803 (1891).

[148] Carter v. Goode, 50 Ark. 155, 6 S. W. 719 (1887); shooting a trespassing mule was not a tort in the Indian Territory, under the circumstances; Le Forest v. Tolman, 117 Mass. 109, 19 Am. R. 400 (1875), action in Massachusetts, under statute of that State, for injury done by a dog in New Hampshire, where no such statute was shown to exist, and the common law did not give the right of action. (Such statute does now exist in New Hampshire; Chickering v. Lord, 67 N. H. 555, 32 Atl. 773 (1893), applying Pub. St. Ch. 118, § 10); Smith v. Condry, 1 How. (U. S.) 28 (1843); Beacham v. Portsmouth Bridge, 68 N. H. 382, 40 Atl 1066 (1896); Phillips v. Eyre, L. R. 6 Q. B. 1, 40 L. J. Q. B. 28 (1870).

[149] McLeod v. Conn., etc., Ry., 58 Vt. 727, 6 At. 648 (1886).

by a criminal proceeding, it will support a tort action, if it amounts to a tort by the *lex fori*. This decision proceeds upon the theory that to support a tort action in England for an act committed abroad, two conditions must concur: First, the act must have been of such a character that it would have been actionable if it had been committed in England. Second, it must not have been justifiable by the law of the place where it was done.[150]

It is to be noted that if the plaintiff brings his action for a common-law tort, he need not allege that the wrong is actionable under the statutes or laws of the State where the wrong was inflicted. The common-law rule will be presumed to obtain there,[151] if the legal system is based upon the common law. While, if he sues for a statutory tort, he must allege and prove the statute.[152]

Injury Which is not Tortious by the Lex Fori. The English courts refuse to entertain a suit for the redress of such an injury.[153] In this country, however, it may be prosecuted, unless its primary object is the enforcement of a penal statute, or unless it is deemed by the courts repugnant to justice or to good morals, or calculated to injure the State where the action is brought, or its citizens.[154] This rule has been most frequently applied in suits

[150] Machado v. Fontes (1897), 2 Q. B. 231. See Ewey v. Mex. C. Ry., 52 U. S. App. 118, 81 Fed. 294, 38 L. R. A. 387 (1897).

[151] Whitford v. Panama Ry. Co., 23 N. Y. 465, 468 (1861); Ill. Cen. Ry. Co. v. Kuhn, 107 Tenn. 106, 64 S. W. 202 (1901).

[152] Kahl v. Memphis, etc., Ry., 95 Ala. 337, 10 So. 661 (1891); Le Forest v. Tolman, 117 Mass. 109, 19 Am. R. 400 (1875).

[153] The Halley L. R., 2 P. C. 193, 37 L. J. Ad. 33 (1868), holding a shipowner not liable in England, for the negligence of pilot whom he was obliged to employ in Belgium.

[154] Higgins v. Cent., etc., Ry., 155 Mass. 176, 29 N. E. 534, 31 Am. S. R. 544, (1892), distinguishing Richardson v. N. Y. C. Ry., 98 Mass. 85 (1867), and Davis v. N. Y. & N. E. Ry., 143 Mass. 301, 58 Am. R. 138 (1887), the latter dealing with a penal statute of Conn.; Wooden v. Western, etc., Ry., 126 N. Y. 10, 26 N. E. 1050, 13 L. R. A. 458, 22 Am. S. R. 803 (1891); Williams v. Pope Mfg. Co., 52 La. Ann. 1417, 27 So. 851 (1900); Herrick v. Minn., etc., Ry., 31 Minn. 11, 16 N. W. 413, 47 Am. R. 771 (1883); Chicago, etc., Ry. v. Doyle, 60 Miss. 977 (1883); Knight v. West Jersey Ry., 108 Pa. 250, 56 Am. R. 200 (1885); Huntington v. Attrill, 146 U. S. 657, 13 Sup. Ct. 224, 36 L. Ed. 1123 (1892); Mexican Nat. Ry. v. Slater, 115 Fed. 593, 53 C. C. App. 239 (1902), affirmed 194 U. S. 920, 24 Sup. Ct. 581 (1904). See dissenting opinion of Fuller, C. J.

for wrongful death. Such actions did not lie at common law. For a time after the enactment of statutes, following Lord Campbell's Act in England,[155] courts of States, where the common law had not been changed, were disposed to exclude suitors whose cause of action arose under a statute of this sort.[156] At present, however, the tendency is to view these statutes as remedial—as " simply taking away a common-law obstacle to recovery for an admitted tort "—and to permit suits for such torts to be brought in any jurisdiction.[157]

Defenses Generally Depend Upon the Lex Loci. This rule follows logically from the principles stated above. A cause of action may have come into existence, but may have been destroyed by subsequent legislation in the place where it arose;[158] or by the operation of well-established rules of law, as in case of the death of the person to whom it belonged.[159] A vested right of defense, it is declared, is a property right, and available to its owner wherever he may be sued.[160] Accordingly, whether the defendant was negligent in a particular situation, and whether the plaintiff was guilty of contributory negligence;[161] whether plaintiff had assumed the risk of the peril which resulted in his injury;[162] whether the negli-

---

[155] *Infra*, Chap. VI.

[156] Richardson v. N. Y. C. Ry., 98 Mass. 85 (1867); Taylor v. Penn. Co., 78 Ky. 348, 39 Am. R. 244 (1880); Woodard v. Mich. So. Ry., 10 Oh. St. 121 (1859).

[157] Dennick v. Central Ry., 103 U. S. 11, 26 L. Ed. 439 (1880); Stewart v. B. & O. Ry., 168 U. S. 445, 18 Sup. Ct. 105, 42 L. Ed. 537 (1897); Bruce v. Cin. Ry., 83 Ky. 174 (1885); Louisville & N. Ry. v. Whitlow, 105 Ky. 1, 43 S. W. 711, 41 L. R. A. 614 (1898).

[158] Phillips v. Eyre, L. R. 6 Q. B. 1, 40 L. J. Q. B. 28 (1870). Cf. Sawyer v. Davis, 136 Mass. 239 (1884).

[159] Higgins v. Cent. Ry. of N. E., 155 Mass. 176, 29 N. E. 534, 31 Am. S. R. 544 (1892); O'Reilly v. N. Y., etc., Ry., 16 R. I. 388, 17 At. 171,

906, 19 At. 244, 5 L. R. A. 364, 6 L. R. A. 719 (1899); " after a cause of action has become extinct where it accrued, it cannot survive elsewhere; " and the law of the place where it accrues determines whether it survives or is assignable, or not.

[160] Pritchard v. Norton, 106 U. S. 124, 1 Sup. Ct. 102, 27 L. Ed. 104 (1882); Hovey v. Elliott, 167 U. S. 409, 17 Sup. Ct. 841, 42 L. Ed. 215 (1896); Bal. & O. Ry. v. Reed, 158 Ind. 25, 62 N. E. 488 (1902).

[161] Louisville & N. Ry. v. Harmon (Ky.), 64 S. W. 640 (1901); Bridger v. Ashville Ry., 27 S. C. 456, 3 S. E. 860, 13 Am. S. R. 653 (1886).

[162] Northern Pac. Ry. v. Babcock, 154 U. S. 190, 14 Sup. Ct. 978, 38 L. Ed. 958 (1894).

gent actor was plaintiff's fellow-servant,[163] and similar questions,
are to be answered by the law of the place where the injury was
inflicted.

§ 6. INDEMNITY BETWEEN WRONGDOERS.

If Free from Fault. We have seen that a master or principal, who has been compelled to pay damages to a third person,
because of his servant's or agent's misconduct, is entitled to indemnity from his wrongdoing representative, if he is himself free from
actual fault.[164] Accordingly, if a railroad company is forced to
pay a passenger for a trunk, lost through the negligence of one of
its baggage masters, it is " entitled to reimbursement at the hands of
the baggage master for the amount which it had paid out." [165] This
principle applies to all cases where one person is liable in tort, as a
constructive wrongdoer only, for the actual tortious misconduct of
another. The fact that they are technically joint tort-feasors does
not prevent the morally innocent one from obtaining indemnity from
the actual wrongdoer.[166]

Indemnity to Agent or Servant. This principle operates,
at times, to secure the agent or servant indemnity from his master
or principal. " Every man, who employs another to do an act which
the employer appears to have a right to authorize him to do, under-

---

[163] Baltimore & O. Ry. v. Reed,
158 Ind. 25, 62 N. E. 488 (1902);
Turner v. St. Clair Tunnel Co., 111
Mich. 578, 70 N. W. 146, 36 L. R. A.
134, 66 Am. S. R. 397 (1897); Rick
v. Saginaw Co.,   Mich.   , 93
N. W. 632 (1903); Ill. Cen. Ry. v.
Harris (Miss.), 29 So. 760 (1901);
Alexander v. Penn. Co., 48 Ohio St.
623, 30 N. E. 70 (1891).

[164] *Supra*, p. 184.

[165] Georgia So. Ry. v. Jossey, 105
Ga. 271, 31 S. E. 179 (1898).

[166] Chesapeake & O. Co. v. County
Comm'rs, 57   Md. 201, 40 Am. R.
430 (1881); Boston v. Worthington,
10 Gray (76 Mass.) 496, 71 Am. Dec.
678 (1858); Westfield v. Mayo, 122
Mass. 100, 23 Am. R. 292 (1877);

Boston & M. Ry. v. Sargeant, 70 N.
H. 299, 47 At. 605 (1900); s. c. again
in — N. H. —, 57 At. 688 (1904);
Boston & M. Ry. v. Brackett, 71
N. H. 494, 53 At. 304 (1902); " It is
only when the party, who is in fault
as to the person injured, is without fault as to the party whose actual negligence is the cause of the
injury, that recovery over can be
had; " Brooklyn v. Brooklyn, etc.,
Ry., 47 N. Y. 475, 7 Am. R. 469
(1872); Gulf, etc., Ry. v. Galveston,
etc., Ry., 83 Tex. 509, 18 S. W. 956
(1892); City of San Antonio v.
Smith, 94 Tex. 266, 59 S. W. 1109
(1900); Culmer v. Wilson, 13 Utah,
129, 44 Pac. 833, 57 Am. S. R. 713
(1896).

takes to indemnify him for all such acts as would be lawful, if the employer had the authority he pretends to have." [167]   The principle has been invoked to secure indemnity, where the plaintiff has been led, by the defendant's misrepresentation of facts, to believe that a course of action was lawful, where it was in truth unlawful.[168]

If not Free from Blame.   Cases of the kind last referred to can rarely occur, for there can be no " valid claim to indemnity where the doer of the act which constitutes the offense has done it with knowledge of all the circumstances necessary to constitute the act an offense, but in ignorance that the act done under those circumstances constituted an offense.   A man is presumed to know the law." [169]   *A fortiori*, whenever the plaintiff has intentionally committed a tort in connection with or for the benefit of another, the courts will not entertain an action in his behalf for indemnity against the other, but leave him where his wrongful act places him.[170]

§ 7.   Contribution Between Wrongdoers.

When Wrong-Doing is Intentional.   This is never allowed wherever the plaintiff's wrongdoing was deliberate and intentional. One who intends to violate the law, or even to do an act which the law conclusively presumes that he knew was wrongful, will be left where his act places him.   Towards him the law imposes no obligation of contribution upon his fellow tort-feasor.[171]

Where no Wrongful Intent.   It often happens, however, that persons join in performing an act which they honestly believe

---

[167] Best, J., in Adamson v. Jarvis, 4 Bing. 66, 72, 29 R. R. 503, 12 Moore, 241 (1827).   In this case, the plaintiff, an auctioneer, to whom defendant had delivered cattle for sale, was obliged to pay to their true owner for their conversion, £1100 damages, £95 costs, and to pay £500 for his own expenses in the action.   He sued for and recovered these sums as damages; Moore v. Appleton, 26 Ala. 633 (1855).

[168] Burrows v. Rhodes (1899), 1 Q. B. 816, 68 L. J. Q. B. 545.   Plaintiff claimed £3000 damages for being induced to take part in the Jameson raid into the South African Re-

public.   Cf.   Simpson v. Mercer, 144 Mass. 413, 11 N. E. 720 (1887).

[169] Kennedy, J., in last cited English case.   See comments on this case in 15 Law Quar. Rev. 236.   Cf. Cumston v. Lambert, 18 Ohio, 81, 51 Am. Dec. 442 (1849).

[170] Nelson v. Cook, 17 Ill. 443 (1856); Culmer v. Wilson, 13 Utah, 129, 44 Pac. 833, 57 Am. St. R. 713 (1896).

[171] Upton v. Times-Democrat, 104 Al. 141, 143, 28 So. 970, 971 (1900); Becker v. Farwell, 25 Ill. App. 432 (1887); Sutton v. Morris, 102 Ky. 613, 44 S. W. 127 (1898); Johnson v. Torpy, 35 Neb. 604, 53 N. W. 575,

to be lawful, but which turns out to be an invasion of the rights of some third party, who sues one of the tort-feasors to judgment and collects the entire damages from him. In this country, there is no doubt that he is entitled to contribution from those who joined him in the wrongdoing.[172] The same rule applies between negligent, as distinguished from willful, tort-feasors.[173] Such is the rule in Scotland.[174] Torts of the kind involved in these cases are, as we have seen,[175] known as *quasi delicts* in Scotch law, and are sharply distinguished from delicts, or intentional torts. In England it is not clear whether the right of contribution exists in this class of torts. The rule laid down in the leading case of Merryweather v. Nixan,[176] seems to negative the right, as does a recent case in the Probate Division.[177] The views of text writers upon this point are not in accord.[178]

---

37 Am. S. R. 447 (1892); Torpy v. Johnson, 43 Neb. 882, 62 N. W. 253, 61 Am. S. R. 267; Cumston v. Lambert, 18 Ohio 81, 51 Am. Dec. 442 (1849); Boyer v. Bolender, 129 Pa. 324, 18 At. 127, 14 Am. S. R. 723 (1889); Spalding v. Oakes, 42 Vt. 343 (1869); plaintiff and defendant were joint owners of a vicious animal.

[172] Vandiver v. Pollak, 97 Ala. 467, 12 So. 473, 19 L. R. A. 628 (1893); s. c. again, 107 Ala. 547, 19 So. 180, 54 Am. S. R. 118 (1895); Bailey v. Bussing, 28 Conn. 455 (1859); Farwell v. Becker, 129 Ill. 261, 21 N. E. 792, 16 Am. S. R. 267, 6 L. R. A. 400 (1889); Ankeny v. Moffet, 37 Minn. 109, 33 N. W. 320 (1887); Achison v. Miller, 2 Ohio St. 203, 59 Am. Dec. 663 (1855); Bartle v. Nutt, 4 Pet. (U. S.) 184, 7 L. Ed. 825 (1830).

[173] Nickerson v. Wheeler, 118 Mass. 295 (1875); Ankeney v. Moffet, 37 Minn. 109, 33 N. W. 320 (1887); Armstrong Co. v. Clarion Co., 66 Pa. 218, 5 Am. R. 368 (1870).

[174] Palmer v. Wick, etc., Co. (1894),

A. C. 318, 71 L. T. 163, 6 R. 245.

[175] *Supra*, Chap. 1.

[176] 8 D. & E. 186, 16 R. R. 810 (1799). See criticism of this case in 17 Law Quar. Rev. 293.

[177] The Englishman and the Australia (1895), P. 212, 64 L. J. P. 74.

[178] Pollock on Torts (6th Ed.), pp. 196, 197: " A negligent wrong-doer has no claim to contribution or indemnity," but the author thinks such claim should be allowed between persons undertaking in concert to abate an obstruction to a supposed highway, but who find themselves adjudged to be trespassers. He adds: " I cannot find, however, that any decision has been given on facts of this kind." Clerk & Lindsell on Torts (2d Ed.) p. 56n; " It is submitted that the view (in The Englishman and the Australia (1895), P. 212) cannot be supported." These writers seem to treat Palmer v. Wick, etc., Co. (1894), A. C. 318, as establishing a rule for England, as well as announcing a rule of Scotch law.

CHAPTER VI.

DISCHARGE OF TORTS.

By Act of Parties. A cause of action for a tort may be discharged either by the act of the parties, or by the operation of law. The most frequent examples of the first species of discharge are afforded by contracts between the parties, by waiver on the part of the injured person or by satisfaction of judgment on the part of the wrongdoer. The principal examples of the second species of discharge are connected with the death of one of the parties, or with the statute of limitations.

Discharge by Contract. To a considerable extent, the law permits parties to contract in advance, that certain conduct by one, causing harm to the other, shall not be an actionable tort, although, but for the contract, the law would treat it as such. Thus, by contract with the shipper, a common carrier may relieve himself from tort liability for the loss of freight by accidental fire.[1] And we have seen, in a former connection, that a servant may contract to take the risks of employment, which the law does not cast upon him, as well as exempt the master from duties of care which are imposed by common law.[2] On the other hand, parties are not absolutely free to contract for exemption from tort liability. In the case of servants, we have seen that legislation has limited very much the

---

[1] Constable v. Nat. Steamship Co., 154 U. S. 51, 14 Sup. Ct. 1032, 38 L. Ed. 903 (1894); Davis v. Cent. Vt. Ry., 66 Vt. 290, 29 At. 313, 44 Am. S. R. 852 (1893). Cf. Stephens v. So. Pac. Co., 109 Cal. 86, 41 Pac. 783, 50 Am. S. R. 17, 29 L. R. A. 751 (1895); Griswold v. Ill. Cent. Ry., 90 Ia. 265, 57 N. W. 843, 24 L. R. A. 647 (1892); Hartford Fire Ins. Co. v. Chic., M., etc., Ry., 70 Fed. 201, 30 L. R. A. 193, 36 U. S. App. 152, 17 C. C. A. 62 (1895).

[2] *Supra*, Chap. iv. Fulton, etc., Mills, v. Wilson, 89 Ga. 318, 15 S. E. 322 (1892); New v. Southern Ry. 116 Ga. 147, 42 S. E. 391 (1902); Pittsburg, etc., Ry. v. Mahoney, 148 Ind. 196, 47 N. E. 464, 40 L. R. A. 101, 62 Am. S. R. 503 (1897).

freedom of contract for the master's exemption.[3] And in the case of carriers, considerations of public policy have led most courts to pronounce invalid most contracts exempting them from liability for their own negligence.[4] Similar considerations have induced decisions annulling other contracts for exemption from the defendant's own negligence, or of those for whom he is personally responsible.[5] Even when contracts exempting tort-feasors from liability are valid, the tendency of the courts is to construe them strictly, and to put upon the wrongdoer the burden of showing that his tort comes within the contract provisions.[6]

Agreement Subsequent to the Tort. After a cause of action has accrued to a person, he is not bound to enforce it. Subject to the rights of his creditors, or of those having a legal interest in his claim, he is free to settle it upon such terms as suit him.[7] If he is capable of binding himself by contract,[8] he may discharge the wrongdoer from tort liability by an agreement upon a valuable consideration, provided it is free from fraud or undue influence.[9]

[3] *Supra*, Chap. iv. Kansas, etc., Ry. v. Peavey, 29 Kas. 169, 44 Am. R. 630 (1883).

[4] Railroad Co. v. Lockwood, 17 Wall. (U. S.) 357, 21 L. Ed. 627 (1873); The New England, 110 Fed. 415 (1901); Louisville & N. Ry. v. Grant, 99 Ala. 325, 13 So. 599 (1892); Welch v. Boston & A. Ry., 41 Conn. 333 (1874); Candee v. N. Y. & H. Ry., 73 Conn. 667, 49 At. 17 (1901); Wabash Ry. v. Brown, 152 Ill. 484, 39 N. E. 273 (1894); Adams Ex. Co. v. Harris, 120 Ind. 73, 21 N. E. 340, 7 L. R. A. 214, 16 Am. S. R. 315 (1889); Louisville & N. Ry. v. Owen, 93 Ky. 201, 19 S. W. 590, 7 L. R. A. 214 (1892); Atchison, etc., Ry. v. Lawler, 40 Neb. 356, 58 N. W. 968 (1894); Willock v. Penn. Ry., 166 Pa. 184, 30 At. 948, 45 Am. S. R. 674, 27 L. R. A. 228 (1895); Missouri Pac. v. Ivy, 71 Tex. 409, 9 S. W. 346, 10 Am. S. R. 758, 1 L. R. A. 500 (1888).

[5] Railway Co. v. Spangler, 44 Ohio St. 471, 8 N. E. 467, 58 Am. R. 833 (1886); Johnson's Adm'x v. Richmond, etc., Ry., 86 Va. 975, 11 S. E. 829 (1890).

[6] St. Louis, etc., Ry. v. Weakly, 50 Ark. 397, 8 S. W. 134, 7 Am. S. R. 104 (1887); Wabash, etc., Ry. v. Brown, 152 Ill. 484, 39 N. E. 273 (1894); Adams Ex. Co. v. Harris, 120 Ind. 73, 21 N. E. 340, 7 L. R. A. 214, 16 Am. S. R. 315 (1889); Baltimore & O. Ry. v. Brady, 32 Md. 333 (1868); Brewer v. New York, etc., Ry., 124 N. Y. 59, 26 N. E. 324, 21 Am. S. R. 647, 11 L. R. A. 483 (1891); Jennings v. Grand Trunk Ry., 127 N. Y. 438, 28 N. E. 394 (1891).

[7] Shaw v. Chic., etc., Ry., 82 Ia. 199, 47 N. W. 1004 (1891).

[8] Gibson v. Western N. Y. Ry., 164 Pa. 142, 30 At. 308, 33 Am. S. R. 586 (1894); Missouri Pac. Ry. v. Brazzil, 72 Tex. 233, 10 S. W. 403 (1888).

[9] Pederson v. Seattle, etc., Ry., 6 Wash. 202, 33 Pac. 351, 34 Pac. 665

Even a voidable agreement may be validated by his subsequent ratification.[10] Hence, a wrongdoer may successfully plead in bar of an action for the tort, a compromise,[11] or an accord and satisfaction,[12] provided the latter has been executed.[13]

At common law a release under seal, if free from fraud, operates to discharge a cause of action for which it is given and received,[14] even though not based on a valuable consideration.[15] In some of our States, however, a " seal imports a consideration, and is *prima facie* evidence of it; but the validity of the instrument may be impeached for want of consideration." [16]

A Covenant not to Sue a tort feasor has a different legal effect from a release under seal. The latter discharges the cause of action; and if there are two or more joint tort-feasors, an unqualified release to one operates as satisfaction of the releasor's claim against each; while the former does not discharge the cause of action. " A covenant not to sue a sole tort-feasor is, to avoid circuity of action, considered a bar to a suit against such tort-feasor." But where there are joint wrongdoers, the covenant is not a bar even in favor of the covenantee, who must resort to his suit for breach of covenant; and clearly the other wrongdoers cannot invoke the covenant as a bar to an action against them.[17]

(1893); Bussian v. Mil., etc., Ry., 56 Wis. 325 (1882); Albrecht v. Mil., etc., Ry., 94 Wis. 397, 69 N. W. 63 (1896).

[10] Drohan v. Lake Shore, etc., Ry., 162 Mass. 435, 38 N. E. 1116 (1894).

[11] Shaw v. Chic., etc., Ry., 82 Ia. 199, 47 N. W. 1004 (1891); Flegal v. Hoover, 156 Pa. 276, 27 At. 162 (1893).

[12] Boosey v. Wood, 3 H. & C. 483, 34 L. R. Ex. 65 (1865); the plaintiff and defendant agreed to accept the publication of mutual apologies in satisfaction and discharge of plaintiff's cause of acton against defendant for libel, and such apologies were published. This executed agreement was held a bar to an action for libel; Oliver v. Phelps, 20 N. J. L. 180 (1843); Guldaker v.

Rockwell, 14 Col. 459, 24 Pac. 556 (1890).

[13] Ogilvie v. Hallan, 58 Ia. 714, 12 N. W. 730 (1882); Burgess v. Denison Paper Co., 79 Me. 266, 9 At. 726 (1887); Hosler v. Hursh, 151 Pa. 415, 25 At. 52 (1892).

[14] Papke v. Hammond Co., 192 Ill. 631, 61 N. E. 910 (1901); Spitze v. Baltimore & O. Ry., 75 Md. 162, 23 At. 307, 32 Am. S. R. 378 (1892).

[15] Phillips v. Cloggett, 11 M. & W. 84, 12 L. J. Ex. 275 (1843); Waln v. Waln, 53 N. J. L. 429, 22 At. 203 (1891), s. c., 58 N. J. L. 640 (1896).

[16] Hobbs v. Electric Light Co., 75 Mich. 550, 42 N. W. 965 (1889); Torrey v. Black, 58 N. Y. 185 (1874).

[17] Duck v. Mayeu (1892), 2 Q. B. 511, 62 L. J. Q. B. 69; City of Chic. v. Babock, 143 Ill. 358, 32 N. E. 271

Discharge by Waiver.   In a former chapter,[18] attention was called to the right, accorded in certain cases to the victim of a tort, to sue the wrongdoer in a contract action.   As this remedy is not concurrent with that which he is entitled to seek in an action *ex delicto,* his final election to pursue it operates to discharge his claim in tort against the same defendant.   Indeed, as was pointed out in the former chapter, some courts hold that this election of remedies discharges the tort *in toto.*[19]   But the better view is that the election " is not strictly a waiver of the tort, for the tort is the only basis of the contract action."   It is a waiver of the damages for the tort and a suing for the value of the property wrongfully taken by the defendant.   " It is simply an election between remedies for an act done, leaving the rights of the injured party against the wrongdoer unimpaired until he has obtained satisfaction." [20]

The victim of a tort does not make a final election to limit himself to a contract remedy, by demanding a sum of money in satisfaction of the wrong, or even by receiving a sum in diminution of damages ; but his acceptance of money or other property to the full amount of his claim discharges his cause of action.[21]   Bringing a suit in contract is evidence of election, but, until judgment is obtained, the election is not considered final.[22]

Discharge by Judgment.   When the victim of a tort sues the wrongdoer to judgment and obtains satisfaction thereof, his cause of action is discharged.   *Nemo debet bis vexari pro eadem causa.*[23]

(1892); Gilbert v. Finch, 173 N. Y. 455, 66 N. E. 133, 61 L. R. A. 807, 93 Am. S. R. 623 (1903).   This case also holds, as does Duck v. Mayeu, that a release to one joint wrongdoer, with a reservation of right to sue the others, is to be construed as a covenant not to sue, rather than as a technical release, in order to carry out the intention of the parties.   *Contra* on this point: Abb. v. Nor. Pac. Ry., 28 Wash. 428, 68 Pac. 954, 58 L. R. A. 293, with valuable note; 92 Am. S. R. 864, with valuable note (1902);   McBride v. Scott, 132 Mich. 176, 93 N. W. 243, 61 L. R. A. 445 (1903).

[18] *Supra,* Chap. II.

[19] Terry v. Munger, 121 N. Y. 161, 24 N. E. 272 (1891);   Carroll v. Fethers, 102 Wis. 436, 78 N. W. 604 (1899).

[20] Huffman v. Hughlett, 11 Lea (Tenn.) 549 (1883);   Keener, Quasi Contracts, chap. III.

[21] Valpey v. Sanders, 5 C. B. 886, 17 L. J. C. P. 249 (1848);   Lythgoe v. Vernon, 5 H. & N. 180, 29 L. J. Ex. 164 (1860);   Smith v. Baker, L. R. 8 C. P. 350, 42 L. J. C. P. 155 (1873);   Bradley v. Brigham, 149 Mass. 141 (1889).

[22] Smith v. Baker, L. R. 8 C. P. 350, 42 L. J. C. P. 155 (1873).

[23] Kitchen v. Campbell, 3 Wils. 304 (1772).

This maxim does not apply, however, where the same conduct of the defendant inflicts two distinct torts upon the plaintiff, for example, false imprisonment and malicious prosecution.[24] The maxim does apply to estop a plaintiff, against whom a judgment on the merits has passed in an action for an alleged tort, from suing again for the same cause.[25] It also estops one, as we have seen in a former connection, from bringing repeated actions from day to day " as the diurnal effects of the one original wrong happen to mature." [26]

Judgment Against One of Several WrongDoers. When a number of persons join in committing a single tort, the victim has his election to sue all of them jointly, or to proceed against each, separately, or to join some and sue the other or others singly.[27] This is " because a tort is in its nature a separate act of each individual." [28] It follows that one joint wrongdoer cannot plead the non-joinder of his fellows in abatement or in bar; [29] nor is it a defense that the plaintiff has another action pending against one of the other wrongdoers.[30] It would seem to follow from this right to pursue each wrongdoer separately, that the victim is entitled to a judgment against each; and that nothing short of the satisfaction of a judgment against one wrongdoer should bar his recovery against the others. And this view prevails generally in this country.[31] In England,[32] however, and in a few of our States,[33] it is

[24] Guest v. Warren, 9 Ex. 379, 23 L. J. Ex. 121 (1854).

[25] Darley & Main Colliery Co. v. Mitchell, 11 A. C. 127, 55 L. J. Q. B. 529 (1885); Horton v. N. Y. C. Ry., 63 Fed. 897 (1894); St. Louis S. W. Ry. v. Moss (Tex. Civ. App.), 28 S. W. 1038 (1894); Blackman v. Simpson, 120 Mich. 377, 79 N. W. 573, 58 L. R. A. 410 (1899).

[26] *Supra*, Chap. V. § 3.

[27] Lovejoy v. Murray, 3 Wall. (U. S.) 1, 18 L. Ed. 129 (1865); The Atlas, 93 U. S. 302, 23 L. Ed. 885 (1876).

[28] Low v. Mumford, 14 Johns. (N. Y.) 426 (1817).

[29] Rich v. Pilkington, Carthew, 171 (1691); Mitchell v. Tarbutt, 5 D. & E. 649 (1794).

[30] McAvoy v. Wright, 137 Mass. 207 (1884).

[31] Lovejoy v. Murray, 3 Wall. (U. S.) 1, 18 L. Ed. 129 (1865); Blann v. Crocheron, 19 Ala. 647, 54 Am. Dec. 203, with note (1851); Dawson v. Schloss, 93 Cal. 194, 29 Pac. 31 (1892); Grundel v. Union Iron Works, 127 Cal. 438, 59 Pac. 826, 78 Am. S. R. 75 (1899); Woodworth v. Gorsline, 30 Col. 186, 69 Pac. 705, 58 L. R. A. (with full note) 417 (1902); Vincent v. McNamara, 70 Conn. 332, 39 At. 444 (1898); Norfolk Lumber Co. v. Simmons, 2 Marv. (Del.) 317, 43 At. 163 (1897); Warnack v. People, 187 Ill. 116, 58 N. E. 242 (1900); Elliot v. Porter, 5 Dana (Ky.), 299, 30 Am. Dec. 689 (1837); Jones v. Lowell, 35 Me. 541

held that the election of the injured party to take judgment against one or more of the wrongdoers puts an end to his claim against the others. If such election were held not to be a defense it would encourage a multiplicity of vexatious actions, it is declared. In case of several joint wrongdoers, it is said, " an unprincipled attorney might be found willing enough to bring an action against each and every of them, and so accumulate a vast amount of useless costs." The maxim, " *interest reipublicæ ut sit finis litium*," is invoked by these tribunals to compel the plaintiff to join all the wrongdoers in one suit, or elect which one he will cast in judgment.

Election by Judgment Creditor. Under the generally prevailing rule, the plaintiff may take several judgments against the various joint tort-feasors, and then elect which judgment he will enforce. This right of election cannot be defeated by a tender of the amount by one of the judgment debtors, nor by a payment into court of the sum adjudged against him.[34] Even after issuing execution upon one judgment and collecting a part, if he fails to collect the whole, he may issue execution upon either of the other judgments, crediting thereon whatever he received under the former executions.[35]

(1852); Cleveland v. City of Bangor, 87 Me. 259, 32 At. 892, 47 Am. S. R. 326 (1895); Corey v. Havener, 182 Mass. 250, 65 N. E. 69 (1902); McReady v. Rogers, 1 Neb. 124, 93 Am. Dec. 333 (1868); Fowler v. Owen, 68 N. H. 270, 39 At. 329, 73 Am. S. R. 588 (1895); Livingston v. Bishop, 1 Johns. (N. Y.) 290, 3 Am. Dec. 330 (1806); Russell v. McCall, 141 N. Y. 437, 36 N. E. 498 (1894); Martin v. Buffaloe, 128 N. C. 305, 38 S. E. 902, 83 Am. S. R. 679 (1901); Maple v. Cin., H. & D. Ry., 40 Ohio St. 313, 48 Am. R. 685 (1883); Hawkins v. Hatton, 1 Nott & McC. 318, 9 Am. Dec. 700 (1818); Turner v. Brock, 6 Heisk (Tenn.), 50 (1871); Sanderson v. Caldwell, 2 Aik. (Vt.) 195 (1827); Griffin v. McClung, 5 W. Va. 131 (1872).

[32] Brown v. Wotton, Cro. Jac. 73,

Yelv. 68, Moore, 762 (1606); King v. Hoare, 13 M. & W. 494, 14 L. J. Ex. 29 (1844); Brinsmead v. Harrison, L. R. 7 C. P. 547, 41 L. J. C. P. 190 (1872).

[33] Hunt v. Bates, 7 R. I. 217, 82 Am. Dec. 592 (1862), but see Parmenter v. Barstow, 21 R. I. 410, 43 At. 1035 (1899); Petticolas v. Richmond, 95 Va. 456, 28 S. E. 566 (1897).

[34] Blann v. Crocheron, 20 Ala. 320 (1852); Power v. Baker, 27 Fed. 396 (1886).

[35] Lovejoy v. Murray, 3 Wall. (U. S.) 1, 18 L. Ed. 129 (1865); Shainwald v. Lewis, 46 Fed. 839 (1889); Ayer v. Ashmead, 31 Conn. 447, 83 Am. Dec. 154 (1863); McVey v. Manatt, 80 Ia. 132, 45 N. W. 548 (1890); U. S. of Shakers v. Underwood, 11 Bush. 265, 21 Am. R. 214 (1875);

The Effect of Satisfying a Judgment for Conversion.
When a person, who has converted the property of another, satisfies a judgment against him therefor, he becomes the legal owner thereof. This title, as between the parties to the action, relates back to the date of conversion, inasmuch as that is the time at which the plaintiff has elected to treat the property as having passed from him.[36] Until the judgment is satisfied, however, it is held generally that the title remains in the plaintiff, and that he may replevy the property or maintain any other action for redress not inconsistent with his first suit.[37] The doctrine of relation is adopted for the purpose of promoting justice, and will not be applied to render innocent third persons liable as trespassers,[38] nor to hold the plaintiff in the trover action liable as indorser of negotiable paper, which he delivered to the converter for a purpose never accomplished by the latter.[39]

Cleveland v. City of Bangor, 87 Me. 259, 32 At. 892, 47 Am. S. R. 326 (1895); Woods v. Pangburn, 75 N. Y. 498 (1878); Brison v. Dougherty, 3 Baxt. (62 Tenn.) 93 (1873); Sanderson v. Caldwell, 2 Aik. (Vt.) 195 (1827). *Contra*, Criner v. Brewer, 13 Ark. 225 (1853); Ashcraft v. Knoblock, 146 Ind. 169, 174, 45 N. E. 69 (1896), holding that the judgment creditor makes a final election when he issues an execution against any one of the judgment debtors.

[36] Hepburn v. Sewell, 5 Har. & J. 211, 9 Am. Dec. 512 (1821); Smith v. Smith, 51 N. H. 571 (1872), 50 N. H. 212 (1870); St. Louis, etc., Ry. v. McKinsey, 78 Tex. 298, 14 S. W. 645, 22 Am. S. R. 54 (1890). In the last case, it is said that the title relates to the date of the judgment.

[37] Spivey v. Morris, 18 Ala. 254, 52 Am. Dec. 224 (1880); Woodworth v. Gorsline, 30 Col. 186, 69 Pac. 705, 58 L. R. A. 417, with note (1902); Miller v. Hyde, 161 Mass. 472, 37 N. E. 760, 42 Am. S. R. 424, with note; 25 L. R. A. 42 (1894). In this case there are two dissenting opinions.

Holmes, J., declares that one whose property has been converted has an election between two courses; he may retake the property or secure a judgment for damages, but that he cannot do both; that his election is determined by judgment. Knowlton, J., was of the opinion that a final election is not made by taking judgment, but is by proceeding to obtain satisfaction by a levy on the defendant's property, especially where he levies on the very property for which he obtained judgment. In *Ex parte Drake*, 5 Ch. D. 866, 46 L. J. Bk. 29 (1877), the court held that a man does not elect himself out of his property by taking a judgment for its value against a converter, nor by proving the claim against the wrong-doer's estate in bankruptcy. Said James, L. J.: "I think it is not the business of any court of justice to find facilities for enabling one man to steal another man's property."

[38] Bacon v. Kimmel, 14 Mich. 201 (1866).

[39] Haas v. Sackett, 40 Minn. 53, 41 N. W. 237, 2 L. R. A. 449 (1889).

§ 2. DISCHARGE BY OPERATION OF LAW.

Death of Either Party. The rule of the common law on this subject is stated by Blackstone [40] in these words: "In actions merely personal, arising *ex delicto,* for wrongs actually done or committed by the defendant, as trespass, battery and slander, the rule is that *actio personalis moritur cum persona;* and it never shall be revived either by or against the executors or other representatives. For neither the executors of the plaintiff have received, nor those of the defendant have committed, in their own personal capacity, any manner of wrong or injury." The primitive rule was even broader than this. "The truth is," to quote the language of a learned judge, "that in the earliest times of English law, survival of causes of action was the rare exception, non-survival was the rule." [41] The first modification of this rule was made by a statute during the reign of Edward III,[42] which enacted that the executors, in case of trespass done to the goods and chattels of their testators, should have an action against the trespassers to recover damages, in like manner as the testators should have had, if they were living. This legislation was construed liberally, so as to give a remedy to the personal representatives of the injured party for all torts except those relating to freeholds, and those where the injury done is of a personal nature.[43] During the early part of the last century,[44] statutory provision was made for suits to recover for injuries to

---

[40] Blackstone's Commentaries, Bk. III, p. 302. Sir Frederick Pollock thinks the maxim *actio personalis moritur cum persona* may have been justified by the vindictive and quasi-criminal character of suits in primitive law for civil injuries. A process, he says, "which is still felt to be a substitute for private war, may seem incapablbe of being continued on behalf of or against a dead man's estate. Some such policy seems to be implied in the dictum, 'If one doth a trespass to me, and dieth, the action is dead also, because it should be inconvenient to recover against one who was not party to the wrong.'" Newton, C. J., in Y. B. 19 Hen. VI, 66, pl. 10 (1440-1441).

[41] Bowen, L. J., in Finley v. Chirney, 20 Q. B. D. 494, 57 L. J. Q. B. 247 (1888), holding that an action for breach of promise to marry does not survive the death of the promisor.

[42] 4 Ed. III, ch. 7 (1330); 25 Ed. III, ch. 5 (1351).

[43] Wilson v. Knubley, 7 East, 128, 134 (1806); Twycross v. Grant, 4 C. P. D. 40, 48 L. J. C. P. 1 (1878); Oakey v. Dalton, 35 Ch. D. 700, 56 L. J. Ch. 823 (1887).

[44] 3 & 4 Will. IV, ch. 42 (1833).

real property, if inflicted within six months before the death of the owner, or if the suit was brought within six months after the personal representatives of the wrongdoer had qualified.

Legislation in this Country. Similar legislation has been enacted in most of our States,[45] with the result, that where the cause of action is in substance an injury to the person, the death of either party will discharge the tort.[46] If the wrong is done to the property rights or interests of another, the action will survive the death of the person wronged,[47] while it will not survive the death of the wrongdoer, unless " property is acquired by him, whereby his estate is benefited." [48] Allowing an action against the personal representatives of the wrongdoer, where his estate has been increased by the tort, has been declared not to constitute an exception to the rule that private wrongs are to be buried with the offender. The executor, it is said, is not made liable for the tort of his testator, " but only for the implied promise which the law raises and allows the injured party to put in the place of the wrong." [49]

---

[45] See "Abatement and Revival," 1 Cyclopædia of Law and Procedure, p. 52. This legislation has been liberally construed, as a rule. Hooper v. Gorham, 45 Me. 209 (1858); Aylesworth v. Curtis, 19 R. I. 517, 34 At. 1109, 61 Am. S. R. 785, 33 L. R. A. 110 (1896).

In some States the statute includes only those cases where the injury is occasioned to property by the direct wrongful act of a party upon real or personal property. Cutting v. Tower, 14 Gray (80 Mass.), 183 (1859); Stebbins v. Dean, 82 Mich. 385, 46 N. W. 778 (1890).

[46] Feary v. Hamilton, 140 Ind. 45, 39 N. E. 516 (1894); Wade v. Kalbfleisch, 58 N. Y. 282 (1874), holding that an action for breach of promise to marry does not survive the promisor. Cf. Pulling v. Great Eastern Ry., 9 Q. B. D. 110, 51 L. J. Q. B. 453 (1882); Webber v. St. Paul City Ry., 97 Fed. 140, 38 C. C. A. 79 (1899). See note in 61 L. R. A.

352–393, on Effect of Death of Either Party after Judgment.

[47] Cregin v. Brooklyn, etc., Ry., 75 N. Y. 192 (1878), action by husband for negligent injuries to his wife, held to be for a wrong to his pecuniary rights and interests and to survive his death; Gorden v. Strong, 158 N. Y. 407, 53 N. E. 33 (1899); Petts v. Ison, 11 Ga. 153 (1852); Curry v. Mannington, 23 W. Va. 18 (1883).

[48] Boor v. Lowry, 103 Ind. 468, 3 N. E. 151, 53 Am. R. 519 (1885), action for malpractice by surgeon does not survive him; Vittum v. Gilman, 48 N. H. 416 (1869); Ott v. Kaufman, 68 Md. 56, 11 At. 580 (1887), *accord*. In some States the statutes go farther than this. See Shafer v. Grimes, 23 Ia. 553 (1867); Hooper v. Gorham, 45 Me. 209, 214 (1858); Geyer v. Douglass, 85 Ia. 935, 52 N. W. 111, (1892).

[49] Mitchell v. Hotchkiss, 48 Conn. 9, 17, 40 Am. R. 146 (1880).

When the plaintiff brings his suit in a Federal court the survival of his action will depend ordinarily upon the common law, as modified by the statutes of the State where the action is brought, or where it might have been brought at the death of the party in question.[50] If, however, the action is founded upon penal provisions of a Federal statute, the question of its survival is determined by Federal Law.[51]

The Dissolution of a Corporation works an abatement of suits against it and prevents the institution of new suits, unless its life is preserved by statute, for the purpose of prosecuting or defending suits, or of settling its affairs.[52] It has been held, in New York, that the rule *actio personalis moritur cum persona* is not to be extended to the civil death of either natural persons or corporations, and that a suit for libel, abated by the dissolution of the corporation, may be continued against the former directors to reach corporation assets in their hands as trustees.[53]

Action for Causing Death. According to the common law, as interpreted by the courts of England and of this country, no civil action could be maintained for the death of a human being, caused by the wrongful act or negligence of another, or for any damages suffered by any person in consequence of such death. Various reasons have been assigned for this rule. In the earliest English cases, it is based upon the doctrine that the civil wrong is drowned or merged in the felony.[54] But we have seen, in a former connection, that this doctrine has never obtained in this country.

Another reason has been sought in the maxim which we have been considering, *actio personalis moritur cum persona*.[55] This, it

---

[50] Martin v. Bal. & O. Ry., 151 U. S. 673, 14 Sup. Ct. 533, 38 L. Ed. 311 (1893); Bal. & O. Ry. v. Joy, 173 U. S. 226, 19 Sup. Ct. 387, 43 L. Ed. 677 (1901); Webber v. St. Paul City Ry., 97 Fed. 140, 38 C. C. A. 79 (1899).

[51] Schreiber v. Sharpless, 100 U. S. 76, 3 S. Ct. 423, 28 L. Ed. 65 (1883).

[52] Nelson v. Hubbard, 96 Ala. 238, 11 So. 428, 17 L. R. A. 375 (1892); Marion Phosphate Co. v. Perry, 74 Fed. 425, 20 C. C. A. 490, 41 U. S. App. 14, 33 L. R. A. 252 (1896);

10 Cyclopædia of Law and Proc. pp. 1310, 1311.

[53] Shayne v. Evening Post Pub. Co., 168 N. Y. 70, 61 N. E. 115, 85 Am. S. R. 654, 55 L. R. A. 777, 10 N. Y. Annot. Cases, 237 (1901), reversing s. c. in 56 App. Div. 426, 101 St. R. 937, 67 N. Y. Supp. 937, 9 N. Y. Ann. Cas. 51, with note (1900).

[54] Higgins v. Butcher, Yelv. 89, Brownlow, 205 (1606).

[55] Green v. Hudson R. Ry., 28 Barb. (N. Y.) 9, 17 (1858), rejected in s. c., when in the court of Ap-

has been replied,[56] " would furnish an adequate reason why no action could be brought by personal representatives, or others, for such damages as the deceased might have recovered for the injury, if death had not ensued, as the action for such damages would not survive. But this reason could have no application whatever to an action brought by a master for loss of services of his apprentice, or by a husband for the loss of his wife," or by a wife or child for the loss of husband or parent.

Still another reason, which has been assigned, is that " the policy of the law refuses to recognize the interest of one person in the death of another," [57]—a reason, it has been replied, " which would make life insurance and leases for life illegal."[58] Others have professed to find the reason of the rule " in that natural and almost universal repugnance among enlightened nations, to setting a price upon human life, or any attempt to estimate its value by a pecuniary standard." Those holding this view, admit, however, that " the necessity which has grown out of the new modes of travel and business in modern times " of making railroad corporations and others, to whom passengers are compelled to trust for safety, more careful to secure a high degree of vigilance in protecting the lives intrusted to their control, has reconciled even the cultivated and enlightened mind of to-day to the idea of compensating the loss of human life in money.[59]

Attempt to Substitute the Scotch Rule. In view of the unsatisfactory character of the reasons assigned for the rule, it is a matter of regret and wonder that the courts of the last century did not reject the rule as barbarous, and, if they could not discover a princple of the common law which would justify them in allowing an action, that they did not borrow one from the law of Scotland.[60] A few judges did make this attempt,[61] but they were overruled by

---

peals, 2 Keyes, 294, 303, 2 Abb. Dec. 277 (1866).

[56] Hyatt v. Adams, 16 Mich. 180, 189 (1867).

[57] Osborn v. Gillett, L. R. 8 Ex. 88, 42 L. J. Ex. 53 (1873).

[58] Pollock on Torts (6th Ed.), 63.

[59] Hyatt v. Adams, 16 Mich. 180, 192 (1867).

[60] Cadell v. Black, 5 Paton's App. Cas. 567 (1812). A recovery was allowed by the civil law as understood in Lower Canada; Ravary v. Grand Trunk Ry., 6 Lower Can. Jur. 49 (1861); Can. Pac. Ry. v. Robinson, 14 Duval (Can. Sup. Ct.), 105, 117 (1887).

[61] Bramwell, L. J., declared such a principle was found in the common law: " The general principle is in the plaintiffs' favor, that *injuria* and *damnum* give a cause of action.

appellate tribunals or overwhelmed by the rising tide of opposing views.[62] The House of Lords in England,[63] and the Supreme Court of the United States [64] carried the barbarous rule into admiralty jurisprudence. Perhaps, the rejection of the more humane and enlightened rule of Scotch jurisprudence was made by our courts with a lighter heart, because of the legislation which began with Lord Campbell's Act in England,[65] giving a cause of action for wrongful death.

Common Law Rule Modified by Statute. Lord Campbell's Act did not abolish the rule that a personal action dies with the person. It gave a totally new action against the person, who would have been responsible to the deceased had he lived.[66] It is entitled, " An Act for compensating the families of persons killed by accidents," and declares that the action against the wrongdoer " shall be for the benefit of the wife, husband, parent (including grand-parent and step-parent) and child (including grand-child and step-child) ; " that it shall be brought by the personal representative of the deceased; that the jury may give such damages as they think the bene-

---

It is for the defendant to show an exception to this rule when the *injuria* causes death; " Osborn v. Gillett, L. R. 8 Ex. 88, 42 L. J. Ex. 53 (1873); Cross v. Guthery, 2 Root (Conn.), 90 (1794); Shields v. Younge, 15 Ga. 349, 60 Am. Dec. 698 (1854); James v. Christy, 18 Mo. 162 (1853); Ford v. Monroe, 20 Wend. (N. Y.) 210 (1838); Sullivan v. Union Pac. Ry., 3 Dillon (U. S. Cir. C.), 335 (1874). In Hawaii, the attempt was successful; Kake v. Horton, 2 Hawaii, 209 (1860); Schooner Robert Lewis Co. v. Kekanoha, 114 Fed. 849 (1902).

[62] Baker v. Bolton, 1 Camp. 493 (1808); Osborn v. Gillett, L. R. 8 Ex. 88, 42 L. J. Ex. 53 (1873); Goodsell v. Hart, etc., Ry., 33 Conn. 55 (1865); Carey v. Berkshire, etc., Ry., 1 Cush. (Mass.) 475 (1848); Hyatt v. Adams, 16 Mich. 180 (1867); Green v. Hudson R. Ry., 2

Keyes (N. Y.), 294 (1866); Insurance Co. v. Brame, 95 U. S. 754, 24 L. Ed. 580 (1877).

[63] Seward v. Vera Cruz, 10 App. Cas. 59 (1884).

[64] The Harrisburg, 119 U. S. 199, 7 Sup. Ct. 140, 30 L. Ed. 358 (1886), overruling numerous decisions in the lower Federal courts, including: The Sea Gull, Chase's Decisions, 145; The Highland Light, Ibid. 150 (1867); Holmes v. Oregon, etc., Ry., 5 Fed. R. 75, 6 Sawyer, 262 (1880); The Columbia, 27 Fed. 704 (1886).

[65] 9 & 10 Vict. c. 93.

[66] Seward v. Vera Cruz, 10 App. Cas. 59 (1884). In this case, it is declared that the action will not lie, unless there is some person answering the description of the widow, parent or child, who suffers pecuniary loss.

ficiaries have sustained by the death, and that the action shall be commenced within twelve calendar months after the death.

Statutes fashioned after this Act have been passed in the District of Columbia and in most of our States and Territories. They differ in many respects, and no attempt will be made in this connection to deal with their provisions in detail. It must suffice, to state the most important principles which have been recognized by the courts in enforcing them.

The Statutes Create a New Cause of Action. In this country, as in England, the legislation upon this topic has been construed by most courts as creating an entirely new cause of action,[67] and not as transferring to the personal representative the right of action, which the deceased person would have had, if he had survived the injury; although the statutes of some states have been differently construed.[68] As the cause of action is thus purely statutory, the plaintiff is bound to show that he is the proper person to bring the action; that at least one of the class named as beneficiaries is in existence and entitled to damages, and that the defendant comes within the class to whom the statute applies.[69] If there are no per-

---

[67] Munroe v. Dredging Co., 84 Cal. 515, 24 Pac. 303, 18 Am. S. R. 248 (1890); Kansas Pac. Ry. v. Miller, 2 Colo. 442 (1874); Donaldson v. Miss. Ry., 18 Ia. 280, 87 Am. Dec. 391 (1865); McKay v. New England Dredging Co., 93 Me. 201, 43 At. 29 (1899); Wooden v. Western N. Y. Ry., 126 N. Y. 10, 26 N. E. 1050, 22 Am. S. R. 803, 13 L. R. A. 458 (1891); Penn. Ry. v. Vandever, 36 Pa. 298 (1860); In re Estate of Mays, 60 S. C. 401, 38 S. E. 684, 54 L. R. A. 660 (1901).

[68] Goodsell v. Hartford, etc., Ry., 33 Conn. 51 (1865); Hennessy v. Bavarian Brewing Co., 145 Mo. 104, 46 S. W. 966, 68 Am. S. R. 554, 41 L. R. A. 385 (1898); Legg v. Britton, 64 Vt. 652, 24 At. 1016 (1890); Brown v. Chic., etc., Ry., 102 Wis. 137, 77 N. W. 748, 44 L. R. A. 579 (1899). Two classes of statutes in this State. See Tiffany, Death by Wrongful Act, Chap. 2, for classification of different American statutes.

[69] Walker v. Vicksburg, etc., Ry., 110 La. 718, 34 So. 749 (1903); Wooden v. Western N. Y. Ry., 126 N. Y. 10, 26 N. E. 1050, 22 Am. S. R. 803, 13 L. R. A. 458 (1891); Myers v. Holborn, 58 N. J. L. 193, 33 At. 389, 30 L. R. A. 345, 55 Am. S. R. 606 (1895); Lewis v. Henlock's, etc., Co., 203 Pa. 511, 53 At. 349, 93 Am. S. R. 923 (1902); Lipscomb v. Houston, etc., Ry., 95 Tex. 5, 64 S. W. 923, 93 Am. S. R. 804 (1901). The plaintiff must show that the death was due to defendant's wrongful act or omission, Rutherford v. Foster, 125 Fed. 187, 60 C. C. A. 129 (1903); Nor. Pac. Ry. v. Adams, 192 U. S. 440, 24 Sup. Ct. 408, 1904).

sons in existence, who are entitled under the statute to take the proceeds of the action as beneficiaries, the action will not lie,[70] except in a few jurisdictions and under peculiar statutory provisions.[71] In case the sole beneficiary dies during the pendency of the action, the action will abate under some statutes,[72] but not under others.[73] The marriage of a widow, it has been held, does not affect the right of action in her behalf for the wrongful death of her former husband.[74]

Construction of the Statutes. While the courts are generally agreed that the plaintiff must show, that the action which he brings is clearly authorized by the statute under which he claims, and, to this extent, insist upon a strict construction,[75] the weight of authority favors the view that the " statutes are not penal but remedial, for the benefit of the persons injured by the death; that their substantial purpose is to do away with the obstacle to a recovery caused by the death." [76]

Damages Recoverable. Upon this topic the statutes are far from uniform. Most of them authorize the recovery of such damages as will compensate the beneficiaries for the pecuniary harm which the evidence shows they have suffered,[77] although a maximum is fixed beyond which the verdict shall not go. In some states, punitive damages are allowed.[78] Generally, the fact that the statutory beneficiaries have received money on policies of insurance on the life of deceased, is inadmissible on the question of damages.[79] Nor

[70] Brown v. Chic., etc., Ry., 102 Wis. 137, 77 N. W. 748, 44 L. R. A. 579 (1899); Wester v. Norwegian Co., 137 Cal. 399, 70 Pac. 276, 92 Am. S. R. 181 (1902).

[71] Florida Cent. Ry. v. Foxworth, 41 Fla. 1, 25 So. 338, 79 Am. S. R. 149 (1899).

[72] Sanders' Admx. v. Louisville, etc., Ry., 111 Fed. 708, (1901).

[73] Cooper v. Shore Elec. Co., 63 N. J. L. 558, 44 At. 633 (1899). But the death affects the quantum of recovery, as his loss is limited to his life-time.

[74] Chic., etc., Ry. v. Lagerkraas, 65 Neb. 566, 91 N. W. 358 (1902).

[75] McMillan v. Spider Lake Co.,

115 Wis. 332, 91 N. W. 979, 60 L. R. A. 589 (1902).

[76] Stewart v. Bal. & O. Ry., 168 U. S. 445, 18 Sup. Ct. 106, 42 L. Ed. 538 (1897); Vetalorio v. Perkins, 101 Fed. 393 (1900); Bonthron v. Phoenix Light Co., (Arizona), 71 Pac. 941, 61 L. R. A. 563 (1903).

[77] See Tiffany, Death by Wrongful Act §§ 153–154, and authorities cited; McKay v. New England Dredging Co., 92 Me. 454, 43 At. 29 (1899); May v. West Jersey Ry., 62 N. J. L. 63, 42 At. 163 (1899).

[78] See Ibid, § 155; Louisville, etc., Ry. v. Lansford, 102 Fed. 62 (1900).

[79] Sherlock v. Alling, 44 Ind. 184 (1873); Althorf v. Wolfe, 22 N. Y.

is the fact admissible that the beneficiaries have inherited a large estate from the deceased.[80]

Whether the plaintiff is entitled to recover nominal damages, in the absence of allegation and proof of special pecuniary harm, is a question upon which the courts are at variance. In England [81] and in some of our states [82] a negative answer has been given. These authorities declare that " the law requires, in this class of cases, that the administrator must show that some person has suffered some pecuniary injury by the death. The statute does not imply that damages and pecuniary loss necessarily flow from the negligent killing. This is a matter that must be made to appear by the proper allegation in the declaration, and proof of fact." [83]

The weight of authority in this Country, however, appears to favor the view that pecuniary damage is presumed from the fact of death; and that the plaintiff is entitled to nominal damages, even though he fails to allege and prove specific pecuniary harm.[84]

Funeral expenses of the deceased are not recoverable under the Statute in England,[85] but are generally in this country, if the law imposes upon any of the relatives, for whose benefit the suit is brought, the obligation to bear such expenses.[86] This is based upon the fact, that the sum, recoverable under the statutes, represents the entire pecuniary loss resulting from the death to each and all the persons mentioned in the statute.

355 (1860); Coulter v. Township, 164 Pa. 543, 30 At. 490 (1894); Lipscomb v. Houston, etc., Ry., 95 Tex. 5, 64 S. W. 923, 93 Am. S. R. 804, 55 L. R. A. 869 (1901).

[80] Stahler v. Phila., etc., Ry., 199 Pa. 383, 49 At. 273, 85 Am. S. R. 791 (1901).

[81] Duckworth v. Johnson, 4 H. & N. 653, 29 L. J. Ex. 25 (1859).

[82] Hurst v. Detroit City Ry., 84 Mich. 539, 48 N. W. 46 (1891); Orgall v. Chic., etc., Ry., 46 Neb. 4, 64 N. W. 450 (1895); McGowan v. International, etc., Ry., 85 Tex. 289, 20 S. W. 80 (1892); Regan v. Chic., etc., Ry., 51 Wis. 599 (1881); In re Calif. Nav. & Imp. Co., 110 Fed. 670 (1901), a decision in admiralty.

[83] Rouse v. Detroit Elec. Ry., 128 Mich. 149, 87 N. W. 68 (1901).

[84] North Chic. Street Ry. v. Brodie, 156 Ill. 317, 40 N. E. 942 (1895); Karrady v. Lake Shore, etc., Ry., 131 Ind. 261, 29 N. E. 1069 (1891); Chic., etc., Ry. v. Thomas, 155 Ind. 634, 55 N. E. 861 (1900); Quinn v. Moore, 15 N. Y. 432 (1857); Hang v. Great Nor. Ry., 8 N. Dak. 23, 77 N. W. 97, 42 L. R. A. 664, 73 Am S. R. 727 (1898); Peden v. Am. Bridge Co., 120 Fed. 523 (1903).

[85] Dalton v. S. E. Ry., 4 C. B. N. S. 296, 27 L. J. C. P. 227 (1858).

[86] Owen v. Brockschmidt, 54 Mo. 285 (1873); Murphy v. N. Y. C. Ry., 88 N. Y. 445 (1882); Penn. Ry. Co.

Effect of Bankruptcy on Tort Actions. This depends upon whether the victim of the tort, or the tort-feasor becomes bankrupt.

(a) If the bankruptcy is that of the victim, it does not operate as a bar to the tort action. In case the tort is a personal one, the bankrupt may bring or continue an action therefor, after bankruptcy, as he could before.[87] In case, however, the tort consists in an injury to property rights, as distinguished from a personal wrong, the right of action passes to the assignee or trustee in bankruptcy, and is to be prosecuted by him.[88]

(b) The bankruptcy of the tort-feasor, although followed by a decree or order of discharge, does not relieve him from liability to an action therefor in England.[89] In this country the language of the statute is not quite so sweeping on this topic. It is as follows: "A discharge in bankruptcy shall release a bankrupt from all of his provable debts, except such as . . . . . . (2) are liabilities for obtaining property by false pretenses or false representations, or for willful and malicious injuries to the person or property of another, or for alimony due or to become due, or for maintenance or support of wife or child, or for seduction of an unmarried female, or for criminal conversation; . . . . . . or (4) were created by his fraud embezzlement, misappropriation, or defalcation while acting as an officer or in fiduciary capacity." [90]

---

v. Bantom, 54 Pa. 495 (1867); Petrie v. Col., etc., Ry., 29 S. C. 303, 7 S. E. 515 (1888).

[87] Howard v. Cruther, 8 M. & W. 601 (1841). Action for seduction of servant. On p. 604, Alderson B. said: "Assignees can maintain no action for libel, although the injury occasioned thereby to the man's reputation may have been the sole cause of his bankruptcy." In re Haensell, 91 Fed. 355 (1899), holding that a cause of action for a malicious prosecution and arrest formed no part of the bankrupt victim's estate. Colwell v. Tinker, 169 N. Y. 536, 62 N. E. 1094, 58 L. R. A. 531, 7 Am. B. R. 344 (1902).

[88] Hodgson v. Sidney L. R., 1 Ex. 313, 35 L. J. Ex. 182 (1866); Mor-gan v. Steble L. R., 7 Q. B. 611, 41 L. J. Q. B. 260 (1872); Tiffany v. Boatman's Bank, 18 Wall. (U. S.) 375, 21 L. Ed. 868 (1873); Wheelock v. Lee, 64 N. Y. 242 (1876); U. S. Bankruptcy Act, 1898, § 70 (a) (b).

[89] Clerk & Lindsell on Torts, (2nd Ed.) 36; 46 and 47 Vict. ch. 52, § 37.

[90] U. S. Bankruptcy Act of 1898, § 17, as amended 1903. For a discussion of this section see Collier on Bankruptcy (4th Ed.) 188--204. Anderson v. Shufeldt, 181 U. S. 575, 21 Sup. Ct. R. 735; 45 L. Ed. 1009 (1901); Dunbar v. Dunbar, 190 U. S. 340; 23 Sup. Ct. 757 (1903); Bryant v. Kinyon, 127 Mich. 152, 86 N. W. 531, 53 L. R. A. 801 (1901).

Statute of Limitations. This statute provides that the various actions for torts shall not be be brought, after the expiration of varying but definite periods. In England the statute [91] divides tort actions into three classes, assigning to the first class a term of limitation of six years; to the second class four years, and to the third class two years. These classes have been briefly described as follows: " Six years. Trespass to land and goods, conversion, and all other common law wrongs (including libel), except slander by words actionable *per se* and injuries to the person. Four years. Injuries to the person (including imprisonment). Two Years. Slander by words actionable *per se*." [92]

In this country, while legislation upon this topic has been fashioned upon the statute of James, the laws of each jurisdiction should be examined by the reader, for they differ in various respects. We can attempt, here, to deal only with the general principles underlying them.

Exemptions from Statutory Bar. It is frequently provided that infants and other persons under legal disability, as well as persons absent from the State, shall be exempted from the running of the statute, during such period of disability or absence. [93] At times, however, no such exemption is found in the statute, and it has been argued in behalf of the person under disability or absent, that he was entitled to exemption by reason of an inherent equity. But this argument has been pronounced unsound, and the rule declared that the exemptions, generally accorded to such persons, do not rest upon any general doctrine of the law that they cannot be subjected to the action of the statutes, but, in every instance, upon express language in those statutes giving them, after the expiration of disability or absence, a definite time to assert their rights. [94] " And where the

---

[91] Ch. 16, 21 James I, as amended by ch. 3, 4 and 5 Anne, ch. 97, §12, 19 and 20 Vict. and ch. 75, §1, 45 and 46 Vict.

[92] Pollock On Torts (6th Ed.) 205.

[93] McFarlane v. Grober, 70 Ark. 371, 69 S. W. 56, 91 Am. S. R. 84 (1902); Jenkins v. Jenson, 24 Utah 108, 66 Pac. 773, 91 Am. S. R. 783

(1901); Parker v. Kelly, 61 Wis. 552 (1884).

[94] Vance v. Vance, 108 U. S. 514, 27 L. Ed. 808 (1882); Murray v. Chic., etc., Ry., 92 Fed. 868, 35 C. C. A. 62 (1899); Carden v. Louisville, etc., Ry., 101 Ky. 113, 39 S. W. 1027 (1897); Bickle v. Chrisman, 76 Va. 678 (1882); Jones v. Lemon, 26 W. Va. 629 (1885).

statute has created specific exceptions, all others must be deemed excluded; the courts are without authority to enlarge or change those specified, or establish others, though in particular cases the ends of justice might seem to be subserved, if it were done." [95]

As soon as the disability is removed, the statute begins to run, and the person has the statutory period thereafter within which to bring the action, although he is not precluded from suing, while the disability lasts.[96] If the statute of limitations once begins to run, however, it does not cease to run on account of any subsequent disability, unless the statute expressly provides for interruption.[97]

Beginning of Statutory Period. The period of limitations dates from the accrual of the cause of action. Wherever the gist of the cause of action is the wrongdoing of the defendant, the date of the act is the beginning of the statutory period.[98] But where the damage to the victim, rather than the misconduct of the tort-feasor, is the gist of the action, the statute does not begin to run until the damage is suffered.[99] In case of seduction, the cause of action accrues at once, although the amount of recovery may be affected by subsequent events.[100] In case of trespass to property, the right of action is com-

---

[95] Powell v. Kohler, 52 Ohio St. 103, 39 N. E. 195, 26 L. R. A. 480, 49 Am. S. R. 705 (1894); cf. Amy v. Watertown, 130 U. S. 320, 9 Sup. Ct. 537, 31 L. Ed. 953 (1888), for discussion of equity rule that the running of the statute is suspended on the ground of fraud. In this case it is said: "True, in a few instances, courts have apparently made exceptions not found in the statute; but they are only such as arise from a state of war, or other imperative necessity, as when courts are shut, or by the act of law one party is forbidden to sue, or the other is rendered incapable of being sued." See Haugher v. Abbott, 6 Wall. (U. S.) 532, 18 L. Ed. 939 (1867). (Courts in States in rebellion closed); St. Paul, etc., Ry. v. Olson, 87 Minn. 117, 91 N. W. 294, 94 Am. S. R. 693 (1902).

(Person prevented from exercising his remedy by paramount authority.)

[96] Powell v. Kohler, supra and cases there cited.

[97] Jenkins v. Jenson, 24 Utah 108, 66 Pac. 773, 91 Am. S. R. 783 (1901).

[98] Herreshoff v. Tripp, 15 R. I. 92, 23 At. 104 (1885).

[99] Mitchell v. Darley Main Colliery Co., 14 Q. B. D. 125; 53 L. J. Q. B. 471 (1884) s. c., sub nom. Darley Main Colliery Co. v. Mitchell, 11 App. Cas. 127, 55 L. J. Q. B. 529 (1886); Lord Blackburn's dissenting opinion is worthy of a careful perusal: St. Louis I. M. & S. Ry. v. Biggs, 52 Ark. 240, 12 S. W. 331, 20 Am. S. R. 174, 6 L. R. A. 804 (1889).

[100] Hutchinson v. Durden, 113 Ga. 987, 39 S. E. 495, 54 L. R. A. 871 (1901); Dunlap v. Linton, 144 Pa.

plete, ordinarily, upon the doing of the act,[101] but in the case of some forms of nuisance or other injury to property interests, there is no actionable wrong, until actual harm is done.[102]

The cause of action against a physician or surgeon for mal-practice accrues at the date of his unskillful act,[103] but if, after doing an improper act, he continues to care for the patient, and during such period continues the unskillful treatment, the statute does not begin to run until the termination of his employment.[104] The cause of action for conversion accrues at the date of the wrongful asportation.[105] If a demand by the owner and refusal by the possessor are necessary to complete the conversion, of course the statute will not begin to run until such demand and refusal.[106] In other torts, a demand may be necessary before the cause of action accrues.[107]

Conflict of Laws. As a rule, statutes of limitations constitute a part of the *lex fori*. Whether the tort is one at common law or depends upon a statute of the jurisdiction where it is inflicted, if the action is brought in another jurisdiction, the statute of limitations applicable to the case is that of the forum; unless the local statute, which creates the right, also limits the duration of the right within a prescribed time.[108]

335, 22 At. 819 (1891). In Davis v. Young, 90 Tenn. 303, 16 S. W. 473, it was held, that where the seduction was effected by a fraudulent promise of marriage, and subsequent acts of illicit intercourse were induced by continuation and renewal of the promise, the statute began to run from the last act of seduction.

[101] St. Louis, etc., Ry. v. Anderson, 62 Ark. 360, 35 S. W. 791 (1896).

[102] St. Louis, etc., Ry. v. Biggs, 52 Ark. 240 (1889); Sherlock v. Louisville, etc., Ry., 115 Ind. 22; 17 N. E. 171 (1888).

[103] Fudden v. Satterlee, 43 Fed. 568 (1890).

[104] Gillette v. Tucker, 67 Ohio St. 106, 65 N. E. 865, 93 Am. S. R. 639 (1902). But see dissenting opinion.

[105] County Board of Education v. State Board of Education, 107 N. C. 366, 12 S. E. 452 (1890).

[106] Haire v. Miller, 49 Ks. 270, 30 Pac. 482 (1892).

[107] In re Tidd: Tidd v. Overell, (1893) 3 Ch. 154; Quinn v. Gross, 24 Or. 147; 33 Pac. 535 (1893).

[108] Williams v. St. L., etc., Ry., 123 Mo. 573, 27 S. W. 387 (1894); Minor's Conflict of Laws, §§ 202, 210.

CHAPTER VII.

§ 1. PARTICULAR TORTS.

Having considered briefly the history of this branch of the law, and having discussed at length the general principles which determine tort liability, as well as the remedies therefor, we proceed to the consideration of the most important classes of torts.

These will be dealt with in the following order: First, torts which are directed principally against the person of the victim. Second, torts which are aimed at the property of the victim. Third, torts which are clear invasions of both the personal and property rights of another.

§ 2. FALSE IMPRISONMENT.

Violates the Right of Personal Liberty. English law has always shown itself solicitous to guard the liberty of the individual. It, therefore, punishes false imprisonment as a crime, and gives to the person unlawfully imprisoned a civil action for damages. It is with the tort action only that we are now concerned. A person is said to be imprisoned " in any case where he is arrested by force and against his will, although it be on the high street or elsewhere, and not in a house." [1]

What Constitute Arrest. " Mere words will not constitute an arrest; and if the officer says, ' I arrest you,' and the party runs away," [2] or having a weapon in his hand, keeps the officer from touching, him and so gets away,[3] there is no arrest. If, however, the officer touches him, in the attempt to take him into custody, there is an

---

[1] Thorpe, C. J., in Year Book of Assizes f. 104, pl. 85 (1348).

[2] Russen v. Lucas, 1 C. & P. 153 (1824); Hill v. Taylor, 50 Mich. 549, 15 N. W. 899 (1883); Hunting-

ton v. Shultz, Harper Law (S. C.) 452, 18 Am. Dec. 660 (1824).

[3] Genner v. Sparks, 1 Salk, 79, 6 Mod. 173 (1704).

arrest, though the officer may not succeed in stopping and holding him.[4]

Neither touching a person, nor actually overpowering him by force is necessary to an arrest. If the officer, or one purporting to act as an officer gives another to understand either by words or acts that the latter is his prisoner, and the party acquiesces in the arrest and submits his will and surrenders his liberty to the officer, there is an imprisonment. One is not obliged to incur the risk of personal violence and insult by resisting.[5] It has even been held that one is imprisoned, while being shadowed by detectives, if it appears "he was in fact deprived of all freedom of action, and that whatever consent he gave to such restraint was an enforced consent."[6] However, a person cannot be imprisoned, who is not cognizant of any restraint,[7] nor whose way is obstructed but who is at liberty to go anywhere else but over this particular way,[8] nor who is induced by false statements to go where he otherwise would not have gone,[9] or to stay where he otherwise would not have remained,[10] nor who voluntarily places himself in a situation where another may lawfully do what results in restraining his liberty.[11]

[4] Whitehead v. Keyes, 3 Allen, (85 Mass.) 495, 81 Am. Dec. 672 (1862); Anonymous, 7 Mod. 8 (1702).

[5] Collins v. Fowler, 10 Al. 859 (1846); Courtoiz v. Dozier, 20 Ga. 369 (1856); Simmons v. Richards, 171 Mass. 281, 50 N. E. 617 (1898); Moore v. Thompson, 92 Mich. 498, 52 N. W. 1000 (1892); Pike v. Hanson, 9 N. H. 491 (1838); Browning v. Rittenhouse, 40 N. J. L. 230 (1878); Gold v. Bissell, 1 Wend. (N. Y.), 210, (1828); Mead v. Young, 2 Dev. & Batt. (17 N. C.) 521 (1837); McCracken v. Ansley, 4 Strob. L. (S. C.) 1 (1849); Smith v. State, 7 Humph. (Tenn.) 43 (1846); Sorensen v. Dundas, 50 Wis. 335 (1880); Wood v. Lane, 6 C. & P. 774 (1834); see note to Hawkins v. Comm. 14 B. Mon. (Ky.) 395 (1854), in 61 Am. Dec. 151--164.

[6] Fotheringham v. Adams Ex. Co., 36 Fed. 252, 1 L. R. A. 474 (1888);

cf. Smith v. State, 7 Humph. (Tenn.) 43 (1846).

[7] Herring v. Boyle, 1 C. M. & R. 377 (1834).

[8] Bird v. Jones, 7 Q. B. 742, 15 L. J. Q. B. 82 (1845). See dissenting opinion of Lord Denman. The majority opinion declares that imprisonment "includes the notion of restraint within some lmits defined by a will or power exterior to our own."

[9] State v. Lemsford, 81 N. C. 528 (1879). Prosecutor voluntarily went with defendant as the result of a practical joke, induced by false statement.

[10] Payson v. Macomber, 3 Allen (85 Mass.) 69. Defendant induced plaintiff to go to Salem and stay there, so as not to be a witness against a third person, but no force or threat of force shown.

Imprisonment may be effected by one who is not an officer,[12] and who does not pretend to act in an official capacity. A person who is locked in a room and forced to stay there against his will,[13] or who is kept in a building by threats of another to hurt him, if he ventures out, is imprisoned.[14]

Unlawfulness of Imprisonment. Any imprisonment which is not legally justifiable is a false imprisonment, and subjects him who is responsible therefor, whether as principal or agent, to an action in tort for damages.[15] The plaintiff in such action need not prove that the defendant acted maliciously or without probable cause, or with any wrongful intention, nor that actual harm of any sort was done to him.[16] He makes out a *prima facie* case by showing the imprisonment, and it then devolves upon the defendant to prove that the imprisonment was lawful and that he was justified in what he did.[17]

Justification Uuder Legal Process. In a former chapter, it was shown that a ministerial officer is not liable in tort for enforcing process fair on its face and issued by a court or magistrate of competent jurisdiction.[18] Accordingly, if he arrests and imprisons a person under such process, the victim cannot maintain an action for false imprisonment, although he may be entitled to an action for malicious prosecution against someone else.[19] If, however,

[11] Moses v. Dubois, Dudley (S. C. Law) 209 (1838); Spooner v. Spooner, 12 Met. (53 Mass.) 281 (1847). Defendant, in each case, carried plaintiff to sea, but the latter had ample opportunity to leave before the ship started.

[12] Price v. Bailey, 66 Ill. 49 (1872); Hildebrand v. McCrum, 101 Ind. 61 (1884).

[13] Woodward v. Washburn, 3 Den. (N. Y.) 369 (1846).

[14] McNay v. Stratton, 9 Bradw. (Ill. App.) 215, 1881).

[15] Bergeron v. Peyton, 106 Wis. 377, 82 N. W. 291, 80 Am. St. R. 33 (1900).

[16] Rich v. McInerny, 103 Ala. 345, 15 So. 663, 49 Am. St. R. 32 (1893); Comer v. Knowles, 17 Ks. 436

(1877); Glazar v. Hubbard, 102 Ky. 68, 42 S. W. 1114, 80 Am. St. R. 340, 39 L. R. A. 210 (1897).

[17] Floyd v. State, 12 Ark. 43, 54 Am. Dec. 250; Mitchell v. State, 12 Ark. 50, 54 Am. Dec. 253 (1851), with noto, pp. 258-271; Jackson v. Knowlton, 173 Mass. 94, 53 N. E. 134 (1899); Snead v. Bonnoil, 166 N. Y. 325, 59 N. E. 899 (1901); Chase v. Ingalls, 97 Mass. 524 (1867).

[18] Supra, Chap. III. O'Shanessy v. Baxter, 121 Mass. 515 (1877); People v. Warren, 5 Hill (N. Y.) 440 (1843).

[19] Rich v. McInerny, 103 Ala. 345, 15 So. 663, 49 Am. St. R. 32 (1893) Marks v. Townsend, 97 N. Y. 590 (1885); Tryon v. Pingree, 112 Mich.

the process is void it will protect no one who is responsible for its enforcement.[20] Moreover, the protection of valid legal process may be lost by its abuse,[21] as when it is wrongfully employed to force the imprisoned person to pay a debt,[22] or to pay illegal fees.[23] In such cases, the one abusing the process is treated as though he were a trespasser *ab initio*. " When the law has given an authority," it is said, " it is reasonable that it should make void everything done by the abuse of that authority, and leave the abuser as if he had done everything without authority." [24] It is deemed to be against " sound public policy to permit a man to justify himself at all under a license or authority allowed him by law, after he has abused it, and used it for improper purposes. The presumption of law is, that he who thus abuses such authority, assumed the exercise of it in the first place for the purpose of abusing it." [25]

Process Under Unconstitutional Statute or Ordinance. An unconstitutional statute or ordinance is for all legal purposes, as if it had never been enacted.[26] All proceedings under it, though nominally conducted in a court of justice, are in truth *coram non judice*. Process issuing from legal tribunals in such circumstances is void, and should afford no defense, either to the parties setting the proceedings in motion, or to the officers enforcing the process. Such

338, 70 N. W. 905, 37 L. R. A. 222, 67 Am. St. R. 399 (1897, with note, pp. 408--427.

[20] Flumoto v. Marsh, 130 Cal. 66, 62 Pac. 303, 509, 80 Am. St. R. 73 (1900); Clyma v. Kennedy, 64 Conn. 310, 29 At. 539, 42 Am. St. R. 194; Comm. v. Crotty, 10 Allen (Mass.) 403 (1865); Wachsmith v. Merch. Nat. Bk. 96 Mich. 427, 56 N. W. 9; 21 L. R. A. 278 (1893); West v. Cabell, 153 U. S. 78; 14 Sup. Ct. 752 (1894). For the distinction between void process, irregular process and voidable process, see Bryan v. Congdon, 86 Fed. 221; 57 U. S. App. 505, 29 C. C. A. 670 (1898); Everett v. Henderson, 146 Mass. 89, 14 N. E. 932, (1888);

Neinitz v. Conrad, 22 Or. 164, 29 Pac. 548 (1892).

[21] Wood v. Graves, 144 Mass. 365, 11 N. E. 567, 59 Am. R. 365 (1887); Caselton v. Taylor, 50 Vt. 220 (1877).

[22] Grainger v. Hill, 4 Bing. N. C. 212 (1838); Holley v. Mix, 3 Wend. (N. Y.) 350, 20 Am. Dec. 702 (1829); Baldwin v. Weed, 17 Wend. (N. Y.) 224, 234 (1837).

[23] Robbins v. Swift, 86 Me. 197, 29 At. 981 (1894).

[24] Allen v. Crofoot, 5 Wend. (N. Y.) 506 (1830).

[25] State v. Moor, 12 N. H. 42 (1841).

[26] Cooley, Principles of Constitutional Law (1st Ed.) 155; Sumner v. Beeler, 50 Ind. 341 (1875).

is the holding in some jurisdictions.[27]   In others, however, it has been held that not only the judicial officers, who have sustained the constitutionality of the statutes or ordinances, are free from liability to tort actions, as upon the principles, heretofore stated, they would be,[28] but that ministerial officers, enforcing process in such cases, are also protected.[29]

Even judicial officers are liable for false imprisonment, when they issue an order of arrest and procure its enforcement, without color of legal authority or jurisdiction.[30]

Arrest Without a Warrant—(a)   By Peace Officers.   In order to prevent the escape of criminals and to bring them to justice promptly, the law permits their arrest without a warrant.   A person who is guilty of a breach of the peace, may be arrested by a peace officer, who is present, even though the latter is " the person upon whom the peace is broken." [31]   Generally speaking the arrest of one who has been guilty of a breach of the peace, is not justified after he has escaped from the place, or peace has been restored.[32] But so long as the conduct of the wrongdoer is such as to show that the public peace is likely to be endangered by his acts, his arrest without a warrant is justifiable.[33]

At common law, petty criminal offenders who are not guilty of a breach of the peace, are not subject to arrest without a warrant,

[27] Sumner v. Beeler, 50 Ind. 341 (1875); State v. Hunter, 106 N. C. 796, 11 S. E. 366, 8 L. R. A. 529 (1890); Barling v. West, 29 Wis. 307, 9 Am. R. 576 (1871); Campbell v. Sherman, 35 Wis. 103 (1874).

[28] *Supra,* Chap. III. *cf.* Roth v. Shupp, 94 Md. 55, 50 At. 430 (1901).

[29] Frammel v. Russellville, 34 Ark. 105, 36 Am. R. 1 (1879); Brooks v. Mangan, 86 Mich. 576, 49 N. W. 633, 24 Am. S. R. 137 (1891); Tillman v. Beard, 121 Mich. 475, 80 N. W. 248 (1899). Persons, called upon by an officer to assist him in enforcing void process, and who do assist in ignorance of the character of the process, are protected in some states. Reed v. Rice, 2 J. J. Marshall (Ky.) 44; 19 Am. Dec.

122 (1829); Firestone v. Rice, 71 Mich. 377, 38 N. W. 885 (1888); but not in others, Oystead v. Shed, 12 Mass. 506, 511 (1815); Elder v. Morrison, 10 Wend. (N. Y.) 128 (1833).

[30] Stephens v. Wilson, 115 Ky. 27, 72 S. W. 336 (1903).

[31] Anonymous Y. B. H. VII, f. 6, pl. 12 (1490).

[32] Regina v. Walker, Dearsley Cr. Cas. 358 (1854); Wahl v. Walton, 30 Minn. 506 (1883); Quinn v. Heisel, 40 Mich. 576 (1879); State v. Lewis, 50 Ohio St. 179, 33 N. E. 405 (1893).

[33] Timothy v. Simpson, 1 C. M. & R. 757, 6 C. & P. 499, 5 Tyrr. 244 (1835); Loggins v. Southern Ry., 64 S. C. 321, 42 S. E. 163 (1902).

and a peace officer who so arrests them is liable to an action for false imprisonment.[34]

By statute, in some jurisdictions, a peace officer is authorized to arrest without a warrant for any crime or public offense committed or attempted in his presence.[35]

He is justified, at common law, in arresting, without a warrant, a person who has committed a felony, although not in his presence. The law goes even further and allows the officer " having reasonable ground to suspect that a felony has been committed, to detain the party suspected until inquiry can be made by the proper authorities." [36] In some states,[37] legislature has limited the officer's authority in this respect to cases where a felony has in fact been committed.

At common law, even a peace officer is not justified in arresting without a warrant, upon suspicion of a misdemeanor,[38] nor for a misdemeanor which was not committed in his presence.[39]

---

[34] Booth v. Hanley, 2 C. & P. 288 (1826), Plaintiff "was turning up to the wall for a particular occasion." Hardy v. Murphy, 1 Esp. 294 (1795), Plaintiff "was noisy in a public street," Wooding v. Oxley, 9 C. & P. 1 (1839), Plaintiff cried, "hear, hear," and asked questions of the speaker, in a public meeting: Palmer v. Maine C. Ry., 92 Me. 399, 42 At. 800, 44 L. R. A. 673, 69 Am. St. R. 513 (1899), Plaintiff charged with fraudulently evading the payment of his fare; Boyleston v. Kerr, 2 Daly (N. Y.) 220 (1867), Plaintiff fraudulently substituted a smaller check for the one first delivered; Kurtz v. Moffit, 115 U. S. 487, 6 Sup. Ct. 148 (1885), A state peace officer has no right to arrest a deserter from the Federal army, as the latter's offence is a breach of the military law, not a felony or breach of the peace. Common law felony defined at p. 499.

[35] Wahl v. Walton, 30 Minn. 506 (1883); New York Code of Criminal Procedure, §177 (1); Claiborne v. Chesapeake & O. Ry., 46 W. Va. 363, 33 S. E. 262 (1899), Plaintiff carried on his person an open knife, a bottle of whiskey and a razor — "a deadly combination," in the opinion of the court, as well as a public offense under a statute.

[36] Beckwith v. Philby, 6 B. & C. 635 (1827); Samuel v. Payne, 1 Doug. 359 (1780); Miles v. Weston, 60 Ill. 361 (1871); Doering v. State, 49 Ind. 56, 19 Am. R. 669, (1874); Burke v. Bell, 36 Me. 317 (1853); Palmer v. Maine C. Ry., 92 Me. 399, 42 At. 800, 44 L. R. A. 673, 69 Am. S. R. 513 (1899); State v. Grant, 76 Mo. 236 (1882); Burns v. Erben, 40 N. Y. 463 (1869); Neal v. Joyner, 89 N. C. 287 (1883); McCarthy v. De Armit, 99 Pa. 63 (1881).

[37] See New York Code of Crim. Proc., § 177 (3).

[38] Palmer v. Maine Cen. Ry., 92 Me. 399, 42 At. 800, 44 L. R. A. 673, 69 Am. S. R. 513 (1899); Comm. v. Carey, 12 Cush. (Mass.) 246

(b) Arrest by a Private Person. The common law authorizes a private person to arrest without a warrant one who is breaking the peace in his presence, or whose conduct shows that the peace is likely to be broken by him.[40] Some modern statutes authorize such arrest for any crime committed or attempted in the presence of the one making the arrest.[41] He is also justified in arresting without a warrant one who, he has probable cause to believe, has committed a felony.[42] His position differs from that of a peace officer, in that he is liable for false imprisonment, if no felony has been committed, though he had probable cause to believe it had been committed.[43] His justification has been narrowed still more in some states, and his right to arrest without warrant for offenses not committed or attempted in his presence, has been limited to persons who have actually committed a felony.[44]

Reasonable and Probable Cause. It has been said by eminent judges,[45] that whether probable cause exists for believing a felony to have been committed, or that the person arrested committed it, is a question of fact for the jury. In England, however, it is well

(1853); Comm. v. McLaughlin, 12 Cush. (Mass.) 615 (1853); Ross v. Leggett, 61 Mich. 445, 28 N. W. 695 (1886); Danovan v. Jones, 36 N. H. 246 (1858); Thomas v. Turck, 94 N. Y. 90 (1883); Snead v. Bonnoil, 166 N. Y. 245, 59 N. E. 899 (1901); San Antonio, etc., Ry. v. Griffin, 29 Tex. Civ. App. 91, 48 S. E. 542 (1898).

[39] Gaillard v. Laxton, 2 B. & S. 363, 31 L. J. M. C. 123 (1862). In this case the officer did not have the warrant with him, when making the arrest, and was held liable for false imprisonment: McCullough v. Greenfield, Mich. , 95 N. W. 532 (1903). Plaintiff was arrested by a deputy sheriff at one place, under the direction of defendant who had the warrant with him, at another place: held a false imprisonment.

[40] Timothy v. Simpson, 1 C. M. & R. 757, 6 C. & P. 499, 5 Tyr. 244 (1835); Palmer v. Maine C. Ry. 92 Me. 399 (1899).

[41] New York Code of Cr. Proc. § 183 (1).

[42] Handcock v. Baker, 2 Bos. & P. 260 (1800). 'It is lawful for a private person to do anything to prevent the perpetration of a felony."

[43] Samuel v. Payne, 1 Doug. 359 (1780); Garnier v. Squiers, 62 Ks. 321; 62 Pac. 1005 (1900); Begley v. Comm. (Ky.) 60 S. W. 847 (1901); Phillips v. Trull, 11 Johns. (N. Y.) 486 (1814); Burns v. Erben, 40 N. Y. 463 (1869); Alabama, etc., Ry. v. Kuhu, 78 Miss. 114, 28 So. 797 (1900).

[44] New York Code of Cr. Proc. § 183 (2).

[45] Lord Tenterden in Beckwith v. Bailey, 6 B. & C. 635 (1827); Gray J. in Snead v. Bonnoil, 166 N. Y. 245, 59 N. E. 899 (1901).

settled that this is a question for the court; [46] and the weight of authority in this country is to the same effect.[47] Probable cause has been defined as " a state of facts actually existing, known to the prosecutor personally or by information derived from others, which would lead a reasonable man of ordinary caution, acting conscientiously upon these facts, to believe a person guilty of an offense justifying his arrest." [48] While these facts are to be considered from the standpoint of the person making the arrest, and not from that of the arrested one,[49] the burden is on the former to show that he had reasonable and probable cause for his belief.[50]

Unreasonable Detention of a Person Arrested.   An officer arresting a person with or without a warrant, or a private individual arresting without a warrant, is not allowed to imprison the suspected criminal indefinitely.   Where the arrest is made without a warrant, it is the duty of the one arresting to take the other party before a magistrate, without unnecessary delay, in order that a judicial examination may be had, for the purpose of determining whether a warrant shall issue, or the prisoner be discharged.[51] " The value of personal liberty is too great, to permit the detention of a suspected fugitive, upon the judgment of a ministerial officer and without a hearing judicial in its character." [52] Even where the arrest is made under a warrant, the officer must take the prisoner, without any

---

[46] Broughton v. Jackson, 18 Q. B. 378, 21 L. J. Q. B. 266 (1852); Lister v. Perryman, L. R. 4 H. L. 521, 39 L. J. Ex. 177 (1870).

[47] Filer v. Smith, 96 Mich. 347, 55 N. W. 999 (1893); Burns v. Erben, 40 N. Y. 463 (1869); McCarthy v. De Armit, 99 Pa. 63 (1881); Wolf v. Perryman, 82 Tex. 112, 17 S. W. 772 (1891); Vinal v. Core, 18 W. Va. 2 (1881).

[48] Claiborne v. Ches. & O. Ry., 46 W. Va.. 363, 33 S. E. 262 (1899). cf. Rich v. McInerny, 103 Ala. 345, 15 So. 663, 49 Am. St. R. 32 (1894).

[49] Brady v. Stiltner, 40 W. Va. 289, 21 S. E. 729 (1895); cf. McCarthy v. De Armit, 99 Pa. 63 (1881).

[50] Jackson v. Knowlton, 173 Mass. 97, 53 N. E. 134 (1899).

[51] Wright v. Court, 4 B. & C. 596, 6 D. & R. 623 (1825); Hall v. Booth, 3 N. & M. 316 (1834); Marsh v. Wise, 2 F. & F. 51 (1860); Lavina v. State, 63 Ga. 513 (1879); Harness v. Steele, 159 Ind. 286, 64 N. E. 875 (1902); Brock v. Stimson, 108 Mass. 520, 11 Am. R. 390 (1871); Twilley v. Perkins, 77 Md. 252, 26 At. 286, 39 Am. St. R. 408, 19 L. R. A. 632 (1893); Linden v. Banfield, 114 Mich. 93, 72 N. W. 1 (1897); Green v. Kennedy, 48 N. Y. 653 (1871); Leger v. Warren, 62 Ohio St. 500, 57 N. E. 506, 78 Am. St. R. 738 (1900).

[52] Simmons v. Van Dyke, 138 Ind. 380, 37 N. E. 973, 26 L. R. A. 33, 46 Am. S. R. 411 (1894).

unnecessary delay, before the magistrate issuing it, in order that the party may have a speedy examination, if he desires it.[53] When any considerable delay ensues, the burden is upon the officer to show that it was reasonably necessary.[54]

Detentions which are not False Imprisonments. The most frequent examples of this class are the temporary detention of pupils as a matter of lawful school discipline,[55] and acts done in behalf of those who are incompetent to take care of themselves, by reason of physical injury,[56] or sudden sickness, or drunkenness, or insanity.[57] The right to restrain the liberty of an insane person, in the absence of a statute,[58] however, depends upon the character of the insanity. If he is harmlessly insane he may not be interfered with; but if his lunacy makes him dangerous to himself or others, he may be confined,[59] although such restraint ought to be followed by judicial proceedings in which a proper order or judgment for confinement may be obtained.

§ 3. MALICIOUS PROSECUTION.

The Nature of this Tort. Blackstone treats it as a species of defamation. His statement is: "A third way of destroying or injuring a man's reputation is by preferring malicious indictments or prosecutions against him, which, under the mask of justice and public spirit, are sometimes made the engines of private spite and enmity."[60] The gist of these actions for malicious prosecution is

[53] Simmons v. Van Dyke *supra;* Anderson v. Beck, 64 Miss. 113 (1886); Francisco v. State, 24 N. J. L. 30 (1853).

[54] Tubbs v. Tukey, 3 Cush (57 Mass.) 438, 50 Am. Dec. 744 (1849); Wiltge v. Holt, 95 Ind. 469 (1884). The delay was caused by the arrested person's drunkenness: Kent v. Miles, 65 Vt. 582, 27 At. 194 (1893). The delay was due to the fact that the court, to which the warrant was returnable, was not in session.

[55] Fertich v. Michener, 111 Ind. 473, 485, 60 Am. R. 709 (1887).

[56] Olle v. Pittsburg, etc., Ry., 201 Pa. 361, 50 At. 1011 (1902).

[57] Porter v. Rich, 70 Conn. 235, 39 At. 169, 39 L. R. A. 353 (1898); Colby v. Jackson, 12 N. H. 526 (1842).

[58] See Washer v. Slater, 67 App. Div. 385, 73 N. Y. Supp. 425 (1901), construing New York Insanity Law, Ch. 545 L. 1896.

[59] Porter v. Rich, 70 Conn. 235; Matter of Oakes, 8 L. Reporter (Mass.) 122 (1845); Look v. Dean, 108 Mass. 116, 11 Am. R. 323 (1871); Van Deusen v. Newcomer, 40 Mich. 90 (1879); Wheal v. W. R., Y. B. 22 Ed. IV, f. 45, pl. 10 (1483).

[60] Blackstone's Commentaries, Vol. III p. 126.

generally acknowledged to be an invasion of the personal rights of the plaintiff, rather than an injury to his property interests;[61] and in most cases, complaint is not made of injury to reputation, but rather of the invasion of one's right of personal liberty.

Indeed, it often happens that the plaintiff has his option of suing either for false imprisonment or for malicious prosecution.[62] If, however, his arrest was made under process valid in form and issued by a competent court upon sufficient complaint, he cannot sue for false imprisonment. His action, if any, is for malicious prosecution.[63]

The Essential Elements of the Tort. A person, who brings his action for this wrong, must prove four things: first, that the prosecution complained of has terminated in his favor: second, that it was instituted maliciously: third, that it was brought without probable cause, and, fourth, that it caused him damage. If he fails to prove either of these propositions he fails in his suit.

Termination in His Favor. The reason for this requirement, given in one of the earliest cases,[64] and repeated in later decisions,[65] is that " it cannot be known until the action is terminated that it was unjust." It has also been declared that if this requirement did not exist " almost every case would have to be tried over again upon its merits." [66]

Whether a prosecution has been terminated is not a difficult question ordinarily. The true test to be applied is: has the particular

---

[61] Lawrence v. Martin, 22 Cal. 174 (1863); Francis v. Burnett, 84 Ky. 23, 35 (1886); Nettleton v. Dinehart, 5 Cush. (59 Mass.) 543 (1850); Porter v. Muck, 50 W. Va. 581, 40 S. E. 459 (1901); Norman v. Orton, 34 Wis. 259, 17 Am. R. 441 (1874). "The personal injury is the *gravamen* of the action, and the effect of the alleged malicious acts of the defendant upon the estate of the plaintiff is incidental merely."

[62] Apgar v. Woolston, 43 N. J. L. 57 (1881).

[63] Whitten v. Bennett, 86 Fed. 405 (1898); Black v. Buckingham, 174 Mass. 102, 54 N. E. 494 (1899); Marks v. Townsend, 97 N. Y. 590 (1885).

[64] Year Book 2 Rich. III, Pl. 9 (1484).

[65] Water v. Freeman, Hob. 267 (1620); Smith v. Cranshaw, W. Jones 93 (1625); Parker v. Langley, 10 Mod. 210 (1714); Fisher v. Bristow, 1 Doug. 215 (1779).

[66] Basebe v. Matthews, L. R. 2 C. P. 684, 36 L. J. M. C. 93 (1867); Frisbie v. Morris, 75 Conn. 637, 55 At. 9 (1903); Quinn v. Rice, 154 Mass. 1, 27 N. E. 772, 12 L. R. A. 288 (1891); Douglass v. Allen, 56 Ohio St. 156, 46 N. E. 707 (1897).

prosecution been " disposed of in such a manner that it cannot be revived, and the prosecutor, if he intends to proceed further, must institute proceedings *de novo?* " [67] It is not necessary that the prosecution be concluded by a trial upon the merits, although this has been declared essential by an eminent judge.[68] Accordingly " a criminal prosecution may be said to have terminated: (1) Where there is a verdict of not guilty; (2) where the grand-jury ignore the bill; (3) where a *nolle prosequi* is entered, and (4) where the accused has been discharged from bail and imprisonment." [69] If the prosecution be one, in which the victim has no opportunity to contest the complaint and obtain a decision, the rule requiring a termination in his favor does not apply.[70] A voluntary abandonment of the original prosecution, with its formal dismissal on that account, is a termination thereof in the victim's favor; but if its dismissal is due to a compromise, the action cannot be said to have terminated in his favor. This is upon the ground that " the termination must be such as to furnish *prima facie* evidence that the action was without foundation." Where there is a compromise, the termination does not furnish evidence that the prosecution was improperly instituted, but indicates that the one prosecuted is in the position of admitting that his antagonist had probably cause for his proceeding.[71]

[67] Apgar v. Woolston, 43 N. J. L. 57, 66 (1881).

[68] Shaw, C. J., in Parker v. Farley, 10 Cush. (64 Mass.) 279 (1852). This view has been modified by later cases in that state: cf. Graves v. Dawson, 133 Mass. 419 (1882).

[69] Lowe v. Wartman, 47 N. J. L. 413, 1 At. 489 (1885); Brown v. Randall, 36 Conn. 56, 4 Am. R. 35 (1869); Hatch v. Cohen, 84 N. C. 602, 37 Am. R. 630 (1881); Douglass v. Allen, 56 Ohio St. 156, 46 N. E. 707 (1897); Driggs v. Burton, 44 Vt. 124 (1871); Rider v. Kite, 61 N. J. L. 8, 38 At. 754 (1897); Craig v. Ginn, 3 Penne. (Del.) 117; 48 At. 192, 94 Am. St. R. 77 (1901).

[70] Steward v. Gormett, 7 C. B. N. S. 191, 29 L. J. C. P. 170 (1859); Hyde v. Grench, 62 Md. 577 (1884);

Bump v. Betts, 19 Wend. 421 (1838). In the first two cases, the malicious proceeding was an *ex parte* application for arrest of the plaintiff, and an order that he give sureties to keep the peace. In the last, there was a malicious attachment of property, with no opportunity to defend.

[71] Wilkinson v. Howell Moo. & Mal. 495 (1830); Marks v. Gray, 42 Me. 86 (1856); Sartwell v. Parker, 141 Mass. 405, 5 N. E. 807 (1886); Rachelman v. Skinner, 46 Minn. 196, 48 N. W. 776 (1891); McCormick v. Sisson, 7 Cow. 715 (1827); Mayer v. Walter, 64 Pa. 283 (1870); Russell v. Morgan, 24 R. I. 134, 52 At. 809 (1902); Craig v. Ginn, 3 Penne. (Del.) 117, 48 At. 192, 94 Am. St. R. 77 (1901).

Malice. This term in its present connection, means something more than " the intentional doing of a wrongful act to the injury of another, without justification or legal excuse therefor." [72] It means malice in fact, as distinguished from malice in law. It means that the conduct of the original prosecutor was actuated by some " improper or sinister motive;" [73] that he instituted the prosecution not " with the mere intention of carrying the law into effect, but with an intention which was wrongful in point of fact," [74] that he did this " from an indirect and improper motive, and not in furtherance of justice." [75]

On the other hand, the term is not to be understood in its popular signification. The plaintiff is not bound to show that the defendant acted from motives of resentment, or ill-will or hatred towards him.[76] He establishes malice by showing that the defendant procured the warrant to be issued by making an intentionally false affidavit; [77] or that, having the opportunity of discovering the facts, he failed to take advantage of it, and recklessly or with culpable negligence instituted the prosecution.[78] Express evidence of malice need not be given. It may be established by circumstantial evidence, and is generally proved in this way. It may be inferred by the jury from a want of probable cause. But its " existence is always a question exclusively for the jury," [79] although when the plaintiff's evi-

[72] Ahrens & Ott. Mfg. Co. v. Hoeher, 106 Ky. 692; 51 S. W. 194 (1899); Vanderbilt v. Mathis, 5 Duer (N. Y.) 559 (1856).

[73] Stewart v. Sonneborn, 98 U. S. 187, 25 L. Ed. 116 (1878).

[74] Abrath v. North E. Ry., 11 Q. B. D. 440, 448-9, 52 L. J. Q. B. 620 (1883).

[75] Ibid, p. 455.

[76] Mitchell v. Jenkins, 5 B. & A. 588, 15 L. J. Q. B. 221 (1833); Pullen v. Glidden, 66 Me. 202 (1877); Wiggin v. Coffin, 3 Story 1, Fed. Cas. No. 17, 204 (1836).

[77] Collins v. Love, 7 Blackf. (Ind.) 416 (1845); Navarino v. Dudrap, 66 N. J. L. 620, 50 At. 353 (1901); Dennis v. Ryan, 63 Barb. 145

(1872); S. C. 65 N. Y. 385, 22 Am. R. 635 (1875).

[78] Hamilton v. Smith, 39 Mich. 222 (1878); Stubbs v. Mullholland, 168 Mo. 47, 67 S. W. 650 (1902).

[79] Stewart v. Sonneborn, 98 U. S. 187 (1878); Wheeler v. Nesbit, 24 How. (U. S.) 545 (1860); Johnson v. Eberts, 11 Fed. 129 (1880); Lunsford v. Dietrich, 93 Ala. 565, 9 So. 308, 30 Am. St. R. 79 (1890); Boyeman v. Shaw, 37 Ark. 160 (1881); Harkrader v. Moore, 44 Cal. 144 (1872); Porter v. White, 5 Mackey (16 Dis. Col.) 180 (1886); Harpham v. Whitney, 77 Ill. 32 (1875); Newell v. Downs, 8 Blackf. (Ind.) 523 (1847); Parker v. Parker, 102 Ia. 500, 71 N. W. 421 (1897); Atchi-

dence fails to make a *prima facie* case of malice, the court should non-suit him.[80]

Probable Cause. This term has been defined as " such a state of facts and circumstances as would lead a man of ordinary caution and prudence, acting conscientiously, impartially, reasonably and without prejudice upon the facts within his knowledge, to believe that the person accused is guilty," [81] or, if the prosecution is a civil suit, to believe " that he had a cause of action " [82] against the one whom he prosecutes. Some courts have declared that the facts and circumstances should be such as would convince a " cautious " man that there was good ground for the prosecution; [83] but the weight of authority is in favor of the statement contained in the definition quoted above.[84] While the law tends to discourage unreasonable invasions of personal rights, it has regard also for the public welfare and for the interests of those who have been wronged. If the test of probable cause is made too strict and severe, persons will be discouraged from setting the wheels of justice in motion.[85]

The question of probable cause is one for the court and not for the jury.[36] Only by reserving it for the court, can anything like cer-

son Co. v. Watson, 37 Ks. 773, (1887); Medcalfe v. Brooklyn Co. 45 Md. 198 (1876); Greenwade v. Mills, 31 Miss. 464 (1856); Johnson v. Chambers, 10 Iredell (32 N. C.) 287 (1849); Gee v. Culver, 12 Or. 228, 11 Pac. 302 (1885); Cooper v. Hart, 147 Pa. 595, 23 At. 833 (1892); Caldwell v. Burnett, 22 S. C. 1 (1884); Evans v. Thompson, 12 Heisk. (Tenn.) 534 (1884); Barron v. Mason, 31 Vt. 189 (1858); Forbes v. Hagman, 75 Va. 168 (1881).

[80] Lauterbach v. Netzo, 111 Wis. 326, 87 N. W. 230 (1901).

[81] Heyne v. Blair, 62 N. Y. 19, 22 (1875); Bacon v. Towne, 4 Cush. (58 Mass.) 217 (1849); Kansas, etc., Co. v. Galloway, — Ark. ——, 74 S. W. 521 (1903).

[82] Ravenga v. Mackintosh, 2 B. & C. 693 (1824).

[83] Munns v. Dupont, 3 Wash. C. C. 31, Fed. Cas. No. 9,926 (1811); Richey v. McBean, 16 Ill. 63 (1855); Cole v. Curtis, 16 Minn. 181 (1870); Ash v. Marlow, 20 O. 119 (1853).

[84] Flam v. Lee, 116 Ia. 289, 90 N. W. 70 (1902); Bank of Miller v. Richmon, 64 Neb. 111, 89 N. W. 627 (1902); McClafferty v. Philp, 151 Pa. 86, 24 At. 1042 (1892); Eggett v. Allen, 106 Wis. 633, 82 N. W. 556, (1900).

[85] Allen v. Flood (1898), A. C. 1, 125, 172, 67 L. J. Q. B. 119, 185, 209; Munns v. Dupont, 3 Wash. C. C. 31, Fed. Cas. No. 9,926 (1811).

[86] Ahrens, etc., Co. v. Hoeher, 106 Ky. 692, 51 S. W. 194 (1899); Bank of Miller v. Richmon, 64 Neb. 111, 89 N. W. 627 (1902); Jones v. Wilmington, etc., Ry., 125 N. C. 227, 34 S. E. 398 (1899).

tainty as to what constitute probable cause be obtained. Of course, if the evidence is conflicting, or, if different inferences may be drawn by reasonable men from uncontradicted evidence, the jury are to determine the facts, or to state their inferences.[87]

Success or Failure of Original Prosecution.

If the termination of the original prosecution was in favor of the prosecutor, and the decision has not been reversed, it furnishes conclusive proof of probable cause for the prosecution.[88] When it has been reversed for legal error, but it is not shown to have been procured by fraud or other unlawful means, the weight of authority is in favor of treating it as still conclusive on the question of probable cause.[89] Indeed, a few courts refuse to inquire, in the suit for malicious prosecution, how the termination of the original proceeding was secured, if it was adverse to the present plaintiff.[90] On the other hand, it has been declared that the true principle to be applied is this: " A conviction is always *prima facie* evidence of the existence of probable cause; but this is a rule of evidence, founded upon the fact that, ordinarily, if a court has proceeded to conviction, it must have had before it such evidence as in the mind of a prudent and reasonable man would convince him of the guilt of the accused; and, therefore, a subsequent reversal, while it may show that the accused was in fact innocent, does not show that there was no probable cause for believing him guilty. Where, however, the conviction is under such circumstances as to deprive it of such naturally evidentiary effect, this presumption ceases." [91]

---

[87] Wiggin v. Coffin, 3 Story, 1, Fed. Cas. No. 17,264 1836); Holliday v. Holliday, 123 Cal. 26, 55 Pac. 703 (1888); Johnson v. Miller, 63 Ia. 529, 50 Am. R. 758 (1884).

[88] Hartshorn v. Smith, 104 Ga. 235, 30 S. E. 666 (1898); Forster v. Orr, 17 Or. 447, 21 Pac. 440 (1889); Swepon v. Davis, 109 Tenn. 99, 70 S. W. 65, 59 L. R. A. 501 (1902).

[89] Crescent City Co. v. Butcher's Union, 120 U. S. 141, 7 Sup. Ct. 472, 30 L. Ed. 614 (1886); Holliday v. Holliday, 123 Cal. 26, 55 Pac. 703 (1898); Adams v. Bicknell, 126 Ind. 210, 25 N. E. 804, 22 Am. S. R. 576

(1890); Morrow v. Wheeler, etc., Co., 165 Mass. 349, 43 N. E. 105 (1896); Cloon v. Gerry, 13 Gray (79 Mass.), 201 (1859); Griffin v. Sellers, 2 Dev. & B. L. (19 N. C.) 492, 31 Am. Dec. 422 (1837).

[90] Clements v. Odorless & Co., 67 Md. 461, 10 At. 442, 1 Am. S. R. 409 (1887); Parker v. Huntington, 7 Gray (73 Mass.), 36, 66 Am. Dec. 455 (1856); Griffin v. Sellers, 4 Dev. & B. L. (20 N. C.) 177 (1838); Herman v. Brookerhoff, 8 Watts (Pa.), 240 (1839). In Griffin v. Sellers it is said, that were the rule otherwise, " the result would be intermi-

The failure of the original prosecution is not conclusive evidence of a want of probable cause. Whether the prosecutor had such cause does not turn upon the actual guilt of the accused, or the state of the case, but upon the honest and reasonable belief of the prosecutor.[92] In most jurisdictions, the failure of the prosecution, while a fact which the plaintiff must establish in order to make out his case, is not evidence tending to show the want of probable cause.[93] In other jurisdictions, it is deemed evidence of a want of probable cause, but does not shift the burden of proof to the defendant.[94] In still others, it is held to make out a *prima facie* case, and casts upon the defendant the burden of showing that he had probable cause.[95]

The holding of an accused person by a committing magistrate, as well as the finding of an indictment by a grand-jury, is generally accounted evidence of probable cause;[96] and his discharge upon a preliminary examination, is treated by some courts as evidence of a want of probable cause.[97]

Advice of Counsel as Evidence of Probable Cause. " Nothing is better settled," an eminent court has declared, " than that when the prosecutor submits the facts to his attorney, who advises they are sufficient, and he acts thereon in good faith, such advice is a defense to an action for malicious prosecution."[98] Not-

---

nable litigation between the parties, alternately changing sides."

[91] Nehr v. Dobbs, 47 Neb. 863, 869, 66 N. W. 864 (1891).

[92] Foshay v. Ferguson, 2 Den. (N. Y.) 617 (1846).

[93] Stewart v. Sonneborn, 98 U. S. 187, 25 L. Ed. 116 (1878); Thompson v. Rubber Co., 56 Conn. 493, 16 At. 554 (1888); Anderson v. Friend, 85 Ill. 135 (1877); Philpot v. Lucas, 101 Ia. 478, 70 N. W. 625 (1897); Stone v. Crocker, 24 Pick. (41 Mass.) 81 (1832); Boeger v. Langenberg, 97 Mo. 390, 11 S. W. 223, 10 Am. S. R. 322 (1888); Apgar v. Woolston, 43 N. J. L. 57 (1881); Willard v. Holmes, 142 N. Y. 492, 37 N. E. 480 (1894); Eastman v. Monastes, 32 Or. 291, 51 Pac. 1095, 67 Am. St. R. 531 (1898); Bekke-

land v. Lyons, — Tex. ——, 72 S. W. 56 (1903); Cullen v. Hanisch, 114 Wis. 24, 89 N. W. 900 (1902).

[94] Rankin v. Crane, 104 Mich. 6, 61 N. W. 1007 (1895); Noblett v. Bartsch, 31 Wash. 24, 71 Pac. 551 (1903); Venal v. Core, 18 W. Va. 1 (1881).

[95] Barhight v. Tammany, 158 Pa. 545, 28 At. 135, 38 Am. S. R. 853 (1893).

[96] Ross v. Hixon, 46 Ks. 550, 26 Pac. 955, 26 Am. S. R. 123 (1891), with valuable note; Perkins v. Spaulding, 182 Mass. 218, 65 N. E. 72 (1903).

[97] Stemper v. Raymond, 38 Or. 16, 62 Pac. 20 (1900).

[98] McClaferty v. Philp, 151 Pa. 86, 24 At. 1042 (1892), *accord.;* Stewart v. Sonneborn, 98 U. S. 187, 25

withstanding this unqualified declaration, several courts of equal
eminence have held that the advice of a duly qualified attorney,
based upon an unfounded or clearly erroneous opinion of the rule
of law involved, does not constitute a defense.[99] " Probable cause,"
say these courts, "may be founded on misinformation as to the
facts, but not as to the law." [100] This view seems indefensible.
Undoubtedly, the blunder of counsel may be so gross as to show
bad faith on his part; [101] but, to quote the language of a distinguished
judge: "though every man being bound to know the law, is
answerable for the legal consequences of his acts, the imputation of
a motive which had no existence in fact is not one of them." [102]

In order that the advice of counsel may establish the existence of
probable cause and thus constitute a defense, the defendant must
show that he made a full and honest disclosure of all the material
facts within his knowledge and belief.[103] He cannot screen himself
behind expert legal advice based upon a fragmentary statement of
facts, nor upon such advice, when, notwithstanding it has been given,
he does not believe that his claim or charge is well-founded.[104]

The defendant is bound to show, too, that the person giving the
advice was a reasonably competent lawyer of good reputation.[105]

L. Ed. 116 (1878); Marks v. Hastings, 101 Ala. 165, 173, 13 So. 297 (1892); Kansas, etc., Co. v. Galloway, — Ark. ——, 74 S. W. 521 (1903); Black v. Buckingham, 174 Mass. 102, 54 N. E. 494 (1899).

[99] Lange v. Ill. Cen. Ry., 107 La. 687, 31 So. 1003 (1902); Nehr v. Dobbs, 47 Neb. 863, 66 N. W. 864 (1896); Hazzard v. Fluny, 120 N. Y. 223, 24 N. E. 194 (1890); Morgan v. Duffy, 94 Tenn. 686, 30 S. W. 735 (1845); Mauldin v. Ball, 104 Tenn. 597, 58 S. W. 248 (1900).

[100] Hazzard v. Fluny, 120 N. Y. 223, 227, 24 N. E. 194 (1890).

[101] Smith v. King, 62 Conn. 515, 26 At. 1059 (1893).

[102] Gibson, C. J., in Herman v. Brookerhoof, 8 Watts (Pa.), 240, 242 (1829).

[103] Black v. Buckingham, 174 Mass. 102, 54 N. E. 494 (1899).

[104] Marks v. Hastings, 101 Ala. 165, 13 So. 297 (1892); Kansas, etc., Co. v. Galloway, — Ark. ——, 74 S. W. 521 (1903); Vann v. McCreary, 77 Cal. 434, 19 Pac. 826 (1888); Johnson v. Miller, 82 Ia. 693, 47 N. W. 903 (1891); Roy v. Goings, 112 Ill. 656 (1886); Lange v. Ill. Cent. Ry., 107 La. 687, 31 So. 1003 (1902); Barhight v. Tammany, 158 Pa. 545, 28 At. 135 (1893); Jackson v. Bell, 5 S. D. 257, 58 N. W. 671 (1894); Stubbs v. Mulholland, 168 Mo. 47, 67 S. W. 651 (1902); Mauldin v. Ball, 104 Tenn. 597, 58 S. W. 248 (1900); Ravenga v. Mackintosh, 2 B. & C. 693 (1824); Hadrick v. Heslop, 12 Q. B. 267, 17 L. J. Q. B. 313 (1848).

[105] Murphy v. Larson, 77 Ill. 172 (1875); Stubbs v. Mulholland, 168 Mo. 47, 67 S. W. 651 (1902). " In this State, where a license to prac-

It is not enough that the adviser be a magistrate, or a layman accustomed to give counsel in legal matters.[106] The attorney should not be biased by any personal interest in the affair;[107] but the better view is that he is not disqualified by the fact that he is the defendant's regular counsel.[108] The rule that professional legal " advice, honestly sought and acted upon, supplies the indispensable element of probable cause " has been judicially declared to originate " in the policy of the law to encourage prosecutions where there is probable cause, actual or constructive, and is founded on the theory that persons, who have made the law their study and followed it as a profession, are well recognized advisers on questions of law, and that the citizen is justified in relying and acting on their advice. The protecting power of the rule is limited to the advice of licensed attorneys in good standing, and of reputed learning and competency. It should not be extended beyond these limitations." [109]

When the defendant establishes the existence of probable cause for his prosecution of plaintiff, he is entitled to judgment, though his motive may have been ever so malicious, and though the prosecution may have terminated in the present plaintiff's favor, and though the latter may have sustained damages.[110]

Legal Damage. The fourth element necessary to constitute a cause of action for malicious prosecution is legal damage to the plaintiff.

tice is obtained almost for the asking, it by no means follows, because a man has been licensed to practice law, that therefore he is qualified to give advice in a matter of such pith and moment as pertains to arresting a suspected man on a criminal charge."

[106] Burgett v. Burgett, 43 Ind. 78 (1873); Olmstead v. Partridge, 12 Gray (82 Mass.) 381 (1860); Beal v. Robson, 8 Ired. L. (N. C.) 276 (1848); Gee v. Culver, 12 Or. 228, 6 Pac. 775 (1883); Sutton v. McConnell, 46 Wis. 269, 50 N. W. 414 (1879). Contra—Ball v. Rawles, 93 Cal. 222, 28 Pac. 937, 27 Am. S. R. 174 (1892).

[107] White v. Cave, 71 Me. 55, 36 Am. R. 533 (1880); Perrenond v. Helm, 65 Neb. 77, 90 N. W. 980 (1902).

[108] Kansas, etc., Co. v. Galloway, — Ark. ——, 74 S. W. 521 (1903), " the objection that he was interested as the attorney of the prosecutor, and, therefore, disqualified under the rule, is untenable, for any lawyer called upon to advise is the attorney for the party asking his advice."

[109] Marks v. Hastings, 101 Ala. 165, 173, 13 So. 297 (1892). Cf. Olmstead v. Partridge, 12 Gray (82 Mass.), 381 (1860).

[110] Stewart v. Sonneborn, 98 U. S.

Such damage, said Chief Justice Holt more than two centuries ago, may be of three sorts, " any one of which is sufficient to support this action. First, damage to his fame, if the matter whereof he be accused be scandalous. Secondly; to his person, whereby he is imprisoned . Thirdly: to his property, whereby he is put to charges and expenses." [111]

Damage to Reputation. The illustrations of this sort of damage, given by Lord Holt, are an indictment for barratry, though the indictment be erroneous or found *ignoramus*,[112] and an indictment of a justice of the peace for doing an act contrary to law.[113] Modern illustrations are afforded by the malicious institution of proceedings in bankruptcy or insolvency,[114] and for proceedings for inquisition of lunacy.[115]

Damage to Person. A criminal prosecution, even though it may not involve scandal to the reputation, subjects the accused to the possible loss of personal liberty, and therefore " necessarily and naturally " causes legal damage to him.[116] Special damages need not be alleged nor proved. Indeed, most text writers and judges omit " legal damage " as a separate element in the cause of action for malicious prosecution, when the original proceeding is a criminal one. But it is submitted that legal damage is always an essential element of this cause of action, although the evidence which establishes the other elements will necessarily establish this, whenever

187, 25 L. Ed. 116 (1878); Frisbie v. Morris, 75 Conn. 637, 55 At. 9 (1903).

[111] Savill v. Roberts, 12 Mod. 208, 5 Mod. 394, 405, 1 Ld. Raym. 374, 1 Salk. 13, 3 Salk. 16, Carth. 416 (1698).

[112] Barns v. Constantine, Cro. Jac. 32, Yelv. 46 (1606).

[113] Henly v. Burnstall, T. Raym, 180, 1 Vent. 23 (1681).

[114] Chapman v. Pickersgill, 2 Wils. 145 (1762); Metropolitan Bank, v. Pooley, 10 App. Cas. 210 (1885); Stewart v. Sonneborn, 98 U. S. 187, 25 L. Ed. 116 (1878); Quartz Hill, etc., Co. v. Eyre, 11 Q. B. D. 674, 52

L. J. Q. B. 488 (1883); petition to wind up a company.

[115] Lockenour v. Sides, 57 Ind. 360, 26 Am. R. 58 (1877); see Wade v. Nat. Bank of Tacoma, 114 Fed. 377 (1902). Injury to reputation done by allegations in the complaint, which injured the present plaintiff's reputation and business.

[116] Quartz Hill Co. v. Eyre, 11 Q. B. D. 674, 52 L. J. Q. B. 488 (1883); Rayson v. South London Co. (1893), 2 Q. B. 304, 62 L. J. Q. B. 593; Saxon v. Castle, 6 A. & E. 652 (1837); Cardinal v. Smith, 109 Mass. 158, 11 Am. R. 682 (1872); Emerson v. Cochran, 111 Pa. 619, 4 At. 498 (1886).

the original prosecution deprives the defendant of personal liberty, or is carried on for the purpose of depriving him of his liberty.[117]

Damage to Property. A case of legal damage is made out, when the plaintiff shows that his property was attached or levied upon,[118] or was interfered with under a search warrant,[119] or his use or control of it was interrupted by an injunction,[120] or *lis pendens*,[121] or a receivership,[122] in proceedings maliciously instituted without probable cause, which have terminated in his favor. In the last cited case, the court said: " Any particular method of interfering with property rights, as by writ of attachment, is not material. An equitable levy upon property, as in garnishee proceedings, or the deprivation of the defendant of his property by means of the appointment of a receiver, or by any other means whereby his property is taken into the custody of the court or taken out of the custody of the owner and out of his free control, which, in the ordinary course of things, causes damage not reached by a mere judgment of vindication or for costs, is sufficient."

Damage to Property Consisting in Charges and Expenses. In commenting on this species of damage, Chief Justice Holt said: " That a man put to answer an indictment is put to

[117] Byne v. Moore, 5 Taunt. 187, 1 Marshall, 121 (1813), declares there must have been an imprisonment, or scandal to reputation; but the case has been criticised as not in accordance with modern law. Clerk and Lindsell, Torts (2d Ed. 557. In Goslin v. Wilcock, 2 Wils. 302 (1766), Lord Camdon said of an action for malicious arrest in a civil suit: " This action has been held to lie because the costs of the cause are not a satisfaction for imprisoning a man unjustly, and putting him to the difficulty of getting bail for a larger sum than is due."

[118] Redway v. McAndrew, L. R. 9 Q. B. 74 1873); Spaids v. Barrett, 57 Ill. 289, 11 Am. R. 19 (1870); Western Co. v. Wilmarth, 33 Ks. 510 (1885); O'Brien v. Barry, 106 Mass. 300, 8 Am. R. 329 (1871);

Fortman v. Rottier, 8 Ohio St. 548 (1858); Tomlinson v. Ward, 9 Ohio, 104 (1839); Mayer v. Walter, 64 Pa. 283 (1879).

[119] Cooper v. Booth, 3 Esp. 135, 144 (1785); Elsee v. Smith, 2 Chitty, 304, 1 D. & R. 97 (1822); Whitson v. May, 71 Ind. 269 (1880); Olson v. Toete, 48 Minn. 225, 48 N. W. 914 (1891); Boeger v. Langenberg, 97 Mo. 390, 11 S. W. 223, 10 Am. S. R. 322 (1888).

[120] Mitchell v. Southwestern Ry., 75 Ga. 398 (1885); Newark Coal Co. v. Upson, 40 Ohio St. 17 (1883).

[121] Smith v. Smith, 56 How. Pr. (N. Y.) 316 (1878), s. c., Aff'd. 20 Hun, 555 (1880).

[122] Luby v. Bennett, 111 Wis. 613, 87 N. W. 804, 56 L. R. A. 261, 87 Am. S. R. 897 (1901).

charges is notorious; and if so, it is an injury to his property; and if this injury be occasioned by a malicious prosecution, it is reason and justice he should have an action to repair him the injury." [123] Later in the same opinion, he notes a great difference between bringing an action maliciously and prosecuting an indictment maliciously. In the latter case, he says, the party maliciously prosecuted has no remedy for the charges to which he is put in defending himself, but that of his action for malicious prosecution. In the former, he declares, costs are given to the defendant as his security against troublesome actions, and these costs are in the stead of pledges required by ancient common law. His conclusion seems to be that one damaged, beyond his costs, by the malicious, groundless, and unsuccessful prosecution of a civil action cannot recover, unless he show that " the action was brought merely for vexation and oppression; but if he show any special matter whereby it appears to the court that it was frivolous and vexatious he shall have an action." [124]

At present, the English courts refuse to entertain an action for the malicious prosecution of a civil suit, unless the special matter alleged as legal damage, consists in the arrest of the person, or in scandal to his business reputation, or in the wrongful interference with his property by attachment or other process. If the only pecuniary damage, which he can show, is the payment of charges and expenses over and above his taxable costs, he will fail. Such expenditures, it is declared, are not legally " necessary to the purposes of the party who has incurred them." " It may be quite reasonable as between the successful party and his solicitor that the extra costs should be paid to the solicitor; but it is unreasonable that the losing party should pay them, they not having been caused by his litigation." As his litigation did not cause them, they cannot be deemed damages inflicted by him. [125]

In the case last cited, Lord Justice Bowen declared: " It is unnecessary to say that there could not be an action for malicious prosecution in the past, and it is unnecessary to say that there may not be such an action in the future, although it cannot be found at the present day. The counsel for the plaintiff company have argued this case with great ability; but they cannot point to a single instance,

[123] Savill v. Roberts, 12 Mod. 208, 209 (1698).
[124] Ibid. at p. 210.

[125] Brett, M. R., in Quartz Hill Co. v. Eyre, 11 Q. B. D. 674, 682.

since Westminster Hall began to be the seat of justice, in which an ordinary action, similar to the actions of the present day, has been considered to justify a subsequent action on the ground that it was brought maliciously and without reasonable and probable cause."

American Courts are Divided. Many courts in this country have approved and followed the English rule, stated in the last paragraph. They hold that the costs, which are allowed by statute, are the only penalty the law gives against a plaintiff for prosecuting a suit in a court of justice, in the regular and ordinary way, and which is not accompanied by the arrest of the person, or seizure of property, or other special injury not necessarily resulting in all suits prosecuted to recover for like causes of action. These tribunals express the opinion that to allow suits for malicious prosecution in such circumstances, would operate to deter an honest suitor from resorting to the courts for the ascertainment of his legal rights, through fear of being obliged to defend a subsequent suit charging him with malicious prosecution. They also insist that if the defendant may sue for extra costs and expenses incurred in defending against an unfounded prosecution, the plaintiff shall be allowed to bring an action when the defendant makes an unfounded defense.[126]

On the other hand, many of our courts reject the English rule, and sustain a recovery for the malicious prosecution of a civil suit, even though not attended with the arrest of the person, or the seizure

[126] Mitchell v. Southwestern Ry., 75 Ga. 398 (1885); Smith v. Mich. Buggy Co., 175 Ill. 619, 51 N. E. 569, 67 Am. S. R. 242 (1898); Wetmore v. Mellinger, 64 Ia. 741, 18 N. W. 870, 52 Am. R. 465 (1884); Supreme Lodge v. Unverzagt, 76 Md. 104, 24 At. 323 (1892); Potts v. Imlay, 4 N. J. L. 330, 7 Am. Dec. 603 (1816); Paul v. Fargo, 84 App. Div. 9, 82 N. Y. Supp. 369 (1903); Terry v. Davis, 114 N. C. 31, 15 S. E. 943 (1894); Cin. Trib. Co. v. Bruck, 61 Ohio St. 489, 56 N. E. 198, 76 Am. S. R. 433 (1900), distinguishing Pope v. Pollock, 46 Ohio St. 367, 21 N. E. 356, 4 L. R. A. 255, 15 Am. St. R. 608 (1889), as arising from the malicious prosecution of suits for forcible entry and detainer. "Judgments in such suits are not conclusive. The proceeding may be commenced and recommenced without limit, unless enjoined, and hence affords an opportunity for the gratification of malice and oppression, and, when this is the case, an action may be maintained by the injured party for the recovery of damages." Muldoon v. Rickey, 103 Pa. 110, 49 Am. R. 117 (1883); Johnson v. King, 64 Tex. 226 (1885); Luby v. Bennett, 111 Wis. 613, 87 N. W. 804, 87 Am. S. R. 897, 56 L. R. A. 261 (1901).

of property or wrongful interference with it. These tribunals declare that the taxable costs in most of our states are small, and are not intended by the legislature to afford full compensation, in cases which are maliciously instituted and are prosecuted without reasonable and probable cause. When a party groundlessly and maliciously sets in motion the formidable machinery of the law, say these courts, to harass and oppress his neighbor, he abuses legal process which was intended for parties acting in good faith, and his wrongdoing is of the same character with that of one who seizes property or interferes with its possession by its true owner. To refuse a remedy for such a wrong is to violate the rule of the common law that no legal injury shall go unredressed. This doctrine seems sound in principle and is gaining in favor.[127]

In some of the cases, cited in the last note, the original prosecution was instituted in a justice's court, where no taxable costs are allowed, and the pecuniary injury to the original defendant was intentionally inflicted in bad faith. The injustice of the English rule in such cases is manifest.

Compensatory and Punitive Damages. As malice on the part of the defendant is an essential element of the cause of action for malicious prosecution, it follows that the plaintiff, if entitled to recover at all, is not limited to compensatory damages, as a rule. Full compensation for obtaining sureties, in case of his arrest, and for the reasonable charges of his counsel, as well as other expenses caused by defendant's wrongful prosecution, should be given him. If his business has been injured, the harm thus suffered is a proper item of damages. Injury to feelings and reputation, indignity and

---

[127] Easton v. Bank of Stockton, 66 Cal. 123, 4 Pac. 1106, 56 Am. R. 77 (1884); Hoyt v. Macon, 2 Colo. 113 (1873); Whipple v. Fuller, 11 Conn. 582 (1836); Woods v. Finnell, 13 Bush (Ky.), 628 (1878); McCordle v. McGinley, 86 Ind. 538, 44 Am. R. 343 (1882); Brand v. Hinchman, 68 Mich. 590, 36 N. W. 664, 13 Am. S. R. 362 (1888); McPherson v. Runyon, 41 Minn. 524, 43 N. W. 392, 16 Am. St. R. 727 (1889); Smith v. Burrus, 106 Mo. 94, 16 S. W. 881, 27 Am. S. R. 329 (1891); McCormick Co. v. Willan, 63 Neb. 391, 88 N. W. 497, 93 Am. S. R. 449, with note (1901); Pangburn v. Bull, 1 Wend. (N. Y.) 345 (1828); Kolka v. Jones, 6 N. Dak. 461, 71 N. W. 558, 66 Am. S. R. 615 (1897); Lipscomb v. Shofner, 96 Tenn. 112, 33 S. W. 818 (1896); Closson v. Staples, 42 Vt. 209, 1 Am. R. 316 (1869; Wade v. Nat. Bank of Commerce, 114 Fed. 377 (1902).

humiliation, abuse by custodians for which the defendant is responsible, suffering due to the bad condition of the jail or other place of imprisonment, may be considered in assessing damages. And, in jurisdictions where punitive damages are allowed, the jury may take into account the wealth of the defendant as well as the character of his misconduct in fixing the sum which he must pay for his malicious prosecution of the plaintiff.[128]

§ 4. MALICIOUS ABUSE OF PROCESS.

Differs from Malicious Prosecution. It is well settled that an action lies for the malicious abuse of lawful process, whether civil or criminal; but such action is not to be confounded with that for malicious prosecution, which we have been considering. If the process, which was abused, was that of arrest, the victim may sue for false imprisonment,[129] or, under the old forms of action, might bring a special action on the case.[130] If the process relates to property, as in the case of an attachment or execution, the party abusing it is remitted to the position of a trespasser *ab initio,* and may be proceeded against in an appropriate action of trespass.[131] There is an abuse of process, where one person serves another with a subpoena, not to secure his attendance as a witness but " to coerce him

---

[128] Brown v. Master, 111 Ala. 397, 20 So. 344 (1895); Foster v. Pitts, 63 Ark. 387, 38 S. W. 1114 (1897); punitive damages not allowed against an innocent principal for the negligence of his agent; Parkhurst v. Masteller, 57 Ia. 474, 10 N. W. 864 (1881); Flan v. Lee, 116 Ia. 289, 90 N. W. 70, 93 Am. S. R. 242 (1902); Spencer v. Cramblett, 56 Ks. 794, 44 Pac. 985 (1896); Drumm v. Cessnum, 61 Ks. 467, 59 Pac. 1078 (1900); Wheeler v. Hanson, 161 Mass. 370, 37 N. E. 382, 42 Am. S. R. 408 (1894); Hlubek v. Pinske, 84 Minn. 363, 87 N. W. 939 (1901); Engleton v. Kabrich, 66 Mo. App. 231 (1896); Minn. Threshing Co. v. Regier, 51 Neb. 402, 70 N. W. 934 (1897); Friel v. Plumer, 69 N. H. 498, 43 At. 618 (1899); Abrahams v. Cooper, 81 Pa. 232 (1876); Fenelon v. Butts, 53 Wis. 344, 10 N. W. 501 (1881); Porter v. Mack, 50 W. Va. 581, 40 S. E. 459 (1901).

[129] Holley v. Mix, 3 Wend. (N. Y.) 350 (1829); Robbins v. Swift, 86 Me. 197, 29 At. 981 (1894); Wood v. Graves, 144 Mass. 365, 11 N. E. 567 (1887).

[130] Grainger v. Hill, 4 Bing. N. C. 212 (1838); Foy v. Barry, 87 App. Div. 291, 84 N. Y. Supp. 335 (1903).

[131] Antcliff v. June, 81 Mich. 477, 45 N. W. 1019 (1890); Sneeden v. Harris, 109 N. C. 349, 13 S. E. 926 (1891); Murray v. Mace, 41 Neb. 60, 59 N. W. 387 (1894).

into paying a debt through the alternative of being obliged to take a long journey " and leave his business.[132]

When a plaintiff sues for malicious prosecution, he must allege and prove that the proceeding complained of was instituted without probable cause, and he must show that it terminated in his favor, save in a few exceptional cases.[133] But " in an action for the abuse of process, the *gravamen* of the complaint is the use of the process for a purpose not justified by law, and to effect an object not within its proper scope ; " and the plaintiff is not bound to allege or prove want of probable cause, nor the termination of the original proceeding.[134]

A Peculiar Form of Abuse of Process is found in cases where the person employing the process is entitled to use it, and the action, to which it is an incident, is properly brought and terminates or must terminate in his favor ; but he uses it in a malicious or reckless way. In Zinn v. Rice,[135] the defendant was sued for such a malicious abuse of process. In a contract action against the present plaintiff, to recover $4,522.15, he laid his damages at $40,000 and levied several attachments on real property of great value and on personal property worth $100,000. " In the case at bar," said the court, " the grievance of the plaintiff is not that the defendant maliciously commenced a groundless suit. He admits that the plaintiff had a good cause of action, and that there is no defense to the suit, and that its termination cannot be in his favor. Nor is the grievance that the defendant abused the process in the former suit, and under color of it, did things not authorized by its terms. His

[132] Dishaw v. Wadleigh, 15 App. Div. 205, 44 N. Y. Supp. 207 (1897).

[133] *Supra*, p. 253; Wood v. Graves, 144 Mass. 365, 11 N. E. 567, 59 Am. R. 95 (1897); Marks v. Townsend, 97 N. Y. 590 (1885); Davis v. Johnson, 101 Fed. 952 (1900); Bucki & Son Co. v. Atlantic Lumber Co., 121 Fed. 233 (1903).

[134] Zinn v. Rice, 154 Mass. 1, 27 N. E. 772, 12 L. R. A. 288 (1891); White v. Ashley Co., 181 Mass 339, 63 N. E. 885 (1902); Antcliff v. June, 81 Mich. 477, 45 N. W. 1019, 21 Am. St. R. 533 (1890); Foy v.

Barry, 87 App. Div. 291, 84 N. Y. Supp. 335 (1903).

[135] 154 Mass. 1, 27 N. E. 772, 12 L. R. A. 288 (1891). *Cf.* Alsop v. Lidden, 130 Ala. 548, 30 So. 401 (1901). In Tisdale v. Major, 100 Ia. 1, 75 N. W. 663 (1898), it was held that mental suffering and anguish, resulting from suing out a wrongful and malicious attachment, as auxiliary to a suit properly brought, do not constitute legal damage; and the case is distinguished from one for malicious prosecution.

grievance is that the defendant having a just cause of action, and a legal suit against the plaintiff, made an excessive attachment of property, which he knew was not needed as security for his debt, and for the purpose of injuring the plaintiff. If the plaintiff has any right of action, which is not controverted, it is idle to say that he must wait until the former action is terminated in his favor."

In Bradshaw v. Frasier,[136] the defendant executed a writ of removal, at a time when the plaintiff's intestate was sick with the measles. The judgment and writ were unassailable, and no specific provision of statute or rule of common law was violated by defendant; but it was alleged, and there was evidence tending to show that the intestate's death was caused by exposure due to defendant's pitiless conduct, in executing the writ while the intestate was too sick to be moved with safety. It was held that " the facts were sufficient to support a finding that there was an abuse of process."

It has been suggested that the wrong in these cases should be called *the malicious use of process,* as it is clearly distinguishable from the ordinary abuse of process.[137]   The only objection to this proposal is, that the phrase, " malicious use of process " has long been employed by the courts as a synonym for malicous prosecution.[138]

§ 5.   WRONGS KINDRED TO MALICIOUS PROSECUTION.

Bringing a Suit in another's Name,   if without authority from that other, is an actionable wrong. When the wrongdoer is sued therefor, it is unnecessary for the victim to allege want of probable cause or malice. The nominal plaintiff in the original suit may have had a perfect cause of action against the defendant, but that will not avail him who took the improper liberty of using the name of another in prosecuting a suit, by which the defendant was injured.[139] If the defendant was arrested, he has a clear case of legal damage.[140] If the nominal plaintiff is a pauper, or can exonerate himself from

---

[136] 113 Ia. 579, 85 N. W. 752 (1901).

[137] Editorial in 30 New York Law Journal, p. 528 (1903).

[138] Wurmser v. Stone (Ks. App.), 40 Pac. 993 (1895); Mayer v. Walter, 64 Pa. 283 (1870); Whitten v. Doolittle's Executor, 57 U. S. App. 145 (1898).

[139] Thurston v. Ummvers, March, N. C. 47 (1640); Foster v. Dow, 29 Me. 442 (1849); Bond v. Chapin, 8 Met. (Mass.) 31 (1844); Holliday v. Sterling, 62 Mo. 321 (1876).

[140] Thurston v. Ummvers, March, N. C. 47 (1640).

the payment of costs, the original defendant is entitled to full compensatory damages,[141] and if the action was groundless and was prosecuted from malicious motives, punitive damages may be recovered.[142] In case the nominal plaintiff is compelled to pay the costs, he can sustain a tort action against the wrongdoer.[143]

Maintenance, as defined by Lord Coke, " is an unlawful upholding of the demandant or plaintiff, tenant or defendant, in a cause depending in suit, by word, writing, countenance or deed." [144] When a stranger intervenes in a pending litigation, either for the plaintiff or the defendant, even though he is free from actual malice and there is probable cause for instituting or defending the suit, he does an unlawful act, and he makes himself liable to the opposite party for all costs and expenses of the proceeding. Blackstone declares that the practice of maintenance was greatly encouraged by the first introduction of uses, and treats it as an offense against public justice, as it keeps alive strife and contention, and perverts the remedial process of the law into an engine of oppression. " A man may, however, maintain the suit," he adds, " of his near kinsman, servant, or poor neighbor, out of charity and compassion, with impuity." [145] This exception to the common law liability for maintenance has received recent judicial recognition.[146] It is also lawful for a person who has an interest in the subject matter of a litigation brought or defended by another, to contribute to its success.[147] But if he has not a common legal interest with such litigant, and cannot bring himself within the exception noted by Blackstone, he will be liable in tort for maintenance.[148] While an action for this wrong is rarely brought, modern decisions, both in England and in this country, show that it is maintainable.[149]

---

[141] Moulton v. Lowe, 32 Me. 466 (1851); Pechell v. Watson, 8 M. & W. 691 (1841).

[142] Bond v. Chapin, 8 Met. (Mass.) 31 (1844).

[143] Metcalf v. Alley, 2 Ired. L. (N. C.) 38 (1841).

[144] Inst. Vol. 2, p. 208.

[145] Commentaries, Vol. 4, p. 135.

[146] Harris v. Brisco, 17 Q. B. D. 504, 55 L. J. Q. B. 423 (1886).

[147] Guy v. Churchill, 40 Ch. D. 481, 58 L. J. Ch. 345 (1889).

[148] Alabaster v. Harness (1895), 1 Q. B. 339, 64 L. J. Q. B. 76.

[149] Bradlaugh v. Newdegate, 11 Q. B. D. 1, 52 L. J. Q. B. 454 (1883); Fletcher v. Ellis, Hemp. (U. S. Superior Ct.) 300, 9 Fed. Cas. No. 4,863a (1836); Goodyear Dental Co. v. White, 2 N. J. Law J. 150 (U. S. C. Ct.), 10 Fed. Cas. No. 5,602 (1879).

CHAPTER VIII.

ASSAULT AND BATTERY.

§ 1. What Constitutes this Tort.

The Right Invaded by an Assault, is the right to live in society without being put in reasonable fear of unjustifiable personal harm. A person who threatens another with immediate personal violence, having the apparent means and opportunity for executing the threat, commits an assault, for which a civil suit will lie,[1] though a criminal prosecution may not.[2] Accordingly, raising a club over the head of another and threatening to strike if the latter speaks, is an assault.[3] It is sometimes said that the intent to inflict violence is essential even to a civil assault; and that when the party threaten-

---

[1] DeS. v. DeS., Y. B. Liber Assisarum, f. 99, pl. 60 (1348). Defendant threw a hatchet, attempting to hit plaintiff, but missed him; Tuberville v. Savage, 1 Mod. 3, 2 Keb. 545 (1669). Plaintiff put his hand upon his sword and said: "If it were not assize time, I would not take such language from you," *held* no assault, as there was no threat of inflicting violence; although the court said: "If one intending to assault, strike at another and miss him, this is an assault; so if he hold up his hand against another in a threatening manner and say nothing, it is an assault;" Martin v. Schoppee, 3 C. & P. 373 (1828). Riding after another, threatening to whip him is an assault, although the person pursued escapes; Stephens v. Myers, 4 C. & P. 349 (1830). Defendant, advancing with clenched fist, was forcibly stopped by others, before getting within striking distance of plaintiff; Read v. Coker, 13 C. B. 850, 22 L. J. C. P. 201 (1853). Defendant and others threatened to break plaintiff's neck, if he did not leave, and advanced upon him.

[2] See Chapman v. State, 78 Ala. 463, 56 Am. R. 42 (1885); but see State v. Shepard, 10 Ia. 126 (1859).

[3] United States v. Richardson, 5 Cranch (C. C.), 348 (1837). "His language showed an intent to strike upon her violation of a condition which he had no right to impose;" French v. Ware, 65 Vt. 338, 26 At. 1096 (1892). "Words never amount to an assault. They frequently characterize accompanying acts."

ing knows that he has not the present ability to execute the threat, the tort of assault is not committed.[4] The better view is, however, that the tort consists not in the wrongdoer's intention, but in his invasion of he plaintiff's right to freedom from being put in fear of bodily harm. A learned court has stated the reason for this view as follows: " One of the most important objects to be attained by the enactment of laws and the institutions of civilized society is, that each of us shall feel security against unlawful assaults. Without such security society loses most of its value. Peace and order and domestic happiness, inexpressibly more precious than mere forms of government, cannot be enjoyed without the sense of perfect security. We have a right to live in society without being put in fear of personal harm. But it must be a reasonable fear of which we complain. And it is surely not unreasonable for a person to entertain a fear of personal injury when a pistol is pointed at him in a threatening manner, when, for aught he knows, it may be loaded, and may occasion his immediate death." [5] Reasonable fear may be inspired by threatening gestures,[6] especially when these are connected with " unlawful, sinister and wicked " conduct on defendant's part.[7]

Absence of intent, on the part of the defendant to put the plaintiff in fear of bodily harm, is pertinent to the defense that the injury was accidental, or due to a practical joke, expressly or impliedly assented to by the plaintiff.[8] But cases of this kind are not common.

The Right Invaded by Battery, is the right to be secure from all unjustifiable interference with one's person. Battery, as dis-

---

[4] Blake v. Barnard, 9 C. & P. 626, 38 E. C. L. 365 (1840). But see R. v. St. George, 9 C. & P. 483 (1840).

[5] Beach v. Hancock, 27 N. H. 223, 59 Am. Dec. 373 (1853); Kline v. Kline, 158 Ind. 602, 64 N. E. 9 (1902); Morgan v. O'Daniel (Ky.), 53 S. W. 1040 (1899); Moran v. Vicray (Ky.), 74 S. W. 244 (1903).

[6] Handy v. Johnson, 5 Md. 450 (1854); Bishop v. Ranney, 59 Vt. 316, 7 At. 820 (1887); Keep v. Quallman, 68 Wis. 451, 32 N. W. 527 (1887).

[7] Newell v. Whitcher, 53 Vt. 589, 38 Am. R. 703 (1880); Leach v. Leach, 11 Tex. Civ. App. 699, 33 S. W. 702 (1895). Soliciting sexual intercourse in a manner " to excite the fear and apprehension of force in the execution of his felonious purpose was an assault; " a " wilful violation of woman's most sacred right of personal security."

[8] Christopherson v. Bare, 11 Q. B. 473, 17 L. J. Q. B. 109 (1848); Fitzgerald v. Cavin, 110 Mass. 153 (1872); Nelson v. Crawford, 122 Mich. 466, 81 N. W. 335, 80 Am. St. R. 577 (1899); Degenhardt v. Heller, 93 Wis. 662, 68 N. W. 411, 57 Am. S. R. 945 (1890).

tinguished from assault, involves the infliction of actual violence upon the person; although the degree of violence is immaterial, and the term "person," in this connection, includes clothing and other articles which are so associated with the body as to partake of its legal inviolability. Accordingly, "the least touching of another in anger," [9] or as a trespasser,[10] or in any manner which amounts to an "unlawful setting upon his person," [11] may subject one to an action for battery. Forcibly cutting the hair of an inmate of the poorhouse, without legal authority,[12] or injuring the clothing of another while on his person,[13] or snatching or striking an article from his hand,[14] or cutting a rope which fastens an article to his body,[15] or striking a horse upon which he is riding, or which is attached to a carriage in which he is seated,[16] or overturning a vehicle or chair in which he is,[17] is an actionable battery.

It is not necessary that the assailant should come into immediate contact with his victim. The force which he sets in motion may be communicated through some instrumentality,[18] as a gun or a whip, If he throws a stone or other missile which hits the plaintiff,[19] or spits in the latter's face,[20] a battery is committed. Fraudulent deception,[21] or recklessness [22] on the defendant's part, may be the legal equivalent of actual force.

---

[9] Cole v. Turner, 6 Mod. 149 (1704).

[10] Richmond v. Fisk, 160 Mass. 34, 35 N. E. 103 (1893). Defendant, without license so to do, entered plaintiff's sleeping room and touched him, so as to awken him, in order to present a milk bill.

[11] Geraty v. Stern, 30 Hun (N. Y.), 426 (1883). Defendant's agent forcibly took an ulster off from plaintiff.

[12] Forde v. Skinner, 4 C. & P. 239, 19 E. C. L. 494 (1830).

[13] Reg. v. Day, 1 Cox. C. C. 207 (1845).

[14] Respublica v. DeLongchamps, 1 Dall. 111 (1784); Dyk. v. DuYoung, 35 Ill. App. 138 (1889).

[15] State v. Davis, 1 Hill L. (S. C.) 46 (1832).

[16] Dodwell v. Burford, 1 Mod. 24 (1669); Spear v. Chapman, 8 Ir. L. R. 461 (1846); Clark v. Downing, 55 Vt. 259, 45 Am. R. 612 (1882); Marentille v. Oliver, 2 N. J. L. (1 Pennington) 379 (1808).

[17] Hopper v. Reeve, 7 Taunt. 698, 1 Moore, 407, 2 E. C. L. 554 (1817).

[18] Bullock v. Babcock, 3 Wend. (N. Y.) 391 (1829); Kendall v. Drake, 67 N. H. 592, 30 At. 524 (1891).

[19] Peterson v. Haffner, 59 Ind. 130, 26 Am. R. 81 (1877).

[20] Alcorn v. Mitchell, 63 Ill. 553 (1872). Damages were assessed at $1,000; Whitsett v. Ransom, 79 Mo. 258 (1883); Draper v. Baker, 61 Wis. 450, 21 N. W. 527, 50 Am. R. 143 (1884). Judgment for $1,200.

[21] Cadwell v. Farrell, 28 Ill. 438 (1862); Carr v. State, 135 Ind. 1,

Extended Signification of Assault. While the common law drew a sharp distinction, as we have seen, between assault and battery, a distinction which is still maintained in many jurisdictions,[23] the modern tendency is to give to the term " assault " an extended signification, making it denote a consummated as well as an inchoate battery.[24] In such signification, the term will be employed throughout the remainder of this section.

Excusable Assaults. For two centuries there has been unquestioned judicial authority for the proposition, that " if two were to meet in a narrow passage, and without violence or design of harm, the one touches the other gently it will be no battery." [25] The law accords a license for all interferences with the persons of others, which are fairly incident to ordinary conduct in the particular circumstances. It does not accord a license, however, for rude, reckless, or unnecessarily dangerous interference with the personal security of others.[26]

Leave and license of the injured party may serve as an excuse to one who otherwise would be liable for an assault.[27] But to have this effect, as we have seen in a former connection, the license must have been obtained without deception, and for a lawful purpose.[28] Inevitable accident is an excuse for what would otherwise be an actionable assault.[29]

Justifiable Assaults. These have been considered at length in a former chapter,[30] and it is not necessary, in this connection, to

34 N. E. 533, 20 L. R. A. 863 (1893); Comm. v. Stratton, 114 Mass. 303, 19 Am. R. 350 (1873); McCue v. Klein, 60 Tex. 168, 48 Am. R. 260 (1883); Bartell v. State, 106 Wis. 342, 82 N. W. 142 (1900).

[22] State v. Monroe, 121 N. C. 677, 28 S. E. 547, 43 L. R. A. 861, 61 Am. S. R. 686 (1897). Druggist dropped croton oil on candy, in order that purchaser might play a joke on some one.

[23] Shapiro v. Michelson, 19 Tex. Civ. App. 615, 47 S. W. 746 (1898).

[24] Pollock on Torts (5 Ed.), 210. New York Penal Code, §§ 217-223.

[25] Holt, C. J., in Cole v. Turner, 6 Mod. 149 (1704).

[26] Mercer v. Corbin, 117 Ind. 450, 20 N. E. 132, 3 L. R. A. 221, 10 Am. S. R. 76 (1889).

[27] *Supra*, p. 76. Fitzgerald v. Cavin, 110 Mass. 153 (1872); Wartman v. Swindell, 54 N. J. L. 589, 25 At. 356, 18 L. R. A. 44 (1892).

[28] *Supra*, p. 77. Markley v. Whitman, 95 Mich. 236, 54 N. W. 763, 20 L. R. A. 55, 35 Am. S. R. 558 (1893); Lund v. Taylor, 115 Ia. 236, 88 N. W. 333 (1901). "When the mutual combat is unlawful, mutual consent is unlawful."

[29] *Supra*, p. 58.

[30] *Supra*, Chap. III.

do more than enumerate the more important classes of such acts. The use of force or violence towards a person is justified on the part of a public officer or his assistants in the performance of a legal duty;[31] or on the part of a private person in lawfully making an arrest,[32] or in the proper defense of himself, his family or his property;[33] or in the enforcement of lawful discipline at home,[34] in school,[35] on board a ship[36] or other public conveyance;[37] or in the lawful restraint or assistance of one mentally or physically incapacitated.[38]

Damages. Every actionable assault entitles the victim to damages, and, even though the trespass is slight, the damages are not necessarily nominal.[39] A different rule obtains in case of an assault necessarily nominal.[39] A different rule obtains in case of an assault upon an animal or other property. There, the owner must allege and prove that the property was actually injured.[40]

In an action for trespass to the person, the plaintiff is not bound to specify in his complaint the various items of damage, unless he seeks to recover for consequential or indirect injuries.[41] All legal harm that is the natural and probable result of the assault, is a proper subject for compensation;[42] and indeed all the harm, which can be shown to have resulted directly from the assault, whether it could have been foreseen by the wrongdoer or not, should enter into the assessment of damages.[43]

[31] *Supra,* p. 242.

[32] *Supra,* p. 246.

[33] *Supra,* p. 52. Higgins v. Minaghan, 78 Wis. 602, 47 N. W. 941, 11 L. R. A. 138, 23 Am. S. R. 428 (1891).

[34] *Supra,* p. 248.

[35] *Supra,* p. 248. Deskins v. Gose, 85 Mo. 485, 55 Am. R. 387 (1885).

[36] *Supra,* p. 155.

[37] *Supra,* p. 155. Montgomery v. Buffalo Ry., 165 N. Y. 139, 58 N. E. 770 (1900).

[38] *Supra,* p. 248. Hoffman v. Eppers, 41 Wiss. 251 (1876).

[39] Richmond v. Fisk, 160 Mass. 34, 34 N. E. 103 (1893). In Dunbar v. Cowger, 68 Ark. 444, 59 S. W. 951 (1900), a verdict of $1.00 was set aside as a travesty on justice.

[40] Slater v. Swan, 2 Stra. 872 (1731); Marentille v. Oliver, 2 N. J. L. (1 Pennington) 379 (1808).

[41] O'Leary v. Rowan, 31 Mo. 117 (1860).

[42] Breezinski v. Tierny, 60 Conn. 55, 22 At. 486 (1891); Morgan v. Kendall, 124 Ind. 454, 24 N. E. 143, 9 L. R. A. 445 (1890); Lund v. Tyler, 115 Ia. 236, 88 N. W. 333 (1901); Andrews v. Stone, 10 Minn. 72 (1865).

[43] Watson v. Rhienderknecht, 82 Minn. 235, 84 N. W. 798 (1901); Vosburg v. Putney, 80 Wis. 523, 50 N. W. 403, 27 Am. S. R. 47, 14 L. R. A. 226 (1891).

In all cases of assault, damages may be given for injuries to the plaintiff's feelings,[44] and if it is willful or reckless, or characterized by deliberate disregard of the plaintiff's rights, or by a disposition to humiliate him, punitive damages are recoverable in most jurisdictions.[45] On the other hand, plaintiff's conduct at the time of the assault, if fairly provocative of defendant's act, may be taken into account in mitigation of exemplary damages,[46] and in some jurisdictions of even compensatory damages.[47] It is proper, in assessing exemplary damages, for the jury to consider the character and standing of the parties and the wealth of the defendant.[48]

Counterclaiming Damages. It is generally held that, in case the person assaulted uses excessive force in repelling the attack and thus becomes liable to an action for assault, he cannot set off or counterclaim the damages which he sustained against those inflicted by him on the plaintiff. Such assaults are deemed distinct and independent wrongs, and not parts of a single transaction.[49]

In a few jurisdictions, however, the opposite view is taken and a counterclaim is allowed.[50]

Assault is Distinguishable from Negligence. Injury inflicted by one upon the person of another as the result of negligence, does not constitute an assault. Hostile or unlawful intent is an

[44] Maisenbacker v. Concordia Society, 71 Conn. 369, 42 At. 67, 71 Am. S. R. 213 (1899); Southern Express Co. v. Platten, 93 Fed. 936, 36 C. C. A. 46 (1899).

[45] Bundy v. Manginess, 76 Cal. 532, 18 Pac. 668 (1888); List v. Miner, 74 Conn. 50, 49 At. 856 (1901); Root v. Sturdivant, 70 Ia. 55, 29 N. W. 802 (1886); Thillman v. Neal, 88 Md. 525, 42 At. 242 (1898); Connors v. Walsh, 131 N. Y. 590, 30 N. E. 59 (1892); Pendleton v. Davis, 46 N. C. (1 Jones L.) 98 (1853). Verdict was for $100 actual damages and $1,000 exemplary damages; and the court refused to disturb it; Spear v. Sweeny, 88 Wis. 545, 60 N. W. 1060 (1894).

[46] Willey v. Carpenter, 64 Vt. 212, 23 At. 630, 15 L. R. A. 853 (1892); Prindle v. Haight, 83 Wis. 50, 52 N. W. 1134 (1892).

[47] Keiser v. Smith, 71 Ala. 481, 46 Am. R. 342 (1882).

[48] Pullman Co. v. Lawrence, 74 Miss. 782, 22 So. 53 (1897); Goldsmith v. Joy, 61 Vt. 488, 17 At. 1010, 4 L. R. A. 500 (1889).

[49] Dole v. Erskine, 35 N. H. 503 (1857); Schnaderbeck v. Worth, 8 Abb. Pr. (N. Y.) 37 (1858); Dooling v. Williams, 35 Ohio St. 58 (1878).

[50] Stone v. Stone, 2 Metc. (Ky.) 339 (1859); Gutzman v. Clancy, 114 Wis. 589, 90 N. W. 1081, 58 L. R. A. 744 (1902).

essential element in this tort,[51] although such intent is often established by the recklessness of the defendant's conduct; and it is not necessary to show an actual intention to do the specific harm which was inflicted.[52]

[51] The Lord Derby, 17 Fed. 265 (1883); Perkins v. Stein, 94 Ky. 433, 22 S. W. 649, 20 L. R. A. 861 (1893).

[52] Welch v. Durand, 36 Conn. 182, 4 Am. R. 55 (1869); Palmer v. Chicago, etc., Ry., 112 Ind. 250, 14 N. E. 70 (1897); Smith v. Comm., 100 Pa. 324 (1882).

CHAPTER IX.

WRONGFUL DISTURBANCE OF FAMILY RELATIONS.

§ 1. The Family Head and Family Rights.

By Primitive Law, the only member of the family who is deemed to be harmed by an unjustifiable disturbance of family relations is the family head. In his capacity as husband, the common law gave him a writ of trespass against one who ravished his wife and carried her away and detained her from him.[1] In his capacity as parent, he was entitled to a writ of trespass " for taking his son and heir, or his daughter and heir, and marrying her." [2] As master, he had " an action of trespass for taking of his apprentice or for taking of his servant." [3]

No such right of action in favor of the wife, or child, or servant, for the abduction or beating or unjustifiable detention of the family head, is recognized by early law. Blackstone observes that the common law, in his time, totally disregarded the loss sustained by the inferior party to the family relation. His explanation of this doctrine is: " that the inferior hath no kind of property in the company, care or assistance of the superior, as the superior is held to have in those of the inferior; and therefore the inferior can suffer no loss or injury. The wife cannot recover damages for beating her husband, for she hath no separate interest in anything during her coverture. The child hath no property in his father or guardian, as they have in him, for the sake of giving him education and nurture. * * * And so the servant, whose master is disabled, does not thereby lose his maintenance or wages. He had no property in his master." [4]

Invasions of Martial Rights. According to Blackstone, these were actionable torts at common law, only when committed against

---

[1] Fitzherbert Nat. Brev. 89 O.
[2] *Ibid.* 90 H.
[3] *Ibid.* 91 I.

[4] Blackstone's Commentaries, Vol. 3, pp. 142, 143.

the husband. And such seems to be the present rule in England.[5]
In the last cited case, Lord Wensleydale said: "The benefit which
the husband has in the *consortium* of the wife, is of a different
character from that which the wife has in the *consortium* of the husband. The relation of the husband to the wife is in most respects
entirely dissimilar from that of the master to the servant, yet in one
respect it has a similar character. The assistance of the wife in the
conduct of the household of the husband, and in the education of his
children, resembles the service of a hired domestic, tutor or gover-
ness; is of material value, capable of being estimated in money; and
the loss of it may form the proper subject of an action, the amount of
compensation varying with the position of the parties. This property is wanting in none. It is to the protection of such material
interests that the law chiefly attends. The loss of such service of
the wife, the husband, who alone has all the property of the married
parties, may repair by hiring another servant; but the wife sustains
only the loss of the comfort of her husband's society and affectionate
attention, which the law cannot estimate or remedy. She does not
lose her maintenance, which he is bound still to supply; and it cannot
be presumed that the wrongful act complained of put an end to the
means of that support, without an averment to that effect. And if
there were such an averment, the recovery of a compensation must
be by joining the husband in the suit, who himself must receive the
money, which would not advance the wife's remedy. The wife is,
in fact, without redress by any form of action for an injury to her
pecuniary interests."

Marital Torts Against the Husband. These "are principally three: abduction, or taking away a man's wife; adultery, or
criminal conversation with her; and beating or otherwise abusing
her."[6]

Abduction may be accomplished either by persuasion, fraud or
violence,[7] and the gist of the wrong is the invasion of the husband's
right of *consortium*—"the right to the conjugal fellowship of the

[5] Holland's Jurisprudence (9th
Ed.), 164, 165; Lynch v. Knight, 9
H. L. C. 577, 5 L. T. N. S. 291, 8
Jur. N. S. 724 (1861).

[6] Blackstone's Commentaries, Vol.
3, p. 139.

[7] Winsmore v. Greenbank, Willes,
577 (1845); Humphrey v. Pope, 122
Cal. 253, 54 Pac. 847 (1898); Hart-
pence v. Rogers, 143 Mo. 623, 45 S.
W. 650 (1898).

wife, to her company, co-operation and aid in every conjugal relation." [8]   According to one class of decisions, this right is invaded whenever the wife's affections are alienated with malice or improper motives, although she may continue to reside under her husband's roof.   "Debauchery and elopement," according to these authorities, are not the essence of the wrong, but only "the immediate and legitimate consequences of the wrong." [9]   According to another class of decisions, the right is not invaded unless there is adultery with the wife, or there is "enticing and procuring, or harboring and secreting her." [10]

Adultery or criminal conversation with the wife is a marital tort to the husband, even though there is no alienation of her affections or abduction of her person.   The gist of this wrong is the shame of the husband and the hazard of having to maintain spurious issue. Hence the recovery of a judgment against the wrongdoer for the enticement of a man's wife from him, is not a bar to an action for criminal conversation with her.[11]   Nor does the husband lose his right of action by his forgiveness of his wife and by living with her thereafter.[12]

An action for damages for criminal conversation is one "for willful and malicious injury to the person and property" of the husband.[13]

Marital Torts Against the Wife.   While the common-law fiction obtained, that the wife's personality is merged in that of her husband, it was not strange that the courts could not see their way to providing a tort remedy for the marital wrongs of the wife.   The enticement of the husband and the alienation of his affections from her, could not harm her material interests, as Lord Wensleydale pointed out in the opinion from which we have already quoted, for

[8] Bigaonette v. Paulet, 134 Mass. 123, 45 Am. R. 307 (1883); Long v. Booe, 106 Ala. 570, 17 So. 716 (1894).

[9] Rinehart v. Bills, 82 Mo. 534, 52 Am. R. 385 (1884); Heermance v. James, 47 Barb. (N. Y.) 120, 32 How. Pr. 142 (1866); Weston v. Weston, 86 App. Div. (N. Y.) 159 (1903).

[10] Houghton v. Rice, 174 Mass.

366, 54 N. E. 843, 75 Am. S. R. 351 (1899); Lellis v. Lambert, 24 Ont. App. 653 (1897).

[11] Schnell v. Blohm, 40 Hun (N. Y.), 378 (1886).

[12] Sikes v. Tippins, 85 Ga. 231, 11 S. E. 662 (1890); Stumm v. Hummel, 39 Ia. 478 (1874).

[13] Tinker v. Colwell, 193 U. S. 473, 24 Sup. Ct. 505 (1904).

she could still compel him to support her. Even if the courts had thought the loss of comfort of her husband's society and affectionate attention susceptible of monetary estimation, a suit for such damages could not have been brought by her alone. The husband must have been a co-plaintiff, and the sum recovered would be his property.

During the latter part of the last century, the fiction of legal unity of husband and wife was greatly modified by legislation. Not only was the wife accorded the ownership and control of property possessed by her at marriage, as well as that acquired by her during coverture, but she was empowered to make contracts, to carry on business, and to maintain actions for the redress of her wrongs, as though she were unmarried.[14] Her legal personality was no longer merged in that of her husband, but, for most purposes, was totally distinct and independent of his. With this change in her legal status, came naturally a change in the judicial conception of her marital wrongs. As she could maintain an action in her own name, and damages recovered would be her sole and separate property, one of the chief objections urged by Lord Wensleydale disappeared. As the law now recognized her legal equality with her husband, Blackstone's reasoning based upon the superiority of one party and the inferiority of the other party to the marital relation, had no longer the foundation of even a fiction. There remained only the view that the wife's " loss of the comfort of her husband's society and affectionate attention," is something so sentimental and ethereal, that " the law cannot estimate or remedy " it.

In reply to this it has been said: " The actual injury to the wife from the loss of *consortium* is the same as the actual injury to the husband from that cause. His right to the conjugal society of his wife is no greater than her right to the conjugal society of her husband. Marriage gives to each the same rights in that regard. Each is entitled to the comfort, companionship and affection of the other. The right of the one and the obligation of the other spring from the

[14] In California, Montana, North Dakota and South Dakota, the Civil Code expressly gives to the wife the same right of action for the abduction or enticement of her husband, that the husband possesses for the wrongful interference with his wife. See Cal. Civ. Code, § 49; North Dakota Civ. Code, § 2718; South Dakota Revised Civ. Code of 1903, § 32.

marriage contract, are mutual in character, and attach to the husband as husband, and to the wife as wife. Any interference with these rights, whether of the husband or of the wife, is a violation not only of a natural right, but also of a legal right arising out of the marriage relation. It is a wrongful interference with that which the law both confers and protects. A remedy, not provided by statute, but springing from the flexibility of the common law and its adaptability to the changing nature of human affairs, has long existed for the redress of the wrongs of the husband. As the wrongs of the wife are the same in principle and are caused by acts of the same nature as those of the husband, the remedy should be the same. Since her society has a value to him capable of admeasurement in damages, why is his society of no legal value to her?"[15]

Action for Enticing Husband. Accordingly, it is held in most American jurisdictions that the wife is entitled to an action in tort against one who entices her husband from her, alienates his affections and deprives her of his society.[16]

In a few states her right to this action is denied. Such a right, it is declared, "would be the most fruitful source of litigation of any that can be thought of." It is also urged that the wife understands,

[15] Bennett v. Bennett, 116 N. Y. 584, 590, 23 N. E. 17, 6 L. R. A. 553 (1889).
[16] Humphrey v. Pope, 122 Cal. 253, 54 Pac. 847 (1898), applying § 49 of the Civ. Code; Williams v. Williams, 20 Col. 51, 37 Pac. 614 (1894); Foot v. Card, 58 Conn. 1, 18 At. 1027, 23 Am. S. R. 258, 6 L. R. A. 829 (1899); Betser v. Betser, 186 Ill. 537, 58 N. E. 249, 51 Am. S. R. 360 (1900); Haynes v. Nowlin, 129 Ind. 581, 29 N. E. 389, 28 Am. St. R. 213, 14 L. R. A. 787 (1891); Price v. Price, 91 Ia. 693, 60 N. W. 202, 51 Am. S. R. 360, 29 L. R. A. 150 (1894); Deitzman v. Mullin, 108 Ky. 610, 57 S. W. 247, 94 Am. S. R. 390 (1900); Wolf v. Frank, 92 Md. 138, 48 At. 132, 52 L. R. A. 102 (1900); Lockwood v. Lockwood, 67 Minn. 476, 70 N. W. 784 (1897);

Warren v. Warren, 89 Mich. 123, 50 N. W. 842, 14 L. R. A. 545 (1891); Clow v. Chapman, 125 Mo. 101, 28 S. W. 328, 46 Am. S. R. 468, with note, 26 L. R. A. 412 (1894); Hodgkinson v. Hodgkinson, 43 Neb. 269, 61 N. W. 577, 47 Am. S. R. 759, 27 'L. R. A. 120 (1895); Seaver v. Adams, 66 N. H. 142, 19 At. 776, 49 Am. S. R. 597 (1889); Bennett v. Bennett, 116 N. Y. 584, 23 N. E. 17, 6 L. R. A. 553, with note (1889); Brown v. Brown, 121 N. C. 8, 27 S. E. 998, 38 L. R. A. 242, 70 Am. S. R. 574 (1897); Westlake v. Westlake, 34 O. St. 621, 32 Am. R. 397 (1878); Gernerd v. Gernerd, 185 Pa. 233, 39 At. 884, 40 L. R. A. 549, 64 Am. S. R. 646 (1898); Beach v. Brown, 20 Wash. 266, 65 Pac. 46, 72 Am. S. R. 98, 43 L. R. A. 114 (1898).

when she enters the marriage relation, that her right to her husband's society is subject to various conditions, including his exposure " to the temptations, enticements and allurements of the world, which easily withdraw him from her society, or cause him to desert or abandon her," and consequently that her right to his society " is not the same in degree and value, as his right to hers" A right of action for his enticement and the alienation of his affections, say these tribunals, must be given by statute in express terms, or they will not recognize it.[17]   Still other courts have defeated the wife in such actions on the ground that she has not shown a loss of *consortium*.[18]

Crim. Con. with Husband.   That the wife can maintain a tort action against another woman for criminal conversation with the husband has been denied, even in a jurisdiction where the abduction of the husband is held actionable.[19]   If the gist of this action, when brought by the husband, is, as we have heretofore stated, the shame to him, and the risk of having to support spurious issue, it would seem that the decision in the last cited case is entirely sound, in the absence of express legislation on the topic.   Certainly the husband's marital infidelity subjects the wife to no risk concerning the legitimacy of her offspring; and it must be confessed that public opinion does not deem her shamed or disgraced by his conduct, if that is limited to criminal conversation.   Of the injury to her feelings or the outrage upon her affections, the law seems not to take cognizance.

Injuries to the Body or Reputation of the Wife.   If these were of such a character as to deprive the husband for any time of the company and assistance of his wife, the common law gave him a separate remedy by action on the case for his damages thus sustained.   For the injuries sustained by her, as an individual, the common law gave an action in the joint names of the husband and wife.[20]   As the common law vested in the husband the recovery

[17] Duffies v. Duffies, 76 Wis. 374, 45 N. W. 522, 20 Am. S. R. 79 (1890); Doe v. Roe, 82 Me. 503, 20 At. 83, 17 Am. S. R. 499, 8 L. R. A. 833 (1890); Lellis v. Lambert, 24 Ont. App. 656 (1897).

[18] Neville v. Gill, 174 Mass. 305, 54 N. E. 841 (1899); Houghton v. Rice, 174 Mass. 366, 54 N. E. 841, 47 L. R. A. 310 (1899).

[19] Kroessin v. Keller, 60 Minn. 372, 62 N. W. 438, 51 Am. S. R. 533, 27 L. R. A. 685 (1895).

[20] Blackstone's Commentaries, Vol. 3, p. 140.

obtained in such a joint suit, he was in a position to discharge the cause of action without her consent,[21] or to prevent her suing, by refusing to join as a plaintiff, or by absenting himself from the jurisdiction.[22]

This has been changed to a considerable but varying extent by modern legislation; and in many jurisdictions the wife is permitted to sue alone for injuries to her person or reputation.[23] Such legislation, however, has not affected the husband's right to sue for those injuries to his wife which are also invasions of his marital rights,[24] or which subject him to expense because of his marital obligations to provide for the comfort and support of the wife.[25] The cases cited in the last two notes show that it is not necessary for the husband to prove that the injured wife sustained the relation of a servant to him. It is enough that he makes out a case of " his loss of *consortium* with her, whether this is caused by assault and battery, by medical or surgical malpractice, or by negligence of any kind." This injury to the husband is deemed generally a personal injury.[26]

§ 2. Abduction.

Torts Against the Parent. Fitzherbert, in the passage quoted on a former page, relating to this topic, speaks only of the abduction of one's son and heir, and of the abduction and marrying of one's daughter and heir. Such invasions of the parent's right in his child rarely come before modern courts for consideration.[27]

[21] Ballard v. Russell, 33 Me. 196, 64 Am. Dec. 620 (1851).

[22] Laughlin v. Eaton, 54 Me. 156 (1866).

[23] *Supra*, 276. Harris v. Webster, 58 N. H. 481 (1878); Harmon v. Old Colony Ry., 165 Mass. 100, 42 N. E. 505, 52 Am. S. R. 499, 30 L. R. A. 658 (1896).

[24] Mewhirter v. Hatten, 42 Ia. 288, 20 Am. R. 618 (1875); Kelley v. N. Y., etc., Ry., 168 Mass. 308, 46 N. E. 1063, 60 Am. S. R. 397, 38 L. R. A. 631 (1897); Riley v. Lidtke, 49 Neb. 139, 68 N. W. 356 (1896); Baltimore, etc., Ry. v. Glenn, 66 O. St.

395, 64 N. E. 438 (1902); Jones v. Utica, etc., Ry., 40 Hun (N. Y.), 349 (1886); Nanticoke v. Warne, 106 Pa. 373 (1884).

[25] Smith v. City of St. Joseph, 55 Mo. 456, 17 Am. R. 660 (1874); Furnish v. Missouri, etc., Ry., 102 Mo. 669, 15 S. W. 315, 22 Am. St. R. 800 (1890).

[26] Maxson v. Del., L. & W. Ry., 112 N. Y. 559, 20 N. E. 544 (1889).

[27] In Hill v. Hobert, 2 Root (Conn.), 48 (1793), the enticement and marrying of a daughter was held actionable in favor of the parent, while in Hervey v. Moseley,

Most of the litigation on this subject in this country is confined to injuries to the child, which deprive the parent of the child's services, or impose upon the parent an increased expenditure of labor or money. They may be divided into two classes: those for the seduction and debauchment of the daughter; and those for any other wrong to a child of either sex.

Ordinary Injuries to Parental Right in Child. These are to be distinguished from invasions of the personal rights of the child. For wrongs of that character, the child may maintain an action;[28] and a recovery therein, even where the action is brought by the parent as next friend, will not affect the parent's action for injuries to him in his parental relation;[29] unless damages for such injuries were recovered in the former suit.[30]

The parent's right of action for ordinary injuries to the child rests upon his right to the child's services and upon his duty of maintenance. Even though the child is too young to render valuable service, the parent is entitled to recover for any extra expense, to which he is put by the defendant's tortious act, in maintaining the child; and in most of our jurisdictions he is entitled to recover for such services of the child as he may lose in the future in conse-

7 Gray (73 Mass.), 479, 66 Am. Dec. 515 (1856), it was held not to be actionable. South Carolina seems to follow the Connecticut doctrine. Kirkpatrick v. Lockhart, 2 Brev. 276 (1809); Dobson v. Cothran, 34 S. C. 518, 13 S. E. 679 (1890); and common-law abduction of the daughter seems to be recognized in Kreay v. Anthus, 2 Ind. App. 482, 28 N. E. 773 (1891); but not in Jones v. Tevis, 4 Litt. (14 Ky.) 25, 14 Am. Dec. 98 (1823).

In Rice v. Nickerson, 9 Allen (91 Mass.), 478, 85 Am. Dec. 777 (1864), compensatory damages were allowed to the father, whose minor son had been wrongfully taken from his custody. In Magee v. Holland, 27 N. J. L. (3 Dutch.) 86, 72 Am. Decc. 341 (1858), it is held that while the parent's right of action is based on the loss of service, or the labor and expense incurred in recovering the child, his recovery is not limited to compensatory damages, but may include a sum for injury to his feelings.

[28] Wilton v. Middlesex Ry. Co., 107 Mass. 108, 9 Am. R. 11 (1871).

[29] Wilton v. Middlesex Ry. Co., 125 Mass. 130 (1898).

[30] Baker v. Flint & P. M. Ry., 91 Mich. 298, 51 N. W. 897, 30 Am. S. R. 298, 16 L. R. A. 154 (1892). "It is undoubtedly true that as a question of law, Oscar had no right in his suit to recover such damages without the consent of his father; but he did recover with the consent of his father; therefore the father is now estopped from setting up a claim for the same damages in this action in his own name."

quence of the injury.[31]   While our courts are coming to treat this action of the parent as based upon the parental relation, rather than on the relation of master and servant, they exclude the elements of affection and sentiment, as well as of parental interest in the future welfare of the child.   Accordingly, they do not permit a recovery in tort by a parent against school officers, who wrongfully expel a child from school;[32] or for wounded feelings and anxiety because of the pain, or distress, or insult, or disfigurement of the child;[33] or for loss of the child's society;[34] or for a libel to a deceased child.[35]

Injury to Parent by Seduction of Daughter.   " The foundation of the action by a father to recover damages against the wrongdoer for the seduction of his daughter, has been uniformly placed, from the earliest time hitherto, not upon the seduction itself, which is the wrongful act of the defendant, but upon the loss of service of the daughter, in which service he is supposed to have a legal right or interest. . . . It has, therefore, always been held that the loss of service must be alleged in the declaration, and that loss of

---

[31] Durden v. Barnett, 7 Ala. 169 (1844); Sykes v. Lawlor, 49 Cal. 236 (1874); Cumming v. Brooklyn, etc., Ry., 109 N. Y. 95, 16 N. E. 65 (1888); Barnes v. Keene, 132 N. Y. 13, 29 N. E. 1090 (1892); Nederlandsch v. Hollander, 59 Fed. 417, 20 U. S. App. 225, 8 C. C. A. 169 (1894). " The evidence showed the child's disability had lasted for more than a year, and still continued, thus raising the presumption that it would continue in the future for a longer or shorter period. Having these facts and the age and sex of the child before them, the jury were as well qualified as an expert could be to form a correct opinion as to the duration of her incapacity, and the value of her services to her father."

[32] Donahue v. Richards, 38 Me. 376, 61 Am. Dec. 256 (1854); Spear v. Cummings, 23 Pick. (40 Mass.)

224, 34 Am. Dec. 53 (1839); Stephenson v. Hall, 13 Barb. (N. Y.) 222 (1852).

[33] Dennis v. Clark, 2 Cush. (Mass.) 347, 48 Am. Dec. 671 (1848); Cowden v. Wright, 24 Wend. (N. Y.) 429, 35 Am. Dec. 633 (1840); Whitney v. Hitchcock, 4 Den. (N. Y.) 461, (1847). But see Magee v. Holland, 27 N. J. L. 86, 72 Am. Dec. 341 (1858), where exemplary damages were held proper, in the case of abduction of children, " for the injury done to his feelings and to prevent similar abuses."

[34] Louisville, etc., Ry. v. Rush, 127 Ind. 545, 26 N. E. 1010 (1890); McGarr v. National, etc., Mills, 24 R. I. 447, 53 At. 320, 60 L. R. A. 122 (1902).

[35] Bradt v. New Nonpareil Co., 108 Ia. 449, 79 N. W. 122, 45 L. R. A. 681 (1899); Sorensen v. Balaban, 11 App. Div. (N. Y.) 164 (1896).

service must be proved at the trial, or the plaintiff must fail. It is the invasion of the legal right of the master to the services of his servant, that gives him the right of action for beating his servant; and it is the invasion of the same legal right, and no other, which gives the father the right of action against the seducer of his daughter."

Such is the language of a learned Chief Justice,[36] and it still embodies the legal rule upon this topic in England. It is true that the father makes out a *prima facie* case of service, by proof that the seduced daughter was a minor and unmarried; and that the courts are astute to discover the relation of master and servant, even where the daughter's service possesses no pecuniary value for the parent.[37] But the " working of the action for seduction in modern practice " is admittedly " capricious " in England.[38] It " affords protection to the rich man whose daughter occasionally makes his tea, but leaves without redress the poor man whose child is sent unprotected to earn her bread amongst strangers." [39]

The Same Subject. American Law. The theory of an injury to the parent, in his character of master, is accepted in most of our states as the basis of his right of action. But, it has been judicially declared, this theory " is little more than a legal fiction used as a peg to hang a substantial award of damages on, as compensation not to the master but to the head of the family. It is accordingly established, in this country at least, that the father may maintain his action for the seduction of his minor daughter, although she is not a member of his household, but is in the actual employ of another, enjoying the fruits of her labor with her father's consent; if he has not relinquished, past the power of recall, his right to control her services." [40] It is sometimes said that the law conclusively presumes the relation of master and servant to exist between the father and a minor daughter; that it is not necessary to show actual service; that constructive service is sufficient.[41] If the

[36] Tindal, C. J., in Grinnell v. Wells, 7 Man. & G. 1033, 14 L. J. C. P. 19 (1844).

[37] Carr v. Clark, 2 Chit. 260, 23 R. R. 748 (1818); Terry v. Hutchinson, L. R. 3 Q. B. 599, 37 L. J. Q. B. 251 (1868); O'Reilly v. Glavey, 32 Ir. L. R. 316 (1892).

[38] Pollock on Torts (6th Ed.), 229.

[39] Sergeant Manning, in note to Grinnell v. Wells, 7 M. & G. 1044.

[40] Simpson v. Grayson, 54 Ark. 404, 16 S. W. 4, 26 Am. S. R. 52 (1891).

[41] White v. Murtland, 71 Ill. 250, 22 Am. R. 100 (1874); Kennedy v.

daughter was of age when seduced, the father must show that "by mutual assent the relation of master and servant did exist" between him and his daughter.[42] It is not necessary, however, to establish a binding contract relation between them.[43]

In some of our States, the fiction of service as the basis of this action has been abolished by statutes in express terms;[44] and in others, the statutory provision that "all fictions in pleading are abolished," has been held to so far modify the common-law rule on this subject, as to permit a "parent to maintain an action for the seduction of the daughter, without averment or proof of loss of services, or expenses of sickness."[45]

It is held, generally, in this country, that the mother, when the actual head of the family by reason of the husband's death or desertion,[46] or any other person, who in fact is *in loco parentis*[47] to the seduced girl, may maintain the action.

Damages in Actions for Seduction. These are not limited, even under the common-law rule, to compensation for loss of ser-

---

Shea, 110 Mass. 147, 14 Am. R. 584 (1872); Middleton v. Nichols, 62 N. J. L. 636, 43 At. 474 (1899); Martin v. Payne, 9 Johns. 387, 6 Am. Dec. 288 (1812); Lipe v. Eisenlerd, 32 N. Y. 229 (1865); Hudkins v. Hudkins, 22 W. Va. 645 (1883); Lavery v. Crooke, 52 Wis. 612, 38 Am. R. 768 (1881).

[42] Beaudette v. Gagne, 87 Me. 534, 33 At. 23 (1895); Mercer v. Walmesley, 5 H. & J. (Md.) 27, 9 Am. Dec. 486 (1820); Vassel v. Cole, 10 Mo. 634, 47 Am. Dec. 136 (1847); Davidson v. Abbott, 52 Vt. 570, 36 Am. R. 767 (1880); Lee v. Hodges, 13 Gratt. (Va.) 726 (1857).

[43] Cases in last note, and Lamb v. Taylor, 67 Md. 85, 8 At. 760 (1887); Sutton v. Huffman, 32 N. J. L. 58 (1866); Lipe v. Eisenlerd, 32 N. Y. 229 (1865); Briggs v. Evans, 5 Ired. L. (27 N. C.) 16 (1844); Hahn v. Cooker, 84 Wis. 629, 59 N. W. 1022 (1893).

[44] Cal. Civ. Code, § 49; Code of Civ. Proc. § 375; Montana Civ. Code, § 35; North Dak. Civ. Code, § 2718; South Dak. Rev. Civ. Code of 1903, § 32; Hill's (Oregon) Code, § 35, applied in Patterson v. Hayden, 17 Or. 238, 21 Pac. 129, 3 L. R. A. 529, 11 Am. St. R. 822 (1889). See other jurisdictions cited in 25 Am. & Eng. Cyc. of Law, p. 209.

[45] Anthony v. Norton, 60 Ks. 341, 56 Pac. 529, 72 Am. S. R. 360, 44 L. R. A. 757 (1899); Hood v. Sudderth, 111 N. C. 215, 16 S. E. 397 (1892).

[46] Hammond v. Corbett, 50 N. H. 501, 9 Am. R. 288 (1871); Furman v. Van Size, 56 N. Y. 435, 15 Am. R. 441 (1874); Davidson v. Abbott, 53 Vt. 570, 36 Am. R. 767 (1880).

[47] Certwell v. Hun, 6 Hun (N. Y.), 575 (1876); Moritz v. Garnhart, 7 Watts (Pa.), 302, 32 Am. Dec. 762 (1838); Maguinay v. Saudek, 5 Sneed (37 Tenn.), 146 (1857).

vices, or for actual expenditures due to the seduction. While the action is in form for loss of service, it is in fact for a personal injury to the parent,[48] and juries are always instructed that they can take into consideration injury to the plaintiff's feelings.[49] "The loss of service is not the rule of damage. It has been said that it is scarcely an item in the account. The real ground of damage is the disgrace of the family. The loss of service in many, in most instances could hardly be accounted anything, and yet often where the least service is or can be performed the highest damages can be given. The loss of service is but one step to that high plane of injury and wrong for which the parent is entitled to compensation. Damages are given to the plaintiff standing in the relation of parent."[50]

Where the common-law rule obtains and damages for loss of service are sought, the plaintiff must show that these are the proximate effect of the seduction. Incapacity to labor caused by pregnancy, or sexual disease, or actual bodily injury resulting directly from the defendant's misconduct, causes a loss of service which is to be recompensed. "But if the loss of health is caused by mental suffering, which is not the consequence of seduction, but is produced by subsequent intervening causes, such as abandonment by the seducer, shame resulting from exposure, or other similar causes, the loss of services is too remote a consequence."[51]

At common law, the assent of the child to the seduction does not bar the parent's action. "In respect to him," it has been declared, "she had no right to consent, and her act in assenting, or even procuring, the criminal connection was a nullity. So the defendant must stand as a wrongdoer, from whose act the plaintiff has suffered damage."[52] In a few jurisdictions, it has been held that her voluntary assent limits the parent's recovery to his actual loss.[53]

---

[48] Hutchinson v. Durden, 113 Ga. 987, 39 S. E. 495, 54 L. R. A. 811 (1901).

[49] Howard v. Crowther, 8 M. & W. 601, 5 Jurist, 914 (1841).

[50] Middleton v. Nichols, 62 N. J. L. 636, 43 At. 575 (1899).

[51] Abrahams v. Kidney, 104 Mass. 222, 6 Am. R. 220 (1870).

[52] McAulay v. Birkhead, 13 Ired.

(35 N. C.) 22, 55 Am. Dec. 427 (1852); Simpson v. Grayson, 54 Ark. 404, 16 S. W. 4, 26 Am. S. R. 52 (1891); Lencker v. Steilen, 89 Ill. 545, 31 Am. R. 104 (1878); Stoudt v. Shepherd, 73 Mich. 588, 41 N. W. 696 (1889); Hein v. Holridge, 78 Minn. 468, 81 N. W. 522 (1900); Lawrence v. Spence, 99 N. Y. 669, 2 N. E. 145 (1885).

[53] Hill v. Wilson, 8 Blacf. (Ind.)

The Supreme Court of Oregon has ruled that the statute of that State, which authorizes a parent to maintain an action for the seduction of a daughter, though the latter be not living at home and there be no loss of service, has entirely changed the character of the action; and that the parent's action will be defeated, if the defendant shows that the daughter voluntarily submitted to illegal intercourse, and was not overcome by the defendant's artifice, promise or persuasion.[54]

§ 3. Torts Against the Master.

Harming or Enticing the Servant. Fitzherbert's statement that "a man shall have an action of trespass for taking of his apprentice, or for taking of his servant,"[55] is preceded and followed by an enumeration of various injuries to property for which trespass would lie. His view, that a wrongful interruption of the relation of master and servant is an interference with the property right of the master, has never been questioned by the courts.[56] One who takes or entices a servant from his master, without justifiable cause, or who wrongfully injures him so that he is disabled from rendering service, commits an actionable wrong against the master; the wrong consisting not in the act itself, but in the consequent loss to the master.[57]

Fitzherbert also notes[58] a "writ of trespass against those who lie near the plaintiff's house, and will not suffer his servants to go into the house, nor the servants who are in the house to come out thereof," so that plaintiff loses "the profits of his land" and "his

123 (1846); Comer v. Taylor, 82 Mo. 341 (1884).

[54] Patterson v. Hayden, 17 Or. 238, 21 Pac. 129, 3 L. R. A. 529, 11 Am. S. R. 822 (1889).

[55] *Natura Brevium*, 91 I.

[56] Grinnell v. Wells, 7 M. & G. 1033, 1041, 14 L. J. C. P. 19 (1844).

[57] Robert Mary's Case, 9 Coke, 111b, 113a (1613); Jones v. Blocker, 43 Ga. 331 (1871). "The master has purchased for a valuable consideration the services of his domestics; " Ames v. Union Ry. Co., 117 Mass. 541, 19 Am. R. 426 (1875); Apprentice injured by defendant's negligence; Bixby v. Dunlop, 56 N. H. 456, 22 Am. R. 475 (1876); Haskins v. Royster, 70 N. C. 601, 16 Am. R. 780 (1874); Huff v. Walkins, 15 S. C. 82, 40 Am. R. 680 (1880).

[58] *Natura Brevium*, 87 N. See Garret v. Taylor, Croke Jac. 567 (1621), where the servants were threatened with mayhem.

service of the same men and servants." Commenting on this writ, a learned writer has said: "It seems, therefore, that 'picketing,' so soon as it exceeds the bounds of persuasion and becomes physical intimidation, is a trespass at common law against the employer." [59] Such is the view generally entertained in this country.[60] If the damage threatened by this intimidation is such as cannot be adequately remedied in a common-law action, equity will enjoin the intimidators, although their acts may be in violation of criminal law.[61]

Whether the moral, as distinguishable from the physical intimidation of servants is an actionable wrong to the master, is a subject upon which the authorities are divided, as we have seen in a former section.[62]

Torts Against the Servant by Wrongfully Influencing the Master. Undoubtedly the servant has no cause of action in tort against one who beats or kills the master, although the assault or death may result in pecuniary harm to the servant. In the language of Blackstone, he hath "no property in the master." [63] And yet, the common law justifies the servant in defending his master against an assault,[64] thus recognizing his interest in the master.

Recently, the question has often arisen, whether the servant has an action in tort against those who wrongfully influence the master to discharge him, or to refuse to give him employment, which but for such wrongful influence he would have obtained. When the conduct of such persons in influencing the master is a violation of the criminal law,[65] or when it takes the form of a conspiracy to

[59] Pollock on Torts (6th Ed.), 230, note k.

[60] *Supra*, 71. Kernan v. Humble, 51 La. Ann. 389, 25 So. 421 (1899); Beck v. Ry., etc., Union, 118 Mich. 497, 77 N. W. 13, 74 Am. S. R. 421, 42 L. R. A. 803 (1893).

[61] Consolidated Steel Co. v. Murray, 80 Fed. 811 (1897); Shoe Co. v. Saxey, 131 Mo. 212, 32 S. W. 1106, 52 Am. S. R. 622 (1895); O'Neil v. Behanna, 182 Pa. 236, 37 At. 843, 61 Am. St. R. 702, 38 L. R. A. 382 (1897).

[62] *Supra*, 72. Vegelahn v. Gunt-ner, 167 Mass. 92, 44 N. E. 1077, 57 Am. S. R. 543, 35 L. R. A. 722 (1896); Allen v. Flood (1898), A. C. 1, 67 L. J. Q. B. 119.

[63] 3 Commentaries, 143.

[64] ———— v. Fakenham, Y. B. 9 Ed. IV, f. 48, pl. 4 (1470); Leward v. Basely, 1 Ld. Raym. 62 (1695).

[65] Old Dominion Steamship Co. v. McKenna, 18 Abb. N. C. 262, 24 Blatch. 244, 30 Fed. 48 (1887); Casey v. Cincinnati Typo. Union, 45 Fed. 135, 12 L. R. A. 193, with note (1891); Quinn v. Leathem (1901), A. C. 495, 70 L. J. Q. B. 76;

accomplish a result which no one of the wrongdoers could effect alone,[66] and results in actual harm to the servant, he can maintain a tort action for damages in most jurisdictions.   If, however, the conduct of the defendants is not positively illegal, and does not exceed the limits of fair competition, it does not amount to a tort, even against the servant who is actually harmed thereby, and whom the defendants actually intended to harm.[67]   Whether the moral intimidation of masters or employers exceeds the limits of fair competition is a point upon which not only different courts, but different members of the same court, have disagreed.[68]

§ 4. Conspiracy as a Tort.

Conspiracy Without Injury.   The cases, which were cited in the notes to the last section, contain much discussion of the controverted question, whether conspiracy is a separate tort.   Some of the judicial opinions answer this question in the negative.   Conspiracy, according to the authors of these opinions, is never the *gravamen* of the action.   They declare that unless the acts, which the conspirators combined to do, would be tortious if done by one

Curran v. Galen, 152 N. Y. 33, 46 N. E. 297, 57 Am. S. R. 496, 37 L. R. A. 802 (1897); Garret v. Taylor, Croke Jac. 567 (1621). See note in 24 Abb. N. C. 260.

[66] Quinn v. Leathem (1901), A. C. 495, 70 L. J. Q. B. 76; Giblan v. Nat. Amalgamated Union (1903), 2 K. B. 600, 72 L. J. K. B. 907; Lucke v. Clothing Cutter's Co., 77 Md. 396, 26 At. 505, 39 Am. S. R. 421, 19 L. R. A. 408 (1893).

[67] Allen v. Flood (1898), A. C. 1, 67 L. J. Q. B. 119; Continental Ins. Co. v. Board of Fire Underwriters, 67 Fed. 310 (1895); National Protec. Assoc. v. Cummings, 170 N. Y. 315, 63 N. E. 639, 88 Am. S. R. 648, 58 L. R. A. 135 (1902); Raycroft v. Tayntor, 68 Vt. 219, 35 At. 53, 54 Am. S. R. 882, 33 L. R. A. 225 (1896).

[68] See cases in last two notes, and Chipley v. Atkinson, 23 Fla. 206, 1 So. 934, 11 Am. S. R. 367 (1887); London Guar. Co. v. Horn, 101 Ill. App. 355 (1902), affd. 206 Ill. 493, 69 N. E. 526 (1904); Perkins v. Pendleton, 90 Me. 166, 38 At. 96, 60 Am. S. R. 252 (1897). In the last cited case, it is declared, that inducing the master to discharge or not to employ a servant, by persuasion or argument however whimsical or absurd, or by threat to do what the defendant has a right to do, is not a tort towards the servant, though the defendant's motives are malicious; but to intimidate the master into discharging the servant, or withholding employment, by fraud or by unlawful threats, is an actionable wrong.

of them, they do not become tortious by reason of the conspiracy; that damage to the plaintiff is the gist of the action.[69]

It is undoubtedly true that a mere conspiracy to injure another is not actionable as a tort. Injury must ensue, or a tort action will not lie. But when one sustains actual harm as the result of concerted action on the part of others, and the harm is such as could not have been inflicted by any of the parties acting singly, it would seem that the distinctive element of the tort is the conspiracy rather than the damage. Damage is an essential element in malicious prosecution, in deceit and in many cases of slander; but no one contends that such fact warrants the assertion that there is no such tort, as malicious prosecution, or deceit, or defamation by slanderous words which are not actionable *per se*.

Concert or Combination. "The essence of conspiracy," to quote from a distinguished jurist, "so far as it justifies a civil action for damages, is a concert or combination to defraud or to cause other injury to person or property, which actually results in damage to the person or property of the person injured or defrauded." [70]

[69] Parker v. Huntington, 2 Gray (68 Mass.), 124, 66 Am. Dec. 455 (1854); Hutchins v. Hutchins, 7 Hill (N. Y.), 107 (1845); Van Horn v. Van Horn, 52 N. J. L. 285, 20 At. 485, 10 L. R. A. 184 (1890); 56 N. J. L. 318, 28 At. 669 (1893); Porter v. Mack, 50 W. Va. 581, 40 S. E. 459, 1901. In the last cited case, it is said: "Owing to its rare character, the law regarding this kind of action has not been well defined, and the decisions of the courts have produced some confusion in regard thereto. The principal authorities maintain that the common law action of conspiracy is obsolete, and that there has been substituted therefor an action on the case in the nature of a conspiracy. That the allegation of conspiracy is mere matter of aggravation, and need not be proven, except to fix the liability of several

defendants; and does not change the nature of the action from one purely on the case, subject to all the settled rules of such action."

[70] Dwight, C., in Place v. Minster, 65 N. Y. 89, 95 (1875). In Bishop on Non-Contract Law, § 362, it is said: "The term 'conspiracy' is in our books oftener misapplied than used correctly. In the just meaning of the word, the title is a considerable one in the criminal law; in our civil jurisprudence it is narrow, yet it exists and is important. It signifies in the true and narrow sense, a wrongful combination of persons to do an act or acts, which when done have brought to another an injury of a sort not admitting of being accomplished alone." Examples of such a tort are afforded by Griffith v. Ogle, 1 Binney (Pa), 172 (1806), holding distinctly that damage is not the

That such a concert or combination " differs widely from an invasion of civil rights by a single individual cannot be doubted." [71] " It may be punished criminally by indictment, or civilly by an action on the case in the nature of a conspiracy, if damage has been occasioned to the person against whom it is directed. It may consist of an unlawful combination to carry out an object not in itself unlawful by unlawful means. The essential elements, whether of a criminal or of an actionable conspiracy, are the same, though to sustain an action special damage must be proved." [72] " The number and compact give weight and cause danger." [73]

The true rule applicable to conspiracies against servants has been well stated as follows: " Every man has a right to employ his talents, industry and capital as he pleases, free from the dictation

gist of the action; and Wilde v. McKee, 111 Pa. 335, 2 At. 108, 56 Am. R. 271 (188).

[71] Lord Macnaghten, in Quinn v. Leathem (1901), A. C. 495, 511. *Cf.* Lord Lindley's statement on p. 539: " But numbers may annoy and coerce where one may not." In Arthur v. Oakes, 63 Fed. 310, at p. 321, Harlan, J., says: " It is one thing for a single individual, or for several individuals, each acting upon his own responsibility and not in co-operation with others, to form the purpose of inflicting actual injury upon the property or rights of others. It is quite a different thing, in the eye of the law, for many persons to combine or conspire together with the intent, not simply of asserting their rights or of accomplishing lawful ends by peaceable methods, but of employing their united energies to injure others or the public."

[72] Lord Brampton, in Quinn v. Leathem (1901), A. C. 495, at p. 528. To the same effect, Carew v. Rutherford, 106 Mass. 1, 10, 8 Am. R. 287 (1870); Giblan v. National

Amalgamated Union (1903), 2 K. B. 600, 621–624. Both of these cases approve of the decision in Gregory v. Duke of Brunswick, 6 M. & G. 205, 6 Scott. N. R. 809, 1 C. & K. 24 (1843), that a conspiracy to hiss another off the stage, and so injure him in his trade or calling, was illegal and actionable.

It has been said that there was no actual decision to the above effect, but Lord Chancellor Halsbury has pointed out that the report of the case, in 6 Scott, N. R. 809, 822, shows that such decision was made. See (1901) A. C. p. 503. Lord Macnaghten referred to the case, as an authority for the proposition that " a conspiracy to injure, resulting in damage, gives rise to a civil liability." It is also treated as an authority for that proposition by Lord Bowen in Mogul Steamship Co. v. McGregor, 23 Q. B. D. 598, 614 (1889), cited approvingly in Allen v. Flood (1898), 1, at p. 74.

[73] Mulcahy v. Reg., L. R. 3 H. L. 306, 317 (1868).

of others; and if two or more persons combine to coerce his choice in this behalf, it is a criminal conspiracy. * * * While such a con-spiracy may give to the individual, directly affected by it, a private right of action for damages, it at the same time lays a basis for an indictment, on the ground that the State itself is directly concerned in the promotion of all legitimate industries and the development of all its resources, and owes the duty of protection to its citizens engaged in the exercise of their callings." [74]

[74] State v. Stewart, 59 Vt. 273, 9   At. 559, 59 Am. R. 710 (1887).

CHAPTER X.

DEFAMATION.

§ I. NATURE OF THE TORT.

The Right Invaded by Defamation. This tort is an invasion of a person's right to enjoy a good reputation, until by his misconduct he has forfeited it. " The law recognizes the value of such a reputation and constantly strives to give redress for its injury." [1] Moreover the law presumes that every person is entitled to enjoy a good reputation, until it is shown that he is not so entitled.[2] Consequently, the plaintiff is not bound to show the falsity of a defamatory statement. On the contrary, the burden of proving its truth is on the defendant.[3]

It is to be borne in mind, too, that the issue tendered in an action

---

[1] Times Pub. Co. v. Carlisle, 94 Fed. 762, 36 C. C. A. 475 (1889); In this case Sanborn, J., said: "'A good name is rather to be chosen than great riches, and loving favor rather than silver and gold.' The respect and esteem of his fellows are among the highest rewards of a well spent life vouchsafed to man in this existence. The hope of them is the inspiration of his youth, and the possession of them the solace of his later years. A man of affairs, a business man, who has been seen and known of his fellowmen in the active pursuits of life for many years, and who has developed a good character and an unblemished reputation, has secured a posssession more useful and more valuable than lands, or houses, or silver or gold. Taxation may confiscate his lands; fire may burn his houses; thieves may steal his money; but his good name, his fair reputation, ought to go with him to the end,—a ready shield against the attacks of his enemies, and a powerful aid in the competition and strife of daily life; " Dixon v. Holden, L. R. 7 Eq. 488, 492 (1869); De Crespigny v. Wellesby, 5 Bing. 392, 406 (1829).

[2] Ibid. Conroe v. Conroe, 47 Pa. 198, 201 (1864); Atwater v. Morning News Co., 67 Conn. 504, 34 At. 865 (1896).

[3] Belt v. Laws, 51 L. J. Q. B. 359, 361 (1882); Ellis v. Buzzell, 60 Me. 209, 211, 11 Am. R. 204 (1872); Lewis v. News Co., 81 Md. 466, 473, 32 At. 246, 29 L. R. A. 59 (1895).

for defamation is not the character of the plaintiff, but the wrong-fulness of the particular statement. Accordingly, "It is not a defense to a libel or slander that the plaintiff has been guilty of offenses other than those imputed to him, or of offenses of a similar character; and such facts are not competent in mitigation of damages. The only tendency of such proof is to show not that the plaintiff's reputation is bad, but that it ought to be bad." [4] The distinction between character and reputation ought to be sharply made and strictly observed, in the discussion of this topic. Reputation is the estimate in which others hold a person,[5] " the common knowledge of the community " [6] in which he lives, based upon " the slow spreading influence of opinion, arising out of his deportment in the society in which he moves." [7] " An existing reputation," it has been declared, " is a fact to which any one may testify who knows it. He knows it because he hears it, and what he hears constitutes the reputation." [8] Character, on the other hand is not built upon hearsay; is not determined by the opinion of others and is not susceptible to harm from scandal. It has been judicially defined as " that which is habitually impressed by nature, traits or habits upon a person." [9]

Injury to Reputation by Means Other than Defamation. The reputation of a person may be harmed by the conduct of another, without a cause of action for libel or slander accruing to him. It may be that the one thus injured has no redress, as where a master refuses to give a servant a " character;" for the law does not recognize a servant's right to a " character " from his

---

[4] Sun Printing Co. v. Schenck, 98 Fed. 925, 40 C. C. A. 163 (1900); when the plaintiff is charged with being a thief, it is competent for defendant to show that he has the general reputation of being a thief; Drown v. Allen, 91 Pa. 393 (1879); See Conroe v. Conroe, 47 Pa. 198 (1864); O'Connor v. Press Pub. Co., 24 Misc. 564, 70 N. Y. Supp. 367 (1901).

[5] Spaits v. Poundstone, 87 Ind. 522, 44 Am. R. 773 (1882); Cooper v. Greely, 1 Den. (N. Y.) 347, 365 (1845).

[6] Chillis v. Chapman, 125 N. Y. 214, 221, 26 N. E. 308, 11 L. R. A. 784 (1891); Smith v. Crompton, 67 N. J. L. 548, 557, 52 At. 386, 58 L. R. A. 480 (1902).

[7] Wright v. City of Crawfordsville, 142 Ind. 636, 642, 42 N. E. 227 (1895).

[8] Bathwick v. Detroit Post, 50 Mich. 629, 642, 45 Am. R. 63 (1883).

[9] Wright v. Crawfordsville, 142 Ind. 636, 642, 42 N. E. (1895).

master.[10] Even when the conduct is tortious and injurious to reputation, it may not amount to defamation, as where a banker, having sufficient funds of his customer, wrongfully dishonors the latter's checks,[11] or where the payee negligently has plaintiff's note protested for non-payment, although it had been paid;[12] or when a creditor institutes legal proceedings against his debtor in a way, and with the view of giving the impression that the debtor is insolvent.[13]

In some jurisdictions, an action is given by statute for insulting words, although they are not defamatory and although they may not be heard or read by a third person.[14]

Publication. As the gist of the tort now under discussion consists in the injury done to reputation, it follows that the defamatory statement must have been published in order to be actionable.[15] No such injury is done when the statement is communicated to the person, concerning whom it is made, without its coming to the knowledge of a third person.[16] Accordingly, a plaintiff does not make out a cause of action for slander by proving that the defendant spoke defamatory words to him. He must go further and show that "they were so spoken as to have been heard by a third

---

[10] Cleveland and etc., Ry. v. Jenkins, 174 Ill. 398, 51 N. E. 811, 66 Am. St. R. 296 (1898); New York, Chic. etc., Ry. v. Schaffer, 65 Oh. St. 414, 62 N. E. 1036, 87 Am. S. R. 628 (1901).

[11] J. M. James Co. v. Cont. Nat. Bank, 105 Tenn. 1, 58 S. W. 261, 80 Am. St. R. 856, 51 L. R. A. 255 (1900).

[12] State Mut. Life v. Baldwin, 116 Ga. 855, 43 S. E. 262 (1903); In May v. Jones, 88 Ga. 308, 14 S. E. 552, 30 Am. S. 154, 15 L. R. A. 154 (1891), it was held libelous to "falsely and maliciously protest" commercial paper.

[13] Brewer v. Dew, 11 M. & W. 625, 12 L. J. Exch. 448 (1843); Odgers Libel & Slander, (3 ed.) p. 13.

[14] Rolland v. Batchelder, 84 Va. 664; 5 S. E. 695 (1888); Sun Life Assur. Co. v. Bailey, 101 Va. 443, 44 S. E. 692 (1903).

[15] Hebditch v. McIlwaine (1894), 2 Q. B. 54; 63 L. J. Q. B. 587.

[16] Clutterbuck v. Chaffers' 1 Stark, 471 (1816); Warnock v. Mitchell, 43 Fed. 428 (1890); Spaits v. Poundstone, 87 Ind. 522 (1882); McIntosh v. Matherly, 9 B. Mon. (48 Ky.) 119 (1848); Lyle v. Clason, 1 Caines (N. Y.) 581 (1804); Wilcox v. Moon, 64 Vt. 450, 24 At. 244 (1892). A sealed letter containing libellous matter, communicated to no one but the party libelled, will sustain an indictment, since such a publication to the party himself tends to a breach of the peace: Edwards v. Wooton, 12 Rep. 351 (1608); Clutterbuck v. Chaffers, 1 Stark, 471 (1816); State v. Avery, 7 Conn. 267, 18 Am. Dec. 105 (1828); Fry v. Mc-

person;"[17] and, if spoken in a foreign language, that they were understood by some one who heard them.[18] Nor is a cause of action established by proof, that a defamatory letter or print was sent by defendant to the plaintiff.[19] Evidence must be given that it was read to or by a third person, and that defendant was responsible for such publication.[20] It is to be noted, however, that plaintiff makes out a *prima facie* case of publication, by showing that the libel was " contained on the back of a postal-card," [21] or by other evidence that " makes it a matter of reasonable inference that the libellous matter was brought to the actual knowledge of any third person." [21 1-4] The burden is then thrown upon the defendant of showing that it did not come to the knowledge of any third person.[21 1-2]

Intention on the part of defendant that third persons shall hear or read the defamatory statement is not essential. He may believe that he and the plaintiff are alone, yet if a secreted third person overhears the slanderous utterance, there is an actionable publication.[22] He may intend to mail a defamatory letter to one about whom it is written, yet, if by inadvertence he mails it to a third

Cord, 95 Tenn. 678, 33 S. W. 568 (1895).

[17] Sheffill v. Van Deusen, 13 Gray (79 Mass.) 304 (1859).

[18] Price v. Jenkins, Croke Eliz. 865 (1601); Mieleng v. Quasdorf, 68 Ia. 726, 28 N. W. 41 (1886); Wormouth v. Cramer, 3 Wend. (N. Y.) 394 (1829).

[19] Clutterbuck v. Chaffers, 1 Starkie 471 (1816).

[20] Delacroix v. Thevenot, 2 Stark. 63 (1817); Kiene v. Ruff, 1 Ia. 482 (1855); Snyder v. Andrews, 6 Barb. (N. Y.) 43 (1849); Fry v. McCord, 95 Tenn. 678, 33 S. W. 568 (1895). If the writer of a defamatory letter locks it in his desk, and a thief takes the letter and makes its contents known, this is not publication by the writer; Pullman v. Hill (1891) 1 Q. B. 524, 60 L. J. Q. B. 299, (opinion of Lord Esher); Weir

v. Hoss, 6 Al. 881, (1844). And if the person to whom the letter is sent makes public its contents, this is not publication by the writer, Wilcox v. Moon, 64 Vt. 450, 24 At. 244 (1892).

[21] Robinson v. Jones, L. R. 4 Ir. 391 (1879); Williamson v. Freer, L. R. 9 C. P. 393, 43 L. J. C. P. 161 (1874). In Fry v. McCord, 95 Tenn| 678, 33 S. W. 568 (1895), it was held that " the sending of a writing in a sealed envelope, to the party himself," is not a publication " in the absence of averment and proof that it was read or heard read by others."

[21 1-4] Clerk and Lindsell, Torts (2 Ed.) p. 490.

[21 1-2] Clutterback v. Chaffers, 1 Stark, 471 (1816).

[22] Desmond v. Brown, 53 Ia. 13, 15 (1871).

person who reads it, there is publication.[23]   So, there is publication,
although the defendant intended to make the statement of another
person than the plaintiff,[24] or intended to make a different statement from that which he actually uttered,[25] or believed the occasion was privileged.[26]

Communicating a defamatory statement to one spouse about the
other is a legal publication,[27] but a communication by one spouse to
the other is privileged,[28] although if it is overheard by a third person the privilege is forfeited and publication is made.[29]

Alleging Publication.   It was settled at an early day, that
no technical words are necessary in alleging publication.   Accordingly, a declaration that defendant spoke the slanderous words in
the presence of others, was held good, although there was no allegation that they were spoken in the hearing of others; the Court
saying, " it shall be necessarily intended that it was in the hearing
when it was in the presence of others." [30]   So an averment that
defendant " openly and publicly promulgated " the statement was
held sufficient.[31]   An allegation, that defendant caused the libel to

---

[23] Fox v. Broderick, 14 Ir. C. L.
453 (1864).

[24] Taylor v. Hearst, 107 Cal. 262,
40 Pac. 392 (1895); S. C. 118 Cal.
366, 50 Pac. 541 (1897); McAllister,
v. Detroit Free Press Co., 76 Mich.
338, 43 N. W. 431, 15 Am. S. R. 339
(1889); Griebel v. Rochester Printing Co., 60 Hun. 319, 14 N. Y. Supp.
848 (1891); Morey v. Morning Journal Assoc., 123 N. Y. 207, 25 N. E.
161, 9 L. R. A. 62 (1890); Warner
v. Press Pub. Co., 132 N. Y. 185, 30
N. E 393 (1892); *Contra*, Hanson v.
Globe News Co., 159 Mass. 293, 34 N.
E. 362 (1893), but see dissenting
opinion of Holmes, Morton and
Barker, J. J.

[25] Shepheard v. Whitaker, L. R. 10
C. P. 502 (1875).

[26] Hebditch v. McIliwain (1894), 2
Q. B. 54, 63 L. J. Q. B. 587, overrul-
ing Tompson v. Dashwood, 11 Q. B.
D. 43, 52 L. J. Q. B. 425 (1883).

[27] Wenman v. Ash, 13 C. B. 836, 22
L. J. C. P. 190 (1853); Schenck v.
Schenck, 1 Spencer (20 N. J. L.)
208 (1844); Wilcox v. Moon, 64 Vt.
450, 24 At. 244 (1892).

[28] Wennhak v. Morgan, 20 Q. B. D.
635, 57 L. J. Q. B. 241 (1888); Ses-
ler v. Montgomery, 78 Cal. 486, 21
Pac. 185 (1889); Trumbull v. Gib-
bons, 3 City H. Rec. (N. Y.) 97
(1818).

[29] State v. Shoemaker, 101 N. C.
690, 8 S. E. 332 (1888).

[30] Hall v. Hennesley, Cro. Eliz. 486
(1596); Miller v. Johnson, 79 Ill. 58
(1875); Burbank v. Horn, 39 Me.
233, 235 (1855), *accord*.

[31] Taylor v. How, Cro. Eliz. 861
(1601); Ware v. Cartledge, 24 Al.
622 (1854); Goodrich v. Warner, 21
Conn. 432 (1852); Hurd v. Moore, 2
Or. 85 (1863); Benedick v. West-
over, 44 Wis. 404 (1878), *accord*.

be printed, charges publication, " because it calls in a third person, an agent, to whom it must have been communicated." [32] For similar reasons, there is actionable publication, when a letter is dictated to a typewriter or stenographer,[33] or a telegram is transmitted.[34] In the latter case, the telegraph company publishes the libel, when one agent communicates it over the wire to another.[35] And it may be laid down as a general proposition, that where two or more persons take part in communicating defamation, there is a publication by each to the other.[36]

Communication Which is not Publication. When the defamatory statement is made to a third person at the plaintiff's request, the publicity is chargeable to the plaintiff, not to the defendant.[37] If, however, the defendant communicates the defamation to a third person, without knowledge that he is an agent of the plaintiff, there is actionable publication. The defendant cannot be heard to say, in such a case, that the publicity is the plaintiff's act.[38]

A person, who voluntarily engages in " the interchange of opprobrious epithets and mutual vituperation and abuse," has been held

---

[32] Baldwin v. Elphinstone, 2 W. Bl. 1037 (1775). Cf. Watts v. Fraser, 7 A. & E. 223, 7 C. & P. 369, 1 M. & Rob. 449 (1835); Sproul v. Pillsbury, 72 Me. 20 (1880).

[33] Gambrill v. Schooley, 93 Md. 48, 48 At. 730, 52 L. R. A. 87, 86 Am. St. R. 414 (1901); Pullman v. Hill (1891), 1 Q. B. 524, 63 L. J. Q. B. 299.

[34] Whitfield v. S. E. Ry., E. B. & E. 115, 27 L. J. Q. B. 229 (1858); Williamson v. Freer, L. R. 9 C. P. 393, 43 L. J. C. P. 161 (1874).

[35] Peterson v. West. U. Tel. Co., 65 Minn. 18, 67 N. W. 646, 33 L. R. A. 302 (1896). If the dispatch does not disclose that its purpose is defamatory, it is the duty of the company, as a *quasi* common carrier, to transmit it: the occasion is privileged, and the company incurs no

liability; Nye v. W. U. T. Co., 104 Fed. 628 (1900).

[36] Spaits v. Poundstone, 87 Ind. 522, 525 (1882).

[37] Warr v. Jolly, 6 C. & P. 497 (1834); Fonville v. McNease, I Dud (S. C.) 303, 32 Am. Dec. 49 (1838); Howland v. Blake Manufacturing Co., 156 Mass. 543, 31 N. E. 656 (1892); Shinglemeyer v. Wright, 124 Mich. 230, 82 N. W. 887 (1900). In the last cited case, the court said: " There is no difference on principle between reading a letter to another, and soliciting a person to make a similar verbal statement. The maxim *volenti non fit injura* applies.

[38] Duke of Brunswick v. Harmer, 14 Q. B. 185 (1849); Byam v. Collins, 111 N. Y. 143, 19 N. E. 75 (1888).

to license his antagonist to a reply in kind.[39] " The right to answer a libel by libel is analagous to the right to defend oneself against an assault upon his person. The resistance may be carried to a successful termination, but the means used must be reasonable ." [40] For any excess of defamation beyond that which is fairly incident to self-defense, the party originally attacked is answerable.[41]

Common carriers,[42] News-vendors,[43] proprietors of circulating libraries [44] and others, who are not responsible for originating defamation, and are merely unconscious vehicles of its distribution, generally escape liability for its publication.[45] But, as pointed out by the courts they are *prima facie* answerable, inasmuch as they have in fact delivered and put into circulation the defamatory matter complained of, and they are therefore called upon to show their ignorance of its existence,[46] and their freedom from negligence in the matter.[47]

[39] Bloom v. Crescioni, 109 La. 667, 33 So. 724 (1903), *Cf.* Laughton v. Bishop of Sudor, L. R. 4 C. P. 495, 42 L. J. C. P. 11 (1872.)

[40] Fish v. St. Louis, etc., Co., 102 Mo. App. 6, 74 S. W. 641 (1903), Koenig v. Ritchie, 3 F. & F. 413 (1862); Shepherd v. Baer, 96 Md. 152, 53 At. 790 (1902); Chaffin v. Lynch, 83 Va. 106, 1 S. E. 803 (1887).

[41] Brewer v. Chase, 121 Mich. 526, 80 N. W 575, 46 L. R. 397, 80 Am. S. R. 527 (1899): " It must not be supposed that when a libellous article is published the person libelled is at once authorized to publish any and all kinds of charges against the offender, upon the theory that they tend to degrade him, and thereby discredit his libellous statements. If this were so, every libel might be answered in this way, and the most disgraceful charges made, the person making them being able to shelter himself behind his belief in their truth. The thing published must be something in the nature of an answer, like an explanation or denial. What is said must have some connection with the charge that is sought to be repelled." See Poissenet v. Reuther, 51 La. Ann. 965, 25 So. 937 (1899), limiting Goldberg v. Dobberton, 46 La. Ann. 1303, 16 So. 192, 28 L. R. A. 721 (1894).

[42] Day v. Bream, 2 Moo. & Rob. 54 (1837).

[43] Emmens v. Pottle, 16 Q. B. D. 354, 55 L. J. Q. B. 51 (1885).

[44] Vizetely v. Mudie's Select Library (1900) 2 Q. B. 170, 69 L. J. Q. B. 645.

[45] Smith v. Ashley, 11 Met. (52 Mass.) 367 (1846). Defendant printed what appeared to be a fancy sketch, without any reason to believe it was a libel on plaintiff.

[46] Day v. Bream, 2 Moo. & Rob. 54 (1837); Staub v. Van Benthuysen, 36 La. Ann. 467, 469 (1884).

[47] Vixetely v. Mudie's Select Library (1900), 2 Q. B. 170, 69 L. J. Q. B. 645.

Repetition of Defamation. There is some authority for the view that in early English law, a person, who, at the time of repeating a defamatory statement, gave the name of its author, could justify his conduct.[48] This doctrine has long been exploded, both in England and in this country. It is now well established that every repetition of a defamatory statement is a new publication, subjecting the repeater to a separate action.[49] The disseminator of scandal cannot take refuge behind rumor, or even the positive assertion of a trusted informant. He must be prepared to establish the truth of the defamatory statement, (not the fact that he has repeated only what he heard and believed to be true), or pay damages for the injury which his scandal-mongering has inflicted upon the plaintiff.[50]

While it is natural, and to be expected, that a defamatory statement will be repeated by those who hear or read it, the rule is settled that one is not liable for a third person's actionable and unauthorized

---

[48] Northampton's Case, 12 Co. 134 (1613). The latter part of the fourth resolution reads: " In a private action for slander of a common person, if J. S. publish that he hath heard J. N. say that J. G. was a traitor or thief; in an action of the case, if the truth be such, he may justify." It will be observed that the name of the informant must have been given when the statement was made, so as to give the plaintiff his action in the first instance against the original author of the slander: Woolworth v. Meadows, 5 East 463 (1803).

[49] McPherson v. Daniels, 10 B. & C. 263, 34 R. R. 397 (1829); Watkin v. Hall, L. R. 3 Q. B. 396, 37 L J. Q. B. 125 (1868); Parker v. McQueen, 8 B. Mon. (47 Ky.) 18 (1847); Nicholson v. Rusk (Ky) 52 S. W. 933 (1899); Staub v. Van Benthuysen, 36 La. Ann.. 467 (1884); Stevens v. Hartwell, 11 Met. (52 Mass.) 542 (1846); Inman v. Foster, 8 Wend. (N. Y.) 602 (1832); Folwell v. Providence Jour-

nal Co. 19 R. I. 551, 37 A. 6 (1896); Sans v. Joerris, 14 Wis. 663 (1861).

[50] Kelley v. Dillon, 5 Ind. 426 (1854); Lehrer v. Elmore, (Ky.) 37 S. W. 292 (1896); Louisville Press Co. v. Tennelly, 105 Ky. 365, 49 S. W. 15 (1899). In the last cited case, it is said: " The public good as well as the usefulness of the press, imperatively demand that no publication injurious to a citizen should ever be made, unless the publisher knows beyond a reasonable doubt that the statements or charges that it publishes are in fact true. It is a matter of public importance that all statements printed and published in the press of the day should be entitled to full faith and credence, and no paper should publish any matter calculated to injure the feelings, business, or standing of any citizen, unless the same be true; and the mere fact that such publisher may believe that the statements or charges made are true, is no defense in law or morals."

repetition of his slander or libel.[51]   Of course, a person who actually authorizes the repetition of a libel or slander which he originates,[52] is liable for such repetition, as he would be for any other tort of his procurement, and it is generally held that when a person publishes defamation to one, who is under a duty to repeat it to another, he is answerable for the repetition.[53]   But where the repetition is not privileged, the burden of proof appears to be upon the plaintiff to show that the defendant actually authorized or requested the repetition.[54]

Joint Publication.   If the publication of a libel is the result of the joint efforts of several persons, each is responsible for the wrong done to the plaintiff.   Accordingly, if A prepares a libel, and B prints it, and C publishes it, the victim may have a joint action against all, or may sue them separately.[55]   The rules apply here which have been set forth in a former connection, relating to joint wrongdoers, to master and servant, to partners, to corporations and their managers.[56]

---

[51] McGregor v. Thwaites, 3 B. & C. 24, 35 (1824); Ward v. Weeks, 7 Bing. 211, 4 M. & P. 796 (1830); Elmer v. Fessenden, 151 Mass. 359, 24 N. E. 208 (1890); Bassell v. Elmore, 48 N. Y. 561 (1872). See Supra p. 90.

[52] Youmans v. Smith, 153 N. Y. 214, 47 W. E. 265 (1897).

[53] Derry v. Handley, 16 L. T. N. S. 263 (1867); Elmer v. Fessenden, 151 Mass. 359, 24 N. E. 208 (1890).

[54] Schoepflin v. Coffey, 162 N. Y. 12, 56 N. E. 502 (1900). The fourth head-note is as follows: " A person whom defendant knew to be a newspaper reporter approached him concerning a report about plaintiff, stating that he understood that defendant had asserted the facts. Defendant repeated the assertion, but there was nothing said about the publication of the statement. Held insufficient to show that defendant intended his remarks to be published." Judge Vann dissented from the conclusion, that the evidence presented no question for the jury, as to whether he intended to cause or promote the publication of the words spoken to the newspaper reporter. According to Clerk & Lindsell's understanding of the English cases, the plaintiff made out a *prima facie* case against the defendant. See their treatise on Torts, (2 ed.) pp. 540-542: also, Clay v. People, 86 Ill. 147 (1877).

[55] Johnson v. Hudson, 7 A. & E. 233 n., 1 H. & W. 680 (1836); Watts v. Fraser, 7 C. & P. 369, 7 A. & E. 223, 1 M. & Rob. 449, 2 N. & P. 157 (1835); Thomas v. Rumsey, 6 Johns (N. Y.) 26 (1810); Youmans v. Smith, 153 N. Y. 214, 47 N. E. 265 (1897.)

[56] Supra, Ch. iv. Also, Abraith v. N. E. Ry., 11 App. Cas. 247, 55 L. J. Q. B. 460 (1886); Johnson v. St. Lous Dispatch Co., 65 Mo. 539, 27 Am. R. 293 (1877); Washington Gas Light Co. v. Lansden, 172 U. S. 534,

Ordinarily, the publication of the same slander by different persons is not a joint tort, but is a separate and distinct wrong done by each slanderer.[57] Hence, if A utters slanderous words of B, which are not actionable *per se*, and C's repetition of them causes B special damage, B can maintain an action only against C.[58]

But there can be no doubt, upon principle, that, if A and C concertedly utter the same slander, at the same time, they are jointly liable; nor, if C utters the slander at A's request, or pursuant to authority from A, or to an understanding between them. And the weight of authority, it is submitted, sustains this doctrine.[59]

§ 2. LIBEL AND SLANDER.

Two Species of Defamation are recognized by English Law. That which is expressed in oral speech, or its equivalent, is called slander;[60] while the term libel is applied to defamation which is expressed in writing or print, or pictures, effigies or other visible and permanent forms.[61]

---

19 Sup. Ct. 296, 43 L. Ed. 543 (1899); Sun Life Asur. Co. v. Bailey, 101 Va. 443, 44 S. E. 692 (1903).

[57] Van Horn v. Van Horn, 56 N. J. L. 318, 29 At. 669 (1893). The statement in this case, following Chamberlain v. White, Cro. Jac. 647 (1623), and Coryton v. Lithebye, 2 Wm. Saund, 117 c. (1682), and in Blake v. Smith, 19 R. I. 476, 34 At. 005 (1896), that "an action for slander will not lie jointly against two, because the words of one are not the words of another," is too broad.

[58] Shurtleff v. Parker, 130 Mass. 293, 39 Am. R. 454 (1881); Gough v. Goldsmith, 44 Wis. 262, 28 Am. R. 579 (1878); Parkins v. Scott, 1 H. & C. 152, 153, 31 L. I. Ex. 331 (1862); Ward v. Weeks, 7 Bing. 211, 4 M. & P. 796 (1830).

[59] Johnson v. Hudson, 7 A. & E. 233 n, 1 H. & W. 680 (1836); and the authorities cited in the three preceding notes; Clerk and Lindsell, Torts (2 Ed.), p. 491. In Cushing v. Hederman, 117 Ia. 637, 91 N. W. 940 (1902); the court appears to assume that a husband and wife might be joint-wrongdoers in the publication of slanderous words. In Haney Mnfg. Co. v. Perkins, 78 Mich. 1, 43 N. W. 1073 (1889), it was declared that if one partner, in the course of the firm's business slanders another "the partnership is liable therefor just as it might be for any other tort," and a joint action against all the partners will lie.

[60] Pollard v. Lyon, 91 U. S. 225 (1875); Gutsole v. Mathers, 1 M. & W. 495, 2 Gale, 64, 5 Dowl. P. C. 69 (1836).

[61] Iron Age Publ'g. Co. v. Crudup, 85 Al. 519, 5 So. 332 (1888). In

The legal distinction between these two species is not limited to their differences in form. It is even more striking and important when their consequences are considered.

Libel is a criminal offense as well as a tort; while the slander of private persons has never been deemed a common-law crime.[62]

Many a statement, which is actionable in the form of a libel, is not actionable as a slander. Sir James Mansfield once declared,[63] that upon principle, he could not " make any difference between words written and words spoken, as to the right which arises on them of bringing the action." He refers to the reasons usually assigned for the distinction in the following passage: " So it has been argued that writing shows more deliberate malignity; but the same answer suffices, that the action is not maintainable upon the ground of malignity, but for the damage sustained. So it is argued that written scandal is more generally diffused than words spoken, and is therefore actionable; but an assertion made in a public place, as in Royal Exchange, concerning a merchant in London, may be much more extensively diffused than a few printed papers dispersed, or a private letter: it is true that a newspaper may be very generally read, but that is all casual." However, he admits that the distinction between written and spoken scandal " has been established by some of the greatest names known to the law, Lord Hardwicke,[64] Hale,[65] I believe Holt, C. J., and others." [66]

Case de Libellis Famosis, 5 Coke, 125 b. (1606), it is said: "Every infamous libel *aut est in scriptis, aut sine scriptis;* a scandalous libel *in scriptis* is, when an epigram, rhyme, or other writing is composed or published to the scandal or contumely of another, by which his fame and dignity may be prejudiced. And such libel may be published: 1. *Verbis aut cantilenis,* as where it is maliciously repeated or sung in the presence of others. 2. *Traditione,* when the libel or any copy of it is delivered over to scandalize the party. *Famous libellus sine scriptis* may be: 1. *Picturis,* as to paint the party in any shameful and ignominious manner. 2. *Signis,* as to fix a gallows, or other reproachful and ignominious signs at the party's door or elsewhere."

[62] Reg v. Holbrook, 4 Q. B. D. 42, 48 L. J. Q. B. 113, 14 Cox C. C. 185 (1878); New York Pen. Code § 242. " It is only when slander is blasphemous, seditious or obscene that the State is concerned to interfere and punish the speaker," Odgers, Libel and Slander (3 Ed.) p. 7.

[63] Thorley v. Lord Kerry, 4 Taunt. 355, 3 Camp. 214 n. (1812).

[64] Bradley v. Methwyn, Selw. N. P. 982 (7 Am. Ed. 1045 n. 1), (1737).

[65] King v. Lake, 2 Vent. 28, Hardr. 470 (1672).

[66] Austin v. Culpepper, 2 Shower,

In accordance with this distinction, words of mere suspicion [67] or which amount to an accusation of dishonest, vicious or immoral conduct which falls short of being criminal,[68] are not actionable, when spoken, although they would be if published in writing or print. An oral charge of false swearing, which does not import perjury in a legal sense, is not actionable; [69] but the same charge becomes actionable when published in a paper.[70] To say of a man in writing that he has the itch and smells of brimstone, is an actionable libel; but to say the same words orally would not be actionable slander.[71] To charge one with being an anarchist is actionable in the form of libel, but not in the form of slander.[72]

Definition of Civil [73] Libel. It has long been established that " scandalous matter is not necessary to make a libel. It is enough if the defendant induces an ill opinion to be held by the plaintiff, or to make him contemptible or ridiculous." [74] Any censorious or ridiculing writing, picture or sign made intentionally and without just cause and excuse is a libel upon its victim.[75] The degree of

313, Skin, 123 (1683). Argued for plaintiff by Holt, who cited King v. Lake, *supra*.

[67] Haynes v. Clinton Printing Co., 169 Mass. 512, 48 N. E. 275 (1897), referring to cases cited by defendant.

[68] Blake v. Smith, 19 R. I. 476, 34 At. 995 (1896): " To say of the plaintiff's wife that ' she is a bad woman, and a disgrace to the neighborhood, and ought not to be allowed on the street,' and that ' she is a damned bitch,' is not to charge her with the commission of any offense known to the law; for, while said language may be suggestive of lewdness, it is also suggestive of drunkenness, of dishonesty, of viciousness, and of other moral infirmities and derelictions."

[69] Ward v. Clark, 2 Johns. (N. Y.) 10 (1806).

[70] Steele v. Southwick, 9 Johns. (N. Y.) 214 (1812).

[71] White v. Nichols, 3 How. (U. S.) 266, 285-6 (1845), citing Villers v. Monsley, 2 Wils. 403 (1769).

[72] Cerveney v. Chic. Daily News, 139 Ill., 345, 13 L. R. A. 864, 28 N. E. 692 (1891); Lewis v. Daily News Co., 81 Md. 466, 32 At. 246 (1895). Cf. Browning v. Comm. — Ky. —, 76 S. W. 19 (1903).

[73] The distinction between civil and criminal libel has not always been observed by judges and writers. Defamation of the memory of the dead is often included in the definition of civil libel; Smith v. Bradstreet Co., 63 S. C. 525, 41 S. E. 763 (1902), but it is well settled that no civil action lies for such defamation; Bradt v. News Nonpareil Co., 108 Ia. 449, 79 N. W. 122 (1899); Wellman v. Sun Publishing Co., 66 Hun, 331, 21 N. Y. Supp. 577 (1892).

[74] Cropp v. Tilney, 3 Salk. 225 (1693).

[75] Villers v. Monsley, 2 Wils. 403 (1769); Riggs v. Denniston, 3

censure or ridicule is not material.[76] " To allow the press to be the vehicle of malicious ridicule of private character, would soon deprave the moral taste of the community and render the state of society miserable." [77]

Oftentimes, a libel is not aimed at one's personal character but affects him chiefly or solely in his office or vocation.[78] In such cases it may be necessary to inquire whether the statement complained of necessarily imports damage to the plaintiff, or whether he must allege and prove, in addition to the publication, special damage. This class of libels involves the distinction, between statements actionable *per se* and those actionable only when they cause special damage, which we shall find of especial importance in cases of slander. Libels upon personal character, however, are always actionable unless privileged. The law assumes that they harm the victim, and relieves him from the necessity of alleging or proving actual damage.[79]

Johns. Cas. 198, 205 (1802); People v. Croswell, 3 Johns. Cas. 337, 354 (1804); Watson v. Trask, 6 O. 531 (1834).

[76] Cooper v. Greeley, 1 Den. (N. Y.) 347 (1845).

[77] Steele v. Southwick, 9 Johns. 214 (1812).

[78] McLoughlin v. Am. Circular Loom Co., 125 Fed. 203, 60 C. C. A. 87 (1903); Lowell, J., said: " We are of the opinion that the language here used is susceptible of a defamatory meaning. In substance it was this: That the plaintiff had installed electric wires contrary to the rules of the New Orleans Board of Underwriters. The letter thus charged the plaintiff with violating the rules of the insurance companies, and it is matter of common knowledge that the owner of a house wired in a manner not permitted by these rules may well be unable to insure it. As most house owners desire insurance, and wish that their electric wires should be so arranged as to make insurance possible, the plaintiff's evidence, admissible under the allegations of his declaration, might warrant a jury in finding that the defendant's letter suggested that the plaintiff so conducted his business as to make inadvisable his employment by one having the ordinary desires of a householder. There is no conclusive presumption that damage results from the language used, and so that language is not libelous *per se*."

[79] Austin v. Culpepper, 2 Shower, 313, Skin, 123 (1683); Bell v. Stone, 1 Bos. & P. 331 (1798); Iron Age Pub. Co. v. Crudup, 85 Al. 519, 5 So. 332 (1888); Wynne v. Parsons, 57 Conn. 73, 17 At. 362 (1889); Bee Pub. Co. v. Shields, — Neb. —, 94 N. W. 1029 (1903); Holmes v. Jones, 147 N. Y. 59, 41 N. E. 409 (1895); Gates v. N. Y. Rec. Co., 155 N. Y. 228, 49 N. E. 769 (1898); Solverson v. Peterson, 64 Wis. 128, 25 N. W. 14 (1885).

Libels Affecting One's Vocation.　In many cases of libels, which affect the victim chiefly or solely in his office or vocation, their tendency to cause legal injury may be so clear, as to render allegation and proof unnecessary. Imputing insanity,[80] or incompetency [81] to a professional man, or insolvency [82] to a trader, or asserting that a merchant has given a chattel mortgage or other security upon his stock,[83] or that a public officer has been guilty of dishonest, corrupt conduct,[84] is a libel actionable *per se*. On the other hand, a false statement that a person, not a trader, owed a debt,[85] or that a judgment had been recovered against a merchant,[86] is not actionable without allegation and proof of special damage, unless the circumstances warrant the inference that the defendant charged the plaintiff with inability to pay his just debts,[87] or with conduct which would "naturally injure his standing in the community and lower him in the esteem of his neighbors." [88]

Libel of a Class.　When a libellous publication is directed against a class or body of persons, such as the commissioners of a county,[89] or the medical staff of a public hospital,[90] any member of the class or body may maintain an action therefor.[91]

A libel upon one, in respect of a vocation which is illegal, is not

---

[80] Morgan v. Lingen, 8 L. T. R. N. S. 800 (1863); Totten v. Sun Pub. Assoc. 109 Fed. 289 (1901); Southwick v. Stevens, 10 Johns (N. Y.) 443 (1813); Moore v. Francis, 121 N. Y. 199, 23 N. E. 1127, 8 L. R. A. 214, 18 Am. S. R. 810 (1890).

[81] Tarleton v. Lagarde, 46 La. Ann. 1368, 16 So. 180, 26 L. R. A. 325, 49 Rm. S. R. 353 (1894); Mattice v. Wilcox, 147 N. Y. 624, 42 N. E. 270 (1895); Krug v. Pitass, 162 N. Y. 154, 56 N. E. 526, 76 Am. St. R. 317 (1900).

[82] Read v. Hudson, 1 Ld. Rayn. 610 (1699); Met. Omnibus Co. v. Hawkins, 4 H. & N. 87, 28 L. J. Ex. 201 (1859); Simons v. Burnham, 102 Mich. 189, 60 N. W. 476 (1894).

[83] Smith v. Bradstreet Co., 63 S. C. 525, 41 S. E. 763 (1902).

[84] Wofford v. Meeks, 129 Al. 349, 30 So. 625 (1901).

[85] Fry v. McCord, 95 Tenn. 678, 33 S. E. 569 (1895).

[86] Woodruff v. Bradstreet, 116 N. Y. 217, 2 N. E. 354 (1889); Searles v. Scarlett (1892), 2 Q. B. 56, 61 L. J. Q. B. 573.

[87] Williams v. Smith, 22 Q. B. D. 134, 58 L. J. Q. B. 21 (1888).

[88] McDermott v. Union Credit Co., 76 Minn. 84, 78 N. W. 967 (1899).

[89] Wofford v. Meeks, 129 Al. 349, 30 So. 625 (1901).

[90] Bornmann v. Star Co., 174 N. Y. 212, 66 N. E. 723 (1903).

[91] Hardy v. Williamson, 86 Ga. 551, 12 S. E. 874, 22 Am. St. R. 479 (1891).

actionable. "The law of libel is not designed to shield one in the practice of an illegal business." [92]

Province of the Court and the Jury. It is sometimes said that it is a pure question of fact for the jury, whether a particular publication comes within the definition of a libel. Such a statement does not accord with the weight of authority either in England or in this country. In civil actions, as distinct from criminal prosecutions [93] for libel, it is the province of the court, not simply to give to the jury a correct definition of libel, but to construe the particular publication.[94] Hence, if, in the opinion of the court, the language is not susceptible of a defamatory meaning, it should nonsuit the plaintiff.[95] On the other hand, if the publication is clearly libellous, in the opinion of the court, it should so charge the jury, leaving to them only the assessment of damages.[96] If, however, the

---

[92] Weltmer v. Bishop, 171 Mo. 110, 71 S. W. 167 (1902), citing Johnson v. Simonton, 43 Cal. 242 (1872), and Perry v. Man, 1 R. I. 263 (1849). Morris v. Langdale, 2 Bos. & P. 284 (1800), Collins v. Carnegie, 1 A. & E. 695, 3 N. & M. 703 (1834) *accord*.

[93] For learned discussions of the province of the court and jury in such prosecutions, see Sparf v. United States, 156 U. S. 51, 15 Sup. Ct. 273, 39 L. Ed. 343 (1895); Roesel v. State, 62 N. J. L. 216, 41 At. 408 (1898); People v. Sherlock, 166 N. Y. 180, 59 N. E. 830 (1901); State v. Burpee, 65 Vt. 1, 25 At. 964 (1892); McCloskey v. Pulitzer Pub. Co., 152 Mo. 339, 53 S. W. 1087 (1899).

[94] Wofford v. Meeks, 129 Al. 349, 30 So. 625 (1901); Haynes v. Clinton Printing Co., 169 Mass. 512, 48 N. E. 275 (1897); Trebby v. Publishing Co., 74 Minn. 84, 76 N. W. 961, 73 Am. S. R. 330 (1898); Alwin v. Liesch, 86 Minn. 281, 90 N. W. 404 (1902); Krug v. Pitass, 162 N. Y. 154, 56 N. E. 526 (1900); Blake v. Smith, 19 R. I. 476, 34 At. 995

(1896); Robertson v. Edelstein, 104 Wis. 440, 443, 80 N. W. 724 (1899); Morgan v. Halberstadt, 60 Fed. 592, 9 C. C. A. 147 (1894).

[95] Capital and Counties Bank v. Henty, 7 App. Cas. 741, 52 L. J. Q. B. 232 (1882); Quinn v. Prudential Ins. Co., 116 Ia. 522, 90 N. W. 349 (1902); Moore v. Francis, 121 N. Y. 199, 23 N. E. 1127, 8 L. R. A. 214, 18 Am. S. R. 810 (1890); Crashley v. Press Pub. Co., 179 N. Y. 27, 71 N. E. 258 (1904).

[96] Trebby v. Pub. Co., 74 Minn. 84, 76 N. W. 961, 73 Am. S. R. 330 (1898); Alwin v. Liesch, 86 Minn. 281, 90 N. W. 104 (1902). In Heller v. Pulitzer Pub. Co., 153 Mo. 205, 54 S. W. 457 (1899), it is said, following the English rule as stated by Lord Blackburn in Capital, etc., Bank v. Henty, 7 App. Cas. 741, 52 L. J. Q. B. 232 (1882). "While the court may sustain a demurrer to the plaintiff's petition, or nonsuit the plaintiff on the trial, or sustain a motion in arrest of a judgment against the defendant, it cannot direct a verdict for the plaintiff

language, or circumstances, of the publication render its defamatory character uncertain, the question of libel or no libel is for the jury.[97]

Liberty of Speech and Press. Constitutional provisions, guaranteeing the liberty of speech and press, do not affect the rules set forth above. It has been judicially declared that, " While the liberty of each is a sacred right, dear to the hearts of the entire Anglo-Saxon civilization, yet the law-makers and the framers of constitutions have all realized that liberty in the exercise of any natural right, when unrestrained by law, leads to licentiousness, and have therefore wisely provided that any one exercising the liberty of speech, or of the press within this State, shall be held responsible for an abuse of such privilege." [98]

Language to be Construed in its Ordinary Sense. In early English law, the rule was observed that, " when the words may have a good construction, you shall never construe them to an evil sense." [99] The purpose of the rule was " to avoid vexatious actions." [100] Later, however, the judges became convinced that the rule was unsound in principle, and harmful in results. Lord Holt announced that, " where words tend to slander a man and take away his reputation, he should be for supporting actions for them, because

---

in a libel case. In this respect, libel cases differ from other cases." It is admitted by the court that this doctrine is not applied in cases of slander, as the provision of the Missouri constitution, making the jury judges of the law as well as the facts, is limited to libel cases.

[97] Press Pub. Co. v. McDonald, 55 Fed. 264 (1893), 63 Fed. 238, 11 C. C. A. 155 (1894); Mosier v. Stoll, 119 Ind. 244, 20 N. E. 752 (1889); Quinn v. Prudential Ins. Co., 116 Ia. 522, 90 N. W. 349 (1902); Bee Pub. Co. v. Shields, — Neb. —, 94 N. W. 1029 (1903); Warner v. Southall, 165 N. Y. 496, 59 N. E. 269 (1901); Bourreseau v. Journal Co., 63 Mich. 425, 30 N. W. 376, 6 Am. S. R. 320 (1886).

[98] Bee Publishing Co. v. Shields, — Neb. —, 94 N. W. 1029 (1903).

[99] Brough v. Dennison, Gold. 143 (1601), holding the words " Thou hast stolen by the highwayside " not actionable; Popham, J., ingeniously suggesting " for it may be taken that he stole upon a man suddenly; " and Fennor, J., with equal ingenuity suggesting. " And it may be intended he stole a stick under a hedge, and these words are not so slanderous that they are actionable."

[100] Pratt, C. J., in Button v. Heyward, 8 Mod. 24 (1722), and Scarlett, *arguendo* in Woolworth v. Meadows, 5 East 463 (1803). This view had been repudiated in some cases, such as Toose v. St., Cro. Jac. 306 (1613).

it tends to preserve the peace."[101] Lord Mansfield declared,[102] " where words from their general import appear to have been spoken with a view to defame a party, the court ought not to be industrious, in putting a construction upon them different from what they bear, in the common acceptance and meaning of them." Early in the last century Lord Ellenborough observed: " The rule which at one time prevailed, that words are to be understood *in mitiori sensu*, has long been superseded: and words are now construed by courts as they always ought to have been, in the plain and popular sense in which the rest of the world naturally understand them." [103]

This principle of construction is now observed by all courts.[104] Accordingly, the inquiry of a judge or jury is not confined to the secret thought of the defendant, but to the effect of his utterance upon the plaintiff's reputation; and that effect is to be determined by the sense, which readers or hearers of common and reasonable understanding would ascribe to it.[105] This sense, it is to be borne in mind, will depend very much upon the circumstances attending the utterance. These may indicate that the statement complained

---

[101] Baker v. Pierce, 2 Ld. Ray. 959 (1703), holding actionable the words " John Baker stole my boxwood, and I will prove it." In Townsend v. Hughes, 2 Mod. 159 (1676), it was held that " words should not be construed either in a rigid or mild sense, but according to the natural and general meaning." In Naben v. Miecock, Skin, 183 (1683); Levinz, J., declared, that he was " for taking words in their natural, genuine, and usual sense, and common understanding, and not according to the witty construction of lawyers."

[102] Peake v. Oldham, Cowp. 275, affirming Oldham v. Peake, 2 Blackstone 959 (1774).

[103] Roberts v. Camden, 9 East 93 (1807). The words spoken by defendant were, " He is under a charge of prosecution for perjury; "

and the court ruled that they were calculated to convey the imputation of perjury actually committed by the plaintiff.

[104] Wofford v. Meeks, 129 Al. 349, 30 So. 625 (1901); Jones v. McDowell, 4 Bibb (Ky.) 188 (1815); Thompson v. Sun Pub. Co., 91 Me. 203, 39 At. 556 (1898); West v. Hanrahan, 28 Minn. 385, 10 N. W. 415 (1881); World Pub. Co. v. Mullen, 43 Neb. 126, 61 N. W. 108 (1894); Turrill v. Dolloway, 17 Wend. (N. Y.) 426 (1837); Reid v. Providence Journal Co., 20 R. I. 120, 37 At. 637 (1897); Clute v. Clute, 101 Wis. 137, 76 N. W. 1114 (1898).

[105] Hankinson v. Bilby, 16 M. & W. 442, 2 C. & K. 440 (1847); Jarnigan v. Fleming, 43 Miss. 710 (1871); Phillips v. Barber, 7 Wend. (N. Y.) 439 (1831).

of was clearly a joke,[106] or was so extravagant by reason of momentary passion, as not to convey its normal meaning;[107] or, on the
other hand, that it was intended to convey a covert or hidden meaning, which would be understood by those to whom it was addressed,
while wearing a harmless appearance to others.[108]

The Office of Innuendo. When the defamatory character
of an utterance is latent, it is necessary for the plaintiff to explain
the disingenuous words and phrases and disclose their true meaning.[109] This he does, by properly alleging those " extrinsic facts
and circumstances in the past and present relations of the parties, or
the facts surrounding the publication, by which the jury shall be
justified in giving to words, not ordinarily actionable, a slanderous
or libelous signification." [110] While this portion of the complaint,
known as the innuendo, is often important, it is to be remembered
that " the meaning of words cannot be extended by innuendo beyond
their natural import, aided by reference to the extrinsic facts with

[106] Donoghue v. Hayes, (Ir. Exch.)
Hayes, 265 (1831): " The principle
is clear that a person shall not be
allowed to murder another's reputation in jest. But if the words be
so spoken that it is obvious to every
bystander, that only a jest is meant,
no injury is done, and consequently
no action will lie." Applying the
same principle, defamation by one
afflicted with " great and notorious
lunacy " should not be actionable,
and such is the view generally held
in this country; Yeates v. Read, 4
Blackf. (Ind.) 463 (1838); Dickinson v. Barber, 9 Mass. 225 (1812);
Bryant v. Jackson, 6 Humph.
(Tenn.) 199 (1845); Horner v.
Marshall, 5 Mumf. (19 Va.) 466
(1817), while in England it has
been judicially declared, that lunacy is not a defense to an action
for libel or slander; Mordaunt v.
Mordaunt, 39 L. J. Prob. & M. 59
(1870).

[107] Austral. Newspaper Co. v. Bennett (1894), A. C. 284, 63 L. J. P. C.

105. Ritchie v. Stenius, 73 Mich.
563, 41 N. W. 687 (1889); Mihojevich v. Badechtel, 48 La. Ann. 618,
19 So. 672 (1896).

[108] Hanchett v. Chiatovich, 101
Fed. 742, 41 C. C. A. 648 (1900);
Hickinbotham v. Leach, 10 M. & W.
361, 2 Dowl. N. S. 270 (1842);
Cooper v. Greely, 1 Den. (N. Y.)
347 (1845).

[109] Sweetapple v. Jesse, 5 B. & Ad.
27, 2 N. & M. 36 (1833); Rawlings
v. Norbury, 1 F. & F. 341 (1851);
Over v. Shiffling, 102 Ind. 191, 26
N. E. 91 (1885); Quinn v. Prud. Ins.
Co., 116 Ia. 522, 90 N. W. 349
(1902); Belknap v. Ball, 83 Mich.
583, 47 N. W. 674, 11 L. R. A. 72, 21
Am. S. R. 622 (1890); Mason v.
Mason, 4 N. H. 110, 113 (1827);
Hemmens v. Nelson, 138 N. Y. 517,
34 N. E. 342 (1893); Crashley v.
Press Pub. Co., 179 N. Y. 27, 71 N.
E. 258 (1904).

[110] Quinn v. Prud. Ins. Co., 116 Ia.
522, 90 N. W. 349 (1902).

which they may be connected." [111]   Moreover, when the plaintiff has assigned a particular meaning to words, by this part of his pleading, he is limited to such meaning,[112] unless the language is clearly libelous.[113]

§ 3. SLANDER.

The Peculiarities of Slander.   Some of these have been stated in preceding paragraphs.   The most striking of them, however, are connected with the distinction which the common law [114] makes between spoken words which are actionable *per se*, and those which are actionable only upon proof that they have caused special damage to the person defamed.   Not a few of these peculiar characteristics are quite arbitrary and not to "be supported upon any satisfactory principle." [115]

Words Actionable Per Se.   These have been classified under four heads by the United States Supreme Court: (1) "Words falsely spoken of a person which impute to the party the commission of some criminal offense involving moral turpitude, for which the party, if the charge be true, may be indicted and punished: (2) Words falsely spoken of a person which impute that the party is infected with some contagious disease, where, if the charge is true, it would exclude him from society: (3) Defamatory words falsely spoken of

---

[111] Camp v. Martin, 23 Conn. 86, 92 (1854); McLaughlin v. Fisher, 136 Ill. 111, 24 N. E. 60 (1890); McFadin v. David, 78 Ind. 445, 41 Am. R. 587 (1881); Simons v. Burnham, 102 Mich. 189, 60 N. W. 476 (1894); Pelton v. Ward, 3 Caines (N. Y.) 73, 2 Am. Dec. 251 (1805); Woodruff v. Bradstreet Co., 116 N. Y. 217, 22 N. E. 354 (1889).

[112] Simmons v. Mitchell, 6 App. Cas. 156, 50 L. J. P. C. 11 (1881); Brown v. Tribune Assoc., 74 App. Div. 359, 77 N. Y. Supp. 461 (1902).

[113] Morrison v .Smith, 177 N. Y. 366, 69 N. E. 725 (1904). In such a case, the defendant is in no worse position, than if the innuendo were not in the complaint.

[114] This distinction does not exist in Louisiana, Sportono v. Fourichon, 40 La. Ann. 424, 4 So. 71 (1888): Civil Code Art. 2315, declares: "Every act whatever of man, that causes damage to another, obliges him, by whose fault it happens, to repair it." Hence, calling a white man a negro in that state is actionable. Sportono v. Fourichon, *supra;* but the words "dirty rat," "thief" and "swindler" applied by an irate and impulsive old woman, in an altercation with her landlord, are not actionable. Mihojevich v. Bodechtel, 48 La. Ann. 618, 19 So. 672 (1896).

[115] Lord Herschell in Alexander v. Jenkins (1892), 1 Q. B. 797, 61 L. J. Q. B. 634.

a person which impute to the party unfitness to perform the duties of an office or employment of profit, or the want of integrity in the discharge of the duties of such office or employment; (4) Defamatory words falsely spoken of a party which prejudice such party in his or her profession or trade." [116]

Words Imputing Crime. The diversity of judicial opinion as to what words imputing the commission of a crime are actionable *per se*, has long been the subject of comment.[117] In the latter part of the fifteenth century the Court of King's Bench declared: " There are divers cases in our law where one shall have *damnum absque injuria;* as for defamation in calling one a thief,[118] or traitor; this is damage in our law, but no tort." Less than a century later, the Court of Common Pleas, in discussing an action brought because the defendant called the plaintiff a heretic,[119] said: " But if it were matter wherein we could decide the main thing, as thief, traitor or the like, for such words an action would lie here, since we have cognizance of what is treason or felony."

The present rule in England is that " spoken words, which impute that the plaintiff has been guilty of a crime punishable with imprisonment, are actionable without proof of special damage." [120] In this country the prevailing rule is that words are actionable *per se*, when the offense which they charge renders the party liable to an indictment for a crime involving moral turpitude, or subjecting him to infamous punishment.[121] The rule has been variously modified,

[116] Pollard v. Lyon, 91 U. S. 225 (1875).

[117] Brooker v. Coffin, 5 Johns. (N. Y.) 188 (1809); Spencer, J., said, " There is not, perhaps, so much uncertainty in the law upon any subject."

[118] Browne v. Hawkins, Y. B. 17 Ed. IV, f. 3 pl. 2 (1477).

[119] Anonymous, Y. B. 27 Hy. VIII, f. 14 pl. 4 (1535). The court assigned this reason for dismissing the action: " If the defendant should justify that the plaintiff is a heretic, and should show in what point, we could not discuss whether it was heresy or not."

[120] Webb v. Beavan, 11 Q. B. D. 609, 52 L. J. Q. B. 544 (1883); Lopes, J., said, " A great number of offenses, which were dealt with by indictment twenty years ago, are now disposed of summarily, but the effect cannot be to alter the law with respect to actions for slander."

[121] Pollard v. Lyon, 91 U. S. 225 (1875); Dudley v. Horne, 21 Al. 379 (1852); Kinney v. Hosen, 3 Harr. (Del.) 77 (1840); Richardson v. Roberts, 23 Ga. 215 (1856); Halley v. Gregg, 74 Ia. 563, 38 N. W. 416 (1888); Lemons v. Wells, 78 Ky. 117 (1879); West v. Hanrahan, 28 Minn. 385 (1881); Hendrickson v.

however, in different States. Some courts hold that words are actionable *per se* if they impute a criminal offense, whether indictable or not, if it is punishable corporally.[122] Others, if the crime imputed involves moral turpitude.[123] Still others, if the crime involves disgrace.[124] And yet others, if it subjects the offender to infamous punishment.[125]

Whether an alleged offender is liable to an infamous punishment, depends upon the opinion, which the public entertains, of the character of the penalty imposable upon him. If the offense may be punished by confinement in a State prison or penitentiary at hard labor, the offender is subject to infamous punishment.[126]

It is well settled that the imputation of a criminal offense need not be made with legal precision; [127] but it must convey the charge, that the one of whom it is spoken had done a wrong, which had been punished,[128] or was punishable, criminally. If the statement, taken as a whole, disclosed the nature of the charge to be one of trespass, or dishonesty, or vice, the employment of such general terms as "thief," "swindler," "robbed," "stole," and the like, will not render the statement actionable.[129]

Sullivan, 28 Neb. 329, 44 N. W. 448 (1889); Johnson v. Shields, 25 N. J. L. 116 (1855); Brooker v. Coffin, 5 Johns. (N. Y.) 188 (1809); Davis v. Brown, 27 O. St. 326 (1875); Davis v. Sladden, 17 Or. 259, 21 Pac. 140 (1889); Davis v. Cary, 141 Pa. 314, 21 At. 633 (1891); Lodge v. O'Toole, 20 R. I. 405, 39 At. 752 (1898); Cage v. Shelton, 3 Rich. L. (S. C.) 242 (1832). Smith v. Smith, 2 Sneed (34 Tenn.) 473 (1855); Payne v. Tancil, 98 Va. 262, 35 S. E. 725 (1900).

[122] Elliot v. Ailsbury, 2 Bibb (Ky.) 473 (1811). Buck v. Hersey, 31 Me. 558 (1850); Wagaman v. Byers, 17 Md. 183 (1861); Birch v. Benton, 26 Mo. 153 (1858).

[123] Frisbie v. Fowler, 2 Conn. 706 (1818); Redway v. Gray, 31 Vt. 292 (1858).

[124] Miller v. Paris, 8 Pick. (25 Mass.) 383 (1829); Zeliff v. Jennings, 61 Tex. 458 (1884); Geary v. Bennett, 53 Wis. 444 (1881).

[125] Harris v. Terry, 98 N. C. 131, 3 S. E. 745 (1887).

[126] Mackin v. United States, 117 U. S. 348, 6 Sup. Ct. 777, 29 L. Ed. 909 (1886).

[127] Odgers, Libel and Slander (3d. Ed.) p. 67, and cases cited. Sherwood v. Chace, 11 Wend. (N. Y.) 38 (1883); Payne v. Tancil, 98 Va. 262, 35 S. E. 725 (1900).

[128] Fowler v. Dowdney, 2 Moo. & Rob. 119 (1838). Krebs v. Oliver, 12 Gray (78 Mass.) 239 (1858).

[129] Murphy v. Olberding, 107 Ia. 547, 78 N. W. 205 (1899). "You damn Irishman! You stole my wire," but the evidence showed that the wire was a part of the realty and not the subject of larceny. Peters v. Booth, 50 S. W. (Ky.) 682

Nor is the charge of an intention to commit a specified crime actionable *per se*.[130]

Imputing Unchastity, even to women, was not actionable slander at common law,[131] but has been made such by legislation in England [132] and in many of our States.[133] In Scotland and in several of our States, the courts have declared such an imputation upon a woman actionable *per se,* because manifestly hindering her advancement in life.[134] These courts refuse to treat an imputation of this sort as mere " brabling words." [135]

Imputing Contagious Diseases. A false imputation of small-

(1899), " She is a damn slut "; Blake v. Smith, 19 R. I. 476, 34 At. 995 (1896), " She is a bad woman and a disgrace to the neighborhood "; Savile v. Jardine, 2 H. Bl. 531 (1795), " You are a swindler." Buller, J., said: " When a man is swindled, it means he is tricked or outwitted."

[130] Mitchell v. Sharon, 59 Fed. 980, 8 C. C. A. 429 (1894); Severinghaus v. Beckman, 9 Ind. App. 388, 36 N. E. 930 (1893); Fanning v. Chase, 17 R. I. 388, 22 At. 275 (1891). If such a charge were written or printed, it would be actionable. Browning v. Comm. — Ky. —, 76 S. W. 19 (1903).

[131] Allsop v. Allsop, 5 H. & N. 534, 29 L. J. Ex. 315 (1860); Pollard v. Lyon, 91 U. S. 225 (1875); Ledlie v. Wallen, 17 Mont. 150, 42 Pac. 289 (1895). See Civil Code of 1895, § 33, Sub. 4, changing the rule and making the imputation of unchastity to a man or a woman actionable.

[132] Slander of Women Act, 1891. (54 & 55 Vict. c. 51).

[133] Preston v. Frey, 91 Cal. 107, 27 Pac. 533 (1891); Dexter v. Harrison, 146 Ill., 169, 34 N. E. 46 (1893); Campbell v. Irwin, 146 Ind. 681, 45 N. E. 810 (1896). Ky. St. § 1,

Nicholson v. Merrit, 109 Ky. 369, 59 S. W. 26 (1900); Hemming v. Elliot, 66 Md. 197, 7 At. 110 (1886); Loranger v. Loranger, 115 Mich. 681, 74 N. W. 228 (1898); Christal v. Craig, 80 Mo. 367 (1883); Hemmens v. Nelson, 138 N. Y. 517, 34 N. E. 342 (1893); Bowden v. Bailes, 101 N. C. 612, 8 S. E. 342 (1888); Freeman v. Price, 2 Bailey Law (S. C.) 115 (1831); Hackett v. Brown, 2 Heisk. (49 Tenn.) 264 (1871); Stewart v. Major, 17 Wash. 238, 49 Pac. 503 (1897).

[134] Cushing v. Hederman, 117 Ia. 637, 91 N. W. 940 (1902); Reitan v. Goebel, 33 Minn. 151, 22 N. W. 291 (1885); Smith v. Minor, 1 N. J. L. 16 (1790); Barnett v. Wood, 36 O. St. 107, 38 Am. R. 561 (1880). In Nicholson v. Rust, (Ky.) 52 S. W. 933, the remarkable statement is made.—" In this State, and, so far as we are advised, throughout the U. S., it is actionable *per se* to impute a want of chastity to a female without allegation or proof of special damage, and it is not necessary that the words should make the charge in express terms."

[135] Oxford v. Cross, 4 Coke, 18 (1599); Hacker v. Heiney, 111 Wis. 313, 87 N. W. 249 (1901).

pox, or measles, or scarlet fever, or diphtheria, or the itch, is not actionable *per se*. " An action for oral slander," according to modern judicial authority,[136] " in charging the plaintiff with disease, has been confined to the imputation of such loathsome and infectious maladies as would make him an object of disgust and aversion, and banish him from human society. The only examples which adjudged cases furnish are of the plague,[137] leprosy,[138] and venereal diseases." [139]

Moreover, if the words relate to time past, they are not actionable. Said a learned English judge: [140] " Charging a person with having committed a crime is actionable, because the person charged may still be punished; it affects him in his liberty.[141] But charging another with having had a contagious disorder is not actionable; for unless the words spoken impute a continuance of the disorder at the time of speaking them, the gist of the action fails; for such a charge cannot produce the effect which makes it the subject of an action, namely, his being avoided by society. Therefore, unless some special damage is alleged in consequence of that kind of charge, the words are not actionable."

Imputation of Unfitness for Office. A false charge of any malversation, or misconduct in his office, is actionable in favor of the incumbent,[142] whether the office be one of profit or of honor.

---

[136] Joannes v. Burt, 6 Allen (88 Mass.) 336 (1863).

[137] Villers v. Monsley, 2 Wils. 403 (1769), *dictum*.

[138] Taylor v. Perkins, Cro. Jac. 144 (1607); Meteye v. Times Pub. Co., 47 La. Ann. 824, 17 So. 314 (1895).

[139] Austin v. White, Cro. Eliz. 214 (1591); Bloodworth v. Gray, 7 M. & G. 334, 8 Scott, N. R. 9 (1844); Watson v. McCarthy, 2 Ga. 57 (1847); Nichols v. Guy, 2 Ind. 82 (1850); Golderman v. Stearns, 7 Gray (73 Mass.) 181 (1856); Williams v. Holdredge, 22 Barb. (N. Y.) 396 (1854); Kaucher v. Blinn, 29 O. St. 62 (1875).

[140] Ashurst, J., in Carslake v. Mapledoran, 2 D. & E. 473 (1788); Nichols v. Guy, 2 Ind. 82 (1850);

Pike v. Van Wormer, 5 How. Pr. (N. Y.) 171 (1850); Irons v. Field, 9 R. I. 216 (1869), *accord.*

[141] In Fowler v. Dowdney, 2 Moo. & R. 119 (1838), it is said, that such a charge is actionable, even though the punishment is alleged to have been suffered, because the " obloquy remains." The obloquy attaching to the victim of venereal disease seems to be disregarded by the courts, when dealing with a charge as to time past; but it is taken into account when the charge relates to existing disorder; Lymbe v. Hockley, 1 Levinz 205 (1667).

[142] Moor v. Foster, Cro. Jac. 65 (1606); Fleetwood v. Curley, Cro. Jac. 557, Hob. 268 (1619); Dole v. Van Rensselaer, 1 Johns. Cas. (N.

Where, however, the imputation is that of unfitness for an office, a distinction is taken between offices of profit and those which are merely honorary.[143] With reference to the former, the law presumes a probability of loss to the incumbent from such defamatory statement.[144] With regard to the latter, it is held, that a charge of unfitness will not sustain an action, without proof of special damage, unless the alleged unfitness or personal misconduct be such as would enable him to be removed from, or deprived of, that office.[145]

Words Which Prejudice a Person in his Profession or Trade. In order that these be actionable *per se*, it must appear that they were spoken of the plaintiff, in relation to a profession, trade, calling or business, in which he was then engaged.[146] Accordingly, a dry-goods merchant does not make out a cause of action, by showing that the defendant falsely asserted, that the plaintiff " made false statements about and misrepresented the lot which he traded to me." Such words are not used of him " with respect to his employment " as merchant, but with respect to an outside transaction.[147] But the statement, " Our school-teacher is a villainous

Y.) 330 (1800). See Forward v. Adams, 7 Wend. (N. Y.) 205, where the charge related to misconduct in an office from which the plaintiff had retired. Also, Prosser v. Callis, 117 Ind. 105, 19 N. E. 735 (1888).

[143] In England, honorary offices include those of Sheriff, Justice of the peace, Alderman, Town-Councillor, Vestrymen, and unbeneficed clergymen of the Church of England.

[144] Booth v. Arnold, (1895), 1 Q. B. 571, 67 L. J. Q. B. 443; O'Shaugnessy v. N. Y. Record Co., 58 Fed. 653 (1893). Gove v. Blethen, 21 Minn. 80 (1874); Cotulla v. Kerr, 74 Tex. 89, 11 S. W. 1058 (1889).

[145] Alexander v. Jenkins (1892), 1 Q. B. 797, 61 L. J. Q. B. 634. The charge was that the plaintiff was " never sober, and not a fit man for the town council."

[146] Bellam v. Burch, 16 M. & W. 590 (1847). " Here the plaintiff was bound to prove that he exercised the so-called profession before and at the time the words were spoken. But the jury have found that the plaintiff's profession, so-called, did not continue at the time the words were spoken; that excludes all presumption on the subject; the defendant's act was nothing more than speaking of the plaintiff as a former contractor."

[147] Winsette v. Hunt, (Ky.) 53 S. W. 522 (1899). Todd v. Hastings, 2 Saund. 307 (1671), " You are a cheating fellow, and keep a false book," without proof that the charge touched the plaintiff in his trade, held not to be actionable. Newman v. Kingerby, 2 Lev. 49 (1672), calling a parson a " fool, ass and goose," was held not actionable as " these are only words of heat, and do not touch him in his profession." Lumby v. Allday, 1 Cr. & Jer. 301, 1 Tyrw. 217 (1831).

reptile. He is not fit to go with decent girls," is clearly aimed at its victim in his vocation; and is actionable *per se*.[148]

The early English cases [149] show a disposition on the part of judges to limit the terms " profession " and " trade " rather narrowly, but the modern " rule,[150] as to words spoken of a man in his office or trade, is not necessarily confined to offices and trades of the nature and duties of which the law can take notice. The only limitation is, that it does not apply to illegal callings." [151]

In cases of the sort now under consideration, the complaint should expressly allege that the defamatory statement was uttered of the plaintiff in the way of his then profession, trade, business or calling, unless this clearly appears from the statement itself.[152]

Whether a particular statement is such as to necessarily harm its victim in his vocation is a question of fact.

It is not strange, therefore, that the verdict of jurors and the rulings of judges, with respect to very similar statements, are quite diverse. There can be no doubt, however, that to falsely charge a trader with insolvency,[153] or a professional man with moral unfit-

---

[148] Bray v. Callihan, 155 Mo. 43, 55 S. W. 865 (1900); Birchley's Case, 4 Coke, 16 *a.* (1595), charging an attorney with being corrupt in his profession; Squire v. Johns, Cro. Jac. 585 (1620), charging a dyer with being a bankrupt knave. Southam v. Allen, T. Ray. 231 (1673); Trimmer v. Hiscock, 27 Hun, (N. Y.) 364 (1882), charging innkeeper with being bankrupt or having no decent accomodations; Buck v. Hersey, 31 Me. 558 (1850), charging a teacher of dancing with drunkenness, vagrancy, etc.; Fitzgerald v. Redfield, 51 Barb. (N. Y.) 484 (1868).

[149] In Terry v. Hooper, T. Ray. 86 (1663), the court was evenly divided as to whether the plaintiff's business of lime-burning " were such a profession of which he may be scandalized." In Fox v. Lapthorne, T. Jones, 156 (1681), it was held

that a renter of lands was not a trader, so as to be " touched in his trade " by the charge that he had cheated in corn. In Barker v. Ringrose, Popham 184 (1626), a wool-winder was held not to be scandalized by the charge that he was a bankrupt knave.

[150] Foulger v. Newcomb, L. R. 2 Ex. 327, 36 L. R. Ex. 169 (1867); DePew v. Robinson, 95 Ind. 109 (1883); Cruikshank v. Gordon, 118 N. Y. 178, 23 N. E. 457 (1890); Morasse v. Brochu, 151 Mass. 567, 25 N. E. 74 (1890).

[151] Hunt v. Bell, 1 Bing. 1 (1822), keeping open rooms for pugilistic encounters; Weltmer v. Bishop, 171 Mo. 110, 71 S. W. 167 (1902).

[152] Ayre v. Craven, 2 Ad. & E. 2 (1834); Jones v. Little, 7 M. & W. 423, 10 L. J. Ex. 171 (1841).

[153] Whittington v. Gladwen, 5 B. & C. 180, 2 C. & P. 146 (1826); Newell

ness [154] or mental incompetence [155] or want of ordinary skill in his calling,[156] or any person with dishonesty in the business whereby he gains his bread,[157] is to utter actionable slander.

Words not Actionable per se, but Causing Special Damage. When defamatory language of this kind is the subject of complaint, the plaintiff must set forth the special loss or injury which he claims to have suffered, and must show that such injury is the natural and proximate consequence of the defamation.[158] It is not enough to allege generally that the plaintiff " has been damaged and injured, in her name and fame," [159] nor that he has " suffered pain of mind, lost the society or good opinion of his neighbors, or the like, unless he has also been injured in his estate or property." [160] It is enough, however, to allege and prove that the slander has prevented the plaintiff from obtaining civil entertainment at a public house,[161] or has led to her being turned away from a private house,

---

v. Howe, 31 Minn. 235, 17 N. W. 383 (1883); Mitchell v. Bradstreet Co., 116 Mo. 226, 22 S. W. 358, 20 L. R. A. 138, 38 Am. St. R. 592 (1893).

[154] Pemberton v. Colls, 10 Q. B. 461, 16 L. J. Q. B. 403 (1847); Irwin v. Brandwood, 2 H. & C. 960, 33 L. J. Ex. 257 (1864); Piper v. Woolman, 43 Neb. 280, 61 N. W. 588 (1895); Hayner v. Cowden, 27 Oh. S. 292 (1875).

[155] Peard v. Jones, Cro. Car. 382 (1635); Watson v. Vanderlash, Hetl. 69, 71 (1628); Botterill v. Whytehead, 41 L. T. 588, 21 A. L. J. 103 (1879); Dennis v. Johnson, 42 Minn. 301, 44 N. W. 68 (1890); St. James Military Acad. v. Gaiser, 125 Mo. 517, 28 S. W. 851, 46 Am. S. R. 502 (1899); Krug v. Pitass, 162 N. Y. 154, 56 N. E. 526, 76 Am. S. R. 317 (1900).

[156] Day v. Butler, 3 Wils. 59 (1770); Edsall v. Russell, 4 M. & Gr. 1090, 5 Scott, N. R. 801, 2 Dowl. N. S. 641, 12 L. J. C. P. 4 (1843); Johnson v. Robertson, 8 Port. (Al.) 486 (1839); Sumner v. Utley, 7

Conn. 257 (1828); Secor v. Harris, 18 Barb. (N. Y.) 425 (1854); Mattice v. Wilcox, 147 N. Y. 624, 42 N. E. 270 (1895); Ganorean v. Superior Pub. Co., 62 Wis. 403, 22 N. W. 726 (1885).

[157] Thomas v. Jackson, 3 Bing. 104, 10 Moore, 125 (1825); Garr v. Selden, 6 Barb. (N. Y.) 416 (1848); Fowler v. Bowen, 30 N. Y. 20 (1864).

[158] Haddan v. Lott, 15 C. B. 411, 29 L. J. C. P. 49 (1860). See Remoteness of Damage, *supra*, p. 90.

[159] Pollard v. Lyon, 91 N. S. 225 (1875); Cook v. Cook, 100 Mass. 194 (1868).

[160] Beach v. Ranney, 2 Hill (N. Y.) 309 (1842); Terwilliger v. Wands, 17 N. Y. 54 (1858); Bassell v. Elmore, 65 Barb. (N. Y.) 627 (1866), 48 N. Y. 561 (1872).

[161] Olmstead v. Miller, 1 Wend. (N. Y.) 506 (1828). In Roberts v. Roberts, 5 B. & S. 384, 33 L. J. Q. B. 249 (1864), it was held that the loss, suffered by the plaintiff in being excluded from a religious society, was

where she was receiving gratuitous entertainment,[162] or has caused the retraction of a pecuniarily valuable, though gratuitous promise,[163] or has caused a woman the loss of a marriage,[164] or has prevented a person from getting or keeping employment,[165] or has caused an injury to the plaintiff's business or avocation.[166] Such loss, however, must be shown to have been the natural and probable consequence of the defamatory statement.[167]

General Damages in Defamation. These may be either nominal, compensatory or exemplary.[168] The amount of damages in each case is peculiarly a question for the jury;[169] but the courts do not hesitate to set aside or modify verdicts, which are either so excessive, or so meager, as to indicate improper motives in the jury.[170]

It is to be borne in mind, that while malice in fact, as distinguished from malice in law, must be shown in order to sustain a verdict for exemplary damages,[171] it is not necessary to establish the existence

---

[162] not temporal damage. Dwyer v. Meehan, 18 L. R. Ir. 138 (1886); Shafer v. Ahalt, 48 Md. 171, 30 Am. R. 456 (1877), accord.

[162] Davies v. Solomon, L. R. 7 Q. B. 112, 41 L. J. Q. B. 10 (1871); Williams v. Hill, 19 Wend. (N. Y.) 305 (1838).

[163] Corcoran v. Corcoran, 7 Ir. C. L. R. 272 (1857), promise to supply plaintiff with means for a trip to Australia.

[164] Davis v. Gardner, 4 Coke, 16 b. (1593); Sheppard v. Wakeman, 1 Lev. 53 (1662).

[165] Sterry v. Foreman, 2 C. & P. 592 (1827).

[166] Brown v. Smith, 13 C. B. 596, 22 L. J. C. P. 151 (1853).

[167] Miller v. David, L. R. 9 C. P. 118, 43 L. J. C. P. 84 (1874). There is "no authority for the proposition that a statement, false and malicious, made by one person in regard to another whereby that other might probably, under some circumstances, and at the hands of some persons, suffer damage, would, if damage resulted in fact, support an action for defamation." Terwilliger v. Wands, 17 N. Y. 34 (1858).

[168] Supra, Ch. V, § 3. Mental suffering as an element of damages, supra, Chap. III, § 11.

[169] Holmes v. Jones, 147 N. Y. 59, 41 N. E. 409 (1896); Minter v. Bradstreet Co., 174 Mo. 444, 73 S. W. 668 (1903).

[170] Peterson v. W. U. Tel. Co., 65 Minn. 18, 67 N. W. 646 (1896).

[171] Peterson v. W. U. Tel. Co., 72 Minn. 41, 74 N. W. 1022 (1898). See Minter v. Bradstreet Co., 174 Mo. 444, 73 S. W. 668 (1903), malice in law is defined as a wrongful act, done intentionally without legal justification or excuse, while malice in fact is defined as an act done with intent to harm the plaintiff or with a wilful and wanton neglect of his rights.

of actual malevolence on the defendant's part towards the plaintiff.[172] It is enough to show that the defendant's conduct in publishing the defamation,[173] or in pleading its truth as a defense,[174] was reckless or wanton. Evidence of such misconduct is always competent for the plaintiff in aggravation of his damages; as is evidence of the extent, to which the defendant has published the defamation; of the number of his repetitions of it, or of his refusal to retract, or of the nature of his apology.[175]

On the other hand, the defendant may absolve himself from exemplary damages or mitigate them, by showing that he acted in good faith, in repeating the defamatory statement as a matter of hearsay, and giving the source of his information,[176] or by showing that the plaintiff provoked the statement,[177] or by showing the plaintiff's bad reputation.[178] By statute in some jurisdictions, various matters may be shown in mitigation of damages, which were not available at common law.[179] Absence of actual malice does not exempt the defamer from liability to compensatory damages [180] except in the cases of qualified privilege, to be considered presently; nor does the fact that the defamation had been published by others, nor that the plaintiff had recovered against such others.[181] Com-

---

[172] Smith v. Matthews, 152 N. Y. 152, 46 N. E. 164 (1897).

[173] Warner v. Pres. Pub. Co., 132 N. Y. 181, 30 N. E. 393 (1892); Morning Journal Assoc. v. Rutherford, 51 Fed. 513, 2 C. C. A. 354, 1 U. S. App. 296 (1892).

[174] Mark v. Pres. Pub. Co., 134 N. Y. 561, 31 N. E. 398 (1892).

[175] Chamberlin v. Vance, 51 Cal. 75 (1875); Thibault v. Sessions, 101 Mich. 279, 59 N. W. 863 (1894); Gribble v. Pioneer Press Co., 34 Minn. 342, 25 N. W. 710 (1885); Enos v. Enos, 135 N. Y. 607, 32 N. E. 123 (1892); Van Derveer v. Sutphin, 5 O. St. 293 (1855); Patten v. Belo, 79 Tex. 41, 14 S. W. 1037 (1890).

[176] Duncombe v. Daniel, 8 C. & P. 222, 2 Jur. 32 (1837); Dole v. Lyon, 10 Johns. (N. Y.) 447 (1813); Republican Pub. Co. v. Mosman, 15 Col.

397, 24 Pac. 1051 (1900); Lothrop v. Adams, 133 Mass. 471 (1882); Upton v. Howe, 24 Or. 420, 33 Pac. 810 (1893).

[177] Tarpley v. Blabey, 2 Bing. N. C. 247, 2 Scott, 642, 7 C. & P. 367 (1836); Stewart v. Tribune Co., 41 Minn. 71, 42 N. W. 787 (1889).

[178] Scott v. Sampson, 8 Q. B. D. 491, 51 L. J. Q. B. 380 (1882); Halley v. Gregg, 82 Ia. 622, 48 N. W. 974 (1891).

[179] Lord Campbell's Act, 6 & 7 Vict. c. 96; New York Code of Civil Procedure, §§ 535, 536.

[180] Odgers, Libel & Slander, (3rd. Ed.) p. 362.

[181] Creevy v. Carr, 7 C. & P. 64 (1835); Enquirer Co. v. Johnston, 72 Fed. 443, 18 C. C. A. 623 (1896); Wilson v. Fitch, 41 Cal. 363 (1873); Sheahan v. Collin, 20 Ill., 325

pensatory damages include loss of reputation, shame and injury to the feelings.[182]

§ 4. DEFENSES IN ACTIONS FOR DEFAMATION.

Classified. These may be classed under three heads: Truth, Privilege, and Fair Comment.

The Truth of the Charge is a complete defense at common law to a civil action for slander or libel, because "the law will not permit a man to recover damages in respect to an injury to a character which he either does not or ought not to possess." [183] It must be specially pleaded, however, in order that evidence of it may be given; for this defense is "not a direct denial of the cause of action, but a collateral matter, which, if established by the defendant, will bar a recovery that otherwise must follow the malicious injury." [184] Moreover, the justification must be as broad as the defamatory charge, and the defendant has the burden of showing that every material part of the charge is true.[185] Again, a plea of the truth should state the charge with the precision of an indictment,[186] and will be construed strictly against the defendant.[187] In some States, the truth of a libel is not a defense, unless the publication was made

(1858); Palmer v. Matthews, 162 N. Y. 100, 56 N. E. 501 (1900); Conroy v. Pittsburg Times Co., 139 Pa. 334, 21 At. 154 (1891).

[182] Hearne v. De Young, 132 Cal. 357, 64 Pac. 576 (1901); Bedkney v. Bedkney, 15 S. D. 310, 89 N. W. 479 (1902); Hacker v. Heiney, 111 Wis. 313, 87 N. W. 249 (1901).

[183] McPherson v. Daniels, 10 B. & C. 270, 5 M. & R. 251, 34 R. R. 397 (1829); Baum v. Clause, 5 Hill (N. Y.) 199 (1843); McCloskey v. Pulitzer Pub. Co., 152 Mo. 339, 53 S. W. 1087 (1899); Castle v. Houston, 19 Ks. 417 (1877).

[184] Atwater v. Morning News Co., 67 Conn. 504, 34 At. 865 (1896); Pokrok Pub. Co. v. Liskovsky, 42 Neb. 64, 60 N. W. 358 (1894); McCloskey v. Pulitzer Pub. Co., 152 Mo. 339, 53 S. W. 1087 (1899).

[185] Miller v. McDonald, 139 Ind. 465, 39 N. E. 159 (1894); Murphy v. Olberding, 107 Ia. 547, 78 N. W. 205 (1899); Rutherford v. Paddock, 180 Mass. 289, 62 N. E. 381 (1902); proof of plaintiff's unchastity is insufficient to establish truth of charge that she was a "dirty, old whore"; Thompson v. Pioneer Press Co., 37 Minn. 285, 33 N. W. 856 (1887); Andrews v. Van Duzer, 11 Johns. (N. Y.) 38 (1814); Dement v. Houston Printing Co., 14 Tex. Civil App. 391, 37 S. W. 785 (1896); Dillard v. Collins, 25 Gratt (Va.) 343 (1874).

[186] Higkinbotham v. Leach, 10 M. & W. 363, 2 Dowl. N. S. 270 (1892); Dennis v. Johnson, 47 Minn. 56, 49 N. W. 383 (1891); Woodbeck v. Keller, 6 Cow. (N. Y.) 118 (1826).

[187] Sunman v. Brewin, 52 Ind. 140 (1875); Buckner v. Spaulding, 127 Ind. 229, 26 N. E. 792 (1890);

in such circumstances as to convince the jury that the defendant acted with good motives and for justifiable ends.[188] Constitutional or statutory provisions to this effect are more frequent, however, with respect to criminal libel.[189]

Privileged Communications. These are of two kinds—absolutely privileged and conditionally privileged. From considerations of public policy, which have been presented in a previous chapter,[190] certain persons are privileged to defame others with impunity. (1) Members of Parliament in England, and Members of Congress and of the State Legislatures in this country, are not to be questioned in any other place for any speech or debate.[191] This exemption does not extend to the members of subordinate assemblies, such as town or county councillors in England,[192] or Boards of Aldermen or Supervisors in this country.[193] Their privilege to defame others is, at most, conditional. Nor does the absolute privilege of legislators attend them, outside of legislative proceedings, in which they are taking an official part.[194] Nor does it permit the circulation of defamatory speeches, even in connection with the official publication of legislative proceedings,[195] in the absence of statutory provision.[196]

Smith v. Buchecker, 4 Rawle (Pa.) 295 (1833); Skinner v. Grant, 12 Vt. 456 (1840); Leyman v. Latimer, 3 Ex. Div. 15, 352, 46 L. J. Ex. 465, 47 L. J. Ex. 470 (1878).

[188] Neilson v. Jensen, 56 Neb. 430, 76 N. W. 866 (1898), applying Art. 1, Sec. 5 of the State Constitution: "The framers of the constitution may have been of opinion that the peace, good order and well being of the state would be best subserved, if every citizen devoted, at least a part of his time to attending to his own business, instead of constituting himself an agent for bruiting abroad the shortcomings of his neighbor;" Perry v. Porter, 124 Mass. 338 (1878), applying the statute of that state; Ross v. Ward, 14 S. D. 240, 85 N. W. 182 (1901), applying Art. 6, Sec. 5 of State Constitution.

[189] New York Constitution, Art. 1, Sec. 8; Lord Campbell's Act, (6 & 7 Vict., c. 96).

[190] Supra, chap. III.

[191] Bill of Rights, 1 Wm. & M., Sess. 2, c. 2; U. S. Constitution, Article 1, Section 6, and similar clauses in the State Constitutions.

[192] Royal Aquarium Society v. Parkinson, (1892), 1 Q. B. 431, 61 L. J. Q. B. 409.

[193] Callahan v. Ingram, 122 Mo. 355, 26 S. W. 1020 (1899); McGaw v. Hamilton, 184 Pa. 108, 39 At. 4 (1898); Buckstaff v. Hicks, 94 Wis. 34, 68 N. W. 403 (1896).

[194] Coffin v. Coffin, 4 Mass. 1, 3 Am. Dec. 189 (1828).

[195] Stockdale v. Hansard, 2 Moo. & Rob. 9, 7 C. & P. 731, 9 A. & E. 1, 2 P. & D. 1, 8 Dowl. 148, 522 (1839); Trebby v. Transcript Pub. Co., 74 Minn. 84, 76 N. W. 961 (1898).

[196] Stockdale v. Hansard, 11 A. &

(2) Judicial officers,[197] counsel engaged in the conduct of proceedings before a court of competent jurisdiction,[198] whether a civil, military or naval court, parties to such litigations,[199] witnesses,[200] and jurors,[201] enjoy in England an absolute privilege from liability to a tort action for defaming others, while engaged in the discharge of their functions. In this country, the rule is not so broad, in the case of counsel, witnesses and parties. Thus, defamatory statements are absolutely privileged, only when they are pertinent and material to the controversy.[202] This "qualification of the English rule is

E. 253, 297 (1840), under 3 & 4 Vict. c. 9.

[197] Scott v. Stansfield, L. R. 3 Ex. 220, 37 L. J. Ex. 155 (1868); Jekyll v. Sir John Moore, 2 B. & P. N. R. 341, 6 Esp. 63 (1806); Yates v. Lansing, 5 Johns. (N. Y.) 282 (1810).

[198] Munster v. Lamb, 11 Q. B. D. 588, 52 L. J. Q. B. 726 (1883); Mackay v. Ford, 5 H. & N. 792, 29 L. J. Ex. 404 (1860), att'y in a county court. In Higginson v. Flaherty, 4 Ir. C. L. 125 (1854), a proctor in an ecclesiastical court was held not privileged in making statements irrelevant to the cause, reflecting on the integrity of the court. For rule as to proceedings before military and naval courts, see Dawkins v. Lord Rockeby, L. R. 7 H. L. 744, 45 L. J. Q. B. 8 (1875).

[199] Hodgson v. Scarlett, 1 B. & Ald. 244 (1818).

[200] Seamen v. Netherclift, 2 C. P. D. 53, 46 L. J. C. P. 128 (1876); Keightley v. Bell, 4 F. & F. 463 (1866). With the possibility of an action for slander hanging over his head, "a witness cannot be expected to speak with that free and open mind, which the administration of justice demands," said Lord Penzance in Dawkins v. Rokeby. L. R. 7 H. L. 744 (1875).

[201] Reg. v. Skinner, Lofft. 55 (1772); Little v. Pomeroy, Ir. R. 7 C. L. 50.

[202] White v. Nichols, 3 How. (U. S.) 266 (1845); Union Mut. Life Ins. Co. v. Thomas, 83 Fed. 803, 28 C. C. A. 96 (1897); Allegation in a pleading; Lawson v. Hicks, 38 Al. 279 (1862); Chambliss v. Blau, 127 Ala. 86, 28 So. 602 (1900); Wyatt v. Buell, 47 Cal. 624 (1874); People v. Green, 9 Col. 506 (1886); Lester v. Thurmond, 51 Ga. 118 (1874); Comfort v. Young, 100 Ia. 627, 69 N. W. 1032 (1897); McDavitt v. Boyer, 169 Ill., 475, 48 N. E. 317 (1897); Gardemal v. McWilliams, 43 La. Ann. 454, 9 So. 108, 28 Am. S. R. 197 (1891); Hunckel v. Vonieff, 69 Md. 179, 14 At. 500 (1888); Maulsby v. Reifsnider, 69 Md. 143, 14 At. 505 (1888); Hoar v. Woods, 3 Met. (44 Mass.) 193 (1841); McAllister v. Press Co., 76 Mich. 338, 43 N. W. 431, 15 Am. S. R. 318 (1889); Hartung v. Shaw, 130 Mich. 177, 89 N. W. 701 (1902); Hastings v. Lusk, 22 Wend. (N. Y.) 410, 34 Am. Dec. 330, and note (1839); Gilbert v. People, 1 Den. 41, 43 Am. Dec. 646, and note (1841); Moore v. Manufacturers' Bank, 123 N. Y. 420, 25 N. E. 1048, 11 L. R. A. 753 (1890); Gattis v. Kilgo, 128 N. C. 402, 38 S. E. 931 (1901); Shadden v. McElwee, 86

adopted in order that the protection given to individuals, in the interest of an efficient administration of justice, may not be abused as a cloak from beneath which to gratify private malice." [203] But, as another learned judge has remarked,[204] the courts are liberal in applying this qualification " even to the extent of declaring that where matter is put forth by counsel, in the course of a judicial proceeding, that may possibly be pertinent, they will not so regard it as to deprive its author of his privilege."

Functions of the Court and of the Jury. Whether an allegation in a pleading, or a statement by counsel, parties or witnesses, is pertinent to the cause, is usually a question for the court.[205] Whether the person making the statement acted in good faith in making it, is a question of fact for the jury.[206]

Conditional or Qualified Privilege. In cases of absolute privilege, as we have seen, neither the falsity of the defamatory statement, nor the bad faith of the defamer, is a subject of inquiry. Granting that the defendant knew his statement was absolutely false, and that he took advantage of his position from the meanest of motives, he still goes scot free.

Where the false, defamatory statement is only conditionally privileged, however, the good or bad faith of the defendant is a very material matter of inquiry. Accordingly, in this country, when counsel, parties or witnesses indulge in false and defamatory statements, which are not material or pertinent to the questions involved in the judicial proceeding in which they are made, the victim may maintain a civil action therefor, by showing that the defendant made the statement in bad faith. In such a case, the question at issue is one of " conduct, of motive, of good faith and honest purpose, or of

---

Tenn. 146, 152, 5 S. W. 604, 6 Am. S. R. 821 (1887); Cooley v. Galyon, 110 Tenn. 1, 70 S. W. 607 (1902); Crookett v. McLanahan, 110 Tenn. 517, 72 S. W. 950 (1903); Torrey v. Field, 10 Vt. 353 (1838); Clemmons v. Danforth, 67 Vt. 617, 32 At. 626 (1895); Johnson v. Brown, 17 W. Va. 71 (1878); Calkins v. Sumner, 13 Wis. 193 (1860).

[203] Lord, J.—in McLaughlin v. Cowley, 127 Mass. 316 (1879).

[204] Vann J.—in Youmans v. Smith, 153 N. Y. 214, 47 N. E. 265 (1897).

[205] Jones v. Brownlee, 161 Mo. 258, 61 S. W. 795, 53 L. R. A. 448 (1901), citing Johnson v. Brown, 13 W. Va. 71 (1878); Forbes v. Johnson, 11 B. Mon. (50 Ky.) 48 (1850); Strauss v. Meyer, 48 Ill., 385 (1868); Carr v. Selden, 4 N. Y. 91 (1850).

[206] Klinck v. Colby, 46 N. Y. 427 (1871); Marsh v. Ellsworth, 50 N. Y. 309 (1872).

bad faith and malicious purpose." [207]   The plaintiff must allege that the statement was not only false and malicious, but that it was not pertinent, and that it was made in bad faith.[208]   And the burden of proof is upon him to establish these allegations.[209]

Good Faith Presumed.   In cases of conditional privilege, it will be observed, the law presumes the defamatory statement to have been made in good faith and for an honest purpose; but such presumption is not conclusive, and the victim is at liberty to establish if he can, bad faith and malicious purpose on the part of his defamer.[210]

This presumption of good faith is based upon the nature of the occasion.   When a person makes a defamatory statement, " in the discharge of some public or private duty, whether legal or moral, or in the conduct of his affairs, in matters where his interest is concerned," the occasion is privileged.   It " prevents the inference of malice which the law draws from unauthorized communications.   If fairly warranted by any reasonable occasion or exigency and honestly made, such communications are protected for the common convenience and welfare of society; and the law has not restricted the right to make them, within any narrow limits." [211]

In order that the occasion be privileged, the duty or interest described above must exist.   No amount of good faith in believing that it existed will avail the defendant.[212]   " Whether the occasion is privileged, if the facts are not in dispute, is a question of law only, for the judge, not for the jury.   If there are questions of fact in dispute upon which the question depends, they must be left to the jury.   But when the jury have found the facts, it is for the

[207] White v. Carrol, 42 N. Y. 161 (1870).

[208] Hartung v. Shaw, 130 Mich. 177, 89 N. W. 701 (1902); Mower v. Watson, 11 Vt. 536, 34 Am. Dec. 704 (1839); Johnson v. Brown, 13 W. Va. 71 (1878).

[209] McDavitt v. Boyer, 169 Ill., 374, 48 N. E. 317 (1897).

[210] Cases in last two notes. Henry v. Moberly, 6 Ind. App. 490, 33 N. E. 981, 48 A. L. J. 34 (1893); Strode v. Clement, 90 Va. 553, 19 S. E. 177 (1894).

[211] Toogood v. Spyring, 1 C. M. & R. 181, 4 Tyr. 582 (1834); Lewis v. Daily News Co., 81 Md. 473, 32 At. 246, 29 L. R. A. 59 (1895); Marks v. Baker, 28 Minn. 162, 9 N. W. 678 (1881); Finley v. Steele, 159 Mo. 199, 60 S. W. 108 (1900); Klinck v. Colby, 46 N. Y. 427 (1871); Briggs v. Garrett, 111 Pa. 404, 2 At. 513 (1886).

[212] Stewart v. Bell (1891), 2 Q. B. 341, 60 L. J. Q. B. 577.

judge to say whether they constitute a privileged occasion." [213] If the occasion is privileged, it matters not whether the privilege is based upon a duty or an interest of the defendant, he is entitled to the presumption that he acted in good faith. "The privilege would be worth very little if a person making a communication on a privileged occasion, were to be required in the first place, and as a condition of immunity, to prove affirmatively that he honestly believed the statement to be true * * * No distinction can be drawn between one class of privileged communications and another."[214]

Defamation in the Performance of a Duty. It is not necessary that the duty be one of positive legal obligation, enforceable by "indictment, action or mandamus; it may be only a moral or social duty of imperfect obligation." [215] When the statement is made in the performance of a duty clearly imposed by a rule of law, courts are everywhere agreed that the occasion is a privileged one.[216] When, however, the duty is one of a social or moral nature, the question, whether it renders the occasion privileged, is one upon which judicial opinion is most discordant.[217]

This is not surprising, because, as a learned judge has pointed out, "the question of moral or social duty being for the judge, each judge must decide it as best he can for himself." [218] On the one hand are judges who hold that the moral duty not to publish matter defamatory of another which he does not know to be true, is stronger than the duty to convey to a third person that which he believes to be true, although such third person would be affected if the matter were true.[219] On the other hand, are judges who hold

---

[213] Hebditch v. McIlwaine (1894), 2 Q. B. 54, 63 L. J. Q. B. 577.

[214] Jenoure v. Delmege (1891), A. C. 73, L. J. P. C. 11.

[215] Harrison v. Bush, 5 E. & B. 344, 25 L. J. Q. B. 25, 99 (1855).

[216] Cooke v. Wildes, 5 E. & B. 328, 24 L. J. Q. B. 367 (1855); Lawless v. Anglo-Egyptian Cotton Co., L. R. 4 Q. B. 262, 10 B. & S. 226, 38 L. J. Q. B. 129 (1869); Byam v. Collins, 111 N. Y. 143, 19 N. E. 75, 2 L. R. A. 129 (1888).

[217] See prevailing and dissenting opinions in Byam v. Collins, *supra*, and the opposing views, in Coxhead v. Richards, 2 M. G. & S. 569, 15 L. J. C. P. 278 (1846), and in Stuart v. Bell (1891), 2 Q. B. 341, 60 L. J. Q. B. 577.

[218] Lindley, L. J. in Stewart v. Bell, *supra*.

[219] Coltman and Cresswell, JJ. in Coxhead v. Richards, 2 M. G. & S. 569, 15 L. J. C. P. 278 (1846); Earl J., in Byam v. Collins, 111 N. Y. 143, 19 N. E. 75, 2 L. R. A. 129, 1888); Joanness v. Bennett, 5 Allen (87 Mass) 169 (1862).

that a person having information materially affecting the interests of another, is under a stronger social and moral duty to communicate that information, than to guard the reputation of the person defamed by such information.[220]

The Performance of a Duty to the Public. Examples of privileged occasions connected with the performance of a public duty are numerous. Charges and communications made in the prosecution of an inquiry into a suspected crime;[221] complaints to superior officials of misconduct on the part of subordinates;[222] arguments presented to legislative committees, or to the executive department, against a bill under consideration;[223] charges and communications in regularly conducted trials before the proper authorities of religious, social and similar organizations,[224] have been repeatedly adjudged to be statements made upon a privileged occasion.

In all of these cases, however, the courts have been careful to point out the limitations of the privilege. The defendant is not allowed to abuse the occasion. His charges, complaints and communications are not to be spread broadcast through the community. Their dissemination is to be restricted to those who have an interest or duty in dealing with them.[225] And the defendant must act in good faith. If he does not know or believe them to be true, or if,

---

[220] Tindal, C. J., and Erle, J., in Coxhead v. Richards, *supra*,—; Danforth, J., in Byam v. Collins, *supra*.

[221] Padmore v. Lawrence, 11 A. & E. 380, 3 P. & D. 209 (1840); Lightbody v. Gordon, ♂ Scotch Sess. Cases (4th Ser.) 934 (1882); Dale v. Harris, 109 Mass. 193 (1872); Klinck v. Colby, 46 N. Y. 427 (1871).

[222] Harrison v. Bush, 5 E. & B. 344, 25 L. J. Q. B. 25, 99 (1855); Proctor v. Webster, 16 Q. B. D. 112, 55 L. J. Q. B. 150 (1885); Jenoure v. Delmege (1891), A. C. 73, 60 L. J. P. C. 11; McIntyre v. McBean, 13 Up. Can. Q. B. 534 (1856); Branaman v. Hinkie, 137 Ind. 496, 37 N. E. 546 (1893); Wieman v. Mabee, 45 Mich. 484, 40 Am. R. 477 (1881).

[223] Woods v. Wiman, 122 N. Y. 445, 25 N. E. 919 (1890).

[224] Etchison v. Pergerson, 88 Ga. 620, 15 S. E. 680 (1891); Redgate v. Roush, 61 Ks. 480, 59 Pac. 1050 (1900); Piper v. Woolman, 43 Neb. 280, 61 N. W. 588 (1895); Shurtleff v. Stevens, 51 Vt. 501 (1879); York v. Pease, 2 Gray (68 Mass.) 282 (1854); Holt v. Parsons, 23 Tex. 9 (1859).

[225] Cases in last four notes, Hocks v. Sprangers, 113 Wis. 123, 87 N. W. 1101 (1902), holding that a statement by one member of a church to another concerning the chastity of a third, over whom such other had no power of discipline, is not made on a privileged occasion.

when stating them, he is not discharging a duty or protecting his legitimate interests, he exceeds the privilege of the occasion, and becomes liable for the harm done to the plaintiff by his defamatory communication.[226] In such circumstances, he is said to act *mala fide;* to be prompted by an indirect and wrong motive; to be impelled by actual malice. " When a defendant claims that the occasion of a libel or slander is privileged, and when it is held by a judge, whose duty it is to decide the matter, that the occasion is privileged, the question arises—under what conditions can the defendant take advantage of the privilege? If the occasion is privileged, it is for some reason, and the defendant is entitled to the protection of the privilege if he uses the occasion for that reason, but not otherwise. If he uses the occasion for an indirect reason or motive, he uses it, not for the reason which makes it privileged, but for another."[227]

Reports of Public Proceedings. It has long been settled that the publication of judicial proceedings is conditionally privileged—the condition being that the proceedings are public, are decent and fit for publication, and that the reports are full and fair, and their publication not inspired by actual malice.[228] The reports of such proceedings are usually made without reference to the individuals concerned, and for the information and benefit of the public. The law, therefore, presumes that they are made in good faith. Moreover, the advantage to the community, from having the proceedings of courts of justice universally known, is deemed to more than counterbalance the inconvenience and hardship to the private persons, whose reputation may be harmed by reports of such pro-

---

[226] Jackson v. Hopperton, 16 C. B. N. S. 829, 12 W. R. 913 (1864).

[227] Brett, L. J. in Clarke v. Molyneux, 3 Q. B. D. 237, 47 L. J. Q. B. 230 (1877).

[228] R. v. Wright, 8 D. & E. 293 (1799); Ryalls v. Leader, L. R. 1 Exch. 296, 4 H. & C. 555, 35 L. J. Ex. 185 (1866); *Re* Evening News, 3 T. L. R. 255 (1886); R. v. Carlile, 3 B. & Ald. 167 (1819). The last two cases involved the publication of obscene and blasphemous libels, as reports of judicial proceedings; Cowley v. Pulsifer, 137 Mass. 392 (1884); and Parke v. Detroit Free Press Co., 72 Mich, 560, 40 N. W. 731 (1888), reports of papers not used in open court; Boogher v. Knapp, 97 Mo. 122, 11 S. W. 45 (1889); Millisch v. Lloyds, 13 Cox C. C. 575, 46 L. J. C. P. 405 (1877), the question was for jury whether the report gave to readers a fair notion of what took place in open court; Stevens v. Sampson, 5 Ex. D. 53, 49 L. J. Q. B. 120 (1879), and Brown v. Prov. Tel. Co., 25 R. I. —;, 54 At. 1061 (1903). Reports were unfair and malicious.

ceedings.[229] This rule, according to the weight of modern authority, both in England and in this country, applies to preliminary investigations, and *ex parte* proceedings, which must result in a final determination.[230]

The full and fair reports of parliamentary and legislative proceedings are also conditionally privileged, for reasons similar to those which apply to the publication of reports of judicial proceedings.[231] No privilege attaches, however, to the publication of a resolution of a city council, which is not within the scope of its official authority.[232]

In this country, the publication of the proceedings of quasi-public bodies, such as the State Medical Societies, has been deemed conditionally privileged;[233] and in England, the official publication by such bodies of their proceedings is conditionally privileged.[234]

Newspaper Reports of Public Meetings. No privilege attaches, at common law, to the reports in the public prints, of other proceedings than those above considered. " Professional publishers of news are not exempt, as a privileged class, from the consequences of damage done by false news. Their communications are not privileged merely because made in public journals." [235] In Eng-

---

[229] Wason v. Walter, L. R. 4 Q. B. 73, 8 B. & S. 671, 38 L. J. Q. B. 34 (1868); Lewis v. Levy, E. B. & E. 537, 27 L. J. Q. B. 282 (1857); Beiser v. Scripps, McRae Pub. Co., 113 Ky. 383, 68 S. W. 457 (1902).

[230] Cases in last note; also, Usill v. Hales, 3 C. P. D. 319, 47 L. J. C. P. 323 (1878); Kimber v. Press Assoc. (1893), 1 Q. B. 65, 62 L. J. Q. B. 152; McBee v. Fulton, 47 Md. 403, 28 Am. R. 465 (1877); Sanders v. Baxter, 6 Heisk. (53 Tenn.) 369 (1871); Metcalfe v. Times Pub. Co., 20 R. I. 674, 78 Am. S. R. 900 (1898).

[231] R. v. Wright, 8 D. & E. 293 (1799); Wason v. Walter, L. R. 4 Q. B. 73, 8 B. & S. 671, 38 L. J. Q. B. 34 (1868); Kane v. Mulvaney, Ir. R. 2 C. L. 402 (1866).

[232] Trebby v. Transcript Pub. Co., 74 Minn. 84, 76 N. W. 961 (1898).

The resolution declared that the plaintiff was a disreputable person and had made an intentionally false and malicious report about the city's credit. The court declared that the council " had no more authority to libel the private character of a private citizen, than an assemblage of private citizens would have," citing Buckstaff v. Hicks, 94 Wis. 34, 68 N. W. 403, 59 Am. S. R. 583 (1896).

[233] Barrows v. Bell, 7 Gray (73 Mass.) 301 (1856); Kirkpatrick v. Eagle Lodge, 26 Ks. 384, 41 Am. R. 316 (1881); Shurtleff v. Stevens, 51 Vt. 501, 31 Am. R. 698 (1879).

[234] Albutt v. Gen. Med. Council, 23 Q. B. D. 405, 58 L. R. Q. B. 606 (1888).

[235] Barnes v. Campbell, 59 N. H. 128 (1879); Davison v. Duncan, 7

land, and in some of our States, statutes have been passed modifying this rule of the common law, and providing that fair and accurate reports of legislative and other public meetings shall be conditionally privileged.[236]

Defamation in the Performance of Private Duty. The commonest example of this species of conditional privilege is afforded by statements of employers about servants. While, as we have seen in a former connection, an employer is under no legal duty to a servant to give him a character,[237] and is under no legal duty, either, to answer inquiries about him by one about to employ him, he is under a private, moral duty of answering such inquiries. Accordingly, the law presumes that in making such answers, he acts in good faith. If they contain defamatory statements about the servant, he cannot recover against the employer without showing that the latter was inspired by actual malice.[238]

In England, it is settled that the employer's statement is conditionally privileged, even when volunteered to one about to employ the servant.[239] This view is sustained by considerable authority in this country [240] and seems sound in principle. A communication, retracting a favorable character,[241] as well as a statement of reasons for dismissing a servant,[242] made to the latter, or his parents, or guardians, or fellow servants, is also conditionally privileged.

E. & B. 229, 26 L. J. Q. B. 104 (1857); Purcell v. Sowler, 2 C. P. D. 215, 46 L. J. C. P. 308 (8177).

[236] Kelly v. O'Malley, 6 T. L. R. 62 (1889); Chalaner v. Landsdown, 10 T. L. R. 290 (1894), applying 51 & 52 VICT. c. 64, sec. 4. (Law of Libel Amendment Act, 1888); Garry v. Bennett, 166 N. Y. 392, 59 N. E. 1117 (1901), under § 1907 N. Y. Code of Civil Procedure.

[237] Supra, Chap. III.

[238] Edmonson v. Stevenson, Bul. N. P. 8 (1766); Child v. Affleck, 9 B. & C. 403, 4 M. & R. 338 (1829); Hollenbeck v. Ristine, 105 Ia. 488; 75 N. W. 355 (1898); Billings v. Fairbanks, 139 Mass. 66 (1885).

[239] Coxhead v. Richards, 2 C. B.

569, 15 L. J. C. B. 278 (1846). Tindal's opinion is now recognized as stating the correct rule. See Stuart v. Bell (1891), 2 Q. B. 341, 60 L. J. Q. B. 577.

[240] Hart v. Reed, 1 B. Mon. (40 Ky.) 166 (1840); Fresh v. Cutter, 73 Md. 87, 20 At. 774 (1890); Noonan v. Orton, 32 Wis. 106 (1873).

[241] Gardner v. Slade, 13 Q. B. 796, 18 L. J. Q. B. 334 (1849); Fowler v. Bowen, 30 N. Y. 20 (1864).

[242] Taylor v. Hawkins, 16 Q. B. 308, 20 L. J. Q. B. 313 (1851); Somerville v. Hawkins, 110 C. B. 590, 20 L. J. C. B. 131 (1885); Hunt v. Great N. Ry. (1891), 2 Q. B. 189, 60 L. J. Q. B. 498; Dale v. Harris, 109 Mass. 193 (1872); Hebner v. Great N. Ry.,

Duty Arising from the Family Relation. Close family relationship imposes a duty upon persons to communicate information to their relatives about third persons, which does not exist in the case of strangers. Accordingly, a son-in-law acts upon a privileged occasion, in giving to his widowed mother-in-law information derogatory to the character of one whom she is about to marry.[243]

Duty of Mercantile Agencies. Statements rendered by such agencies to persons, making inquiries about persons with whom they propose to deal, are clearly privileged.[244] Whether the circulation among all of their subscribers of a sheet containing such statements, is privileged, is a question upon which authorities differ.[245] In a leading case, the majority of the court held it was not privileged.[246] The English view appears to be that it is privileged, " as being a reasonable and usual method of conveying to the subscribers the information which they needed, for the safe conduct of their business." [247] It is quite important, however, that the agency reports only the information which it has received, and reports that with substantial accuracy. If it carelessly makes a mistake in reporting, its privilege may be forfeited.[248]

---

78 Minn. 289, 80 N. W. 1128 (1899); Missouri Pac. Ry. v. Richmond, 73 Tex. 568, 11 S. W. 555 (1889).

[243] Todd v. Hawkins, 8 C. & P. 88, 2 M. & R. 20 (1837), cited approvingly in Byam v. Collins, 111 N. Y. 143, 19 N. E. 75, 2 L. R. A. 129 (1888); Baysett v. Hire, 49 La. Ann. 904, 22 So. 44 (1897).

[244] Howland v. Blake M'f'g. Co., 156 Mass. 543, 31 N. E. 656 (1892); Ormsby v. Douglass, 37 N. Y. 477 (1868); S. P. in Waller v. Lock, 7 Q. B. D. 622, 51 L. J. Q. B. 274 (1882); Robshaw v. Smith, 38 L. T. 423 (1878).

[245] See Douglass v. Daisey, 114 Fed. 628, 52 C. C. A. 324, 57 L. R. A. 475 (1902), and authorities cited. Also Odgers, Libel and Slander (3d Ed.) 273.

[246] King v. Patterson, 49 N. J. L. 417, 9 At. 705, 60 Am. R. 622 (1887).

See also Johnson v. Bradstreet, 77 Ga. 172 (1886); Newbold v. Bradstreet, 57 Md. 38, 40 Am. R. 426 (1881); Pollasky v. Michener, 81 Mich. 208, 46 N. W. 5 (1890); Mitchell v. Bradstreet, 116 Mo. 226, 22 S. W. 358 (1893); Sunderlan v.Bradstreet, 46 N. Y. 188, 7 Am. R. 322 (1871); Bradstreet v. Gill, 72 Tex. 115, 9 S. W. 753, 2 L. R. A. 405 (1898); State v. Lonsdale, 48 Wis. 348, 4 N. W. 390 (1879); Trussell v. Scarlett, 18 Fed. 214 (1882), with note; Locke v. Bradstreet, 22 Fed. 771 (1885).

[247] Boxsins v. Goblet Frères (1894), 1 Q. B. 842, 63 L. J. Q. B. 401; Andrews v. Nott Bower (1895) 1 Q. B. 888, 64 L. J. Q. B. 536.

[248] Douglass v. Daisey, 114 Fed. 628, 52 C. C. A. 324, 57 L. R. A. 475 (1902). In this case the information received was that Daisey had

Volunteered Statements for the Benefit of Recipient.
The older view in England, and that which obtains in some of our States, as we have seen, is that one who volunteers information to another, who has not asked for it, and with whom the volunteer has no confidential relations, nor common interests, acts at his peril. If the information is defamatory of a third person and false, he is liable for the damage done to such person's reputation. He is not acting upon a privileged occasion.[249]

The present English rule, and that which seems to be gaining favor in this country, has been stated as follows: " Where a person is so situated that it becomes right in the interests of society that he should tell to a third person certain facts, then if he *bona fide* and without malice does tell them, it is a privileged communication." [250] " It is not necessary in all cases that the information should be given in answer to an inquiry." [251] The difficulty in applying this rule, it will be observed, arises in the answer to the question, " Was it right in the particular case, to volunteer to the third person the statement complained of?" As this question is for the judges, " each judge must decide it as best he can for himself." [252]

Defamation in Self-Defense. The rule on this topic has been formulated as follows: " Every statement made with the object of protecting some interest of the writer or speaker, and reasonably necessary for such purpose, is conditionally privileged." [253] This interest may relate to the writer's or speaker's

---

assigned certain property to T., to secure him for indorsing a note. The report made by the agency was that he had assigned to T. for the benefit of his creditors. *Held* that it was a question for the jury, whether the mistake was due to carelessness, so as to destroy the privilege.

[249] King v. Watts, 8 C. & P. 614 (1838); Buisson v. Huard, 106 La. 768, 31 So. 293 (1901) is based upon the fact that the defendant did not volunteer the statement complained of, but made it in response to inquiries.

[250] Davies v. Snead, L. R. 5 Q. B. 608, 39 L. J. Q. B. 202 (1870) Blackburn J., followed in Stuart v. Bell (1891), 2 Q. B. 341, 60 L. J. Q. B. 577.

[251] Jessel M. R. in Waller v. Lock, 7 Q. B. D. 621, 51 L. J. Q. B. 274 (1882).

[252] Lindley L. J., in Stuart v. Bell (1891), 2 Q. B. 291, 60 L. J. Q. B. 577.

[253] Fraser's Law of Libel and Slander, (3d. Ed.) p. 135.

reputation,[254] or to his property,[255] and it may be an interest belonging to him exclusively,[256] or to him in common with others.[257]

Fair Comment. This defense has been confounded at times with that of conditional privilege; [258] but the distinction between the two is perfectly clear and well settled. When a defendant sets up the defense of conditional privilege he asserts and must prove that he stands in such a relation to the facts of the case, that he is justified in saying or writing what would be slanderous or libelous in any one else. When his defense is fair comment, he asserts that he has done only what every one has a right to do, and that his utterance is not a libel, or slander, and would not be a libel or slander by whomsoever published.[259]

Subjects of Fair Comment. Speaking generally, any matter of public interest is a proper subject of fair comment. " Nothing is more important," in the language of an eminent English judge, " than that fair and full latitude of discussion should be allowed to writers upon any public matter, whether it be the conduct of public men or the proceedings in courts of justice, or in Parliament, or the publication of a scheme, or a literary work." [260] This principle has found expression in various constitutional provisions in this country. For example, the Maryland Declaration of Rights asserts, " that any citizen of the State ought to be allowed to speak, write and publish his sentiments on all subjects, being responsible for the abuse of that privilege." [261]

---

[254] Koenig v. Ritchie, 3 F. & F. 413 (1862), Langton v. Bishop of Sudor, L. R. 4 P. C. 495, 42 L. J. P. C.. 11 (1872; Shepherd v. Baer, 96 Md. 152, 53 At. 790 (1902).

[255] Squires v. Wason Mfg. Co., 182 Mass. 137, 65 N. E. 32 (1902). In Browning v. Comm.—Ky.—; 76 S. W. 19 (1904), it was held that defendant must show, that he had reasonable ground to believe, that his property was in danger from the plaintiff's misconduct.

[256] Smith v. Smith, 73 Mich. 445, 41 N. W. 499, 3 L. R. A. 52 16 Am. S. R .594 (1889); Livingston v Bradford, 115 Mich. 140, 73 N. W. 135 (1897).

[257] Caldwell v. Story, 107 Ky. 10, 52 S. W. 850 (1899); Finley v. Steele, 159 Mo. 299, 60 S. W. 109 (1900); Warner v. Mo. Pac. Ry., 112 Fed. 114 (1901).

[258] Henwood v. Harrison, L. R. 7 C. P. 606, 41 L. J. C. P. 206 (1872); Ross v. Ward, 14 S. D. 240, 85 N W. 182 (1901).

[259] Blackburn L. J. in Campbell v. Spotteswoode, 3 B. & S. 769, 32 L. J. Q. B. 185 (1863).

[260] Crompton J. in Campbell v. Spotteswoode, 3 B. & S. 769, 32 L. J. Q. B. 185 (1863).

[261] Quoted and explained in Coffin v. Brown, 94 Md. 190, 50 At. 567 (1901).

The subjects of fair comment which are most frequently involved in actions for defamation, are (1) the character and conduct of public men or candidates for office, and (2) literary, artistic or commercial productions, offered to the public.[262]

The Criticism of Public Men. "The full liberty of public writers to comment on the conduct and motives of public men has only in very recent times been recognized.[263] Comments on government, on ministers and officers of State, on members of both houses of parliament, on judges and other public functionaries are now made every day, which half a century ago would have been the subject of actions, or of *ex officio* informations, and would have brought down fine and imprisonment on publishers and authors. Yet who can doubt that the public are gainers by the change, and that, though injustice may often be done, and though public men may often have to smart under the keen sense of wrong inflicted by hostile criticism, the nation profits by public opinion being thus freely brought to bear on the discharge of public duties." [264]

That there is a clear distinction between the publication of personal abuse, and of fair comment upon the conduct and official character of men, engaged in managing public or semi-public affairs, is now well settled. Judge Cooley, speaking for the Supreme Court of Michigan,[265] once declared: "It is very certain that no declaration of this or any other court can convince the common reason, that this distinction is not plain and palpable. Few wrongs can be greater than the public detraction which has only abuse, or profit from abuse, for its object. Few duties can be plainer than to challenge public attention to official disregard of principles which protect public and personal liberty."

What Comment on Personal Conduct is Fair. Whether a particular statement is an unfair aspersion of personal character,

---

[262] Odgers, Libel and Slander (3d Ed.) p. 46. classifies these topics as follows: "1. Affairs of State. 2. The Administration of Justice. 3. Public Institutions and Local Authorities. 4. Ecclesiastical Matters. 5. Books, Pictures and Architecture. 6. Theaters, Concerts and other public entertainments. 7. Other Appeals to the Public."

[263] It was established in this country much earlier than in England. See Hogg v. Dorrah, 2 Porter (Ala.) 212 (1835); Sillars v. Collins, 151 Mass. 50, 23 N. E. 723 (1890).

[264] Cockburn C. J. in Wason v. Walter, L. R. 4 Q. B. 73, 8 B. & S. 671, 38 L. J. Q. B. 34 (1868).

[265] Miner v. Tribune Co., 49 Mich. 358, 13 N. W. 773 (1882).

or a fair comment upon public conduct, is generally a question for the jury.[266] In the Kentucky case cited in the last note, a publication appeared in the Courier-Journal charging that Vance had violated his oath of office as a supervisor of election, and with interfering with and bribing voters. The court instructed the jury to award the plaintiff damages, if they believed the publication false and was made maliciously; and that malice was to be inferred or presumed from the falsity of the publication, but that if they believed the statements contained in the publication were substantially true, as published, or were reasonable and fair criticism of the acts and conduct of the plaintiff as supervisor, and were made in good faith and without malice, they should find for the defendants; and the court held that these instructions were substantially correct, and that the jury were the judges of the truth of the matter put in issue, and were also the judges of the reasonableness of the grounds upon which the newspaper's charges were based; that animadversions upon the conduct of a public officer, however severe were not libelous if confined within the limits of fair and reasonable criticism, and based on facts." [267]

Another court has defined fair comment in the following terms; " Real comment is merely the expression of opinion. Misdescription is a matter of fact. If the misdescription is such an unfaithful representation of a person's conduct as to induce people to think that he has done something dishonorable, disgraceful and contemptible, it is clearly libelous. To state accurately what a man has done, and then to say that in your opinion such conduct is dishonorable, or disgraceful, is comment which may do no harm, as every one can judge for himself whether the opinion expressed is well founded or not. Misdescription of conduct, on the other hand, only leads to one conclusion detrimental to the person whose conduct is misdescribed, and leaves the reader no opportunity of judging for himself of the conduct condemned, nothing but a false picture being presented for judgment.[268]

At times, however, the statement is clearly an aspersion of private character, and the court does not hesitate to declare that it is not

[266] Merivale v. Carson, 20 Q. B. D. 275, 58 L. T. 331, (1887); Vance v. Courier Journal Co., 95 Ky. 41, 23 S. W. 591 (1893).

[267] Approved and followed in Evening Post Co. v. Richardson, 113 Ky. 641, 68 S. W. 665 (1902).

[268] Christie v. Robertson, 10 New S. Wales L. R. 157, 161 (1889).

fair comment.[269] On the other hand, the statement may be unquestionably fair as a comment or criticism, and the court may dispose of the case without submitting to a jury.[270]

Criticism of Candidates for Public Office. There is some authority for the view that defamatory statements concerning a candidate for public office are conditionally privileged, when made by electors or when made to them; that in such a case the defamed candidate, in order to recover, must prove not only the falsity of the statement but also that the defendant published it in bad faith.[271] The weight of authority, however, is opposed to this view. Most courts have approved of the rule, announced by Chief Justice Parsons, in an early Massachusetts case, as follows: "When any man shall consent to be a candidate for a public office conferred by the election of the people, he must be considered as putting his character in issue, so far as it may respect his qualifications and fitness for the office; and publications of the truth on this subject, with the honest intention of infoming the people, are not a libel, for it would be unreasonable to conclude that the publication of truths, which it is the interest of the people to know, should be an offense against the law. For the same reason, the publication of falsehood and calumny against public officers, or candidates for public offices, is an offense most dangerous to the people, and deserves punishment, because the people may be deceived, and reject the best citizens to their great injury, and, it may be, to the loss of their liberties." [272]

It is not always easy to apply this rule in a given case, but the dis-

---

[269] Coffin v. Brown, 94 Md. 190; 50 At. 567 (1901).

[270] Kilgour v. Evening Star Co., 96 Md. 16, 53 At. 716 (1902).

[271] Ross v. Ward, 14 S. D. 240, 85 N. W. 182 (1901); Mott v. Dawson, 46 Ia. 533 (1877); Bays v. Hunt, 60 Ia. 251, 14 N. W. 785 (1882); State v. Balch, 31 Ks. 465 (1884); Marks v. Baker, 28 Minn. 162, 9 N. W. 678 (1881); Briggs v. Garrett, 111 Pa. 404, 2 At. 513 (1886); Express Co. v. Copeland, 64 Tex. 354 (1885). In State v. Haskins, 109 Ia. 656, 80 N. W. 1063 (1899), it was held that this privilege did not ex-

tend to the publication in a newspaper, circulated outside the district in which the candidate was running; following on this point, Buckstaff v. Hicks, 94 Wis. 34, 68 N. W. 463 (1896), and Duncombe v. Daniell, 1 W. W. & H. 101, 8 C. & P. 222 (1838).

[272] Comm. v. Claps, 4 Mass. 163, 3 Am. Dec. 212 (1808), Jarman v. Rea, 137 Cal. 339, 70 Pac. 216 (1902); Jones v. Varnum, 21 Fla. 431 (1885); Rearick v. Wilcox, 81 Ill. 77 (1876); Belknap v. Ball, 83 Mich. 583, 47 N. W. 674 (890); Aldrich v. Press Printing Co., 9 Minn. 133, 86 Am.

tinction which is to be borne in mind is that between comment and criticism, on the one hand, and statements of fact, on the other. " It is one thing to comment upon or criticise, even with severity the acknowledged or proved acts of a public man, and quite another to assert that he has been guilty of particular acts of misconduct." [273] Or to put it in another way: " An elector may freely canvass the character and pretensions of officers and candidates, but he has no right to calumniate one who is a candidate for office with impunity." [274] " A public journal or an individual, who indulges in defamatory assertions about candidates for office, is equally liable for his acts with those who commit the same offense against private individuals."[275]

Criticism of Literary, Artistic or Commercial Productions and Displays. Every one who publishes a book,[276] or publicly exhibits a picture or other work of art,[277] or presents or takes part in a theatrical or other public performance,[278] or advertises or offers to the public an article for sale,[279] or engages in the construction and management of a railroad,[280] " commits himself to the judgment of the public, and any one may comment upon his performance. If the commentator does not step aside from the work, or introduce fiction for the purpose of condemnation, he exercises a fair and legitimate right."

Dec. 84 (1864); Smith v. Burrus, 106 Mo. 94, 16 S. W. 881, 13 L. R. A. 59, 27 Am. S. R. 329 (1891); King v. Root, 4 Wend. (N. Y.) 113, 21 Am. Dec. 102 (1829); Hamilton v. Eno, 81 N. Y. 116 (1880); Mattice v. Wilcox, 147 N. Y. 624, 42 N. E. 270 (1895); Post Pub. Co. v. Molony, 50 O. St. 71, 33 N. E. 92 (1893); Brewer v. Weakley, 2 Overt. (2 Tenn.) 99, 5 Am. Dec. 656 (1807); Sweney v. Baker, 13 W. Va. 158, 31 Am. R. 757 (1879).

[273] Davis v. Shepstone, 11 App. Cas. 187, 55 L. J. P. C. 51 (1886); Burt v. Advertiser Co., 154 Mass. 238, 28 N. E. 1 (1891); Hallam v. Post Pub. Co., 59 Fed. 530, 8 C. C. A. 201, 16 U. S. App. 613 (1893).

[274] Aldrich v. Press Printing Co., 9 Minn. 133, 86 Am. Dec. 84 (1864).

[275] Seeley v. Blair, Wright (O.) 358 (1833).

[276] Carr v. Hood, 1 Camp. 355, n. (1808); Cooper v. Stone, 24 Wend. (N. Y.) 434 (1840).

[277] Soam v. Knight, Moo. & M. 74 (1827); Gott v. Pulsifer, 122 Mass. 235, 23 Am. R. 322 (1877).

[278] Dibdin v. Swan, 1 Esp. 28 (1793); Green v. Chapman, 4 Bing. (N. C.) 92; 5 Scott 340 (1837) Fry v. Bennett, 28 N. Y. 324 (1863).

[279] Hunter v. Sharpe, 4 F. & F. 983 (1866); Paris v. Levy, 9 C. B. N. S. 342, 30 L. J. C. P. 11 (1861); Boynton v. Remington, 3 Allen, (85 Mass.) 397 (1862).

[280] Crane v. Waters, 10 Fed. 619 (1882).

If, however, the commentator or critic does step aside from expressing his opinion of the book, or the work of art, or the performance, or the wares of the plaintiff, and indulges in defamation of the plaintiff himself, he is no longer exercising a fair and legitimate right; he is no longer exercising the function of a guardian of public morals or of correct literary or artistic taste; he is not engaging in fair discussion in order to promote " the truth of history or the advancement of science," but he is committing a tort and must answer in damages for his injury of the plaintiff.[281]

What Comment on Literary and other Displays is Fair?
This question is generally for the jury. The court ordinarily leaves it to them to say " whether they think the limit of fair criticism has been passed." [282] The jury are to be informed that " every latitude must be given to opinion and prejudice, and then they are to say whether any fair man would have made the comment or criticism in question on the work. * * * If it is no more than fair, honest, independent, bold, even exaggerated criticism, then their verdict will be for the defendant. * * * The court should give a very wide limit to the jury. Mere exaggeration or even gross exaggeration may not make the comment unfair. However wrong the opinion expressed may be in point of truth, or however prejudiced the writer, it may still be within the prescribed limits. The question which the jury must consider is this: Would any fair man, however prejudiced he may be, however exaggerated or obstinate his views, have said that which this criticism has said of the work criticised? If it goes beyond that, then they must find for the plaintiff; if they are satisfied that it does not, then it falls within the allowed limit, and there is no libel at all." [283] Applying these tests, it is clear that one who, under the pretense of criticism, makes a personal attack on the character of the author, the artist, the performer or the vendor, or who imputes to him something which he has never presented to the public, goes beyond the limits of fair comment and criticism.

---

[281] Tabert v. Tipper, 1 Camp. 350 (1808); Strauss v. Francis, 4 F. & F. 939 (1866); Duplany v. Davis, 3 T. L. R. 184 (1887); Whistler v. Ruskin, Times, Nov. 26th, 27th, 1878; Hunter v. Sharpe, 4 F. & F. 983 (1866); Gott v. Pulsifer 122 Mass. 235, 23 Am. R. 322 (1877); Cooper v. Stone, 24 Wend. (N. Y.) 434 (1840).

[282] Bowen L. J. in Merivale v. Carson, 20 Q. B. D. 275 (1887).

[283] Lord Esher, M. R. in Merivale v. Carson, *supra*.

CHAPTER XI.

TRESPASS TO PROPERTY.

Definition of Trespass. Blackstone defines " trespass in its largest and most extensive sense," as, " any transgression or offense against the law of nature, of society, or of the country in which we live, whether it relates to a man's person or to his property." [1] We are not now concerned with trespass, in any such large and extensive sense, but with the tort which consists in the unlawful disturbance of another person's possession of lands or goods. [2]

Trespass to Realty. " Every unauthorized, and, therefore, unlawful entry into the close of another is a trespass." [3] The technical designation of it, at common law, is " trespass *quare clausum fregit*;" from the language of the old writ, which called upon the defendant to show cause *quare clausum querentis fregit*—why he had broken into plaintiff's close. " For, every man's land is in the eye of the law, inclosed and set apart from his neighbor's; and that, either by a visible and material fence, or by an ideal, invisible boundary, existing only in the contemplation of law, as when one man's land adjoins another's in the same field." [4]

A personal, bodily entry upon the land is not necessary to constitute a trespass. One who stands on his own land and throws stones or other missiles upon his neighbor's property, [5] or kicks or strikes it, [6] or removes a line fence which rests partly on the neighbor's land, [7] or turns water upon his neighbor's land, [8] or constructs

---

[1] Commentaries, Vol. 3, p. 208.

[2] Kent's Commentaries Vol. 4, p. 120.

[3] Dougherty v. Stepp, 1 Dev. & Bat. (18 N. C.) 371 (1835); Brown v. Manter, 22 N. H. 468, 472 (1851).

[4] Commentaries Vol. 3, p. 209.

[5] Pickering v. Rudd, 4 Camp. 219, 221, 1 Stark 56 (1815); Prewitt v.

Clayton, 5 Mon. (21 Ky.) 4, 5 (1827) Hay v. The Cohoes Co., 2 N. Y. 159, 51 Am. Dec. 279 (1849).

[6] Ellis v. Loftus Iron Co., L. R. 10 C. P. 10, 44 L. J. C P. 24 (1874).

[7] Garrett v. Sewell, 108 Al. 521, 18 So, 737 (1895).

[8] Byrnes v. City of Cohoes, 67 N. Y. 204 (1876); Jutt v. Hughes, 67

eaves or other projection over the neighbor's land,[9] is clearly liable for breaking the close of his neighbor. So, it is submitted, throwing or firing a missile, or sending a balloon through the air, over the land of another, amounts to a legal breaking of his close.[10]

Intention of Trespasser. It is also to be borne in mind, that the intent, with which an act is done, is not the test of liability of a party to an action for trespass.[11] A person may be ever so innocent of an intention to cross the invisible boundary of his neighbor's land, or he may believe that he has a perfect right to cross it, and yet his innocence and good faith will not protect him.[12] His conduct may be marked by the utmost civility,[13] and even be actuated by a desire to benefit, or it may in fact benefit the owner.[14] Still, if his entry was unauthorized, he is a trespasser, and liable accordingly. Mere inadvertence or accident in crossing the line will not save him from trespass; [15] nor will plaintiff's failure to prove that defendant's act caused substantial damage. The law implies damage from the trespass.[16] Even though the harm be so trifling, that plaintiff's witnesses are unable to place any estimate upon the injuries inflicted, yet, it is said, if no recovery could be had, the trespasser, by repetition of the act and the lapse of time, might acquire an easement in plaintiff's land, in spite of anything that could be done to prevent it.[17]

N. Y. 267, 273 (1876); Mairs v. Manhattan Real Estate Assoc. 89 N. Y. 498, 505 (1882).

[9] Smith v. Smith, 110 Mass. 302 (1872); *Contra*, Pickering v. Rudd, 4 Camp. 219, 1 Stark 56 (1815).

[10] *Dicta* in Kenyon v. Hart, 6 B. & S. 249, 252 (1865); Wandsworth Board v. United Tel. Co., 13 Q. B. D. 904, 53 L. J. Q. B. 449 (1884).

[11] Guille v. Swan, 19 Johns (N. Y.) 381, 10 Am. Dec. 234 (1822); Higginson v. York, 5 Mass. 341 (1809).

[12] Pfeiffer v. Grossman, 15 Ill. 53 (1853); Baltimore etc. Ry. v. Boyd 67 Md. 32, 10 At. 315, 1 Am. S. R. 362 (1887); De Camp v. Bullard 159 N. Y. 450, 54 N. E. 26 (1899); Murphy v. City of Fond du Lac 23 Wis. 365 (1868).

[13] Cannon v. Overstreet, 2 Bax. (61 Tenn.) 464 (1872).

[14] Ketcham v. Newman, 141 N. Y. 205, 22 N. E. 1052, 24 L. R. A. 102 (1894).

[15] Basely v. Clarkson, 3 Levinz, 37 (1681); Newsom v. Anderson, 2 Ired. (24 N. C.) 42, 37 Am. Dec. 406 (1841.). *Contra*, Keller v. Mosser, Tappan (Ohio) 43 (1816).

[16] Dixon v. Clow, 24 Wend. (N. Y.) 188 (1840); Kiel v. Chartiers Valley Gas Co., 131 Pa. 466, 19 At. 78, 17 Am. St. R. 823 (1890); Carter v. Wallace, 2 Tex. 206 (1847).

[17] Norvell v. Thompson, 2 Hill (S. C.) 470 (1834). In this case,

Mitigation and Aggravation of Damages.   While the good faith of the trespasser can never bar an action, it may and often does operate to lessen the award of damages.   In such a case as that cited in the last note, it would limit the recovery to a nominal sum. In the case of taking minerals,[18] or trees,[19] it reduces the recovery, in most jurisdictions, to the value of the property when first taken. On the other hand, the bad faith of the trespasser may enhance the award of damages.   If a telephone company unlawfully cuts the limbs of trees belonging to plaintiff, with knowledge that they are his, and especially if he does this after warning from the plaintiff not to do it, punitive damages may be awarded against him.[20]

The Right to Damages for Trespass to Land, vests in the owner, as soon as the trespass is committed, and descends to his heirs.[21]   It does not merge in the title to the land subsequently acquired by the trespasser.[22]   Even though the trespasser be a disseizor, at the time of his trespass, he will still be liable after reentry by the true owner.[23]

It is to be borne in mind that the gist of the tort, which we are now considering, is the disturbance of the possession, and that whatever is done, after the breaking and entry, is but an aggravation of damages.[24]   Even if the plaintiff declares for breaking his close

---

the trial judge charged the jury, that, if there were actually no damage done, or if it were so inconsiderable that it could not be estimated, as the defendant set up no claim to the land, and supposed he had permission of the real owner, they might find a verdict for the defendant; and they did so. This charge was held to be erroneous.

[18] Livingstone v. Rawyards Coal Co., 5 App. Cas. 25, 42 L. T. N. S. 334 (1880); Dougherty v. Chestnut, 86 Tenn. 1, 5 S. W. 444 (1888).

[19] Wooden Ware Co. v. U. S., 106 U. S. 432, 1 Sup. Ct. 398, 27 L. Ed. 230 (1882); Striegel v. Moore, 55 Ia, 88, 7 N. W. 413 (1880); Holt v. Hayes, 110 Tenn. 42, 73 S. W. 111 (1902).

[20] Memphis Telephone Co. v. Hunt,

16 Lea (84 Tenn.) 456, 1 S. W. 159 (1886); Cumberland Tel. Co. v. Poston, 10 Pickle (94 Tenn.) 696, 30 S. W. 1040 (1895); Telephone Co. v. Shaw, 102 Tenn. 313, 52 S. W. 163 (1899).

[21] Mountz v. Railroad Co., 203 Pa. 128, 52 At. 15 (1902).

[22] McClintock v. Railroad Co. 66 Pa. 404 (1870).

[23] Emerich v. Ireland, 55 Miss. 390 (1877); Alliance Trust Co. v. Nettleton Hardware Co., 74 Miss. 584, 21 S. W. 396, 36 L. R. A. 155 (1897), and cases cited therein.

[24] Taylor v. Cole, 3 D. & E. 292 (1789); Curtis v. Groat 6 Johns. (N. Y.) 168, 5 Am. Dec. 204 (1810); Smith v. Ingram, 7 Iredell (29 N. C.) 175, (1847); Carter v. Wallace, 2 Tex. 206 (1847).

and cutting his trees, he may recover, although he fails to prove that any trees were cut.[25]

Injuries Which are not Trespass. A person's land may be injured by materials belonging to another, or by forces set in motion by another, and yet a trespass not be committed. If stones and other materials, are carried upon plaintiff's land from defendant's, by a violent storm, or by other natural forces, plaintiff's possession is disturbed, but that disturbance is not due to trespass by defendant. It is due to an accident.[26] Again, the plaintiff's realty may be harmed " through the jarring of the ground or the concussion of the atmosphere, caused by explosions " of blasts set off on defendant's adjoining premises. If, however, such injuries are not due to materials hurled upon the land: if they are not due to the direct application of force, but are merely consequential, plaintiff cannot maintain an action for trespass. His remedy is an action on the case for negligence.[27]

The Possession of Plaintiff, which entitles him to maintain an action for trespass to land, is not limited to a possession attendant upon his personal occupation of the premises. It is enough that there was an actual possession in the plaintiff, when the trespass was committed, or a constructive possession in respect of the right being actually vested in him.[28] This is true even of uninclosed and unimproved lands,[29] unless there is an adverse possession or right in some

[25] Mundell v. Perry, 2 Gill. & J. (Md.) 193 (1830); Brown v. Manter, 22 N. H. 468 (1851). In Bailey v. Chic. M. & St. Paul Ry., 3 S. Dak. 531, 54 N. W. 596, 19 L. R. A. 653, with valuable note, it is held that where trees are destroyed or taken by a trespasser, the owner may sue for the injury to the realty, in which case the measure of damages is the diminished value of the realty; or he may sue for the value of the trees, when the measure of damages will be their market value.

[26] Snook v. Town Council of Bradford, 14 Up. Can. Q. B. 255 (1856). Had these materials been so placed by plaintiff, as naturally to slide down upon plaintiff's land, there would have been a good case of trespass. Gregory v. Piper, 9 B. & C. 591, 4 M. & R. 500 (1829).

[27] Sullivan v. Dunham, 161 N. Y. 290, 55 N. E. 923, 47 L. R. A. 715 76 Am. St. R. 274 (1901); Holland House Co. v. Baird, 169 N. Y. 136, 62 N. E. 119 (1901.

[28] Kent's Commentaries, Vol. 4, p. 120; Bulkley v. Dolbeare, 7 Conn. 232 (1828); McColman v. Wilkes, 3 Strob. (S. C.) 465 (1849); Wilson v. Phœnix Co., 40 W. Va. 413, 21 S. E. 1035, 52 Am. St. R. 890, (1895).

[29] Baltimore etc., Co. v. Boyd, 67 Md. 32, 10 At. 315, 1 Am. St. R. 362, (1887); Irvin v. Patchin, 164 Pa. 51, 30 At. 436, (1894).

other person, by contract or by operation of law, to the actual exclusion of the plaintiff.[30]

Trespass may be maintained by a reversioner, when the breaking of the close results in injury to his interest in the lands.[31] Accordingly, the unauthorized interference with trees in the highway, or the erection of telegraph poles, or other structures in the highway, which interfere with the reasonable use of his premises by the adjoining owner, and impose a new burden upon them, is generally treated as a trespass against such owner, when the fee to the highway at the point in question, is in him.[32]

Trespass by Animals. The common law held the owner [33] and the custodian [34] of cattle liable for their trespasses. He was under an absolute duty to keep them upon his own premises; and, if they wandered therefrom, and broke into the close of another, their owner was liable for all the damages which they inflicted, whether he had notice or not of their propensity to do the particular mischief.[35]

This has been modified by general custom,[36] or by statute [37] in

[30] Storrs v. Feick, 24 W. Va. 606, (1884).

[31] Bigelow's Leading Cases on Torts, p. 355; Develin v. Snellinburg, 132 Pa. 186, 11 At. 1119 (1890).

[32] Chesapeake etc., Co. v. Mackenzie, 74 Md. 36, 21 At, 690, 28 Am. St. R. 219, (1891); Broome v. N. Y. etc., Co., 42 N. J. Eq. 141, 7 At. 851 (1886); Western Union Tel. Co. v. Williams, 86 Va. 696, 11 S. E. 106, 19 Am. St. R. 908, 8 L. R. A. 429 (1890); Kreuger v. Wis. Tel. Co., 106 Wis. 96, 81 N. W. 1041, 50 L. R. A. 298 (1900).

[33] Gresham v. Taylor, 51 Al. 501, (1874); Crawford v. Hughes, 3 J. J. Marsh (26 Ky.) 433 (1830); Noyes v. Colby, 30 N. H. 143 (1855); Wells v. Howell, 19 Johns. (N. Y.) 385 (1822); Rossell v. Cottom, 31 Pa. 525 (1858).

[34] Tewksbury v. Bucklin, 7 N. H. 518 (1834).

[35] Decker v. Gammon, 44 Me. 322, 69 Am. Dec. 99 (1857); Lyons v. Merrick, 105 Mass. 71 (1870); Angus v. Radin, 5 N. J. L. 815, 8 Am. Dec. 626, (1820); Malone v. Knowlton, 15 N. Y. Suppl. 506, 39 N. Y. S. R. 901 (1891); Morgan v. Hudnell, 52 O. St. 552, 40 N. E. 716, 27 L. R. A. 862, 49 Am. St. R. 741 (1895); Dolph v. Ferris, 7 W. & S. (Pa.) 367, 42 Am. Dec. 246 (1844); Mosier v. Beale, 43 Fed. 358 (1890).

[36] Logan v. Gedney, 38 Cal. 579 (1869); Seely v. Peters 5 Gilman (Ill.) 130 (1848); Kerwhacker v. Cleveland etc., Ry., 3 O. St. 172, 62 Am. Dec. 246 (1854); Buford v. Houtz, 133 U. S. 320, 10 Sup. Ct. 305, 33 L. Ed. 618 (1890);, affirming S. C. 5 Utah 591, 18 Pac. 633 (1888).

[37] Lazarus v. Phelps, 152 U. S. 81, 14 Sup. Ct. 477, 38 L. Ed. 363 (1894).

many of our jurisdictions, and the rule has become established that the land-owner must fence against the cattle of his neighbor running at large. Under such custom or statutes, however, no privilege accrues to the cattle owner to drive his animals upon the unfenced land of another, and appropriate their pasturage to himself. If he does this he becomes a trespasser [38] and makes himself liable for the fair rental of the land thus used.[39] Even when his cattle accidentally stray upon unfenced land, although he is not answerable for their trespass, the land-owner may drive and keep them off: [40] and the latter is under no duty to keep such premises in a safe condition for them.[41] His duty is only to refrain from inflicting upon them wanton or willful injury.

In an early English case, Lord Holt declared that the liability for trespasses of animals, is limited to beasts in which the defendant has a valuable property.[42] Although this statement is mere dictum, it has been accepted by many courts as a correct statement of the law.[43] Accordingly these courts have held that the owner of dogs and cats is not answerable for their trespasses upon land, as he is for those of his cattle. These animals, it is said, are not so absolutely the chattels of the owner as to be the subject of larceny; their wanderings ordinarily cause but slight damage, and common usage accords them a wider liberty than is permitted to cattle, horses, sheep, and the like.[44]

---

[38] Cosgriff v. Miller, 10 Wy. 190, 68 Pac. 206 (1902); Poindexter v. May, 98 Va. 143, 34 S. E. 971 (1900).

[39] Lazarus v. Phelps, 152 U. S. 81, 14 Sup. Ct. 477, 38 L. Ed. 363 (1894); Monroe v. Cannon, 24 Mont. 316, 61 Pac. 863, 81 Am. St. R. 439 with valuable note (1900).

[40] Addington v. Canfield, 10 Okl., 204, 66 Pac. 355 (1901).

[41] Beinhorn v. Griswold, 27 Mon. 79, 59 L. R. A. 771, 69 Pac. 557 (1902); Knight v. Albert, 6 Pa. 472, 47 Am. Dec. 478 (1847); Clarendon Land Co. v. McCleland Bros., 89 Tex. 483, 34 S. W. 98, 59 Am. S. R. 70, (1896).

[42] Mason v. Keeling, 12 Mod. 332, 1 Ld. Ray. 606 (1700).

[43] Brown v. Giles 1 C. & P. 188, 12 E. C. L. 79 (1823); Saunders v. Teape 51 L. T. N. S. 263, 48 J. P. 757, 29 A. L. J. 321 (1884). In Dewell v. Sandars, Cro. Jac. 490, (1619), it was declared that the owner of a dovecote is liable if his pigeons eat his neighbors' grain. In Woolf v. Chalker, 31 Conn., 121, 81 Am. Dec. 175 (1862), it was held that "if the owner trespass and his dog attend him, and do mischief unbidden, the owner is liable.

[44] Willes J. in Read v. Edwards, 17 C. B. N. S. 245, 260, 34 L. J. C. P.

Other courts have declined to accept Lord Holt's dictum, and have held the owner of a dog to the same responsibility for its trespasses, as attaches to the owner of an ox or horse.[45]

Trespasses by Animals Driven Along Highways. For these, the owner or custodian is not liable, unless they are due to his negligence. This exception has been described by a learned judge as "absolutely necessary for the conduct of the common affairs of life."[46]

Duty of Land-Owner to Trespassers. Although as we have seen in a previous connection, a trespasser is not an outlaw[47] he is not entitled to have the premises, upon which he is trespassing kept in a safe condition. The only legal duty which the land-owner owes him, is to abstain from inflicting upon him willful or wanton injury.[48] A different view is held in some jurisdictions, when the trespasser is an infant, especially if there is ground for finding that he has been enticed upon the dangerous premises, by the land-owner.[49]

Trespass to Chattels. This consists, ordinarily, in wrongfully taking or destroying personal property. It has been said that trespass does not lie for an assault upon a ship, or other insensate thing,[50] but that it does for beating and wounding a beast.[51] The

31 (1864); Smith v. Donohue, 49 N. J. L. 548, 60 Am. R. 652 (1887).

[45] Doyle v. Vance, 6 Vict. L. R. (Cases at Law) 87 (1880); Churnot v. Lawson, 43 Wis. 536, 28 Am. R. 567 (1878), Ryan, C. J., dissented; cf. Crowley v. Grovnell, 73 Vt. 45, 50 At. 546, 55 L. R. A., 876 (1901), where the owner of a dog was held liable for his jumping against the plaintiff and knocking him down, even though he jumped in playfulness. The test laid down is: had the owner, as an ordinarily prudent person, reason to anticipate the injury, which actually occurred—?

[46] Tillett v. Ward, 10 Q. B. D. 17, 52 L. J, Q. B. 61 (1882); Hartford v. Brady, 114 Mass. 466, 19 Am. R. 377 (1874); Barnum v. Turpening 75 Mich. 557, 42 N. W. 967 (1874); Moynahan v. Wheeler 117 N. Y. 285, 22 N. E. 702 (1889).

[47] *Supra* 88.

[48] Jordan v. Grand Rapids Ry., 162 Ind.—, 70 N. E. 524, (1904); Daniels v. New York etc., Ry., 154 Mass. 349, 28 N. E. 283, 13 L. R. A. 248, 26 Am. S. R. 253 (1891); Christian v. Illinois Cent. Ry., 71 Miss. 237, 12 So. 710 (1894); Beinhorn v. Griswold, 27 Mon. 79, 69 Pac. 557, 59 L. R. A. (1902).

[49] Union Pac. Ry. v. McDonald, 152 U. S. 262, 14 Sup. Ct. 619, 38 L. Ed. 434 (1894).

[50] Marlow v. Weekes, Barnes' Notes of Cases, 452 (1744). The decision in Paul v. Slason, 22 Vt. 231, 54 Am. Dec. 75 (1850), accords with the above dictum, but it was based upon the maxim, *De minimis non curat lex.*

[51] Marlow v. Weekes, *supra;* Dand v. Sexton, 3 D. & E. 37 (1789).

better view seems to be, however, that any wrongful disturbance of another's possession, whether amounting to an asportation or destruction or not, and whether depriving the plaintiff of the valuable use of the property or not, is an actionable trespass.[52]

It is not necessary that actual force be applied to the property. If the defendant intentionally frightens plaintiff's horse so that it runs away and is injured, he is liable in trespass as he would have been, had he beaten and wounded the animal by the direct application of force.[53] So, if an officer unlawfully levies upon plaintiff's property, he is a trespasser, although there is no manual taking or removal.[54] And if one sets fire upon his land, he is liable in trespass, if it escapes and harms another's goods.[55]

Intention to Inflict Harm is not material; the same rule applying to trespasses to goods, that we have found applying to real-property trespasses. One, who interferes with the possession of goods, acts at his peril,[56] and is answerable " not only for the bare act of trespass, but also for the natural, immediate and direct consequences of that act." [57]

---

[52] Pollock's Torts, (6th Ed.) pp. 334, 335; Alderson, B. in Fouldes v. Willoughby, 8 M. & W. 540, 549 (1841); Bull v. Cotton 22 Barbour (N. Y.) 94 (1856). No allegation that plaintiff lost the use of the horse. In Fullam v. Stearns, 30 Vt. 443, 456 (1857), the opinion is expressed that there may have been a trespass in Paul v. Slason, *supra; cf.* Pope v. Cordell, 47 Mo. 251 (1871). Fitzherbert's Natura Brevium, 88 M. and 89, L. shows that the writ of trespass could be had for breaking one's mill-stone, or chasing his sheep or swine to their injury.

[53] Cole v. Fisher, 11 Mass. 137 (1814); Louby v. Hofner, 1 Dev. L. (12 N. C.) 185 (1827); James v. Caldwell, 7 Yerg. (15 Tenn.) 38, (1834); Waterman v. Hall, 17 Vt. 128, 43 Am. Dec. 484 (1844).

[54] Miller v. Baker, 1 Met. (42 Mass.) 27 (1840); Wintringham v.

Lafoy, 7 Cow. (N. Y.) 735, (1827); Philips v. Hall, 8 Wend. (N. Y.) 610, 24 Am. Dec. 108 (1832).

[55] Jordan v. Wyatt, 4 Gratt. (45 Va.) 151, 47 Am. Dec. 720 (1847).

[56] Dexter v. Cole, 6 Wis. 319, 70 Am. Dec. 465 (1858); defendant attempted to separate plaintiff's sheep from his own flock, but inadvertently drove off four belonging to plaintiff.

It is not trespass for one, lawfully driving cattle or sheep on the highway, to drive animals, which mix with his, to a convenient place for separating them. VanValkenburg v. Thayer, 57 Barb. (N. Y.) 196 (1870); but it is trespass for him to drive them away with his, without taking reasonable precautions to discover and separate them; Young v. Vaughan, 1 Houst., (Del.) 331 (1857); Brooks v. Olmstead, 17 Pa. 24, (1851).

[57] Bruch v. Carter, 32 N. J. L. 554

Possession of Plaintiff. This may be either actual or constructive. "It is established law, that he, who has the general property in a personal chattel, may maintain trespass for the taking of it, by a stranger, although he never had the possession in fact; for the general property in a personal chattel, draws to it possession in law."[58]

It is also established, that one, who illegally interferes with the possession of a chattel, is liable in trespass to the one whose actual possession is invaded[59] although such possession is illegal. A successful defense to the action of trespass must rest upon the rightfulness of the defendant's conduct, not upon defects in the plaintiff's title, or in his right to possession.[60] One may be a trespasser, even against a thief.[61]

Excusable Trespasses. These have been dealt with, at considerable length, in a previous chapter,[62] and their consideration need not be renewed here.

It will be recalled that a very extensive head of excuse, in cases of trespass, is that of license. When that license is abused it becomes

(1867). Defendant untied plaintiff's horse, led him to another post and hitched him. Here, he became entangled in his halter, was thrown to the ground and killed. Judgment upon verdict for plaintiff for the value of the horse affirmed.

[59] Bulkley v. Dolbeare, 7 Conn. 232, 235 (1828); Haythorn v. Rushforth 16 N. J. L. 160, 38 Am. Dec. 540 (1842); Putnam v. Wyley, 8 John. (N. Y.) 432, 5 Am. Dec. 346 (1811); Edwards v. Edwards, 11 Vt. 587, 34 Am. Dec. 711 (1839).

[59] Gutter v. Pac. Steam Whaling Co., 96 Fed. 617 (1899). Seamen on board an abandoned whaling bark successfully maintained trespass against the defendant, whose servants took the stores from the bark, although the seamen had bare possession and no ownership. "The peace and good order of society," it is declared, "require that persons thus in the possession of property, even without any title, should be enabled to protect such possession, by appropriate remedies against mere naked wrongdoers," citing Jeffries v. G. W. Ry., 5 E. & B. 802, 25 L. J. Q. B. 1071 (1856); Wheeler v. Lawson, 103 N. Y. 40, 8 N. E. 360, (1886).

[60] Brown v. Ware, 25 Me. 411 (1845); Commonwealth v. Rourke, 10 Cush. (64 Mass.) 397 (1852); Ewings v. Walker, 9 Gray (75 Mass.) 95 (1857); Odiorne v. Colley, 2 N. H. 66, 9 Am. Dec. 39, (1819); Potter v. Washbun, 13 Vt. 558, 37 Am. Dec. 615 (1840).

[61] Commonwealth v. Coffee, 9 Gray, (75 Mass.) 139 (1857); Ward v. People, 3 Hill, (N. Y.) 395 (1842); Fletcher v. Cole, 26 Vt. 170, 177, (1853).

[62] Chapter 111.

important to inquire whether it was accorded to the defendant by the law, or by consent of the plaintiff.

Trespass Ab Initio. When the license is accorded by law, it is said that the law should make void everything done by the abuse of its authority, and leave the abuser as though he were a trespasser from the beginning. But where a man, who is under no necessity to give a license to another, does give it, and the licensee abuses the authority, there is no reason why the law should interpose to make void everything done by such abuse, because it was the man's folly to trust another with an authority, who was not fit to be trusted.[63]

Accordingly, where one distrains property,[64] or takes up an estray,[65] and converts or abuses it, he is liable as a trespasser *ab initio*. So is an officer who seizes property or arrests a person under legal process, and then abuses the authority given him by the law—as by unreasonable delay in removing the property,[66] or by charging illegal fees.[67] So is one who secures entrance upon plaintiff's land by authority of the law, and then abuses the license.[68]

On the other hand, if the license proceeds from the plaintiff, an abuse of it will not make the original entry upon the land a trespass, although the abuser's act may be in itself a trespass.[69] And it is to be borne in mind, that the abuse of the authority of law, which makes a man a trespasser *ab initio,* is the abuse of some special and particular authority, and has no reference to the general rule which makes acts lawful which the law does not forbid.[70]

---

[63] Allen v. Crofoot, 5 Wend. (N. Y.) 506 (1830).

[64] Duncombe v. Reeve, Croke Eliz., 783 (1601).

[65] Bagshaw v. Goward, Croke Jac., 147, 1 Yelv. 96, Noy, 119 (1606); Adams v. Adams, 13 Pick., (30 Mass.) 384 (1832).

[66] Williams v. Powell, 101 Mass. 467 (1869).

[67] Robbins v. Swift, 86 Me. 197, 29 At. 981 (1894), and cases cited.

[68] Gardner v. Rowland, 2 Ire. (24 N. C.) 247 (1842); Adams v. Rivers, 6 Barb. (N. Y.) 390 (1851); Harrison v. Duke of Rutland (1893) 1 Q. B. 142, 62 L. J. Q. B. 117, 47 A. L. J. 329.

[69] Hubbell v. Wheeler, 2 Aik. (Vt.) 359 (1827); Jewell v. Mahood 44 N. H. 47 (1863); Allen v. Crofoot, 5 Wend. (N. Y.) 506 (1830); The Six Carpenters's Case, 8 Coke 146, a. (1610).

[70] Esty v. Wilmot, 15 Gray (81 Mass.) 168 (1860).

CHAPTER XII.

TROVER AND CONVERSION.

The Fiction of Finding.   Originally, the action of trover was " an action of trespass on the case for the recovery of damages against a person who had found goods, and refused to deliver them to the owner upon demand, but had converted them to his own use."[1]   The allegation of finding was often fictitious, but the defendant was not allowed to deny the fiction; and in modern times the allegation is treated as unnecessary.[2]   The substance of the action, to-day, is for the wrongful interference with the plaintiff's dominion over the property in question.[3]

In many cases, the plaintiff has his option to sue for trespass or for conversion.[4]   This is true, whenever the defendant's conduct is a wrongful interference with the plaintiff's possession and with his right as owner.[5]

---

[1] Smith v. Grove, 10 Mo. 51 (1848); Cooper v. Chitty, 1 Burr. 20 (1756).

[2] Royce v. Oakes, 20 R. I. 252, 38 At. 371, 39 L. R. A. 845 (1897); Burroughs v. Bayne, 5 H. & N. 296, 29 L. J. Ex. 188 (1860).

[3] Cases in last two notes; Davis v. Hunt, 114 Al. 146, 21 So. 468 (1896); Payne v. Elliott, 54 Cal. 339, (1880); Platt v. Tuttle, 23 Conn. 233 (1854); Harris v. Saunders, 2 Strob. Eq. (S. C.) 370 (1835); approving of the following definition: " A conversion seems to consist in any tortious act, by which the defendant deprives the plaintiff of his goods, either wholly or for a time."

[4] In Montgomery etc., Co. v. Chapman & Co., 126 Fed. 68 (1903) the court said; " The distinction between trespass and conversion is this: that trespass is an unlawful taking—as, for example, the unlawful removal of the property— while conversion is an unlawful taking or keeping in the exercise, legally considered, of the right of ownership. A mere seizure or unlawful handling may amount to a trespass, while conversion is usually characterized by a usurpation of ownership."

[5] Bassett v. Maynard, 1 Rolle Abd. 105 M. pl, 5 (1601); Bishop v. Montague, Cro. Eliz., 824 (1601), S. C. Cro. Jac. 50 (1604); Leverson v. Kirk. 1 Rolle Abd. 105, M. pl. 10 (1610); Dexter v. Cole, 6 Wis. 320 (1858).

Subject Matter of Trover. While the fiction of finding remained an essential element of the cause of action, trover could be brought only for tangible chattels. At present, however, it lies for any species of personal property [6]—for bank bills; [7] or other negotiable instruments; [8] for certificates of stock; [9] for copies of book accounts; [10] for timber or crops converted after severance from the realty; [11] for domestic animals,[12] as well as for animals of a wild nature which have been tamed,[13] or reduced to the legal ownership and control of the plaintiff; [14] and even for property which the plaintiff had no legal right to possess. [15] It does not lie, however, to protect the ownership of counterfeit money, or any other chattel, which the law treats as a nuisance, and outside the pale of legal toleration.[16]

Against Whom the Tort May be Committed. It is not necessary that the plaintiff be the true owner of the goods in question. If he has a special property therein, as bailee,[17] or as receiver under an order of the court,[18] or, if he is in actual possession at the time of their conversion by the defendant,[19] although that possession may be in the nature of a disseisin of the true owner,[20] he can suc-

---

[6] State v. Omaha, Nat. Bank, 59 Neb. 483, 81 N. W. 483 (1899).

[7] Moody v. Keener, 7 Porter (Al.) 218 (1838); Royce v. Oakes, 20 R. I. 252, 38 At. 371, 39 L. R. A. 845 (1897).

[8] Comparet v. Burr, 5 Blackf. (Ind.) 419 (1840); Griswold v. Judd, 1 Root (Conn.) 221 (1790).

[9] Payne v. Elliot, 54 Cal. 339 (1880).

[10] Fullam v. Cummings, 16 Vt. 697 (1844).

[11] Sampson v. Hammond, 4 Cal. 184 (1854); Nelson v. Burt, 15 Mass. 204 (1818). In Platner v. Johnson, 26 Miss. 142 (1853), the court held that trover would not lie, because the severance and asportation were one transaction.

[12] Drew v. Spaulding, 45 N. H. 472 (1864).

[13] Amory v. Flyn, 10 Johns, (N. Y.) 102, 6 Am. Dec. 316 (1813).

[14] Taber v. Jenny, 1 Sprague (U. S. Adm. Dec.) 315 (1856).

[15] Averill v. Chadwick, 153 Mass. 171, 26 N. E. 441 (1891).

[16] Spalding v. Preston, 21 Vt. 9, 14, 50 Am. Dec. 68 (1848).

[17] Buxton v. Hughes, 2 Bing. 173 (1824); Smith v. James, 7 Cow. (N. Y.) 328 (1827); National Surety Co. v. United States, 129 Fed. 70 (1904); The Beaconsfield, 158 U. S. 30, 15 Sup. Ct. 869, 39 L. Ed. 993 (1894).

[18] Kehr v. Hall, 117 Ind. 405, 20 N. E. 279 (1888).

[19] Wheeler v. Lawson, 103 N. Y. 40, 8 N. E. 360 (1886); Cook v. Thornton, 109 Al. 523, 20 So. 14 (1895).

[20] Disseisin of Chattels, by Professor Ames, 3 Harv. L. R. 23, 313, 337 (1889).

cessfully maintain the action. In such cases, the defendant does not make out a defense, as a rule, by showing that the true ownership is in a third person. He must go further and connect himself with such title.[21]

When the plaintiff is not in possession at the time of the defendant's conversion, he must show property in himself and his right to immediate possession. In such cases, it is proper to say that he must recover upon the strength of his legal right and not upon the defects in the defendant's title.[22]

How Conversion is Committed. The tort of conversion ordinarily assumes one of four forms:[23] (1) A wrongful taking under a claim of ownership, or a claim inconsistent with the plaintiff's ownership. (2) An exclusion of the plaintiff from his rightful exercise of dominion, although the defendant's taking was lawful. (3) A wrongful use of the property. (4) Its wrongful detention. Let us consider these in detail:—

Wrongful Asportation in the Exercise of Dominion. If the asportation, or wrongful taking, is not of a character inconsistent with the plaintiff's ownership, it may be trespass, but it does not amount to conversion.

Accordingly, a person who removes the goods of another, for his own convenience, and does not restore them to their original position, may be liable in trespass, but not in conversion, for he makes no claim to their ownership or possession; he does no act which amounts to an exercise of ownership or right of property inconsistent with the real owner's right of possession.[24] If, however, he

---

[21] Stowell v. Otis, 71 N. Y. 36 (1866); Cook v. Patterson, 35 Al. 102 (1859); Jeffries v. Great Western Ry., 5 E. & B. 802, 25 L. J. Q. B. 107 (1856).

[22] Union Stockyard Co. v. Mallory, 157 Ill. 554, 41 N. E. 888, 48 Am. St. R. 341 (1895).

[23] Kennet v. Robinson, 2 J. J. Marsh. (25 Ky.) 84 (1829); Fernald v. Chase, 37 Me. 289 (1853); State v. Haley, 2 Hask. (U. S. Cir. Ct.) 354, Fed. Cases No. 8,977 (1879); Glover v. Riddick, 11 Ired. (33 N. C.) 582 (1850); Harris v. Saunders, 2 Strob. Eq. (S. C.) 370 (1848).

[24] Bushel v. Miller, 1 Strange 128 (1718); Fouldes v. Willoughby, 8 M. & W. 540, 5 Jur. 534 (1841). The defendant put plaintiff's horses off his steamboat, because of the plaintiff's misconduct, though not with any view to appropriating them to his own use or to deprive defendant of them, but to get rid of him. Shea v. Milford, 145 Mass. 525, 14 N. E. 769 (1888). Defendant's officers requested plaintiff to

removes them to a place to which he refuses the owner access,[25] or does any other act in exclusion or defiance of the owner's right; makes any assumption of property and of the right of disposition, or intermeddles in a way which indicates a claim of ownership; or makes any assertion of the control which belongs to the owner, his conduct may be treated as amounting to a conversion.[26]

Intention to Convert, unless followed by some act which amounts to an exclusion of the owner from his exercise of dominion over the goods, is not a conversion.[27] Accordingly, a threat, by one not in possession of goods, to resist their removal by the owner, may be actionable as slander of title, but not as conversion.[28] The same is true of a pretended purchase or sale of goods, by one who neither takes nor delivers possession of them.[29] If, however, the goods are in the defendant's possession, his refusal to allow the plaintiff to remove them may constitute a conversion.[30]

Conversion without Physical Taking. The asportation necessary to constitute a conversion, where the tort is founded upon a wrongful taking, need not be actual; it may be constructive. A person, who wrongfully transfers a bill of lading or a warehouse

remove his property from the parcel of land where they were stored; and upon his refusal to do so, removed it to another parcel. Nothing was done in derogation of plaintiff's dominion. Mattice v. Brinkham, 74 Mich. 705, 42 N. W. 172 (1889). Articles were removed from one room to another: Sparks v. Purdy, 11 Mo. 219 (1847), similar to preceding case.

[25] Fosdick v. Collins, 1 Stark, 173 (1816).

[26] Nelson v. Whetmore, 1 Rich. (S. C.) 318 (1845.) In this case, the defendant permitted plaintiff's slave, who represented himself to be a free mulatto, to travel with him, and was held not liable for a conversion as he did not use the slave as property.

[27] England v. Cowley, L. R. 8 Ex. 126, 42 L. J. Ex. 80 (1873); Penny v. State, 88 Al. 105, 7 So. 50 (1889); Herron v. Hughes, 25 Cal. 555 (1864); Irish v. Cloyes, 8 Vt. 30 (1836).

[28] Boobier v. Boobier, 39 Me. 406 (1855); Polley v. Lenox Iron Works, 2 Allen (84 Mass.) 182, 184 (1861); Platner v. Johnson, 26 Miss. 142, 143 (1853).

[29] Traylor v. Horrall, 4 Blackf. (Ind.) 317 (1837); Fuller v. Tabor, 39 Me. 519 (1855); Burnside v. Twichell, 43 N. H. 390 (1861).

[30] Badger v. Batavia etc., Co., 70 Ill. 302 (1873); *Contra*—Town v. Hazen, 51 N. H. 596 (1872). In Thorogood v. Robinson, 6 Q. B. R. 769, 14 L. J. Q. B. 87 (1845), a verdict for defendant was sustained, chiefly on the ground that plaintiff did not send some one with proper authority to demand and receive the goods.

receipt, and thereby enables a third person to get the goods to the exclusion of the owner, is liable as for an asportation.[31] So, too, is the one receiving such a document of title and claiming the property under it.[32] And, of course, a buyer of chattels, which are in his presence, is guilty of asportation, when he asserts that they are his and repudiates the owner's title and possession, although he does not touch them.[33] Moreover, a taking by an agent, for which the principal is legally responsible, is his taking.[34] Again, one who shuts up his neighbor's trespassing fowls and refuses to turn them loose; [35] a lessor, who insists that articles belonging to a lessee are his own, and forbids the lessee from taking them,[36] and a public official who unlawfully prevents the owner from taking his property from a warehouse,[37] is guilty of their asportation. So is a sheriff, constable or marshal, who levies upon goods without lawful right, although he does not actually touch them. It is enough that he "assumes such a control over the property, by a possession actual or constructive, as deprives the owner of his dominion over them for any purpose." [38] If, however, he does not assume their custody or control, but contents himself with asserting his intention to do so in the future, he is not able for conversion.[39]

Goods Obtained By Fraud. Even though the owner of goods voluntarily delivers them to another, the latter is guilty of a wrongful taking, if he obtains them by such a fraud as justifies the owner in avoiding the sale, or other transaction, to which his assent was obtained.[40] Upon its avoidance, the owner may insist that no

[31] Hiort v. Bott, L. R. 9 Ex. 86, 43 L. J. Ex. 81 (1874).

[32] McCombie v. Davies, 6 East. 538, 8 R. R. 534 (1805).

[33] Chamberlin v. Shaw, 18 Pick. (36 Mass.) 278 (1836). The same doctrine was applied to a land owner, who refused to permit a mortgagee to take a boiler from his premises. Badger v. Batavia etc., Co., 70 Ill. 302 (1873).

[34] Kayworth v. Hill, 3 B. & Ald. 685 (1820). Taking was by the wife, and husband held liable with the wife; Chambers v. Lewis, 28 N. Y. 454 (1863).

[35] Leonard v. Belknap, 47 Vt. 602 (1874).

[36] Vilas v. Mason, 25 Wis. 310 (1870).

[37] Bristol v. Burt, 7 Johns. (N.Y.) 254 (1810).

[38] Johnson v. Farr, 60 N. H. 426 (1880); Abercrombie v. Bradford, 16 Al. 500 (1849); Stuart v. Phelps, 39 Ia. 14 (1874); Wintringham v. Lafoy, 7 Cow. (N. Y.) 735 (1827).

[39] Mallalieu v. Laugher, 3 C. & P. 551 (1828); Herron v. Hughes, 25 Cal. 555 (1864); Fernald v. Chase, 37 Me. 289 (1853).

[40] Thompson v. Rose, 16 Conn. 71,

title or right of possession ever passed to the defrauder. Of course if the owner does not avoid the transaction, until after the goods have been transferred to a *bona fide* purchaser, he cannot proceed against the latter for conversion.[41] Nor, according to the better authorities, can he maintain conversion against an innocent transferee of such defrauder, although not one for value, without demand and refusal.[42]

Excluding the Rightful Owner, or Possessor. The most frequent examples of this form of conversion are afforded by the destruction, or sale of personal property.

It is not necessary to show that the defendant actually converted to his own use the property of the plaintiff, nor that he derived any benefit therefrom. It is enough that, by an intended act, he deprived the plaintiff of the property. Accordingly, one commits conversion by killing animals, or burning up property, or melting ice, or cancelling a certificate, or by so dealing with a chattel that its identity is destroyed.[43]

Nonfesance, Or Negligent Omission. If the deterioration or destruction of the article, however, is due to the mere nonfeasance of the defendant, he can successfully defend against an action of conversion, although he may be liable in an action for negli-

41 Am. Dec. 141 (1844); Lovell v. Hammond, 66 Conn. 500, 34 At. 511 (1895); Holland v. Bishop, 60 Minn. 23, 61 N. W. 681 (1895); Thurston v. Blanchard, 22 Pick. (40 Mass.) 18, 33 Am. Dec. 700 (1839); Baird v. Howard, 51 O. St. 57, 36 N. E. 732, 40 Am. St. R. 550, 22 L. R. A. 846, (1894).

41 Trott v. Warren, 11 Me. 226 (1824); Bradley v. Obeare, 10 N. H. 477 (1839); Mowrey v. Walsh, 8 Cow. (N. Y.) 238 (1828).

42 Goodwin v. Wertheimer, 99 N. Y. 149, 1 N. E. 404 (1885); but see Farley v. Lincoln, 51 N. H. 577 (1872).

43 Keyworth v. Hill, 3 B. & Ald. 685 (1820), opinion of Abbott C. J.; Atchinson etc., Ry. v. Tanner, 19 Col. 559, 36 Pac. 541, (1894), seventh count for destruction of grass; Frost v. Plumb, 40 Conn. 111, 16 Am. R. 18 (1873); Olds v. Chicago Open Board of Trade, 33 Ill. App. 445 (1889); Simmons v. Sikes, 3 Ire. (24 N. C.) 98 (1841); Ascherman v. Philip Best Co., 45 Wis. 462 (1878); Richard v. Atkinson, 1 Strange, 576 (1723); Dench v. Walker, 14 Mass. 500 (1780); Sanderson v. Haverstick, 8 Pa. 294 (1848.) In Bryne v. Stout, 15 Ill. 180 (1853), it is held that the castration of a trespassing hog does not amount to conversion. Cf. Simmons v. Lillystone, 8 Exch. 431, 22 L. J. Exch. 217 (1853), cutting a spar.

gence.[44] For example, a warehouseman, or common carrier fails to guard properly articles which have been confided to him, and they become worthless,[45] or are lost or stolen.[46] He is not liable in trover, although he may be answerable either for a breach of his contract, or of his common law duty, to keep safely. " Conversion " it is said, " upon which recovery in trover may be had, must be a positive, tortious act. Nonfeasance or neglect of duty, mere failure to perform an act obligatory by contract, or by which property is lost to the owner will not support the action."[47]

When, however, the property is rendered worthless, or its nature is changed, or it is lost or destroyed as the proximate result of the defendant's act, or misfeasance, trover may be maintained, even though the defendant is a bailee,[48] or an agent.[49]

Sale of Property, as a Conversion.   A person, who engages in selling and delivering property, thereby asserts ownership, either in himself, or in the person for whom he professes to act. If the ownership is in another, the act of selling is a distinct repudiation of that other's dominion, and an exclusion of him from possession. It is, therefore, actionable conversion, no matter

[44] Central etc., Co. v. Lampley, 76 Al. 357 52 Am. R. 334 (1884); Thompson v. Moesta, 27 Mich. 182 (1873); Salt Springs Bank v. Wheeler, 48 N. Y. 492, 8 Am. R. 504 (1872); Tinker v. Morrill, 39 Vt. 477, 94 Am. Dec. 345 (1866).

[45] Mulgrave v. Ogden, Croke Eliz. 219 (1591); Emory v. Jenkinson, Tappan (O.) 219 (1818); Jones v. Allen, 1 Head (38 Tenn.) 626 (1858).

[46] Ross v. Johnson, 5 Burr. 2825 (1772); Williams v. Gesse, 3 Bing. N. C., 849, 32 E. C. L. R. 389 (1837); Bowlin v. Nye, 10 Cush. (64 Mass.) 416 (1852); Scovill v. Griffith, 12 N. Y. 509 (1855); Walmsley v. Atlas S. S. Co., 168 N. Y. 533, 61 N. E. 896, 85 Am. St. R. 699 (1901); Louisville etc., Ry. v. Campbell, 7 Heisk. (54 Tenn.) 253 (1872).

[47] Davis & Son v. Hurt, 114 Al. 146, 21 So. 468 (1896); Smith v. Archer, 53 Ill. 241 (1870); Savage v. Smythe & Co., 48 Ga. 562 (1873).

[48] Munford v. Taylor, 2 Met. (59 Ky.) 599 (1859); Hay v. Connor, 2 Har. & J. (Md.) 347 (1808); Wentworth v. McDuffie, 48 N. H. 402 (1869); Hawkins v. Hoffman, 6 Hill (N. Y.) 586, 41 Am. Dec. 768 (1844); Weakley v. Pearce, 5 Heisk. (52 Tenn.) 401 (1871); Ry. Co. v. O'Donnell, 49 O. St. 489, 32 N. E. 476, 34 Am. St. R. 579 (1892); Marshall etc. Co. v. Kansas etc. Ry., 176 Mo. 480, 75 S. W. 638, 98 Am. St. R. 508 (1903).

[49] Donahue v. Shippee, 15 R. I. 543, 8 At. 541 (1887); plaintiff's grass was cut by defendant, while working for a third person.

whether the seller believed the property to be his or not. In attempting to transfer the ownership he acted at his peril.[50]

The same rule applies to an auctioneer, broker or other agent, when he sells and delivers property for a principal who is not its owner and has no legal authority to dispose of it.[51] Wrongful intent is not an essential element of the tort of conversion in such cases. Its gist is the rightful owner's deprivation of his property, by some unauthorized act of another asserting dominion or control over it.[52]

Purchaser is also Liable for Conversion. As one, who buys and receives possession of property, does thereby assert dominion over it, to the exclusion of everyone else, his act of purchasing and taking possession amounts to conversion, as against the true owner. His good faith in the transaction does not save him,[53] and, in most jurisdictions, it does not entitle him even to a demand for the property from the true owner, before a suit in trover can be brought.[54]

[50] Hutchins v. King, 1 Wall. (68 U. S.) 53, 17 L. Ed. 544 (1863); May v. O'neal, 125 Al. 620, 28 So. 12 (1899); Merchants Bank v. Meyer, 56 Ark. 499, 20 S. W. 406 (1892); Horton v. Jack, 126 Cal. 521, 58 Pac. 1051 (1899); Brown v. Campbell Co., 44 Ks. 237, 24 Pac. 492 (1890); Lafeyth v. Emporia Bank, 53 Ks. 51, 35 Pac. 805 (1894); Gore v. Izer, 64 Neb. 380, 90 N. W. 758 (1902); Pease v. Smith, 61 N. Y. 477 (1875); Croft v. Jennings, 173 Pa. 216, 33 At. 1026 (1896); Morril v. Moulton, 40 Vt. 242 (1867).

[51] Stephens v. Elwall, 4 M. & S. 259 (1815); Hollins v. Fowler, L. R. 7 H. L. 757, 44 L. J. Q. B. 169 (1875); Consolidated Co. v. Curtis, (1892) 1 Q. B. 495, 61 L. J. Q. B. 325; Swim v. Wilson, 90 Cal. 126, 127 Pac. 33 13 L. R. A. 605, 25 Am. St. R. 110 (1891); Kimball v. Billings, 55 Me. 147, 92 Am. Dec. 581 (1867); Robinson v. Bird, 158 Mass. 357, 33 N. E. 291, 35 Am. St. R. 495 (1893); Berchich v. Marye, 9 Nev. 312 (1874); *contra*—Frizzell v.

Rundle, 88 Tenn. 396, 12 S. W. 918, 17 Am. St. R. 998 (1890).

[52] Boyce v. Brockway, 31 N. Y. 490 (1865); Reid v. Colcock, 1 Nott & McCord (S. C.) 592 (1819).

[53] Cooper v. Willomatt, 1 C. B. 672, 14 L. C. J. P. 219, 50 E. C. L. R. 672 (1845); Scott v. Hodges, 62 Al. 337 (1878); Sims v. James, 62 Ga. 260 (1879). Gilmore v. Newton 9 Allen (91 Mass.) 171, 85 Am. Dec. 749 (1864); Trudo v. Anderson, 10 Mich. 357 (1862); Hyde v. Noble, 13 N. H. 494, 38 Am. Dec. 508 (1843); Velzian v. Lewis, 15 Or. 539, 16 Pac. 631, 3 Am. St. R. 184 (1888); Carey v. Bright, 58 Pa. 70 (1868); Riford v. Montgomery, 7 Vt. 411 (1835).

[54] In N. Y., it is held that "an innocent purchaser of personal property from a wrong-doer shall first be informed of the defect in his title, and have an opportunity to deliver the property to the true owner, before he shall be liable as a tort-feasor for a wrongful conversion." Gillett v. Roberts, 58 N. Y. 28, 34 (1874.)

Even in jurisdictions, where an innocent purchaser from a wrongful holder is entitled to a demand, he forfeits that right by selling the property. Until the sale, it is said, his mere possession is not inconsistent with the plaintiff's ownership, but the sale estops him from denying that he was dealing with it adversely to the plaintiff.[55]

The pledgee or mortgagee of personal property, who asserts a right to it, in defiance of the claim of the true owner, is guilty of converting it.[56]

Wrongful Use of Property as a Conversion. Perhaps the most common example of this form of conversion is afforded by the bailee who deals with property, of which he has lawful possession, in a manner inconsistent with the purposes of the bailment. Some instances of this class have been given, under previous headings, such as destruction[57] and loss,[58] due to the culpable acts of the hirers of property or of carriers.

Other examples are afforded by the bailees of various descriptions, who sell or pledge property without authority therefor from their bailors;[59] or who, having it lawfully in their possession for one purpose, use it for a different[60] and unjustifiable[61] purpose. In cases of this class, the bailee, having converted the property,

[55] Pease v. Smith, 61 N. Y. 477 (1875).

[56] McCombie v. Davies, 6 East. 558, 8 R. R. 534 (1805); Newcomb-Buchanan Co. v. Baskett, 14 Bush. (77 Ky.) 658 (1879); Hotchkiss v. Hunt, 49 Me. 213, 224 (1860); Stanley v. Gaylord, 1 Cush. (55 Mass.) 536, 48 Am. Dec. 643 (1848); Thrall v. Lathrop, 30 Vt. 307, 73 Am. Dec. 306 (1858).

[57] Frost v. Plumb, 40 Conn. 111, 16 Am. R. 19 (1873).

[58] Marshall etc. Co. v. Kansas etc. Ry., 176 Mo. 480, 75 S. W. 638, 98 Am. St. R. 508 (1903). *Accord*, Youl v. Harbottle, 1 Peake 49 (1791); Devereaux v. Barclay, 2 B. & Ald. 702, 21 R. R. 457 (1819).

[59] Powell v. Sadler, Paley, Prin. & Agent (3 Ed.) 80 (1806); Mulliner v. Florence, 3 Q. B. D. 484, 47 L. J. Q. B. 700 (1878); Hooks v. Smith, 18 Al. 338 (1850); McPartland v. Read, 11 Allen (93 Mass.) 231 (1865).

[60] Welch v. Mohr, 93 Cal. 371, 28 Pac. 1060 (1892); Wheelock, v. Wheelwright, 5 Mass. 104 (1809); Disbrow v. Tenbroeck, 4 E. D. Smith (N. Y.) 397 (1855); Woodman v. Hubbard, 25 N. H. 67, 7 Am. Dec. 310 (1852); Hart v. Skinner, 16 Vt. 138, 42 Am. Dec. 560 (1844).

[61] Doolittle v. Shaw, 92 Ia. 343, 60 N. W. 621, 26 L. R. A. 366 and note; 54 Am. St. R. 562 (1894); Spooner v. Manchester, 133 Mass. 270, 43 Am. R. 514 (1882). These cases hold that a slight deviation from, or extension of, the proposed route, may be justifiable. Cf. Alvord v. Davenport, 43 Vt. 30 (1870).

becomes liable for its value, without regard to the degree of care which he may have taken of it, and regardless also of the immediate cause of its injury or destruction.[62] He may be liable, too, although an infant and thus in a position to defend successfully an action for breach of his contract as bailee,[63] or, although the contract of bailment was made on Sunday, and, therefore, invalid.[64] In the case of an infant bailee, it is generally held that any willful and positive act on his part, in violation of the bailment, amounts to an election on his part to disaffirm the contract, and constitutes him, thereafter, a converter of the property.[65]

Conversion of Principal's Property by Agent. An agent is guilty of conversion, as against his principal, when he sells or exchanges the latter's property without authority,[66] or applies its proceeds to an unauthorized purpose,[67] or refuses to return it or its proceeds upon a seasonable demand.[68]

If the agent's default, however, consists in a simple omission to act,[69] or in a mere breach of duty, as in selling goods (which he is authorized to sell) for a lower price than that named by his principal, or on different terms,[70] or, as, in using railroad bonds, in effect-

[62] Ledbetter v. Thomas, 130 Al. 299, 30 So. 342 (1901); Malone v. Robinson, 77 Ga. 719 (1886); Murphy v. Kaufman, 20 La. Ann. 559 (1868); Fisher v. Kyle, 27 Mich. 454 (1875); Perham v. Coney, 117 Mass. 102, 9 Am. R. 30 (1875); Lane v. Cameron, 38 Wis. 603 (1875); DeVain v. Mich. Lumber Co., 64 Wis. 616, 25 Am. St. R. 552, 60 N. W. 621, 26 L. R. A. 366 (1885).

[63] Homer v. Thwing, 3 Pick. (20 Mass.) 492 (1826); Freeman v. Boland, 14 R. I. 39, 51 Am. R. 340 (1882); Towne v. Wiley, 23 Vt. 355, 56 Am. Dec. 85 (1854).

[64] Frost v. Plumb, 40 Conn. 111, 16 Am. R. 18 (1873); Hall v. Corcoran, 107 Mass. 251, 9 Am. R. 30 (1871).

[65] Campbell v. Stakes, 2 Wend. (N. Y.) 137, 19 Am. Dec. 561 (1828); Wentworth v. McDuffie, 48 N. H. 402 (1869).

[66] Haas v. Damon, 9 Ia. 589 (1859); Etter v. Bailey, 8 Pa. 442 (1848).

[67] McNear v. Atwood, 17 Me. 434 (1840); Murray v. Burling, 10 Johns, (N. Y.) 172 (1813); Laverty v. Snethen, 68 N. Y. 522, 23 Am. R. 184 (1877); Cotton v. Sharpstein, 14 Wis. 226, 80 Am. Dec. 774 (1861).

[68] Britton v. Ferrin, 171 N. Y 235, 63 N. E. 954 (1902).

[69] McMorris v. Simpson, 21 Wend. (N. Y.) 610, 614 (1839).

[70] Loveless v. Fowler, 79 Ga. 134, 11 Am. St. R. 407, 4 S. E. 103 (1887); Serjeant v. Blunt, 16 Johns. (N. Y.) 73 (1819).

ing a reorganization, without following all the directions of the principal,[71] he is not guilty of conversion.

Asportation or Detention by a Mere Custodier. The courts, both in England and in this country, are disposed to treat the acts of agents, servants and bailees as not amounting to conversion, when they are limited to the mere custody or transportation of property, and are done without any intention of interfering with the title of the true owner, or of antagonizing his dominion. The difficulty lies, in fixing the limits of this exception to the general rule of liability, for wrongful intermeddling with another's property.

Perhaps the following statement fairly expresses the prevailing view upon this topic: The reception of property by delivery from one, whom the receiver is justly entitled to regard as its owner, and its return to him, or delivery over to a third person upon his order, without notice of an adverse claim in another, and without reference to the question of ownership of the property, are not tortious acts.[72]

Accordingly, it has been held that if a bailee have the temporary possession of property, holding the same as the property of the bailor and asserting no title in himself, and in good faith restores the property to the bailor, before he is notified that the true owner will look to him for it, no action will lie against him, for he has only done what it was his duty to do.[73]

Some courts have gone further, and have held, that the bailee of goods, known by him to have been stolen by the bailor, is not liable for conversion to the true owner for taking custody and delivering them back to the thief.[74] They have also held that the mortgagee [75]

---

[71] Indust. & Gen. Trust v. Tod, 170 N. Y. 233, 63 N. E. 285 (1902). See dissenting opinion.

[72] Burditt v. Hunt, 25 Me. 419, 44 Am. Dec. 289 (1845); Greenway v. Fisher, 1 C. & P. 190 (1824); Brett J. in Fowler v. Hollins, L. R. 7 Q. B. at p. 630 (1872); Frome v. Dennis, 45 N. J. L. 515 (1883).

[73] Nelson v. Iverson, 17 Al. 216 (1850); Hill v. Hayes, 38 Conn. 532, (1871); Parker v. Lombard, 100 Mass. 405 (1868); Hodgson v. St. Paul Plow Co., 78 Minn. 172, 80 N. W. 956, 50 L. R. A. 644, with valuable note, (1899); Nanson v. Jacob,

93 Mo. 331, 6 S. W. 246, 3 Am. St. R. 531 (1887); Walker v. First Nat. Bank, 43 Or. 102, 72 Pac. 635 (1903). In Hudmon v. Dubois, 85 Al. 446, 5 So. 162, 2 L. R. A. 475 (1888), constructive notice, by the registration of a chattel mortgage, was held sufficient to make the bailee's act of delivery a conversion.

[74] Loring v. Mulcahy, 3 Allen, (85 Mass.) 575 (1862).

[75] Leonard v. Tidd, 3 Met. (44 Mass.) 6 (1841); Spackman v. Foster, 11 Q. B. D. 99, 52 L. J. Q. B. 418 (1883).

or pledgee [76] is not guilty of conversion, when he does not assume to hold the property adversely to the true owner. It is difficult to see, however, why the very act of taking possession as mortgagee or pledgee is not a repudiation of the true owner's dominion. In a recent Minnesota case,[77] the court enunciated the following rule: "An agent or servant, who, acting solely for his principal or master, and by his direction, and without knowing of any wrong, or being guilty of gross negligence in not knowing it, disposes of or assists the master in disposing of property which the latter has no right to dispose of, is not thereby rendered liable for a conversion of the property." The same court, however, has shown a tendency to limit the doctrine thus announced, and has refused to apply it to a commission merchant, who receives warehouse receipts from his debtor, and applies the grain to the payment of the debt, believing that the grain belongs to the debtor, while in fact it is the property of another.[78]

It is clear, too, that the doctrine is not to be applied, when the agent or servant takes an active, though *bona fide,* part with his master, or principal, in actually converting the property.[79]

Conversion by a Finder. In dealing with the topic just discussed, a learned English judge [80] said: "I cannot find it anywhere distinctly laid down, but I submit to your lordships that, on principle, one who deals with goods, at the request of a person who has the actual custody of them, in the *bona fide* belief that the custodier is the true owner, or has the authority of the true owner, should be excused for what he does, if the act is of such a nature as would be excused if done by the authority of the person in possession, if he was the finder of goods, or intrusted with their custody."

Just what a finder may do with goods which he takes into his possession, without being guilty of conversion, may not be clearly settled. Certainly he is not liable for conversion, when the property

---

[76] Leuthold v. Fairchild, 35 Minn. 99, 27 N. W. 503, 28 N. W. 218 (1886).

[77] *Ibid.*

[78] Doliff v. Robins, 83 Minn. 498, 86 N. W. 772, 85 Am. St. R. 466 (1901).

[79] Miller v. Wilson, 98 Ga. 567, 25 S. E. 578 (1896); Shearer v. Evans, 89 Ind. 400 (1883); Wardner-Bushnell Co. v. Harris, 81 Ia. 153, 46 N. W. 859 (1890); D. M. Osborne Co. v. Piano Mfg. Co., 51 Neb. 562, 70 N W. 1124 (1897).

[80] Blackburn L. J. in Hollins v. Fowler, L. R. 7 H. L. 757 (1875).

becomes worthless, or is lost, by reason of his nonfeasance,[81] although he may be liable in some other form of action for the proximate consequences of his gross negligence.[82] It is also clear, that if he abuses the property,[83] or takes upon himself its delivery to some third person who is not entitled to it,[84] his act amounts to a conversion. But, is it a conversion for him, after taking the property into his possession, to place it back where he found it, provided this act of dispossession subjects it to no greater peril than it was in, when he found it?

Undoubtedly there are dicta to the effect that, though a finder is not bound to take possession, if he does, he is bound to keep safely for the true owner, and to make reasonable effort to discover him; that, after taking possession, there is no *locus penitentiae*.[85] This, it is submitted, tends to deter finders from taking temporary possession of property, the quality of which is not apparent at a glance, and is opposed to the weight of authority.[86] The Supreme Court of Massachusetts has held that one, who takes up a horse going at large in the highway, does not convert it by turning it back again into the highway;[87] and the Supreme Court of Tennessee has

[81] Mulgrave v. Ogden, Croke Eliz. 219, Owen 141 (1591); Nelson v. Merriam, 4 Pick. (21 Mass.) 249 (1826).

[82] Ross v. Johnson, 5 Burr. 2825 (1772).

[83] Murgoo v. Cogswell, 1 E. D. Smith (N. Y.) 359 (1852).

[84] Coke J. in Isaack v. Clark, 2 Bulstrode 306 (1615). In this case there was no actual finding. The finding alleged was a fiction of the pleader, and it is not clear whether Lord Coke's dictum was intended to apply to the case of actual finding, or to the fictitious finding, in the case then before the court.

[85] Sovern v. Yoran, 16 Or. 269, 20 Pac. 100, 8 Am. St. R. 293 (1888); Smith v. Nashua & L. Ry., 27 N. H. 86, 90, 50 Am. Dec. 384 (1853).

[86] Dougherty v. Posegate, 3 Ia. 88 (1856). In this case, defendant's legal advisers had told him to put the money, which he had found, back where he found it. The court does not intimate that this was unsound advice, and the liability of the defendant, the jury were instructed, depended upon whether he had been guilty of gross negligence. Cf. analogous cases, Roulston v. McClelland, 2 E. D. Smith (N. Y.) 60 (1853); Griswold v. Boston & M. Ry., 183 Mass. 434, 67 N. E. 354 (1903); Doxtator v. Chic. & M. Ry. 120 Mich, 596, 79 N. W. 922 (1899); Dyche v. Vicksburg etc., Ry., 79 Miss. 361, 30 So. 711 (1901).

[87] Wilson v. McLaughlin, 107 Mass. 587 (1871). It is true, the court says, that the defendant's act, in turning the horse into the highway, was due to the refusal of his employer to let the horse remain on his land. But, if the law im-

declared that one, who finds in his pasture the cow of another, ought to turn her out and let her find her owner.[88]

Conversion by Unlawfvl Detention.

Not every wrongful detention of goods amounts to a conversion. If a person is bailee of an article, he may be bound by the terms of the bailment to return it to the bailor. Still, his mere failure to return it at the end of the bailment period is a breach of contract, not a tort. Nor can his contract liability be turned into conversion, by a demand from the bailor, that he return the article, and by his refusal to comply with the demand.[89] Such refusal does not amount to an assertion of dominion over the article. If the demand is for its surrender, however, and the bailee refuses to comply therewith, this is evidence of conversion.[90] " For what is conversion," said Lord Holt, " but an assuming upon one's self the property and right of disposing of another man's goods, and he that takes upon himself to detain another man's goods from him without cause, takes upon himself the right of disposing of them."[91]

Uncondtional Refusal.

In order to make out a case of conversion by demand and refusal, where there is no evidence of unlawful taking or use, the refusal must be unqualified,[92] or the qualification must have been made in bad faith, or upon a legally untenable ground.[93] Moreover, when one ground has been assigned by the

poses upon the finder the positive duty of keeping the article, this command of the master to violate the aefendant's legal duty would not avail him. He would be bound to take the horse off from his employer's premises, but he could have kept the animal in some other place.

[88] Medlin v. Balch, 102 Tenn. 710, 52 S. W. 140 (1899).

[89] Fifield v. Maine Co., 62 Me. 77 (1873); Bassett v. Bassett, 112 Mass. 99 (1873); Farrar v. Rollins, 37 Vt. 295 (1864).

[90] Dent v. Chiles, 5 Stew. & P. (Al.) 383, 23 Am. Dec. 360 (1832); Dame v. Dame, 38 N. H. 429, 75 Am. Dec. 195 (1859); Wykoff v. Stevenson, 46 N. J. L. 326 (1884); McCormick v. Penn. Ry., 49 N. Y. 303

(1872); s. c. 99 N. Y. 65, 52 Am. R. 6 (1885); Claflin v. Gurney, 17 R. I. 185, 20 At. 932 (1890); Sibley v. ctory, 8 Vt. 15 (1836).

[91] Baldwin v. Cole, 6 Mod. 212 (1704); Davies v. Nicholas 7 C. & P. 339 (1836), accord.

[92] Rushworth v. Taylor, 3 Q. B. 699, 12 L. J. Q. B. 80 (1842); McLain v. Huffman, 30 Ark. 428 (1875); Moore v. Fitzpatrick, 7 Baxt. (66 Tenn.) 350 (1874); Nay v. Crook, 1 Pin. (Wis.) 546 (1845).

[93] Borroughs v. Bayne, 5 H. & N. 296, 29 L. J. Ex. 188 (1860); Briggs v. Haycock, 63 Cal. 343 (1883); Johnson v. Lindstrom, 114 Ind. 152, 16 N. E. 400 (1888); Williams v. Smith, 153 Pa. 463, 25 At. 1122 (1893); Roberts v. Yarboro, 41 Tex. 449 (1874).

defendant for his refusal, and suit is brought for conversion, he cannot justify by evidence that he had a legally tenable ground for refusal. Such ground was waived by his choosing to stand upon another ground.[94]

Qulified Refusal. When there has been neither wrongful taking nor use of the property by the defendant, and it is demanded from him by one whose right to demand and receive it is not known to him, he may safely refuse to surrender, until he has had a fair opportunity to clear up his doubts on the subject. Such a refusal is a qualified one, and if made in good faith and upon reasonable grounds, it does not constitute a case of conversion.[95] Whether the defendant has acted reasonably, either in assigning the qualification, or in the time taken for resolving his doubts, is a question of fact, and, whenever different inferences may be drawn from the evidence, is for the jury.[96]

The doctrine, which we have been considering, is most frequently invoked in behalf of a common carrier or other bailee. When a demand is made upon him for the goods, by another than the bailor, or some one claiming under him, the bailee is not bound to act upon the instant, but is entitled to a reasonable time for investigation; and, during such period, his detention of the property is not a conversion.[97] As soon, however, as he becomes satisfied, or had he acted reasonably, would have become satisfied, that the claimant is entitled to the possession of the property, he should surrender it.

[94] Boardman v. Sill, 1 Camp. 410 (1809); Marine Bank v. Fiske, 71 N. Y. 353 (1877); Singer Mfg. Co. v. King, 14 R. I. 511 (1884); 24 Am. L. Reg., N. S. 51 (1885).

[95] Green v. Dunn, 3 Campb. 215 (1811); Alexander v. Southey, 5 B. & Ald. 247, 24 R. R. 348 (1821); Zachary v. Pace, 9 Ark. 212, 47 Am. Dec. 744 (1848); Witherspoon v. Blewett, 47 Miss. 570 (1873); Robinson v. Burleigh, 5 N. H. 225 (1830); Mount v. Derrick, 5 Hill, (N. Y.) 455, (1843); Ball v. Liney, 48 N. Y. 6, 8 Am. R. 511 (1871); Blankenship v. Berry, 28 Tex. 448.

[96] Vaughan v. Watt, 6 M. & W.

492 (1840); Pilott v. Wilkinson, 3 H. & C. 345, 34 L. J. Ex. 22 (1864); Ingalls v. Buckley, 15 Ill. 224, (1853); Entee v. N. J. S. Co., 45 N. Y. 34 (1871); Felcher v. McMillan, 103 Mich. 494, 61 N. W. 791 (1895); Dowd v. Wadsworth, 13 N. C. 130, (2 Dev.) 18 Am. Dec. 567 (1829); Watt v. Potter, 2 Mason, (U. S. C. C.) 77 (1820).

[97] Merz v. Chic. etc., Ry. Co., 86 Minn. 33, 90 N. W. 7 (1902); Hett v. R. R., 69 N. H. 139, 44 At. 910 (1897); Holbrook v. Wight, 24 Wend. (N. Y.) 169, 177, 35 Am. Dec. 607 (1840); Smith v. Durham, 127 N. C. 417, 37 S. E. 473 (1900).

Such a surrender is justifiable even against his bailor.[98] If he cannot decide upon the merits of the adverse claimants, he should demand a bond of indemnity from the one to whom he delivers, or should interplead them.[99]

Conversion by a Tenant in Common.   The mere refusal of one tenant in common of personalty, to permit his co-tenant to use or possess it, is not a conversion, ordinarily. When two persons have an equal title to an indivisible chattel, such as an ox, a horse or a cow, it is said, neither can enjoy his moiety without actual and exclusive possession of the chattel. Hence, neither can lawfully compel the other to surrender possession. The one excluded from possession has no legal remedy, except to take it when he can see fit.[100]

If, however, one tenant in common destroys the property, or does an act equivalent to its destruction, he is guilty of conversion.[101] When he sells and delivers it as his sole property, he commits conversion, according to the weight of authority in this country.[102] It is submitted that this is the correct view, because he is doing an act which he intends as a repudiation of his co-tenant's title and a defiance of his dominion. In England, such a sale is not treated as a conversion [103] unless possibly it is a sale in market overt.[104] In the latter case, the purchaser becomes the legal owner of the

---

[98] The Idaho, 93 U. S. 575, 23 L. Ed. 278 (1876); Nat. Bank of Commerce v. Chic. etc., Ry., 44 Minn. 224, 46 N. W. 342, 560, 9 L. R. A. 263, 20 Am. St. R. 566 (1890). In Kohn v. Richmond, etc., Ry., 37 S. C. 1, 16 S. E. 396, 24 L. R. A. 100, 34 Am. St. R. 734, with valuable note, it was held, that a common carrier, receiving goods for transportation, is liable for conversion in failing to deliver to their true owner upon a demand, only when such demand is made under and accompanied by legal process.

[99] Ball v. Liney, 48 N. Y. 6, 8 Am. R. 511 (1871); Hutchinson on Carriers, (2 Ed.) 407.

[100] Coke on Littleton, § 323;

Southworth v. Smith, 27 Conn. 355, 71 Am. Dec. 72 (1858); Hudson v. Swan, 83 N. Y. 552 (1881).

[101] Morgan v. Marquis, 9 Ex. 145, 148, 23 L. J. Ex. 21 (1853); Jacobs v. Seward, L. R. 5 H. L. 464, 475, 41 L. J. C. P. 221 (1871); Osborn v. Schenck, 83 N. Y. 201 (1880).

[102] Perminter v. Kelly, 18 Al. 716, 54 Am. Dec. 177 (1851); Goell v. Morse, 126 Mass. 480 (1879); White v. Osborn, 21 Wend. 72 (1839).

[103] Mayhew v. Herrick, 7 C. B. 229, 18 L. J. C. P. 179 (1849); Sanborn v. Morrill, 15 Vt. 700, 40 Am. Dec. 701, (1843), *accord*.

[104] Parke B. in Farrar v. Beswick, 1 M. & W. 682, 688, Tyrwh. & Gr. 1053 (1836).

entire chattel, which is thereby lost to the non-consenting co-owner.

In this country, an exception has been made to the general rule stated above, with respect to fungible goods. As they are alike in quality and value, and divisible by weight, measure or number, one co-tenant may sever and take out his share, without interfering with the other co-tenant's right of enjoyment of his share. Accordingly, if the tenant in possession refuses to permit a division, he exercises an unjustifiable dominion over the property and is guilty of conversion.[105]

Conversion by Pledgee. It is admitted, both in England and in this country, that in case of a bailment other than a pledge, a sale by the bailee without authority " determines the contract, the right of possession at once reverts to the owner, and he can treat the sale as a conversion." [106] In England, however, it is held that a sale of the property by the pledgee does not amount to a conversion, because the pledgor has no right of possession until he tenders what is due on the pledge.[107] In this country, it has been held that when a pledgee sells the collateral, without authority from, notice to, or an accounting with the pledgor, he is guilty of conversion, and the pledgor's right of action is consummate.[108] This, it is submitted, is the better view.

Tender of Converted Goods by Defendant. Since Lord Mansfield's time, the English courts have allowed the converter to bar the cause of action by a return of the goods, and, if a suit has been commenced, by the payment of costs; when the goods are of

---

[105] Pickering v. Moore, 67 N. H. 533, 32 At. 828, 68 Am. St. R. 695, 31 L. R. A. 698 (1894); Gates v. Bowers, 169 N Y. 14, 61 N. E. 993, 88 Am. St. R. 530 (1901).

[106] Clerk & Lindsell, Torts, (2 Ed.) 223; Cooper v. Willomat, 1 C. B. 672, 14 L. J. C. P. 219 (1845).

[107] Donald v. Suckling, L. R. 1 Q. B. 585, 35 L. J. Q. B. 232 (1866); Holliday v. Holgate, L. R. 3 Ex. 299, 37 L. J. Exch. 174 (1868).

[108] Richardson v. Ashby, 132 Mo. 238, 247, 33 S. W. 806 (1895); Waring v. Gaskell, 95 Ga. 731, 22 S. E. 659 (1894); Fay v. Gray, 124 Mass. 500 (1877); Stevens v. Wiley, 165 Mass. 402, 407, 43 N. E. 198 (1896); Upham v. Barbour, 65 Minn. 364, 68 N. W. 42 (1896); Woodword v. Hascall, 59 Neb. 124, 80 N. W. 483 (1899); Stearns v. Marsh, 4 Den. 227, 47 Am. Dec. 248 (1847); Toplitz v. Bauer, 161 N. Y. 325, 55 N. E. 1059 (1900); Blood v. Erie Dime Co., 164 Pa. 95, 105, 30 At. 362 (1899); Walley v. Deseret Nat. Bank, 14 Utah 305, 320, 47 Pac. 147 (1896), *accord.*

" an ascertained quantity and value, and there are no circumstances that can enhance the damages above the real value." [109]　This course was admitted by Lord Kenyon [110] to be inconsistent with the earlier decisions,[111] and is not followed when the plaintiff is entitled to punitive damages, or the value of the converted property is in dispute.[112]　The defendant is always allowed, however, to return the property, and to have it applied in mitigation of damages.[113]

This doctrine has been accepted by some of our courts,[114] but the prevailing rule is that of the early common law, which permits the owner of converted property to abandon it to the converter and recover its value, as well as any special or punitive damages to which he can show himself entitled.[115]

---

[109] Fisher v. Prince, 3 Burr, 1363 (1762).

[110] Pickering v. Truste, 7 D. & E. 53 (1796).

[111] Wilcock's Case, 2 Salk. 597 (1704); Bowington v. Parry, 2 Strange 822 (1729); Olivant v. Perineau, 2 Strange 1191, 1 Wil. 23 (1743).

[112] Pickering v. Truste, 7 D. & E. 53, 54 (1796); Tucker v. Wright, 3 Bing. 601 (1826).

[113] Plevin v. Henshall, 10 Bing. 24 (1833); Hiort v. L. & N. W. Ry. 4 Ex. D. 188, 48 L. J. Ex. 545 (1879).

[114] Ward v. Moffett, 38 Mo. App. 395 (1889); Bigelow Co. v. Heintze, 53 N. J. L. 69, 21 At. 109 (1890), return allowed when conversion not willful and property unchanged; Rutland Ry., v. Bank 32 Vt. 639 (1860); Farr v. State Bank, 87 Wis. 223, 58 N. W. 377, 41 Am. St. R. 40 (1894), tender allowed before suit, if the conversion resulted from mistake.

[115] Norman v. Rodgers, 29 Ark. 365 (1874); Carpenter v. Dresser, 72 Me. 377, 39 Am. 337 (1881); Northrup v. McGill, 27 Mich. 234 (1873); Stickney v. Allen, 10 Gray (76 Mass.) 352 (1858); Gilbert v. Peck, 43 Mo. App. 577 (1890); denying the right to return, when the conversion is willful; Comm. Bank v. Hughes, 17 Wend. (N. Y.) 91 (1837); Brewster v. Silliman, 38 N. Y. 423 (1868); Baltimore Ry. v O'Donnell, 49 O. St. 489, 32 N. E. 476, 21 L. R. A. 117 (1892); Weaver v. Ashcroft, 50 Tex. 427 (1878); Hofschulte v. Panhandle Co., 50 S. W. (Tex. Civ. App.) 608 (1899).

CHAPTER XIII.

DECEIT AND KINDRED TORTS.

§ I. DECEIT.

As a Tort. Our discussion of this prolific source of litigation will be comparatively brief, for it is limited to deceit as a tort; that is, as a cause of action at common law for damages. Neither the right of the party deceived to rescind a contract induced thereby, nor his right to equitable relief comes within the scope of the present work. Although deceit, as a tort, is a much narrower topic than fraud, in its various relations to the law of contracts, to the law of property and to equity jurisprudence, it is much more extensive than it was three centuries,[1] or even a hundred and fifty years ago.[2]

Deceit Defined. " Where one person makes a statement to another which (1) is untrue; and which (2) the person making it does not believe to be true, whether knowing it to be untrue, or being ignorant whether it is true or not; and which (3) the person making it intends or expects to be acted upon, in a certain manner by the person to whom it is made, or with ordinary sense and prudence would expect it to be so acted upon; and (4) in reliance on which

---

[1] If the reader would compare the modern limits of this topic with those of three and a half centuries ago, he need only refer to Fitzherbert's Natura Brevium, published in 1534. He says, " This writ (*de disceit*) lieth properly when one man doeth anything in the name of another, by which the person is damnified and deceived." He then gives several pages of precedents, nearly every one of which involves a case of false personation or a case of the improper use of legal process. At 99*k* he gives a precedent for the writ in case of a false " warranty of the length of cloaths."

[2] The anonymous author of Actions on the Case for Torts and Wrongs (London 1720) devotes Chapter IX to " Actions on the case for Disceits and on Warranties." It contains but little matter of value to the lawyer of today, but it shows that the judicial conception of deceit as a tort was quite different, at the opening of the 18th Century, from that which is entertained at the opening of the twentieth century.

the person to whom it is made does act in that manner to his own harm; then the person making the statement is said to deceive the person to whom it is made." [3]

Statement of Fact. It is not every untrue statement, connected with a transaction, which will sustain an action for deceit, although it be shown to have induced the plaintiff to act to his harm. A mere promise to do an act in the future is an illustration. A broken promise, although causing harm to the promisee, is not a tort. If it were, the distinction between breaches of contract and torts would disappear. [4]

It is to be born in mind, however, that a statement may be a representation of fact although it takes the form of a promise. Accordingly, if A is induced to accept bills, drawn on him by B, by C's statement that no part of the proceeds shall be applied to B's indebtedness to C. and if A shows that C intended, when the statement was made, to apply the proceeds to his claim against B, and did so apply them to A's harm, C is liable in an action for deceit. [5] A man, who buys goods on credit, not only promises to pay for them, but either expressly or impliedly represents that he intends to pay for them. If, in truth, he has no such intention, then his lan-

---

[3] Sir Frederick Pollock's Draft of a Civil Wrongs Bill for India, sect. 40; Taylor v. Commercial Bank, 174 N. Y. 181, 185, 66 N. E. 726, 95 Am. St. R. 564 (1903).

[4] Union Pac. Ry. v. Barnes, 64 Fed. 84 (1894): A promise to sell land and convey a perfect title by one who believes his title is good, when in fact it is defective; Smith v. Parker, 148 Ind. 127, 45 N. E. 770 (1897): A promise to furnish the money for a specified business; Ayers v. Blevins, 28 Ind. App. 101, 62 N. E. 305 (1901): A promise to make certain machinery work up to a stated capacity; Long v. Woodman, 58 Me. 49, (1870): A promise to give bond for the reconveyance of certain property; Syracuse Knitting Co. v. Blanchard, 69 N. H. 447, 43 At. 637 (1899): A

promise that the dealings of defendant and plaintiff "should be more satisfactory than last season"; Gray v. Palmer, 2 Robt. (N. Y.) 500 (1864): A promise to collect a draft and apply the proceeds in a specified manner; Taylor v. Commercial Bank, 174 N. Y. 181, 66 N. E. 726, 95 Am. St. R. 564 (1903): An assurance that plaintiff would get his pay, if he made a loan to a third person.

[5] Clydesdale Bank v. Paton (1896) A. C. 381, 394, 65 L. J. P. C. 73. In this case, there was no evidence either that the bank did not have the intention of keeping its promise, or that it broke it. Cockrill v. Hall, 65 Cal. 326 (1884): A promise to return a note the next day, or pay it, inducing plaintiff to act to his harm.

guage, or his conduct, or both amount to a false representation of fact, for which deceit will lie.[6] The mere facts, however, that the buyer is insolvent and fails in business, before the term of credit expires, and never pays for the goods, do not make out a case of deceit. The plaintiff must go further and show that the defendant bought the goods, with the preconceived design of not paying for them.[7] Undoubtedly " it is very difficult to prove what the state of a man's mind at a particular time is, but, if it can be ascertained, it is as much a fact as anything else; as much a fact as the state of his digestion." [8]

Deception by Silence. Mere silence, unaccompanied by language or conduct which renders the silence beguiling, or by circumstances which impose upon the defendant a duty to speak, will not sustain an action for deceit, however reprehensible it may be morally.[9] But it often happens that the previous conduct of the defendant, or his relations to the other party to a transaction, impose upon him a duty to speak. Where there is such " a duty or obligation to speak, and a man in breach of that duty or obligation holds his tongue and does not speak, and does not say the thing he is bound to say, if that be done with the intention of inducing the other party to act upon the belief, that the reason why he did not speak was because he had nothing to say, there is fraud." [10] Accordingly, a banker who receives deposits, after he knows he is hopelessly insol-

---

[6] Morville v. Blackman, 42 Conn. 324 (1875); Burrill v. Stevens, 73 Me. 395, 398 (1892); Leather Co. v. Flynn, 108 Mich. 91, 65 N. W. 519 (1895); Nichols v. Pinne, 18 N. Y. 295 (1858); D. Adler & Sons v. Thorpe, 102 Wis. 70, 78 N. W. 184 (1899); Biggs v. Barry, 2 Curtis, (U. S. C. C.) 259 (1855); Swift v. Rounds, 19 R. I. 527, 35 At. 45, 61 Am. St. R. 791 (1896).

[7] Cases in last note; Hart v. Moulton, 104 Wis. 349, 80 N. W. 599 (1899); in Whitten v. Fitzwater, 129 N. Y. 626, 29 N. E. 298, (1891), it was held fraudulent for the purchaser to receive goods, knowing he

could not pay for them, although he intended to pay when he contracted for them.

[8] Bowen, L. J., in Edgington v. Fitzmaurice, 29 Ch. D. 549, 583, 55 L. J. Ch. 650 (1884).

[9] Pratt Land Co. v. McLain, 135 Al. 452, 33 So. 185, 93 Am. St. R. 35 (1902); Kirtley's Administratrix v. Shinkle, (Ky.) 69 S. W. 723 (1902); Wiser v. Lawler, 189 U. S. 260, 23 Sup. Ct. 624 (1902); Rothmiller v. Stein, 143 N. Y. 581, 38 N. E. 718, 26 L. R. A. 148 (1894).

[10] Blackburn L. J., in Brownlie v. Campbell, 5 App. Cases, 925, 950 (1880).

vent, is guilty of deceiving his depositors.[11] So is a father, who induces another to give credit to his son, by a letter from which he omits the statement that the son is a minor. Such silence is designed to mislead.[12]

Opinion as Distinguished From Fact. In order to make out a case of deceit, the plaintiff must show that the defendant's false statement was one of fact, as distinguished from one of opinion, or belief.[13] "If," said a learned judge, "the defendant went no further than to say that the bond was an A No. 1 bond, which we understand to mean simply that it was a first-rate bond, or that the railroad was good security for the bond, we are constrained to hold that he was not liable under the circumstances of this case, even if he made the statement in bad faith. The rule of law is hardly to be regretted, when it is considered, how easily and insensibly, words of hope or expectation are converted by an interested memory into statements of quality and value, when the expectation has been disappointed."[14]

Hence, statements by a seller, relative to the value or quality of goods, are generally treated as expressions of opinion.[15] If, how-

[11] Anonymous, 67 N. Y. 598 (1876); Cassidy v. Uhlman, 170 N. Y. 505, 63 N. E. 554, 79 Am. S. R. 596 (1902).

[12] Kidney v. Stoddard, 7 Met. (48 Mass.) 252 (1843). "Such a partial and fragmentary statement of fact, as that, the withholding of that which is not stated makes that which is stated absolutely false," will sustain an action for deceit, Lord Cairns, in Peek v. Gurney, R. 6 H. L. 377, 403, 43 L. J. Ch. 19 (1873). "To tell half a truth only is to conceal the other half," Mitchell J. in Newell v. Randall, 32 Minn. 171, 50 Am. R. 562 (1884); Croyle v. Moses, 90 Pa. 250, 35 Am. R. 654 (1879); an artful and evasive answer, intended to deceive and actually deceiving the plaintiff.

[13] In Hedin v. Minn. etc. Inst., 62 Minn. 146, 64 N. W. 158, 35 L. R. A.

417, with vlauable note, 62 Am. St. R. 146 (1895), an action for deceit was sustained for false and fraudulent representations that the defendant's disease was curable and would be cured by the defendant for five hundred dollars The liability for deceit, it was held, "may arise where one has or assumes to have knowledge upon a subject of which the other is ignorant, and knowingly makes false statements, on which the other relies."

[14] Holmes J., in Deming v. Darling, 148 Mass. 504, 505, 20 N. E. 107, 2 L. R. A. 743 (1889).

[15] Harvey v. Young, Yelv. 21 (1597); Ekins v. Tresham, 1 Lev. 102 (1675); Gustafson v. Rustemeyer, 70 Conn. 125, 39 At. 104, 39 L. R. A. 644, 66 Am. St. R. 92 (1898); Williams v. McFadden, 23 Fla. 143, 148, 1 So. 618, 11 Am. St.

ever, the seller, goes beyond the limits of mere puffing and makes assertions of fact upon which the opinion is represented to rest, as that the goods are new and fresh, when they are old and shop-worn, he makes himself liable for deceit.[16]   At times, it may be difficult to determined whether the statement involves an assertion of fact as well as an axpression of opinion. In such cases the question is for the jury.[17]

Statements as to the price paid or offered for property are held by some courts to be " so manifestly statements of opinion on the part of the seller, or mere evidence of the opinion of others respecting its value, that they cannot be deemed statements of material facts which will lay the foundation for an action for deceit, even if the statements are false and intended to deceive." [18]   These courts, however, are ready to lay hold of any additional statements or circumstances, indicative of the defendant's fraudulent purpose, as a club with which to beat him, when he has lied about the price paid or offered.[19]

R. 345 (1887), " Human opinion is so various and discordant, and what it really is, is so difficult of proof, that the law allows great latitude of statements which are properly traceable to it; " Gordon v. Parmelee, 2 Allen (84 Mass.) 212 (1861); Gordon v. Butler, 105 U. S. 553, 26 L. Ed. 1166 (1881).

[16] Strand v. Griffith, 97 Fed. 854, 38 C. C. A. 444 (1899); Stewart v. Stearns, 63 N. H. 99, 56 Am. R. 496 (1884); cf. Martin v. Jordan, 60 Me. 531 (1872), false statement, as to the amount of hay cut the previous year, on the land sold by the defendant to the plaintiff; Savage v. Stevens, 126 Mass. 207 (1879), false statements as to the location and condition of a farm.

[17] Andrews v. Jackson, 168 Mass. 266, 47 N. E. 412, 60 Am. St. R. 390, 37 L. R. A. 402 (1897); Simar v. Canady, 53 N. Y. 298, 13 Am. R. 523 (1873).

[18] Cole v. Smith, 26 Col. 506, 58 Pac. 1068 (1899); Hemmer v. Cooper, 8 Allen (90 Mass.) 334 (1864); Holbrook v. Connor, 60 Me. 578, 11 Am. R. 212 (1872), see dissenting opinion; Bishop v. Small, 63 Me. 12 (1874).

[19] Braley v. Powers, 92 Me. 203, 42 At. 362 (1898): An action for deceit was sustained, for false statements as to the cost of producing buckles, under a patent which defendant sold plaintiff; Manning v. Albee, 11 Allen (93 Mass.) 520, 92 Am. Dec. 736 (1866): The statement was that certain bonds were selling in the market at a given price; Way v. Ryther, 165 Mass. 226, 42 N. E. 1128 (1896): Statement, that the property was billed to the defendant at a certain price, together with the false statement that he could not find the bill, may constitute deceit. " We have no disposition," said the court, " to extend the decisions in favor of vendors' representations beyond the limit to which they have

Other courts do not hesitate to declare that the statement of a vendor that he paid or had been offered a certain price for the property he sells, is a statement of fact; and if the purchaser, without knowing or having reason to know what price was paid or offered, relies upon the false statement to his injury, he is entitled to maintain an action for deceit.[20] They also declare, that false statements as to value may often take the form of false assertions of fact, and thus amount to actionable deceit;[21] especially where they are grossly and palpably false, or where their utterer has better means of knowing their truth or falsity than has the one to whom they are made.[22] So, inducing one to sell goods at a certain price, by the false statement of the purchaser, that the seller's rivals in trade offer the same goods at such a price, is a fraud.[23]

Statement as to a Person's Credit. This, undoubtedly, involves to some extent an expression of opinion, but ordinarily it contains an assertion of fact. If the defendant is asked, by one who is considering whether to give financial credit to him or to a third person, for the pecuniary standing of himself or of the third person, and answers that he is a person " safely to be trusted and given credit to in that respect,"[24] or that he is " as good as any

---

gone;" Kilgore v. Bruce, 166 Mass. 136, 44 N. E. 108 (1896). Representation, that all the stock, which the defendant was selling, was being sold at the price asked of the plaintiff.

[20] Dorr v. Cory, 108 Ia. 725, 78 N. W. 682 (1899); Johnson v. Cavitt, 114 Ia. 183, 80 N. W. 256 (1901); Stony Creek Woolen Co. v. Smalley, 111 Mich. 321, 69 N. W. 722 (1896); Conlan v. Roemer, 52 N. J. L. 53, 18 At. 858 (1889); Fairchild v. McMahon, 139 N. Y. 290, 34 N. E. 779, 36 Am. St. R. 701 (1893).

[21] Wilson v. Nichols, 72 Conn. 173, 43 At. 1052 (1899); Shelton v. Healy, 74 Conn. 265, 50 At. 742 (1901); Leonard v. Springer, 197 111, 532, 64 N. E. 299 (1902), " Where false statements of value are made with an intention that

they shall be understood as statements of fact, and not as expressions of opinion, they will constitute fraud; " Coulter v. Clark, 160 Ind. 311, 66 N. E. 739 (1903); Bish v. Beatty, 111 Ind. 403, 12 N. E. 523 (1887); statement that certain notes were as good as government bonds; Smith v. Countryman, 30 N. Y. 655 (1864); Rothschild v. Mack, 115 N. Y. 1, 21 N. E. 726 (1889); Assertion that a note was as good as the Bank of England.

[22] Hedin v. Minn. etc. Ints., 62 Minn. 146, 64 N. W. 158, 62 Am. St. R. 146, 35 L. R. A. 417 (1895) and cases cited in the note at pp. 418, 427-429.

[23] Smith Kline & Co. v. Smith, 166 Pa. 563, 31 At. 343 (1895).

[24] Pasley v. Freeman, 3 D. & E. 51, 1 R. R. 638 (1789).

man in the country for that sum," [25] he certainly assumes to state a matter of fact. If his statement was consciously false, was made for the purpose of inducing the plaintiff to give credit, and such credit was given to the plaintiff's harm, most courts have not hesitated to hold him liable for deceit.[26] In England, and in some of our jurisdictions, statutes have been passed providing that no action shall be brought upon such representations, unless made in writing and signed by the party to be charged therewith.[27]

Misrepresentation of Law. The general rule, upon this topic, is that " a false or mistaken representation of what the law is upon an admitted state of facts is no basis of an action in deceit, especially when there are no confidential relations between the parties." [28] Or to put it in another form, " A statement of opinion upon a question of law, when the facts are equally well known to both the parties, cannot constitute a false representation or deceit."[29]

---

[25] Upton v. Vail, 6 Johns. 181, 5 Am. Dec. 210 (1810); Boyd's Executors v. Browne, 6 Pa. 310 (1847); Robbins v. Barton, 50 Ks. 120, 31 Pac. 686 (1892).

[26] Endsley v. Johns, 120 Ill. 469, 60 Am. R. 572 (1887); Patten v. Gurney, 17 Mass. 182, 9 Am. Dec. 141 (1821); Morehouse v. Yeager, 71 N. Y. 594, (1877); Gainsville Natl. Bank v. Bamberger, 77 Tex. 48, 13 S. W. 959 (1890); Lang v. Lee, 3 Rand, (Va.) 410 (1825).

In Rhode Island, the court is not inclined to hold the defendant for statements about his own financial standing as strictly as for those about a third person. Lyons v. Briggs, 14 R. I. 222, 57 Am. R. 372 (1893); White & Co. v. Fitch, 19 R. I. 687, 36 At. 425 (1897); Vermont is not disposed to hold a person answerable in deceit for false assertions as to credit. Fisher v. Brown, 1 Tyler 387, 4 Am. Dec. 726; Jude v. Woodburn, 27 Vt. 415 (1855). See also Savage v. Jackson, 19 Ga. 305

(1856), criticising Pasley v. Freeman, 3 D. & E. 51 (1789).

[27] Lord Tenderten's Act, 9 Geo. IV. ch. 14, § 6 (1829); Nevada Bank v. Portland Natl. Bank, 59 Fed. 338 (1894); applying the statute of Oregon;—1 Hill's Code, § 786, p. 594; Kimball v. Comstock, 14 Gray (80 Mass.) 508 (1860), applying the Massachusetts statute.

[28] Gormley v. Gym. Ass'n., 55 Wis. 350, 13 N. W. 242 (1882); defendant, when leasing a hall to plaintiff, said, " If you lease the hall you can retail liquors, etc., at the bar, under licenses held by me." Plaintiff was bound to know that such licenses would not protect him; Fish v. Cleland, 33 Ill. 238, 243 (1864); Thompson v. Phoenix Ins. Co., 75 Me. 55, 46 Am. R. 357 (1883); Ins. Co. v. Reed, 33 O. St. 283, 294 (1877).

[29] Mutual Life Co. v. Phinney, 178 U. S. 327, 20 Sup. Ct. 906 (1900); Upton v. Tribelock, 91 U. S. 45, 50 (1875); Davis v. Betz, 66 Al. 206,

Where, however, there is a misrepresentation of fact as well as of law,[30] or where "any peculiar relationship of trust or confidence exists between the parties, and one avails himself of such a trust or confidence to mislead the plaintiff by a misrepresentation as to the legal effect of the transaction," we have an exception to the general rule stated above, and an action for deceit may lie.[31] Perhaps, the distinction between a misrepresentation of law, and a misrepresentation of mixed law and fact, has never been stated more clearly than by a learned English judge [32] in these words: "A misrepresentation of law is this, when you state the facts, and state a conclusion of law, so as to distinguish between facts and law. The man who knows the facts is taken to know the law. But when you state that as a fact which no doubt involves, as most facts do, a conclusion of law, that is still a statement of fact and not a statement of law."

Knowledge of the Untruth.   Bad faith is the very essence of the common law tort of deceit. Accordingly, it is generally held that the plaintiff, who asks damages for deceit, must show, that the defendant knew that the false statement complained of was untrue, or that he made it without belief in its truth, or recklessly, careless whether it was true or false. It is not enough for him to show that the statement was false, and was made negligently, or without reasonable ground for belief in its truth. He must go further and show that it was actually fraudulent, that is, that the defendant did not have an honest belief in its truth.[33]

---

210 (1880); Platt v. Scott, 6 Blackf. (Ind.) 389, 39 Am. Dec. 436 (1843); Mayhew v. Phoenix Ins. Co., 23 Mich. 105 (1871); Starr v. Bennett, 5 Hill (N. Y.) 303 (1843).

[30] Westervelt v. Demarest, 46 N. J. L. 37, 50 Am. R. 400 (1884); Moreland v. Atchison, 19 Tex. 303 (1857); Hubbard v. McLean, 115 Wis. 9, 90 N. W. 1077 (1902).

[31] Townsend v. Cowles, 31 Al. 428, 436, (1858); "So, if the plaintiff was in fact ignorant of the law, and defendant took advantage of such ignorance, to mislead him by a false statement of the law, it would constitute a fraud;" Cooke v. Nathan,

16 Barb. (N. Y.) 342 (1853); Hirshfield v. London Ry., 2 Q. B. D. 1, 46 L. J. Q. B. 94 (1876).

[32] Jessel, M. R., in Eaglesfield v. Londonberry, L. R. 4, Ch. D. 693, 702, 35 L. T. 822 (1876).

[33] Derry v. Peek, 14 App. Cases, 337, 58 L. J. Ch. 864 (1889), reversing Peek v. Derry, 37 Ch. D. 541, 57 L. J. Ch. 347 (1887). In Angus v. Clifford, (1891), 2 Ch. 449, 463, 60 L. J. Ch. 443, Lindley, L. J. said; "Speaking broadly of Peek v. Derry, I take it, that it has settled, once and for all, the controversy which was well known to have given rise to very considerable difference

It should be borne in mind, however, that evidence of negligence on the part of defendant in making the false statement, as well as the want of reasonable ground for his belief in its truth, is always admissible in an action for deceit. To quote from the principal opinion in Peek v. Derry; [84] " I desire to say distinctly that when a false statement has been made, the question whether there were reasonable grounds for believing it, and what were the means of knowledge in the possession of the person making it, are most weighty matters for consideration. The ground upon which an alleged belief was founded is a most important test of its reality. I can conceive many cases where the fact, that an alleged belief was destitute of all reasonable foundation, would suffice of itself to convince the Court that it was not really entertained, and that the representation was a fraudulent one. So, too, although means of knowledge are a very different thing from knowledge, if I thought that a person making a false statement had shut his eyes to the facts, or purposely abstained from inquiring into them, I should hold that honest belief was absent, and that he was just as fraudulent as if he had knowingly stated what was false."

On the other hand, it is admissible for the defendant to give evidence, tending to show his honest belief in the truth of the statement, which was in fact false, and even to show the meaning, which he actually intended to convey by equivocal language. [35]

of opinion, as to whether an action for negligent representation, as distinguished from fraudulent representation, could be maintained. There was considerable authority that it could, and there was considerable authority that it could not."

Wilman v. Mizer, 60 Ark. 281, 30 S. W. 31 (1895); Watson v. Jones, 41 Fla. 241, 25 So. 678 (1899); Boddy v. Henry, 113 Ia. 462, 85 N. W. 771, 53 L. R. A. 769 (1901); Wilkins v. Standard Oil Co., 70 N. J. L. —, 57 At. 258 (1904); Daly v. Wise, 132 N. Y. 306, 312, 30 N. E. 837, 16 L. R. A. 236 (1892); Johnson v. Cate, 75 Vt. 100, 53 At. 329, (1902); Cooper v. Schlesinger, 111 U. S. 148, 152, 4 Sup. Ct. 360, 28 L. Ed. 382

(1883); Iron Co. v. Bamford, 150 U. S. 665, 14 Sup. Ct. 219, 37 L. Ed. 1215 (1893); Simon v. Goodyear Co., 105 Fed. 573, 581 (1900).

[34] Herschell L., in Derry v. Peek, 14 App. Cas. 337, 370, 58 L. J. Ch. 864 (1889).

[35] Angus v. Clifford, (1891) 2 Ch. 541, 57 L. J. Ch. 347, opinion of Lindley L. J.; Nash v. Minn. etc., Co., 163 Mass. 574, 40 N. E. 1039, 28 L. R. A. 753, 47 Am. St. R. 489 (1895), " Inasmuch as the question involved is what was his state of mind, and his actual intent as distinguished from his apparent intent, he is entitled to explain his language as best he can, if it is susceptible of explanation, and to tes-

Other Remedies Available for Negligent Misrepresentation.
Many of the courts, which hold most steadfastly to the doctrine that
actual fraud must be shown to sustain an action for deceit, are careful to point out, that the law affords other remedies to the victim of
innocent misrepresentation. He may maintain an action for breach
of warranty,[36] or for rescission of the contract,[37] or even for damages caused by the defendant's negligent discharge of some duty
owing to the plaintiff.[38]

In some jurisdictions, he is allowed to maintain an action for
deceit, wherever the misrepresentation is of a character which would
entitle him to rescission of the transaction.[39] In others, the rule is
declared to be that " if a statement of fact which is susceptible of
actual knowledge is made as of one's own knowledge, and is false,
it may be made a foundation of an action of deceit, without further
proof of an actual intent to deceive." [40]

Intended to Induce Plaintiff. Not only must the plaintiff
show that the defendant dishonestly made a false statement of fact,
but there must be evidence that he made it with the intention of
inducing the plaintiff to act upon it. " A mere naked falsehood is

---

tify what was in his mind in reference to the subject to which the
alleged fraud relates. In this respect
his expressions, whether spoken or
written, are not dealt with in the
same way, as when the question is,
what contract has been made between two persons, who were mut-
ually relying upon the language
used in their agreements ";Kountze
v. Kennedy, 147 N. Y. 129, 41 N. E.
414, 49 Am. St. R. 651, 29 L. R. A.
363 (1895).

[36] Kountze v. Kennedy, *supra*,
Stone v. Denny, 4 Met. (45 Mass.)
151, 156 (1842); Watson v. Jones,
41 Fla. 241, 25 So. 678 (1899).

[37] Smith v. Bricker, 86 Ia. 285, 53
N. W. 250 (1892); Foard v. Mc-
Comb, 12 Bush. (75 Ky.) 723
(1877).

[38] Houston v. Thornton, 122 N. C.
365, 29 S. E. 827, 65 Am. St. R. 699
(1898).

[39] Walters v. Eaves, 105 Ga. 584,
32 S. E. 609 (1899); Gerner v.
Mosher, 58 Neb. 135, 78 N. W. 384,
46 L. R. A. 244 (1899); Shea v.
Mabry, 1 Lea (69 Tenn.) 319, 342
(1878), " Culpable negligence in
making false statements, to induce
action by others, is in law equivalent to fraud; " Seale v. Baker, 70
Tex. 283, 7 S. W. 742, 8 Am. St. R.
592 (1888); Hoffman v. Dixon, 105
Wis. 315, 81 N. W. 491 (1900).

[40] Weeks v. Currier, 172 Mass. 53,
55, 51 N. E. 416 (1898), citing with
other cases Chatham Furnace Co.
v. Moffat, 147 Mass. 403, 18 N. E.
168, 9 Am. St. 727 (1888), holding
that " forgetfulness of the existence
of a fact after a former knowledge,
or a mere belief on the subject, will
not excuse a statement of actual
knowledge; " but see Nash v. Minn.
etc. Co., 163 Mass. 574 at page 578.

not enough to give a cause of action; the falsehood must have been told with the intention that it should be acted upon by the party injured."[41] It is not necessary, however, that the falsehood be communicated directly to the plaintiff by the defendant. It is enough that the false statement was intended to reach the plaintiff and operate upon his mind.[42] One, who puts into circulation a bill of exchange, with a forged acceptance, thereby makes a representation of its genuineness to every one to whom it is presented.[43] One, who makes a false statement of his financial standing to a mercantile agency, intends that it shall be repeated by the agency to third persons who may be interested in his credit.[44] Whether a false statement by the directors of a financial institution, contained in a report which the law requires to be filed in a public office, may subject them, or the corporation for which they are acting, to a suit for deceit, should depend upon the facts of the case. If the statute requires this statement for the benefit of all, who may deal with the institution, or purchase its stock, then, the statement must be deemed intended to influence any of that class.[45] Even if the statute has no such object, and requires the statement only for the information of

<hr />

[41] Langridge v. Levy, 2 M. & W. 519 (1837), citing Pasley v. Freeman, 3 D. & E. 51 (1789); Thorp v. Smith, 18 Wash. 277, 51 Pac. 381 1897); Steiner Brothers v. Clisby, 103 Al. 181, 192, 15 So. 612 (1893). " If the false representation is made to A to induce him to part with his money, and he does part with it, A must sue; but if made to him to induce B to part with his, and B is thereby induced to do so, he and not A is the party injured who may maintain the action," following Wells v. Cook, 16 O. St. 67, 88 Am. Dec. 436 (1865).

[42] Comm. v. Call, 21 Pick. (38 Mass.) 515, 523, 32 Am. Dec. 284 (1839); Henry v. Dennis, 95 Me. 24, 49 At. 58, 85 Am. St. R. 365 (1901).

[43] Polhill v. Walter, 3 B. & Ad. 114, 37 R. R. 344 (1832); same principle applied, in Denton v. G. N. Ry., 5 E.

& B. 850, 25 L. J. Q. B. 129 (1856), to false statements in a railroad time table.

[44] Eaton, Cole & Co. v. Avery, 83 N. Y. 31, 38 Am. R. 389 (1880); Tindle v. Birkett, 171 N. Y. 520, 64 N. E. 210 (1902); Hinchman v. Weeks, 85 Mich. 535, 48 N. W. 790 (1891); Gainsville Nat. Bank v. Bamberger, 77 Tex. 48, 13 S. W. 959 (1890).

[45] Gerner v. Mosher, 58 Neb. 135, 78 N. W. 384, 46 L. R. A. 244 (1899); cf. Bedford v. Bagshaw, 4 H. & N. 538, 29 L. J. Ex. 59 (1859), statements made to a committee of the London Stock Exchange; Peek v. Gurney, L. R. 6 H. L. 377, 43 L. J. Ch. 19 (1873), false statements, intended to deceive only the original allottees of shares, and not those who bought them from such allottees.

public officials, the question still remains, should the defendant have foreseen that reliance would be placed upon such a statement by the plaintiff, who is not a public official, but a creditor of the corporation or a purchaser of its stock? The prevailing view is, that such a consequence is too remote, and that the plaintiff has no action for deceit.[46]

Corrupt Motive Unnecessary. If the defendant makes the false statement, with the intention of inducing the plaintiff to act upon it, and he does so act to his harm, the motive of the defendant becomes immaterial.[47] Misrepresentations of this character are frequently made from inconsiderate good nature, prompted by a desire to benefit a third person and without a view of advancing the utterer's own interests. But the motive by which he was actuated does not enter into the inquiry. If he made representations productive of loss to another, knowing such representations to be false, he is responsible as for a fraudulent deceit."[48]

Inducing Plaintiff to Act. If the false statement of fact, knowingly made by the defendant, really induces the plaintiff to act upon it to his harm, the defendant may escape liability for deceit by showing that the assertion was of such a character as not to justify the plaintiff in placing confidence in it. It is quite clear that a dealer in spectacles has no right to rely on the statement by the manufacturer, that the glasses were of a superior quality, and treated by a chemical process which was known only to a person in the employ

---

[46] Hunnewell v. Duxbury, 154 Mass. 286, 28 N. E. 267, 13 L. R. A. 733 (1891); Merchant's Nat. Bank v. Armstrong, 65 Fed. 932 (1895); Hindman v. 1st Nat. Bank, 86 Fed. 1013 (1898), s. c., 112 Fed. 931, 941, 50 C. C. A. 623 (1902); cf. English cases in last note; also, Clerk and Lindsell, on Torts (2 Ed.) pp. 466-469; McCracken v. West, 17 O. 16 (1848), holding that if a person write a letter to another, desiring him to introduce the bearer to such merchants as he may desire, and describing him as a man of property and the bearer does not deliver it to the addressee, but uses it to obtain credit elsewhere, the person so giving credit cannot maintain an action for deceit, though the representations in the letter are untrue;" Barry v. Crosky, 2 Johns. & H. 1 (1861).

[47] Pasley v. Freeman, 3 D. & E. 51 (1798); Foster v. Charles, 7 Bing. 105 (1830); Rothmiller v. Stein, 143 N. Y. 581, 38 N. E. 718, 26 L. R. A. 148 (1894).

[48] Boyd's Exec. v. Browne, 6 Pa. 310 (1847); Allen v. Addington, 7 Wend. (N. Y.) 9 (1831); N. Y. Imp. Co. v. Chapman, 118 N. Y. 288, 292, 23 N. E. 187 (1890); Endsley v. Johns, 120 Ill. 479, 12 N. E. 247, 60 Am. R. 572 (1887).

of the company; that this process imparted a quality to the glass that made it fit the eye indefinitely; that the glasses once fitted would always adapt themselves to the eye.[49]

Some courts, as we have seen, treat false assertions concerning the cost of property, or of the price paid or offered for it, as statements, so commonly made by persons having property for sale, that the buyer has no right to rely and act upon them.[50]   Other courts [51] declare that wherever the interests of the plaintiff and defendant are adverse, it is the duty of the former to distrust the truthfulness of statements made by the latter.

As a rule, however, the plaintiff is not to be turned out of court, because a shrewd, keen, skeptical bargainer would not have been deluded by the intentionally false statement of the defendant.   " It is as much actionable fraud willfully to deceive a credulous person, with an improbable falsehood, as it to deceive a cautious, sagacious person with a plausible one." [52]   Or, in the language of another court, " The design of the law is to protect the weak and credulous, as well as those whose vigilance and sagacity enable them to protect themselves. * * * The law is not blind to the fact that communities are composed of individuals of several degrees of intelligence and capacity." [53]   Or, again, " No rogue should enjoy his ill-gotten plunder for the simple reason that his victim is, by chance, a fool." [54]

Means of Knowledge Immaterial.   While the law requires men in ordinary business transactions to use their wits, and not to confide implicitly in trader's talk on the part of one whose business

[49] Hirschberg Optical Co. v. Michaelson, (Minn.) 95 N. W. 461 (1901).

[50] Vernon v. Keys, 12 East 632, 4 Taunt. 488, 11 R. R. 499, (1810). Lord Mansfield is reported as saying that a purchaser is at liberty to do " what every seller in this town does every day, who tells every falsehood he can to induce the purchaser to purchase; " Holbrook v. Connor, 60 Me. 578 (1872), cf. Whiting v. Price, 169 Mass. 576, 48 N. E. 772, 61 Am. St. R. 307 (1897), holding that the representation, that the bond in question was secured by particular property worth half a million dollars, could not be excused as one of those generalities, which, whether true or not, are to be expected from a man who wants to sell his goods.

[51] Aetna Ins. Co. v. Reed, 33 O. St. 283 (1877).

[52] Barnot v. Frederick, 78 Wis. 1, 47 N. W. 6 (1890).

[53] Ingalls v. Miller, 121 Ind. 188, 22 N. E. 995 (1889.)

[54] Chamberlin v. Fuller, 59 Vt. 256, 9 At. 832 (1886).

interests are antagonistic to theirs,[55] it is not inclined to ignore or protect positive, intentional fraud, successfully practiced upon even the simple-minded and unwary. It is not disposed to look with favor upon the defense that the plaintiff was guilty of contributory negligence, in not presuming that the defendant's statement was false, and untrustworthy.[56] Even when the defendant refers the plaintiff to a source of information, which would disclose the falsity of his statement, the plaintiff is not bound to avail himself of that source. He is entitled to stand upon the defendant's assurance of its truthfulness.[57]

Of course, if he does pursue the investigation, suggested by the defendant, and acts upon its results, he cannot afterwards insist that he relied upon the defendant's representations.[58] Nor can he be heard to say, that he was induced by the false representation to act to his harm, where he discovers the fraud before he acts.[59] Nor will a deliberate falsehood avail him, though made by the defendant, with a view to deceiving him, if it was not known to him when he acted,[60]

---

[55] Slaughter's Admin. v. Gerson, 13 Wall. (80 U. S.) 379 (1871); Salem India Rubber Co. v. Adams, 23 Pick. (40 Mass.) 256, 265 (1839); Long v. Warren, 68 N. Y. 426 (1877).

[56] Graham v. Thompson, 55 Ark. 296, 18 S. W. 58 (1892); Oakes v. Miller, 11 Col. App. 374, 55 Pac. 193 (1898); Maxfield v. Schwartz, 45 Minn. 150, 47 N. W. 448, 10 L. R. A. 606 (1890); Whiting v. Price, 172 Mass. 240, 51 N. E. 1084, 70 Am. St. R. 262 (1898); Arnold v. Teel, 182 Mass. 1 64 N. E. 413 (1902); Warder v. Whitish, 77 Wis. 430, 46 N. W. 540 (1890); Strand v. Griffith, 97 Fed. 854, 38 C. C. A. 444 (1897); Reynell v. Sprye, 1 Deg. M. & G. 660, 21 L. J. Ch. 633 (1852).

[57] Wheeler v. Baars, 33 Fla. 696, 15 So. 584 (1894); Thorne v. Prentiss, 83 Ill. 99 (1876); David v. Park, 103 Mass. 501 (1870); Holst v. Stewart, 161 Mass. 516, 37 N. E. 755 (1894); Redding v. Wright, 49 Minn. 322, 51 N. W. 1056 (1891); Cotrill v. Krum,

100 Mo. 397, 13 S. W. 753 (1890); Albany Savings Bank v. Burdick, 87 N. Y. 40 (1881); Blacknall v. Rowland, 108 N. C. 554, 13 S. E. 191 (1891); Castenholz v. Heller, 82 Wis. 30, 51 N. W. 432 (1892).

[58] Enfield v. Colburn, 63 N. H. 218 (1884); Halls v. Thompson, 1 Sm. & M. (Miss.) 443 (1843).

[59] Selway v. Fogg, 5 M. & W. 83, 8 L. J. Ex. 199 (1839); Kingman v. Stoddard, 85 Fed. 740, 57 U. S. App. 397, 29 C. C. A. 413 (1898); Fitzpatrick v. Flannagan, 106 U. S. 648, 660, 1 Sup. Ct. 369 (1882); Schmidt v. Mesmer, 116 Cal. 267, 48 Pac. 54 (1897); McEacheran v. Western etc. Co., 97 Mich. 479, 56 N. W. 860 (1893); Vernol v. Vernol, 63 N. Y. 45 (1875).

[60] Horsfall v. Thomas, 1 H. & C. 90, 31 L. J. Ex. 322 (1862), a defect in a gun was artfully plugged and concealed, but the gun was bought without inspection; Brackett v. Griswold, 112 N. Y. 454, 20 N. E. 376 (1899).

nor if, although it were known to him, it did not cause him damage.[61]

Need Not be Sole Inducement. While the plaintiff, in an action of deceit, is bound to show that he had a right to rely and did rely upon the defendant's false statement and was damaged as a proximate consequence thereof, it is not necessary for him to show that the falsehood was the sole inducement to his action, nor even the predominant motive. It is enough that the falsehood had a material influence upon him, although it operated in connection with other motives or inducements.[62]

Functions of Court and Jury. The rule upon this subject has been laid down as follows:[63] " Most of the questions involved in an action for deceit are questions of fact for the jury. Whether the defendant made the alleged false representation, and whether, if he made it, he knew it to be false, and whether the plaintiff was ignorant of its falsity, and whether he relied upon it, and was thereby damaged, are undoubtedly questions of fact for the jury. But, assuming all these facts to be proved, the materiality of the representation is a question of law for the court." Applying the rule to the facts of the case then before the court, it was held that the false statement by the defendant, that as agent of the company, whose stock he was offering to the plaintiff, he had sold several hundred shares to specified persons for the price which he named to the plaintiff, and which the latter paid, was a material statement of fact and legally sufficient to maintain the suit, if the other elements of fraud were proved.

False Statement by Agent or Servant. Whether an action of deceit will lie against a morally innocent principal, whose agent or servant has fraudulently deceived the plaintiff, has been much discussed. Some judges have held that, as conscious wrongdoing on

---

[61] Nye v. Merriam, 35 Vt. 438 (1862); Freeman v. Venner, 120 Mass. 424 (1876).

[62] Tatton v. Wade, 18 C. B. R. 371, 25 L. J. C. P. 240 (1856); Matthews v. Bliss, 22 Pick. (39 Mass.) 48 (1839); Light v. Jacobs, 183 Mass. 206, 66 N. E. 799 (1903); Morgan v. Skiddy, 62 N. Y. 319 (1875); Bristol v. Bristol Water Works, 19 R. I.

618, 35 At. 884, 49 Am. St R. 794 (1896).

[63] Caswell v. Hunton, 87 Me. 277, 32 At. 899 (1895); Polland v. Brownell, 131 Mass. 138 (1881); Powers v. Fowler, 157 Mass. 318, 32 N. E. 166 (1892); Estell v. Myers, 54 Miss. 174, 185 (1876); *accord.* Davis v. Davis, 97 Mich. 419, 56 N. W. 774 (1893), holds that the materiality is for the jury.

the part of the defendant is of the essence of the tort of deceit, the action is not maintainable against a principal who has not authorized or ratified the agent's falsehood, and who is not morally culpable with respect to it. The victim may sue the agent for deceit, say the judges, but his remedies at law against the principal are limited to the rescission of any contract induced by it, and the recovery of any money paid, or property transferred to the principal, or of which he has had the benefit.[64]

The prevailing view is, however, that the principal is liable for the deceit of his agent or servant, as he is for any other tort of such representative. Provided the agent or servant made the false representation in the course of his employment,[65] the master is liable though he may not have authorized it, or known that it was made, or be morally responsible for it. Having put the agent or servant "in his place to do that class of acts, he must be answerable for the manner, in which the representative has conducted himself in doing the business, which it was the act of the master to place him in." [66]

§ 2. SLANDER OF TITLE.

Nature of the Tort. This wrong differs from Deceit in that the falsehood is intended not to induce the plaintiff to act to his

---

[64] Udell v. Atherton, 7 H. & N. 172, 30 L. J. Ex. 337 (1861); Western Bank of Scotland v. Addie, L. R. 1 H. L. Sc. 145 (1867); Kennedy v. McKay, 43 N. J. L. 288 (1881).

[65] Taylor v. Commercial Bank, 174 N. Y. 181, 66 N. E. 726, 95 Am. St. R. 564 (1903), holding that a bank cashier is not acting within the scope of his authority in making a representation as to a customer's solvency.

[66] Barwick v. Eng. Joint Stock Bk., L. R. 2 Ex. 265, 36 L. J. Ex. 147 (1867); Swire v. Francis, 3 App. Cas. 113, 47 L. J. P. C. 18 (1877); Strang v. Bradner, 114 U. S. 555, 5 Sup. Ct. 1038, 29 L. Ed. 248 (1884); Hindman v. 1st. Nat. Bank, 112 Fed. 931, 50 C. C. A. 623 (1902); Am. Nat. Bk. v. Denver, 25 Col. 367, 55 Pac. 1090 (1898); Wheeler v. Baars, 33 Fla. 696, 15 So. 584 (1894); Rhoda v. Annis, 75 Me. 17, 46 Am. R. 354 (1883); Haskell v. Starbird, 152 Mass. 117, 25 N. E. 14, 23 Am. St. R. 809 (1890); Busch v. Wilcox, 82 Mich. 336, 47 N. W. 328, 21 Am. St. R. 563 (1890); N. Y. Imp. Co. v. Chapman, 118 N. Y. 288, 23 N. E. 187 (1890); Chester v. Dickerson, 54 N. Y. 1 (1873); Brundage v. Mellon, 5 N. D. 72, 63 N. W. 209 (1895); Peckham Iron Co. v. Harper, 41 O. St. 100 (1884); Erie City Iron Works v. Barber, 106 Pa. 125 (1884).

harm, but to induce third persons to refrain from buying the plaintiff's property or from patronizing his business. It takes its name from the form which it most frequently assumed in early English law, that of slandering the plaintiff's title to goods [67] or to land,[68] for the purpose of preventing his sale of them. At present, however, it assumes a variety of forms and may be said to consist in the publication of false statements, disparaging the title or property interests of the plaintiff, with the intention of causing him damage and resulting in actual damage to him.[69]

Falsity and Malice. These are not to be inferred from the fact of publication, as they are in the case of personal defamation,[70] but must be established by evidence.[71] There is some authority for the proposition that one, who disparages the title of another to his damage, is liable therefor, although he did not intend any injury;[72] but this view appears to have originated in the disposition of certain

[67] In the Court Baron, (Selden Soc. Pub. Vol. 4) at p. 130 (1320) judgment is noted against "Alice Balle (3 d.) for that she defamed the lord's corn, whereby the other purchasers forebore to buy the lord's corn, to the lord's damage." At p. 136 (1323), "It is found by inquest that John Curteys and John Cordhant have slandered the hedge of Hugh Seld in the fen, whereby the said Hugh has lost the sale of the said hedge to his damage at 2s."

[68] Mildmay's Case, 1 Coke 177b. (1584); Gerard v. Dickerson, Cro. Eliz. 196 (1589); Pennyman v. Robanks, Cro. Eliz. 427 (1596).

[69] Pater v. Baker, 3 C. B. 868, 16 L. J. C. P. 124, 32 E. C. L. 161 (1847); Burkett v. Griffith, 90 Cal. 532, 27 Pac. 527, 25 Am. St. R. 151 (1891); Webb v. Cecil, 9 B. Mon. (48 Ky.) 198, 48 Am. Dec. 423 (1848); Kendall v. Stone, 5 N. Y. 15, 18 (1851); Wier v. Allen, 51 N. H. 177 (1871), false statement that a breeding stallion was diseased; Paul v.

Halferty, 63 Pa. 46 (1869), false assertion that ore in plaintiff's land would soon run out; Ratcliffe v. Evans, (1892) 2 Q. B. 524, 61 L. J. Q. B. 535, false statement that plaintiff had ceased to carry on his business.

[70] Supra, Chap. X. But the complaint neeα not set out words, used by the defendant, that are actionable. It is enough that the defendant's conduct intimidated customers from buying plaintiff's goods by threats of prosecution; McElwee v. Blackwell, 94 N. C. 261 (1886).

[71] Hatchard v. Mège, 18 Q. B. D. 771, 56 L. J. Q. B. 397 (1887); Steward v. Young, L. R. 5 C. P. 122, 39 L. J. C. P. 85 (1870); Daniel v. Baca, 2 Cal. 326, 56 Am. Dec. 339 (1852); Cardon v. McCormall, 120 N. C. 461, 27 S. E. 109 (1897).

[72] Ross v. Pynes, 3 Call (5 Va.) 568, Wythe 69 (1790)), "R. though he is believed not to have designed any injury, ought to make reparation for the loss."

judges to treat slander of title, as a species of personal defamation, and has long been thoroughly discredited.[73]

There is also some authority for the proposition that a rival trader is guilty of slandering the title, whenever he disparages the property of his competitors, by false assertions of the superiority of his own.[74] Most courts, however, have repudiated this doctrine on the ground that it " would open a very wide door to litigation, and might expose every man, who said his goods were better than another's, to the risk of an action." [75] Dealing with a case of this character, Lord Chancellor Herschell wisely remarked: " That this sort of puffing advertisement is in use is notorious; and we see rival cures advertised for particular ailments. The court would then be bound to inquire, in an action brought, whether this ointment, or this pill, better cured the disease which it was alleged to cure—whether a particular article of food was in this respect, or that, better than another. Indeed, the courts of law would be turned into a machinery for advertising rival productions, by obtaining a judicial determination which of the two was the better." [76]

Rival Claimants to Property. Where the false statement in disparagement of the plaintiff's title is made by one, who believes in good faith that he has a lawful claim upon the property in question, the occasion is privileged, and he is not liable for the damage which his misrepresentation causes to the plaintiff.[77] If, however,

[73] Pitt v. Donovan, 1 M. & S. 639, 14 R. R. 535 (1813); Pater v. Baker, 3 C. B. 868, 16 L. J. C. P. 124, 32 E. C. L. 161 (1847); Hill v. Ward, 13 Al. 310 (1848); Walkley v. Bostwick, 49 Mich. 374, 13 N. W. 780 (1882); Harrison v. Howe, 109 Mich. 476, 67 N. W. 527 (1896); Andrew v. Deshler, 45 N. J. L. 167 (1883); Hovey v. Rubber Tip Co., 57 N. Y. 119, 15 Am. R. 470 (1874); Hopkins v. Drowne, 21 R. I. 20, 41 At. 567 (1898).

[74] Western Counties Co. v. Lawes Chem. Co., L. R. 9 Ex. 218, 43 L. J. Ex. 171 (1874).

[75] Evans v. Harlow, 5 Q. B. 624, 13 L. J. Q. B. 130 (1843); Tobias v. Harland, 4 Wend. (N. Y.) 537, 541

(1830); Johnson v. Hitchcock, 15 Johns (N. Y.) 185 (1818).

[76] White v. Mellen, (1895) App. Cases. 154, 165, 64 L. J. Ch. 308.

[77] Hill v. Ward, 13 Al. 310 (1848); McDaniel v. Baca, 2 Cal. 326, 56 Am. Dec. 339 (1852); Everett Piano Co. v. Brent, 60 Ill. App. 372 (1895); Stark v. Chetwood, 5 Ks. 141 (1869); Duncan v. Griswold, 92 Ky. 546, 18 S. W. 354 (1892); Gent v. Lynch, 23 Md. 58, 87 Am. Dec. 558 (1865); Swan v. Tappan, 5 Cush. (59 Mass.) 104 (1849); John C. Lovell Co. v. Houghton, 116 N. Y. 520, 23 N. E. 1066, 6 L. R. A. 363 (1889); Feiten v. Milwaukee, 47 Wis. 494, 2 N. W. 1148 (1879).

his claim is a sham, and his falsehood is intended to injure the plaintiff and not to benefit his own legitimate interests, he is liable.[78] While actual malice on the part of the defendant must be shown,[79] it is not necessary to give direct proof of an intention to impair the value of the property. It is enough to show, (at least to take the case to the jury on the question of fraudulent intention,) that the defendant's false statements were recklessly uttered, in disregard of the plaintiff's rights.[80]

Slander of Title and Damage. The rule has long been settled that " in the action for slander of title, there must be an express allegation of some particular damage resulting to the plaintiff from such slander." [81] Accordingly, if the plaintiff makes no such allegation, or, having made it, fails to prove some particular damage which is the proximate result of the slander, he must fail in his suit.[82] Nor will it avail him to aver that the statement complained of was " false, scandalous, malicious and defamatory." [83] These are but epithets, and the law requires the plaintiff to show, in what respect he has been actually harmed, by the defendant's disparagement of his property.

---

[78] Walden v. Peters, 2 Rob. (La.) 331, 38 Am. Dec. 213 (1842) ; Chesebro v. Powers, 78 Mich. 472, 44 N. W. 290 (1889) ; Gore v. Condon, 87 Md. 368, 739, 39 At. 1042, 46 L. R. A. 382, 67 Am. St. R. 352 (1898).

[79] Andrew v. Deshler, 45 N. J. L. 167 (1883) ; Squires v. Wason Mfg. Co., 182 Mass. 137, 65 N. E. 32 (1902).

[80] McDaniel v. Baca, 2 Cal. 326, 56 Am. Dec. 339 (1852) ; Gott v. Pulsifer, 122 Mass. 235, 23 Am. R. 332 (1877).

[81] Malachy v. Soper, 3 Bing. N. C. 371, 3 Scott 373 (1836) ; Ratcliffe v. Evans (1892) ; 2 Q. B. 524, 532, 61 L. J. Q. B. 535, " The necessity of alleging and proving actual temporal loss, with certainty and precision, in all cases of this sort, has been insisted upon for centuries. But it is an ancient and established rule of pleading, that the question of generality of pleading must depend upon the subject matter."

[82] Burkett v. Griffith, 90 Cal. 532, 27 Pac. 527, 13 L. R. A. 707 and note, 25 Am. St. R. 151 (1891) ; Dooling v. Budget Pub. Co., 144 Mass. 258, 10 N. E. 809, 59 Am. R. 83 (1887) ; Wilson v. Dubois, 35 Minn. 471, 29 N. W. 68 (1886) ; Haney Mfg. Co. v. Perkins, 78 Mich. 1, 43 N. W. 1073, (1889) ; Marlin Fire Arms Co. v. Shields, 171 N. Y. 384, 64 N. E. 163, 59 L. R. A. 310 (1902). In Dodge v. Colby, 108 N. Y. 445, 15 N. E. 703 (1888), the allegations of falsity, malice and special damage were admitted by the demurrer.

[83] Evans v. Harlow, 5 Q. B. 624, 13 L. J. Q. B. 130 (1843) ; White v. Mellen (1895), App. Cas. 154, 64 L. J. Ch. 308,

§ 3. UNFAIR COMPETITION.

The Term is Modern. In a leading English case, the opinion was expressed that " to draw a line between fair and unfair competition, between what is reasonable and unreasonable passes the power of the courts." But the learned judge, who expressed that opinion, was careful to limit it to " mere competition; for I have no doubt," he added, " that it is unlawful and actionable for one man to interfere with another's trade by fraud or misrepresentation." [84] It is interference of this exceptional character that has come to be characterized as " unfair competition."

The term is quite modern. Sir Frederick Pollock assures us that it " is hardly known as yet in English courts." [85] During the last quarter of a century it has come into very general use among judges,[86] and writers upon legal topics, in this country.[87]

The Nature of This Tort. As a wrong, remediable in a common law action for damages, unfair competition consists in intentionally inducing third persons to buy the defendant's property or patronize his business, by false representations that the property or the business is that of the plaintiff.[88] In equity, the term may be

[84] Fry, L. J., in Mogul Steamship Co. v. McGregor, 23 Q. B. D. 598, 626, 58 L. J. Q. B. 465 (1898).

[85] Law of Torts (6 Ed. 1901) 307. There is no reference to the term in the first edition of this work. In the last edition of Kerr, on Fraud and Mistake, (1902), it is used at p. 379, but the cases cited, one of them as late as 1900, do not employ the term. A very interesting article on " The New German Law of Unfair Competition " appeared in the Law Quarterly Rev., p. 156, Vol. 13, (London, 1897).

[86] Lawrence Mfg. Co. v. Tenn. Mfg. Co., 138 U. S. 537, 549, 11 Sup. Ct. 396, 34 L. Ed. 997 (1890); Gray v. Taper-Sleeve Pulley Works, 16 Fed. 436, (1883), " Their complaint is against what they assert to be

unfair competition; " Hostetter Co. v. Martinoni, 110 Fed. 524 (1901); Sterling Remedy Co. v. Spermine Med. Co., 112 Fed. 1000, (1901); Bissell Chilled Plow Works v. T. M. Bissel Plow Co., 121 Fed. 357, 366 (1902); Kyle v. Perfec. Mattress Co., 127 Al. 39, 28 So. 545, 85 Am. St. R. 78 (1899).

[87] " Certain cases analogous to Trade Marks," 4 Harv. Law Rev. 321 (1891); " Prevention of Unfair Competition in Business," 5 Harv. Law Rev. 139 (1891); " Unfair Competition," 10 Harv. L. R. 275 (1896; " Unfair Competition in Trade," note in 30 C. C. A. Reports, 376 (1898); Hopkins, Law of Unfair Trade, (Chicago, 1900).

[88] Sykes v. Sykes, 3 B. & C. 541, 5 D. & R. 292, 3 L. J. K. B. 46

even broader, including conduct of the defendant which is unjustifiably harmful to the plaintiff, but which is not intentionally dishonest.[89] We shall not undertake to discuss, here, the equity side of this subject, as we are dealing with a branch of the common law, and not with equity jurisdiction. If the learned reader would pursue further his investigations of this rapidly expanding topic, he is referred to treatises on Trade Marks, Trade Names, and Unfair Trade.

The tort, now under consideration, is frequently, indeed most commonly brought before the courts, in connection with a claim for the infringement of a trade-mark, but the two are quite distinct. When the plaintiff shows that he has an absolute right to the use of a particular word or words as a trade-mark, an infringement of that right is an invasion of his right of property, wthout regard to the intention of the infringer. Accordingly, he is entitled to at least nominal damages in a suit at law,[90] and to an injunction in equity against the further violation of his right of property.[91] " But where the alleged trade-mark is not in itself a good trade-mark, yet the use of the word has come to denote a particular manufacturer or vendor, relief against unfair competition or perfidious dealing will be awarded, by requiring the use of the word by another to be confined to its primary sense, by such limitations as will prevent misapprehension on the question of origin. In the latter class of cases, such circumstances must be made out as will show wrongful intent in fact, or justify that inference, from the inevitable consequences of the act complained of." [92]

Infringement of Trade-Marks.   When the plaintiff brings his action for violation of his right of property in a trade-mark or

---

(1824); Marsh v. Billings, 7 Cush. (61 Mass.) 322 (1852).

[89] Orr, Ewing & Co. v. Johnston & Co., 40 L. T. N. S. 307 (1879); Vulcan v. Myers, 139 N. Y. 364, 368, 34 N. E. 904 (1893).

[90] Blofield v. Payne, 4 B. & Ad. 410, 1 N. & M. 353, (1833); Thomson v. Winchester, 19 Pick. (36 Mass.) 214 (1837); Morison v. Salmon, 2 M. & G. 385, 2 Scott 449 (1841); Rodgers v. Nowill, 5 C. B. 109, 17 L. J. C. P.

52 (1847); Coffeen v. Brunton, 4 McLean (U. S. C. C.) 516 (1849); Marsh v. Billings, 7 Cush. (61 Mass.) 322 (1852).

[91] McLean v. Fleming, 96 U. S. 245, 24 L. Ed. 828 (1877); Lawrence Mfg. Co. v. Tenn. Mfg. Co., 138 U. S. 537, 549, 11 Sup. Ct. 396, 34 L. Ed. 997 (1890).

[92] Elgin Nat. Watch Co. v. Ill. Watch Co., 179 U. S. 665, 675, 21 Sup. Ct. 270, 45 L. Ed. 365 (1900).

trade name, he is required to show that he has acquired an exclusive right to its use. In order to show this he must prove [93] that the " name, device or symbol was adopted for the purpose of identifying the origin or ownership of the article to which it is attached," or he business with which it is associated; or " that it points distinctly, either by itself or by association, to the origin, manufacture or ownership of the article on which it is stamped. It must also appear to be designed, as its primary object and purpose, to indicate the owner or producer of the commodity, and to distinguish it from like articles manufactured by others." He must also establish his priority of appropriation of the name, symbol or device; that is to say, he must " have been the first to use or employ the same on like articles of production." [94] " If the device, mark or symbol was adopted or placed upon the article for the purpose of identifying its class, grade, style or quality, or for any purpose other than a reference to or indication of its ownership, it cannot be sustained as a valid trade-mark. [95] Such trade-mark cannot consist of words in common use as designating locality, section or region of country," or of an ordinary surname. [96]

---

[93] Columbia Mill Co. v. Alcorn, 150 U. S. 460, 463, 14 Sup. Ct. 151, 37 L. Ed. 1144 (1893), citing Canal Co. v. Clark, 13 Wall. 311, 20 L. Ed. 581 (1871); McLean v. Fleming, 96 U. S. 245, 24 L. Ed. 828 (1877); Mfg. Co. v. Trainor, 101 U. S. 51, 25 L. Ed. 993 (1880); Goodyear India Rubber Glove Co. v. Goodyear Rubber Co., 128 U. S. 598, 9 Sup. Ct. 166, 32 L. Ed. 535 (1898); Lawrence Mfg. Co. v. Tenn. Mfg. Co., 138 U. S. 537, 11 Sup. Ct. 396, 34 L. Ed. 997 (1890).

[94] Derringer v. Platt, 29 Cal. 292, 87 Am. Dec. 170 (1865); Herman v. Solis Cigar Co., 4 Col. App. 475, 36 Pac. 444 (1894); Menendez v. Holt, 128 U. S. 54, 9 Sup. Ct. 143, 32 L. Ed. 526 (1888); George v. Smith, 52 Fed. 830 (1892); Ayer v. Rushton, 7 Daly (N. Y.) 9 (1877); Schneider v. Williams, 44 N. J. Eq.

391, 14 At. 812 (1888). " Three things are requisite to the acquisition of a trade-mark. First, the person desiring to acquire the title must adopt some mark not in use to distinguish goods of the same class or kind, already on the market, belonging to another trader. Second, he must apply his mark to some article of traffic. Third, he must put his article marked with his mark on the market."

[95] Oakes v. Candy Co., 146 Mo. 391, 48 S. W. 467 (1898); Speiker v. Lash, 102 Cal. 38, 36 Pac. 362 (1894); Larabee v. Lewis, 67 Ga. 561, 44 Am. R. 735 (1881); Ball v. Siegel, 116 Ill. 137, 4 N. E. 667, 56 Am. R. 766 (1886); C. F. Simmons Med. Co. v. Mansfield Co., 93 Tenn. 84, 23 S. W. 165 (1893).

[96] Glendon Iron Co. v. Uhler, 75 Pa. 467, 15 Am. R. 599 (1874);

It is not necessary to the validity of a trade-mark, that it be registered, even in a jurisdiction where there is statutory provision for registration. " Property in trade-marks does not derive its existence from an act of Congress," [97] nor from any other legislative act,[98] in this country. In England, however, " The right to trade-marks now mainly depends upon statutes," [99] and no person is entitled to institute proceedings to prevent, or to recover damages, for the infringement of a trade-mark, capable of being registered under the statutes, unless it has been duly registered.

When a valid trade-mark exists, " it is a property right for the violation of which damages may be recovered in an action at law, and the continued violation of it will be enjoined by a court of equity, with compensation for past infringement." [100] In the language of another court, " while competition is essential to the life of commerce, and is the consumer's certain defense against extortion, it should be fair and honest; and the manufacturer who produces an article of recognized excellence in the market, and stamps it with the insignia of his industry, integrity and skill, makes his trade-mark a part of his capital in business, and thus acquires a property right in it, which a court of equity will protect, against all forms of commercial piracy."[101]

Brown Chem. Co. v. Meyer, 139 U. S. 540, 11 Sup. Ct. 625, 35 L. Ed. 247 (1891).

[97] LaCroix v. May, 15 Fed. 236 (1883), quoting from Trade-Mark Cases, 100 U. S. 82, 92, 25 L. Ed. 550 (1879).

[98] Oakes v. Candy Co., 146 Mo. 381, 399, 48 S. W. 467 (1898); the opposite doctrine in Whittier v. Dietz, 66 Cal. 78 (1884), has been nullified by Sec. 3199 of the Political Code enacted in 1885. In Hennessy v. Braunschweiger & Co., 89 Fed. 665, 668 (1898), it is said, " Registration under the act of Congress is of but little, if any, value except for the purpose of creating a permanent record of the date of adoption and use of the trade-mark, or in cases where it is necessary to give

jurisdiction to the Federal courts."

[99] Clerk & Lindsell, Torts (2 Ed.) 625, referring to 46 & 47 Vict., Ch. 57; and 51 and 52 Vict., Ch. 50.

[100] Trade-Mark cases, 100 U. S. 82, 92, 25 L. Ed. 550 (1879); Bradley v. Norton, 33 Conn. 157, 87 Am. Dec. 200 (1865).

[101] Vulcan v. Myers, 139 N. Y. 364, 34 N. E. 904 (1893); Blackwell v. Wright, 73 N. C. 310 (1875)); Saxlehner v. Eisner & Mendelson Co., 179 U. S. 19, 21 Sup. Ct. 7, 45 L. Ed. 60 (1900); Kyle v. Perfec. Mattress Co., 127 Al. 39, 28 So. 545, 85 Am. St. R. 78, with valuable note (1900); Burt v. Tucker, 178 Mass. 493, 59 N. E. 1111, 52 L. R. A. 112, 86 Am. St. R. 499 (1901); Regis v. J. A. Jayne & Co., 185 Mass. 458, 70 N. E. 480 (1904), " If at common

Words, Symbols, and Devices Which are not Trade Marks. To these a person cannot acquire a right to exclusive use, in the nature of a property right, no matter how long, or how widely, he has employed them, in connection with his property or his business. " But it is nevertheless true that even without any strict proprietary interest, as a trade-mark, in the terms or device employed, a party is entitled to protection against the unfair use of them by another, in the effort to take away from him the trade or custom which he has built up." [102] Anyone who uses such terms or devices, not for the honest purpose of fair competition with a business rival, but for the purpose of palming off his goods or representing his business as the goods or the business of that rival, in the hope of finding " more profit and less trouble in trading on another man's reputation than on his own," [103] perpetrates a fraud, and is liable in damages to the rival who is injured by such unfair competition.[104]

Deceit is the Basis of a suit brought to redress this wrong,[105] whether it takes the form of a common-law action for damages, or

law, an action for damages caused to a manufacturer whose goods were put upon the market under a trade-mark and had acquired a distinctive value and reputation, could be maintained against another trader, who fraudulently copies and places upon the goods made by him a similar mark or label, in equity, relief can be granted not only as to damages already suffered, but an injunction can be awarded restraining such unlawful use in the future."

[102] Draper v. Skerrett, 116 Fed. 206 (1902), holding that " French Tissue " was not a valid trade-mark, but that defendant's imitation of plaintiff's symbols, devices and display, was intended to deceive the public into buying defendant's emollient paper for plaintiff's.

[103] Lord Macnaghton in Reddaway v. Banham, (1896) App. Cas. 199, 217, 65 L. J. Q. B. 381. In this case, " Camel Hair Belting " was held not

a valid trade-mark because not a fanciful term but fairly descriptive of the material used in the belting, but its use by the defendant was fraudulent.

[104] Reddaway v. Banham, *supra,* " The fundamental rule is that one man has no right to put off his goods for sale as the goods of a rival trader; " Sterling Remedy Co. v. Gory, 110 Fed. 372 (1901). " Unless the defendant intended to infringe upon the rights of the complainant, he has gone to extraordinary pains in imitating the package of the complainant for no purpose," Sterling Rem. Co. v. Spermine Med. Co. 112 Fed. 1000, 50 C. C. A. 657, (1901). " There was here manifest attempt to put upon the public the goods of the defendant, as those of the complainant."

[105] Allen B. Wrisley Co. v. Iowa Soap Co., 122 Fed. 796, 59 C. C. A. 54 (1903), holding that " one who so names and addresses his product

a suit in equity for an injunction as well as for pecuniary compensation. Accordingly, if the plaintiff fails to make out a clear case of deceitful representation or perfidious dealing, either by direct or circumstantial evidence, he cannot recover.[106] Where deception is the natural result of the defendant's simulation of the plaintiff's labels or other devices, however, positive proof of fraudulent intent need not be proved.[107]

The Fraudulent Use of a Proper or Corporate Name.

While the law does not permit a natural or artificial person to convert his name into a trade-mark, and thus monopolize its use, even in a particular business,[108] it does protect him against the fraudulent employment of the same name by another, however valid may be the other's right to the name. The following statement of the

that a purchaser, who exercises ordinary care to ascertain the sources of its manufacture, can readily learn that fact by a reasonable examination of the boxes or wrappers that cover it, has fairly discharged his duty to the public, and to his rivals, and is guiltless of that deceit which is an indispensable element of unfair competition."

[106] Lawrence Mfg. Co. v. Tenn. Co., 138 U. S. 537, 551, 11 Sup. Ct. 396, 34 L. Ed. 1005 (1891), the letters " L. L." did not constitute a valid trade-mark, and the defendant's brand was entirely dissimilar in appearance to the plaintiff's; French Republic v. Saratoga Vichy Co., 191 U. S. 427, 24 Sup. Ct. 145, 49 L. Ed. 247 (1903). "The essence of the wrong consists in the sale of the goods of one manufacturer or vendor as those of another; and it is only when this false representation is directly or indirectly made, that the party who appeals to the court of equity can have relief. Applying this doctrine to the case under consideration, we are clearly of the opinion that there is no such

similarity in the labels as at present used, and that there is no such fraud shown in the conduct of the defendant, as would authorize us to say that the plaintiffs are entitled to relief; " Postum Cereal Co. v. Health Food Co., 119 Fed. 848, 56 C. C. A. 360 (1902), name and package so dissimilar as not to mislead; Barrett Chem. Co. v. Stern, 176 N. Y. 27, 68 N. E. 65 (1903).

[107] Am. Wal. Watch Co. v. U. S. Watch Co., 173 Mass. 85, 53 N. E. 141, 43 L. R. A. 826, 73 Am. St. R. 263 (1899); Wirtz v. Eagle Bottling Co., 50 N. J. Eq. 164, 24 At. 658 (1892); Drake Med. Co. v. Glessner, 68 O. St. 337, 358, 67 N. E. 722 (1903).

[108] Robinson v. Storm, 103 Tenn. 40, 52 S. W. 880 (1899), "The law is settled that no one can acquire the right of a trade-mark, either in his own name or in that of another person, so as to exclude one of the same name from using it to identify goods which he sees proper to put upon the market, so long as in doing so the latter perpetrates no fraud thereby, or is guilty of no unfair artifice."

principle, taken from a decision of the U. S. Sup. Court, is in accord with the views which generally prevail, both in England, and in this country: " Every one has the absolute right to use his own name honestly in his own business, even though he may thereby incidentally interfere with and injure the business of another having the same name. In such case, the inconvenience or loss to which those having a common right are subjected, is *damnum absque injuria*. But although he may thus use his name, he cannot resort to any artifice or do any act calculated to mislead the public as to the identity of the business firm or establishment, or of the article produced by them, and thus produce injury to the other beyond that which results from the similarity of name. Where the name is one which has previously thereto come to indicate the source of manufacture of particular devices, the use of such name by another, unaccompanied with any precaution or indication, in itself amounts to an artifice calculated to produce the deception alluded to in the foregoing adjudications. Indeed the enforcement of the right of the public to use a generic name, dedicated as the results of monopoly, has always, where the facts required it, gone hand in hand with the necessary regulation, to make it accord with the private property of others, and the requirements of public policy. The courts have always, in every case without exception, treated the one as the co-relative or resultant of the other." [109]

As intimated in the foregoing paragraph, a corporation cannot monopolize the name which it assumes, upon its organization. If, however, it has built up a business and gained a reputation which

---

[109] Singer Mfg. Co. v. June Mfg. Co., 163 U. S. 169, 187, 16 Sup. Ct. 1002, 41 L. Ed. 118 (1896); Staurt v. F. G. Stewart Co., 33 C. C. A. 484, 91 Fed. 247, 63 U. S. App. 561 (1889); Russia Cement Co. v. Le Page, 147 Mass. 206, 17 N. E. 304 (1888); Higgins Co. v. Higgins Soap Co., 144 N. Y. 462, 39 N. E. 490, 27 L. R. A. 42, 43 Am. St. R. 769 (1895); Montgomery v. Thompson, (1891) App. Cas. 217, 60 L. J. Ch. 757; Wyckoff v. Howe Scale Co., 110 Fed. 521 (1901), "That all persons have respectively the right to use their own names in their own business, is entirely clear; but this right is subject to the limitation, common to all rghts, that it is to be so used as not to injure the rights of others." Hence persons named Remington were enjoined from making and selling typewriters as "Remington-Sholes" typewriters, on the ground that it "would make confusion in the plaintiff's trade, and tend to pass off the new machines for the regular Remington machines of the plaintiff."

goes with that name, such priority of use may put another corporation, which selects the same name, to a disadvantage. The newcomer into the field of competition must not palm off its goods, as those of the old and well known corporation.[110] " Courts demand a high order of commercial integrity, in the use by competitors of a name under which a rival has gained a business reputation, whether that name is strictly a trade-mark or is descriptive of quality merely; and frown upon all filching attempts to obtain the reputation of another." [111] Hence, it does not matter that the name of the newcomer is not precisely that of the established corporation. Indeed, " similarity and not identity is the usual recourse, when one party seeks to benefit himself by the good name of another." [112]

Imitating Packages and Buildings. Unfair trade consists, oftentimes, in imitating the bottles or packages, in which a rival manufacturer or dealer of established reputation puts up his goods;[113] or the livery, or insignia worn by the servants, or agents of one conducting a particular business.[114] It has even resorted to the erection of a duplicate building alongside the mercantile house of a successful trader.[115] But however protean its form, or ingenious

---

[110] Am. Wal. Watch Co. v. U. S. Watch Co., 173 Mass. 85, 53 N. E. 141, 43 L. R. A. 826, 72 Am. St. R. 263 (1899); Elgin Nat. Watch Co. v. Ill. Watch Case Co., 179 U. S. 665, 21 Sup. Ct. 270, 45 L. Ed. 365, (1900).

[111] Hostetter Co. v. Martinoni, 110 Fed. 524, 525 (1901); Higgins Co. v. Higgins Soap Co., 144 N. Y. 462, 39 N. E. 470, 27 L. R. A. 42, 43 Am. St. R. 769 (1895).

[112] Celluloid Mfg. Co. v. Cellonite Mfg. Co., 32 Fed. 94 (1887); Peck Bros. & Co. v. Peck Bros. Co., 113 Fed. 291, 51 C. C. A. 251 (1902); Bissell Chilled Plow Works v. T. M. Bissell Plow Co., 121 Fed. 357 (1902).

[113] VanHoboken v. Mohns, 112 Fed. 528 (1901), gin put up in bottles of distinctive color, size and shape; Centaur Co. v. Neathery, 91 Fed.

891, 34 C. C. A. 118 (1899); Centaur Co. v. Link, 62 N .J. Eq. 147, 49 At. 828 (1901), " In the present case, notwithstanding the difference in the printed matter on the labels, I am unable to resist the conclusion, that the size and the shape of the bottles, and the color and form of the label were selected by the defendant, for the purpose of leading some purchasers to take their compound, under the supposition that they were getting what they had always got, namely the medicine made by the complainant." Robinson v. Storm, 103 Tenn. 40, 52 S. E. 880 (1899).

[114] Knott v. Morgan, 2 Keen 213 (1836); Marsh v. Billings, 7 Cush. (61 Mass.) 322 (1851); Stone v. Carlan, 13 Law Reporter (N. Y.) 360 (1850).

[115] Weinstock v. Marks, 109 Cal.

its tricks may be, it falls under the condemnation of the law, whenever the plaintiff can convince the proper tribunal, that its object is to induce the public to patronize the defendant, under the mistaken supposition, that it is patronizing the plaintiff.

False and Misleading Trade Marks. When a person seeks an injunction or damages against one who has hurt his business by making false representations to the public, it is essential that he should not, in his trade-mark, or trade name, or in his advertisements or descriptions of his goods or business, be himself guilty of any false or misleading representations. A court will not protect him against a competitor, however unfair, if he is engaged in deceiving and defrauding the public. In such a case it does not take into account the attitude of the defendant. It beats the plaintiff on the ground that the privilege of deceiving the public is not a legitimate subject of commerce; that one has no legal right to complain, that, by the fraudulent rivalry of others, his own fraudulent profits are diminished.[116]

But it is not every misstatement on the part of the plaintiff, in his trade-mark, or his advertisements, that will defeat him. He may claim for his wares qualities which they do not possess. In the case of medicines, he may exaggerate their curative qualities. Still, if his conduct does not transgress the limits of ordinary mercantile dealing, and cannot fairly be characterized as fraudulent towards the public, he will be entitled to relief.[117]

529, 42 Pac. 142, 50 Am. St. R. 57 (1895), "In its facts, we apprehend, no case like it can be found, either in this country or in England. * * * The fact that the question comes to us in an entirely new guise, and that the schemer had concocted a kind of deception heretofore unheard of in legal jurisprudence, is no reason why equity is either unwilling or unable to deal with him." Accordingly, the court commanded the defendant to distinguish his place of business from that in which plaintiff was carrying on his business, so as to sufficiently indicate to the public, that it was a different place of business from the plaintiff's."

[116] Worden v. Cal. Fig. Syrup Co., 187 U. S. 516, 23 Sup. Ct. 161, 47 L. Ed. 282 (1902); Manhattan Med. Co. v. Wood, 108 U. S. 218, 2 Sup. Ct. 436, 27 L. Ed. 706 (1882); Joseph v. Macowsky, 96 Cal. 518, 31 Pac. 914, 19 L. R. A. 53 (1892); Prince Mfg. Co. v. Prince's Metallic Paint Co., 135 N. Y. 24, 31 N. E. 990, 17 L. R. A. 129 (1892).

[117] Marshall v. Ross, L. R. 8 Eq. 651, 39 L. J. Ch. 225 (1869); Samuel Bros. v. Hostetter Co., 118 Fed. 257, 55 C. C. A. 111 (1902). "Much of the evidence in the case, taken on

Abandonment and Laches. A person may lose his right to a valid trade-mark, or to words and devices analogous to a trade-mark, by voluntary abandonment; as, by dismissing a suit brought to restrain its use by others;[118] or, by disuse for a considerable period.[119] But abandonment is not established by evidence of temporary discontinuance of its use, or of failure to enforce the plaintiff's rights under it.[120] The intent accompanying the discontinuance is important, and if the jury or trial court finds that the plaintiff, during the period of discontinuance, intended to resume business and the use of the trade-mark or name, abandonment is negatived[121] " Simple laches, without more," it is said in a recent carefully considered decision,[122] " is not sufficient to interfere with a

behalf of the appellant, was for the purpose of showing that the appellee's preparation is a quack medicine and an alcoholic stimulant, and, therefore, not entitled to the protection of a court of equity. Upon the evidence in the case, this contention cannot be sustained. The record contains the testimony of many physicians, who have prescribed the preparation in their practice for the ailments mentioned on the label. It is argued, that no one preparation can possibly be a remedy for the numerous and divers ills, for which the label declares this preparation to be adapted. The court will not attempt minute investigation of this field of inquiry. It is one upon which the experts differ. It is enough to advert to the fact, that the preparation purports to be a general tonic, and, as such, efficacious in restoring strength to those weakened by various ailments; and that it has become widely known and largely manufactured and used, and that it has a commercial value. The argument that it is a quack medicine, and that it is injurious to the human system, and is containdicated for some of

the ailments which it purports to cure, comes with ill grace from those who imitate it, as closely as they may, without possessing a complete knowledge of its formula, and, by unfair trade, sell the simulated article as and for the genuine." Newbro v. Undeland, Neb. 96 N. W. 635 (1903).

[118] Browne v. Freeman, 12 W. R. 305, 4 N. R. 476 (1864).

[119] Blackwell v. Dibrell, 3 Hughes (U. S. Cir. Ct.) 151, 14 Off. Gaz. 633 (1878).

[120] Taylor v. Carpenter, 2 Wood & M. (U. S. C. C.) 1 (1846); Chappell v. Sheard, 2 K. & J. 117, 1 Jur. N S. 996 (1855); Lazenby v. White, 41 L. J. Ch. 354 (1871); Saxlehner v. Eisner & Mendelson Co., 179 U. S. 19, 21 Sup. Ct. 7, 45 L. Ed. 60 (1900).

[121] Burt v. Tucker, 178 Mass. 493, 59 N. E. 1111, 54 L. R. A. 112, 86 Am. St. R. 499. In Menendez v. Holt, 128 U. S. 514, 9 Sup. Ct. 143, 32 L. Ed. 526 (1888), it is said, that " abandonment requires proof of non-user by the owner, or general surrender to the use of the public."

[122] Bissell Chilled Plow Works v. T. M. Bissell Plow Co., 121 Fed. 357,

complainant's right to injunctive relief, though it may affect his right to damages for past infringement." In the case then before the court a delay of nearly six years was held not to defeat the complainant's right to damages for past infringement.

375 (1902), citing McLean v. Fleming, 96 U. S. 245, 24 L. Ed. 828 (1877), holding the plaintiff's delay so great as to forfeit his right to an acount; Menendez v. Holt, 128 U. S. 514, 9 Sup. Ct. 143, 32 L. Ed. 526 (1888), delay such as to preclude recovery of past damages; Saxlehner v. Eisner & Mendelson Co., 179 U. S. 19, 21 Sup. Ct. 7, 45 L. Ed. 60 (1900), holding that laches as to bottle and label did not defeat plaintiff's right to injunction and damages.

CHAPTER XIV.

NUISANCE.

§ 1. PRIVATE NUISANCE.

Definition. This tort consists in wrongfully disturbing one in the " reasonably comfortable use and enjoyment of his property," [1] or in the enjoyment and exercise of a common right.[2] Particular conduct of the defendant may entitle the plaintiff to sue either for trespass or for nuisance.[3] If he chooses the former action, the gist of his complaint is the defendant's wrongful disturbance of his

[1] Lowe v. Prospect Hill Cem., 58 Neb. 94, 78 N. W. 488, 46 L. R. A. 237 (1899).

[2] Harrop v. Hirst, L. R. 4 Ex. 43, 38 L. J. Ex. 1 (1868); McCartney v. Londonderry & Co., (1904) App. Cas. 301, cases where a riparian owner took more water from a running stream than he was entitled to; Lynn v. Hooper, 93 Me. 46, 44 At. 127, 47 L. R. A. 752 (1899) and cases cited in the opinion; Morton v. Moore, 15 Gray (81 Mass.) 573, 576 (1860), " This right of the public confers upon every individual the privilege of traveling upon, using and enjoying a common highway for any and all lawful purposes, and consequently no one can be deprived of the enjoyment of such an easement by any adverse or unlawful use or occupation of the way by an individual for his private purposes "; Haag v. Board of Com-

missioners, 60 Ind. 511, 28 Am. R. 654 (1878), applying the following statutory definition, " Whatever is injurious to health, or indecent, or offensive to the senses, or an obstruction to the free use of property, so as essentially to interfere with the comfortable enjoyment of life or property, is a nuisance, and the subject of an action," Ind. Civ. Proc. § 289; Parke v. Kilham, 8 Cal. 77, 68 Am. Dec. 310 (1859), and Sec. 3479 of the Cal. Civ. Code.

[3] Fay v. Prentice, 1 C. B. 829, 14 L. J. C. P. 298 (1845), a cornice on defendant's building, which overhung plaintiff's garden. Blackstone speaks of such overhanging constructions, as a species of trespass, 3 Comm. 217; Miles v. Worcester, 154 Mass. 511, 28 N. E. 676, 26 Am. St. R. 264, 13 L. R. A. 841 (1891).

possession. If he chooses the latter, the gist of his complaint is the discomfort caused him by the defendant.

According to Bracton, actionable nuisances, in his day, were confined to annoyances to freeholders in the enjoyment of their property;[4] and Blackstone defines private nuisance as "anything done to the hurt or annoyance of the lands, tenements or hereditaments of another."[5] At present, as appears from the definition and authorities given above, the term has a more extended meaning, and is no longer limited to discomforts to freeholders.

Ordinarily the motive of the defendant is not material, in determining whether he is maintaining a nuisance. Under some modern statutes, however, structures erected by a person are a nuisance or or not, according to the purpose for which he put them up.[6]

Legalizing Nuisances. Modern legislation frequently attempts to legalize that which at common law would be an actionable nuisance. In Britain, where Parliament is practically omnipotent, the validity of such legislation cannot be questioned.[7] In this country, the courts may be, and often are called upon to decide whether such statutes exceed the constitutional bounds of legislative authority.[8] Both there and here, such statutes are subjected to a strict construction.[9]

---

[4] De Legibus Angliae, Vol. 3, chs. 28, 43-46. In chapter 43, this author points out the distinction, then existing, between nuisances which are tortious and hurtful, and those which are hurtful, but not tortious.

[5] Commentaries, Vol. 3, p. 216.

[6] Lovell v. Noyes, 69 N. H. 263, 46 At. 25 (1898), applying the following statutory provision: "Any fence, or other structure in the nature of a fence, unnecessarily exceeding five feet in height, erected or maintained for the purpose of annoying the owners or occupants of adjoining property, shall be deemed a private nuisance. Any owner or occupant injured, either in his comfort, or the enjoyment of his estate, by such nuisance,

may have an action of tort for the damage sustained thereby." Pub. St. c. 143, §§ 28, 29.

[7] London & Brighton Ry. v. Truman, 11 App. Case. 45, 55 L. J. Ch. 354 (1895).

[8] Supra p. 45. Western Granite Co. v. Knickerbocker, 103 Cal. 111, 37 Pac. 192 (1894); Beach v. Sterling Iron Co., 54 N. J. Eq. 65, 33 At. 286 (1895).

[9] Met. Asylum Dist. v. Hill, 6 App. Cas. 193, 50 L. J. Q. B. 253 (1881); Att'y Gen. v. Gaslight Co., 7 Ch. D. 217, 47 L. J. Ch. 534 (1877). In Morton v. City of New York, 140 N. Y. 207, 35 N. E. 490, 22 L. R. A. 241 (1893), it is said: "But the statutory sanction which will justify an injury to private property must be express, or must be given

Turning Lawful Acts Into Nuisances. Modern legislation also attempts to put under the ban of nuisance many a thing, which was perfectly justifiable at common law. Here, again, the inquiry is important, in this country, whether the legislation is constitutional.[10] In a carefully considered case,[11] upon this subject, it is declared; " Generally it is for the legislature to determine what laws and regulations are needed to protect the public health and secure the public comfort and safety, and while its measures are calculated, intended, convenient and appropriate to accomplish these ends, the exercise of its discretion is not subject to review by the courts. But they must have some relation to these ends. A law enacted in the exercise of the police power must in fact be a police law. If it be a law for the promotion of the public health, it must be a health law, having some relation to the public health."

Oftentimes, the declaration of a nuisance is found in the ordinance of a municipal corporation. In such cases, the further inquiry is to be made, has the legislature undertaken to confer upon the municipality in question authority to extend the list of nuisances, or only to prohibit those things which are nuisances at common law. If the authority is of the latter kind, any ordinance declaring that to be a nuisance, which was not such at common law, is invalid.[12] If the authority is of the former kind, the true test to be applied has been judicially stated [13] as follows: " Nuisances may thus be classi-

---

by clear and unquestionable implication from the powers expressly conferred, so that it can fairly be said that the legislature contemplated the doing of the very act which occasioned the injury "; Kobbe v. Village of New Brighton, 48 N. Y. Supp. 990, 23 App. Div. 243 (1897); Holmes v. City of Atlanta, 113 Ga. 961, 39 S. E. 458 (1901).

[10] Supra, 43; Fischer v. St. Louis, 194 U. S. 361, 24 Sup. Ct. 611 (1904), holding a city ordinance valid, which prohibited dairies within the city limits, without permission of the municipal assembly.

[11] Matter of Jacobs, 98 N. Y. 96, 50 Am. R. 636 (1885), holding an act entitled " An Act to improve the public health, by prohibiting the manufacture of cigars and preparations of tobacco in any form in tenement houses, in certain cases etc." unconstitutional.

[12] Board of Aldermen v. Norman, 51 La. Ann. 736, 25 So. 401 (1899); Pye v. Peterson, 45 Tex. 312, 23 Am. R. 608 (1876); State v. Mott, 61 Md. 297, 48 Am. R. 105 (1883).

[13] Laugel v. City of Bushnell, 179 Ill. 20, 63 N. E. 1086, 58 L. R. A. 266 (1902); City of Carthage v. Mansell, 203 Ill. 474, 67 N. E. 831 (1903); Ex Parte Lacey, 108 Cal. 326, 41 Pac. 411, 38 L. R. A. 640, 49 Am. St. R. 93 (1895), ordinance held constitutional; Beiling v.

fied: First those which in their nature are nuisances *per se,* or are so denounced by the common law, or by statute; second, those which in their nature are not nuisances, but may become so by reason of their locality, surroundings, or the manner in which they may be conducted, managed, etc.; third, those which in their nature may be nuisances, but as to which there may be honest differences. of opinion in impartial minds. The power, granted by the statute to the governing bodies of municipal corporations, to declare what shall be nuisances, and to abate the same, etc., authorizes such bodies to conclusively denounce those things, falling within the first and third of these classes, to be nuisances; but, as to those things falling within the second class, the power possessed is only to declare such of them to be nuisances as are in fact so."

Nuisances Per Se. This class includes all wrongful disturbances of one's enjoyment of property or common rights, which have been constitutionally declared to be nuisances by statute or by judicial decision, or which are clearly actionable torts under established principles of the common law. " There are certain things and certain trades which are considered as nuisances of themselves; as a slaughter-house in a thickly populated town, a pig-sty near a dwelling house," [14] a house of ill-fame,[15] conduct amounting to

Evans, 144 Ind. 644, 142 N. E. 621, 35 L. R. A. 272 (1895); ordinance as to slaughter houses constitutional; Comm. v. Parks, 155 Mass. 531, 30 N. E. 174 (1892), ordinance as to blasting constitutional; *Ex Parte* O'Leary, 65 Miss. 80, 3 So. 144, 7 Am. St. R. 640 (1887), ordinance as to hogs unconstitutional; St. Louis v. Heitzeberg Packing Co., 141 Mo. 375, 42 S. W. 954, 64 Am. St. R. 516 39 L. R. A. 551 (1897), smoke ordinance held unconstitutional; *In re* Hong Wah, 82 Fed. 623 (1897), ordinance prohibiting public laundries within city limits held unconstitutional. " To make an occupation indispensable to the health and comfort of civilized man, and the use of the property necessary to carry it on, a nuisance, by

a mere arbitrary declaration in a city ordinance, and suppress it as such, is simply to confiscate the property and deprive the owner of it without due process of law. It also abridges the liberty of the owner to select his own occupation, and his own methods in the pursuit of happiness; and thereby prevents him from enjoying his rights, privileges and immunities and deprives him of the equal protection of the laws, secured to every person by the constitution of the United States."

[14] Att'y Gen. v. Steward, 20 N. J. Eq. 415, 417 (1869); Evans v. Fertilizing Co., 160 Pa. 209, 213, 28 At. 702 (1894).

[15] Givens v. VanStuddiford, 86 Mo. 149, 56 Am. R. 421 (1885);

public indecency,[16] the fouling of springs, wells and streams,[17] keeping a large quantity of explosives near dwellings,[18] or keeping animals or other property dangerous to human life.[19] In such cases the tort is established by proof of the existence of the thing, the prosecution of the trade, the maintenance of the establishment, or the acts and conduct in question.

Lawful and Laudable Business. When a business of this character is attacked as a nuisance, the plaintiff must show that it is conducted in an improper manner, or at an improper place. "The building of a limekiln is good and profitable," declared an English court, three hundred years ago, "but if it be built so near a house that, when it burns, the smoke enters into the house, so that none can dwell there, an action lies for it.[20] Even though the smoke and gases incident to such a commendable business do not drive the dwellers from the house, the business will still be adjudged a nuisance, if it renders the house uncomfortable, or if it materially injures trees, shrubs or vines growing upon the premises.[21]

The erection and maintenance of a hospital may be a work of the highest philanthropy, but if it operates to destroy the peace, quiet and comfort of those in adjoining residences, and seriously and injuriously affects their health and depreciates their property, the

---

Hamilton v. Whitridge, 11 Md. 128 (1857); Neaf v. Palmer, 103, Ky. 496, 45 S. W. 506 (1898); Cranford v. Tyrell, 128 N. Y. 341, 28 N. E. 514 (1891).

[16] Hayden v. Tucker, 37 Mo. 214 (1866); Nolin v. Franklin, 4 Yerg. (12 Tenn.) 163 (1833).

[17] State v. Taylor, 29 Ind. 517 (1868); Beach v. Sterling Iron Co., 54 N. J. Eq. 65, 33 At. 286 (1895).

[18] McAndrews v. Collerd, 42 N. J. L. 189, 36 Am. R. 508 (1880); Wilson v. Phoenix Powder Co., 40 W. Va. 413, 21 S. E. 1035, 52 Am. St. R. 890 (1895).

[19] Muller v. McKesson, 73 N. Y. 195, 29 Am. R. 123 (1875).

[20] Aldred's Case, 9 Coke, 59a, (1610).

[21] Campbell v. Seaman, 63 N. Y. 568, 20 Am. R. 567 (1876), "The fact that the trees and vines are for ornament, or for luxury, entitles them no less to the protection of the law. Every one has the right to surround himself with articles of luxury, and he will be no less protected than one who surrounds himself only with articles of necessity. The law will protect a flower or a vine as well as an oak. * * * The fact that the nuisance is not continued and that injury is only occasional, furnishes no answer to the claim. The nuisance has occurred often enough, within two years, to do the plaintiffs large damage."

court will not hesitate to adjudge it a private nuisance to those who are in no way responsible for its location and operation.[22]

Public Cemeteries are most desirable but if " it can be clearly proved that a place of sepulture is so situated that the burial of the dead there will injure property or health, either by corrupting the surrounding atmosphere or the water of wells or springs," it will be adjudged a nuisance.[23] It will not be adjudged a nuisance, however, simply because it offends the fancy, delicacy or fastidiousness of neighbors, or even depreciates the market value of adjoining property.[24]

Injury to Property. When the gist of the nuisance consists of injury to property, the plaintiff is required to show a " tangible and appreciable injury,"[25] an " injury which is certain and substantial and not slight or theoretical." [26] The damage must be such " as can be shown by a plain witness to a plain common juryman. * * * If the plaintiff is obliged to start with scientific evidence, such as the microscope of the naturalist or the tests of the chemist,

---

[22] Deaconess Home and Hospital v. Bontjes, 207 Ill. 553, 69 N. E. 748, 64 L. R. A. 215 (1904), To the objection of the defendant that the question of nuisance had not been submitted to a jury, the court replied, that if there was doubt upon the evidence, whether a nuisance existed or not, the question should be submitted to a jury, but as there was "no evidence tending to show that a nuisance does not exist," the court would grant an injunction without a finding by a jury.

[23] Lowe v. Prospect Hill Cem. Ass'n., 58 Neb. 94, 78 N. W. 488, 46 L. R. A. 237 (1889). "A use made by one of his property which works an irreparable injury to the property of his neighbor; the use made by one of his property whereby the unwritten, but accepted, law of decency is violated; the use made by one of his property whereby his neighbor is deprived of the reason-

ably comfortable use and enjoyment of his own property; the use made by one of his own property which will probably or likely endanger the health and the life of his neighbor—is a private nuisance."

[24] Monk v. Packard, 71 Me. 309, 36 Am. R. 315, 43 A. L. J. 366 (1880).

[25] Campbell v. Seaman, 63 N. Y. 568, 577, 20 Am. R. 567 (1876); Lano v. City of Concord, 70 N. H. 485, 49 At. 687 (1900).

[26] Downing v. Elliott, 182 Mass. 28, 64 N. E. 201 (1902), " The fair import of the master's findings is, that, while he cannot say that no soot and cinders were deposited on the plaintiff's ice, if any were deposited they contributed only slightly, if at all, to the injury to the ice, and the damage done by them was insignificant as compared with that resulting from other causes."

for the purpose of establishing the damage itself, that evidence will not suffice." [27]

When the plaintiff presents proof that the defendant's locomotive cast upon his land and salt vats such quantities of soot, cinders, dust and dirt as to injure the quality and quantity of his salt product, he is entitled to damages.[28] On the other hand, if he complains of a cemetery as a nuisance to his water supply, but fails to prove any contamination from that source, his action must fail.[29] So, if he complains of vibrations or shocks communicated to his property by machinery or blasting, on defendant's land, he must show not only sensible and certain harm to his property, but also unreasonable conduct on the defendant's part. "In the strict sense" remarked a learned judge, "the use of machinery producing noise or vibration injures neighboring property. But to some extent such results must come to all who live in a busy, prosperous city. The hum and throb of mechanical life cannot be wholly confined to the walls of any structure. Hence the true test must be whether the use by the owner of the industry is reasonable, having due regard to all the interests affected, and the requirements of public policy." [30] Again, it is not a private nuisance to resort to blasting on one's own land, when this is necessary to fit it for a lawful business. If such blasting is done without negligence, and the injury sustained by the plaintiff is consequential, he has no redress.[31] Whether oil or gas wells are a nuisance to adjoining

[27] Salvin v. North Brancepeth Co., L. R. 9 Ch. 705, 709, 44 L. J. Ch. 149 (1874).

[28] Syracuse Solar-Salt Co. v. Rome etc., Ry., 60 N. Y. Supp. 40; 43 App. Div. 203 (1899), affirmed 168 N. Y. 650 (1901).

[29] Wahl v. Meth. Ep. Cem., 197 Pa. 197, 46 At. 913 (1900).

[30] Russell J. in Bowden v. Edison Elec. Co., 60 N. Y. Supp. 835 (1899).

[31] Booth v. R. W. & O. Ry., 140 N. Y. 267, 35 N. E. 592, 24 L. R. A. 105 (1893); "The fundamental proposition, upon which the plaintiff's counsel rests his argument in support of the recovery, is that the use of the explosives constituted a nuisance, and that one who creates or maintains a nuisance is liable for any special injury resulting therefrom. * * * Whether a particular act done upon, or a particular use of one's premises constitutes a violation of the obligations of vicinage would seem to depend upon the question whether such act or use was a reasonable exercise of the right of property, having regard to time, place and circumstances. It is not everything in the nature of a nuisance which is prohibited. * * * The rule governing the rights of adjacent landowners in the use of

property depends on their location, capacity and management. If such wells and their necessary accompaniments subject neighboring buildings to constant danger of destruction by fire, they are a nuisance, and if their owner wishes to gain the profit which they bring to him, he must pay to his neighbor the damages sustained by that neighbor for his pecuniary benefit, or stop his business.[32]

Personal Discomfort.   It is well settled that the acts of the defendant, or a condition of things for which he is responsible, may amount to a nuisance, although actual sickness is not caused or threatened thereby. It is enough that they produce material physical discomfort and annoyance to persons of ordinary sensibility,[33] having regard to the locality in which the alleged nuisance exists. " Everything is to be looked at from a reasonable point of view." [34] Noises, odors, smoke or dust may constitute an actionable nuisance in one locality, when the same amount of either or all of them in another locality would not create a nuisance. " The reasonable use of one's property depends on the circumstances of each case. What would be permissible in one locality might be unlawful in another." [35]

their property seeks an adjustment of conflicting interests through a reconciliation by compromise, each surrendering something of his absolute freedom, so that both may live. To exclude the defendant from blasting to adapt his lot to the contemplated uses, at the instance of the plaintiff, would not be a compromise between conflicting rights, but an extinguishment of the rights of the one for the benefit of the other." See other cases and comments thereon, supra, p. 44.

[32] McGregor v. Camden, 47 W. Va. 193, 34 S. E. 936 (1899).

[33] Bishop v. Banks, 33 Conn. 118 (1865); bleating of calves kept overnight in a slaughter-house near plaintiff's dwelling; Dittman v. Repp, 50 Md. 517, 33 Am. R. 325 (1878), noise resulting from a lawful business; Catlin v. Valentine, 9 Paige (N. Y.) 575 (1842), slaughter-house in a city; Ross v. Butler, 19 N. J. Eq. 294 (1868), smoke, cinders, noise or odors, although not in a degree injurious to health, may amount to a nuisance; Rhodes v. Dunbar, 57 Pa. 274 (1868), noises disturbing sleep; Snyder v. Cabell, 29 W. Va. 48, 1 S. E. 241 (1886), roller-skating rink; Crump v. Lambert, L. R. 3 Eq. 409 (1867), "the real question is whether the annoyance is such as materially to interfere with the ordinary comfort of human existence."

[34] St. Helen's Smelting Co. v. Tipping, 11 H. L. C. 642, 35 L. J. Q. B. 66 (1865); Gaunt v. Fynney, L. R. 8 Ch. App. 8, 42 L. J. Ch. 122 (1872).

[35] *In re* Mulligan, Lord v. DeWitt, 116 Fed. 713 (1902); Hurlbut v. McKone, 55 Conn. 31, 10 At. 164, 3 Am. St. R. 17, 36 A. L. J. 168 (1887);

Moreover, the source of noises, when these are complained of as a nuisance, is to be taken into account. If they proceed from ordinary musical instruments in the dwelling of a neighbor, or from his children, and are only such as are to be expected in the particular neighborhood, they must be put up with. While the same amount of noise caused by horses in the basement of an adjoining house, will be an actionable nuisance.[36]

Discomfort to Ordinary Persons. The test to be applied, in such cases as we are now considering, is whether the conduct of the defendant, or the state of things for which he is responsible subject ordinary persons in the neighborhood to material and unreasonable discomfort. It may be very unkind, or even inhuman, for one to continue a noise or a business on his premises, which shocks the nerves or sensibilities of his sick or fastidious neighbors. But, legal rights to the use of property are not to be determined by such a fluctuating standard, as the personal peculiarities, or state of health of one's neighbor. The standard to be applied is the effect of such use upon the comfort of ordinary people in the vicinity.[37]

Norcross v. Thoms, 51 Me. 503 (1863); Craven v. Hodenhausen, 141 Pa. 546, 21 At. 774 (1891), "What is a nuisance is very largely a question of fact, in determining which all the circumstances must be taken into consideration, with the right of the plaintiff and defendant to the use of their property." The court held that the evidence fully justified the finding, that defendant's stable and carpet cleaning establishment were a nuisance, in a residential neighborhood.

[36] Ball v. Ray, L. R. 8 Ch. App. 467 (1873).

[37] Rogers v. Elliott, 146 Mass. 349, 15 N. E. 768, 4 Am. St. R. 316 (1888), "Plaintiff's claim rests upon the injury done him on account of his peculiar condition. However this request should have been treated by the defendant, upon consider-

ations of humanity, we think he could not demand as of legal right that the bell should not be used." Wescott v. Middleton, 43 N. J. Eq. 478, 37 A. L. J. 93 (1887), defendant's business as undertaker affected the tender sensibilities of the plaintiff; but the court found that it would not affect ordinary persons uncomfortably, and, hence was not an actionable nuisance; In re Mulligan, 116 Fed. 713 (1902), "The plaintiff's contention is that he is suffering from a disease and an operation which have left him in such an exceedingly enfeebled condition, that his heart has become very weak, and himself extremely sensitive to any shake or jar; that, in the opinion of his physicians, a jar such as might be occasioned by the slightest possible blast on the defendant's lot might cause his

Temporary Annoyance. The courts are agreed that " there is a manifest distinction between acts and uses which are permanent and continuous, and temporary acts, which are resorted to in the course of adapting premises to some lawful use. For example, the erection of an iron building adjacent to a dwelling might, for the time being, cause as much noise and discomfort as would arise from conducting the business of finishing steam boilers on adjacent premises; but this would not constitute a nuisance, and the owner of the dwelling would have no remedy." [38]

Even in the case of temporary annoyance, incident to the reasonable improvement or use of premises, the annoyer must act reasonably. He cannot blast rock, or hammer metal, or operate noisy steam drills or hoisting machines, at all hours of the day and night. He must conform to the habits of the community, and not unreasonably disturb his neighbors, during ordinary non-working hours.[39] Moreover, it is important to distinguish between acts, which merely annoy, and those which injure, or are calculated to injure seriously, adjoining property. As a rule, the latter will amount to an actionable nuisance, although their continuation for an indefinite period may not be intended by the defendant. The principle applicable to a temporary disturbance has been stated by an eminent judge as follows: " Those acts necessary for the common and ordinary use and occupation of land and houses may be done, if conveniently done, without subjecting those who do

death; wherefore he contends that the defendant should be enjoined from using his property in the usual way, by excavating for a building, until plaintiff dies or recovers sufficiently to move away. This is a startling proposition and one which finds no support in the authorities. * * * Plaintiff has mistaken his forum. The only real basis for his contention is common humanity, and to defendant's humanity, not to legal tribunals, his appeal must be made."

[38] Booth v. R. W. & O. Ry., 140 N. Y. 267, 35 N. E. 592, 24 L. R. A. 105 (1893). In this case, blasting was held not to be a nuisance, although had it been continuous and permanent, it would have amounted to a nuisance; Harrison v. Southwork etc., Co., (1891) 2 Ch. 409, 60 L. J. Ch. 630.

[39] Peacock v. Spitzelberger, (Ky.) 29 S. W. 877 (1895), work in blacksmith shop prohibited between 8 P. M. and 6 A. M.; McDonald v. Newark, 42 N. J. Eq. 136 (1886); Stevenson v. Pucce, 66 N. Y. Supp. 712 (1900), defendant was restrained from commencing noise before 7 A. M. and from continuing after 6 P. M.; Dennis v. Eckhart, 3 Grant's Cases (Pa) 390 (1862).

them to an action. * * * There is an obvious necessity for such a principle. It is as much for the advantage of one owner as another; for the very nuisance the one complains of, as the result of the ordinary use of his neighbor's land, he will create in the ordinary use of his own, and the reciprocal nuisances are of a comparatively trifling character. The convenience of such a rule may be indicated by calling it a rule of give and take, live and let live." [40]

Negligence Not Necessary. If the plaintiff proves that he has been harmed by a nuisance, for which the defendant is responsible, it is unnecessary for him to show that the defendant was negligent in the matter. "As a general rule, the question of care, or want of care, is not involved in an action for injuries resulting from a nuisance." [41] If a person stores on his land explosives, in such quantities and in such proximity to his neighbors, as to amount to a nuisance, it will be no answer for him when sued for damages caused by their explosion, that he exercised the greatest possible care in guarding them. Though their explosion may be due to a fire for which he is in no way responsible, or to lightning, or to the criminal act of a third person, he is legally answerable for the harm. [42]

---

[40] Bramwell B. in Bamford v. Turnley, 3 B. & S. 62, 83 (1862). The majority of the court held that this rule did not include the burning of bricks on defendant's land, although the business was to be limited to bricks for use on the land. Approved in Colwell v. St. Pancras Borough Council, (1904) 1 Ch. 707, 73 L. J. Ch. 275, where the defendant claimed that the vibration, caused by an electric generating station, could be avoided after a time by experiment and alteration of machinery.

[41] Laflin & Rand Powder Co. v. Tearney, 131 Ill. 322, 23 N. E. 390, 7 L. R. A. 262, 19 Am. St. R. 34 (1890).

[42] Rudder v. Koopman, 116 Al. 332, 22 So. 601, 37 L. R. A. 489 (1896); Kleebauer v. Western Fuse Co., (Cal.) 69 Pac. 246, 60 L. R. A. 377 (1902); Cameron v. Kenyon-Cornell Co., 22 Mont. 312, 56 Pac. 358, 74 Am. St. R. 602, 44 L. R. A. 508, (1899); McAndrews v. Collerd, 42 N. J. 189, 36 Am. R. 508, (1880); Heeg v. Licht, 80 N. Y. 579, 36 Am. R. 654 (1880); Prussak v. Hutton, 30 App. Div. 66, 51 N. Y. Supp. 761 (1898); Bradford Glycerine Co. v. St. Mary's Woolen Co., 60 O. St. 560, 54 N. E. 528, 45 L. R. A. 658, 71 Am. St. R. 740 (1899); Cheatham v. Powder Co., 1 Swan (31 Tenn.) 213, 55 Am. Dec. 734 (1851); Fort Worth Ry. v. Beauchamp, 95 Tex. 496, 500, 68 S. W. 502, 93 Am. St. R. 864, 58 L. R. A. 716 (1902); Wilson v. Phoenix Powder Co., 40 W. Va. 413, 21 S. E. 1035, 52 Am. St. R. 890 (1895).

If, however, the storing of explosives at the particular place does not amount to a nuisance, the defendant is not liable for damages caused by their explosion, in the absence of evidence that he was negligent in collecting or guarding them.[43]

When a business is carried on,[44] or structures are erected or excavations are made, for which defendant is responsible, and which are private nuisances to the plaintiff, the defendant is liable for damages caused by them, whether he exercised due care in their construction and maintenance or not.[45] The same rule applies in the case of a savage and dangerous animal, so kept as to be a nuisance.[46]

As negligence is not the gist of the action in such cases, contributory negligence on the plaintiff's part is no defense.[47]

Coming to a Nuisance. Blackstone declared [48] that if one fixes his habitation near a nuisance, he has no remedy for the damage which the nuisance causes him, on the ground of *"volenti non fit injuria."* This view has long been discarded, both in England [49] and in this country.[50] If one property owner by devoting

---

[43] Kenney v. Koopman, 116 Al. 310, 22 So. 593, 67 Am. St. R. 119, with note, 37 L. R. A. 497 (1896); Kleebauer v. Western Fuse Co., 138 Cal. 497, 71 Pac. 617, 94 Am. St. R. 62, 60 L. R. A. 377 (1903); Tuckashinsky v. Lehigh etc. Co., 199 Pa. 515, 49 At. 308 (1901); Fort Worth Ry. v. Beauchamp, 95 Tex. 496, 68 S. W. 502, 93 Am. St. R. 864, 58 L. R. A. 716 (1902).

[44] Bohan v. Port Jervis Gas Co., 122 N. Y. 18, 25 N. E. 246 (1890).

[45] Hazeltine v. Edgmond, 35 Ks. 202, 10 Pac. 544, 57 Am. R. 157 (1886); Cork v. Blossom, 162 Mass. 330, 38 N. E. 495, 44 Am. St. R. 362, 26 L. R. A. 256 (1894). In this case, it was held that the structure was not a nuisance, unless unfit to withstand ordinary gales. If so unfit, it was maintained by the defendant at his peril. Davis v. Rich, 180 Mass. 235, 62 N. E. 375 (1902);

Cahill v. Eastman, 18 Minn. 324, 10 Am. R. 184 (1874); Davis v. Niag. Falls Power Co., 25 App. Div. 321 (1898), 171 N. Y. 336, 64 N. E. 4, 89 Am. S. R. 817, 57 L. R. A. 545 (1902).

[46] Smith v. Pelah, 2 Strange, 1264 (1748); Card v. Case, 5 C. B. (57 Eng. C. L.) 622 (1848); Woolf v. Chalker, 31 Conn. 121, 130, 81 Am. Dec. 175 (1860); Muller v. McKesson, 73 N. Y. 195, 29 Am. R. 123, (1878); Twigg v. Ryland, 67 Md. 380, 50 Am. R. 226 (1884); McCaskell v. Elliott, 5 Strob. (S. C.) 196, 53 Am. Dec. 706 (1850). In Hayes v. Smith, 62 O. St. 161, 56 N. E. 879 (1900), the court holds that negligence in keeping even a vicious animal must be shown.

[47] Authorities cited in preceding note.

[48] Commentaries, Vol. 2, p. 403.

[49] St. Helen's Smelting Co. v.

his premises to a particular trade, at a time when the surrounding property is vacant, can acquire a right to continue the business, however offensive it may be to dwellers coming into the neighborhood, then he has it in his power to virtually control the uses to which such property may be put, or to destroy its value.

Nor is it any answer for the defendant, whose use of his premises amounts to a nuisance, that the place is a convenient one for him and for the public. "In the eye of the law, no place can be convenient for the carrying on of a business which is a nuisance, and which causes substantial injury to the property of another. Nor can any use of one's land be said to be a reasonable use, which deprives an adjoining owner of the lawful use and enjoyment of his property." [51]

Undoubtedly, when a court of equity is asked to enjoin a useful and lawful business as a nuisance in a particular locality, regard will always be had to the inquiry whether the business has been carried on for a considerable period, and the erection of buildings and growth of population have been due to its existence. [52] If the development of the locality is due largely to the offensive business, and the thing complained of is not positively noxious but only disagreeable, an injunction may be denied. [53] If, however, the

Tipping, 11 H. L. C. 642, 35 L. J. Q. B. 66 (1865); Bamford v. Turnley, 3 B. & S. 62, 66 (1862).

[50] Hurlbut v. McKone, 55 Conn. 31, 10 A. R. 164, 3 Am. St. R. 17, 36 A. L. J. 168 (1887); Laflin & Rand Powder Co. v. Tearney, 131 Ill. 322, 23 N. E. 390, 19 Am. St. R. 34 (1890); Susquehanna Fertilizer Co. v. Malone, 73 Md. 268, 20 At. 900, 25 Am. St. R. 595 (1890); Bushnell v. Robinson, 62 Ia. 540, 18 N. W. 888 (1883); King v. Morris etc. Ry., 18 N. J. Eq. 397 (1867); Campbell v. Seaman, 63 N. Y. 584, 20 Am. R. 567 (1876); Sherman v. Langham, (Tex.) 13 S. W. 1042 (1890).

[51] Susquehanna Fertilizer Co. v. Malone, 73 Md. 268, 277 (1890). A contrary doctrine seems to be applied in Dolan v. Chicago etc. Ry., 118 Wis. 362, 95 N. W. 385 (1903).

But see Anderson v. Chicago etc. Ry., 85 Minn. 337, 88 N. W. 1001 (1902).

[52] Wier's Appeal, 74 Pa. 230, 241 (1873).

[53] Ballentine v. Webb, 84 Mich. 38, 47 N. W. 485, 13 L. R. A. 321 (1890). James, L. J. said in Salvin v. Brancepeth Coal Co., L. R. 9 Ch. 705, 44 L. J. Ch. 149 (1874), "If some picturesque haven opens its arms to invite the commerce of the world, it is not for this court to forbid the embrace, although the fruit of it should be the sights and sounds and smells of a common seaport and shipbuilding town, which would drive the Dryads and their masters from their ancient solitudes." See Dolan v. Chicago etc. Ry., 118 Wis. 362, 95 N. W. 385 (1903).

business is actually harmful to health or destructive of property, it will be enjoined, although the cessation or removal, may entail a heavy burden upon the defendant.[54]

§ 2. PUBLIC NUISANCE.

Private Action For. The earliest and most frequent cases of public nuisances, which also subject the wrongdoer to a private action, involve obstructions to highways. Such an obstruction " is a common nuisance, and, being a wrong of a public nature, the remedy is by indictment. It is not in itself a ground of civil action by an individual, unless he has suffered from it some special and particular damage which is not experienced in common with other citizens. In such a case, the actual damage to the plaintiff constitutes the gist of the action." [55]

The difficulty in this class of cases has been to determine whether the plaintiff has sustained damage in his individual capacity, or only as one of the public.[56] If the nuisance interferes with the rights of travel common to him and the public, his inconvenience and consequential injury are not deemed special damage.[57] If, however, it compels him to unload goods and carry them around the obstruction in a more expensive way,[58] or if it compels him to travel back and take a more circuitous route, with an obvious loss of time and profit, or to forego his business altogether;[59] or if it

[54] Bohan v. Port Jervis Gas. Co., 122 N. Y. 18, 25 N. E. 246 (1890); Sullivan v. Jones & Laughlin Steel Co., 208 Pa. 540, 57 At. 1065 (1904). The dissenting opinions in this case are worthy of careful perusal.

[55] Houck v. Wachter, 34 Md. 265, 6 Am. R. 332 (1870).

[56] Knowles v. Penn. Ry., 175 Pa. 623, 629-630, 34 At. 974, 52 Am. St. R. 860 (1896); Brayton v. Fall River 113 Mass. 218, 18 Am. R. 470 (1873).

[57] Fineux v. Hovenden, Cro. Eliz. 664 (1600); Winterbottom v. Lord Derby, L. R. 2 Ex. 316, 36 L. J. Ex. 194 (1867); Dennis v. Mobile etc.

Ry., 137 Al. 649, 35 So. 30, 97 Am. St. R. 69 (1902); Griffith v. Holman, 23 Wash. 347, 63 Pac. 239, 83 Am. St. R. 831, 54 L. R. A. 178 (1900).

[58] Rose v. Miles, 4 M. & S. 101.

[59] Creasly v. Codling, 2 Bing. 263 (1824); Piscataqua Nav. Co. v. N. Y. etc. Ry., 89 Fed. 362, (1898); Dudley v. Kennedy, 63 Me. 465 (1874); Farmers' Co-op. Co. v. Albermarle etc. Ry., 117 N. C. 579, 23 S. E. 43 (1895); Hughes v. Heiser, 1 Binn. (Pa.) 463, 2 Am. Dec. 459 (1808); Knowles v. Penn. Ry., 175 Pa. 623, 34 At. 974, 52 Am. St. R. 860 (1896), plaintiff had a contract to haul dirt at 15c. a load; with

blocks up the only or principal means of ingress and egress to plaintiff's land or place of business;[60] or if it unreasonably diverts custom from the plaintiff's place of business;[61] or if it invades the plaintiff's easement of light and air in the highway,[62] a private action will lie.

The rule that the law does not permit private actions to be brought for the abatement of public nuisances, or for damages caused thereby, unless special damage to the plaintiff is also shown, distinct not only in degree but in kind from that which is done to the whole public, " has never been extended to cases where the alleged wrong is done to private property, or the health of individuals is injured, or their peace and comfort in their dwellings is impaired, by the carrying on of the offensive trades and occupations." [63] Moreover, it is the tendency of courts in this country to sustain a private action whenever the plaintiff can show that he has sustained a clear injury as an individual, however slight that may be.[64]

§ 3. PARTIES TO NUISANCE ACTIONS.

Who may Bring the Action. Originally, as we have seen, only the owner of a freehold interest in lands could maintain an

highway as obstructed by defendant, the cost of hauling would be 40c. a load; nuisance was held a special injury to plaintiff.

[60] Iveson v. Moor, 1 Ld. Ray 486, 1 Salk. 15, Carth. 451, Comber. 480, Holt. 10 S. C. as Jeveson v. Moor, 12 Mod. 262, (1698); Roberts v. Mathews, 137 Al. 523, 34 So. 624, 97 Am. St. R. 56 (1902); Venard v. Cross, 8 Ks. 248 (1871); Brayton v. Fall River, 113 Mass. 218 (1873); Smith v. Mitchell, 21 Wash. 536, 58 Pac. 667, 75 Am. St. R. 858 (1899).

[61] Wilkes v. Hungerford Mark. Co., 2 Bing. N. C. 281, 1 Hodges 281, 2 Scott 446 (1835); Fritz v. Hobson, 14 Ch. D. 42, 49 L. J. Ch. 321 (1880); Flynn v. Taylor, 127 N. Y. 596, 28 N. E. 418, 14 L. R. 556 (1891).

[62] First Nat. Bank. v. Tyson, 133 Al. 459, 32 So. 144, 91 Am. St. R. 46, 59 L. R. A. 399 (1902); Townsend v. Epstein, 93 Md. 537, 49 At. 629, 86 Am. St. R. 441, 52 L. R. A. 409 (1901).

[63] Wesson v. Washburn Iron Co., 13 Allen (95 Mass.) 95, 90 Am. Dec. 181, (1866); Roberts v. Mathews, 137 Al. 523, 34 So. 624, 97 Am. St. R. 56 (1902); Adams Hotel Co. v. Cobb, (Ind. Terr.) 53 S. W. 478 (1899); Reinhart v. Sutton, 58 Ks. 726, 51 Pac. 221 (1897); Downs v. City of High Point, 115 N. C. 182, 20 S. E. 385 (1894), *accord*.

[64] Callahan v. Gilman, 107 N. Y. 360, 14 N. E. 264, 1 Am. St. R. 831 (1887); Pierce v. Dart, 7 Cowen (N. Y.) 609 (1827), holding that the delay and expense of plaintiff, in

action for a nuisance. This doctrine was long ago modified, and now a tenant in possession of premises, injuriously affected by a nuisance, is entitled to sue therefor, even though he became tenant after the nuisance was instituted. The measure of his damages will be, ordinarily, the depreciation in the rental value of the premises caused by the nuisance.[65]

If the nuisance operates to permanently injure the leased premises, or create an easement over them, the reversioner has a right of action also. Indeed, for any injury to his rights as reversioner the owner may sue, although the same nuisance may be actionable in favor of a tenant as well.[66]

Nuisance to Health. When the nuisance does not operate to injure property, but affects the health or personal comfort of individuals, who have no estate or legal interest in adjoining premises, the courts are not agreed as to whether such individuals can maintain an action for nuisance. On the one hand it is held, that a private action on the case for nuisance consisting in offensive and noxious odors, smoke or noises, can be brought only by one who is the owner of, or has some legal interest, as lessee or otherwise, in land, the enjoyment of which is affected by the nuisance.[67]

On the other hand it is held, that any one who has sustained special damage, such as sickness, by reason of a nuisance, whether public or private, is entitled to sue for such damage, in an action on the case for nuisance, although he has no property rights in the premises, where he lawfully is when the injury is inflicted,[68]

---

abating the nuisance, was sufficient special damage to sustain the action. *Contra,* Winterbottom v. Lord Derby, L. R. 2 Ex. 316, 36 L. J. Ex. 194 (1867).

[65] Bly v. Edison Elevtric Light Co., 172 N. Y. 1, 64 N. E. 745, 58 L. R. A. 500 (1902); Smith v. Phillips, 8 Phil. (Pa.) 10 (1871). See Broder v. Saillard, 2 Ch. D. 692, 45 L. J. Ch. 414 (1876).

[66] Jones v. Chappell, L. R. 20 Eq. 539, 44 L. J. Ch. 658 (1875); Baker v. Sanderson, 3 Pick. (20 Mass.) 348 (1825); Francis v. Schoelkopf, 53 N. Y. 152 (1873); Hine v. N. Y.

Elec. Ry., 128 N. Y. 571, 29 N. E. 69 (1891).

[67] Kavanagh v. Barber, 131 N. Y. 211, 30 N. E. 235, 15 L. R. A. 689 (1892); Ellis v. Kansas City Ry., 63 Mo. 131, 21 Am. Rep. 436 (1876).

[68] Fort Worth etc. Ry. v. Glenn, —— Tex. ——, 80 S. W. 992, 65 L. R. A. 818 (1904). " It seems to us that the conflict of opinion has arisen from confusing the damage, which results to property from a nuisance, with that special damage which may result to the individual from the nuisance." *Cf.* Shipley v. Fifty Associations, 106 Mass. 194, 8

There can be no doubt that the plaintiff would be entitled to recover, upon proof of negligence on the part of the defendant, in the performance of any duty owing by him to the plaintiff.[69]

Municipal Corporation as Plaintiff. As a property owner, a municipal corporation may maintain an action for a nuisance, precisely as though it were a private corporation or a natural person.[70] When it is clothed with authority to keep highways in proper condition and to abate nuisances, it may be the plaintiff in an action for nuisance, without regard to special damage having been caused to its corporate interests, or to those of any of its citizens.[71]

Who May be Sued for a Nuisance. Certainly the person who creates and maintains a nuisance is liable to a suit therefor.[72] It does not matter that his acts or omissions give rise to a nuisance on the land of a third person, whither he has no legal right to go, in order to abate it. He must still answer for its consequences.[73] Nor does it matter that the defendant is a corporation, or a master, and that the nuisance is due to the acts or omissions of officers, agents or servants; although these various representatives may be liable also.[74]

Am. R. 318 (1870), an action for damages caused by the falling of snow from defendant's building upon plaintiff, while walking along the street. The court said: "For the purpose for which plaintiff was walking along the street, her rights were exactly the same as though she owned the soil in fee simple. * * * In contemplation of law, the person is at least as much entitled to protection as the estate."

[69] Hunt v. Lowell Gas Light Co., 8 Allen (90 Mass.) 169, 85 Am. Dec. 697 (1864).

[70] U. S. v. Cole, 18 D. C. 504 (1889); Dayton v. Roberts, 1 Oh. Dec. 385 (1894).

[71] Burlington v. Schwartzman, 52 Conn. 181, 52 Am. R. 571 (1884); Nor. Cen. Ry. v. Baltimore, 21 Md. 93 (1863); Town of Hutchinson v. Filk, 44 Minn. 536, 47 N. W. 255 (1890); City of Llano v. Llano County, 5 Tex. Civ. App. 132, 23 S. W. 1008 (1893), and authorities digested; Waukesha Hygeia Min. Spring Co. v. Waukesha, 83 Wis. 475, 53 N. W. 675 (1892).

[72] Dorman v. Ames, 12 Minn. 451 (1867); McDonald v. Newark, 42 N. J. Eq. 136 (1886); East Jersey Water Co. v. Bigelow, 60 N. J. L. 201, 38 At. 631 (1897).

[73] Thompson v. Gibson, 7 M. & W. 456, 9 Dowl. P. C. 717 (1841); Miles v. Worcester, 154 Mass. 511, 28 N. E. 676, 26 Am. St. R. 264 (1891); Smith v. Elliott, 9 Pa. 345 (1848).

[74] Supra, Chap. IV. § 3. Also Miles v. Worcester, 154 Mass. 511, *supra;* Jersey City v. Kiernan, 50 N. J. L. 246, 13 At. 170 (1888); Winn v. Rutland, 52 Vt. 481 (1880).

The creator of a nuisance cannot escape liability for its consequences, in most jurisdictions, by leasing or selling it to another.[75] In an early American case on this subject it is said, " If the question, which this case presents, were now to be decided for the first time, it seems to us, that it would be very difficult to find a good reason, why the original wrongdoer should be discharged by conveying the land. The injury has no connection with the ownership of the land. * * * We are not aware, that in any action against an individual for a tort, it can be a good defense to show that a third person has assented to the wrong and thus become liable." [76]

The view has been expressed by some courts, however, that even the creator of a nuisance will not be answerable for its continuance, after he has parted with the possession of the land; unless he derives a benefit from the nuisance, as by devising the premises and receiving rent, or unless in the conveyance of the property, he covenants for its continuance.[77]

Liability of Grantee. Although the author of a nuisance may not rid himself of liability by parting with the ownership of property with which it is connected, the tenant or grantee of such property may subject himself to liability therefor.[78] Ordinarily, however, he does not become liable by simple failure to remove the nuisance, nor even by the enjoyment of " adventitious, accidental advantages from it." [79] Nor will his repair of a structure which constitutes a nuisance, as distinguished from rebuilding it render him liable.[80] There must be some active participation in the continuance of the nuisance, or some positive act done evi-

---

[75] Roswell v. Prior, 2 Salk. 459, 1 Lord Raym. 713, 12 Mod. 635 (1699); Dorman v. Ames, 12 Minn. 451 (1867); Hyde Park etc. Co. v. Porter, 167 Ill. 276, 47 N. E. 206 (1897).

[76] Plumer v. Harper, 3 N. H. 88, 92, 14 Am. Dec. 333 (1824).

[77] Hanse v. Cowing, 1 Lans. (N. Y.) 288 (1869), citing Mayor of Albany v. Cunliff, 2 N. Y. 165 (1849); Waggoner v. Jermaine, 3 Den. (N. Y.) 306 (1846), and Blunt v. Aiken, 15 Wend. (N. Y.) 522, 30

Am. Dec. 72 (1836). These cases are cited with approval in East Jersey Water Co. v. Bigelow, 60 N. J. L. 201, 38 At. 631 (1897).

[78] Cobb v. Smith, 38 Wis. 21 (1875).

[79] Hughes v. Mung. 3 H. & Mc. 441 (1796). A stream had been diverted by defendant's grantee, and defendant had permitted his cattle to drink from it.

[80] Donough v. Gilman, 3 Allen (85 Mass.) 264 (1861).

dencing its adoption by the grantee.[81] Such acts were shown in a leading English case.[82] Defendant's husband diverted water from plaintiff's conduit by means of "a little pipe and a cock, drawing thereby water to serve his house, and to stop it again at his pleasure." After his death, the defendant while occupying the house continued to use the water, and the court held that she was guilty of a new diversion, "because the portion of the water turned aside had not continual course or running, but was sometimes stopped by the cock, and opened again at defendant's pleasure."

When the grantee has not become an active participant in the maintenance of the nuisance, it is well settled both in England and in this country, that he cannot be held liable until he has notice of its existence.[83] If the nuisance is not such *per se,* there is much authority for the view that the grantee will not be liable until he has been requested to abate it. "This rule," it is declared, "is a very reasonable one. The purchaser of property might be subjected to great injustice, if he were responsible for consequences of which he was ignorant and for damages which he never intended to occasion." [84]

Landlord and Tenant. In accordance with the principles stated in the foregoing paragraph, the owner of property having a

[81] Walter v. County Comm'rs, 35 Md. 385, 392 (1871); Curtice v. Thompson, 19 N. H. 471 (1849).

[82] Moore v. Brown, Dyer 319b (1573); Leahan v. Cochran, 178 Mass. 566, 569, 60 N. E. 382, 53 L. R. A. 891, 86 Am. St. R. 506 and note, (1901). Defendant maintained a conductor pipe from roof to side-walk, which was a public nuisance, of whose continuance defendant must be presumed to have known; Morris Canal Co. v. Ryerson, 27 N. J. L. 457 (1859); Meyer v. Harris, 61 N. J. L. 83, 101, 38 At. 690 (1897), *accord.* In the last case the defendant held a lease of the land for 999 years, and the court said, he should be considered for all practical purposes the owner.

[83] Penruddock's Case, 5 Coke 100b;

Ray v. Sellers 1 Duv. (62 Ky.) 257 (1864)); Pillsbury v. Moore, 44 Me. 154, 69 Am. Dec. 91 (1857); Nichols v. Boston, 98 Mass. 39, 93 Am. Dec. 132 (1867); Thompson v. Smith, 11 Minn. 15 (1865); Pinney v. Berry, 61 Mo. 359 (1875); Conhocton Stone Road v. Buff. etc. Ry., 51 N. Y. 573, 10 Am. R. 646 (1873); Dodge v. Stacey, 39 Vt. 558, 577 (1867); Slight v. Gutzlaff, 35 Wis. 675, 17 Am. R. 476 (1874); Phil. & C. Ry. v. Smith, 64 Fed. 679 (1894).

[84] Johnson v. Lewis, 13 Conn. 303, 397, 33 Am. Dec. 405 (1839); West v. Louisville etc. Ry., 8 Bush. (71 Ky.) 404 (1871); Pierson v. Glean, 14 N. J. L. 36 (1833); Plumer v. Harper, 3 N. H. 88, 14 Am. Dec. 333, with note, (1824).

nuisance thereon, is liable for the damages which it occasions, even after he has leased it to a tenant.[85] So he is, if he covenants to repair; and the nuisance arises during the tenancy, because of his omission to repair; or if he leases the premises to be used as a nuisance.[86] As a general rule, if there is no nuisance when the property is leased, and the tenancy is not for purpose of maintaining one, and the landlord does not covenant to repair, the liability for a nuisance rests solely on the occupant and author of the nuisance.[87]

Landowner and Licensee. While a landowner is not liable for a nuisance created and maintained on his land by a stranger, whose acts or omissions are in no way attributable to him,[88] he is liable for a nuisance resulting from a licensee's use of his property.[89] Indeed, it has been held that if one, without the landowner's consent, attaches a wire to a chimney and thus converts it into a nuisance to passers-by, the landowner will be liable for consequent damages, if knowingly he permits the nuisance to continue.[90]

Joint Liability. The grantor and grantee, or the landlord and tenant, or licensor and licensee, or the master and servant may be sued jointly for the nuisance, in cases where the plaintiff has his option of suing either. So other persons, whatever their legal relations, who co-operate in causing or in continuing a nuisance, may be sued jointly therefor.[91]

---

[85] Patterson v. Jos. Schlitz Brewing Co., 16 S. D. —, 91 S. W. 336 (1902); Schwalbach v. Shinkle etc. Co., 97 Fed. 483 (1899) and cases cited. In Riley v. Simpson, 83 Cal. 217, 23 Pac. 293 (1890), the landlord furnished material used by the tenant in erecting the nuisance, and was held liable.

[86] Ahern v. Steele, 115 N. Y. 203, 209, 22 N. E. 193, 5 L. R. A. 449, 12 Am. St. R. 778 (1889), and cases cited in prevailing and dissenting opinions; Timlin v. Stand. Oil Co., 126 N. Y. 514, 27 N. E. 786, 22 Am. St. R. 845 (1891), the same liability rests upon a subletting tenant.

[87] Pretty v. Bickmore, L. R. 8 C. P. 401, 28 L. J. N. S. 835, (1873); Lufkin v. Zane 157 Mass. 117, 31

N. E. 757, 34 Am. St. R. 262, 17 L. R. A. 251 (1892); Harris v. Cohen, 50 Mich. 324 (1883); Wunder v. McLean, 134 Pa. 334, 19 At. 749, 19 Am. St. R. 749 (1890.)

[88] Wolf v. Kilpatrick, 101 N. Y. 146, 4 N. E. 188, 54 Am. R. 672 (1886).

[89] Rockport v. Rockport Granite Co., 177 Mass. 246, 58 N. E. 1017, 51 L. R. A. 779.

[90] Gray v. Boston Gas L. Co., 114 Mass. 149, 19 Am. R. 324 (1873).

[91] Hyde Park etc. Co. v. Porter, 167 Ill. 267, 47 N. E. 206, (1897); Simmons v. Everson, 124 N. Y. 319, 26 N. E. 911, 21 Am. St. R. 676 (1891); Comminge v. Stevenson, 76 Tex. 642, 13 S. W. 556 (1890); Rogers v. Stewart, 5 Vt. 215, 26 Am. Dec. 296 (1833); Marine Ins. Co. v.

Where, however, the acts of various parties are entirely independent and without the element of concert, although of a similar character and producing like harm to the plaintiff, the wrongdoers cannot be joined as defendants in an action at law; [92] Although there is authority for uniting them in an equity action, when the only relief sought is that of an injunction. [93] It has been suggested, that the proper course would seem to be, to bring separate equity actions and apply to have them tried together. [94]

At times a person, whose acts are connected with the creation of a nuisance, escapes liability on the ground that their causal connection is too remote. If one constructs a lawful work on his land, such as a mill pond, which becomes a nuisance only by reason of the acts of third persons, or by the operation of natural forces, not reasonably to be anticipated, he is not answerable for the nuisance. [95]

Defendant's Misconduct not the Sole Cause of Harm. It is no defense for one who fouls a stream, or the air, or indulges in disturbing noises, that others had been doing the same things before he began. [96] Said a learned English judge: [97] " Where there are many existing nuisances, either to the air or to water, it may be very difficult to trace to its source the injury occasioned by any one of them; but if the defendants add to the former foul state of the water, and yet are not to be responsible on account of its previous

St. Louis etc. Ry., 41 Fed. 643 (1890). But see Dutton v. Borough of Lansdowne, 198 Pa. 563, 48 At. 494, 82 Am. St. R. 214, 53 L. R. A. 469 (1901).

[92] Keyes v. Little York Gold Co., 53 Cal. 724 (1879); Ferguson v. Fermenich Co., 77 Ia. 576, 42 N. W. 448, 14 Am. St. R. 319 (1887); Evans v. Wilmington etc. Ry., 96 N. C. 45, 1 S. E. 529 (1887); Chipman v. Palmer, 77 N. Y. 51, 33 Am. R. 566 (1879); Lull v. Fox, etc. Co., 19 Wis. 100 (1865); Sadler v. Great Wes. Ry., (1895) 2 Q. B. 688, 65 L. J. Q. B. 26, affirmed (1896) A. C. 450.

[93] Draper v. Brown, 115 Wis. 361, 91 N. W. 966 (1902), distinguishing Lull v. Fox etc. Co., 19 Wis. 100;

Thorpe v. Brumfitt, L. R. 8 Ch. App. 650 (1873).

[94] Garrett, Law of Nuisances (2 Ed.) p. 240 (1897).

[95] State v. Rankin, 3 S. C. 438, 450, 16 Am. R. 736 (1872); Brimberry v. Savannah etc. Ry., 78 Ga. 641, 3 S. E. 274 (1887); Covert v. Cranford, 141 N. Y. 521, 36 N. E. 597, 38 Am. St. R. 826 (1894).

[96] Harley v. Merrill Brick Co., 83 Ia. 73, 80, 48 N. W. 1000, (1891); Euler v. Sullivan, 75 Md. 616, 23 At. 845, 32 Am. St. R. 420 (1892); Beach v. Sterling Iron & Zinc Co., 54 N. J. Eq. 65, 33 At. 286 (1895); and cases cited.

[97] Lord Chelmsford, in Crossley v. Lightowler, L. R. 2 Ch. App. 478, 481 (1867).

condition, this consequence would follow; that if the plaintiffs were to make terms with other pollutors of the stream, so as to have water free from impurities produced by their works, the defendants might say: "We began to foul the stream at a time when, as against you, it was lawful for us to do so, inasmuch as it was unfit for your use, and you cannot now by getting rid of the existing pollutions from other sources, prevent our continuing to do what, at the time when we began, you had no right to object to." It may be that the defendant's misconduct, if operating simply would not amount to an actionable nuisance. If, however, a nuisance results from its combination with noise, smoke or obstructions caused by others, the victim is entitled to relief against each of the wrongdoers.[98]

§ 4. REMEDIES FOR NUISANCE.

Three Classes. Our law sanctions three forms of remedy for the tort of nuisance—abatement by self-help; an action at law for damages; and equitable relief by injunction.

The first of these remedies has been discussed in a former connection.[101] It is, perhaps, well to add, that, even when a statute confers the power of self-help upon a municipal corporation, the corporation is not bound to resort to such remedy. It may resort to the courts for judicial redress against the maintainer of the nuisance.[102]

[98] Lambton v. Mellish, (1894) 3 Ch. 163, 63 L. J. Ch. 929, Thorpe v. Brumfit, L. R. 8 Ch. App, 650 (1875). Said James L. J., "Suppose one person leaves a wheel-barrow standing on a way, that may cause no appreciable inconvenience; but if a hundred do so, that may cause a serious inconvenience, which a person entitled to the use of the way has a right to prevent; and it is no defense to any one person among the hundred to say, that what he does causes of itself no damage to the complainant."

[99] Supra, Chap. V, § 2.

[100] Am. Furniture Co. v. Town of Batesville, 139 Ind. 77, 38 N. E. 408 (1894).

[101] Goldsmith v. Tunbridge Wells Co., L. R. 1 Ch. 349, 355, 35 L. J. Ch. 382 (1866); Gaunt v. Fynney, L. R. 8 Ch. App 8, 42 L. J. Ch. 122 (1872); Nelson v. Milligan, 151 Ill. 462, 38 N. E. 239 (1894); Edwards v. Allonez Mining Co., 38 Mich. 46 (1878); Wahl v. M. E. Cem., 197 Pa. 197, 46 At. 913 (1900), and cases cited.

[102] Learned v. Castle, 78 Cal. 454, 18 Pac. 872, 21 Pac. 11 (1889), damages fixed by the jury at $1.00;

Action For Damages. This is the form of remedy most frequently resorted to by the nuisance victim. Indeed, if the nuisance is of temporary or intermittent character, or if its interference with a clear legal right of the plaintiff is comparatively trifling, he may be limited to this form of action.[103]

The damages recoverable may be either nominal, compensatory or punitive. Oftentimes, nominal damages are all that the plaintiff seeks, in the way of money recovery. His primary object is to secure a judicial affirmance of the legal right, which defendant is invading by the particular nuisance.[104]

When compensatory damages are sought, for a nuisance that is continuing, the plaintiff is usually limited to such damages as he shows he had sustained, at the time of bringing the action; for " every continuance or repetition of the nuisance gives rise to a new cause of action, and the plaintiff may bring successive actions as long as the nuisance lasts." [105]

Compensatory damages in the case of a permanent nuisance depreciating the value of property, will be measured ordinarily by the difference between the value of the property without the nuisance and with it.[106] If the nuisance is temporary, or if a tenant is the plaintiff, the ordinary measure of damages is the diminution of rental value during its continuance.[107] In case special damages are

Watson v. New Milford Water Co., 71 Conn. 442, 42 At. 265 (1899), diversion of water; Watson v. Town of New Milford, 72 Conn. 561, 45 At. 167 (1900), nuisance of sewage, but no proof of personal discomfort, or depreciation of property; Farley v. Gate City Gas L. Co., 105 Ga. 323, 31 S. E. 193 (1898), " If a nuisance is shown, the law imports damages; " Tootle v. Cliflin, 22 O. St. 247 (1871); Casebeer v. Mowry, 55 Pa. 419, 93 Am. Dec. 766 (1867), the amount of damages awarded was three cents.

[103] Joseph Schlitz Brewing Co. v. Compton, 142 Ill. 511, 32 N. E. 693 (1892); Bowers v. Miss. etc. Co., 78 Minn. 398, 81 N. W. 208, 79 Am. St. R. 395 (1899); Uline v. N. Y. C. etc. Ry., 101 N. Y. 98, 4 N. E. 536 (1886).

[104] Bungenstock v. Nishnabotna Draining Dist., 163 Mo. 198, 64 S. W. 149 (1901).

[105] Swift v. Broyles, 115 Ga. 885, 42 S. E. 277 (1902); Bly v. Edison Electric Co., 172 N. Y. 1, 64 N. E. 745, 58 L. R. A. 500 (1902); Herbert v. Rainey, 162 Pa. 525, 29 At. 725 (1894).

[106] Lockett v. Ft. Worth etc. Ry., 78 Tex. 211, 14 S. W. 564 (1890).

[107] Robb. v. Carnegie Bros. & Co., 145 Pa. 324, 341, 22 At. 649, 14 L. R. A. 329 (1891); Ducktown Sulphur etc. Co. v. Barnes, (Tenn.) 60 S. W. 593 (1900).

shown, as the natural and proximate result of the nuisance, these may be recovered. For example, if members of the property owner's family are made sick and services are lost as well as medical expenses are incurred, these form proper items of damage.[108] So, if crops or trees are destroyed, their value may be recovered.[109] If patronage is turned away from a hotel by the nuisance, the consequent loss to the proprietor, whether owner or tenant, is a proper item of damage.[110]

Punitive damages may be recovered, when the defendant persists in continuing an unmistakable nuisance, or when his misconduct in connection with it is in any other way willful or wanton.[111] Mere negligence on the defendant's part, or a mistake of judgment, or a *bona fide* assertion of his right to maintain what is thereafter adjudged to be a nuisance, will not warrant punitive damages.[110]

Relief by Injunction. The power of a court of equity to command the destruction of a nuisance,[111] or to restrain its continuance,[112] is so well established and so frequently and effectively exercised, that the practicing lawyer of today is apt to forget "that the jurisdiction of this court over nuisance by injunction at all is of recent growth."[113] Less than a century ago, Lord Eldon expressed the view that an injunction should never be issued, until the existence of the nuisance had been established by a trial.[114]

This view no longer obtains, but a court of equity, when asked

---

[108] Keiser v. Mahoney City Gas Co., 143 Pa. 276, 22 At. 759 (1891).

[109] Paddock v. Sowers, 51 Mo. App. 320 (1892); Keiser v. Mahoney, 143 Pa. 276, 291, 22 At. 759 (1891).

[110] Morford v. Woodworth, 7 Ind. 83 (1855); Willett v. St. Albans, 69 Vt. 330, 38 At. 72 (1897).

[111] Kelk v. Pearson, L. R. 6 Ch. 809 (1871).

[112] Henderson v. N. Y. C. Ry., 78 N. Y. 423 (1879). In this case, plaintiff sought damages, an abatement of the use of the railroad and an injunction restraining its operation.

[113] Ripon, Earl of, v. Hobart, 3 M. & K. 169, 180 (1834). Lord Brougham added, that this "jurisdiction had not till very lately been much exercised, and has at various times found great reluctance on the part of learned judges to use it, even in cases," where plaintiff's injury was clear and great.

[114] Att'y Gen. v. Cleaver, 18 Ves. 211 (1811), "The instances of the interposition of this court," said Lord Eldon, "upon the subject of nuisance are very confined and rare." In Att'y Gen. v. Nichol, 16 Ves. 338 (1809), the injunction was dissolved upon defendant's giving an undertaking to remove the nuisance, if the case at law went against him.

to prevent a threatened nuisance, or to enjoin an existing one, or to command its destruction or abatement, requires the complainant to make out " a case of strong and clear injustice, of pressing necessity, and imminent danger of great and irreparable damage, and not of that nature for which an action at law would furnish a full and adequate remedy." [115] It has been judicially declared to be " the rule in equity that where the damages sustained can be measured and compensated, equity will not interfere where the public benefit greatly outweighs private and individual inconvenience." [116]

In cases where the plaintiff goes into equity to enjoin the existence and continuance of a nuisance, he may claim and recover damages also. If his complaint enables the court to take jurisdiction of his entire controversy with the defendant, and settle and adjust all matters of difference between them touching the nuisance, a decree abating the nuisance, but making no provision for damages, will bar a subsequent action at law to recover such damages. In such cases, it is held that the plaintiff may recover, in the equity suit, damages down to the time of trial.[117]

[115] Eastman v. Amoskeag Mfg. Co., 47 N. H. 78 (1866); Health Dep't of N. Y. v. Purdon, 99 N. Y. 237, 52 Am. R. 22 (1885); Penn Lead Co's Appeal, 96 Pa. 116, 20 Am. L. Reg. 649, 23 A. L. J. 209 (1881).

[116] Daniels v. Keokuk Water Works, 61 Ia. 549, 16 N. W. 705 (1883); Gallagher v. Flury, —— Md. ——, 57 At. 672 (1904); Upjohn v. Board of Health, 46 Mich. 542, 9 N. W. 845 (1881). In Att'y Gen. v. Doughty, 2 Ves. Sr. 455 (1752), Lord Hardwicke said, " I know of no general rule of common law which says that building so as to stop another's prospect is a nuisance. Was that the case, there would be no great cities; and I must grant injunctions to all the new buildings in this town."

[117] Gilbert v. Boak Fish Co., 86 Minn. 365, 90 N. W. 767, 58 L. R. A. 735, and cases cited in note, (1902).

CHAPTER XV.

NEGLIGENCE.

§ I. NATURE OF THE TORT.

Negligence is Relative. A learned court has recently declared that "negligence is not a thing but a relation. It implies a duty to use diligence, and such a duty may be owed to one person and not to another."[1] Another court has said: "Negligence is a violation of the obligation which enjoins care and caution in what we do. But this duty is relative, and when it has no existence between particular parties, there can be no such thing as negligence in the legal sense of the term."[2] Still another court has said: "In order to maintain an action for an injury to person or property by reason of negligence or want of due care, there must be shown to exist some obligation or duty towards the plaintiff, which the defendant has left undischarged or unfulfilled."[3]

Accordingly, a plaintiff does not make out a cause of action for negligence by showing that the defendant has acted carelessly, or violated a duty towards some one, and that the plaintiff has suffered

---

[1] Boston & M. Ry. v. Sargeant, 72 N. H. 455, 57 At. 688 (1904), quoting from Rigby L. J. in Mowbray v. Merryweather (1895), 2 Q. B. 640, 647, 65 L. J. Q. B. 50.

[2] Towanda Ry. v. Munger, 5 Den. (N. Y.) 255, 49 Am. Dec. 239 (1848). In this case the animals of plaintiff below trespassed upon the R. R. track, and were killed. In Morris v. Brown, 111 N. Y. 318, 326, 18 N. E. 722, 7 Am. St. R. 751 (1888), it is said: "But the duty

to be actively cautious and vigilant is relative, and where that duty has no existence between particular parties, there can be no such thing as negligence in the legal sense of the term."

[3] Sweeny v. Old Col. etc. Ry., 10 Allen (92 Mass.) 368 (1865). Defendant was held to have induced plaintiff to cross the tracks, and was thereby under a duty of care towards him.

damage therefrom. He must show that he had a legal right to care and caution on the part of the defendant, which right was violated to his injury by the defendant.[4] That violation, it is true, may result either from omission or commission;[5] but neither doing nor failing to do a particular thing is a tort, unless it invades some person's legal rights.[6]

Distinguishable from Intentional Wrongdoing. Negligence is of a negative character. It does not involve the idea of a willful or intentional act or omission on the part of another. The harm which it causes is not designed but inadvertent. The distinction between negligence and fraud has been stated as follows: " Fraud is a deceitful practice or willful device, resorted to with intent to deprive another of his right, or in some way to do him an injury. It is always positive; the mind concurs with the act; what is done, is done designedly and knowingly. But in negligence, whatever may be its grade, there is no purpose to do a wrongful act, or to omit the performance of a duty. There is, however, an absence of proper attention, care or skill. Negligence, in its various degrees, ranges between pure accident and actual fraud, the latter commencing where negligence ends; "[7] though it is said, that " an act may be so grossly negligent that it may be presumed to have been willfully or intentionally done." [8] It has also been said, " While the term ' willful and wanton negligence ' means something more than simply ' negligence,' or even ' gross negligence,' it does

---

[4] Smith v. Tripp, 13 R. I. 153 (1880).

[5] Railroad Co. v. Jones, 95 U. S. 439, 24 L. Ed. 506 (1887). In this case, the railroad company's negligence of omission was held not to avail Jones, because the company did not owe him any duty of diligence.

[6] Smith v. Trimble, (Ky.) 64 S. W. 915 (1901); McCaughna v. Owosso etc. Co., 129 Mich. 407, 89 N. W. 73 (1902); Kelly v. Mich. Cen. Ry., 65 Mich. 186, 31 N. W. 904, 8 Am. St. R. 876 (1887), " Negligence is in law a relative term, and implies the non-observance or omis-

sion to perform a duty which is prescribed by law, or it arises from the situation of the parties and circumstances surrounding the transaction; " Sias v. Rochester Ry., 169 N. Y. 118 62 N. E. 132, 56 L. R. A. 850 (1901); Baltimore & O. Ry. v. Cox, 66 O. St. 276, 64 N. E. 119 (1902); Dobbins v. M. K. & T. Ry., 91 Tex. 60, 41 S. W. 62, 38 L. R. A. 573, 66 Am. St. R. 856 (1897).

[7] Beardsley J, in Gardner v. Heartt, 3 Den. (N. Y.) 232, 236 (1846).

[8] Hays v. Railway, 70 Tex. 602, 606, 8 S. W. 491, 8 Am. S. R. 624 (1888).

not include the element of malice, or an actual intent to injure another."[9]

Degrees of Negligence. Whether negligence is divisible into degrees, corresponding to degrees of care incumbent on the defendant, is a question which has elicited much discussion and a great variety of opinions. Speaking broadly, the various theories may be reduced to three classes. First, that there are three degrees of care required by the law, slight, ordinary and great; and consequently there are three degrees of negligence,—gross, or the failure to exercise even slight care; ordinary, or the the failure to exercise ordinary care; and slight, or the failure to exercise great care.[10]

Second, that but two degrees of care are required; the care ordinarily exercised by a specialist in the matter in hand, and the care ordinarily exercised by a non-specialist in the same matter. A failure to exercise the former of these degrees of care is termed ordinary negligence, while a failure to exercise the latter kind of care is termed slight negligence.[11]

Third, that there are no degrees of care or of negligence; that "negligence is, in all cases, the same thing, namely, the absence of due care." According to this view, "it is in each case practically a question of fact for the jury, whether the proper degree of care has been taken—the jury being guided by considerations of what a reasonable and prudent man would have done under the circumstances."[12]

---

[9] Sloniker v. Great Nor. Ry., 76 Minn. 306, 79 N. W. 168 (1899). "Where a person discovers another in a position of peril, although the latter is a trespasser, and negligently placed himself in such position, and the former, after so discovering him, can by the exercise of ordinary care avoid injuring him, but omits to do so, he evinces such reckless disregard of the safety of others as to constitute, in law, willful and wanton negligence."

[10] Sherman and Redfield, Negligence (5 Ed.) Chap. 111; Whittaker's Smith, Negligence (2 Ed.) pp. 22-25.

[11] Wharton, Negligence, (2 Ed.) § 636.

[12] Clerk and Lindsell, Torts (2 Ed.) p. 393. In Wilson v. Brett, 11 M. & W. 115, 12 L. J. Ex. 264 (1843), Rolfe B. said, "I can see no difference between negligence and gross negligence—it is the same thing, with the addition of a vituperative epithet." Similar views are expressed by Willes and Montague Smith JJ. in Griff v. Gen. Iron Screw Collier Co., L. R. 1 C. P. 612, 35 L. J. C. P. 321 (1866); by Curtis J., in Steamboat New World v. King, 16 How. (U. S.) 464, 14 L. Ed. 1019 (1853); and by Bradley J., in Railroad v. Lockwood, 17

While many courts have expressed themselves, during the last half century, in terms similar to those quoted in the last note, others have expressed their approval of the theory, which recognizes three degrees of negligence. This theory was accepted without question by judges and legal writers, until recently.[13] It commands the support of some of the best courts in this country,[14] and is recognized in various statutory provisions in many of our States.[15] This classification, it is submitted, is a desirable one, and one that accords with the various gradations of legal right, invaded by the tort of negligence. Accordingly, in our further discussion of this topic, we shall use slight negligence to designate the want of great diligence, gross negligence to designate the want of slight diligence, and ordinary negligence to designate the want of diligence between these two extremes, that is, the want of ordinary diligence.[16]

Wall. (U. S.) 357, 21 L. Ed. 627 (1873); and by Sanborn J., in Purple v. U. P. Ry., 114 Fed. 123, 51 C. C. A. 564 (1902); and by Ragan C., in Village of Culbertson v. Holliday, 50 Neb. 229, 69 N. W. 853 (1897).

[13] Coggs v. Bernard, 2 Ld. Ray. 909, Com. 133, Salk. 26, Holt, 13 (1704); Sir William Jones, Bailments, p. 21; Story, Bailments (9 Ed.) § 17.

[14] Redington v. Pos. Tel. Co., 107 Cal. 317, 40 Pac. 432, 48 Am. St. R. 132 (1895); Chicago etc. Ry. v. Johnson, 103 Ill. 512, 522-523 (1882); French v. Buffalo etc. Ry., 4 Keyes 108, 114, 2 Abb. App. Dec. (N. Y.) 201 (1868); First Nat'l Bank of Carlisle v. Graham, 85 Pa. 91, 27 Am. R. 628 (1885); I. & G. N. Ry. v. Cocke, 64 Tex. 151 (1885).

[15] Galbraith v. West End Ry., 165 Mass. 572, 43 N. E. 501 (1896), citing several statutes, and declaring that it has never been the law of that state, that gross negligence means no more than a want of ordinary care; Sullivan v. Boston Elec. Co., 181 Mass. 294, 63 N. E. 904 (1902); Davis v. Atlantic etc. Ry., 63 S. C. 370, 41 S. E. 468 (1902).

[16] Chicago etc. Ry. v. Johnson, 103 Ill. 512, 522-3 (1882); Ill. Central Ry. v. Stewart, (Ky.) 63 S. W. 596 (1901), defining gross negligence as "the failure to take such care as a person of common sense and reasonable skill in business, but of careless habits, would observe in avoiding injury to his own person, or life, under circumstances of equal danger;" Louisville & N. Ry. v. Walden, (Ky.) 74 S. W. 694 (1903.) "This court has repeatedly decided that gross negligence is the absence of slight care;" Lockwood v. Belle City Ry., 92 Wis. 97, 111-112, 65 N. W. 66 (1896), citing earlier cases in that state and approving the three classes, slight, ordinary and gross negligence. See also National Bank v. Graham, 100 U. S. 699, 25 L. Ed. 750, (1879), affirming judgment in the same case in 85 Pa. 91 (1877); and declaring the bank guilty of gross negligence,

Examples of the three degrees. The case of National Bank v. Graham, referred to in the last note, was dealt with by the Supreme Court of Pennsylvania as one involving the liability of a gratuitous bailee. Against such an one, whether a banker, or a common carrier, the bailor has not the legal right which he possesses against a bailee for hire. His right is limited to exacting slight care, and if the property is harmed or lost while under the control of the bailee, the bailor is bound to show, in a suit for negligence, that the bailee did not exercise slight care or diligence in guarding it.[17] Another example of this class, in which gross negligence must be proved, is afforded by the bare licensee. He has not the right to the exercise of more than slight care or diligence by the licensor. As a general rule "a licensee goes upon land at his own risk, and must take the premises as he finds them."[18]

An example of liability for slight negligence is afforded by the common carrier of passengers for hire;[19] by the owner of dangerous animals;[20] and by him who employs dangerous agencies, such as guns, explosives and the like.[21] These persons are not absolute insurers of the safety of those, who are likely to be harmed by the prosecution of their business; but they are bound to exercise an extraordinary degree of care, as we shall see hereafter—a degree of care commensurate with the risk to which their business subjects others.

An example of liability for ordinary negligence is afforded by the landowner who impliedly invites persons upon his premises. The measure of his duty is to exercise reasonable prudence and care.[22]

---

and holding that gross negligence on the part of a gratuitous bailee is a tort.

[17] Giblin v. McMullen, L. R. 2 P. C. 317, 337, 38 L. J. P. C. 25 (1868); Louisville & N. Ry. v. Gerson, 102 Al. 409, 14 So. 873 (1894).

[18] Reardon v. Thompson, 149 Mass. 267, 21 N. E. 369 (1889).

[19] Treadwell v. Whittier, 80 Cal. 574, 585, 22 Pac. 266, 5 L. R. A. 498, 13 Am. St. R. 175 (1889); Warren v. Fitchburg Ry., 8 Allen (90 Mass.) 227, 85 Am. Dec. 700 (1864); Phil. & Reading Ry. v. Derby, 14 How.

(U. S.) 468, 486, 14 L. Ed. 502 (1852).

[20] Ficken v. Jones, 28 Cal. 618, 625 (1865); Baird v. Vaughn, (Tenn.) 15 S. W. 734 (1890).

[21] Dixon v. Bell, 5 M. & S. 198, 17 R. R. 308 (1816); Carter v. Towne, 98 Mass. 567, 96 Am. Dec. 682 (1868); Thomas v. Winchester, 6 N. Y. 397, 58 Am. Dec. 455 (1852).

[22] Griffen v. Manice, 166 N. Y. 188, 198, 59 N. E. 925, 52 L. R. A. 922, 82 Am. St. R. 630 (1901), distinguishing the liability of a landowner for defects in a passenger elevator,

§ 2. PROVING NEGLIGENCE.

Burden of Proof. The litigant who bases his case or his defense upon negligence, is bound to prove that his opponent was negligent. The presumption of law is that every person performs his legal duty.[23] Accordingly, the burden of proving negligence, in any litigation, rests throughout the case on the party asserting it; although, as in other cases, the burden of giving evidence may shift from one side to the other, during the progress of the trial. If an ordinary bailee of goods for hire is sued for their loss, the bailor makes out a *prima facie* case of negligence by evidence of the bailee's failure to return the goods upon demand. If the bailee then shows that the goods were stolen from him or destroyed, the *prima facie* case is met, and plaintiff must go further and prove that the loss was due to " some negligence or want of care, such as a prudent man would take under similar circumstances of his own property."[24]

Presumption, when Contract is Broken. The same evidence may or may not establish a *prima facie* case of negligence on the part of the defendant, according as it shows a breach of contract on the defendant's part or not. For example, a stage coach upsets;[25] or a railroad train is suddenly jolted;[36] or a steamship is

used for the convenience of those visiting the building, from the liability or the common-carrier of passengers.

[23] Huff v. Austin, 46 O. St. 386, 387, 21 N. E. 864, 15 Am. St. R. 613 (1889).

[24] Claflin v. Meyer, 75 N. Y. 260, 31 Am. R., 467 (18/8). In Tex. & P. Ry. v. Barrett, 166 U. S. 617, 619, 17 Sup. Ct. 707, 41 L. Ed. 1136 (1896), it is said of an employee, who sues his employer for failure to provide suitable appliances: " The burden of proof is on the plaintiff throughout the case to show, that the boiler and engine, which exploded, were improper appliances to

be used on its railroad by defendant; and that by reason of the particular defects, pointed out and insisted on by plaintiff, the boiler exploded and injured him; " Norfolk etc. Ry. v. Cromer, 99 Va. 763, 40 S. E. 54 (1901).

[25] Stokes v. Saltonstall, 13 Pet. (U. S.) 181, 10 L. Ed. 115 (1839); Boyce v. Cal. Stage Co., 25 Cal. 460 (1864); Wall. v. Livezay, 6 Col. 465 (1882).

[26] Railroad Co. v. Pollard, 22 Wall. (U. S.) 341, 22 L. Ed. 877 (1874). In Loudon v. Eighth Ave. Ry., 162 N. Y. 380, 56 N. E. 988 (1900), the plaintiff joined two street car comanies in an action for injuries sustained in a collision. The court

thrown with extraordinary force against a wharf;[27] or a train is derailed by obstacles on the track, or by defective rails or defective rolling stock;[26] and a passenger is injured. The accident itself affords *prima facie* evidence of the carrier's negligence, for he contracted to carry the passenger safely. Had a servant of the carrier been harmed in the same accident, " a different rule would obtain in his case. The fact of accident would carry with it no presumption of negligence, on the part of the employer "; and the employee would be bound to establish, as an affirmative fact, that the employer had been guilty of negligence.[29]

A similar difference is generally recognized " between actions founded in negligence, where a contract relation existed between the parties, and those in which the defendant owed no duty, other than to use such ordinary care and caution, as the nature of the business demanded to avoid injury to others." [30]

Res Ipsa Loquitur. Except in cases, where the defendant has bound himself by contract to do something safely, or where a valid statute imposes a similar obligation,[31] the phrase, *res ipsa*

---

held that a presumption of negligence was raised against the Eighth Ave. Co., by the fact of the collision, as the plaintiff was its passenger; but no such presumption arose against the other company.

[27] Inland etc. Co. v. Tolson, 139 U. S. 551, 11 Sup. Ct. 653, 35 L. Ed. 270 (1890).

[28] Gleeson v. Virginia Mid. Ry., 140 U. S. 435, 11 Sup. Ct. 859, 35 L. Ed. 458 (1890); Virginia C. Ry. v. Sanger, 15 Gratt. (Va.) 230 (1859).

[29] Patton v. Texas & P. Ry., 179 U. S. 658, 21 Sup. Ct. 275, 45 L. Ed. 361 (1900); Mountain Copper Co. v. VanBuren, 123 Fed. 61, 59 C. C. A. 279 (1903).

[30] Cosulich v. Standard Oil Co., 122 N. Y. 118, 126, 25 N. E. 259, 19 Am. St. R. 475 (1890); Huff v. Austin, 46 O. St. 386, 21 N. E. 864, 15 Am. St. R. 613, (1889); Thompson, S. D., in 10 Cen. L. J. 261 (1880); Spees v. Boggs, 198 Pa. 112, 47 At. 875, 52 L.

R. A. 833, 82 Am. St. R. 792 (1901); Veith v. Hope Salt Co., 51 W. Va. 96, 41 S. E. 187, 57 L. R. A. 410 (1902).

[31] Atchison etc., Ry. Matthews, 174 U. S. 96, 19 Sup. Ct. 609, 43 L. Ed. 909 (1898); Clark v. Russell, 97 Fed. 900 38 C. C. A. 541 (1899), referring to statutes imposing liability upon railroad companies wholly independent of negligence; Stewart v. Ferguson, 164 N. Y. 553, 58 N. E. 622 (1900); Marino v. Lehmaier, 173 N. Y. 530, 66 N. E. 572, 61 L. R. A. 811 (1903); True & True Co. v. Woda, 201 Ill. 315, 66 N. E. 369 (1903), violation of city ordinance as to height of lumber piles; Chesley v. Nantasket etc. Co., 179 Mass. 469, 61 N. E. 50 (1901), violation of act of Congress as to sounding bell or fog-horn; Jones v. Ill. Central Ry., 75 Miss. 970, 23 So. 358 (1898) violation of ordinance as to speed of train; Elmore v. Sea-

loquitur, is rarely to be applied literally. In other words, the plaintiff rarely makes out a case of negligence by merely showing that some harm has been inflicted upon him by an accident, in connection with the defendant's affairs. To quote from a modern decision; [32] " in no instance can the bare fact that an injury has happened, of itself and divorced from all surrounding circumstances, justify the inference that the injury was caused by negligence. It is true that direct proof of negligence is not necessary. Like any other fact, negligence may be established by the proof of circumstances from which its existence may be inferred. . . . This phrase (*res ipsa loquitur*), which literally translated means that the ' thing speaks for itself,' is merely a short way of saying that the circumstances attendant upon an accident are themselves of such a character as to justify a jury in inferring negligence as the cause of that accident." [33]

A plaintiff who shows that he was injured by the falling of a building into the street,[34] or by the falling of the pole of a toll-gate as he was passing thereunder,[35] makes out a *prima facie* case of negligence; while one who proves that he was injured by the bursting of a fly-wheel used by the defendant,[36] or the bursting of a boiler or engine,[37] or the fall of an elevator [38] does not make out such a

board etc. Co., 132 N. C. 865, 44 S. E. 620 (1903), violation of statute requiring automatic couplings; Kelly v. Anderson, 15 S. D. 107, 87 N. W. 579 (1901), violation of statute as to setting stubble fires in certain months; Norfolk Ry. v. Corletto, 100 Va. 355, 41 S. E. 740 (1902), violation of statute as to speed of train. In all of these cases it was held, that a *prima facie* case of negligence is made out, by evidence of the violation of the statute or ordinance.

[32] Benedict v. Potts, 88 Md. 52, 40 At. 1067, 41 L. R. A. 478 (1898).

[33] City of Atlanta v. Stewart, 117 Ga. 144, 43 S. E. 443, (1903); Byrne v. Boodle, 2 H. & C. 722, 33 L. J. Ex. 13 (1863); Kearney v. London etc. Ry., L. R. 5 Q. B. 441 (1870),

L. R. 6 Q. B. 759, 40 L. J. Q. B. 285 (1871); Cummings v. Nat'l Furnace Co., 60 Wis. 602, 18 N. W. 742, 20 N. W. 665 (1884), *accord.*

[34] Mullen v. St. John, 57 N. Y. 567, 15 Am. R. 530 (1874); Murray v. McShane, 72 Md. 217, 36 Am. R. 369 (1879), a brick fell on plaintiff from defendant's dilapidated wall.

[35] Hyde's Ferry Turnpike Co. v. Yates, 108 Tenn. 428, 67 S. W. 69 (1902).

[36] Piehl v. Albany Ry., 162 N. Y. 617, 57 N. E. 1122 (1900).

[37] Losee v. Buchanan, 51 N. Y. 476, 10 Am. R. 623 (1873); Marshall v. Wellwood, 38 N. J. L. 339, 20 Am. R. 394 (1876).

[38] Griffen v. Manice, 166 N. Y. 188, 59 N. E. 925, 52 L. R. A. 922, 82 Am. St. R. 630 (1901).

case. In the one set of cases, the circumstances are such as to afford just ground for a reasonable inference that according to ordinary experience, the accident would not have occurred except for want of due care; while in the other set, they do not warrant such an inference.[39]

Functions of Court and Jury. A learned English writer, after alluding to the fact that the discussions concerning the several functions of the court and the jury, in negligence cases, have not been carried on by modern judges in the manner best fitted to promote the clear statement of principles, and declaring that it is difficult to sum up the results of these discussions or to reconcile them, expresses the opinion that the tendency of modern judicial rulings in England has been, if not to enlarge the province of the jury, to arrest the process of curtailing it.[40]

It is doubtful whether the same tendency exists in this country.[41] True, courts will not lightly take cases from the jury. " Jurors are the recognized triers of questions of fact, and, ordinarily, negligence is so far a question of fact as to be properly submitted to and

---

[39] Judson v. Giant Powder Co. 107 Cal. 549, 40 Pac. 1020, 5 L. R. A. 498 (1895); Wadsworth v. Boston El. Ry., 182 Mass. 572, 66 N. E. 421 (1903); Johnson v. Walsh, 83 Minn. 74, 85 N. W. 910 (1901); Paynter v. Bridgeton etc. Co., 67 N. J. L. 619, 52 At. 367 (1902); Cole v. N. Y. Bottling Co., 23 App. Div. 177 (1897); Weidmer v. N. Y. El. Ry., 114 N. Y. 462, 21 N. E. 1041 (1889); Volkmar v. Man. Ry., 134 N. Y. 418, 31 N. E. 870, 30 Am. St. R. 678 (1892); Shafer v. Lacock, 168 Pa. 497, 32 At. 44, 29 L. R. A. 254 (1895); Stearns v. Ontario Spinning Co., 184 Pa. 519, 39 At. 292, 63 Am. St. R. 807 (1898); Richmond etc. Co. v. Hudgins, 100 Va. 409, 41 S. E. 736 (1902); The Joseph B. Thomas, 86 Fed. 658, 30 C. C. A. 333, 56 U. S. App. 619, 46 L. R. A. 58 (1898).

[40] Pollock, Torts (6 Ed.) p. 426.
[41] Hunter v. Cooperstown & S. V.

Ry., 112 N. Y. 371, 19 N. E. 820, 8 Am. St. R. 75, 2 L. R. A. 832 (1889); s. c. again 126 N. Y. 18, 26 N. E. 958, 12 L. R. A. 429 (1891). The judgment on a verdict for the plaintiff was reversed, because in the opinion of a majority of the Court of Appeals, (a majority of four to three when the case was before that court the second time), the evidence failed to make out a case of negligence on the part of the defendant, and did clearly establish contributory negligence on plaintiff's part. Gavett v. Man. & L. Ry., 12 Gray (82 Mass.) 501, 77 Am. Dec. 422 (1860), affirming a judgment on a verdict directed by the trial court in defendant's favor, on the ground that there was no proof of due care, and no facts were shown from which an inference of such care could by any possibility be drawn by reasonable men.

determined by them. At the same time the judge is primarily liable for the just outcome of the trial. He is not a mere moderator of a town meeting, submitting questions to the jury for determination, nor simply ruling on the admissibility of testimony, but one who in our jurisprudence stands charged with full responsibility. He has the same opportunity that the jurors have for seeing the witnesses, for noting all those matters in a trial not capable of record, and when in his deliberate opinion there is no excuse for a verdict save in favor of one party, and he so rules by instruction to that effect, an appellate court will pay large respect to his judgment." [42]

An admirable discussion of this topic is to be found in a modern Connecticut case,[43] an outline of which is presented in the head-notes as follows: " The conception of negligence involves the idea of a duty to act in a certain way towards others and a violation of that duty by acting otherwise. It involves the existence of a standard with which the given conduct is to be compared and by which it is to be judged.[44]

Where this standard is fixed by law, the question whether the conduct in violation of it is negligence, is a question of law. And where the standard is fixed by the general agreement of men's judgments, the court will recognize and apply the standard for itself.[45]

But where it is not so prescribed or fixed, but rests on the particular facts of the case and is to be settled for the occasion by the exercise of human judgment upon these facts, as where the standard is the conduct in the same circumstances of a man of ordinary prudence, there the question is one of fact and not of law." [46]

[42] Brewer J., in Patton v. Texas etc. Ry., 179 U. S. 658, 21 Sup. Ct. 275, 45 L. Ed. 361 (1900), affirming a judgment upon a verdict for defendant, directed by the trial judge, and affirmed by the Circuit Court of Appeals.

[43] Farrell v. Waterbury Horse Ry., 60 Conn. 239, 21 At. 675, 22 At. 544 (1891).

[44] Detroit & M. Ry. v. Van Steinburg, 17 Mich. 99, 119-123, (1868);

Fernandez v. Sac City Ry., 52 Cal. 45, 50 (1877).

[45] Solomon v. Manhattan Ry., 103 N. Y. 437, 442, 9 N. E. 430, 57 Am. R. 760 (1886). " It is, we think, the general rule of law, that the boarding or alighting from a moving train is presumably and generally a negligent act *per se;*" Fleming v. Wes. Pac. Ry., 49 R. 633 (1874). Cleveland etc. Ry. v. Crawford 24 O. St. 651, 15 Am. R. 633, (1874).

§ 3. CONTRIBUTORY NEGLIGENCES.

Consequences of. At common law, contributory negligence on the part of the plaintiff is an absolute bar to his recovery. In the language of a learned judge;[47] "In an action for injuries arising from negligence, it always was a defense that the plaintiff had failed to show that, as between him and the defendant, the injury had happened solely by the defendant's negligence. If the plaintiff by some negligence on his part directly contributed to the injury, it was caused by the joint negligence of both, and no longer by the sole negligence of the defendant, and that formed a defense."

Such is not the consequence of contributory negligence in an admiralty action. "In the case of a collision between two vessels by the fault of both, the maritime law everywhere, by what has been called the *rusticum judicium,* apportions equally between both vessels the damages done to both."[48] It often happens that the plaintiff has his option of suing, either in a common law tribunal or in an admiralty court. In such cases he should not hesitate to go into admiralty, if there is any possibility of contributory negligence on his part.[49]

---

[46] McCully v. Clarke, 40 Pa. 399, 80 Am. Dec. 584 (1861). "When the standard of care shifts with the circumstances of the case, it is in its very nature incapable of being determined as a matter of law and must be submitted to a jury."

[47] Lord Esher, M. R., in Thomas v Quatermaine, L. R. 18 Q. B. 685, 688, 56 L. J. Q. B. 340 (1887).

[48] Ralli v. Troop, 157 U. S. 386, 406, 15 Sup. Ct. 657, 39 L. Ed. 742 (1894), citing The North Star, 106 U. S. 17 (1882), which held that if the losses were unequal, the entire damage was to be divided equally between the vessels, and half the difference between their respective losses was to be decreed in favor of the one that suffered most, so as to equalize the burden;

and the Max Morris, 137 U. S. 1, 11 Sup. Ct. 29, 34 L. Ed. 586 (1890), which left open the question whether the decree should be for exactly one-half the damages, where the defendant suffered no harm, or whether a greater or less portion might bo decreed, according as the plaintiff was more or less negligent than defendant. See The Victory, 68 Fed. 395, (1895), and Wm. Johnson Co. v. Johansen, 86 Fed. 886 (1898), approving the view, that the liability of a marine tortfeasor should be measured by his degree of fault.

[49] In Atlee v. Packet Co., 21 Wall. (U. S.) 389, 495, 22 L. Ed. 619 (1874), the court said: "The plaintiff has elected to bring his suit in an admiralty court, which has juris-

Burden of Proof. Whether contributory negligence is an affirmative defense, or whether the plaintiff is bound to show, as a part of his case, that he was free from contributory negligence, is a question upon which the courts are divided. In England, it is well settled " that the onus of proving affirmatively that there was contributory negligence on the part of the person injured, rests, in the first instance, upon the defendant, and that in the absence of evidence tending to that conclusion, the plaintiff is not bound to prove the negative in order to entitle " him to recovery.[50] The same rule has been laid down by the Supreme Court of the United States [51] and by the courts of last resort in a majority of our States.[52]

---

diction of the case notwithstanding the concurrent right to sue at law. In this court, the course of proceeding is, in many respects, different and the rules of decision are different. The mode of pleading is different; the proceeding more summary and informal, and neither party has a right to trial by jury. An important difference, as regards this case, is the rule for estimating damages. ᵛ * * This rule of the Admiralty commends itself quite as favorably in its influence in securing practical justice, as the common law rule." In some States, the admiralty rule, or its equivalent, has been adopted by statute. See, Ala. etc. Ry. v. Coggins, 88 Fed. 455 (1898), applying §§ 2972, 3034, of the Georgia Code.

[50] Lord Watson in Wakelin v. London & S. W. Ry., 12 App. Cas. 41, 47, 56 L. J. Q. B. 229 (1886). It is said that Lord Esher is the only English judge, who has supported the opposite doctrine. Clerk & Lindsell, Torts (2 Ed.) p. 438 n. (i).

[51] Inland etc. Co. v. Tolson, 139 U. S. 551, 11 Sup. Ct. 653, 35 L. Ed. 270 (1890).

[52] See Chap. XV., Beach, Contrib-utory Negligence (2 Ed.), where the authorities are classified, analyzed and discussed with ability. Alabama, Arizona, Arkansas, California, Colorado, Georgia, Idaho, Kansas, Kentucky, Maryland, Minnesota, Missouri, Nebraska, New Hampshire, New Jersey, Ohio, Oregon, Pennsylvania, Rhode Island, South Carolina, Texas, Vermont, West Virginia, Utah and Wisconsin follow the U. S. Supreme Court. In Weiss v. Penn. Ry., 79 Pa. 387, 390 (1875), Sharswood J. says, "The presumption of law is that the plaintiff has done all that a prudent man would do under the circumstances" to save himself from harm. Mr. Beach declares (§ 423) that the statistics of litigation show that no such presumption ought to be indulged in by the courts. "When the average plaintiff comes into court with his action of negligence, the mathematical chance is more than six to one, at the very lowest, that when the evidence is all in, it will give the defendant the verdict on the ground of plaintiff's own concurring and participating default."

In many jurisdictions, however, the burden is held to be upon the plaintiff of showing affirmatively, either by direct evidence or by the drift of surrounding circumstances, his freedom from contributory negligence. The reasoning leading to this conclusion is fairly indicated in the following extract from a Connecticut case; "It is necessary for the plaintiff to prove, first, negligence on the part of the defendant; and second, that the injury to the plaintiff occurred in consequence of that negligence. But in order to prove this latter point, he must show that such injury was not caused, wholly, or in part by his own negligence; for although the defendant was guilty of negligence, if the plaintiff's negligence contributed essentially to the injury, it is obvious that it did not occur by reason of defendant's negligence. Hence, to say that the plaintiff must show the absence of contributory negligence, is only saying that he must show that the injury was owing to the negligence of the defendant." [53]

Of course, in either class of jurisdictions, if the plaintiff's own evidence discloses contributory negligence on his part, his case breaks down, and the defendant is entitled to a verdict or nonsuit.[54]

What amounts to Contributory Negligence within the rule which bars the plaintiff's recovery, in cases where it exists, is a question which gave the courts considerable trouble for a time, but which appears to be fairly well settled now, on both sides of the Atlantic. The older view in England [55] and one which still obtains

[53] Park v. O'Brien, 23 Conn. 339, 345 (1852). In Brackett v. Fair Haven & W. Ry., 73 Conn. 428, 433-4, 47 At. 763 (1900), it is said, "When an injury to one results from the fault of both, the equitable rule would be that each should suffer in proportion to his wrong. But, on grounds of public policy, the law has established an arbitrary rule that when the injury complained of has been caused by the culpable negligence of both plaintiff and defendant, it has not been caused by the defendant, and so the plaintiff cannot recover for the injury. This arbitrary rule not only affects a right of action, but operates as a

rule of evidence." Other States following this doctrine are, Illinois, Indiana, Iowa, Louisiana, Maine, Massachusetts, Michigan, Mississippi, New York and North Carolina.

[54] Ryan v. Louisville etc. Ry., 44 La. Ann. 806, 11 So. 30 (1892); Baltimore etc. Ry. v. Whitacre, 35 O. St. 627, (1880); Tolman v. Syracuse etc. Ry., 98 N. Y. 198, 50 Am. R. 649 (1885); Weiss v. Penna. Ry., 79 Pa. 387 (1875).

[55] Martin v. Great Nor. Ry., 16 C. B. 179, 3 C. L. R. 817 (1855); Brett J.'s charge to the jury, in Radley v. London etc. Ry., as given in 1 App. Cas., at p. 755 (1876).

in a few jurisdictions in this country,[56] is that any negligence on the part of the plaintiff which can be said to have a causal connection with his injury, whether remote or proximate, is to be deemed contributory negligence within the rule. In other words the plaintiff is bound to prove that the harm was due solely to defendant's negligence.

The present view is, that contributory negligence which defeats the plaintiff is negligence on his part, which is a proximate cause of his harm. In a leading English case,[57] the following charge to the jury was held to contain an accurate statement of the true doctrine: " If both parties were equally to blame, and the accident was the result of their joint negligence, the plaintiff could not be entitled to recover; that, if the negligence or default of the plaintiff was in any degree the proximate cause of the damage, he could not recover, however great may have been the negligence of the defendant; but that, if the negligence of the plaintiff was only remotely connected with the accident, then the question was whether the defendant might not, by the exercise of ordinary care, have avoided it." [58]

The Supreme Court of the United States has recently declared; [59] that the generally accepted and most reasonable rule of law applicable to actions in which the defense is contributory negligence, may be thus stated: Although the defendant's negligence may

[56] Norfolk & W. Ry. v. Cromer, 99 Va. 763, 40 S. E. 54 (1901); " The question to be determined in every case is not whether the plaintiff's negligence caused, but whether it contributed to the injury of which he complains."

[57] Tuff v. Warman, 2 C. B N. S. 740 (1857), 5 C. B. N. S. 573, 27 L. J. C. P. 322 (1858).

[58] Approved in Radley v. London etc. Ry., 1 App. Cas. 754, 46 L. Ex. 573 (1876), declaring incorrect, Mr. Justice Brett's direction to the jury, that plaintiff must satisfy them, that the harm happened solely by defendant's negligence. In Spaight v. Tedcastle, 6 App. Cas. 217, 219 (1891), Selborne L. C. said: " Great injustice might be done, if in applying the doctrine of contributory negligence to a case of this sort, (a collision between a ship and a tug,) the maxim, *causa proxima, non remota, spectatur*, were lost sight of. * * * An omission ought not to be regarded as contributory negligence if it might, in the circumstances which actually happened, have been unattended by danger, but for the defendant's fault; and if it had no proper connection, as cause, with the damage which followed as its effect."

[59] Grand Trunk Ry. v. Ives, 144 U. S. 408, 429, 12 Sup. Ct. 679, 36 L. Ed. 485 (1892).

have been the primary cause of the injury complained of, yet an action for such injury cannot be maintained, if the proximate and immediate cause of the injury can be traced to the want of ordinary care and caution in the person injured; subject to this qualification, which has grown up in recent years, that the contributory negligence of the party injured will not defeat the action, if it be shown that defendant might, by the exercise of reasonable care and prudence, have avoided the consequences of the injured party's negligence." [60]

The Last Clear Chance. The qualification, mentioned in the foregoing extract, is often spoken of as the " doctrine of the last clear chance." A recent writer,[61] after an exhaustive examination of modern decisions, summarizes the results as follows: " The foregoing review of authorities, while disclosing much difference of opinion with reference to the ultimate question as to defendant's liability to one guilty of negligence, under a given set of facts and circumstances, seems nevertheless, when proper distinctions are observed, to show a decided tendency on the part of the courts to apply the doctrine of the last clear chance to any omission of duty on the part of defendant, whether before or after discovering the peril in which the plaintiff or deceased had placed himself, or his property, by his antecedent negligence, if the breach of duty intervened or continued after the negligence of the other party had ceased. The criticism that is often made, that the doctrine of the last clear chance in effect abrogates the doctrine of contributory negligence, does not seem to be well founded." [62]

[60] The following are a few of the cases which hold that contributory negligence must be the proximate cause of the harm; Purcell v. Chicago etc. Ry., 109 Ia. 629, 80 N. W. 682, 77 Am. St. R. 557 (1899); Ward v. Maine C. Ry. 96 Me. 136, 51 At. 947 (1902); Holwerson v. St. Louis etc. Ry., 157 Mo. 216, 57 S. W. 770, 50 L. R. A. 850 (1900); Oates v. Met. St. Ry., 168 Mo. 535, 68 S. W. 906, 58 L. R. A. 447, (1902); Costello v. Third Ave. Ry., 161 N. Y. 317, 55 N. E. 897 (1900); Rider v. Syracuse, etc., Ry., 171 N. Y. 139, 63 N. E. 836, 58 L. R. A. 125 (1902),

see dissenting opinion; Wheeler v. Grand Trunk Ry., 70 N. H. 607, 50 At. 103 (1901); Doolittle v. Southern Ry., 60 S. C. 130, 40 S. E. 133 (1901); Cooper v. Georgia C. & N. Ry., 61 S. C. 345, 39 S. E. 543 (1901); Chatanooga Light & Power Co. v. Hodges, 109 Tenn. 331, 70 S. W. 616 (1902); Internat. etc. Ry. v. Williams, 20 Tex. Civ. App. 587, 50 S. W. 732 (1899); Mauch v. City of Hartford, 112 Wis. 40, 87 N. W. 816 (1901).

[61] Note in 55 L. R. A. pp. 418-465.

[62] Harrington v. Los Angeles Ry., 140 Cal. 514, 74 Pac. 15, 63 L. R. A.

Cause of Danger Distinguished from Cause of Harm.

It often happens that a person puts himself in a place which he knows to be dangerous, or conducts himself without due care in a position of danger, and yet is not guilty of contributory negligence with respect to an injury which befalls him. A person drives an unsafe horse near a train of cars;[63] or becomes a railroad passenger, while intoxicated;[64] or takes a place on a scaffold,[65] or in a car,[66]

238 (1903); Western & A. Ry. v. Ferguson, 113 Ga. 708, 39 S. E. 306 (1901); Bogan v. Carolina Ry., 129 N. C. 154, 39 S. E. 808, 55 L. R. A. 481 (1901), *accord*. Chicago, B. & Q. Ry. v. Lilley,—Neb.—, 93 N. W. 1012 (1903), *contra*. " To adopt the doctrine of the so-called ' last clear chance ' decisions, would be to require, not only of railway enginmen, but of all other users of dangerous or ponderous machinery, the constant exertion of that extreme degree of vigilance and care, which ordinarily prudent men employ only in cases of extreme and unusual peril. To our minds, such a requirement would be impracticable and unjust; but if the ' last clear chance ' rule is to be adopted it should be done frankly and openly, without any of the delusive limitations and qualifications of the jurisdiction of its origin, which, in practice, do not limit or qualify; and the hitherto prevailing rule as to contributory negligence ought to be explicitly and decisively abrogated and set aside. The rule of law is not difficult of statement, and business men, litigants, and lawyers have a right, if it is adopted, to its unequivocal announcement."

[63] Nashua Iron Co. v. Worcester, etc., Ry., 62 N. H. 159 (1882), If due care on the part of either at the time of the injury would prevent it, the antecedent negligence of one or both parties is immaterial,

except it may be as one of the circumstances by which the requisite measure of care is to be determined. In such a case, the law deals with their behavior in the situation in which it finds them, at the time the mischief is done, regardless of their prior misconduct. The latter * * * is the cause of the danger; the former is the cause of the injury."

[64] Wheeler v. Grand Trunk Ry., 70 N. H. 607, 50 At. 103 (1901). In Smith v. Norfolk, etc., Ry., 114 N. C. 728, 19 S. E. 863, 25 L. R. A. 287 (1894), the plaintiff's intestate had fallen on the defendant's track while intoxicated, but defendant could not avoid the accident after discovering him; Bageard v. Consol T. Co., 64 N. J. L. 316, 45 At. 620, 49 L. R. A. 424, 81 Am. St. R. 498 (1900).

[65] Smithwick v. Hall, 59 Conn. 261, 21 At. 924, 12 L. R. A. 279, 21 Am. St. R. 104 (1890). Plaintiff was warned not to stand at a particular place on a scaffold, because it had no railing there. He was knocked from that point by the falling of a wall, due to defendant's negligence. His conduct was held not a cause of his injury, but a condition. " If he had not changed his position, he might not have been hurt. And so, too, if he had never been born, or had remained at home, on the day of the injury."

[66] Ky. Cen. Ry. v. Thomas, 79 Ky. 160, 164, 42 Am. R. 208 (1880).

or elsewhere [67] which he is notified is dangerous, and is injured through the defendant's negligence. If at the time the mischief is done, the defendant was under a duty of care towards the plaintiff, notwithstanding the latter's misconduct; and, had he discharged that duty, no injury would have befallen the plaintiff, then it is clear that the proximate cause of the injury was defendant's negligence. Any precedent fault, on the part of the plaintiff, was at most a cause of the danger, not a cause of the harm.[68]

At times, it is very easy to apply this doctrine, and courts are able in such cases to declare that there was,[69] or was not,[70] contributory negligence on the plaintiff's part. At other times the members of the court will draw such diverse inferences from the same evidence, as to lead to their disagreement, not only about the plaintiff's contributory negligence, but about the propriety of sending that question to a jury.[71]

Careless Conduct Induced by Defendant. When a person's safety is imperiled by the negligence of another, and he is forced to act upon the spur of the moment, without time for reflection or the exercise of cool judgment, all that is required of him is, that he shall act with reasonable prudence under the conditions and cir-

Dunn v. Grand Tr. Ry., 58 Me. 187, 4 Am. R. 267 (1870); Jones v. Chicago etc. Ry., 43 Minn. 279, 45 N. W. 444 (1890). N. Y. etc. Ry. v. Ball, 53 N. J. L. 283, 21 At. 1052 (1893); Webster v. Rome, etc. Ry., 115 N. Y. 112, 21 N. E. 725 (1889).

[67] Fickett v. Lisbon Falls Co., 91 Me. 268, 39 At. 996 (1898); Gray v. Scott, 66 Pa. 345, 5 Am. R. 371 (1870).

[68] In Fla. So. Ry. v. Hirst, 30 Fla. 1, 11 So. 506, 16 L. R. A 631 (1892). it was held, however, that it is contributory negligence for a passenger to ride in an express car, in violation of a known rule of the company.

[69] Davis v. Cal. etc. Ry., 105 Cal. 131, 38 Pac. 647 (1894); Balt. Consol. Ry. v. Foreman, 94 Md. 226, 51 At. 83 (1902); Mearns v. Cen. Ry.

N. J., 163 N. Y. 108, 57 N. E. 292 (1900); Houston etc. Ry. v. Clemmons, 55 Tex. 88, 40 Am. R. 799 (1881); Gahagan v. Bos. & M. Ry., 70 N. H. 441, 50 At. 146, 55 L. R. A. 426 (1900); Sewell v. N. Y., etc., Ry., 171 Mass. 302, 50 N. E. 541 (1898); Seyfer v. Otoe County, 66 Neb. 566, 92 N. W. 756 (1902); Gilbert v. Erie Ry., 97 Fed. 747 (1899).

[70] Internat'l etc Ry. v. Williams, 20 Tex. Civ. App. 587, 50 S. W. 732 (1899); Martin v. W. U. Ry., 23 Wis. 437, 99 Am. Dec. 189 (1868). Mather v. Rillston, 156 U. S. 391, 15 Sup. Ct. 464, 39 L. Ed. 414 (1895).

[71] Rider v. Syracuse, etc. Ry. 171 N. Y. 139, 63 N. E. 836, 58 L. R. A. 125 (1902); Hord v. Southern Ry., 129 N. C. 305, 40 S. E. 69 (1901).

cumstances, as they appear to him at the moment. If he so acts, " his conduct is recognized by the law as a consequence of the defendant's mismanagement, for which the latter is responsible."[72] Even though the plaintiff's conduct is of such a character as to be clearly negligent, but for the choice of risks unjustifiably put upon him by the defendant, and though that conduct be the proximate cause of his harm, it is not chargeable to him as contributory negligence.[73]

The same rule is applied, when the defendant's misconduct has imperiled the lives of others than the plaintiff. " The law has so high regard for human life that it will not impute negligence to an effort to preserve it, unless made under circumstances constituting rashness, in the judgment of prudent persons." [74] And when the danger is imminent, a deliberate balancing of chances is not to be expected. " The attendant circumstances must be regarded; the alarm, the excitement and confusion usually present on such occasions; the uncertainty as to the proper move to be made; the promptness required, and the liability to mistake as to what is best to be done, suggest that much latitude of judgment should be allowed to those who are thus forced by the strongest dictates of humanity to decide and act in sudden emergencies." [75] The Supreme Court of Nebraska,[76] referring to the attempt of a servant, in charge of a hand-car, to remove it from the railroad track and

[72] Gannon v. N. Y. etc. Ry., 173 Mass. 40, 52 N. E. 1075, 43 L. R. A. 833 (1899); Mobus v. Town of Waitsfield, 75 Vt. 122, 53 At. 775 (1902).

[73] L. Wolff Mfg. Co. v. Wilson, 152 Ill. 9, 38 N. E. 694, 26 L. R. A. 229 (1892); Sears v. Dennis, 105 Mass. 310 (1870); Ellick v. Wilson, 58 Neb. 584, 79 N. W. 152 (1899); Chic. etc. Ry. 1. Winfrey, — Neb. —, 93 N. W. 526 (1903); Coulter v. Am. etc. Co., 56 N. Y. 585 (1874). Jans v. Boyce, 1 Stark. 493, 18 R. R. 812 (1816).

[74] Eckert v. Long Is. Ry., 43 N. Y. 502, 3 Am. R. 731 (1871).

[75] Penn. Co. v. Langendorf, 48 O. St. 316, 28 N. E. 172, 13 L. R. A. 190, 29 Am. St. R. 553 (1891). *Accord.* Cen. Ry. v. Crosby, 74 Ga. 737, 58 Am. R. 463 (1885); Penn. Co. v. Raney, 89 Ind. 453, 46 Am. R. 173, (1883); Peyton v. Tex. etc., Ry., 41 La. Ann. 861, 6 So. 690 (1889); Md. Steel Co. v. Marney, 88 Md. 482, 42 At. 60, 71 Am. St. R. 441, 42 L. R. A. 842 (1898); Linnehan v. Sampson, 126 Mass. 506, 30 Am. R. 692 (1879); Donahoe v. Wabash etc., Ry., 83 Mo. 560, 53 Am. R. 594 (1884); Corbin v. Philadelphia, 195 Pa. 461, 45 At. 1070, 49 L. R. A. 715, 78 Am. St. R. 825 (1900); Cottrill v. Chic. etc. Ry., 47 Wis. 634, 32 Am. R. 796 (1879).

[76] Omaha etc., Ry. v. Krayenbuhl, 48 Neb. 553, 67 N. W. 447 (1896).

thus obviate a possible train wreck, costing many lives, said: " Such conduct was not negligence but heroism." And the New York Court of Appeals,[77] dealing with a case where the father had plunged into a canal to save his child who had fallen through a defective bridge, declared; " It would have been in contradiction of the most common facts in human experience, if the father had not plunged into the canal to save his child."

Attempts to Save Property, are not encouraged by the courts, when they subject the rescuer to grave personal danger.[78] And where the defendant has not been guilty of actionable negligence, plaintiff acquires no right of suit against him, by sacrificing himself for the benefit of a third person.[79]

Forgetfulness of Danger. The fact, that one has known that a particular source of danger exists, is admissible against him as evidence of contributory negligence, in case he voluntarily subjects himself to the danger and incurs harm therefrom. Such evidence, however, does not show conclusively that he has been guilty of contributory negligence. If the source of danger is a defect in the highway, the traveler is entitled to presume that it has been repaired. Even if he knows that it still exists, he is not bound to

---

[77] Gibney v. State, 137 N. Y. 1, 33 N. E. 142, 33 Am. St. R. 690, 19 L. R. A. 365 (1893). The court added, " But while the immediate cause of the peril to which the father exposed himself was the peril of the child, for the purpose of administering legal remedies, the cause of the peril in both cases may be attributed to the culpable negligence of the State, in leaving the bridge in a dangerous condition."

[78] Cook v. Johnson, 58 Mich. 437, 25 N. W. 388, 55 Am. R. 703 (1885); McGill v. Me. etc. Co., 70 N. H. 125, 46 At. 684, (1900); Morris v. R. R. Co., 148 N. Y. 182, 186, 42 N. E. 574 (1898); Chattanooga Light Co. v. Hodges, 109 Tenn. 331, 70 S. W. 616 (1902); Seale v. Gulf etc. Ry., 65 Tex. 274, 57 Am. R. 602 (1886). Cf. Berg v. Great Nor. Ry., 70 Minn.

272, 73 N. W. 648, 68 Am. St. R. 524 (1897); Linning v. Ill. etc. Ry., 81 Ia. 246, 47 N. W. 66 (1890); Pullman Car Co. v. Laack, 143 Ill. 242, 32 N. E. 285, 18 L. R. A. 215 (1892); Wasmer v. D. L. & W. Ry., 80 N. Y. 212, 36 Am. R. 608 (1880), where the injured person, or his representative, recovered; his effort to save property being reasonably prudent in the circumstances.

[79] Evansville etc. Ry. v. Hiatt, 17 Ind. 102 (1861), defendant was guilty of no negligence whatever; Kelley v. Boston, 180 Mass. 233, 62 N. E. 259 (1902), the Massachusetts statute imposes liability upon cities, for defective highways, in favor only of travelers, and plaintiff was not a traveler, when she descended into an open catch-basin, to rescue her child.

keep his thoughts fixed at all times on such defect. Momentary forgetfulness does not necessarily establish contributory negligence,[80] although there is now and then a case which seems to hold that it does.[81]

Assumption of Risk. The distinction, between this defense and that of contributory negligence, has been pointed out in a former connection. That distinction has not always been observed by the courts, and not a few tribunals, as we saw, have deliberately ignored or repudiated it. Two Minnesota cases,[82] reported in the same volume, will illustrate the distinction. In the earlier of these cases, the plaintiff, with full and present knowledge of the defective condition of a sidewalk, and of the risks incident to its use, voluntarily attempted to walk upon it, when she could have gone around the defective part easily. The court held that she took her chances of injury—she voluntarily assumed a known risk—and injury having ensued, she had only herself to blame.[83]

[80] Kelly v. Blackstone, 147 Mass. 448, 18 N. E. 217, 9 Am. St. R. 730 (1888); Maloy v. City of St. Paul, 54 Minn. 398, 56 N. W. 94 (1893); Weed v. Ballston Spa, 76 N. Y. 329 (1879); Knoxville v. Cox, 103 Tenn. 368, 53 S. E. 734 (1899); McQuillan v. City of Seattle, 10 Wash. 464, 38 Pac. 1119, 45 Am. St. R. 799 (1895); Simonds v. Baraboo, 93 Wis. 40, 67 N. W. 40, 57 Am. St. R. 895 (1896).

[81] Davis v. Cal., etc., Ry., 105 Cal. 131, 38 Pac. 647 (1894).

[82] Wright v. City of St. Cloud, 54 Minn. 94, 55 N. W. 819 (1893); Maloy v. City of St. Paul, 54 Minn. 398, 56 N. W. 94 (1893). In Burns v. Bos. El. Ry., 183 Mass. 96, 60 N. E. 418 (1903), it was held that a passenger, who rode on the front platform, knowing that there was a sign on the car, that "passengers riding on the front platform do so at their own risk," accepted the risk. There was no evidence that the rule had been waived by the company, as in Sweetland v. Lynn & B. Ry., 177 Mass. 574, 59 N. E. 443, 51 L. R. A. 783 (1801). Risk was assumed in McGorty v. Southern etc. Co., 69 Conn. 635, 38 At. 359, 61 Am. St. R. 62 (1897); Lamson v. Am. Ax. & T. Co., 177 Mass. 144, 58 N. E. 585 (1900); Phelps v. Chic. etc. Ry., 122 Mich. 171, 81 N. W. 101 (1899); Dillenberger v. Weingartner, 64 N. J. L. 292, 45 At. 638 (1900); Langlois v. Dunn Worsted Mills, 25 R. I. — 57 At. 910 (1904); Norfolk etc., Ry. v. Marpole, 97 Va. 594, 34 S. E. 462 (1899).

[83] Cf. Jones v. Canal etc. Co., 109 La. 213, 33 So. 200 (1902); Cattano v. Met. Ry., 173 N. Y. 565, 66 N. E. 563 (1903). The majority opinion proceeds upon the theory that plaintiff did not take the risk; Cincinnati etc. Ry. v. Lohe, 68 Oh. St. 101, 67 N. E. 161 (1903); Smith v. City of New Castle, 178 Pa., 298, 35 At. 973 (1896), plaintiff, it was held, did not take the risk, reversing decision of trial court; Phillips v. Ritchie Co., 31 W. Va. 477, 7 S. E.

In the latter case; the defect (a hole in the sidewalk) was temporarily concealed by a light snow, and the plaintiff testified that she was not thinking of the defect when she stepped into it and fell. The court held that the case presented a question for the jury, whether the plaintiff's inattention to the known defect amounted to contributory negligence on her part.[84]

Comparative Negligence. It is well settled that where both the plaintiff and defendant are equally guilty of a mere want of ordinary care, the plaintiff cannot recover.[85] The negligence in such cases is often spoken of as concurrent. Where the negligence of the plaintiff, however, is small in comparison with that of the defendant, although operating concurrently with it to produce the harm, courts have often remarked upon the harshness of the common law rule of contributory negligence, and some have substituted for it a doctrine known as that of comparative negligence. It has been stated as follows: " The degrees of negligence must be measured and considered, and whenever it shall appear that the plaintiff's negligence is comparatively slight and that of the defendant gross, he shall not be deprived of his action." [86]

The doctrine has been rejected in the State of its origin,[87] and probably does not obtain now in any jurisdiction.[88] It appears to have been the result of an unsuccessful attempt to state the doctrine of decisive or proximate negligence, already discussed.[89]

427 (1888); Bormann v. City of Milwaukee, 93 Wis. 522, 67 N. W. 924 (1896); Reed v. Stockmeyer, 74 Fed. 186, 20 C. C. A. 381, 34 U. S. App. 727 (1896).

[84] Cf. Moshenvel v. Dist. Columbia, 191 U. S. 247, 24 Sup. Ct. 57 (1903); Van Duzen Gas Co. v. Schelies, 61 O. St. 298, 55 N. E. 998 (1899).

[85] Little v. Supervior etc. Ry., 88 Wis. 402, 60 N. W. 705 (1894).

[86] Galena etc. Ry. v. Jacobs, 20 Ill. 478 (1858); Chicago v. Stearns, 105 Ill. 554 (1883).

[87] City of Lanark v. Dougherty, 153 Ill. 163, 166, 38 N. E. 892 (1894).

[88] It was adopted in Union Pac. Ry. v. Rollins, 5 Ks. 167, (1869), but repudiated in Atchison etc. Ry. v. Morgan, 57 Ks. 154, 45 Pac. 576 (1896). Possibly it obtains in Nebraska, Village of Orleans v. Perry, 24 Neb. 831, 836, 40 N. W. 417 (1888). In a few states, a similar doctrine has been enunciated in statutes. See Fla. So. Ry. v. Hirst, 30 Fla. 1, 11 So. 506, 32 Am. St. R. 17, 16 L. R. A. 631 (1892); Ala. etc., Ry. v. Coggins, 88 Fed. 455 (1898).

[89] In Inland etc. Co. v. Tolson, 139 U. S. 551, 559, 11 Sup. Ct. 653, 35 L. Ed. 270 (1891) it is said; "The jury might well be of the opinion that while there was some negligence on his part, in standing

Young Children and other Incapables. A minor may be guilty of contributory negligence, whenever it is shown that he is capable of taking ordinary care of himself in the situation in question. Whether he has such capacity is a question of fact, although the undisputed evidence in a particular case may show to the satisfaction of the court, either that he was,[90] or that he was not,[91] capable of contributory negligence. Generally speaking, " the standard of responsibility is the average capacity of others of the same age and experience, and to this standard a child should be held, in the absence of evidence on the subject." [92]

One, who is so devoid of intelligence, as to be unable to apprehend apparent danger, and to avoid exposure to it, cannot be guilty of contributory negligence; because he is incapable of exercising care. Still, other persons are not bound to observe special precautions for the safety of such an incapable, unless they have notice of his incapacity, or mental deficiency.[93] When the incapacity comes from voluntary intoxication, it is no excuse for contributory negligence; [94] although, if the defendant knew of the intoxication,

where and as he did, yet, that the officers of the boat knew just where and how he stood, and might have avoided injuring him, if they had used reasonable care to prevent the steamboat from striking the wharf, with unusual and unnecessary violence. If such were the facts, the defendant's negligence was the proximate, direct, and efficient cause of the injury."

[90] Killelea v. Cal. H. Co., 140 Cal. 602, 74 Pac. 157 (1903); Evans v. Josephine Mills, 119 Ga. 448, 46 S. E. 674 (1904); Shelley v. City of Austin, 74 Tex. 608, 12 S. W. 753 (1889).

[91] Carney v. Concord St. Ry., 72 N. H. 364, 57 At. 218 (1903); O'Brien v. Wis. C. Ry., 119 Wis. 7, 96 N. W. 424 (1903); Kunz v. City of Troy, 104 N. Y. 344, 10 N. E. 442, 58 Am. R. 508 (1887).

[92] Parker v. St. Ry., 207 Pa. 438, 441, 56 At. 1001 (1903); Lafferty v.

Third Ave. Ry., 85 App. Div. 592, 598, 83 N. Y. Supp. 405, 176 N. Y. 594 (1903); Stone v. Dry Dock etc. Ry., 115 N. Y. 107, 21 N. E. 712 (1889); Cleveland Rolling M. Co. v. Corrigan, 46 O. St. 283, 20 N. E. 666, 3 L. R. A. 385 (1889); Robinson v. Cone, 22 Vt. 213, 54 Am. Dec. 67 (1850); Kucera v. Merrill L. Co., 91 Wis. 637, 65 N. W. 374 (1895).

[93] Worthington v. Mencer, 96 Al. 319, 11 So. 72, 17 L. R. A. 407 (1892).

[94] Johnson v. Louisville etc. Ry., 104 Al. 241, 16 So. 75, 53 Am. St. R. 39 (1893); Burke v. Chic. etc., Ry., 108 Ill. App. 565 (1903); Meyer v. Pac. Ry., 40 Mo. 151 (1867); Bageard v. Consol. Tr. Co., 64 N. J. L. 316, 45 At. 620, 49 L. R. A. 424, 81 Am. St. R. 498 (1900); Smith v. Norfolk etc. Ry., 114 N. C. 728, 19 S. E. 863, 25 L. R. A. 287 (1894).

and could have avoided harming the plaintiff (by the exercise of due care, his failure to exercise such care will constitute decisive negligence, and be the proximate cause of the harm.[95]

§ 4. IMPUTED NEGLIGENCE.

Master and Servant. We have seen, in an earlier chapter, that the negligence of the servant, using that term in its generic sense, is imputable to the master, when the latter is a defendant. It is likewise imputable to him when he is a plaintiff, provided, as in the former case, that the negligence of the servant is within the apparent scope of his authority.[96] Accordingly, a person who sues for the value of his slave, killed by defendant's negligence, may be defeated by evidence of contributory negligence on the slave's part.[97]

Moreover, a husband who sues for damages for the loss of the society and services of his wife, as well as for the medical expenses, due to injuries caused by the defendant's negligence, is subject to the defense of contributory negligence by the wife.[98] Whether an action by the wife for personal injuries is subject to the defense of contributory negligence on the husband's part, depends upon the question whether he was acting as her representative at the time; at least, in jurisdictions where she is entitled to sue alone, and is also entitled to the recovery.[99] If the husband must join as a plaintiff, and especially if the recovery belongs to him, his contributory negligence will bar a recovery.[100]

Carrier and Passenger. There is some authority for the proposition that a passenger is so far identified with the carrier, that the negligence of the latter, or of his servants, is to be imputed to

[95] Edgerly v. Union St. Ry., 67 N. H. 312, 36 At. 558 (1892).

[96] St. Louis etc. Ry. v. Hecht, 38 Ark. 35*l* (1882); Louisville etc. Ry. v. Stommel, 126 Ind. 35, 25 N. E. 863 (1890); La Riviere v. Pemberton, 46 Minn. 5, 48 N. W. 406 (1891); Puterbaugh v. Reasor, 8 O. St. 484 (1859).

[97] Sims v. Macon etc. Ry. 28 Ga. 93 (1859).

[98] Chicago etc. Ry. v. Honey, 63 Fed. 39, 12 C. C. A. 190, 27 U. S. App. 196, 26 L. R. A. 42 (1894); Winner v. Oakland, 158 Pa. 405, 12 At. 1110 (1893).

[99] Davis v. Guarnieri, 45 O. St. 470, 15 N. E. 350, 4 Am. St. R. 548 (1887); Bailey v. City of Centerville, 115 Ia. 271, 88 N. W. 379 (1901).

[100] Penn. Ry. v. Goodenough, 55 N. J. L. 577, 28 At. 3, 22 L. R. A. 460 (1893).

the passenger; although neither the carrier nor his employees sustain the relation of servants to the passenger, but are independent contractors.[101] This doctrine has been repudiated, however, in most of the jurisdictions, which once enforced it, and never found much favor in this country.[102] A learned English judge, referring to the reasoning in Thorogood v. Bryan, said;[103] " I do not think it well grounded either in law or in fact. What kind of control has the passenger over the driver (*cf.* an omnibus or street car) which would make it reasonable to hold the former affected by the negligence of the latter?—And when it is attempted to apply this reasoning to passengers travelling in steamships or on railways, the unreasonableness of such a doctrine is even more glaring."

Parent and Child. Whether the negligence of the parent, or of one *in loco parentis*, should be imputed to a child who is incapable of exercising care on his behalf, is a question upon which the courts

[101] Thorogood v. Bryan, 8 C. B. 115, 18 L. J. C. B. 336 (1849); Payne v. Chic. etc. Ry., 39 Ia. 523 (1874); Lockhart v. Lichtenthaler, 46 Pa. 151 (1863); Carlisle v. Sheldon, 38 Vt. 440, 447 (1886). In Cuddy v. Horn, 46 Mich. 596, 41 Am. R. 178 (1881), and Prideaux v. Mineral Point, 43 Wis. 513, 28 Am. R. 558 (1878), the doctrine is laid down that a passenger in a private conveyance is identified with the driver, because if the latter does not obey the former's directions, the passenger can refuse to commit his safety any longer to the driver's care.

[102] The Bernina, 12 Prob. Div. 58, 56 L. J. P. D. & A. 17 (1887), aff'd *sub nom.* Mills v. Armstrong, 13 App. Cas. 1, 57 L. J. P. D. & A. 65 (1888); Little v. Hackett, 116 U. S. 366, 6 Sup. Ct. 391, 29 L. Ed. 652 (1886); Mo. Pac. Ry. v. Tex. Pac. Ry., 41 Fed. 316 (1890); Little v. Rock. etc. Ry., 58 Ark. 454, 25 S. W. 117 (1894); Larkin v. Burlington etc. Ry., 85 Ia. 492, 52

N. W. 480 (1892); Pittsburg etc. Ry. v. Spencer, 98 Ind. 186 (1884); Danville etc. Turnpike Co. v. Stewart, 2 Met. (Ky.) 119 (1859); Holzab v. New Orleans etc. Co., 38. La. Ann. 185, 58 Am. R. 177 (1886); Randolph v. O'Riordon, 155 Mass. 331, 29 N. E. 583 (1892); Cuddy v. Horn, 46 Mich. 596, 41 Am. R. 178 (1881); Flaherty v. Minn. etc. Ry., 39 Minn. 328, 40 N. W. 160, 12 Am. St. R. 654, 1 L. R. A. 680 (1888); Koplitz v. City of St. Paul, 86 Minn. 373, 90 N. W. 794 (1902); Becke v. Mo. Pac. Ry., 102 Mo. 544, 13 S. W. 1053, 9 L. R. A. 157 (1890); N. Y. C. Ry. v. Steinbrenner, 47 N. J. L. 161, 54 Am. R. 126 (1885); Chapman v. New Haven Ry., 19 N. Y. 341, 75 Am. Dec. 344 (1859); Dean v. Penn. Ry., 129 Pa. 514, 18 At. 718 (1889); Covington Tr. Co. v. Kelly, 36 O. St. 86 (1880); Markham v. Houston etc. Co., 73 Tex. 247, 11 S. W. 131 (1889).

[103] Lord Herschell in Mills v. Armstrong, 13 App. Cas. at p. 8.

of this country are divided. The argument in favor of imputing the parent's contributory negligence to the child, as stated in the leading case on this topic is as follows: The law enjoins the duty of mutual care upon persons, who are in the highway or in similar positions, where the presence of either limits to some extent the freedom of action of the other. Small children are not exempt from this rule when they bring actions for redress of injuries, and the only way to enforce the rule is to require due care from those, to whom the law and the necessity of the case have delegated the exercise of that discretion, which the small child does not possess. Such a child, it is said, is not *sui juris*. He belongs to another, to whom discretion in the care of his person is exclusively confided. That person is keeper and agent for this purpose; and in respect of third persons, his act must be deemed that of the infant; his neglect, the infant's neglect. When the infant complains of wrongs to himself, the defendant has a right to insist that he should not have been the heedless instrument of his own injury. If his proper agent and guardian has suffered him to incur mischief, it is much more fair that he should look for redress to that guardian, than that the latter should negligently allow his ward to be in the way of travellers, or like persons, and then harrass them in courts of justice, recovering heavy verdicts for his own misconduct.[104]

This argument has been deemed unsound by the majority of our courts which have dealt with this question. It is admitted that the law puts the infant under the care of an adult, but how, it is asked, can this right to care for and protect be construed into a right to waive or forfeit any of his legal rights? If the parent or guardian were to contract with the defendant, that the latter should not be liable to the infant for any harm inflicted upon him by the joint negligence of the parent and defendant, such engagement, it is declared, would be invalid, both because it would be against good morals, and, also, beyond the legal authority of the parent. More-

[104] Hatfield v. Roper, 21 Wend. (N. Y.) 615 (1839); followed in Daly v. Hintz, 113 Cal. 366, 45 Pac. 693 (1896); Atch. etc., Ry. v. Calvert, 52 Ks. 547, 552, 34 Pac. 976, (1893); Leslie v. Lewiston, 62 Me. 468 (1873); Baltimore etc. Ry. v. McDonnell, 43 Md. 534, 551 (1875); Holly v. Bos. Gaslight Co., 8 Gray (74 Mass.) 123, 69 Am. Dec. 233 (1857); Fitzgerald v. St. Paul etc. Ry., 29 Minn. 336, 13 N. W. 168, 43 Am. R. 212 (1882); Decker v. McSorley, 111 Wis. 91, 86 N. W. 554 (1901); D. L. & W. Ry. v. Devore, 114 Fed. 155, 52 C. C. A. 77 (1902).

over, if the parent's negligence is imputable to the infant, so as to defeat an action for injuries sustained by him, it is equally imputable, for the purpose of subjecting him to actions for the harmful consequences to third persons from such negligence; a conclusion for which there is no shadow of legal authority. And, finally, it is said, the conversion of the infant, who is entirely free from fault, into a wrongdoer by imputation, is a logical contrivance uncongenial with the spirit of jurisprudence; while there is no injustice, no hardship in requiring all wrongdoers to be answerable to a person, who is incapable either of self-protection, or of being a participant in their misfeasance.[105]

Of course, when the parent sues, in his own right, for his loss of the child's services, or for expenditures rendered necessary by the child's injuries, his own negligence in caring for and guarding the child is a valid defense.[106]

§ 5. LIABILITY OF LANDOWNER OR OCCUPIER; AND OF OTHERS ENGAGED IN EXTRA HAZARDOUS UNDERTAKINGS.

Doctrine of Rylands v. Fletcher. In this leading English

[105] Newman v. Phillipsburg, etc. Co., 52 N. J. L. 446, 19 At. 1102, 8 L. R. A. 842 (1890). Accord, Govt. St. Ry. v. Hanlon, 53 Al. 70 (1875); St. Louis etc. Ry. v. Rexroad, 59 Ark. 180, 26 S. W. 1037 (1894); Daley v. Norwich etc. Ry. 26 Conn. 591, 68 Am. Dec. 413 (1858); Chic. City Ry. v. Wilcox-, 138 Ill. 370, 27 N. E. 899, 21 L. R. A. 76 (1889); City of Evansville v. Senhenn, 151 Ind. 42, 47 N. E. 634, 68 Am. St. R. 218, 41 L. R. A. 728 (1897), overruling Pittsburg etc. Ry. v. Vining, 27 Ind. 513, 92 Am. Dec. 269 (1867); Westerfield v. Lewis, 43 La. Ann. 63, 9 So. 52 (1891); Westbrook v. Mobile etc. Ry., 66 Miss. 560, 6 So. 321, 14 Am. St. R. 587 (1889); Winters v. Kan. City. Ry., 99 Mo. 509, 12 S. W. 652, 6 L. R. A. 536, 17 Am. St. R. 691 (1889); Huff v. Ames, 16 Neb. 139,

19 N. W. 623, 49 Am. R. 716 (1884); Warren v. Manchester St. Ry., 70 N. H. 352 47 At. 735, with full collection of authorities, (1900); Bottoms v. Seaboard etc. Ry., 114 N. C. 699, 19 S. E. 730, 25 L. R. A. 784, 41 Am. St. R. 799 (1894); Bellefontaine etc. Ry. v. Snyder, 18 O. St. 399, 98 Am. Dec. 175 (1868); Galveston etc. Ry. v. Moore, 59 Tex. 64, 46 Am. R. 265 (1883); Dicken v. Liverpool etc. Co., 41 W. Va. 511, 23 S. E. 582 (1895); Robinson v. Cone, 22 Vt. 213, 54 Am. Dec. 67 (1850); Chicago etc. Ry. v. Kowalski, 92 Fed. 310, 34 C. C. A. 1, with note classifying decisions, (1899).

[106] Belefontaine etc. Ry. v. Snyder, 24 O. St. 670 (1874; Erie City Ry. v. Schuster, 113 Pa. 412, 6 At. 269, 57 Am. R. 471 (1886); Williams v. Tex. etc., Ry., 60 Tex. 205 (1883).

case, it was judicially declared;[107] "That the true rule of law is that the person who for his own purposes brings on his lands, and collects and keeps there anything likely to do mischief if it escapes, must keep it at his peril; and if he does not do so, is *prima facie* liable for all the damage which is the natural consequence of its escape. He can excuse himself by showing that the escape was owing to the plaintiff's default; or, perhaps, that the escape was the consequence of *vis major,* or the act of God.[108] * * * The general rule, as above stated, seems on principle just. The person whose grass or corn is eaten down by the escaping cattle of his neighbor, or whose mine is flooded by the water from his neighbor's reservoir,[109] or whose cellar is invaded by the filth of his neighbor's privy, or whose habitation is made unhealthy by the fumes and noisome vapors of his neighbor's alkali works, is damnified without any fault of his own; and it seems but reasonable and just that the neighbor, who has brought something on his own property, which was not naturally there, harmless to others so long as it is confined to his own property, but which he knows to be mischievous, if it gets on his neighbor's, should be obliged to make good the damage which ensues if he does not succeed in confining it to his own property. But for his act in bringing it there, no mischief could have accrued, and it seems but just that he should at his peril keep it there, so that no mischief may accrue; or, answer for the natural, and anticipated consequences. And upon authority, this we think is established to be the law, whether the things so brought be beasts, or water, or filth or stenches."

This bold generalization of Mr. Justice Blackburn, has been ex-

[107] Blackburn J. in Fletcher v. Rylands, L. R. 1 Ech. 265, 279-280, 35 L. J. Ex. 154 (1866)), approved in Rylands v. Fletcher, L. R. 3 H. L. 330, 339-340, 37 L. J. Ex. 161 (1868), by Cairns, Ld. Ch., and Cranworth, L. J.; also in Smith v. Giddy. (1904) 2 K. B. 448.

[108] Nichols v. Marsland, L. R. 2 Ex. 1, 46 L. J. Ex. 174 (1876), so holds; and in Box v. Jubb, 4 Ex. D. 76, 48 L. J. Ex. 417 (1879), it was held that a reservoir owner is not liable for the escape of water due to the act of a stranger, which defendant had no reason to anticipate.

[109] In Rylands v. Fletcher, the plaintiff's harm came from water percolating through an ancient coal shaft, long filled up and not known to defendant or his agents, from a reservoir built by defendant on his land.

travagantly praised [110] and extravagantly censured.[116] Having been accepted by the House of Lords, it has fixed the rule for England; and yet, we are assured, "the tendency of later decisions has been rather to encourage the discovery of exceptions than otherwise. * * * No case has been found, not being closely similar in its facts, or within the same previously recognized category, in which the unqualified rule of liability without proof of negligence has been enforced." [112]

Rylands v. Fletcher not Generally Approved in America.

While the decision has been cited frequently by our courts, few of them have given it unqualified approval, while many have emphatically rejected its doctrine. Perhaps the supreme judicial court of Massachusetts has given it countenance beyond most of our tribunals, but even in that jurisdiction, the rule is limited, apparently, to cases of trespass and nuisance.[113] As thus limited, it is neither novel nor objectionable.[114]

[110] Professor Wigmore, in 7 Harv. Lew Rev. pp. 454, 455 speaks of Mr. Justice Blackburn's generalization as "epochal in its consequences." He adds; "The practical effect of that great jurist's opinion has been to furnish us with three main categories of acts to which responsibility is affixed with reference to specific harm, viz. (1) acts done willfully with reference to that harm; (2) acts done at peril with reference to that harm; (3) acts done negligently with reference to that harm."

[111] Mr. Bishop, in his Non-Contract law, § 839, note 3, after quoting the passage given above, remarks; "It is needless to say that such is *not* the law in any common law country. * * * The reasoning so far as it proceeds on grounds, other than negligence, is the individual reasoning of the judges, and not the reasoning of the law."

[112] Pollock, Torts (6 Ed.) 472, 473.

[113] Fitzpatrick v. Welch, 174 Mass. 486, 55 N. E. 178, 48 L. R. A. 278 (1899), where defendant collected water on his roof and discharged it into a gutter, from which it necessarily flowed upon plaintiff's land, unless diverted by defendant. Said Holmes C. J.; "The danger is so manifest, so constant and so great as to impose upon defendant the duty of preventing, at his peril, harm from coming to pass." He cited Shipley v. Fifty Associates, 106 Mass. 194, 8 Am. R. 318 (1870), where defendant maintained a French roof, so near the street, as to cause snow and ice to fall upon travellers; and Jutte v. Hughes, 67 N. Y. 267, (1876), where defendant's drains and privies discharged water and filth upon plaintiff's land.

[114] Supra, Chaps. 11 and 14. Also, Berger v. Minn. Gaslight Co., 60 Minn, 296, 301, 62 N. W. 336 (1895); "It is only those things, the natural tendency of which is to become a nuisance, or to do mischief, if they escape, which the owner keeps

In a recent Massachusetts case, the Rylands v. Fletcher rule, it is said, applies only " to unusual and extraordinary uses of one's property which are so fraught with peril to others, that the owner should not be permitted to adopt them for his own purposes, without absolutely protecting his neighbors from injury or loss by reason of the use; * * * unless he provides safeguards whose perfection he guarantees." [115] Such a rule, it was declared, is not applicable to the construction and maintenance of the walls of an ordinary building near the land of an adjacent owner. " As it is desirable that buildings and fences should be put up, the law does not throw the risk of that act, any more than of other necessary conduct, upon the actor, or make every owner of a structure insure against all that may happen, however little to be foreseen." [116] The duty of a land owner, or occupier, in such case of lawful use, is to make the conditions safe, so far as it can be done by the exercise of ordinary care.

If, however, the walls of a building become ruinous and thus a nuisance to neighbors, or those lawfully near them, the owner is under the duty of not suffering the structure to remain, without using such care in the maintenance of it as will absolutely prevent injuries, except from such causes as *vis major*, acts of public enemies, or wrongful acts of third persons, which human foresight could not reasonably be expected to anticipate and prevent.[117]

The New York Court of Appeals has refused to accept the rule laid down in Rylands v. Fletcher, declaring that it is in direct conflict with the law as settled in this country.[118] Similar disapproval of the rule has been expressed by the courts of last resort in other States.[119] In the New Jersey case, cited in the last note, it is said; " The fallacy in the process of argument by which judgment is

---

at his peril; " thus limiting Cahill v. Eastman, 18 Minn. 324, 10 Am. R. 184 (1872), which followed Rylands v. Fletcher.

[115] Ainsworth v. Lakin, 180 Mass. 397, 62 N. E. 746, 57 L. R. A. 132 (1902).

[116] Quinn v. Cummings, 171 Mass. 255, 50 N. E. 624, 42 L. R. A. 101, 68 Am. St. R. 420 (1898).

[117] Ainsworth v. Lakin, 180 Mass. 397, 62 N. E. 748, 57 L. R. A. 132 (1902); Simmons v. Everson, 124 N. Y. 319, 26 N. E. 911, 21 Am. St. R. 677 (1891).

[118] Losee v. Buchanan, 51 N. Y. 476, 487, 10 Am. R. 623 (1873).

[119] Brown v. Collins, 53 N. H. 442, 16 Am. R. 372, and note (1873); Marshall v. Welwood, 38 N. J. L. 339, 20 Am. R. 394 (1876).

reached, in the case of Fletcher v. Rylands, appears to consist in this : that the rule mainly applicable to a class of cases, which should be regarded as, in a great degree exceptional, is amplified into a general if not universal principle." Let us consider these exceptional cases.

Liability for Cattle and Nuisances. We have seen in a former chapter [120] that a person acts at his peril in maintaining a nuisance; and, in another chapter,[121] that the owner of trespassing cattle is answerable for all the harm done by them, whether he have notice of their disposition to do the particular harm or not. But we also saw, that the owner of cattle is not liable for harm done by them while driven along the highway without negligence on his part, and without notice of their viciousness; nor is he liable for mischief done by them to the person or personal property of another, at other times, when the action is not one of trespass *quare clausum fregit*, without proof that he had notice of their viciousness, or that he was otherwise negligent.[122]

Clearly it cannot be said that the common law imposed upon the owner of cattle the liability of an insurer against all damage done by them, if they escaped from his land.[123]

Vicious Animals. When these are not useful for any lawful purpose, or are so kept, as to be a menace to human beings, while engaged in lawful pursuits, they are fairly classed as a nuisance. Hence they may be killed without incurring liability; and, if they do damage, their owner or responsible keeper must answer therefor.[124]

When, however, the vicious animal, such as a watch-dog, may be lawfully kept for useful purposes, the liability of the owner or keeper is for negligence in the manner of keeping it.[125] He is, of

[120] Chapter XIV.

[121] Chapter XI.

[122] Van Leuven v. Lyke, 1 N. Y. 515, 516, 49 Am. Dec. 346 (1848); Annapolis etc. Ry. v. Baldwin, 60 Md. 88, 45 Am. R. 711 (1892).

[123] In Chapter XI, it was shown that custom and legislation have modified the common law liability of cattle owners materially.

[124] Jones v. Carey, 9 Houst. (Del.)

214, 31 At. 976 (1891); Aldrich v. Wright, 53 N. H. 398, 16 Am. R. 329 (1873); Muller v. McKesson, 73 N. Y. 195, 29 Am. R. 129 (1878).

[125] Knickerbocker Ice Co. v. Finn, 80 Fed. 483 (1897); Baldwin v. Ensign, 49 Conn. 113, 44 Am. R. 205 (1881); Hahnke v. Friederick, 140 N. Y. 224, 35 N. E. 487 (1893); Duval v. Barnaby, 75 App. Div. 154, 77 N. Y. Supp. 337, 11 N. Y. Anne-

course, bound to exercise a degree of care, commensurate with the
danger to others which will follow the dog's escape from his custody, to so secure it that it will not injure anyone who does not unlawfully provoke or intermeddle with it," or invite an attack from
it.[126]

Care of Fire and Electricity. The common law held the person starting a fire, even for necessary and lawful purposes, to an
absolute responsibility for its consequences. The doctrine of a carefully considered case, decided in 1400 A. D.,[127] is thus stated in
Rolle's Abridgment: " If my fire by misfortune burns the goods of
another man, he shall have an action against me. * * * If my servant put a candle or other fire in a place in my house and it falls and
burns my house and the house of my neighbor, an action on the
case lies against me." [128] The only defense available to the one, on
whose premises a fire originated, was that the fire was due to the
unauthorized act of a stranger, or of one for whose act defendant
was not legally answerable.

This doctrine was modified by statute in 1707,[130] so as to exempt
land holders from liability for accidental fires; but for the consequences of fire negligently or intentionally started for any purpose,
the originator is absolutely liable still,[131] save in cases where he has
received statutory authority to maintain a fire, as in the case of
railroad companies.[132]

---

tated Cas. 227 and note (1902);
Benoit v. Troy etc. Ry., 154 N. Y.
223, 48 N. E. 524 (1897); Hayes v.
Smith, 62 O. St. 161, 182, 56 N. E.
879 (1900); Crowley v. Groonell, 73
Vt. 45, 50 At. 546, 55 L. R. A. 876,
86 Am. St. R. 790 (1901), a big dog
whose assault may have been play-
ful, but was dangerous.

[126] DeGray v. Murray, 69 N. J. L.
458, 55 At. 237 (1903); Worthen v.
Love, 60 Vt. 285, 14 At. 461 (1888).
In some states the liability of the
owner or keeper of dogs has been
made nearly absolute. See Dillehay
v. Hickey, (Ky.) 71 S. W. 1 (1902);
Carroll v. Marcoux, 98 Me. 259, 56
At. 848 (1903); Riley v. Harris, 177
Mass. 163, 58 N. E. 584 (1900);

Jenkinson v. Coggins, 123 Mich. 7,
81 N. W. 974 (1900); Peck v. Williams, 24 R. I. 583, 54 At. 381
(1903).

[127] Beaulieu v. Finglam, 2 H. IV.,
18 pl. 6.

[128] Action Sur. Case, Pur. Fewe,
B. 1 and 3.

[129] Allen v. Stephenson, 1 Lutw. 90
(1700).

[130] Chap. 31, Sec. 6, of 6 Anne, sup-
erceded by 14 Geo. 3, Chap. 78, Sec.
86.

[131] Filliter v. Phippard, 11 Q. B.
347, 17 L. J. Q. B. 89 (1847), rejecting Blackstone's and Lord
Lyndhurst's understanding of the
statutes.

[132] Jones v. Festiniog Ry., L. R. 3

The same extraordinary liability rests upon one, who brings electricity upon his premises, whence it escapes to the harm of his neighbors.[133]

In this country, the common law liability for fire has never been enforced. A person does not start a fire on his land at his peril. If it spreads beyond his premises and harms others, his liability for the harm must be grounded on his negligence. The same is true of his liability for electricity escaping from his control. In both cases, however, the care which he must exercise in guarding the dangerous element, varies with the hazard to which it exposes others.[134]

In some states, the liability for the consequences of fire is regulated by statute.[135]

Liability for Explosives. This, under the doctrine of Rylands v. Fletcher, should be absolute, and such seems to be the holding in England.[136] In this country, the liability is absolute, only when the defendant's conduct amounts to the maintenance of a nuisance.[137] Otherwise, his liability is for negligence. If he is ignorant of the character of the explosive, and his ignorance is not due to fault on his part, his duty of care is fixed by the apparent character of the article.[138] Otherwise, he is bound to exercise a degree

Q. B. 733, 37 L. J. Q. B. 214 (1868); Powell v. Fall, 5 Q. B. D. 597, 49 L. J. Q. B. 423 (1880).

[133] Nat. Tel. Co. v. Baker, (1893) 2 Ch. 186, 62 L. J. Ch. 699.

[134] St. Louis etc. Ry. v. Youley, 53 Ark. 503, 14 S. W. 800 (1890); Burroughs v. Housatonic Ry., 15 Conn. 124, 38 Am. Dec. 64 (1842); Hauch v. Hernandez, 41 La. Ann. 992, 6 So. 783 (1889); Batchelder v. Heagan, 18 Me. 32 (1840); Hewey v. Nourse, 54 Me. 257 (1866); Clark v. Foot, 8 Johns. (N. Y.) 421 (1811). Liability for electricity, Southern Bell Tel. Co. v. McTyer, 137 Al. 601, 34 So. 1020 (1903); Knowlton v. DesMoines etc. Co., 117 Ia. 451, 90 N. W. 818 (1902); Thomas v. Maysville Gas Co., 108 Ky. 224, 56 S. W. 154 (1900); Gerrish v. Whitfield, 72 N. H. 222 55 At. 551 (1903); Mitchell v. Raleigh Elec. Co., 129 N. C. 166, 39 S. E. 801 (1901); Daltry v. Media Elec. Co., 208 Pa. 403, 57 At. 833 (1904); Cumberland etc. Co. v. United Elec. Ry., 93 Tenn. 492, 29 S. W. 104, 27 L. R. A. 236 (1894); Joyce, Electric Law, Chap. 22.

[135] Shearman & Redfield, Negligence (5 Ed.) Sec. 671, and authorities there cited.

[136] Clerk and Lindsell, Torts (2 Ed.) 375.

[137] Heeg v. Licht, 80 N. Y. 579, 36 Am. R. 654 (1880); and authorities cited in the chapter on Nuisance.

[138] The Nitro-Glycerine case, 15 Wall. (U. S. 524, 21 L. Ed. 206 (1872). The third head note is as follows: "Where there is nothing to excite the suspicion of a com-

of care commensurate with the hazard to which his possession, use or sale of the explosive subjects others,[139] who are free from contributory fault.[140]

Poisons and Other Dangerous Articles. Here, again, the liability of the manufacturer, seller, lender or user is not that of an insurer of safety. He does not act at his peril in lawfully making, selling, lending, or using such articles. He does incur liability, however, even to persons with whom he has no contract relations, when he fails to exercise such care as is fairly necessary to the protection of others against the extraordinary hazard to which these articles subject them.[141] Accordingly, if a drug dealer sells to a

mon carrier as to the contents of a package, it is not negligence * * * to handle it in the same manner as other packages, of similar outward appearance, are handled." At p. 538, after referring to cases arising from fire, blasting and similar causes, the court says: "The rule deducible from them is, that the measure of care against accident, which one must take to avoid responsibility, is that which a person of ordinary prudence and caution would use, if his own interests were to be affected, and the whole risk were his own."

[139] Carter v. Towne, 98 Mass. 567, 96 Am. Dec. 682 (1868); Wellington v. Downer Ker. Oil Co., 104 Mass. 64 (1870); Weiser v. Holzman, 33 Wash. 87, 73 Pac. 797 (1903). In the last cited case, plaintiff alleged "negligence in the manufacture and bottling of a dangerous explosive, called champagne cider;" and the complaint was held upon demurrer to state a good cause of action. In Walker v. Chic. etc. Ry., 71 Ia. 658, 33 N. W. 224 (1887), plaintiff failed, because she did not give evidence of negligence on defendant's part. See Binford v. Johnson, 82 Ind. 426, Am. R. 508 (1882);

Waters-Pierce Oil Co. v. Davis, 24 Tex. Civ. App. 508, 60 S. W. 453 (1900); Smith v. Clark Hardware Co., 100 Ga. 163, 28 S. E. 73, 39 L. R. A. 607 (1897).

[140] Birmingham Water Works Co. v. Hubbard, 85 Al. 179, 4 So. 607 (1887); the jury exonerated the plaintiff from contributory negligence. In Carter v. Towne, 103 Mass. 507 (1870), it appeared that the plaintiff, a child of eight, had handed gun-powder to her mother, after buying it from the defendant, and thus the latter escaped the liability, which he was held in 98 Mass. 567, *supra*, to have incurred; his negligent sale, and delivery to the child was not the proximate cause of the child's injury from the explosion. See Gartin v. Meredith, 153 Ind. 16, 63 N. E. 936 (1897).

[141] Salisbury v. Erie Ry., 66 N. J. L. 233, 50 At. 117, 55 L. R. A. 578, 88 Am. St. R. 480 (1901); defendant held liable for negligent use of handcar, by one to whom foreman had loaned it; Winkler v. Car. & N. W. Ry., 126 N. C. 370, 35 S. E. 621, 78 Am. St. R. 663 (1900); defendant held liable for negligently maintaining a barbwire fence.

druggist a jar of belladonna, negligently labeled "'extract of dandelion," he is liable to any one who sustains injury by using the drug as dandelion.[142]   Again, a person, who sells or rents an article, which he knows, or is legally bound to know, is imminently dangerous to life or limb, to another, without giving notice of its qualities, is liable to any person who suffers injury therefrom, which might have been reasonably anticipated.[143]   Especially is this true, when the defendant has been guilty of fradulent or unjustifiable concealment of dangerous defects.[144]

Cases coming within these principles are to be distinguished from those falling within the general rule that a contractor, manufacturer, vendor or bailor is not liable to third parties, who have no contractual relations with him, for negligence, as distinguished from fraudulent or wanton conduct in the construction, manufacture, sale or bailment of property.[145]   It is frequently difficult to determine

[142] Thomas v. Winchester, 6 N. Y. 397, 57 Am. Dec. 455 (1852); Accord, Mood-Balm Co. v. Cooper, 83 Ga. 457, 10 S. E. 118, 5 L. R. A. 612, 20 Am. St. R. 324 (1889); Norton v. Sewall, 106 Mass. 143, 8 Am. R. 298, (1870); Davis v. Guarnieri, 45 O. St. 470, 15 N. E. 350, 4 Am. St. R. 548 (1887); Wise v. Morgan, 101 Tenn. 273, 48 S. W. 971 (1898); Peters v. Johnson, 50 W. Va. 644, 41 S. E. 190 57 L. R. A. 428 (1902); George v. Skivington, L. R. 5 Ex. 1, 38 L. J. Ex. 8 (1869).

[143] Lewis v. Terry, 111 Cal. 39, 43 Pac. 398, 31 L. R. A. 220, 52 Am. St. R. 146 (1896),a folding bed; Hayes v. Phil. etc. Ry., 150 Mass. 457, 23 N. E. 225 (1890); Necker v. Harvey, 49 Mich. 517, 14 N. W. 503 (1883); Barrett v. Lake Ont. Co., 174 N. Y. 310, 66 N. E. 968, 61 L. R. A. 829 (1903); Schutte v. United Elec. Co., 68 N. J. L. 435, 53 At. 204 (1902); Carson v. Godley, 26 Pa. 111, 67 Am. Dec. 404 (1856); Elkins v. McKean, 79 Pa. 493 (1875); Elliott v. Hall, 15 Q. B. D. 315, 54 L. J. Q. B. 518

(1885); Parry v. Smith, 4 C. P. D. 325, 48 L. J. G. P. 731 (1879).

[144] Langridge v. Levy, 2 M. & W. 519, 46 R. R. 693 (1837); Schubert v. J. R. Clark Co., 49 Minn. 331, 51 N. W. 1103, 15 L. R. A. 818, 32 Am. St. R. 559 (1892); Kahner v. Otis, Elevator Co., 96 App. Div. 169, 89 N. Y. Supp. 185 (1904); contra, Kuelling v. Roderick Lean Mfg. Co., 88 App. Div. (N. Y.) 309 (1903).

[145] Heizer v. Kingsland etc. Co., 110 Mo. 605, 19 S. W. 630, 15 L. R. A. 821, 33 Am. St. R. 481 (1892); Curtin v. Somerset, 140 Pa. 70, 21 At. 244, 12 L. R. A. 322, 23 Am. St. R. 220 (1891); McCaffrey v. Mossberg etc. Co., 23 R. I. 381, 50 At. 651, 55 L. R. A. 822 (1901); Bragdon v. Perkins- Campbell Co., 87 Fed. 109, 58 U. S. App. 91, 30 C. C. A. 567, (1898); Stand. Oil Co. v. Murray, 119 Fed. 572, 57 C. C. A. 1, with valuable note (1902); Huset v. J. I. Case etc. Co., 120 Fed. 865, 57 C. C. A. 237 (1903), a very valuable case. See also Ulshowski v. Hill, 61 N. J. L. 375, 39 At. 904 (1898); Styles v.

to which of the foregoing classes a particular case belongs, and different courts have drawn inconsistent inferences from similar states of fact. But the rule of law applicable when the question of fact has been settled, is not in dispute.

Common Carriers, Liverymen, Caterers, etc. Persons engaged in the foregoing and similar callings, whose business directly involves the personal safety and lives of others, and who assume to be specially skilled in their occupations,[146] are bound, it is said,[147] to exercise "the most watchful care and the most active diligence; anything short of this is negligence and carelessness, and would furnish clear ground of liability if an injury was thereby sustained." This doctrine has been applied with no little rigor to common carriers, who employ modern methods of transportation. While they are not insurers of the safety, even of passengers with whom they have contracted, they are bound to exercise a degree of care and vigilance, commensurate with the risk which their route, their rate of speed, and the other conditions, for which they are responsible, subject third persons, whether passengers or those having no contract relation with them. At times, this requires from them the "exercise of extraordinary vigilance aided by the highest skill," and they are liable for "the slightest negligence or fault in this regard."[148] At other times "a less degree of care is required," they

F. R. Long Co., ——N. J. L. —— 57 At. 448 (1904); Slattery v. Colgate, 25 R. I. 220, 55 At. 639 (1903).

[146] Bishop v. Weber, 139 Mass. 411, 1 N. E. 154, 52 Am. R. 715, (1885), case of Caterer. Physicians are bound to exercise such skill and care, as are exercised generally by physicians of ordinary care and skill, in similar circumstances. Burk v. Foster, 114 Ky. 20, 69 S. W. 1096 (1902); Gillette v. Tucker, 67 O. St. 106, 65 N. E. 865 (1902).

[147] Hadley v. Cross, 34 Vt. 586, 588, 80 Am. Dec. 699 (1861); liverymen are not insurers, however, of the safety of their patrons. They are liable only for negligence; Copeland v. Draper, 157 Mass. 558, 39 N. E. 944, 19 L. R. A. 283, 34 Am. St. R. 314 (1893). Although slight

negligence may be enough, Horne v. Meakin, 115 Mass. 326 (1874).

[148] Penn. Co. v. Roy, 102 U. S. 451, 456, 26 L. Ed. 141 (1880); Ingalls v. Bills, 9 Met. (59 Mass.) 1, 43 Am. Dec. 346 (1845); Hegeman v. Western Ry 13 N. Y. 9, 64 Am. Dec. 517 (1855); B. & O. Ry. v. Wightman, 29 Gratt (Va.) 431, 445, 26 Am. R. 384, (1877); "The slightest neglect, against which human prudence and foresight might have guarded, and by reason of which his death may have been occasioned, renders such company liable in damages for such death;" Searle v. Kanawha Ry., 32 W. Va. 370, 9 S. E. 248 (1884); Redhead v. Midland Ry., L. R. 4 Q. B. 379, 38 L. J. Q. B. 169 (1869); Hyman v. Nye, 6 Q. B. D. 685, 44 L. T. 919 (1881).

are " bound simply to exercise ordinary care in view of the dangers to be apprehended." [149]

Liability of Landowners to Lawful Passers-By. In the absence of a statute imposing specific duties upon landowners and occupiers,[150] they are not absolutely liable to persons lawfully passing by their premises, for harm sustained by such persons from causes originating thereon, unless these sources of harm are nuisances,[151] or unless the harm is due to an act of trespass for which the landowner is responsible.[152] The measure of duty resting upon the landowner, in other than these exceptional cases, is to make a reasonable and proper use of his land. Whether he has been negligent in the performance of this duty; whether his use of his land is an unnecessary interference with the rights of passers-by, and subjects them to unnecessary danger, must depend upon the facts of each case.[153] When he has been thus negligent, and his misconduct has caused harm to a lawful passer-by, he must answer for it.[154]

Liability of Landowner to Invited Persons. Towards those expressly or impliedly invited upon one's premises, for mutual advantage, the inviter owes the duty of ordinary care. He is not the

[149] Kelly v. Manhattan Ry., 112 N. Y. 443, 450, 20 N. E. 383, 3 L. R. A. 443 (1889). *Accord*, Ark. Mid. Ry. v. Canman, 52 Ark. 517, 13 S. W. 280 (1889). In the New York case, the negligence consisted in allowing the steps of a station stairway to become slippery. In the Arkansas case, the plaintiff contended that it was negligence, to run mixed passenger and freight trains.

[150] Smith v. Milwaukee etc. Exchange, 91 Wis. 360, 64 N. W. 1041, 30 L. R. A. 504, 51 Am. St. R. 912 (1895).

[151] Parker v. Union Woolen Co., 42 Conn. 399, 402 (1875).

[152] Smethurst v. Barton Square Church, 148 Mass. 261, 19 N. E. 387, 2 L. R. A. 695, 12 Am. St. R. 550 (1889).

[153] Wolf v. DesMoines Elec. Co., 124 Ia. ——, 98 N. W. 301 (1904);

Morris v. Whipple, 183 Mass. 27, 69 N. E. 199 (1903); Fielders v. Nor. Jersey Ry., 68 N. J. L. 343, 53 At. 404, 59 L. R. A. 455, 96 Am. St. R. 552 (1902); Brendle v. Spencer, 125 N. C. 474, 34 S. E. 635 (1899). Defendant blew a locomotive whistle, near the highway, for the purpose of frightening plaintiff's horses, and thereby caused them to run away. Jury found this conduct was willful and wanton.

[154] Crogan v. Schiele, 53 Conn. 186, 55 Am. R. 88 (1885); Haughey v. Hart, 62 Ia. 96, 17 N. W. 189 (1883); Detzur v. Stroh Brewing Co., 119 Mich. 282, 77 N. W. 948, 44 L. R. A. 500 (1899); Jager v. Adams, 123 Mass. 26, 25 Am. R. 7 (1877); Weller v. McCormick, 52 N. J. L. 470, 19 At. 1101, 8 L. R. A. 798 (1890); Beck v. Carter, 68 N. Y. 283, 23 Am. R. 175 (1877).

insurer of their safety, nor is he bound to exercise extraordinary care in guarding them from harm, unless the nature of his enterprise subjects them to extraordinary danger. Nor is he bound to guard them against harm, to which they unnecessarily expose themselves. But he is under the duty of having those parts of his premises to which they are invited, in a reasonably safe condition for them.[155]

This class of persons includes those who enter stores, or hotels, or other business places, in accordance with ordinary usage; [156] tenants of portions of a building and their business callers; [157] persons calling to pay or collect debts, or make estimates for work in the customary manner; [158] and others of like sort. Whether a person is within this class, or upon premises as a mere licensee, appears to depend upon the application to the facts of the particular case of " the principle that invitation is inferred, where there is a common interest or mutual advantage, while a license is inferred, where the object is the mere pleasure or benefit of the person using the premises." [159]

Liability to Licensees. Inasmuch as a licensee is upon the premises of another for his own benefit or pleasure, we should ex-

---

[155] Indemauer v. Dames, L. R. 1 C. P. 274, 35 L. J. C. P. 274 (1866); L. R. 2 C. P. 311, 36 L. J. C. P. 181 (1867); Crogan v. Schiele, 53 Conn. 186, 1 At. 899, 55 Am. R. 88 (1885); D'Amico v. City of Boston, 176 Mass. 599, 58 N. E. 158 (1900); Land v. Fitzgerald, 68 N. J. L. 28, 52 At. 229 (1902).

[156] Sweeney v. Old Colony Ry., 10 Allen (Mass.) 368, 87 Am. Dec. 644 (1865); Brotherton v. Manhat. Beach Co., 48 Neb. 563, 67 N. W. 479 (1896), S. C. 50 Neb. 214, 68 N. W. 757 (1897); public bathing beach; Dinnihan v. Lake Ont. Co., 8 App. Div. 509, 40 N. Y. Supp. 764 (1896); toboggan slide at a bathing resort; Houston etc. Ry. v. Phillio, 96 Tex. 18, 69 S. W. 994, 59 L. R. A. 392 (1902); Hupfer v. Nat'l Dist. Co., 114 Wis. 279, 90 N. W. 191 (1902).

[157] Crane Elev. Co. v. Lippert, 63 Fed. 942 (1894); Wilcox v. Zane, 167 Mass. 302, 45 N. E. 923 (1897); Swords v. Edgar, 59 N. Y. 28, 17 Am. R. 295 (1874); Stenberg v. Wilcox, 96 Tenn. 163, 33 S. W. 917, 34 L. R. A. 615 (1896); Miller v. Hancock, (1893) 2 Q. B. 177. In Hart v. Cole, 156 Mass. 475, 31 N. E. 645, 6 L. R. A. 557 (1892), it was held that a person attending a wake, without special request, was not an invited person within the rule.

[158] Peake v. Buell, 90 Wis. 508, 63 N. W. 1053, 48 Am. St. R. 946 (1895).

[159] Campbell, Negligence § 33, quoted with approval in Bennett v. Ry. Co., 102 U. S. 577, 26 L. Ed. 235 (1880).

pect the licensor to be liable only for gross negligence. And such is the view taken in England, and, generally, in this country. He who is receiving the gratuitous favors of another has no such relation to him, it is said, as to create a duty to make safer or better, than it happens to be, the place where hospitality is tendered. The licensee must take the premises as he finds them.[160] At most, he can claim only that the licensor shall abstain from entrapping him to his harm;[161] shall not create new and undisclosed sources of danger, without warning him of the change of situation.[162]

Whether the invited private guest is to be classed with licensees, or with invited persons, is a question upon which judicial opinion is somewhat at variance. In England it is well settled that he is a

[160] Hounsel v. Smith, 7 C. B. N. S. 731, 29 L. J. C. P. 303 (1860); Gautret v. Egerton, L. R. 2 C. P. 371, 36 L. J. C. P. 191 (1867); Rooney v. Woolworth, 74 Conn. 720, 52 At. 411 (1902); Ill. C. Ry. v. Eicher, 202 Ill. 556, 67 N. E. 376 (1903); Lary v. Clev. etc. Ry., 78 Ind. 323, 41 Am. R. 572 (1881); Cumberland etc. Co. v. Martin, —— Ky. ——, 76 S. W. 394 (1903); Settoon v. Tex. etc., Ry., 48 La. Ann. 807, (1896); Dixon v. Swift, 98 Me. 207, 56 At. 761 (1903); Reardon v. Thompson, 149 Mass. 267, 21 N. E. 369 (1889); Taylor v. Haddonfield etc. Co., 65 N. J. L. 103, 46 At. 707 (1900); Larmore v. Crown Pt. Co., 101 N. Y. 391, 4 N. E. 752 (1886); Ann Arbor Ry. v. King, 68 O. St. 210, 67 N. E. 479 (1903); Paolino v. McKendall, 24 R. I. 432, 53 At. 268, 60 L. R. A. 133, 96 Am. St. R. 736 (1902); Clapp v. LaGrill, 103 Tenn. 164, 52 S. W. 134 (1899); Felton v. Aubrey, 74 Fed. 350 (1896); Ellsworth v. Metheney, 104 Fed. 119 (1900).

[161] Corby v. Hill, 4 C. B. N. S. 556, 27 L. J. C. P. 318 (1858); Gallagher v. Humphrey, 6 L. T. R. N. S. 684, 10 W. R. 664 (1862); Byrne v. N.

Y. C. Ry., 104 N. Y. 362, 10 N. E. 539 (1887); Harriman v. Pittsburg etc. Ry., 45 O. St. 11, 12 N. E. 451, 4 Am. St. R. 507 (1887), torpedoes placed on track by defendant's servants, in mere wantonness; Campbell v. Boyd, 88 N. C. 129, 43 Am. R. 740 (1883); Davis v. Chic. etc. Ry., 58 Wis. 646, 17 N. W. 406, 46 Am. R. 667 (1883), repudiating the distinction between active and passive negligence in such cases.

[162] Beck v. Carter, 68 N. Y. 283, 23 Am. R. 175 (1877). The case of Lepnick v. Gaddes, 72 Miss. 200, 16 So. 213, 26 L. R. A. 686, with note, 48 Am. St. R. 547 (1894), was decided on the pleadings, the defendant having demurred to the declaration; and the court held that a cause of action against the licensor was set forth. When the case came to trial, however, the plaintiff failed to show that he had been entrapped, by any inducement of the defendant. The evidence disclosed that the defendant was not invited, or even licensed, to cross defendant's vacant lot, upon which was an uncovered cistern. See S. C. 18 So. 319 (1895).

licensee.[163]   This, it is submitted, is the true doctrine, whenever he is enjoying gratuitous hospitality.[164]   In some of our jurisdictions, however, there is a disposition to work out a species of estoppel against even the private host.[165]   It is well settled, that the guest of a tenant has no greater rights against the landlord than the tenant has [166] and one invited upon premises for a particular purpose, becomes either a licensee or a trespasser, if he uses it for any other purpose.[167].

Liability of Trespassers. We have seen in a previous chapter that a trespasser is not an outlaw. The landowner is bound not to attack him; nor set spring guns or similar dangerous traps for him, without proper warning; [168] nor subject him to harm by wilful, reckless or wanton conduct.[169]   He is under no duty, however, to anti-

---

[163] Southcote v. Stanley, 1 H. & N. 247, 25 L. J. Ex. 339 (1856); Pollock C. B. said; " The same principle applies to the case of a visitor at a house; whilst he remains there, he is in the same position as any other member of the establishment, so far as regards the negligence of the master or his servants; and he must take his chance with the rest;" Bramwell, B., rested his opinion upon the fact, that the falling, of the glass from a door upon the plaintiff was due to defendant's omission, as distinguished from commission.

[164] Shearman and Redfield, Negligence (5 Ed.) § 706; Thompson's commentaries on Negligence (2 Ed.) Vol. 1, § 971; Plummer v. Dill, 156 Mass. 426, 31 N. E. 128, 32 Am. St. R. 463 (1892), semble.

[165] Barman v. Spencer, (Ind.) 49 N. E. 9, 44 L. R. A. 815 (1898). Cf. Atlanta Oil Mills Co. v. Coffey, 80 Ga. 145, 4 S. E. 759, 12 Am. St. R. 244 (1887), where plaintiff was on defendant's land to take away goods, given by the latter to the former; Phillips v. Library Co., 55 N. J. L. 307, 27 At. 478 (1893);

Davis v. Cent. Cong'l. Soc., 129 Mass. 367, 37 Am. R. 368 (1880).

[166] McConnell v. Lemley, 48 La. Ann. 1443, 20 So. 887, 34 L. R. A. 609, 55 Am. St. R. 319 (1896); Roche v. Sawyer, 176 Mass. 71, 57 N. E. 216 (1900).

[167] Ryerson v. Bathgate, 67 N. J. L. 537, 51 At. 708, 57 L. R. A. 307 (1902).

[158] Supra, Chap. 3. But a trespasser who goes upon land, knowing it is thus defended against unlawful intruders, takes the risk of the situation. Magar v. Hammond, 171 N. Y. 377, 64 N. E. 150, 59 L. R. A. 315 (1902).

[469] Marble v. Ross, 124 Mass. 44 (1878), defendant kept a vicious stag in a pasture; held to be reckless misconduct. In Quigley v. Clough, 170 Mass. 429, 53 N. E. 884, 45 L. R. A. 500 (1899), the court held that a barb-wire fence, put up to prevent persons from taking a short cut across his lawn, was to be distinguished from an active source of harm, such as a spring-gun or a vicious animal; and a verdict, directed by the trial judge for the defendant, was sustained.

cipate the presence of trespassers, or to regulate his business conduct with a view to safeguarding them. His duty to a trespasser, it is generally agreed, " is merely negative. He must not go on maliciously, or with disregard for obvious consequences, when he knows of the peril. He is not required to use care to anticipate and discover the peril of such a person, but only to do so after the discovery of the danger. Until then, no legal duty is imposed, because no one by a wrongful act can impose a duty upon another." [170]

Examples of wilful, reckless, or wanton conduct towards a known, or anticipated trespasser, are afforded by the cases noted below.[171]

Alluring Infant Trespassers. An exception to the rule of nonliability to trespassers has developed in several jurisdictions, in favor of children. It is stated as follows in a leading case : [172] " Although a child of tender years, who meets with an injury upon the premises of a private owner, may be a technical trespasser, yet the owner may be liable, if the things causing the injury have been left

---

[170] Louisville & N. Ry. v. Hocker, 111 Ky. 707, 64 S W. 638, 65 S. W. 119 (1901); Christian v. Ill. C. Ry., 71 Miss. 237, 15 So. 71 (1894); Buch v. Amory Mfg. Co., 69 N. H. 257, 44 At. 809 (1898); Cleveland etc. Ry. v. Marsh, 63 O. St. 236, 245, 58 N. E. 821 (1900); Rathbone v. Oregon Ry., 40 Or. 225, 66 Pac. 909 (1901); Singleton v. Felton, 101 Fed. 526 42 C. C. A. 57 (1900).

[171] Western & A. Ry. v. Bailey, 105 Ga. 100, 31 S. E. 547 (1898), running a train at a reckless rate of speed, and without sounding whistle or bell, after discovering the trespasser; Ill. C. Ry. v. Leiner, 202 Ill. 24, 67 N. E. 398 (1903), no attempt made to avoid a collision; the terms willful and wanton are discussed, at length, in this case; Palmer v. Gordon, 173 Mass. 410, 53 N. E. 909 (1899), defendant spilled water on a hot stove to frighten plaintiff, and scalded him; Carney v. Concord St. Ry., 72 N. H. 364, 57 At. 218 (1903); starting a car, under which a child nad been caught, instead of lifting it; Smith v. Savannah Ry., 100 Ga. 96, 27 S. E. 725 (1896); Kansas City Ry. v. Kelly, 36 Ks. 655 14 Pac. 172 (1887); Smith v. Louisville & N. Ry., 95 Ky. 11, 23 S. W. 652 (1893); Farber v. Mo. etc. Ry., 139 Mo. 272, 40 S. W. 932 (1897); Southern Ry. v. Shaw, 86 Fed. 865, 31 C. C. A. 70 and note (1898). In the last five cases, trespassers were recklessly eejcted from moving cars.

[172] City of Pekin v. McMahon, 154 Ill. 141, 39 N. E. 484, 45 Am. St. R. 114, 27 L. R. A. 206 (1895). The city owned unenclosed lots, whereon were water and timbers, with which children were accustomed to play. The city was held liable for the drowning of a trespassing child, in this alluring flood.

exposed and unguarded, and are of such a character as to be an attraction to the child, appealing to his childish curiosity and instincts. Unguarded premises, which are thus supplied with dangerous attractions are regarded as holding out implied invitations to such children." The argument in favor of this exception rests chiefly upon the assumption that the child is allured by the landowner, and hence cannot be regarded as a voluntary trespasser. But it rests to some extent upon the feeling that landowners ought to have a special regard for the safety of children.[173]

In reply to this argument it is urged that, if carried to its logical conclusion, it would render the owner of a fruit tree liable for damages to a trespassing boy, who, in attempting to get the fruit, should fall from the tree and be injured, or who should be made sick by eating green, or harmful fruit; that it would charge the duty of protecting children upon every member of the community, except upon their own parents.[174]

Authorities for the Infant. These begin with Lynch v. Nurdin,[175] in England, and Stout v. Sioux City Ry.,[176] in this country.

---

[173] In Keffe v. Mil. etc. Ry., 21 Minn. 207, 18 Am. R. 393 (1875); the court said; " Now, what an express invitation would be to an adult, the temptation of an attractive play ground is to a child of tender years. If the defendant had left its turntable, unfastened, for the purpose of attracting young children to play upon it, knowing the danger into which it was alluring them, it would certainly be no defense to an action by the plaintiff, who had been attracted upon the turntable and injured, to say, that the plaintiff was a trespasser, and that his childish ' instincts were no excuse for his trespass." In Thompson's Commentaries on on Negligence (2 Ed.) 1026, the learned author says; " One doctrine under this head is, that if a child trespasses upon the premises of the defendant, and is injured in consequence of something that befalls

him while trespassing, he cannot recover damages, unless the injury was wantonly inflicted, or was due to the recklessly careless conduct of the defendant. This cruel and wicked doctrine, unworthy of a civilized jurisprudence, puts property above humanity, leaves entirely out of view the tender years and infirmity of understanding of the child, indeed his inability to be a trespasser in sound legal theory, and visits upon him the consequences of his trespass, just as though he were an adult."

[174] Brinkley Car Works v. Cooper, —Ark. — 67 S. W. 752 (1902).

[175] 1 Q. B. 29, 10 L. J. Q. B. 73 (1841).

[176] Stout v. Sioux City etc. Ry., 2 Dillon (U. S. C. C.) 294, Fed. Cases, 13, 504 (1872). Affirmed as Ry. Co. v. Stout, 17 Wall, (U. S.) 657, 21 L. Ed. 745 (1873).

In the English case, the defendant's carman went into a house, leaving his horse and cart unwatched and unfastened in the street for half an hour. During this period, the plaintiff, a lad of seven, and several other children began playing with the outfit. He got upon the cart; and was thrown under the wheel and run over, by reason of one of his companions starting the horse. At the trial, defendant's counsel asked the court to direct the jury that the plaintiff could not recover, as his own negligence brought the mischief upon him. This was refused, and the jury were told that it was for them to say, first, whether it was negligent to leave the horse and cart as they were left; and, second, whether that negligence occasioned the accident. This refusal and direction were upheld by the appellate court. The Lord Chief Justice declared, that the case presented more than the want of care on the plaintiff's part. " We find in it," he said, " the positive misconduct of the plaintiff—an active instrument towards the effect. We have here express authorities for our guidance." He then proceeds to discuss the spring-gun [177] and dog-spike [178] cases, as the proper authorities for the case in hand. After stating them, he proceeds; " A distinction may be taken between the willful act done by the defendant in those cases, in deliberately planting a dangerous weapon in his ground with the design of destroying trespassers, and the mere negligence of the defendant's servant in leaving his cart in the open street. But between willful mischief and gross negligence, the boundary line is hard to trace; I should say, impossible." Accordingly he concludes, it was for the jury to say whether the defendant's misconduct amounted to gross negligence and so brought him within the doctrine of Bird v. Holbrook.[179] He says, " They would naturally inquire whether the horse was vicious or steady; whether the occasion required the servant to be so long absent from his charge, and whether in that case no assistance could have been procured to watch the horse; whether the street was at that hour likely to be clear or thronged with a noisy multitude; especially whether large parties of young children might be reasonably expected to resort to the spot. If this last mentioned fact were probable, it would be hard to say that a case of gross negligence was not fully established."

[177] Ilott v. Wilkes, 3 B. & Ald. 304, 22 R. R. 400 (1820); Bird v. Holbrook, 4 Bing. 628, 29 R. R. 657 (1828).

[178] Deane v. Clayton, 7 Taunt. 489, 18 R. R. 553 (1817).

Although this case has been approved recently in England,[180] it has also been doubted by eminent judges,[181] and its doctrine is certainly inconsistent with some later cases,[182] unless it is to be limited to misconduct toward trespassing children, which is positively unlawful or wanton.[183]

Railroad Company v. Stout. In this case, it appeared that the railroad company maintained a turntable on its land, which had been constructed and was used in the ordinary way, in the company's business. It was about a quarter of a mile from the company's station-house, in an unfenced lot. There were but few houses in the neighborhood, and plaintiff's house was three quarters of a mile away. He, a boy of six years, with two other boys a little older, went to the turntable and finding it unlocked and unwatched, began playing with it. His comrades turned it, and his foot was caught and crushed, while he was attempting to step from the main track upon it. The trial judge charged the jury, that they were to

[179] 4 Bing. 628, 29 R. R. 657 (1828).

[180] In Harrold v. Watney, (1898) 2 Q. B. 320, 67 L. J. Q. B. 771, one of the judges spoke of Lynch v. Nurdin, as never having been questioned; and cited it as authority for the court's decision in the case at bar. This judge unhesitatingly declared, that defendant's fence adjoining the highway was so insecure as to be a nuisance; that had an adult leaned against it to tie his shoe-string and it had fallen on him, as it fell on plaintiff, while trying to scale it, the adult would have had an action. The case does not range itself on the side of the turn-table and similar cases in this country.

[181] Alderson B., in Lygo v. Newbold, 9 Exch. 302, 305, 23 L. J. Ex. 108 (1854).

[182] Hughes v. Macfie, 2 H. & C. 744, 33 L. J. Ex. 177 (1863). Defendant had raised his cellar-flap against the wall of his house and plaintiff, a child of seven, wrongfully played with it and was injured. No recovery was allowed; Mangan v. Atterton, L. R. 1 Ex. 239, 35 L. J. Ex. 161 (1866). A machine for crushing oil cake was left in a public place, and plaintiff, a child of four, had his fingers smashed, while playing with it. No recovery was allowed.

[183] Clark v. Chambers, 3 Q. B. D. 327, 47 L. J. Q. B. 427 (1878), defendant unlawfully obstructed with chevaux-de-frise plaintiff's road. Plaintiff stumbled over the obstruction in the dark and put out an eye. Defendant was held liable. See Clerk and Lindsell, Torts (2 Ed.) pp. 436-437, where it is declared, that Lynch v. Nurdin cannot be regarded as law in opposition to Hughes v. Macfie and Mangan v. Atterton. Beven Negligence (2 Ed.) Vol. 1, pp. 183-190, and Pollock, Torts (6 Ed.) 43, 457, support the doctrine of Lynch v. Nurdin, as to trespassing children.

decide whether the turntable in the situation, condition and place where it was, was a dangerous machine; that if it was not dangerous, the company was not liable for negligence; that they were to further consider whether, situated as it was on defendant's property in a small town, somewhat remote from habitations, there was negligence in not anticipating that injury might occur, if it was left unlocked and unguarded; that if the company did not have reason to anticipate that children would be likely to resort to it, or that they would be likely to be injured if they did resort to it, then there was no negligence. The jury found a verdict for $7,500 for the plaintiff. Upon appeal, the judgment entered upon this verdict was affirmed by the supreme court of the United States. Mr. Justice Hunt, delivering the unanimous judgment of this court, declared that "while a railway company is not bound to the same degree of care in regard to mere strangers, who are unlawfully upon its premises, that it owes to passengers conveyed by it, it is not exempt from responsibility to such strangers for injuries arising from its negligence." He also said; "That the turntable was a dangerous machine, which would be likely to cause injury to children who resorted to it, might be fairly inferred from the injury which actually occurred to the plaintiff. There was the same liability to injure him, and no greater, that existed with reference to all children. When the jury learned from the evidence that he had suffered a serious injury by his foot being caught between the fixed rail of the road-bed and the turning rail of the table, they were justified in believing that there was a probability of the occurrence of such accidents. So, in looking at the remoteness of the machine from inhabited dwellings, when it was proved to the jury that several boys from the hamlet were at play there on this occasion, and that they had been at play upon the turntable upon other occasions, and within the observation and to the knowledge of the employees of the defendant, the jury were justified in believing that children would probably resort to it, and that the defendant should have anticipated that such would be the case. As it was in fact upon this occasion, so it was to be expected that the amusement of the boys would have been found in turning this table while they were on or about it. This could certainly have been prevented by locking the turntable when not in use by the company. It was not shown that this would cause any considerable expense or inconvenience to the defendant. It could probably have been prevented by the repair of the broken latch. This was a heavy catch, which by dropping into a socket, prevented the revolution of the turntable. There had been one on this table, weighing some eight or ten pounds, but it had been broken off and had not been replaced. It was proved to have been usual with railroad companies to have upon their turn-tables a latch or bolt, or some similar instrument. The jury may well have believed that if the defendant had incurred the trifling expense of replacing this latch, and had taken the slight trouble of putting it in its place, these very small boys would not have taken the trouble to lift it out, and thus the whole difficulty would have been avoided. Thus reasoning, the jury would have reached the conclusion that the defendant had omitted the care and attention it ought to have given; that it was negligent, and that its negligence caused the injury to the plaintiff."

The doctrine of this case has been repeatedly affirmed by the supreme court,[184] and has been adopted by many state tribunals. In one of the earliest and ablest opinions [185] upon this side of the controversy, it is said, that " what an express invitation would be to an adult, the temptation of an attractive plaything is to a child of tender years "; that while the defendant did not leave the turn-table unfastened for the purpose of injuring young children, yet " the defendant knew that by leaving this turntable unfastened and unguarded, it was not merely inviting young children to come upon the turntable, but was holding out an allurement which, acting upon the natural instincts by which such children are controlled, drew them by those instincts into a hidden danger; and having thus knowingly allured them into a place of danger, without their fault (for it cannot blame them for not resisting the temptation it has set before them), it was bound to use care to protect them from the danger into which they were thus led; and from which they could

---

[184] Hayes v. Railroad Co., 111 U. S. 228, 4 Sup. Ct. 369, 28 L. Ed. 410 (1884); Union P. Ry. v. McDonald, 152 U. S. 262, 14 Sup. Ct. 619, 38 L. Ed. 484 (1893). In the latter case, the Railroad Co., had failed to fence the slack-pit, as it was required by statute to do; and its servants deliberately frightened plaintiff into running over the unfenced slack-pit, where he received his injuries.

[185] Keefe v. Mil. etc. Ry., 21 Minn. 207, 18 Am. R. 393 (1875). The opinion of the trial judge who granted a motion for judgment for defendant on the pleadings, may be read in 2 Cent. L. J. 170.

not be expected to protect themselves.—the difference between the plaintiff's position and that of a voluntary trespasser, capable of using care, consists in this, that the plaintiff was induced to come upon the defendant's turntable by the defendant's own conduct, and that, as to him, the turntable was a hidden danger,—a trap."

Alluring Nuisances. Situations of this kind are often spoken of as attractive or alluring nuisances. "One may not bait his premises," it is said, "with some dangerous instrument or quality, alluring to the incautious or vagrant, and then deny responsibility for the consequences of following the natural instincts of curiosity or amusement aroused thereby, without taking reasonable precautions to guard against the accidents liable to ensue. Rights can only be enjoyed subject to those limitations which regard for the weaknesses and deficiencies of others dictate to be humane and just. This rule has been applied, not only in the turntable cases, but to others in which dangerous situations have been negligently maintained, and especially to cases of death or injury by falling into unguarded pools or vats of water." [186]

Converting Trespassers into Baited Victims. It will be observed that the foregoing doctrine rests upon the conversion of the infant trespasser into an innocently baited victim. And this conversion is wrought by the magic of a legal fiction. The landowner does not construct the turntable, or reservoir, nor make the excavation or other change in his premises, with a view to bait [187] children

---

[186] Price v. Atchinson Water Co., 58 Ks. 551, 50 Pac. 450, 62 Am. St. R. 625 (1897). Plaintiff's son of eleven years was drowned while fishing in defendant's reservoir. The trial court non-suited the plaintiff, but the appellate court held that whether the defendant was negligent, in maintaining dangerous reservoirs, and whether plaintiff was guilty of contributory negligence were questions for the jury. In Consol. Elec. Co. v. Healy, 65 Ks. 798, 70 Pac. 884 (1902), the court defined an attractive nuisance as "a place which, though patently dangerous to those of ordinary knowledge and prudence, is so enticing to others excusably lacking in intelligence and caution as to induce them to venture into it;" and declared, that the rule of liability for resulting injuries "applies to one, who maintains on his own premises a dangerous instrumentality, not in itself attractive, but placed in such immediate proximity to an attractive situation, on the premises of another, as to form with it a dangerous whole, notwithstanding the attractive situation on the other premises may not of itself be dangerous."

[187] Townsend v. Wathen, 9 East.

to their destruction, but with a view to the beneficial use of his land. Nothing is further from his wish or thought than alluring anybody to his premises. And yet, if the lawful changes in his property do allure vagrant infants, whose parents are unable or unwilling to properly control them, the law imposes upon him a duty of care towards them which, it is admitted, he owes to nobody else.

In rejecting this doctrine, the supreme court of Michigan [188] recently said; "We have only to add that every man who leaves a wheelbarrow, or lawnmower, or spade, upon his lawn; a rake with its sharp teeth pointing upward, upon the ground, or leaning against a fence; a bed of mortar prepared for use in his new house; a wagon in his barnyard, upon which children may climb, and from which they may fall; or who turns in his lot a kicking horse or a cow with calf—does so at the risk of having the question of his negligence left to a sympathetic jury. How far does this rule go? Must his barn door, and the usual apertures through which the accumulations of the stable are thrown, be kept locked and fastened, lest 12 year old boys get in and be hurt by the animals, or by climbing into the haymow and falling from the beams? May a man keep a ladder or a grindstone or a scythe or a plow or a reaper without danger of being called upon to reward trespassing children, whose parents owe and may be presumed to perform the duty of restraint? Does the new rule go still further and make it necessary for a man to fence his gravel pit or quarry? And if so, will an ordinary fence do, in view of the known propensity and ability of boys to climb fences? Can a man safely nowadays own a small lake or fish pond? and must he guard ravines and precipices upon his land? Such is the evolution of the law, less than twenty years after the decision of Railroad Company v. Stout, when with due deference, we think some of the courts

---

277 (1808), is usually cited on this point. But in that case, plaintiff alleged, and gave evidence tending to prove, that the defendant deliberately set the traps "wrongfully intended to catch, maim and destroy the plaintiff's dogs." No one would say that a landowner who actually intended to entrap and injure trespassing children, or adults, would not be liable for injuries resulting from such intentional traps. In Ponting v. Noakes (1894) 2 Q. B. 281, 63 L. J. Q. B. 549, defendant was held not liable for the death of plaintiff's horse, due to the latter's eating from a yew tree, which was wholly on defendant's land; the court distinguishing Townsend v. Wathen, as a case where the wrongful intention was the gist of the action.

left the solid ground of the rule, that trespassers cannot recover for injuries received, and due merely to negligence of the persons trespassed upon."

Hardship for the Landowner. The courts which impose upon the landowner a special guardianship over vagrant infants, trespassing upon his alluring premises, declare that there is no real hardship in this doctrine. When such a trespasser is a mere " hoodlum, disregarding property rights from mere love of mischief, and taking risks out of mere bravado, or in conscious defiance of moral and legal restraint, and is thus injured, we may pity his folly, but justly say, as the law says, that having intelligently assumed the risk, he ought not to recover damages." [189]   But, who is to say whether the trespassing infant comes within the category of " hoodlum " or of " baited victim."?   The jury, say these courts.   The jury will also be called upon to determine whether the premises are dangerously alluring, and whether the defendant has used proper care in guarding his alluring premises.   As a practical result, the landowner is saddled with the responsibility of an insurer of infants, who are curious and agile enough to trespass upon lands, having alluring improvements, which may be dangerous for them.[190]

Reaction from Railroad Company v. Stout. In a number of states, whose courts followed the lead of the supreme court, in the turntable cases, a halt has been called, and a disposition is shown to limit the doctrine of those cases, rather than to extend it.   The su-

[188] Ryan v. Tower, 128 Mich. 463, 87 N. W. 644, 92 Am. St. R. 481, 55 L. R. A. 310 (1901).

[189] Edgington v. Burl. etc. Ry., 116 Ia. 410, 90 N. W. 95, 57 L. R. A. 561 (1902). *Accord,* Ala. G. S. Ry. v. Crocker, 131 Al. 584, 31 So. 561 (1901); C. B. & Q. Ry. v. Krayenbuhl, 65 Neb. 889, 91 N. W. 880 (1902).

[190] Professor Jeremiah Smith, Landowner's Liability to Children, 11 Harv. L. R. 349, 434, At. p. 438, he says: " Suppose even that the judge goes still further, (much further indeed it is believed than judges have usually gone) and tells the jury that, in determining what is reasonable care, they should take into account not only the desirability of preserving innocent children from harm, but also the desirability of making beneficial use of land. How much weight will the jury allow to the latter consideration, when put in competition with the former, in a concrete case, appealing to their sympathies? How much consideration will they give to the general impolicy of hampering the use of land with troublesome and expensive restrictions, when they have before them a maimed child, or the mourning relatives of a deceased infant? "

preme court of Georgia has frankly avowed this purpose; and has ruled, that even a railroad company is not bound to fence or guard an excavation upon its premises, so as to prevent injuries to children trespassing thereon, although the excavation and its surroundings have an alluring attraction for children.[191]

A similar reaction is observable in California,[192] Missouri [193] and Texas.[194]

In the last cited case, the supreme court of Texas said of the " turntable cases ";[195] " This line of decisions has not been uniformly followed, and has met with much adverse criticism, and it seems to us that, with respect to the care which the owner of land is required to exercise, in order to secure from injury children who may trespass upon it, they go to the limit of the law. They proceed upon the ground that turn-tables are attractive to children. In

[191] Savannah etc. Ry. v. Beavers, 113 Ga. 398, 39 S. E. 82, 54 L. R. A. 314 (1901). The court quotes at length from Prof. Jeremiah Smith's articles, in 11 Harv. L. R. 349, 434, and commends them as a learned and exhaustive treatise upon the subject of the liability of landowners to children. The court had committed itself to the doctrine of Ry. Co. v. Stout, in a turntable case, Ferguson v. Col. etc. Ry., 75 Ga. 637, 77 Ga. 102 (1886)—but expressed its determination to " limit the doctrine to the turntable cases." The same determination was stated, again, in O'Connor v. Brucker, 117 Ga. 451, 453, 43 S. E. 731 (1903), a case where a trespassing child was allured into a vacant house, by reason of its being unlocked.

[192] In Barrett v. Southern Pac. Ry., 91 Cal. 296, 27 Pac. 666, 25 Am. St. R. 186 (1891), the Supreme Court followed Ry. Co. v. Stout, in a turntable case, but declined to extend the doctrine to an alluring pond, in Peters v. Bow-

man, 115 Cal. 345, 47 Pac. 114, 598 56 Am. St. R. 106, (1896), and to alluring street cars left unat-the car tracks at the end of the line, in George v. Los. Angeles Ry., 126 Cal. 357, 58 Pac. 819, 46 L. R. A. 829 (1899).

[193] Koons v. St. Louis etc. Ry., 65 Mo. 592 (1877), committed the court in a turntable case; but in Overholt v. Veiths, 93 Mo. 422, 6 S. W. 74 (1887), the court refused to apply the doctrine against the owner of an abandoned but alluring quarry; and in Barney v. Hannibal, etc. Ry., 126 Mo. 372, 28 S. W. 1969, 26 L. R. A. 847 (1894), it refused to apply the doctrine against a railroad company which failed to fence in its freight yard.

[194] Missouri K. & T. Ry. v. Edwards, 90 Tex. 65, 36 S. W. 430, 32 L. R. A. 825 (1896), reversing S. C. in 32 S. W. 815 (1895).

[195] Evanisch v. Gulf etc. Ry., 57 Tex. 126, 44 Am. R. 586 (1882); and Ry. Co. v. Stout, 17 Wall. 657, 21 L. Ed. 745 (1873), were cited as samples of this class of cases.

both of the cases cited, stress was laid upon this fact, and also upon the fact that the use of turn-tables by the children was known to the servants of the defendants. The ruling in these cases, we think, must be justified upon one of two grounds; either that the turntables possess such peculiar attractiveness, as playthings for children, that to leave them exposed should be deemed equivalent to an invitation to use them, or that, when unsecured, they are so obviously dangerous to children that, when it is discovered that they are using them, it is negligent on the part of the owner not to take some steps to guard them against the danger. But when it is said that it is enough that the object or place is attractive or alluring to children, and when it is said, as has been intimated, that the fact that they resort to a peculiar locality is evidence of its attractiveness, the question suggests itself, what object or place is not attractive to very young persons who are left free to pursue their innate propensity to wander in quest of amusement? What object at all unusual is exempt from infantile curiosity? What place, conveniently accessible for their congregation, is free from the restless feet of adventurous truants?"

Repudiation of Railroad Company v. Stout. In many jurisdictions,[196] the doctrine announced by Railway Company v. Stout has been squarely repudiated, and the rule has been laid down, that " no distinction exists between adults and infants when entering uninvited upon lands of another, with relation to the duty which the owner or occupier of such lands owes to them." [197] The learned judge, writing the opinion in the case last cited, said; " It must be conceded, I think, that the rule which imposes liability upon the landowner is a hard one, so far as he is concerned in this respect; that no matter how carefully he may endeavor to protect himself by discharging the duty which the law places upon him, the probability of failure is great. When contemplating the alteration of his land, from the condition in which nature left it, for the purpose of ob-

---

[196] Some of the cases not heretofore nor hereafter cited are the folowing: Brinkley Car Works v. Cooper, 70 Ark. 331, 67 S. W. 752, 57 L. R. A. 724 (1902); Schauf's Admin'r v. City of Paducah, 106 Ky. 228, 50 S. W. 42, 90 Am. St. R. 220 (1899); Turess v. N. Y. etc. Ry.,

61 N. J. L. 314, 40 At. 614 (1898); McAlpin v. Powell, 70 N. Y. 126 (1877); Cooper v. Overton, 102 Tenn. 211, 52 S. W. 183, 45 L. R. A. 591 (1899).

[197] D. L. & W. Ry. v. Reich, 61 N. J. L. 643, 40 At. 682, 41 L. R. A. 831, 68 Am. St. R. 727 (1898).

taining a more beneficial user therefrom, he must first consider whether the alteration will render it attractive to children of tender years, and, if so, whether they will be subjected to danger if they succumb to the attraction. If he honestly concludes that the change will not operate to attract children, and that, therefore, although it may make his property dangerous, he is under no obligation to provide for their safety, or if he concludes that, although the alterations may render his property attractive to children, they will not incur danger by coming upon it, and for either of these reasons fails to take precautions for their safety, it will be for the jury to say whether he must answer for the result, if injury to a child follows upon his omission; and their verdict will depend upon whether, in their opinion, he had a reasonable ground for his conclusion. So too, if he appreciates that the change which he proposes to make will render his premises dangerously attractive to children, and takes precautions to exclude them therefrom, it is still possible that they may elude his vigilance, and receive hurt while trespassing; and when that occurs, it at once becomes a question for the jury to say, whether or not the injury was the result of the care, on the part of the landowner, in affording that protection which his duty required. What the conclusion of the jury would be in any given case, of course, no one can tell. The fact, however, is suggestive that in every reported case, so far as I have examined them (and I have examined many), where this doctrine has been under consideration, it has always been the landowner, and never the injured child, who was trying to avoid the result of the verdict of the jury. It is only in those cases, where the action of the jury has been controlled by the trial court, that the injured child has sought a review. The probability that the landowner will not be able to avoid liability for injuries to children who come upon his lands without invitation, no matter how careful he may have been, while it affords no reason for denying the existence of the rule which holds him to responsibility, certainly requires that we should not accept it as sound unless it rests upon a solid foundation."

Similar views have been announced by the courts of other states.[198] It is quite apparent, therefore, that the tide of judicial

[198] Daniels v. N. Y. etc. Ry., 154 Mass, 349, 28 N. E. 283, 13 L. R. A. 248, 26 Am. St. R. 253 (1891); Frost v. Eastern etc. Ry., 64 N. H. 220, 9 At. 790, 10 Am. St. R. 396 (1886); Walsh v. Fitchburg Ry.,

opinion is setting strongly against the doctrine of Railroad Company v. Stout. This has been admitted by one of the most enthusiastic advocates of the doctrine.[190] The present writer does not share that learned and lamented author's regret over this change in the tide. On the other hand, he views it as the result of the sober, second thought of the bench and the bar.

145 N. Y. 301, 39 N. E. 1068, 27 L. R. A. 724, 45 Am. St. R. 615 (1895); Gillespie v. McGowan, 100 Pa. 144, 45 Am. R. 365 (1882); Paolino v. McKendall, 24 R. I. 432, 53 At. 268, 60 L. R. A. 133, (1902); Uther-malen v. Boggs Run Co., 50 W. Va. 457, 40 S. E. 410, 55 L. R. A. 911, 88 Am. St. R. 884 (1901).

[190] Thompson, Commentaries on Negligence, Vol. 1, § 1031 (1901).

INDEX.

473